HUMAN SOCIETIES

An Introduction to Macrosociology

HUMAN SOCIETIES
An Introduction to Macrosociology

SIXTH EDITION

Gerhard Lenski
Jean Lenski
Patrick Nolan

McGraw-Hill, Inc.
New York   St. Louis   San Francisco   Auckland   Bogotá   Caracas
Hamburg   Lisbon   London   Madrid   Mexico   Milan   Montreal   New Delhi
Paris   San Juan   São Paulo   Singapore   Sydney   Tokyo   Toronto

HUMAN SOCIETIES
An Introduction to Macrosociology

1 2 3 4 5 6 7 8 9 0 DOC DOC 9 5 4 3 2 1 0

ISBN 0-07-037242-X

This book was set in Palatino by the College Composition Unit
in cooperation with Ruttle Shaw & Wetherill, Inc.
The editors were Phillip A. Butcher and Edwin Hanson;
the production supervisor was Diane Renda.
The cover was designed by Amy Becker.
R. R. Donnelley & Sons Company was printer and binder.

Library of Congress Cataloging-in-Publication Data

Lenski, Gerhard Emmanuel, (date).
    Human societies: an introduction to macrosociology / Gerhard
Lenski, Jean Lenski, Patrick Nolan.—6th ed.
        p.   cm.
    ISBN 0-07-037242-X (text).—ISBN 0-07-037243-8 (instructor's manual)
    1. Macrosociology.   2. Social evolution.   3. Social systems—
History.   I. Lenski, Jean.   II. Nolan, Patrick.   III. Title.
HM51.L357   1991
301—dc20   90-6418

To the memory of
Andrei Dmitrievich Sakharov

Contents in Brief

PART THREE INDUSTRIAL SOCIETIES AND INDUSTRIALIZING SOCIETIES

Contents

ix

CHAPTER **4.** _____
Types of Human Societies   69

PART **TWO**   PREINDUSTRIAL SOCIETIES

CHAPTER **5.** _____
Hunting and Gathering Societies   87

CHAPTER **6.** _____
Horticultural Societies   120

PART **THREE** INDUSTRIAL SOCIETIES AND INDUSTRIALIZING SOCIETIES

CHAPTER 13. _____

Industrial Societies: Social Stratification   316

CHAPTER 14. _____

Industrial Societies: The Family, the Media, and More   338

CHAPTER 15. _____

Industrializing Agrarian Societies   361

FOREWORD

In the academic division of labor, the task of sociology is to explain the way the totality of social patterns works together, whether well, not so well, or badly indeed. Sociologists study how patterned ways of behaving in various arenas (political, economic, and religious, for example) interact as people try to provide for themselves and reproduce the next generation of workers.

Thus, the study of sociology should help students to understand the public and private issues they will have to confront in a world changing at an accelerating rate. However, students can get a handle on interpreting social change only if sociology provides a meaningful map of the world, a theory that explains how and why societies change. Such a theory must be based on a comparison of different societies at different times and places. The root question is, What factors in the course of human history have shaped the social organization of tribes, nations, and states?

Unfortunately, all too often in the United States, sociology is introduced as a descriptive account of only one society at basically one point in time: the United States in the last years of the twentieth century. The picture is familiar but it yields no understanding. Although the account is larded with little ad hoc blobs of theory, its relation to the rest of an interconnected world is obscure. Presenting sociology as a compendium of contemporary life in the United States has two consequences. First, because so many sociological concepts have seeped into public consciousness through the mass media, many students feel they already know what sociology is about. They had all that stuff in high school. Or so they say. Second, and of far greater importance, a descriptive account at one point in time cannot explain the origins of a society nor can it suggest what to expect in the future. It is as if someone tried to explain geography by using isolated examples from Nairobi, Chicago, and the Himalayas.

In order to map human societies, one must begin with the most basic element in the way they are organized: the kind of work men and women must do each day to put bread on the table to maintain themselves and their children. But subsistence work doesn't exist in a vacuum. It is strongly affected by ecology and technology: climate, rainfall, terrain, soil conditions, and the tools that have been invented to enable people to produce more widgets in a given time period. Although ecology and technology set limits on the ways that humans can organize themselves, humans make their own history because it is they who ultimately determine what form their organizations will take. And, in turn, the way humans organize themselves affects ecological conditions and the development of new tools.

Thus, the intellectual challenge of developing a macrolevel theory of human organization is sociology's primary reason for existence. And a good macrolevel theory of human societies has never been more needed than right now. During most of human history, predicting the shape of human society one hundred years hence was not so difficult. Ecology and technology changed slowly. The future looked much like the past. Slowly, over many generations, the hoe replaced hunting and gathering as the major subsistence tool. And, after many, many generations had passed, the hoe was replaced by the plow. But the plow was followed by the Industrial Revolution, a term that in itself signifies the quickened pace of change.

Now the pace of technological change has so accelerated that we hardly know what to call our "age" in human history. The word "post-industrial," like "post-modern," conveys little information. It says only that we seem to have got beyond modern, but into what? No one knows for certain. A basic problem is that the human race, owing to technological development, now has the capacity to change the ecological setting we have long taken for granted. This leaves us with an unprecedented challenge in charting the future of human life on this planet.

In meeting this challenge the Lenski, Lenski, and Nolan text far surpasses all other introductory texts. To my knowledge it is the only text that undergirds the discipline with a theory. It is a mistake to think of it as just another classification scheme. Instead, the ecological–evolutionary approach is a theory of societal organization that takes in the whole of human history. It provides startling insights into major questions that no other text even tries to address. With this approach, sociological concepts can be introduced in a theoretical context, providing intellectual nourishment that isn't available elsewhere.

An example, painfully brief, will illustrate the depth of the questions raised, as well as the answers suggested, by the ecological–evolutionary approach. What makes social inequality vary from one society to another? *Human Societies* highlights the importance of two factors: enough "wealth" to tempt alert entrepreneurs to seize it and conditions that make it possible to monopolize the use of force. The level of social inequality is therefore low in societies whose subsistence is based on hunting and gathering: there isn't enough surplus food (or anything else) for anyone to hoard.

In contrast, inequality is high in plow societies. A fantastic surplus (compared to that in foraging or hoe societies) coupled with the availability of iron weapons tempts those who can, to make peasants, serfs, and slaves out of nearly everybody else. Common people were probably worse off than were their hunting and gathering ancestors.

In industrial societies, the level of social inequality tends to fall. A huge surplus ensures that incentive to control it will be high, but it is harder for elites to monopolize the use of force over the long run. Mass education (without which industrialization has not occurred) makes people "uppity." Governmental stability requires a measure of popular support.

And what about social equality in post-industrial societies? Now the world is interdependent. But the various nations are at vastly different levels of well-being, which makes for political instability. Ecological crisis is a threat. Knowledge of advanced military technology is widespread, giving many nations, large and small, rich and poor, awesome power to destroy. The unanticipated consequences of technological change should make the twenty-first century interesting indeed. The task of sociology to provide a map to interpret social change has never been as important as it is now. This book provides that map.

Joan Huber
The Ohio State University

PREFACE

This volume differs from most textbooks written for the introductory course in sociology. It is neither a survey of contemporary American society nor an encyclopedia-like introduction to the different specialties that have developed in the discipline. Instead, it is a comparative and historical analysis of human societies—the largest, most powerful, and most important social systems humans have created—written from the perspective of a systematic, macrochronic, macroorganizational theory of change.

Human Societies has three basic objectives. First, it seeks to provide students with a comprehensive and meaningful "map" of the social world *as a whole*—a map that will help them see their own society in a new and broader perspective. For this reason, we focus primarily on the various types of societies that have evolved over the course of history, and on the major historical eras.

Second, *Human Societies* seeks to heighten awareness of change. In our experience, younger people seldom appreciate how profoundly the world they have come to know in the first twenty years of their lives is likely to change during the rest of their lifetime. We seek to sensitize them to the major forces that have shaped the direction of change in the past and are shaping it today. In our opinion, sociology has not done a good job in this respect, ignoring or minimizing the importance of several of the most powerful forces of all.

Third, *Human Societies* seeks to prepare students for their role as citizens in a democratic society. We do not provide prepackaged answers to tomorrow's problems, but we do provide the conceptual "tools" that they will need if they are to act in an informed and responsible manner.

This volume is the sixth edition of *Human Societies* and possibly the last in which the original authors will play the major role. We welcome Patrick Nolan, who joins us for the first time in this edition and who will play an increasingly important role in the future. A reviewer of previous editions, he has used *Human Societies* for many years and brings a wealth of new classroom experience to the task. Among his contributions to this edition are the all-new *Student Study Guide,* the substantially expanded and improved *Instructor's Manual,* and the reworking of all of the statistical analyses of preindustrial societies.

No chapter is entirely unchanged in the present edition. In a few chapters, the changes are largely stylistic and not substantively significant. In most chapters, however, there are important substantive changes. All of the changes are identified in the *Instructor's Manual* (available on request from the publisher), and we recommend that both instructors who have used previous editions and those using *Human Societies* for the first time obtain a copy.

Acknowledgments

It is not possible to acknowledge adequately all our intellectual debts in the brief space available here. But many who read this volume will recognize our debt to Thomas Malthus, Charles Darwin, Herbert Spencer, Karl Marx, Max Weber, Thorstein Veblen, Albert Keller, William Ogburn, V. Gordon Childe, George Peter Murdock, R. H. Tawney, Sir Julian Huxley, George Gaylord Simpson, Leslie White, Julian Steward, Amos Hawley, Marvin Harris, and William H. McNeill, among others. The citations that appear at the end of this volume should be regarded as further acknowledgments of indebtedness and appreciation.

Many social scientists and a few biologists have been kind enough to provide critical comments on, and suggestions for, one or more of the six editions of *Human Societies* thus far. The social scientists include Brian Aldrich, Francis R. Allen, E. Jackson Baur, Rae Lesser Blumberg, Robert Carroll, William R. Catton, Jr., Ronald Cosper, Timothy Crippen, David Featherman, Thomas Feucht, George Furniss, Walter Goldschmidt, Robert Bates Graber, Gareth Gustafson, Thomas D. Hall, Amos Hawley, Paul Heckert, John Hofley, Joan Huber, Holly Hughes, Larry Hunt, Donald Irish, Philip Marcus, Robert Miller, Ross Purdy, Leo Rigsby, Norman Storer, Wout Ultee, Charles K. Warriner, Norbert Wiley, and Everett K. Wilson. The biologists include Alfred E. Emerson, Richard E. Lenski, and Edward O. Wilson. We extend sincere thanks to each of them for valuable suggestions, but remind readers that the final responsibility for the contents is ours alone.

We also thank Phillip Butcher, our editor at McGraw-Hill; Edwin Hanson, senior editing supervisor; Sylvia Shepard, development editor; and Safra Nimrod, photo department manager, for their many contributions. Finally, we extend our special thanks to Lois McKoy who helped us in so many ways in the preparation of the manuscript.

Gerhard Lenski

Jean Lenski

Patrick Nolan

HUMAN SOCIETIES

An Introduction to Macrosociology

PART ONE

THEORETICAL FOUNDATIONS

1

The Human Situation

Imagine that we have in front of us an enormous album filled with photographs of the human scene beginning 100,000 years ago. Each of its 1,000 pages offers glimpses of a different century.

Throughout the first three-quarters of the album, the pictures are of people physically indistinguishable from ourselves, naked or clad in animal skins. There are shots of these people huddled around fires in front of caves, nursing infants beside rude shelters made of branches and leaves, and fashioning simple tools and weapons from stone, wood, and bone. Other photographs show them hunting with wooden spears and foraging for edible plants. Fascinating though these pictures are, we find ourselves turning hundreds of pages to discover there is little or nothing to distinguish one century from another.

Early in the second half of the album, however, we see a scene that is strikingly different: a small group of people is burying a child. Soon after page 700, there is evidence of other new activities. In some photographs, men are painting scenes of animals and hunters on the walls of caves; in others, people are engaged in strange rituals. Other innovations gradually appear: spoons, saws, needles, bows and arrows, even crude dugout canoes. Shortly before page 900, we begin to see people trapping and netting fish, harvesting wild grains with stone sickles, weaving baskets, taming wild dogs and sheep—and, yes, drinking beer.

Not until the last hundred pages, however, are there any photographs of people farming, and it is another twenty or thirty pages before there are any real towns. Somewhere around page 950, we see people using the earliest systems of writing to record important events of their day, the time historians refer to as "the dawn of history." Several pages later there is a view of men constructing one of the great pyramids of Egypt. Further on, we begin to see occasional pictures of individuals whose names we recognize: Moses on page 967, Aristotle on 976, Cleopatra on 979, Jesus on 980.

Although change is far more evident throughout these late pages of the album than in earlier ones, adjacent pages still look remarkably similar to one another. Then,

3

near the bottom of page 998 we see a picture of an early factory filled with machines and, on the very next page, steam locomotives, steamships, and gaslit city streets filled with horses and buggies.

Now, the final page. Enormous buildings thrust through the clouds, jets streak across oceans, and Hiroshima and Nagasaki vanish in incredible bursts of heat and light....

Although this journey through the past is only an amusing exercise in imagination, it makes us wonder why humans were so long emerging from the Stone Age. Were they so happy with their way of life that they were not motivated to try new ways of doing things?

The historical record also raises questions about the human situation today and in the future. What caused the tremendous acceleration in the rate of change in the recent past? How much more change can we expect in the future, and will the benefits of that change outweigh the costs? In short, what kind of world awaits us in the twenty-first century? And, most important of all, can we do anything to increase the chances that it will be the kind of world we want it to be?

Questions like these force us to recognize how much we resemble poorly prepared astronauts on a fleet of spaceships, hurtling at fantastic speeds on an uncharted course that is filled with unknown hazards. These ships are the societies of which each of us is a member—American society, Canadian society, Dutch society, Chinese society, Soviet society, Nigerian society, Brazilian society, and all the rest. These extraordinarily complex social systems are moving rapidly into uncharted realms, and we, like ill-trained astronauts, have only the most limited understanding of the systems on which our survival and well-being depend.

Presidents, prime ministers, and other leaders constantly seek to reassure us. Sometimes they even manage to create the illusion that they understand, and can control, the forces of change. But a moment's reflection reminds us that neither they nor their predecessors planned or willed the world that exists today. Like the rest of us, they have repeatedly been caught off guard by unanticipated changes and developments.

In a world like this, each one of us has a vested interest in learning as much as we can about human societies. Above all, we need to prepare ourselves for the changes that lie ahead.

Fortunately, we are not without resources. The branch of modern science known as *sociology** has as its chief concern the study of human societies. Its aim is to understand societies and the forces that have made them what they are. Although many important questions remain to be answered, substantial progress has already been made.

Much of the work of sociologists is devoted to the study of one or another of the many different component parts of societies (e.g., individuals, families, communities, classes) and to specific features and problems (e.g., crime, race relations, re-

---

*For definitions of this and other terms used in this volume, see the Glossary, the blue pages from 433 to 440.

ligion, politics). The study of these components and features of societies is sometimes called *micro*sociology.

*Macro*sociology, in contrast, focuses on human societies themselves. It, too, is concerned with individuals, families, classes, social problems, and all of the other parts and features of societies, but it analyzes them *in relation to the larger social systems— the societies—of which they are part.* The difference between macrosociology and microsociology is the same as the difference between the study of complex mechanical systems, such as spaceships, and the study of one of their component parts, such as their booster engines or life-support systems.

This volume takes the *macro*sociological approach. Our primary concern, and the focus of our analysis, will be human societies themselves. This does not mean that we will ignore their components: that would be impossible. It does mean, however, that when we consider their component parts and various features we will treat them as what they are: parts of larger and more inclusive social systems.

Two other characteristics of this book should be noted. First, its approach to the study of human societies is *historical.* We must examine societies over an extended period of time if we hope to understand the critical processes of societal change and development. Experience has shown, moreover, that the broader the span of time we consider, the better we can understand the most basic processes of change in human life.

Second, our approach to the study of human societies is *comparative.* Comparison is the basis of science. An understanding of *anything* depends on comparing it with other things. To understand an individual chimpanzee, for example, scientists compare it with other chimpanzees. To understand chimpanzees as a species, they compare them with other apes, and to understand apes, they compare them with other primates and other mammals. In every comparison the similarities and the differences are used to draw inferences about why things are as they are. Only by repeated comparisons is it possible to build a reliable store of knowledge about the world of nature and all that it contains. This is true whether our concern is with atoms, galaxies, robins, chimpanzees—or human societies.

In making comparisons, the most important task for scientists is to discover *differences that make a difference.* In medicine, for example, the aim is to discover the actual causes of diseases, not just their symptoms. The same is true in other sciences: the goal is to discover the causes of things.

This search for the causes of things leads to the development of theory. *Scientific theories* are explanations of various aspects of the world of nature; they are explanations of why things are as they are. Theories also provide a coherent set of principles that form the basic frame of reference for a field of inquiry.

One of the most important characteristics of scientific theories is that they are *falsifiable.* This means that they are stated in such a way that they can be tested and shown to be wrong, if indeed they are wrong. To win acceptance in the scientific community, a theory must withstand repeated tests and must be supported by a substantial body of observations that are consistent with its explanation of relationships.

Sometimes it seems as though science is merely the patient accumulation of facts. But facts by themselves are meaningless; they explain nothing. For scientists, the collection of facts is the means to a much more important end, namely, the development and testing of theories designed to explain some aspect of the world of nature.

Our study of human societies in this volume will be guided by such a theory—*ecological–evolutionary theory*. As its name suggests, this theory is concerned with two things. First, it is concerned with the relation of societies to their environments and with the relations of the parts of a society to one another. Second, the theory is concerned with the evolution of societies—how and why they change and how these changes create differences among societies.

HUMAN SOCIETIES: THEIR PLACE IN NATURE

Often in the past, and still today, many people have thought of human societies as though they stood apart from the world of nature that science studies. This is easy to do, because modern industrial societies are much like giant cocoons that stand between us and the surrounding environment. As a result, we seldom encounter anything that has not been processed and transformed by human actions. Nevertheless, the first premise of ecological–evolutionary theory is that *human societies are a part of the global ecosystem and cannot be adequately understood unless this fact is taken fully into account.*[1]

As many scholars have observed, the world of nature is structured like a system of wheels within wheels. Larger things are made up of smaller things, and these in turn are made up of still smaller things. Figure 1.1 provides a greatly oversimplified view of the structure of the world of nature as understood by modern science. Subatomic particles, such as protons and electrons, form the lowest level. These are combined in various ways to form atoms, such as carbon and radium. Atoms in turn are organized into molecules, such as water, salt, amino acids, and proteins. Though Figure 1.1 does not show it, molecules constitute multiple levels in the hierarchy, because some of the simpler molecules, the amino acids, for example, are building blocks for more complex and more inclusive molecules such as proteins.

Once we go beyond the level of molecules, we encounter the important division between living and nonliving things. Since our concern is with human societies, there is no need to consider all the levels of nonliving matter. Suffice it to note that the structure leads by degrees to the level of the giant galaxies that wheel through space and ends with the universe itself.

Societies, however, are part of the biotic world: they are one of the ways in which *living* things are organized. More specifically, they are a form of organization found in many species of multicellular organisms.

This brings us to the question of why some species are organized into societies while others are not.

Societies as Adaptive Mechanisms

The development of the societal mode of organization has been called "one of the great steps in evolution, as important as the emergence of the cell, the multicellular

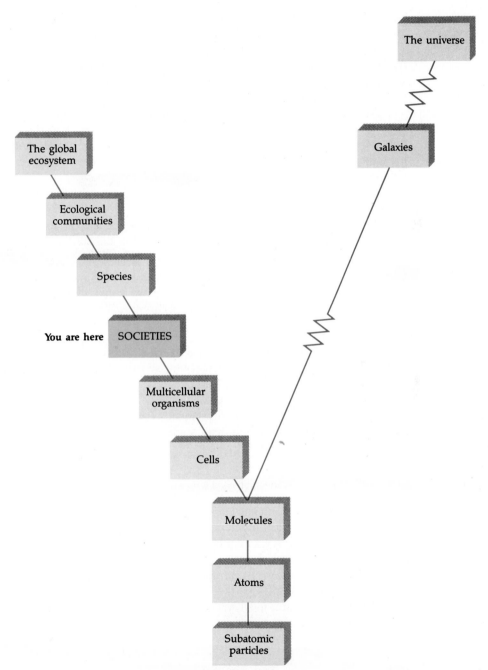

FIGURE 1.1 Levels of organization in the world of nature.

organism, and the vertebrate system."[2] Actually, societies evolved not once but a number of times, independently, and in widely scattered parts of the animal kingdom. They are concentrated in three areas: (1) many species of vertebrates, especially among mammals, birds, and fish; (2) the social insects (ants, termites, and many species of wasps and bees); and (3) the colonial invertebrates (such as corals, sponges, and Portuguese man-of-war).[3]

Why did so many and such diverse species develop this particular mode of organization? Quite simply, because being organized this way helped the members of these species survive. In other words, the societal mode of life became common in the animal kingdom for the same reason that wings, lungs, and protective coloring became common: they are all valuable *adaptive mechanisms.*

But societal organization is different from adaptive mechanisms that enable species to perform some particular activity—the way wings, for example, enable creatures to fly, or lungs enable them to exchange oxygen and other gases with the air. What distinguishes social species from all the rest is a characteristic that has the potential for being used in a great variety of ways: *an enhanced capacity for cooperation.*

To those who study animal behavior, "cooperation" means simply that the individuals in a given species associate with and interact with one another for their mutual benefit. It does not mean they cooperate in every activity, nor does it imply an absence of competition and conflict.

The types of cooperative activities in which the various social species engage include reproduction, nurture of their young, securing food, and defense against predators and other dangers.* Some social species rely on cooperative behavior in almost every area of life; others are less involved in, or less dependent on, social activities. But every social species benefits substantially from the fact that its members are genetically programmed to solve at least some of their problems by acting together instead of individually.

A Definition of Human Societies

Once we recognize that human societies are adaptive mechanisms involving cooperative activities among their members, we are close to a definition of these important entities. There is, however, one other essential consideration that must be taken into account.

Human societies have within them many kinds of smaller groups, such as families, communities, political parties, and religious groups, and these subgroups are *also* adaptive mechanisms involving cooperative activities among their members. Thus, our definition needs to specify that human societies are *autonomous* groups—groups that are not subject to the authority or political control of any larger, more inclusive group. In short, *a human society is a politically autonomous group of people which engages in a broad range of cooperative activities.*

---

*Even *non*social animals display cooperative activity in the area of reproduction (i.e., they reproduce sexually). But a species is not classified as "social" if its cooperative activity is limited to this single, though important, area.

FIGURE 1.2 Cooperative activities in which social species may engage include reproduction, nurture of the young, and defense against predators: elephant society in Tanzania.

This definition obviously applies to American society, Soviet society, or Brazilian society, but not to an American labor union, Soviet Jews, or the city of Rio de Janeiro. None of the latter is autonomous; each is subordinate to the larger society of which it is a part. Similarly, the population of the Federal Republic of Germany (West Germany) constitutes a society, but German-speaking people as a whole, scattered among several societies (West Germany, East Germany, Austria, Switzerland), do not; the population of Saudi Arabia constitutes a society, but Arabs as a whole and Muslims do not.

Sometimes unusual circumstances make it difficult to say whether a group of people is or is not a society at a particular point in its history. Uncertainty is most likely to arise when a small society is gradually absorbed by a larger and more powerful one. Consider the Eskimos of northern Canada, for example. Not long ago these people lived in numerous small settlements, each one largely self-sufficient and each one free of outside political control. Gradually, however, the Canadian government began asserting authority over these groups. At the same time, the Eskimos were becoming increasingly involved in economic relationships with Canadians and were drawn into the complex web of cooperative ties that is Canadian society. Because these developments occurred slowly over an extended period, it is impossible to say precisely when a given Eskimo group ceased being a society and became, instead, part of Canadian society. But the precise date when the balance tipped is far less important than the overall pattern of change that occurs when small societies are absorbed by larger ones.

UNDERSTANDING HUMAN SOCIETIES: BASIC ASSUMPTIONS

That human societies are part of the larger world of nature is not simply a truism to be acknowledged and then forgotten; it is a fundamental fact that must be reckoned with and taken fully into account in any serious effort to understand them. At the same time, however, human societies are not merely one more kind of society with a few new wrinkles added. On the contrary, many of their most important characteristics are unique.

In studying human life and human societies, it is easy to emphasize one of these aspects of the human situation to the neglect of the other. Ecological–evolutionary theory, the theory that will guide our study of human societies, avoids this by starting with three basic assumptions. First, because human societies are part of the world of nature, they are all influenced by their *environments* in a variety of ways. Second, because human societies are part of the world of nature, their members, like the members of every other species, are endowed with a *genetic heritage* that profoundly influences their actions. Third, this human heritage enables the members of human societies—and them alone—to create *cultural* heritages, and it is this that gives human life its unique qualities. If we neglect or ignore *any* of these three factors, our understanding of human societies will necessarily be flawed.

Human Societies and the Environment

To say that every human society is dependent on its environment and that this environment profoundly influences it raises an important question. Exactly what does the term "environment" mean?

This term refers to *everything that is external to a specified population and that has any effect on it.* Thus, for whales, the oceans and the varied forms of life they contain, together with the air above them, the ships that sail on them, and the toxic wastes that pour into them, constitute the environment, just as tropical forests and the countless species of plants and animals they contain are the environment of monkeys.

For a human society, the environment includes such things as the soil, mineral and water resources, climate, terrain, plants, animals, and other features of the territory it occupies. In addition, its environment includes any other human societies with which its members come into contact or which influence it in any way. In other words, every human society must adapt not only to a *biophysical* environment but to a *human social* environment as well. Its welfare and even its survival depend on its success in adapting to *both*.

In thinking about the environment, we need to recognize at the outset that it is not only *an essential resource* for human societies but also *the source of many of their problems*. Thus, while a society depends on its environment for all the material necessities of life (i.e., food, water, shelter, etc.), that same environment also harbors deadly enemies. The biophysical environments of some human groups have contained many kinds of large and deadly predators, and the environments of even the most advanced modern societies harbor countless species of viruses, bacteria, insects, and rodents.

The *social* environment presents threats of other kinds. In the twentieth century alone, hundreds of millions of people have lost their lives, been wounded, or been driven from their homes as a result of war. And even when war is avoided, one society can be threatened and harmed by another through other means, such as atmospheric or other pollution, economic competition, or political subversion.

Human Societies: Their Genetic Heritage

In the efforts of societies to cope with the challenges of their environments, their most basic resource has always been *the vast store of information contained in the genes of their members*. For the genes with which each of us is endowed at the moment of conception contain the information that is essential for life itself, and for everything we do from breathing and walking to learning and communicating.

Until the present century, however, no one even knew of the existence of genes, far less imagined the enormous influence they exert on every living thing from the simplest one-celled animals to humans. Even today many people fail to recognize, or badly underestimate, their importance.

As biologists have discovered, every species has a genetic heritage uniquely its own. This heritage is the product of an evolutionary process that has been going on for more than 3 billion years. Because of it, each member of a species is endowed with a vast store of *chemically coded information* which it receives from its parents or parent.*

Individuals have no control over the information stored in their genes. Yet this information guides and shapes the life of every living thing, in much the same way that the information built into the design of a modern computer influences the computer's operations and the information stored in our brains affects our feelings and our actions.

Like every other species, we humans possess a unique and distinctive heritage that influences every aspect of our lives. Like the information we carry in our brains, the information stored in our genes is *a product of experience* that influences all subsequent actions. Unlike the kinds of information we learn, however, it does not result from our personal experience. Rather, it is the result of the experiences of countless generations of our ancestors. Through the interaction of the biological processes of mutation, sexual recombination, and natural selection, every species gradually accumulates its own distinctive store of useful genetic information.

To understand our species' genetic heritage, we need to bear in mind the nature of our ancestry. We are members of the anthropoid suborder (which also includes the great apes and monkeys), which is part of the primate order, which is part

---

*Some species reproduce asexually and these individuals therefore have only a single parent.

of the mammalian class, which, in turn, is part of the vertebrate division of the animal kingdom. This means that we are more closely related and genetically more similar to other anthropoids than to the rest of the primate order, to other primates than to other mammals, to the rest of the mammalian class than to other vertebrates, to the rest of the vertebrate division than to other animals, and to other animals than to plants. It also means that our basic adaptations resemble those of primates and mammals more closely than those of other, less closely related species.

When we compare ourselves with the other anthropoids and especially with our closest kin of all, the great apes (e.g., chimpanzees and gorillas), the range of common traits is striking. To begin with, there are the many traits that we and they share with most other mammals, such as warm-bloodedness, body hair, lungs, four limbs, a relatively elaborate brain, the ability to learn and communicate, and, in the female, mammary glands that secrete milk for the nurturance of offspring. In addition, we and the other anthropoids share such traits as upright posture, flexible arms and hands, separated fingers and opposable thumbs, year-round sexual readiness, prolonged immaturity of our young, greater reliance on the sense of sight than of smell, and a high order of intelligence.

One cannot compare humans with other species in this way without recognizing the extent to which basic patterns of human life are rooted in our genetic system. For it is not just a matter of similarities between our anatomy and physiology and that of the other primates: it is also a matter of behavioral tendencies and predispositions. If we humans are capable of cooperation and live in societies, it is not because we choose to be social creatures, but because of our genetic heritage. Similarly, if we rely on learning as a basic mode of adaptation to the world we live in, it is not because we decided it was the best thing to do, nor did we invent learning. Rather, it is an expression of our mammalian and primate heritage.

Learning is the process by which an organism acquires, through experience, information with behavior-modifying potential.[4] This means that when it comes to solving problems, an animal that can learn is not completely dependent on instinct (i.e., the behavioral repertoire provided by its genetic heritage). Instead, its own experiences become a factor shaping its behavior. In the case of humans and some of the higher primates, the evolution of the forebrain has reached the point where they are able to store such a wide range of memories that they can learn by *insight*; in other words, they can analyze a situation in their minds and thereby avoid the time-consuming, costly, and often painful process of trial and error.[5]

The adaptive value of the ability to learn is greatly enhanced when animals live together in groups. This gives the individual more opportunity to observe, and to communicate with, others of its kind. In effect, social animals benefit from the experience of their fellows as well as from their own personal experience. Social life thus multiplies the amount of information available to a population. In the words of two leading students of primate life, "The [primate] group is the locus of knowledge and information far exceeding that of the individual member. It is in the group that experience is pooled."[6]

The adaptive value of the ability to learn is also greatly enhanced among primates by the prolonged physical immaturity of their young. The young of most species are genetically equipped to fend for themselves from the moment of birth. For

FIGURE 1.3 All mammalian species have a marked capacity for learning. Among anthropoids, this is enhanced by the prolonged physical immaturity of the young: chimpanzee family, with older sister nuzzling younger brother in mother's arms.

mammals, however, there is a period during which the young depend on sustained contact with one or both parents. In the case of the anthropoids, this period of dependence is especially prolonged, a fact that is linked both with their enhanced capacity for learning and with their dependence on the societal mode of life.

But what makes us so different from those anthropoid apes—chimpanzees and gorillas—with whom we share more than 99 percent of our genes?[7] After all, only we build skyscrapers, set off nuclear explosions, philosophize, compose symphonies, and travel in space. The explanation is that at some point in the evolution of one anthropoid line there occurred a series of genetic changes that, although few in number, had revolutionary consequences for behavior. The most critical changes altered the structure of the brain and shifted the center of vocalization to the neocortex, or newer part of the brain, where learning takes place and learned information is stored. Thus, thanks to relatively minor genetic changes, our remote ancestors acquired the capacity to create a radically new mode of adaptation—culture.*

---

*This is a classic example of what is known as the "threshold effect," in which a small change in one thing has a big effect on something else—as when someone walks for miles in a pouring rain without any improvement in his situation and then takes one or two additional steps and enters a building and completely escapes the downpour.

Culture: A New Mode of Adaptation and a New Kind of Heritage

Unlike the genetic heritages of other species, ours enables us to create culture. This makes it possible for us to adapt to our environments and satisfy our needs in totally new and remarkably varied ways.

Because culture is such a basic and critical part of human life, we need to understand precisely what it is. Unlike the information that every species passes from one generation to the next through its genes, culture is *learned* information, and it is passed from person to person and from generation to generation by means of *symbols*.

What are symbols that they have made such a difference to our species? After all, the members of other species also communicate among themselves, using *signals* to share information. Both signals and symbols are *information conveyers*. But there is a vital difference: the meaning of a signal is wholly or largely determined by the genetic makeup of the individuals who use it; the meaning of a symbol is not.

The best way to understand this distinction is to look at examples of the two kinds of information conveyers, beginning with signals.[8] Animals signal with movements, sounds, odors, color changes, and so on, and the signals they produce vary greatly in the amount of information they convey. The simplest type of signal is one that is used in only a single context and that has only one possible meaning—the sexually attractive scent released by a female moth, for example. In contrast, some species are able to transmit more complex information by varying the frequency or intensity of a signal or by combining different signals simultaneously or in sequence. Thus, a foraging honeybee returns to her hive and performs the "waggle dance" to direct fellow workers to the food source she has located.[9] By varying the movements and vibrations that comprise the dance, she communicates enough information about direction and distance to enable her sisters to land remarkably near the target, and at the same time adds a comment on the quality of the food supply and the state of the weather.

In some species, especially birds and mammals, the use of and response to signals are partially learned. The young of certain species of birds, for example, must learn some elements of their territorial songs from adults.[10] We, too, learn to modify and use genetically based signals in different ways. Thus, we learn to pretend to yawn to indicate boredom. But whether simple or complex, and whether or not learning is involved, a signal is an information conveyer whose basic form and meaning are genetically determined.

Symbols, by contrast, are not genetically determined. The ability to create and use symbols does depend on genetics, but the form of a symbol and the meaning attached to it do not. Thus, a symbol is *an information conveyer whose form and meaning are determined by those who use it*.

Humans share the ability to create symbols with no other species. Various kinds of animals from plow horses to circus seals have been trained to recognize, respond to, and even use, after a fashion, a number of symbols. Chimpanzees and gorillas have proved to have a remarkable ability in this regard, learning to use up to 750 different symbols, even combining a few of them to convey more complex meanings.[11] None of these animals, however, has ever *created* a symbol, that is, has ever deliberately assigned its own meaning to a gesture, sound, or object. Rather, the symbols they use were designed by humans and taught to them. What is more, these creatures show no prelanguage features in the wild.[12] Thus, while their accomplishments are impressive, they cannot compare with humans. For we not only quickly master the language of the group into which we are born but we are capable at a very early age of devising new symbols and even entire symbol systems. Small children invent names for their stuffed animals and sometimes go on to make up "secret codes." And at least one case has been documented in which a set of twins, first thought to be retarded because no one understood their speech, proved to have invented an entirely original and complex language by which they communicated with one another.

We can appreciate the significance of symbols only when we understand their "genetic independence." Take the sound of the third letter of our alphabet, for example. We use that sound to refer to the act of perceiving (to see), to a bishop's jurisdiction (a see), and to a large body of water (a sea), as well as to the letter itself. Spanish-speaking people, meanwhile, use it to say "yes" and "if," and French-speaking people to say "yes," "if," "whether," and "so." Obviously there is no logical connection between these various meanings, nor is there any genetically determined connection between the meanings and the sound. They are simply arbitrary usages adopted by the members of certain societies.

Further evidence that symbols are determined by their users and not by genes is the ease with which we alter them. When Chaucer wrote "Hir nose tretis, hir yen greye as glas," he meant to say—in fact, he did say—"Her nose well-formed, her eyes gray as glass." English-speaking people have simply altered many of their symbols since his day. Slang is created by the reverse procedure: the symbol itself remains unchanged, but it is given a new meaning. The words "bread" and "dough," for example, have both come to be used to refer to money.

Although linguistic symbols are the most basic and important, they are not the only kind we use. Anything to which humans assign a meaning becomes a symbol. Thus, the cross has become a symbol of Christianity, the hammer and sickle a symbol of Russian communism. Every nation in the world today has a flag to represent it, and standardized symbols communicate basic traffic directions on highways.

Because they are not genetically determined, symbols can be combined and recombined in countless ways to form symbol systems of fantastic complexity, subtlety, and flexibility. The only limits are set by the physical characteristics of those who use them, that is, by the efficiency and capacity of the human brain and nervous system and the accuracy of our senses. And symbol systems help to overcome even these limitations. For example, our species' memory (i.e., its capacity for storing information) has been greatly increased by the use of written symbols and written records.

In the final analysis, the importance of symbol systems lies not in what they are, but in what they have made it possible for our species to become. Although we are all born into the human family, we become fully human only through the use of symbols. Without them, we are unable to develop the unique qualities we associate with humanness. For symbols are more than a means of communication: they are tools

Fifteen Ways to Say "I Love You"

Because there is no necessary connection between the sounds people make
and their meaning, different languages use different combinations of sounds
to express the same idea. Thus, every language has its own distinctive way
of saying "I love you." In some languages, the phrase varies slightly when
a woman addresses a man; these variants are shown in parentheses.

Arabic: Ana b'hibbik (Ana b'hibbak)
Cambodian: Bon sro lanh oon
Chinese: Wo ai ni
Danish: Jeg elsker Dig
English: I love you
French: Je t'aime
German: Ich liebe dich
Hebrew: Ani ohev otakh (Ani ohevet otkhah)
Hindi: Maiñ tumheñ piyar karta huñ
Hungarian: Szeretlek
Italian: Ti voglio bene
Japanese: Watakushi-wa anata-wo aishimasu
Korean: Tangsinŭl sarang hä yo
Navaho: Ayór ánósh'ní
Russian: Ya tebya liubliu

Source: Charles Berlitz, *Native Tongues* (London: Panther, 1984), p. 54.

with which we think and plan, dream and remember, create and build, calculate, speculate, and moralize.

The difference between a human mind without symbols and that same mind
with them is eloquently described in Helen Keller's account of her early life.[13] Miss
Keller became both deaf and blind before she learned to talk. By the age of seven,
after years without meaningful communication with other people, she had become
very much like a wild animal. Then, a gifted teacher, Anne Sullivan, began trying to
communicate with her by spelling words into her hands. Helen learned several words,
but she did not yet comprehend the real significance of symbols. Finally, in a moment
that both women later described in moving terms, Helen suddenly realized that *everything* had a name, that *everything* could be communicated with symbols! In her
own words, she felt "a thrill of returning thought." At last, the world that exists only
for symbol users began to open to her.

Miss Keller's experience helps us understand why the ancients, in their accounts
of creation, so often linked the beginning of language with the beginning of the world.
One of the oldest written texts from Egypt, for example, tells how Ptah, the creator of

the world and the greatest of the gods, "pronounced the names of all things" as a central part of his act of creation.[14] Language also figures prominently in Chinese and Hindu creation myths. The book of Genesis tells us that the first thing Adam did after he was created was to name all the beasts and birds; and the Gospel According to St. John opens with the lines "In the beginning was the Word, and the Word was with God, and the Word was God." Significantly, the original Greek for "word" was *logos*, which meant not merely word, but meaning and reason. And *logos* is the root of our own word "logic," and of the suffix *-logy*, used to denote science, as in biology or sociology.

The German scientist Alexander von Humboldt once said, "No words, no world," and it is true that the human world, the world of human societies, would not exist without words. Without words and other symbols, human societies would differ little from the societies of other primates, for they would lack their most distinctive feature: culture. *With* symbols, every society has developed its own rich and distinctive heritage to supplement its genetic heritage.

In the chapters that follow, we will explore in detail the impact of these cultural heritages and see how they have influenced human life. First, however, we need to pull together the several elements of our analysis to this point.

HUMAN SOCIETIES: THE BASIC MODEL

The aim of ecological–evolutionary theory, as we have seen, is to understand why human societies are the way they are. Like every theory, it starts with certain assumptions. It assumes that human societies are, on the one hand, part of the world of nature and, at the same time, unique in a number of fundamental ways.

One of the tools that can help us in analyzing societies and in constructing theories about them is a technique known as *modeling*, which expresses hypothesized cause and effect relationships in a detailed and explicit manner. Modeling compels us to be precise about the relationships involved in a theory—more precise than we might otherwise be. One way of doing this is to construct models in the form of mathematical equations that express these relationships. This method is used widely in physics and economics, and sometimes also in sociology. Another method, and one that is especially well suited to *macro*sociology, expresses relationships by means of visual diagrams.

In the chapters that follow, we will present a number of models in diagrammatic form as a means of summarizing various aspects of ecological–evolutionary theory. Since some of the relationships involved are complex, some of the models will also be complex.

Our first model, however, is quite simple. But it is extremely important because it identifies the most basic determinants, or causes, of the characteristics of human societies as understood by ecological–evolutionary theory. As Figure 1.4 indicates, this theory asserts that all of a society's characteristics are ultimately due to just three things: (1) the influence of its biophysical and social environments, (2) the influence of our

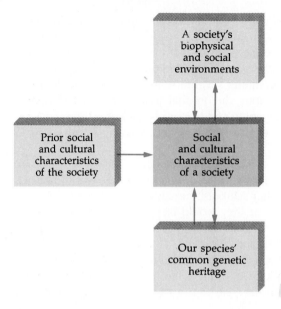

FIGURE 1.4 Ecological–evolutionary model of the determinants of the characteristics of human societies.

species' genetic heritage, and (3) the influence of prior social and cultural character- istics of the society itself. The model also indicates that human societies have an effect both on their environments and on our species' genetic heritage.

In the chapters that follow, we will *amplify and extend* this basic model, adding greater detail. In Chapter 2, for example, we will examine the middle box on the right side of Figure 1.4 to see just what those characteristics are. In Chapter 3 we will see why and how human societies change. This will provide us with the information we will need in Chapter 4 to "map" the principal types and varieties of societies that have evolved over the course of the last 100,000 years.

From that point on we will examine each of the major types of societies and see how the forces of change have transformed human societies over the course of his- tory. Throughout the process, we will gradually extend our basic model by incorpo- rating into it, and into our theory, the more interesting features and complexities of human life.

2

Human Societies as Sociocultural Systems

One of the fascinations of human societies is their diversity. In any other social species, one society is remarkably like the next in size, complexity, and the activities of its members. This is hardly surprising, of course, in view of the fact that one society is also remarkably like the next in its genetic heritage and that this heritage determines the great majority of the species' characteristics.

Why, then, are human societies, which *also* have similar genetic heritages, so different from one another in so many ways? Why are some huge and organizationally complex, while others are small and simple? And why are the activities of their members often so varied? Why, for example, are the members of some societies warlike, while the members of others are relatively peaceful? Why are some puritanical in relations between the sexes, while others are much more permissive?

The explanation of the tremendous variations among human societies is that their common genetic heritage enables them to develop very different cultural heritages. Without their cultures, human societies, too, would all be essentially alike. But with culture comes an extraordinary potential for diversity.

Because our societies, unlike those of other species, are both social *and* cultural units, sociologists and other social scientists often refer to them as *sociocultural* systems. This contraction of the two words is partly a convenience. But it is more than that: it is a reminder that the social and cultural aspects of human life are inextricably intertwined.

HUMAN SOCIETIES AS SYSTEMS

The term *system*, which we have just linked with "sociocultural" and which appears frequently in sociological writing, is a simple word with a profound meaning. It can be applied to a wide variety of things, many of them in the world of nature. There are physical systems, such as the solar system, star systems, weather systems, and systems of lakes and rivers. Every living organism is a system. And there are systems *within* organisms (digestive, reproductive, etc.), systems *of* organisms (populations, societies), and systems that include organisms and their environments (ecosystems). Then there are the systems created by humans: mechanical systems (cars, pianos), political systems, linguistic systems, mathematical systems, irrigation systems, and transportation systems. In every instance, the term refers to *an entity made up of interrelated parts*.

The key word in this definition is "interrelated." In the words of one expert, a system is a "bundle of relations."[1] For this reason, what happens to one of the component parts of a system has implications for other parts and for the system as a whole. Too much beer in the stomach has repercussions for the brain, for example, just as the alignment of an automotive system's wheels affects its steering. Francis Thompson, the poet, captured the systemic qualities of the universe itself in his line, "Thou canst not stir a flower without troubling of a star."[2]

The meaning of the concept *system* is best understood, however, if we focus on a smaller, more specific "bundle of relations," such as the mechanism of a watch. In working order, this entity is a mechanical system. Each of its components (gears, dial, hands, etc.) is also an entity—and each remains an entity even if the mechanism is dismantled. But when the relations among these components have been destroyed, the entity that is *the system* ceases to exist. A system, then, is clearly more than the sum of its parts: it is the sum of its parts *plus all of the relations among them*.

Systems vary greatly in the degree to which the functions of the parts are coordinated with one another and with the functioning of the system as a whole. Using this as a criterion, mechanical systems are some of the most nearly "perfect" systems known. Consider the watch mechanism again. Each component exists, and each functions, for one purpose only: the purpose for which *the system* exists and functions (i.e., to mark the passage of time). Moreover, each component relates only to the other parts of its own system, and its operation is totally dependent upon theirs.

It should come as no surprise, then, to note that, insofar as *systemic* qualities are concerned, the societies of some species resemble a watch more than they resemble human societies. The activities that go on in the honeybee's social system, for example, are as beautifully coordinated as gears and dials: they all serve the interests of the system (i.e., the society as a whole) and demonstrate a nearly total interdependence among the parts. The bees' genetic heritage is clearly a blueprint for a harmonious social system.

The situation is quite different in human societies. For one thing, the coordination among their component parts is often poor. For another, their components do not always function in ways that are conducive to the well-being of the system itself (i.e., the society). For example, their members are individualistic and often self-assertive, resist efforts to coordinate and control their behavior, and do not readily subordinate their needs to the needs of the group. In short, a genetic blueprint that is very different from the honeybee's, but just as compelling, *prevents* human societies from achieving the strict ordering of relations that characterizes some systems.

FIGURE 2.1 Mechanical devices, such as a watch, are nearly "perfect" systems.

There must, however, be enough cooperation among the members of a human society, and the various parts of the system must function smoothly enough, for *the basic needs of the system itself* to be met. The alternative is the dissolution of that "bundle of relations" that is the society.

This creates problems, because the needs of the system and those of its members are not necessarily the same. For example, an individual does not have to have children in order to satisfy his or her basic survival needs, but a society is doomed if it fails to produce new members to replace each older generation as it dies off. Similarly, individuals can violate their society's laws and moral codes and survive, even prosper; but no society can endure unless it fights such violations and keeps antisocial and disruptive behavior in check.

In response to the multiplicity of needs of both individuals and societies, untold numbers of social and cultural answers have evolved. Although these answers have always been imperfect, they are fascinating in their diversity and complexity.

THE FIVE BASIC COMPONENTS OF HUMAN SOCIETIES

To understand how these social and cultural answers develop, we need to consider the five basic components that are present in every human society: (1) population, (2) culture, (3) material products, (4) social organization, and (5) social institutions. Although we will examine each one separately, these components cannot actually be isolated from one another. Because they exist only in interaction with one another in a society, it is impossible to discuss any one of them without reference to the rest. We will, however, disentangle them as best we can.

Population

Population, the first basic component of society, is a term that refers to *the members of a society considered collectively*. In analyzing human societies, there are three aspects of population that must be taken into account: (1) the genetic constants, (2) the genetic variables, and (3) the demographic variables.

Genetic Constants   The genetic constants of a population are those characteristics that reflect our species' *common genetic heritage*. As the word "constants" implies, these traits are the same for every society and, for all practical purposes, the same from one generation to the next.

Specifying the genetically based traits that are shared by people everywhere is not an easy task. First, there is simply no way that scientists can observe and study the biological component of human life without cultural influences getting in the way.

The second problem in drawing up a list of our common genetic traits lies in the complexity of genetics itself. Scientists are still a very long way from fully understanding the subject. One thing that is clear, however, is that most observable traits—for example, a physical characteristic or behavioral tendency—do not result from the action of a single gene, but rather from the interaction of *a number of different genes*. Any given gene, meanwhile, usually affects not just a single trait, but *a number of different traits*. To compound the problem further, the influence of genes can be modified by environmental factors.

Several illustrations may help to make the complexity of the problem clear. First, despite much debate it is still not clear whether the difference in performance of men and women on certain kinds of aptitude tests is the result of early cultural influences, of genetics, or of some combination of the two. Similarly, homosexuality, long considered to be entirely the product of cultural influences, is now suspected of being, at least in part, the result of hormonal influences on the fetus at a critical point in pregnancy. And schizophrenia, autism, and other mental and emotional illnesses once blamed entirely on poor parenting and other cultural factors have now been found to have genetic bases.

Obviously, there is a great deal we do not understand about the influence of genetics on human life. We know enough, however, to put to rest the once-popular "tabula rasa" hypothesis.[3] Proponents of this view claimed that the minds of newborn infants are like blank slates, totally devoid of content, and that human thought and action are due entirely to social and cultural influences experienced after birth.

This idea has long had great appeal because, if it were true, it should be possible for careful social planning to eliminate most of the ills of the world. If societies can make people selfish, cruel, and aggressive, they should also be able to make them kind, compassionate, and caring.

Today, however, after more than a century of disappointments resulting from efforts to transform "human nature," and thanks to insights provided by the new sciences of genetics and primatology, it is clear that people and their societies are profoundly influenced by the genetic heritage of our species *as well as* by their cultures.[4] The unattractive aspects of human life, no less than the attractive ones, inevitably reflect this ancient evolutionary heritage and seem destined to remain a part of the human scene for a long time to come.*

With these cautions and considerations in mind, what can be said about the genetic constants?

First, it is clear that *our species' common genetic heritage confronts the members of every society with the same basic physical needs*. These include needs—for food, water, sleep, warmth, and oxygen—that must be satisfied if we are merely to survive. In addition, there are a variety of other needs that vary in intensity from individual to individual, and from stage to stage within an individual's life. Among these are sexual needs, the need for play, the need for new experience, and the need for social experience, all of which have been shown to have a genetic basis.†[5]

Second, *humans everywhere develop a variety of derivative needs and desires that reflect their social and cultural experiences as well as their genetic heritage*. Because these experiences vary from society to society and among individuals within the same society, the nature and intensity of the needs also vary. But all of us tend to develop at least minimally the need or desire to control the people and events that affect us; to possess things; to give and receive affection; to express ourselves; to be respected and admired; to have emotional, aesthetic, or spiritual experiences; and to discern order and meaning in life.

Third, *the members of every society have the same basic physiological resources to use in satisfying their needs*. These include such obvious physical equipment as legs, fingers, teeth, ears, bowels, heart, brain, and so on. Of these, the brain is an especially impressive resource: it provides us with the means of recording information equivalent to the content of a thousand twenty-four-volume sets of the *Encyclo-*

---

*This does not mean, of course, that nothing can be done about the unpleasant aspects of human behavior. Every society takes steps to discourage and suppress them, and always with some success. But both modern history and our knowledge of genetics indicate that there are limits to what societies can achieve in this regard.

†Newborn infants, for example, have a decided preference for visual variety and contrast in their surroundings and a "bias to explore" that is manifest from the moment of birth. Newborns also have such a powerful need for social contact and the stimulation it provides that when this is denied, their health often suffers and they may even die.[6]

FIGURE 2.2 Human infants are born with a powerful need for the stimulation of social contact, for new experience, and even for play.

paedia Britannica and is far more densely packed with information than any computer.[7] In addition, we are genetically programmed for the automatic performance of a variety of activities (e.g., digestion, ovulation, circulation, growth) and have many valuable reflex actions and response sets (e.g., we automatically draw back without conscious thought when touching something hot).

Fourth, *humans are all dependent on the societal mode of life, especially during the formative years.* The human infant is born in a condition of extreme immaturity and helplessness compared with other animals. In fact, for its first year its development includes processes such as brain growth and bone hardening that are part of *fetal* development in other primates.*[8] Maturation proceeds at an unusually slow pace, and humans require much longer to reach maturity than the young of other species. Even as adults, most of us are unable to satisfy our basic needs except as members of some society.

Fifth, as we have already seen, *we humans have an immense capacity for learning, and for modifying our behavior in response to what we learn.* The result is a remarkable flexibility and adaptability of behavior, and freedom from the constraints of genetically programmed behavior which so restricts the lives of most other ani-

---

*The reason humans enter the world in this immature state is apparently due to brain size. If infants were to develop in the womb the additional months it would take for them to become more mature, their greater head size would make birth impossible.

| Motor | Visual | Somatic sensory |
| Auditory | Olfactory | Cerebral cortex |

Ground shrew   Tree shrew   Tarsius   Chimpanzee   Human

FIGURE 2.3 The human brain is an impressive resource: it can record as much information as 1,000 twenty-four-volume sets of the *Encyclopaedia Britannica*. Compare the size of the cortex of humans with that of other primates.

mals. Thus, we can devise a variety of alternative patterns of action for virtually any situation confronting us.

Sixth, *humans everywhere have the capacity to create and use symbol systems and cultures*. This uniquely human ability is dependent on a variety of genetically based attributes, including such organs of speech as lips, tongue, palate, sinuses, and vocal cords. Equally important, however, are peculiarities of the human brain, specifically those areas of the cerebral cortex that control speech and abstract thought.[9] Most linguists now believe that, despite the many differences among the 3,000 spoken languages humans employ, there is a single underlying structure that is shared by all and is part of our common genetic heritage.[10]

Seventh, *humans have a highly developed awareness of self and an acute consciousness of their situation with respect to the rest of the world*. This is both a blessing and a curse. Because of it, we are able to picture ourselves in situations we have never experienced, and thus plan for the future and develop goals. But with this awareness and foresight comes the realization that we are responsible for our actions, and thus we acquire the capacity for making moral judgments and creating a moral order. A famous geneticist once observed that no other animal has to bear anything comparable to the tragic discord that self-awareness has created for humans.[11]

Eighth, *our species' heritage includes powerful emotions and appetites inherited from remote prehuman ancestors*. These are preserved in the portion of our brain that physiologists refer to as "the old brain" or "the animal brain." The precise nature of the relation of the old brain to the cerebral cortex, the reasoning part of the brain, has yet to be determined. But it is obvious that under conditions of stress our emotions often take control of our actions and rationality is sacrificed—or forced to serve ends dictated by our emotions.

Ninth, and finally, *humans are powerfully motivated to put their own needs and desires ahead of those of others, especially when the stakes are high*.[12] The genetic basis of this becomes obvious when we compare human societies with the societies of the social insects. Social relations in the latter are invariably harmonious because these creatures are genetically programmed to respond to other members of their society in a totally cooperative and altruistic manner. Individuality in these insects is genetically suppressed.

From an evolutionary standpoint, individuality, self-awareness, and self-serving behavior all appear to be by-products of our species' tremendous dependence on learning. Learning, by its very nature, is a differentiating and individuating experience. No two individuals can possibly share exactly the same set of experiences over the course of their lives, and since experience shapes both our values and our perceptions of ourselves, a highly developed awareness of self and self-serving behavior become unavoidable. This does not prevent us from cooperating with one another, since most of us discover in infancy and early childhood that the benefits of cooperation usually exceed the costs. Thus, enlightened self-interest ensures a substantial amount of cooperation in every human society.

The late Abraham Maslow, a psychologist, once theorized that there is a genetically based hierarchy of needs that each of us possesses. Our physiological needs are the most basic, followed by the need for safety, and then, in turn, by the need to belong and be loved, the need for esteem and respect, and the need for self-actualization.[13] The more basic needs, according to Maslow, remain dominant in a person's life until they are satisfied, but the more fully they are met, the more compelling the higher needs become. Thus, the most urgent need of one accustomed to having all of his or her physical and safety needs met will be the need to be loved and accepted by others. And the person whose needs are satisfied in every other respect may be driven by the need for "self-actualization"—the need for self-expression, perhaps, or for power, or for esthetic experience. Although Maslow's theory is still unproven, it suggests how a common genetic heritage could produce such varied values and behavior as we find in human societies.

As many great novelists and poets have recognized, a powerful tension is built into the very fabric of human life: Homo sapiens is, by nature, both a social animal and an individualistic, self-centered animal. It is this more than anything else that creates the drama in human life, and the uncertainties. And it is this which justifies one early sociologist's characterization of human societies as systems of "antagonistic cooperation."[14]

Genetic Variables In addition to the core of traits which all humans share and which make up the major portion of everyone's genetic heritage, each of us also has thousands of genes that are absent, or occur in somewhat different forms, in other individuals. Because these genes are not distributed equally among societies and their populations, there are *variable* aspects to the genetic heritage of human societies. These include skin color, hair texture, eye shape, blood type, incidence of color blindness, taste sensitivity, and susceptibility to various diseases, to name a few of those that have been identified thus far.[15] The *direct* impact of these variables on the life of human societies appears to have been of limited importance. However, because of social and cultural responses to them, such as ethnic stereotyping and prejudice, their *indirect* effects have often been substantial.

Although prior to the modern era human populations in different regions of the world had no direct contact with one another and therefore could not interbreed for long periods, no fully human group was ever isolated long enough, or became genetically differentiated enough, to become a separate species. During prolonged pe-

FIGURE 2.4 Human populations became genetically differentiated in a number of highly visible ways during prolonged periods when interbreeding was not possible: compare the height, body build, hair type, and skin color of the Eskimo with the Masai tribesman from Kenya.

riods of isolation, however, human populations did become genetically differentiated in a number of highly visible ways, such as skin, hair, and eye color; hair type; body build; and shape of face and head. These differences, which tend to be interrelated, eventually became the basis of our modern concept of race. A *race* is simply a part of the human population in which some combination of these highly visible traits occurs with a frequency that is appreciably different from that of other parts of the human population. Racial differences, it may be noted, are found in many species, not just in humans.[16]

Members of modern societies often have difficulty appreciating the adaptive value of racial characteristics, because we no longer depend on them for our survival or well-being. When we encounter unpleasantly strong sunlight, for example, we adapt *culturally*: we create artificial shade or we apply artificial "pigment" to our eyes (sunglasses) and to our skin (suntan oil). Throughout most of human history, however, a population's *genetic* attributes were its primary means of adapting to the hazards of its environment, and even minor variations in relevant characteristics, such as the ability to store body fat as an insulation against extreme cold, could determine which individuals survived and which did not.

This explains why many genetic variables, from skin color to body and facial form, are not randomly distributed across the globe, but occur in discernible geographical patterns.[17] For example, the pigment in our skin determines how dark it is and protects underlying cells from exposure to ultraviolet light. Darker skin is universal in hot, sunny regions, with the heaviest pigmentation of all in the African Sudan, where solar radiation is the most intense and constant.[18] In contrast, light pigmentation in countries with limited sunshine facilitates the synthesis of vitamin D, which protects a person against rickets.[19]

The "sickling gene," found chiefly in populations of Africa, the Middle East, and India, in areas where a particularly deadly form of malaria occurs, provides a somewhat different illustration of the adaptive value of genetic variables. An individual who inherits this gene from *both* parents will develop sickle-cell anemia, a disease that is normally fatal before adulthood. But a far greater number of people in the population inherit the gene from only one parent, develop only mild symptoms of the anemia, and are highly resistant to certain virulent forms of malaria. Thus, in areas with a high incidence of malaria, the sickling gene has had great adaptive value: its benefits have clearly outweighed its costs.[20]

Most genetic variables are not as easy to identify as the ones we have discussed so far. This is because most of our characteristics result from the action of more than one gene and are not determined by genes alone. Genes provide the *potential*, but the reality is determined by the interaction of genes and environment. Complicating matters, environment also includes the intrauterine environment of the prenatal period, even the preconception experience of sperm and egg. This interaction of genetics and environment has been dramatically illustrated many times, as in the case of Jewish children born in Israeli kibbutzim and Japanese children born in America who, because of better diets, tower over parents born in the ghettos of Europe and in Japan. It is clear that most biological characteristics, from longevity to musical aptitude, are shaped by both genes and environment. But so far, at least, efforts to separate the two and measure their relative influence have proved frustrating and unprofitable.

One thing has been clarified, however: the relation between racial and nonracial genetic variables. Studies have been made, for example, of color blindness and blood characteristics, which are variables that can be precisely identified and are minimally affected by environmental factors, and whose gene frequency in a population can therefore be accurately calculated. When the distributions of these genes are plotted geographically, they cut across racial lines. For example, the frequency of the gene for type B blood is essentially the same among the south Chinese, Russians, and west Africans.[21] Findings like these make it clear that the traits used to define race are an extremely limited set of variables that are not correlated to any appreciable degree with other genetic variables that have been carefully analyzed.

Demographic Variables The demographic properties of a population include such things as its size, its density, how it is dispersed or concentrated (e.g., to what extent its members are concentrated in a few areas or spread out more evenly over its entire territory), the patterns of migration into and out of the society, its composition in terms of age and sex, and its birth and death rates. These characteristics, like certain clusters of genes, vary from one society to another. But these variations, unlike most genetic variations, have direct, demonstrable, and far-reaching consequences for human societies.

Population size is the most variable of the demographic properties of human societies, which have ranged in numbers from 20 members or less (in some preliterate societies of the recent past) to more than 1 billion (China's current population). Variations in other demographic characteristics often appear insignificant beside such variations in size. For example, two societies with stable populations (i.e., neither growing in size nor declining) and with annual death rates of 14 per 1,000 and 40 per 1,000, respectively, may not seem very different. But this variation actually means that the average life expectancy at birth of the members of the first society is seventy-one years, and of the second only twenty-five years!

In later chapters we will have frequent occasion to consider demographic variables, since they play an important part in the evolution of human societies. By contrast, we will have very little to say from here on about the genetic variables discussed in the previous section, since there is little to indicate that they have played a significant role in societal evolution.

Culture

The second basic component of every sociocultural system is culture, a *society's symbol systems and the information they convey*. As we saw in Chapter 1, symbols are information conveyers that enable us to handle information in ways that are impossible for other creatures. We can *extract* more information from an experience (i.e., *learn* more) because symbols permit us thought processes denied other species. We can also *share* more information, because symbols enable us to express so much of the subtlety, complexity, and diversity of our experiences. We can, in fact, do more with information *whatever* is involved: in recording it, accumulating it, storing it, combining it, or applying it, symbol users have a fantastic advantage over signal users.

The symbol systems and store of information that comprise a society's culture are like a foundation laid down by previous generations. Because each new generation has this base on which to build, it can avoid repeating many of the experiences of earlier generations. If a group has already learned how to make and use fire, or invented the plow, or devised a system of numbers, its members need not repeat the time-consuming and often difficult process by which that particular element of culture was first acquired. Instead, they can address new challenges, which may result in further enrichment or modification of their culture.

We will examine both of the basic parts of culture in some detail, beginning with symbol systems.

Symbol Systems The most basic symbol systems in any society are its *spoken languages.** No matter how many other symbol systems a society creates, these are the ones its members use in their basic thought processes, and the ones that bear the major burden of transmitting information among them.

At the heart of every spoken language is an enormous set of social conventions, or customary practices, that constitute its vocabulary and grammar. The vocabulary is a set of sounds with meanings attached to them, and the relationship between a sound and its meaning is embedded in the history of its use by those who share that language. To those who speak English, the word "bed" means a place to sleep, not because of any logical or necessary connection between the sound and the activity, but because this is the convention that has evolved in English-speaking populations. Similarly, grammatical conventions tell us how words must be combined if they are to be meaningful and intelligible to others. Thus, it means one thing to say, "The bear ate Jack," something quite different to say, "Jack ate the bear," and nothing at all to say, "The ate bear Jack."

Until we study a foreign language, most of us have the impression that there is something natural—even inevitable—about the way our own society and its language separate experience and thought into the bits of meaning we call words, and that learning another language is only a matter of learning the sounds another society applies to those same "units of experience." Yet as people conversant in two or more languages are well aware, words in one do not necessarily have an equivalent in the other. Americans and Russians were reminded of this some years ago during talks between President Kennedy and Chairman Khrushchev. Kennedy repeatedly said that the Russians should not miscalculate the will and intentions of the American people, and every time the word "miscalculate" was translated, Khrushchev flushed angrily. Kennedy later learned that the Russian language has no precise equivalent of this word, and the translator had seized on a Russian word, normally applied to a small child or uneducated person, meaning "unable to count." Khrushchev naturally assumed that Kennedy was implying he was not very bright![22]

One reason languages separate experience into different units is because the experiences of the people who *create* and *use* the languages are so different. For example, gauchos, the famous horsemen of the Argentine prairies, have 200 words to denote the different colors of horses, but only 4 for all the plants known to them: *pasto*, fodder; *paja*, bedding; *cardo*, wood; and *yuyos*, all others.[23] Meanwhile, the Eskimos have numerous terms to refer to the various phenomena that we call simply "snow." They have one word for dry-wind-driven snow, one for dry-packed-suitable-for-cutting-into-blocks-and-building-igloos snow, another for ice-crust-surface snow, and so on.[24] In yet another part of the world, the Dugum Dani, Stone Age horticulturists on the island of New Guinea, have seventy different words that refer to sweet

---

*Many societies have, or have had, two or more languages. Even those with a single language have often had multiple dialects that were mutually unintelligible.

potatoes, their staple crop,[25] and in the Middle East, Arabic is reputed to have a thousand words for sword, indicative of that culture's stress on poetry and emphasis on synonyms and figures of speech.[26] English is a language rich in numbers and units of measurement, perfect for describing and recording mathematical and scientific data. In short, a language reflects the needs, concerns, and experiences of those who use it.

Another reason languages differ in the way they categorize and classify experience is the haphazard and spontaneous manner in which they evolve. Consider the evolution of the word "bureau," for example. A bureau was originally something made of baize, a thick green cloth. Because these bureaus were often put on writing tables and chests of drawers, the word was eventually extended to mean the furniture as well as the cloth. Later, because many government offices were equipped with bureaus, or writing tables, the offices themselves came to be known by that term (e.g., the Federal Bureau of Investigation).[27]

This process of change in language is so much a matter of chance that it is unlikely that the same pattern would occur in two societies. Even if two societies begin with the same language, as when a small group separates from the parent group to settle a new territory, linguistic differences are bound to develop unless an extremely high level of communication is maintained between them. There is no better example of this in the modern era than in the differences between English as it is spoken in England, Australia, Canada, Jamaica, and the United States. To Australians, for example, "Don't come the raw prawn," means "Don't try to put one over on me," and "Fair and dinkum" means "True and honest."

So far we have discussed spoken language as if it were merely a neutral and passive vehicle for transmitting information. But as political leaders, propagandists, and advertisers have long recognized, individual words often acquire, through the process of association, powerful emotional connotations that enable them to convey more than is embodied in their formal definitions. Words like "communist," "racist," and "sexist," for example, have such strong negative associations for many Americans that they respond unthinkingly to the emotional content of these symbols. Words can also acquire strong positive associations, and these, too, may be used to manipulate emotions. For example, linking kinship terms with organizations, as in "Mother Russia," "Mother Church," or "Uncle Sam," can stimulate warm feelings of affection.

A leading linguist of the last generation, Edward Sapir, went so far as to claim that the way people perceive reality "is to a large extent unconsciously built upon the language habits of the group," and that, as a result, different societies live in different worlds, "not merely the same world with different labels attached."[28] Though few scholars would go this far, they recognize that language is a vital part of human experience and helps to determine what we feel, what we perceive, and what we do.[29]

Supplementing its spoken language, every society uses conventional gestures and facial expressions whose meanings are evident to members of the group. This second kind of symbol system, *body language*, should not be confused with such facial expressions and body movements as our involuntary reaction when we touch something hot, or the way we pucker up when we taste something bitter. These are genetically determined signals. True body language is symbolic, just as words are, for the form and meaning of the gestures and expressions are determined by those who use them. Consider, for example, the shrug of the shoulders. Various groups use it to convey indifference, uncertainty, or a lack of information on the subject in question, with the specific meaning being indicated by the context in which it is used.

Body language may be the oldest type of symbol used by our species, and it probably once played a greater role in communication than it does today. Yet even now it can be an invaluable source of information: people convey so much with a smile or frown, a tilt of the head, a movement of the hands. This is one reason many of us avoid the telephone when we have an emotionally charged message to deliver, such as news of the death of a loved one. We know we can communicate our own feelings more effectively and read those of others more clearly when we combine words, body language, and signals.

A third kind of symbol system in many societies is *written language*, a relatively recent development in human history. Some of the oldest written records in existence today were prepared thousands of years ago by temple authorities in Mesopotamia to enable them to keep a record of business transactions.[30] These priests were stewards of their god's resources, and when they loaned out his animals or grain, it was imperative to get them back again. Even though the priest who made a loan might die, the god expected it to be repaid. To keep track of their god's property and thereby avoid his wrath, the priestly community devised a primitive system of writing that involved a mixture of numerals, pictographs, and ideograms.

The arbitrary and symbolic nature of this writing is clear. Even when a pictograph (essentially a picture) was used to represent a bull, it was a stylized representation that excluded many of the animal's features that might have been included. Moreover, the same features were used consistently, indicating that conventional forms of notation had already been established. From a very early date, the pictograph of a jar came to represent a certain quantity of grain, rather than the jar itself. And finally, among these early examples of writing are a number of ideograms, which are "pure" symbols, since they are completely arbitrary and based solely on convention. They lack any visual resemblance to the objects they represent, just as the dollar sign bears no resemblance to the currency it symbolizes.

FIGURE 2.5 Two sides of a limestone tablet found in Iraq, bearing some of the oldest known writing (about 3500 B.C.). Included are symbols for head, hand, foot, threshing sledge, and several numerals.

As new uses for writing were discovered, new efforts were made to translate spoken language into written form. At an early date kings and princes recorded their military triumphs for posterity, priests their sacred rites and traditions. At first, as the Mesopotamian priests' experience makes clear, a society's written symbols could express only a small part of what was possible with its verbal symbols. Gradually, however, written languages developed until they were able to convey the same information as spoken ones, and writing came into its own as a means of storing information, for communication across the barriers of space and time, and eventually as a medium of artistic expression, education, and entertainment.

As societies have acquired more information, it has often become necessary to go beyond such basic symbols as letters and numerals. Thus, new symbol systems have evolved that greatly facilitate the handling of specialized kinds of information. For example, musicians devised musical notation so they could express the information that they create and use, and mathematicians and scientists developed a wide variety of symbol systems to express abstract ideas, complex numbers, and so on. The specialized symbol systems now found in modern societies include languages for the deaf, the blind, engineers, stenographers, computer scientists, and others too numerous to mention.

Over the course of history, the relative importance of the three basic types of language—body, spoken, and written—has altered considerably. Body language, including symbolic gestures and facial expressions, may well have been dominant among our very early ancestors, declining only when true speech evolved. Then, until quite recently, verbal symbols remained the primary means of transmitting information from one person to another and from one generation to the next. With the invention of the printing press and the subsequent spread of literacy, written language steadily increased in relative importance, largely because it could overcome space and time, the historic barriers to communication. During the last century, thanks to such devices as the telephone, radio, motion pictures, and television, spoken language, too, has overcome those barriers, altering the balance once again. And in the most recent, most dramatic development of all, a great variety of languages have been created for computers, enabling them to handle fantastic amounts of information of diverse kinds. More important than these shifts in the relative importance of different types of language, however, is the fundamental trend that has persisted from early prehistoric times: *the continuing expansion of old symbol systems and the creation of new ones has steadily increased the capacity of human societies to handle information.*

Information Cultural information is *knowledge acquired through experience and conveyed through symbols.* A society's information, is, in effect, a product of its experience: its experiences in the remote past and in the recent past; its experiences with its environment and within itself. Needless to say, no society's culture preserves every experience of every member throughout its entire history. Rather, a society gleans what it or its more influential members consider valuable and attempt to preserve it.

Because every society has a unique past, every culture is unique. We can say this another way: out of diverse experience, diverse information emerges. This means that human societies not only have different amounts of information on a given subject; they frequently have different "facts" as well. Since we know that human senses and intellect are limited and fallible, this should be no surprise. Even hard scientific "facts" must often be revised in the light of later research.

Cultural information is not limited to the kinds of ideas whose truth or accuracy is capable of being proved or disproved, however. It includes a group's total perception of reality: its ideas about what is real, what is true, what is good, what is beautiful, what is important, what is possible. When we discussed symbol systems, we saw that they, too, are so rooted in subjective experience that even individual symbols may become "units of experience"—which explains why a word like "mother" can be so emotionally charged. We also saw that the kind of information conveyed by symbol systems ranges from historical and statistical data to concepts of deity, attitudes toward horses and plants, characteristics of snow, poetic inclinations, even music itself. Cultural information includes, quite literally, *everything humans are capable of experiencing and able to convert into symbolic form*.

Because all human societies have certain fundamental kinds of experiences in common, because their members all have the same basic needs to satisfy, and because all societies have the same system needs, all cultures include information on certain basic subjects:

- Every culture has a substantial store of information about the biophysical environment to which the society must adapt, including its plant and animal life, its soils and terrain, its mineral resources and water supply, its climate and weather conditions.
- Every culture includes information about the group's social environment, the other human societies with which the group has contact.
- Every culture contains information about the society itself: its origin, its people, its heroes, its history.
- Every culture contains information that seeks to explain the ultimate causes of things and events.
- Every culture has information that enables the members to cope with recurring problems, from feeding themselves to resolving intragroup conflict.
- Every culture contains information that guides individuals in making judgments about what is good and what is right and what is beautiful.
- Every culture has information created solely to satisfy culturally activated and intensified needs, such as the desire for artistic expression, for example, or for ritual.

Although this list is neither exhaustive nor detailed, it conveys something of the breadth of culture.

Much of the information contained in cultures is ideological in nature and results from efforts to make sense out of human experience.[31] For *ideology is information used to interpret experience and help order societal life*. Because humans are users of symbols and creatures of culture, life can be overwhelming. We think, feel, hope, enjoy, and suffer as no other creatures can. We imagine what we cannot know and yearn for what may not exist. We live simultaneously in three worlds: the past, the present, and the future. We alone, apparently, live out our lives aware that death

FIGURE 2.6 All cultures contain information created solely to satisfy culturally activated and intensified needs, such as the desire for artistic expression and social rituals: Balinese dancers performing the sacred dance drama of The Witch and The Dragon.

is inevitable. To make things more difficult, we create for ourselves a profusion of cultural alternatives, in the face of which our genetic heritage is an inadequate guide. It is not surprising, therefore, that as individuals we need help in interpreting experience, finding meaning, and making choices. And, as we have seen, societies need help in regulating and ordering their collective life.

Medieval Christianity is a good example of a highly developed and comprehensive ideology, the kind that answers virtually all of these individual and societal needs. At its center was a vision of a universe inhabited by many kinds of spiritual beings (seraphim, cherubim, humans, demons, devils, etc.) mostly under the dominion of God. God was perceived as the King above all earthly kings, but because His authority was challenged by Satan, the prince of evil, people were confronted with a choice as to which to serve. Those who chose God (who would ultimately prevail) were obliged to accept the Church's doctrines and conform to its code of morality. The latter enjoined Christians to be charitable to one another, honest, sober, hardworking, monogamous (better yet, celibate), obedient to all in authority, and regular in devotions and worship. Since no one could adhere perfectly to these requirements, the Church provided opportunities for people to confess their sins, do penance, and obtain absolution.

When we look closely at medieval Christianity, we find the three basic elements that comprise *every* ideology. First, there is a system of *beliefs* about the kind of world we inhabit. Second, there is a system of general *moral values* that emanate from, or are justified by, those beliefs. Finally, there is a system of *norms* that apply those general values to specific situations and spell out how the members of the group are to act in various circumstances, what they should and should not do.

There are two basic kinds of norms in every society, and they have evolved in very different ways. Some are part of official or legal codes of conduct that are enforced by an authority, such as a government, a church, or other organization. We refer to such norms as *laws, regulations*, or *rules*, and they are sometimes accompanied by explicit statements of the sanctions that will be used to punish those who violate them. A city ordinance, for example, may specify a fine of $25 for littering streets or sidewalks.

In contrast, many norms are informal and unofficial, and violations of them are not officially sanctioned. Thus, every society and every subgroup in a society, from corporations to families, has many informal rules, or *customs*, which define for the members acceptable and unacceptable behavior. Customs apply to such diverse things as modes of dress, hairstyles, food preparation, the selection of marriage partners, the performance of various tasks, proper grammar, and attitudes toward children or older people—to name only a few. These informal norms are as important in shaping behavior as more formal ones. Norms and their related *sanctions* (i.e., rewards and punishments) are basic components of every system of social control.

Sometimes it is difficult to determine, or even to imagine, how certain elements of ideology originated, or what they can possibly tell us about the past experience of a society. This is true, for example, of one of the central beliefs of Hinduism, the belief in the sacredness of the cow. The boxed insert explains how this seemingly strange belief has, for centuries, helped the members of Indian society cope with some of their basic and recurring problems in a highly adaptive way.

In very small societies, all of the members usually have common beliefs and values. In larger and more complex societies, however, this is rarely the case. People in different occupational groups, different kinds of communities, and different classes have different interests and different experiences, and these inevitably lead to different beliefs, different values, and different norms. Not infrequently, these differences cause conflicts between the people involved. In extreme cases, as in modern Lebanon and the United States at the time of the Civil War, such conflicts may threaten the very existence of a society.

Another crucial body of information in every culture is *technology*. This is *information about how to use the material resources of the environment to satisfy human needs and desires*. Compared to ideology, technology seems rather prosaic and uninteresting. Historians and social scientists have tended to ignore it,[32] and until recently people seldom came to blows over the relative merits of different technologies. As we will see in coming chapters, however, the influence of technological information on the course of history and on the process of societal change and development has been greatly out of proportion to the recognition usually accorded it.

In every society, a large component of technological information concerns food: where and how to grow it or get it and how to process it for consumption or storage. There is also information about the other material resources available to the society

India's Sacred Cows: The Adaptive Value of an Ideology

In a society where tens of millions of people go to sleep hungry every night, devout Hindus, who constitute the vast majority of India's population, would not dream of killing any of that country's 54 million cows. To a Hindu, even murder is not as great a sacrilege as killing a cow.

Marvin Harris, a leading proponent of ecological–evolutionary theory, examined this seeming paradox in an effort to find a rational explanation. He rejected the view that an ideology evolves arbitrarily, unrelated to the rest of societal life or to the experiences of its members in the past. Rather, he suspected that any belief that has been as widespread and as persistent as the Indian taboo against cow slaughter must have significant adaptive value for the society.

In a volume titled *Cows, Pigs, Wars and Witches: The Riddles of Culture*, Harris reported the results of an analysis of this subject. He found that the cow is of enormous economic value to the members of Indian society. A peasant's cow is, in effect, a factory that provides food (milk, butter); fertilizer; fuel for cooking (dried manure is excellent for this purpose, producing a clean, low heat); flooring material (a paste of manure and water hardens into a smooth surface that holds down dust and can be swept clean); and, most important of all, oxen to pull the peasant's plow. Harris also found that less than 20 percent of the food consumed by Indian cattle is edible by humans. In short, the cow converts substances of little worth to the peasant into extremely valuable products.

Although Indian peasants recognize that a living, productive cow is vastly more valuable to them and to their children than the same cow consumed as food, it would be only natural for them to ignore this fact when they are desperately hungry. The religious taboo against killing cows is a powerful cultural mechanism that helps to protect these animals even in times of famine and thereby preserves an invaluable resource. In short, Hinduism's conception of the cow as sacred is based on the experience of countless generations of the Indian people and continues to serve them well.

and how they may be converted into useful forms—into fuel for heat, cooking, and other purposes; into clothing and shelter; into tools, weapons, ornaments, houses, factories, toys, and other things the group or its members need or value.

Because a distinctive body of information tends to build up in response to each set of human needs, we sometimes speak of various technologies in the same society, such as a military technology or a communications technology. Often, however, we speak of a society's technology in the singular, because there is an underlying unity to this store of information. The principles of metallurgy, for example, are used in virtually every area of technological activity in a modern industrial society.

Material Products

The third component of human societies consists of *the things they produce or obtain through trade*. These products of technology range from perishable items that are consumed within days or even hours, as with many foods, to things that endure for centuries, such as pyramids, cathedrals, and plastic containers. They range, too, from utilitarian objects like hammers and houses to frivolous items like boom boxes and Frisbees.

Energy is easily the most vital product of societal activity, since without a continuous input of it, all activity would come to a halt: even thought requires energy! Food is the most basic source of energy. In societies today the energy resources of food are supplemented by energy obtained from animals, from wind and water, and, in modern industrial societies, from mineral sources (coal, petroleum, natural gas, and uranium).

Many of the material products of human labor are meant only for consumption. Some, however, are created to facilitate the production of other products. These are known as *capital goods* and are a major determinant of a society's wealth. The more capital goods a society possesses, the more goods it is able to produce.

The first capital goods were simple tools and weapons made of stone, wood, and bone which enabled our early ancestors to produce such essentials as fire, food, shelter, and more tools and weapons. Later, as the store of cultural information increased and as new environmental resources became available, the character of tools changed. Metals became especially important because they combined strength and

FIGURE 2.7 The more capital goods a society possesses, the more goods it is able to produce and the wealthier it tends to become: the Krupp steel works at Rheinhausen, West Germany.

durability with malleability. With the domestication of animals, an important new kind of capital good was created. In more recent times, new and enormously productive capital goods have been created in the form of large industrial complexes that utilize sophisticated machines and instruments and are powered by the recently discovered, inanimate forms of energy.

Social Organization

The fourth component of every society is *the network of relationships among its members*. These relationships make it possible for members to satisfy both their own individual needs and the needs of the society as a whole. The latter include the need to replace members who die or leave the group and to equip their successors with the many skills needed to make them productive, contributing members of the group; the need to produce and distribute essential goods and services; the need to hold in check conflicts within the group so that vital relationships can be maintained; and the need to protect members from external threats, whether from the biophysical environment or from other human societies.

Systems of social organization are influenced to some extent by biological differences among the members. Social relationships in all mammalian societies, for example, are organized to take account of age and sex differences. Human societies, however, rarely stop there. In most instances they go much further, developing elaborate kinship networks and other complex social arrangements that reflect cultural influences. Thus, when we think of social organization we must think of it as a product of the interaction of culture and people.

Individuals Every society must cope with a constant turnover in its membership. Older members die and are replaced with newborn infants.* This creates a major problem: although these infants have the same basic genetic resources as the individuals who died, they lack their cultural resources. In other words, none of them knows anything about their society's store of information on matters ranging from religion to technology. Everything must be learned. To put it another way, raw, ignorant "recruits" must somehow be transformed into productive and responsible people who can work cooperatively with others and make a contribution to the group's welfare.

The means by which societies do this is known as *the socialization process*. This is a complex process that begins as soon as the infant is capable of discerning that its actions generate *re*actions by others, and that some of those reactions are pleasant while others are not. Sometimes these reactions are conscious, purposive efforts by parents and others to influence or train the child. But often they are simply unplanned, spontaneous responses—the response, for example, of weary parents who are awakened repeatedly by a cranky baby.

---

*To varying degrees, membership turnover also involves individuals who migrate from one society to another. Emigration and immigration, however, do not alter the basic nature of the problem of member turnover discussed in this section.

Over time, even very young children begin to anticipate the responses of other people and to adjust their behavior accordingly. At this point, they have begun to absorb the culture of their society and to internalize its norms and values. This process continues throughout an individual's life, and comes to include the conscious acquisition of countless skills that can range from brushing one's teeth to programming computers.

The socialization process is never entirely successful in any society. The "concern for self" which is part of our genetic heritage, together with the individuating nature of learning, combine to limit the extent to which people are able to subordinate their personal interests to those of society. All of us are able to rationalize at least some violations of our society's norms. ("It was just a little white lie." "Everybody exceeds the speed limit here.")

Most of the time, however, most individuals, by the time they reach adulthood, conform to their society's standards, partly because of their desire to obtain the rewards and avoid the penalties that can be expected, and partly because they have come to accept their society's standards as their own. In short, they have become contributing members of their society, individuals who are able to fill its various roles.

Roles Roles are *positions in a society that can be filled by individuals*. They develop in response to the recurring needs of the society. Young children, for example, require care and attention, and the roles of mother and father have evolved in response to this need. In large and complex societies, there is a continuing need for political leadership, and a variety of roles, ranging from school board member to president or prime minister, have developed in response.

Roles in society, like roles in the theatre, have distinctive behavioral expectations and requirements attached to them.[33] Thus, just as a man may play the role of Romeo on the stage, so he may "play" the roles of husband, father, and doctor in his home and community. In both instances, people expect him to act in certain ways and not in others, simply because of the roles he occupies. When he meets those expectations, he is applauded or rewarded. When he fails to meet them, he is criticized, or worse.

The behavioral requirements and expectations that are attached to "real life" roles are the norms we discussed on page 36. As we saw then, they may be quite formal, as in the laws forbidding theft and murder, or they may be informal, as in a neighborhood's expectations concerning property maintenance. They may involve fundamental moral issues, or they may involve the minutiae of etiquette. Norms also vary in their scope. Some apply to everyone, as in the law forbidding bigamy in the U.S.; others apply to only a few, as in rules governing the conduct of members of the Canadian Parliament.

As we will see in later chapters, roles change as societies change. New roles are added and older ones disappear. Even when roles persist, their content often changes. Thus, prior to the development of modern technology, the feeding of infants was entirely the work of women. Today, this is a responsibility often shared with men.

Groups In most societies, individuals are organized into a variety of units we call groups. These range from small family units and cliques to giant corporate entities of

FIGURE 2.8 Roles in society are like roles in the theatre: both have distinctive behavioral expectations attached to them. Balcony scene from Shakespeare's *Romeo and Juliet*.

various kinds. In popular usage, the term "group" is often applied to any aggregation of people, regardless of their other characteristics. Sociologists, however, limit the term to *an aggregation whose members (1) cooperate to satisfy common, or complementary, needs; (2) have shared norms; and (3) have a sense of common identity.*

As this definition suggests, human aggregations differ in their *degree* of "groupishness." While some aggregations clearly qualify as groups (e.g., Jehovah's Witnesses) and others just as clearly do not (e.g., all redheads in the United States), many are borderline (e.g., Americans of Irish descent). This last example reminds us that the degree of "groupishness" of an aggregation is not permanently fixed. Aggregations may take on more of the qualities of a group, or they may lose some. Their members may come to work together more closely; develop new, stronger, and more generally shared norms; and acquire a stronger sense of common identity; or just the opposite may occur, as has happened with Irish-Americans during the last hundred years.

Even after we exclude such aggregations as redheads, the concept "group" still includes such a wide variety of organizations that it is necessary to differentiate among them. The most familiar way of doing this is by their basic function in society. Thus, we differentiate between families, churches, schools, political parties, and so forth.

Sociologists have also found it useful to differentiate among groups on the basis of their size and the intensity of the social ties among their members. Small groups in which there are face-to-face relations of a fairly intimate and personal nature are known as *primary groups*. Primary groups are of two basic types, *families* and *cliques*. In other words, they are organized around ties of either kinship or friendship. Larger, more impersonal groups are known as *secondary groups*.

Classes Inequality is a fact of life in every human society. Some individuals always control more of the society's resources than others do and enjoy more than their share of its benefits.

Human societies differ greatly, however, in the amount of inequality present among their members. In some it is minimal, in others it is enormous. In larger and more complex societies, where inequality is always substantial, individuals can be divided into *classes,* or strata, on the basis of their relationship to various social and cultural resources, such as political office, wealth, occupational skills, education, and legal status (e.g., free persons versus slaves). Viewed as a whole, the classes of a society constitute its system of stratification, or class system.[34]

Sociologists and others often find it is enough simply to distinguish between the upper, middle, and lower classes of a society. For some purposes, however, more precise distinctions are needed. Thus, in discussing societies of the past, we often distinguish between nobles and commoners or between free persons and slaves. Similarly, in discussing contemporary societies, we often refer to the working class, the professional class, political elites, and others. In each instance the class or stratum is defined on the basis of *some important attribute* (e.g., legal status, type of job, education) *that is the same for all members of the class and that influences their access to power, privilege, and prestige.*

Not surprisingly, inequality is one of the major sources of conflict within societies. No system of stratification can satisfy everyone, since there is no obviously "right" or "fair" way to distribute power, privilege, and prestige. For example, it is equally reasonable to assert that a given product should be distributed on the basis of (1) how much a person needs it, (2) how much effort a person invests in producing it, or (3) how much skill a person contributes, to name only three of the possibilities.

Even if a society settled on one of these principles in allocating its rewards, disputes are still likely. If members applied the principle of effort, for example, they would still have to decide how to measure effort. Should it be calculated by the hours spent on the job, by the foot-pounds of energy expended, or by how hard a person tries? Or, if the group adopts a different criterion, how do they measure and compare such dissimilar skills as those of a nurse, a computer programmer, and a statesman? In brief, there is no one "right" way to allocate rewards in human societies, and arbitrary standards are inevitable. But arbitrary or not, there must be standards and this leads to inequality and to systems of stratification.

Because of systems of inequality, not everyone has an equal voice in decision making within societies. On the contrary, in many societies a few individuals have vastly more influence on societal policies than others. We need to keep this in mind whenever we discuss the policies and actions of such societies: while leaders make decisions on behalf of, and in the name of, the entire society, most members of the society have often never been consulted. This is a problem even in societies with multiparty political systems and free elections.

Social Institutions and Institutional Systems

Social institutions and institutional systems are the last of the five basic components of human societies. These differ from the other components we have considered in one important respect: they are *combinations of the other four components*. In other words, they bring together population, culture, the material products of culture, and social organization (see Figure 2.9 on page 44).

A British sociologist once described social institutions as "frozen answers to fundamental questions."[35] Although it is an exaggeration to call them "frozen" answers, institutions are durable and persisting elements of sociocultural systems. For purposes of definition, we may think of them as *durable answers to important and persistent problems.*

One reason for their durability is that their value to society is impressed on individuals at an early age. Thus, we grow up thinking of them as natural and inevitable. Another reason for their durability is that the different elements of institutional systems are intricately intertwined and it is often impossible to change one element without being compelled to change countless others, making the cost of change too great.

Modern industrial societies have literally thousands of these "durable answers." Their institutions include such things as marriage, the jury system, secret ballot elections, the rights of private property, the freedom to practice religion or not to practice it as one sees fit, the right to privacy, and many more.

For many purposes, sociologists are less interested in specific social institutions than in institutional systems. As the name implies, *institutional systems* are *systems of interrelated institutions*. Five such systems are of major importance in the study of human societies, and much of our analysis in later chapters, especially Chapters 5 to 16, will be organized around them. They are: (1) kinship, (2) the economy, (3) the polity, (4) religion, and (5) education. These are like major slices of the sociocultural "pie." Each provides answers to a set of interrelated, important, and persistent problems that confront every society. Kinship is the oldest of these systems, but all of them have existed for thousands of years and all seem likely to continue for as long as human societies endure.

THE WORLD SYSTEM OF SOCIETIES

Before we conclude this discussion of human societies as sociocultural systems, there is one more system that needs to be considered. Every human society is, itself, part of

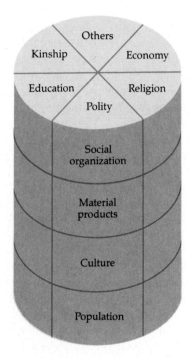

FIGURE 2.9 Relations among the basic components of human societies. Each major institutional system brings together people, culture, the material products of culture, and social organization.

a larger and more inclusive sociocultural system that sociologists have come to call the *world system of societies*.

Throughout history, human societies have established and maintained relations with one another. They have exchanged ambassadors, carried on trade and commerce, sent out missionaries, translated books, exacted tribute, and in countless other ways developed and maintained a network of social and cultural ties. During much of the past, direct ties were limited to neighboring societies, since direct relations with distant societies were not possible. But even then, *indirect* relations existed. Society A maintained ties with Society B, which, in turn, maintained ties with Society C, and so on throughout the system. No society was ever totally cut off from the world system of societies for long, since even the most isolated societies had occasional contacts with others. With advances in transportation and communication during the last 5,000 years, relations between societies increased greatly and direct relations have been established between societies far removed from one another. As a result, the world system of societies has grown more integrated and more complex and has come to exercise an ever-increasing influence on the life of individual societies.

3

The Evolution
of Human Societies

Human life has changed tremendously in recent millennia. Ten thousand years ago all human societies were tiny nomadic groups obliged to forage for the basic necessities of life. The practice of farming had not yet begun, and there were very few permanent settlements of any kind. Most societies were compelled to move every few weeks or months in order to obtain sufficient food. The largest societies at that time had only a few hundred members at most, and the average society had only 25 or 30 members. Recent research indicates that the total human population at that time numbered no more than a few million, divided among 100,000 to 300,000 tiny societies.[1]

Today, conditions are remarkably different. The human population has increased *a thousandfold*, numbering more than 5 billion. The average size of societies has increased *a millionfold* to 25 or 30 million, while the number of societies has dropped precipitously to less than 200. For the vast majority of societies, farming long ago replaced hunting wild animals and foraging for edible plants as the basic means of subsistence. Permanent settlements are almost universal, and there are now a number of cities with populations of 15 million or more.

These are only a few of the more obvious changes that have occurred. There have been thousands of others just as remarkable—changes in ideology and technology and all the other kinds of cultural information; changes in the material products created and used by societies; changes in social organization; and changes in institutions and institutional systems. These changes, which we often forget or take for granted, are especially remarkable if we compare the experience of human societies with that of other primate or other mammalian societies during the same period. Chimpanzee societies today, for example, are hardly distinguishable from chimpanzee societies of 10,000 years ago, and the same is true of insect societies, fish societies, and the rest. Where significant changes have occurred, such as the growth of rat populations or the decline of wolf populations, they are largely the result of human activity, by-products of the changes that have occurred in human societies.

FIGURE 3.1 Ten thousand years ago all human societies were tiny groups obliged to forage for food and other necessities. A few such groups have survived into the twentieth century: Bushmen of southwestern Africa.

Ten thousand years is an enormous amount of time from the perspective of a single human life span, but it is a very short time by evolutionary standards. What has caused such rapid and far-reaching change?

THE GREAT PARADOX

Before we attempt to answer this question, there is a puzzling paradox that must be considered. *Despite the tremendous changes that have occurred in human life during the last 10,000 years, the majority of societies changed very little during their entire existence.* In other words, contrary to what we might infer from the changes that have occurred in the world system of societies—or from our own experience of life in the twentieth century—rapid social and cultural change has been the exception rather than the rule until recently. In most societies, life changed very little from one generation to the next, or even from one century to the next.

When first considered, this paradox seems to be a contradiction, but actually it is not. A system can change greatly even if most of its parts do not change—if the parts that fail to change are simply eliminated from the system.

This is exactly what has happened in the world system of societies. The great majority of individual societies changed very little during the course of their exist-

TABLE 3.1 The Great Paradox Illustrated: While the Majority of Societies Have Remained Unchanged throughout Their Existence, the World System of Societies Has Changed Tremendously

Societies	Population Size			
	Time 1	Time 2	Time 3	Time 4
A	100	1,000	2,000	5,000
B	100	500	1,000	2,500
C	100	100	100	100
D	100	100	100	100
E	100	100	100	*
F	100	100	100	*
G	100	100	*	*
H	100	100	*	*
I	100	*	*	*
J	100	*	*	*
World system total	1,000	2,100	3,400	7,700

*This society no longer exists.

ence, but almost none of those societies survived into the present century. Almost all of the societies that *have* survived have been that small minority that have changed, and changed greatly.

Table 3.1 provides a simplified illustration of what has happened in the last 10,000 years. Of the ten hypothetical societies in the illustration, only two changed from Time 1 to Time 4. During the course of their existence, the other eight did not change at all in terms of size. Nevertheless, as the bottom line of the table shows, the size of this hypothetical world system steadily increased, and by Time 4 it was almost eight times larger than it had been in Time 1.

As this illustration suggests, *a process of selection has been at work in the world system of societies, favoring innovative societies at the expense of those that resisted change.* As we will see later in this chapter and elsewhere, this process has favored those societies that have been most successful in accumulating useful information relevant to subsistence activities. When societies have come into conflict with one another over territory and other vital resources, those that have been technologically more advanced have usually prevailed.* Thus, even though the vast majority of individual societies have resisted social and cultural change, the world system of societies has been dramatically transformed.

It is obvious, therefore, that we have to consider both change and continuity (i.e., the absence of change) if we are to understand human societies. Both have been profoundly important in the evolution not only of the world system of societies but of individual societies as well.

*There have been exceptions, of course, as when more advanced societies have waged wars far from home and when their vital interests were not involved. This happened in the American war in Vietnam, for example.

CONTINUITY AND CHANGE IN INDIVIDUAL SOCIETIES

As we have seen, human societies are essentially adaptive mechanisms by means of which human populations strive to satisfy their varied needs and desires.* Sometimes this is accomplished by preserving traditional ways of doing things, and sometimes by adopting new and innovative ways. In human societies we find ample evidence of both continuity and change.

Social and Cultural Continuity

Change in a society is largely a *cumulative* process. In other words, it is a process in which new elements are added to the sociocultural system far more often than older elements are eliminated. This is why sociocultural systems have grown so much more complex over the course of history.

Even in a society that appears to be changing rapidly, most elements of culture and social organization remain unchanged for extended periods. In modern industrial societies, for example, where rates of change are among the highest the world has ever known, many elements of culture are hundreds of years old, and some, such as the alphabet, the calendar, the numeral system, certain religious beliefs and practices, and basic techniques of farming and metallurgy, are thousands of years old. The same is true of many elements of social organization, such as the roles of prime minister, king, queen, priest, and rabbi, and the even older roles of mother, father, husband, wife, child, cousin, and grandparent.

There are a number of reasons for the persistence of social and cultural elements in a society, but one of the most important is *the conscious recognition of their adaptive value.* People are naturally reluctant to do away with something they depend on when they have nothing better to take its place. Thus, every society preserves its spoken language, its basic medical, military, and subsistence technologies, and many of its norms and customs because they are recognized as workable ways of satisfying some very important needs of the society as a whole. Cultural elements are also preserved if they are perceived by enough people as useful in answering their individual or personal needs. This explains the persistence of many elements of art, music, literature, and religion, and the persistence of a great variety of customs and norms, including even such antisocial patterns of behavior as speeding or illicit drug use.

Sometimes elements of culture are preserved not because they are superior solutions to problems but simply because they ensure *standardized behavioral responses* in situations where these are essential. For example, although driving a car on the right side of the road is inherently neither safer nor easier than driving on the left, this choice cannot be left to individuals. Every society must have a norm to ensure that all of its drivers follow the same procedure.

---

*This does not mean that human societies strive to satisfy the needs and desires of all their members equally or impartially. On the contrary, as we have seen (page 43), all societies are more responsive to the needs of some of their members than to the needs of others.

FIGURE 3.2 Although rates of change in modern industrial societies are among the highest the world has ever known, many elements of their cultures are hundreds or even thousands of years old: Jewish boy reading from scriptures more than 2,000 years old.

Another cause of continuity is *the cost involved in changing*. Change can be expensive; it would cost billions of dollars, for example, for Americans to change to the metric system. Change can also be costly in terms of time and energy, since it takes both to learn new rules and techniques and new ways of relating to others and performing one's job.

Change also exacts a *psychic* toll. This can affect people at any age when they encounter new environments, as when a child moves to a new neighborhood or a young woman enters military boot camp. *New information* can be even more threatening. People in the past were reluctant to believe the world was round because it contradicted the evidence of their senses; people today are often just as loath to part with the comfortable thought that our earth is the center of the universe or that the world was created in six days. New information can threaten one's view of life, making it necessary to restructure one's thinking on many other subjects in order to accommodate it.

Not surprisingly, the longer one lives with a set of ideas and beliefs, the more difficult and traumatic such "restructuring" becomes. This is why older people may be more conservative—that is, less open to new information and less eager for change—than young people. The *biological process of aging* is thus a very real force for continuity in every society, and its effects are magnified by the fact that older people often have greater power and influence than younger people.

But aging is not the only process that can make the members of a society conservative. The *socialization process* is probably the greatest force of all for continuity
within societies. As we saw on page 39, this is the process by which individuals learn
the culture of their group and acquire the skills that enable them to become functional members of their society. Through this process the members of a society acquire the belief that their culture is a precious resource and worth preserving. During their prolonged immaturity, children are obliged to master many of the most basic
elements of their culture. This is essential for their survival, and their only road to any
degree of independence. Before they learn to talk, for example, children are almost
totally dependent on other people; after they master their society's language, they
have an invaluable tool to help them get what they want. The same is true of other
elements of culture: it pays the child to master them. Thus, the desire of members of
the adult generation to preserve their culture by transmitting it to their offspring is
more than matched by their offspring's eagerness to learn it, especially during the
formative years. Since this cycle necessarily repeats itself as each generation matures,
the result is a tremendous force for continuity.

These efforts to pass culture on to the next generation are reinforced by *ideologies*. One of the chief functions of ideology is to preserve valued insights of the past.
Since these insights usually include the belief that the existing social order is a moral
order that ought to be preserved, a society's values, norms, and leadership acquire an
aura of the sacred and thus become less vulnerable to efforts to alter them. Ironically,
even revolutionary ideologies like Marxism eventually acquire a sacred and conservative character: once they win acceptance, they too become a force for continuity
and for resistance to change.

Finally, *the systemic nature of human societies* is a major force for continuity.
This is because most of the elements in a sociocultural system are linked to other
elements in such a way that change in one area often makes change in other areas
necessary. As a result, the members of a society do not adopt change casually, especially when they are aware of how extensive—and expensive—that change may ultimately be. When Sweden shifted to driving on the right-hand side of the road, for
example, this "simple" change meant not only that cars and other vehicles had to be
redesigned, but that traffic signals and road signs throughout the country had to be
relocated, traffic laws revised, and the deeply ingrained habits of millions of people
altered. Similarly, as more women with young children have become employed in
many societies, it has been necessary to create expensive new child care systems.

A society naturally hesitates to make changes that might have such far-reaching
consequences, and this in itself is a considerable force for preserving the status quo.
As we saw in Chapter 2, the systemic nature of human societies is especially evident
in its institutions and institutional systems, and it is there that we can see most clearly
many of the basic forces for continuity and conservatism.

Social and Cultural Change

In spite of the strength of the forces promoting social and cultural continuity, some
change eventually occurs in every society. Even in the simplest and most tradition-

minded societies, gradual changes occur in such things as the pronunciation of words, and legends are altered inadvertently as they are transmitted by word of mouth from one generation to the next.

Social and cultural change is of two basic types. Sometimes it involves the addition of new elements to the existing system; sometimes it involves the elimination of older elements. In the first instance, we refer to social and cultural *innovation*; in the second, we speak of social and cultural *extinction*.

Forms of Innovation Social and cultural innovation takes various forms. Often it takes the form of borrowing from other societies, a process known as *diffusion*. This occurs more often than most of us realize. In fact, there is good reason to believe that most elements in most sociocultural systems have been borrowed from other societies.

Many innovations, of course, are independently produced within society. These are of several types. *Alterations* are the least important. These are innovations whose adaptive value is no greater than that of the things they replaced, as in new styles of dress or new musical fashions. Alterations are often unintentional, as in gradual changes in the pronunciation of words or inadvertent errors in the transmission of stories and legends.

Discoveries and inventions are much more important types of innovations. *Discoveries* provide the members of a society with new information that has adaptive value, while *inventions* are new combinations of already existing information.[2] Thus, Columbus was a discoverer, while Gottlieb Daimler, who built the first automobile, was an inventor. What Daimler did was to combine in a new way a number of things that were already part of the technological heritage of western societies (e.g., the gasoline engine, the carriage body, running gears, the drive shaft, brakes). The "only" thing that was new about the automobile was the automobile itself. As we will see shortly, we must understand the nature of inventions if we are to understand why societies differ in their rates of innovation and change, and why these rates have changed over the centuries.

Causes of Innovation Persius, a Roman poet, once wrote of hunger as "the teacher of the practical arts and the bestower of invention." Plato put the matter even more succinctly when he described necessity as the mother of invention.

One does not need to be a social scientist to recognize the stimulus that *hunger and other human needs* provide. Throughout the ages, men and women, prodded by unfulfilled needs and desires, have dreamed of ways of satisfying them. Most dreams have remained just dreams, but sometimes individuals have transformed them into realities and something new and useful has been added to the sum of human knowledge.

While most of us have no trouble recognizing how unsatisfied needs influence the innovative process, we are likely to overlook the role of *chance*, or accident. Based on our experience as members of a modern industrial society, we tend to think of inventions and discoveries as products of planning and forethought. Yet from earliest times to the present, chance has been an important factor in the innovative process.

FIGURE 3.3 "If this doesn't result in one or two first-class inventions, nothing will."

Thus, in a primitive society, someone with a high fever may dream of a visit by a long-dead grandmother and awaken to find the fever abated. Nothing would be more natural under the circumstances than for the individual to assume that the "visit" was the cause of the cure and, in future illnesses, to pray to the grandmother for help. Should such prayers sometimes be followed by cures, the practice might well spread and eventually become a permanent feature of the society's culture.

Chance has also played an important role in *technological* innovation. Random strikes by lightning, for example, were almost certainly an important part of the process by which humans first learned about fire and became aware of its uses and dangers. More recently, the great scientist Louis Pasteur discovered the principle and technique of immunization only after he accidentally injected some animals with a stale bacterial culture of chicken cholera. When the animals unexpectedly survived, it occurred to Pasteur that weakened bacteria might immunize against the very disease that the bacteria, at full strength, were responsible for. Similarly, a key problem in the development of modern photography was solved when Louis Daguerre put a bromide-coated silver plate into a cupboard where, unknown to him, there was an uncovered container of mercury. When he returned the following day, he found that a latent image had begun to develop and correctly surmised that fumes from the mercury were responsible.[3]

While these and many other examples illustrate the role that chance has played in the innovative process, it would be a mistake to suppose that chance *alone* is responsible in most of these cases. Conscious, purposive action is also involved. Not just anyone could have made the discoveries made by Pasteur and Daguerre. Each man was already working on a problem about which he was highly knowledgeable, and each was a member of a society that already possessed a substantial store of relevant information.

It is difficult to exaggerate the importance of that *existing store of relevant information* where technological and scientific innovations are concerned. This can be demonstrated by the fact that two or more individuals, working independently, but with knowledge of the same body of information, have often made the same invention or discovery at about the same time. More than half a century ago, two sociologists compiled a list of 148 of these independent inventions and discoveries, and there have been more since then.[4] Examples from their list included:

Sunspots: Fabricius, Galileo, Harriott, Scheiner, 1611
Logarithms: Napier, 1614; Buergi, 1620
Calculus: Newton, 1671; Leibnitz, 1676
Nitrogen: Rutherford, 1772; Scheele, 1773
Oxygen: Priestley, Scheele, 1774
Water as H_2O: Cavendish, Watt, 1781; Lavoisier, 1783
Telegraph: Henry, Morse, Steinheil, Wheatstone and Cooke, 1837
Photography: Daguerre and Niepce, Talbot, 1839
Natural selection: Darwin, Wallace, 1858
Telephone: Bell, Gray, 1876

Because of culture, human needs and desires seem limitless. Each problem that is solved and each need that is satisfied seems to generate new needs and new desires as people come increasingly to take the satisfaction of their former needs and desires for granted. This is the basis of the so-called "revolution of rising expectations" that is such a striking feature of life in the twentieth century. Despite the fact that standards of living have risen more in the last century than in any previous century, discontent and dissatisfaction have probably never been greater. Recognition of this important aspect of human nature has led some observers to note that while Plato was certainly correct in his observation that necessity is the mother of invention, it is also true that *invention is the mother of necessity*. In other words, the process of innovation and change seems to feed on itself so that once it is set in motion it tends to continue, and even to accelerate.

One of the reasons for this is *the systemic nature of sociocultural systems*. Because the various components of these systems are interdependent, a change in any one of them generates pressure for change in others. The invention of the automobile, for example, created the need for many new laws and for the construction of a vast new highway system. More important still, it led to the transformation of cities by encouraging the growth and spread of suburbs and the construction of thousands of new suburban shopping centers, which often have weakened or destroyed older business districts in the centers of cities. In addition, the automobile spawned a tremendous number of other changes in the business world, including the fast-food industry, motels, and the trucking industry, to name but three.

Not all cultural innovations generate the same degree of pressure for change in the rest of the system. Some create very little pressure for further change, while others generate tremendous pressure. A new style of painting, for example, may have no

impact on society outside a small circle of artists and critics. A new political movement, on the other hand, can have far-reaching consequences, depending on the number of people who join it and the seriousness with which they take it. But one kind of
innovation that never fails to have far-reaching consequences is change in a society's
basic subsistence technology. For reasons that will become clear shortly, changes in
subsistence technology have ramifications that are felt in almost every other area of
life.

Many changes in human societies arise in response to *changes in either their
biophysical or social environments*. Archaeologists have found, for example, that
changes in climate in the past (e.g., at the end of the last Ice Age) led to changes in
diet, in technology, and probably in other societal characteristics as well.[5] Similarly,
changes in the social environment (e.g., increasing contacts among societies or the
rise of expansionistic and militaristic neighbors) can create new problems for societies and lead to social and cultural innovations of various kinds.

Finally, one of the most neglected causes of change has been *human fecundity*.
Human populations, like other populations, are able to produce many more offspring
than environmental resources can sustain. In other species, this merely leads to high
death rates among the young, except in those rare instances when a genetic mutation
or environmental change enables a population to utilize some new resource. Human
societies, however, are able to respond to population pressures with cultural innovations. *Ideological* changes in customs or in laws, for example, may cause people to
delay the age at which they marry, or legitimate such practices as abortion. Alternatively, *technological* changes may provide the population with better methods of contraception, or enable them to produce more food to keep a growing number of children alive and well.

Variations in the Rate of Innovation   When we compare different societies, we find
that they produce innovations at greatly different rates. Some, such as American society, have had extremely high rates of innovation. In many others, the rate of innovation has been negligible.

There are a number of reasons for such variations, but one of the most important is *the amount of information a society already possesses.*[6] One of the most important forms of innovation—invention—is the act of combining already existing elements of culture. This means that a society's potential for invention is a mathematical
function of the number of elements, or amount of information, already present. Table
3.2 illustrates this principle. It shows how various numbers of units, or elements, of
information can be combined. Although two units can be combined in only one way,
three units can be combined in four ways, and four units in eleven ways. In other
words, *the addition of each new unit more than doubles the number of possible combinations*. Thus, a mere fivefold increase in the number of units from two to ten leads
to a *thousandfold* increase in the number of possible combinations, and when the
number of units reaches twenty, over a million combinations are possible!

Of course, not all elements can be combined in a useful way. It is difficult, for
example, to imagine a useful combination of the hammer and the saw. The number
of potential combinations, therefore, is much greater than the number of fruitful ones.

TABLE 3.2 Number of Combinations Possible for Various Numbers of Units

No. of Units	Total Number of Combinations									Total
	2 at a Time	3 at a Time	4 at a Time	5 at a Time	6 at a Time	7 at a Time	8 at a Time	9 at a Time	10 at a Time	
2	1	0	0	0	0	0	0	0	0	1
3	3	1	0	0	0	0	0	0	0	4
4	6	4	1	0	0	0	0	0	0	11
5	10	10	5	1	0	0	0	0	0	26
6	15	20	15	6	1	0	0	0	0	57
7	21	35	35	21	7	1	0	0	0	120
8	28	56	70	56	28	8	1	0	0	247
9	36	84	126	126	84	36	9	1	0	502
10	45	120	210	252	210	120	45	10	1	1,013

This does not affect the relationship between the number of units and the number of combinations, however. Thus, the amount of available technological information is a major factor in a society's rate of innovation.

A second cause of variations in the rate of innovation is *population size.*[7] Because every member of a society has somewhat different needs and abilities, the more people there are, the more new ideas and information are likely to be produced. Larger populations, because they tend to be organizationally more complex, are also likely to generate more varied patterns of social interaction, leading to more new customs, norms, laws, and other kinds of information required to control and regulate relationships. In the case of technological innovations, the more people who are aware of a problem and looking for a solution, the more quickly it will be found, other things being equal. Since societal populations vary so greatly in size, this is another factor of considerable importance.

A third factor affecting the rate of innovation is *the stability of the environment to which a society must adapt*. The greater the rate of environmental change, the greater the pressure for change in culture and social organization. This is true with respect to both the biophysical and the social environment. And any change in the latter that upsets the balance of power among societies (e.g., large-scale migrations, empire building, a new weapons system) is an especially potent force for further innovation and change.

A fourth factor influencing the rate of innovation in a society is *the extent of its contact with other societies*. The greater its interaction, the greater its opportunities to appropriate their innovations. In effect, contact enables one society to take advantage of the brainpower and cultural information of other societies through the process of diffusion.

The importance of diffusion was beautifully illustrated some years ago by an anthropologist, Ralph Linton, who wrote:

> Our solid American citizen awakens in a bed built on a pattern which
> originated in the Near East but which was modified in Northern Europe

before it was transmitted to America. He throws back covers made from
cotton, domesticated in India, or linen, domesticated in the Near East, or
wool from sheep, also domesticated in the Near East, or silk, the use of
which was discovered in China. All of these materials have been spun and
woven by processes invented in the Near East. He slips into his moccasins,
invented by the Indians of the Eastern woodlands, and goes to the
bathroom, whose fixtures are a mixture of European and American
inventions, both of recent date. He takes off his pajamas, a garment invented
in India, and washes with soap invented by the ancient Gauls. He then
shaves, a masochistic rite which seems to have been derived from either
Sumer or ancient Egypt. . . .

Linton followed this individual as he went through his daily round of activities using
cultural elements most of which originated in other societies. As the day comes to a
close and "our friend has finished eating," Linton wrote,

he settles back to smoke, an American habit, consuming a plant domesticated in Brazil in either a pipe, derived from the Indians of Virginia, or a
cigarette, derived from Mexico. If he is hardy enough he may even attempt a
cigar, transmitted to us from the Antilles by way of Spain. While smoking he
reads the news of the day, imprinted in characters invented by the ancient
Semites upon a material invented in Germany. As he absorbs the accounts of
foreign troubles, he will, if he is a good conservative citizen, thank a Hebrew
deity in an Indo-European language that he is 100 per cent American.[8]

A fifth factor in a society's rate of innovation is *the character of its biophysical
environment.* As we have seen, the potential for development and change in some
societies has been severely limited by environmental factors over which they have no
control. Thus, desert and arctic societies have been unable either to develop the techniques of plant cultivation themselves or to learn them from others. The absence of
vital resources, such as an adequate water supply or accessible metallic ores, can also
hinder innovation, as can endemic diseases and parasites that deplete people's energy.[9]
Topography has played an important role in shaping patterns of intersocietal communication. Oceans, deserts, and mountain ranges have all prevented or seriously
impeded the flow of information between societies, while navigable rivers and open
plains have facilitated it. Considering the importance of diffusion, enormous differences in the rate of innovation can be explained by this factor alone.

Sixth, the rate of innovation is greatly influenced by *"fundamental" innovations.*
Not all discoveries and inventions are of equal importance: a few pave the way for
thousands more, while the majority have little effect.[10] The invention of the plow and
the steam engine and the discovery of the principles of plant cultivation, animal domestication, and metallurgy were all fundamental innovations. So, too, were the inventions of writing and money.

Sometimes a fundamental innovation will cause the rate of innovation to rise
because it involves a principle that can be applied, with minimum effort and imagination, in hundreds, even thousands, of different areas. This was true, for example, of
the steam engine, metallurgy, printing, and the silicon chip. Sometimes, however, an

invention or discovery is considered "fundamental" because it so drastically alters the conditions of human life that hundreds or thousands of other changes become either possible or necessary. This was the case with the principle of plant cultivation, which, as we shall see in a later chapter, led to revolutionary changes in every area of human life.

A seventh factor influencing the rate of innovation is *the society's attitude toward innovation*. In many societies there has been such a powerful ideological commitment to tradition that innovation of any kind has been discouraged.[11] In contrast, most modern societies have a strongly positive attitude toward innovation and change.

Though the problem has not been studied as carefully as it deserves, a society's attitude toward innovation seems to be greatly influenced by its prior experience. A society that has benefitted from change in the past is usually more receptive to innovation than a society that has not. Attitudes toward innovation also vary according to the nature of the dominant ideology in a society. Some ideologies generate a very conservative outlook and oppose change; Confucianism is an example of such a faith. Capitalism, in contrast, has been much more supportive of innovation and change.

Before we leave the subject of the rate of innovation, it is important to note a tendency that is especially evident where technological innovation is concerned: *it tends to occur at an accelerating pace.* Figure 3.4 illustrates this speedup for human

FIGURE 3.4 The number of important technological innovations by century, 1000 A.D. to 1900 A.D. Technological innovation tends to occur at an accelerating rate, because each new element increases the probability of acquiring more. See also Table 5.1, page 96.

Source: Adapted from Ludwig Darmstaedter and Rene DuBois-Reymond, *4000 Jahre Pionier-Arbeit in den Exakten Wissenschaften* (Berlin: Stargardt, 1904).

societies as a whole during the period from 1000 A.D. to 1900 A.D. . The majority of societies have never experienced such an acceleration. But those that have experienced it have influenced human history out of all proportion to their numbers.

The explanation of the acceleration is that *each new bit of useful technological information acquired by a society increases the probability it will acquire still more*. This is partly a function of the potential of technological elements for being recombined in new ways. But more than that, technological advance tends to reinforce several of the other basic factors that influence the rate of innovation. Throughout history, for example, advances in a society's subsistence technology have typically led to an increase in the size of its population, which, in turn, contributed to further innovation because there were more people aware of problems and alert to possible solutions. Similarly, technological advance has led to increased intersocietal contact, resulting in greater diffusion and thus enhancing the rate of technological innovation.

In short, technological innovation and advance tend to make *further* innovation and advance increasingly likely. It is hardly surprising, therefore, that societies in which this happens come to be increasingly different from societies in which it does not.

Social and Cultural Extinction   Because of social and cultural innovations, societies are often faced with choices between competing alternatives, and this leads to a *process of selection*. Earlier in this century, for example, the members of many societies were confronted with a choice between the horse and carriage and the new "horseless carriage." Gradually, the horseless carriage, or automobile, as it came to be known, replaced the older means of transportation.

The process of selection is like the process of innovation in that it too can be rational and deliberate, as in the adoption of the automobile and the rejection of the horse and buggy. But, again, as in the process of innovation, chance and irrational factors may play a part.

Although it is, of course, the members who make the choices which shape and alter their society, everyone does not have an equal voice. "Who decides" depends on the kind of decision involved and the nature of the power structure involved. For example, the teenaged members of an industrial society may choose, at one level, which songs become hits, but their range of choices has already been substantially narrowed by the people who control the music industry and who pay disc jockeys to promote certain records and otherwise manipulate the selective process. Similarly, all of the members of a democratic society may have equal opportunities to cast their votes for public officials, but the choice among candidates has already been substantially narrowed by elites in the mass media and the political system.

This raises the question of whether or not a society's culture and social organization can be considered truly adaptive. While much of it *is* adaptive for the society as a whole (i.e., it helps satisfy basic needs of the system or its members), many elements have been selected by and for the benefit of special segments of the society and are "adaptive" only, or largely, for them. Thus, the process of selection may result in the retention of many elements that are *nonadaptive* or even *maladaptive* for the society as a whole. Drug pushers and users select elements which they find reward-

FIGURE 3.5 Intrasocietal selection often occurs imperceptibly, as one element of technology gradually replaces another: in the early decades of the present century, the horseless carriage gradually replaced the horse-drawn carriage in industrial societies.

ing, but which create serious problems for society as a whole (e.g., crime and illness). Similarly, major corporations make decisions that lead people to adopt maladaptive or harmful products, such as sugar-coated cereals, tobacco, and alcohol.

SOCIETAL GROWTH AND DEVELOPMENT

Most societies, as we have seen, changed little during the course of their existence. Moreover, most of the changes that occurred were of little importance—gradual changes in the pronunciation of words, minor alterations in the content of rituals and legends, changes in etiquette, and so on.

Occasionally, however, more significant changes have occurred. Some societies have grown substantially. Some have shifted from a nomadic way of life to permanent settlements in villages, and some have shifted from a predominantly rural mode of life to a predominantly urban one. Such changes have usually been accompanied by important changes in social organization—substantial increases in organizational complexity, marked increases in the division of labor, and significant increases in social inequality. In short, some societies have experienced a process of substantial growth and development while others have not.

How can we explain such a profound difference in the experience of societies?

We have already considered the basic factors that cause innovation in a society and those that affect the rate of innovation. Now we need to look at cultural innovation from a somewhat different angle and ask the further question: do *all* kinds of new information have the same potential for societal growth and development, or do certain kinds of innovations have a greater potential than others?

Technology's Role in Societal Growth and Development Technology, as we have seen, is that part of a society's store of cultural information that is used to transform the resources of the biophysical environment into the material products its members need or desire. *Subsistence* technology is the most critical part of this store of information, since it is information used to produce the food and other sources of energy on which all of the activities of a society ultimately depend.[12] Without energy, not even thinking or planning are possible. Thus, it is not surprising that *an advance in subsistence technology is a necessary precondition for a significant increase in the size and complexity of a society*.

Societies that depend on hunting and gathering as their chief means of subsistence cannot sustain populations nearly as large as those that depend on farming; and those that depend on slash-and-burn horticulture, a more primitive method of farming, cannot sustain populations as large as those that depend on plow agriculture. These differences in the limits set on the size of a society by its subsistence technology are matched by differences in the limits set on other aspects of societal development, such as the extent of the division of labor, the degree of social inequality, the size and complexity of communities, the wealth of the society and its standard of living, and the power of the society over its biophysical environment and over other societies. In short, *technology defines the limits of what is possible for a society*.[13]

Within the range of options made possible by its technology, a society's choices are often influenced by the relative economic costs of the various alternatives. China's technology, for example, makes the production of automobiles and the construction of a highway system *possible*, but its decision makers have opted instead for less costly solutions to their society's transportation needs: mass public transport and private bicycles. In a world in which resources are never sufficient to meet all of the demands for goods and services, differences in cost can never be ignored by societies, and they are compelled to adopt one of the less expensive solutions much of the time. Thus, in addition to determining the limits of the possible for a society, *technology also affects the choices that are made by influencing the costs of various alternatives*.

Advances in a society's subsistence technology are also important because *they stimulate advances in other kinds of technology*. For example, advances in subsistence technology tend to be accompanied or followed by advances in other productive technologies and in the technologies of transportation, communication, and defense, all of which contribute to societal growth and development (see Figure 3.6).

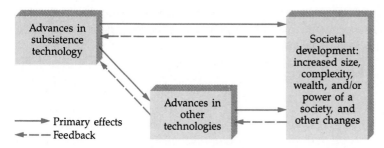

FIGURE 3.6 Model of the effects of advances in subsistence technology on other technologies and on societal development.

Technology's critical role in societal growth and development is not surprising when we consider that a society's tools and machines are, in effect, the functional equivalent of improvements in the basic organs with which its members are endowed—eyes, ears, voice box, arms, legs, brain, nervous system, and the rest. Microscopes, telescopes, and television all extend the range of our vision, just as telephones and radios extend the range of our hearing, and bicycles, automobiles, and airplanes increase our mobility. Where technological advances have occurred, they have enabled the members of societies to act as if they had acquired a new and improved genetic heritage—improved sight, more acute hearing, new powers of locomotion, and so forth. Thus, technological advances—especially advances in subsistence technology—are functionally equivalent to the important kinds of changes that occur in the course of biological evolution.

One important feature of the process of societal development that should not be overlooked is indicated by the feedback* loops shown in Figure 3.6. Advances in subsistence technology stimulate advances in other technologies and lead to growth in the size and complexity of a society. But these developments, once they have occurred, usually increase the probability of further advances in subsistence technology.† Population growth, for example, increases the number of potential innovators and, although few individuals ever make an invention or discovery of practical value, the greater the number of potential innovators in a society, the greater tends to be the rate at which innovations occur. Thus, as this example suggests, *once the process of societal development is set in motion, it tends to become self-sustaining.* While this is not inevitable, the probabilities of continued development clearly increase.

Societal growth and development, while advantageous to societies in many ways, are not unmixed blessings. They create new problems and these often lead to changes that many members of society would prefer not to make—changes in beliefs and values, changes in patterns of social organization, changes in institutional arrangements. Among preliterate societies, for example, technological advance often leads to pop-

---

*Feedback is a special kind of causal relationship. It is one in which a part of the effect produced by the initial cause or event reverts back to, and alters, its source. For example, illness may cause a loss of appetite, and the resulting failure to eat may then aggravate the illness.
†There are exceptions, as we will see in Chapter 7.

ulation growth, and population growth necessitates changes in social organization. Such societies must choose either to split up into smaller independent groups in order to preserve their traditional kin-based system of governance, or to remain united but adopt a more authoritarian political system that is dominated by a small elite minority.[14]

Ideology's Role in Societal Growth and Development   Whenever its technology presents it with a range of options, a society's beliefs and values—the core elements of ideology—always come into play. These often have little or no effect on societal growth and development, as when people choose one style of clothing in preference to another, one form of entertainment rather than another, or even one form of marriage over another. Sometimes, however, ideologies do have a substantial effect, as when they dispose people to accept and even welcome change or, conversely, to view it negatively.[15] Western capitalism, for example, is far more supportive of new ideas and innovation of all kinds than is Islamic fundamentalism.

When the beliefs and values involved are felt to be sufficiently important, a society may reject the most economic solution to its needs in favor of a solution that is ideologically preferable. The United States, for example, has chosen to make private automobiles and an extensive system of superhighways a major part of its solution to its transportation needs, reflecting, at least in part, the individualism of its members and their desire for ease and freedom of movement.

Ideologically based decisions that affect a society's basic institutions may have extremely grave consequences. In eastern Europe, for example, countless decisions by Communist leaders over the years eventually led to a political and economic crisis of such proportions that the members of these societies rose up in mass revolt. And in a number of Third World societies, deeply ingrained beliefs about the value of large families have resulted in such high rates of population growth that it has been virtually impossible to improve living conditions for the majority of people.

Since one of the important consequences of technological advance is that it increases the range of options available to societies and their members, such advance leads to greater scope for the exercise of beliefs and values. Advanced societies today have far more choices available to them than societies of the past, and they are much freer to apply diverse ideologies in making their decisions. This does not guarantee happy results, of course, as the bitter experiences of Nazi Germany and the Soviet Union remind us.

CHANGE IN THE WORLD SYSTEM OF SOCIETIES

As we have seen, change has been a basic characteristic of the world system of societies for the last 10,000 years. In that period, the human population has grown a thousandfold and the average size of individual societies has increased a millionfold. Meanwhile, the number of societies in existence has declined dramatically. These changes have been accompanied by countless other changes in the conditions of human life and in the characteristics of human societies—changes in family life, in the social roles of both men and women, in religion, in politics, in art, and more. Today, in the latter part of the twentieth century, we are witnessing what appears to be the emergence of a single global culture, as societies around the world increasingly adopt similar patterns of dress, similar tastes in music, similar ambitions and aspirations, and, increasingly, a single language for intersocietal communication (i.e., English).

Societal Variation and Intersocietal Selection

The key to the major changes that have occurred in the world system of societies in the last 10,000 years is the process of intersocietal selection that has drastically reduced the number of societies.[16] Were it not for this process, in which the units that survive (or become extinct) are entire societies, human life would not have changed nearly as rapidly as it has.

This process of selection presupposed the existence of differences among societies. Such differences were inevitable once the human population began to spread out geographically and occupy new and different kinds of environments. Chance also contributed to the process of societal differentiation, so that even when two societies confronted similar environmental challenges, they did not respond in exactly the same way. Differences in vocabulary provide a good example of this: even when all societies were confronted with identical experiences, such as birth and death, or the differences between males and females, they created different symbols to represent them. More important still, different beliefs developed to explain and interpret these experiences, and varied norms evolved to guide behavioral responses.

Not all the differences that have developed among societies have been equally important from the standpoint of intersocietal selection. Differences that influenced societal growth and development have been especially important, because *societies that have grown in size and developed in complexity and military power have been much more likely to survive and transmit their cultures and institutional patterns than societies that have preserved traditional social and cultural patterns and minimized innovation* (see Figure 3.7).

The reasons for this are obvious. To survive, societies must be able to defend their populations and territories against a variety of threats. These include the ravages of epidemics, natural disasters of other kinds, and, above all, threats from other societies. One only need consider the history of the United States, Canada, Australia, Brazil, or the Soviet Union to see what happens to smaller and less developed indigenous societies (i.e., the American Indians, the Australian aborigines, and various tribal groups in Siberia and Soviet Asia) when they compete for territory with larger and more developed societies. Larger societies have greater manpower and can more easily absorb military casualties. In addition, their more advanced technology has military applications, so that their soldiers have more deadly weapons, better logistical support, and greater mobility. Finally, their more complex patterns of social organization can easily be adapted to military needs and this, too, provides an important competitive advantage. Thus, while it would be a mistake to suppose that more developed societies always prevail over their less developed rivals, the odds are strongly in their favor.

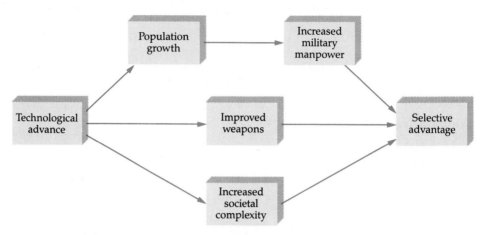

FIGURE 3.7 Model of the effects of technological advance on the process of intersocietal selection.

Intersocietal selection is not always a violent process. Sometimes societies collapse simply because of insufficient support from their members. This is especially likely to occur when a less developed society comes into contact with one that is much more highly developed. Many members of the less developed society become impressed with the wealth and power of the more advanced society and either migrate to it or begin to adopt its customs. If these tendencies become widespread, the institutional fabric of the less developed society begins to fray and a process of societal disintegration begins. There are a number of well-documented cases of this in India, where primitive tribes in the hill country have simply disintegrated and their former members have been absorbed into Indian society.[17]

A Model of the Evolution of the World System of Societies

Building on what we have learned about the process of intersocietal selection, we can now construct a model of the evolutionary process that explains the basic trends in the world system of societies in recent millennia. As Figure 3.8 indicates, the model is based on two premises. First, it assumes the existence of variation, or differences, among societies. Second, it assumes an inherent tendency of societies to develop an increased need for resources, either because of growth in population or because of the growth of their members' culturally generated needs and desires. The combination of these two conditions sets the stage for a deadly process of competition that has resulted in the survival of a small minority of societies and the extinction of the vast majority.

Because technologically advanced societies have had the advantage in this process of intersocietal selection, *their characteristics have increasingly come to be the characteristics of the world system as a whole*. Thus, because technologically advanced societies tend to be larger than other societies, the average size of societies has been increasing for the last 10,000 years. Similarly, because technologically advanced societies are structurally more complex than other societies, the trend in the world sys-

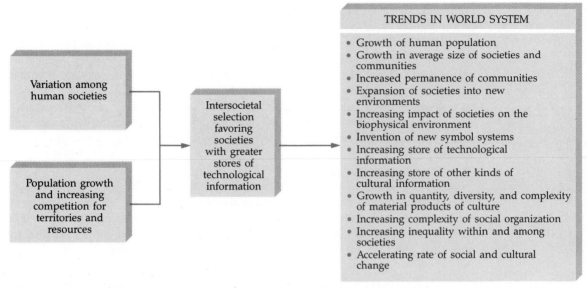

FIGURE 3.8 Model of the causes of the evolution of the world system of societies.

tem has been in the direction of increasingly complex societies. The same logic applies to all of the trends shown in Figure 3.8.

There is, of course, nothing inevitable or unalterable about these trends. A number of factors could disrupt them. For example, a deadly new disease could sweep through human societies and, in a short period of time, reverse most of the trends of the last 10,000 years. The Black Plague of the fourteenth century had this effect in a number of societies, and it is not inconceivable that something comparable could happen on a global scale. An unpredictable catastrophe involving the biophysical environment could also reverse the trends of history, as could a war fought with modern military technology. Both nuclear and biochemical warfare have the potential for producing a global catastrophe, and there is no technological antidote for either. Ecological–evolutionary theory clearly provides no grounds for complacency regarding the future.

Although we cannot predict the future, we can say that, so far, the process of intersocietal selection has favored technologically advanced societies. Like the old game of musical chairs, it has eliminated first one, then another, of the less developed societies. The result is a world system that, with the passage of time, increasingly consists of what were once the exceptions—innovative and developing societies.

SOCIOCULTURAL EVOLUTION DEFINED

By now it is clear that *sociocultural evolution is the process of change and development in human societies that results from cumulative growth in their stores of cultural information*. Although sociocultural evolution is an extraordinarily complex phenomenon, it is easier to understand once we recognize that it includes both continuity and change.

It is also important to recognize that sociocultural evolution operates on two distinct levels simultaneously. First, it occurs within individual societies. Second, it occurs within the world system of societies. While these two processes are separate and distinct, they are also related, because the changes that occur in individual societies produce the variations on which the process of intersocietal selection operates. This is the process that determines which societies and which cultures survive and which become extinct, and the role that each of the survivors plays within the world system.

The consequences of sociocultural evolution have been very different for different human societies: when we look at them individually, we see a variety of patterns of development. But when we look at the world system, we see that at that level sociocultural evolution has produced *one dominant pattern* for at least the last 10,000 years. In the chapters that follow, we will explore both the diversity of patterns in individual societies and the dominant pattern of the world system.

Excursus: A Comparison of Biological and Sociocultural Evolution

During recent decades, our understanding of biological evolution and sociocultural evolution has advanced dramatically. It is now clear for the first time that *both types of evolution are based on records of experience that are preserved and transmitted from generation to generation in the form of coded systems of information.* In the case of biological evolution, the record of experience is preserved and transmitted by means of the genetic code. In the case of sociocultural evolution, the record is preserved and transmitted by means of symbol systems. Both the genetic "alphabet" and symbol systems provide populations with the means of acquiring, storing, transmitting, and using enormous amounts of information on which their welfare and, ultimately, their survival depend. Thus, *symbol systems are functional equivalents of the genetic alphabet.*

It is hardly surprising, therefore, that there is a fundamental similarity in the way the two evolutionary processes operate. Continuity and change are present in both, and change takes the form of both innovation and extinction. Both processes also involve variation and selection.

Despite these similarities, there are a number of important differences in the way the two systems of evolution operate. Some of these are of special significance for students of human societies, such as the difference that results from the way information is

transferred and spread in the two evolutions. The only way genetic information can be transmitted is through the process of reproduction. Because different species cannot interbreed, they cannot share genetic information with one another.* Thus, biological evolution is characterized by continued differentiation and diversification, a process much like the branching of a tree or shrub. Cultural information, by contrast, is easily exchanged between the members of different societies. Not only can human societies exchange information, but two or more can merge into a single system—the equivalent, were it possible, of the merging of separate species in biological evolution. Thus, sociocultural evolution is likely to eventuate in even fewer and less dissimilar societies than exist today.

This is related to a second important difference. In biological evolution, the emergence of more complex species of plants and animals has not had the effect of eliminating, or reducing the number of, simpler species. One-celled organisms thrive alongside, and in-

---

*Closely related species do occasionally interbreed, as when lions and tigers produce "ligers" or "tiglons." These hybrids are usually sterile, however, at least in the animal kingdom, and therefore their importance in the process of biological evolution has been minimal.

deed *inside*, complex multicellular organisms. In sociocultural evolution, on the other hand, the emergence of new and more complex kinds of societies has usually led to the extinction of older, simpler ones, as illustrated by the destruction of thousands of small American Indian societies since 1492. Thus, while biological evolution produces the pattern of a richly branched shrub, sociocultural evolution approximates

FIGURE 3.9 Biological evolution, like sociocultural evolution, is based on records of experience that are preserved and transmitted from generation to generation in coded systems of information: model of the DNA molecule in which vast amounts of information are transmitted genetically from parents to offspring. *(Omikron/Photo Researchers)*

the pattern of a pine tree that gradually loses its lower branches as new, higher branches appear and overshadow them.

A third basic difference involves a population's ability to incorporate into heritable form the useful information its members have acquired through the process of individual *learning*. In sociocultural systems, this is easily done; it is, as we have seen, the basis of their evolution. But it has no counterpart in biological evolution. Most biologists prior to Darwin believed that something analogous *did* occur in the biotic world. Jean Baptiste Lamarck, Darwin's most famous predecessor, argued that if an organism continually repeated a certain action, not only would this produce structural change in the organism, but the change would be inherited by its offspring.[18] It has long since been clear that biological evolution does not work that way: giraffes do not have long necks because their ancestors stretched day after day to reach high leaves, but because short necks were a liability in their ancestors' environment; animals with the genes for short necks were unable to survive and reproduce. In the cultural world, however, a kind of Lamarckian evolution *does* occur. Just about anything a population learns and considers worth preserving can be incorporated into its cultural heritage.

Springing from the easy flow of cultural information among societies and the ease with which it is incorporated into heritable form is yet another way in which sociocultural evolution differs from biological: it has a capacity for much higher rates of change in our species. An evolution whose mechanism is genetic change is necessarily a slow process in a species that has a long generation span and relatively few offspring. But cultural information, relative to genetic, can be rapidly acquired, exchanged, recombined, and accumulated, with the result that substantial alterations in a society's culture may occur within a single generation. Moreover, sociocultural evolution does not require that every society go through step-by-step sequential stages of development, which are the essence of biological evolution. Rather, a society may compress or even skip stages.[19] In the Third World today, for example, some nations have gone directly from human porters and pack animals to trucks and airplanes as the primary movers of goods, bypassing the stage of dependency on wagons and railroads that was part of the evolutionary experience of those societies in which the newer methods of transportation were first developed.

One other important difference involves the conditions under which major evolutionary change occurs. In the biotic world, most *major* change happens when a population becomes reproductively isolated and cannot exchange genetic information with other populations of its species. In contrast, human societies that are isolated almost invariably experience a *low* rate of cultural change. In short, isolation tends to have opposite effects in the two modes of evolution.

Finally, sociocultural evolution may have a greater potential than biological evolution for being brought under rational human control. So far, however, this process has hardly begun. One of humanity's most urgent tasks in the years ahead is to increase our understanding of the dynamics of sociocultural evolution so that we can find ways to control its direction and make it more responsive to human needs and ideals.

4

Types of Human Societies

The basic aim of science, as we have seen, is to explain how the world works. To this end, scientific research—whether it is focused on butterflies, galaxies, or human societies—looks for patterns and regularities in the world around us. This requires countless observations designed to reveal how things resemble one another, how they differ, and why—*a process of systematic comparison.*

CLASSIFYING HUMAN SOCIETIES

Over the years this process of comparison has given rise to many systems of classification in the various sciences. The periodic table in chemistry and the Linnaean taxonomy and its successors in biology are two of the more familiar. Such systems help us to make sense of the wealth of data generated by research and serve as guides to scientists, suggesting new comparisons for study and new lines of research. But most important of all, each of these systems of classification has stimulated the development of theories that explain the patterns and regularities that have been discovered.

The system of classification that we will use in studying human societies is based on the *subsistence technologies* they employ. The origin of this system, like the origin of ecological–evolutionary theory itself, lies in the work of seventeenth- and eighteenth-century European scholars who responded to the discovery of less developed societies in the New World, Africa, and Asia by rethinking age-old questions about human origins and history. This led some of them to compare societies and try to classify them. A number of them even recognized the crucial importance of subsistence technology and based their systems of classification on it.[1]

The system of classification used in this volume grows out of that early work. It divides human societies into ten basic categories, with individual societies classified on the basis of their primary mode of subsistence:[2]

Hunting and gathering societies
Simple horticultural societies
Advanced horticultural societies
Simple agrarian societies
Advanced agrarian societies
Fishing societies
Maritime societies
Simple herding societies
Advanced herding societies
Industrial societies

A system of classification is most useful when it is kept simple, so that the classification of cases is as unambiguous as possible. Thus, a society is classified as a hunting and gathering society only if the hunting of wild animals and foraging for uncultivated plant foods are its primary means of subsistence. Horticultural societies are societies which practice farming, but do not have plows.[3] Advanced horticultural societies use metal tools and weapons, while simple horticultural societies have only wood and stone ones. Agrarian societies also engage in farming, but they use plows. Advanced agrarian societies use iron tools and weapons, while simple agrarian soci-

FIGURE 4.1 Members of a twentieth-century society of hunters and gatherers: Australian aborigines singing sacred songs in preparation for important ritual ceremony.

eties have only copper and bronze, which are softer metals and less plentiful. (See Table 4.1.)

Fishing, herding, and maritime societies are different from the other types of societies in that they are *environmentally specialized* types. Each of them is distinguished from other societies at roughly the same level of development, not so much on the basis of the body of technological information they *possess*, but rather in terms of what they *use* in their subsistence activities. Each relies disproportionately on those elements in its technology that are especially suited to the distinctive features of its particular environment. Thus, a fishing society relies primarily on those elements of its technology that are most useful to people located on a body of water. A herding society relies disproportionately on those elements of its technology that enable it to subsist on open grasslands with sparse rainfall. Maritime societies, like fishing societies, utilize their proximity to water, though in a different way: being technologically more advanced, they have been able to adapt their technology to the use of waterways for trade and commerce at a time when the movement of most goods was much cheaper by water than by land (see page 183).

Technologically, there is more variation among herding societies than among either of the other specialized types.[4] For this reason, the category is divided into simple and advanced types. The basic distinction is that the latter have horses or camels for transportation in work and warfare, while the former lack this important resource.

Industrial societies are the newest type of society and technologically the most advanced. The distinguishing feature of these societies is their heavy dependence on machine technology and on the inanimate sources of energy—coal, petroleum, natural gas, and nuclear power—that drive the various machines. Because of their highly advanced technology, industrial societies are the most powerful and productive societies the world has ever seen.

Not all societies fit neatly into the ten types of societies listed above. Some are *hybrids* that combine in roughly equal proportions the characteristics of two or more of the basic types. Often—though not always—hybrid societies are in a state of transition from one mode of production to another and from one level of development to another. Thus, many Third World societies today are beginning to industrialize, but

TABLE 4.1 Criteria for Classifying Primary Types of Human Societies

Type of Society	Plant Cultivation*	Metallurgy*	Plow*	Iron*	Inanimate Energy Sources*
Hunting and gathering	−	−	−	−	−
Simple horticultural	+	−	−	−	−
Advanced horticultural	+	+	−	−	−
Simple agrarian	+	+	+	−	−
Advanced agrarian	+	+	+	+	−
Industrial	+	+	+	+	+

The symbol + means that the trait is widespread in the type of society indicated; the symbol − means it is not.

FIGURE 4.2 Hybrid societies depend on elements of technology from two or more basic societal types: contemporary India, an industrializing agrarian society, combines elements of the older agrarian technology with elements of modern industrial technology.

still depend heavily on preindustrial technology. These industrializing agrarian and industrializing horticultural societies will be examined in detail in Chapters 15 and 16.

SOCIETAL TYPES AND ENVIRONMENT

Human societies have had to adapt to many kinds of environments. Some have had to adapt to near-desert conditions where food resources have been hard to obtain, while others have had the good fortune to be located close to large bodies of water where they have had access to abundant supplies of fish in addition to all the resources of the land they occupied.

The great majority of societies, however, have occupied territories that were neither as rich in resources as the latter nor as impoverished as the former. In most cases the major part of their land has been suitable for plant cultivation of one kind or another. Many, however, have occupied territories that have been suitable only for the less productive form of cultivation known as horticulture.[5] In many tropical and

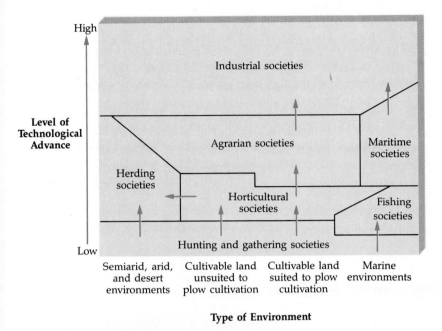

FIGURE 4.3 An ecological–evolutionary taxonomy of societies.

semitropical regions, poor soils, inappropriate crops, and other factors have made plow agriculture impossible or unprofitable until recently.*

In summary, then, *the two most basic causes of fundamental differences among societies over the course of human history have been: (1) differences in their subsistence technologies, and (2) differences in their environments.*

Figure 4.3 illustrates how these two factors have combined to produce the various types of societies we have identified. The *vertical dimension* indicates how differences in the level of subsistence technology lead to differences among societies. For example, maritime societies occupy environments similar to those of fishing societies, but they differ from fishing societies because they are technologically more advanced. The *horizontal dimension* of Figure 4.3 indicates how differences in environmental conditions lead to further differences among societies. Thus, although maritime societies and agrarian societies are quite similar in their levels of technological development, they differ in important ways because of differences in the environments to which they have adapted.

---

*In recent years, heavy use of chemical fertilizers and other products of modern industrial technology has begun to make plow agriculture possible and profitable in some of these areas, but even now horticulture still remains the more profitable form of farming in most tropical areas.

The arrows in Figure 4.3 indicate the usual patterns of societal evolution. Thus, we see that fishing societies and horticultural societies have evolved from hunting and gathering societies. On the other hand, some herding societies, which are roughly similar in level of technological advance to horticultural societies, may have evolved from horticultural societies.[6] Usually, however, technologically more advanced types of societies have evolved from less advanced types.

One feature of Figure 4.3 that requires special comment is the absence of arrows flowing upward from herding and horticultural societies in areas that are not suitable for plow cultivation. Further development of these societies seems to have been blocked by environmental constraints. When a more advanced kind of society is found in one of these environments, it is the result of societal *expansion* rather than societal evolution. An industrial society exists in the arid regions of the southwestern United States, for example, because an industrial society that originated in the eastern part of North America, an area well suited to plow cultivation, expanded into that area.

SOCIETAL TYPES THROUGH HISTORY

Throughout most of human history, everyone lived in hunting and gathering societies. This period of relative social and cultural uniformity ended only within the last 10–12,000 years.

The first new type of society to emerge was fishing society (see Figure 4.4). Though the practice of fishing seems to have begun thousands of years earlier, fishhooks, nets, traps, boats, and paddles had to be invented before any society could make the shift from hunting and gathering to fishing as its *primary* means of subsistence.[7]

Simple horticultural societies probably came next, first appearing in the Middle East around 7000 B.C.[8] Though people began to use copper within the next 1,500 years,[9] it was not until nearly 4000 B.C. that metal tools and weapons became common enough in any of these societies to permit us to call them *advanced* horticultural.[10]

The plow was invented late in the fourth millennium, and this innovation also occurred in the Middle East.[11] By 3000 B.C. it was used widely enough by societies in Mesopotamia and Egypt to justify labeling them simple agrarian.

Iron was discovered early in the second millennium B.C. but, like copper, did not become the dominant material in tools and weapons for a long time.[12] Thus, the first *advanced* agrarian societies did not appear until the early years of the first millennium B.C.

The origin of herding societies remains something of a mystery. Evidence of animal domestication dates from about 9000 B.C., but evidence from the earliest site suggests a hybrid technology.[13] While we cannot say for certain when any society first came to depend on herding as its chief means of subsistence, it was probably sometime after horticultural societies appeared.

Maritime societies date from the end of the third millennium B.C. Minoans on the island of Crete were apparently the first people to rely on overseas commerce as

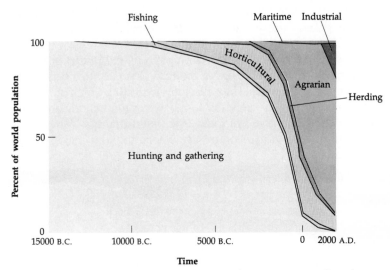

FIGURE 4.4 Societal types through history: changes in size reflect the growth or decline in numbers of each of the societal types.

their primary economic activity.[14] Maritime societies emerged first in the Mediterranean world around 2000 B.C. and flourished in Europe during the Middle Ages. Currently, Singapore is the only maritime society.

The last major societal type is industrial. The inventions that mark the beginning of the modern technological revolution occurred in the eighteenth century. But it was not until early in the nineteenth that Britain, which pioneered in industrialization, reached the point where it could be classified as a truly industrial society. Since then, more than twenty others have followed Britain's lead.

Historical Eras

As Figure 4.4 makes clear, the types of human societies in the world system have changed greatly in the last 10–12,000 years. There was a time when every society was at the hunting and gathering level of development; today, we have everything from hunting and gathering to industrial societies.

To understand a given society, past or present, it is not enough to know what type of society it is or was. It is equally important to know when it existed, since this tells us a great deal about its *social* environment. For example, the situation of hunting and gathering societies in the last hundred years has been far more precarious than it was 10,000 years ago. Such groups have found themselves in the unenviable position of interacting with far more advanced and far more powerful societies. No matter where hunting and gathering societies have been located, members of industrial societies have penetrated, using vast resources in ways that have transformed the conditions of life for less advanced groups. This has often been done with the best of intentions—as in the establishment of medical, educational, or religious missions—

but their good intentions have made little difference. The ultimate effect has been to transform and eventually destroy the social and cultural systems of technologically primitive peoples.

In studying a society, therefore, it is important to specify the historical era involved. The various eras are named according to the type of society that was politically and militarily dominant at the time. Thus, the long period in which all human societies were hunting and gathering societies is designated as the hunting and gathering era, while the period in which we live today is the industrial era.

From the standpoint of ecological–evolutionary theory, the four major eras in human history have been:*

1. The hunting and gathering era (from human beginnings to about 7000 B.C.)
2. The horticultural era (from about 7000 B.C. to about 3000 B.C.)
3. The agrarian era (from about 3000 B.C. to about 1800 A.D.)
4. The industrial era (from about 1800 A.D. to the present)

As Figure 4.5 suggests, the best way to understand what sociocultural evolution has meant is to examine in sequence the four types of societies whose dominance in successive eras has defined the upper limits of technological advance. In them we can trace all the basic trends in population, culture, the material products of culture, social organization, and social institutions.

The reason for these trends, as Figure 4.5 reminds us, is that the rise of technologically more advanced societies contributed directly to the decline of those less advanced. For when horticultural societies appeared, the chances for survival of neighboring hunting and gathering societies were substantially reduced unless they too adopted the new technology. The same was true for both hunting and gathering and horticultural societies after agrarian societies appeared. The less advanced societies lacked both the numbers and the weapons needed to defend themselves against the more advanced societies that coveted their territories and other resources. Those that managed to survive did so only in remote and isolated areas protected by oceans or other geographical barriers, or in territories judged undesirable by members of the more advanced societies (e.g., deserts, tropical rain forests, mountainous areas). In recent times, the pattern of military conquest and expansion has greatly declined, but the pattern of cultural penetration by technologically more advanced nations has increased tremendously, as we will see in later chapters.

DIFFERENCES AMONG TYPES OF SOCIETIES

One of the most important propositions in ecological–evolutionary theory asserts that advances in subsistence technology are a necessary condition for any significant increase in the size and complexity of a society (see page 60). Beginning in Chapter 5, we will put this proposition to the test as we examine each of the major types of societies.

---

*These dates are for the world as a whole. In many parts of the world, the horticultural and agrarian eras began later. For example, the agrarian era did not begin in the New World until the sixteenth century A.D., after European colonization and settlement.

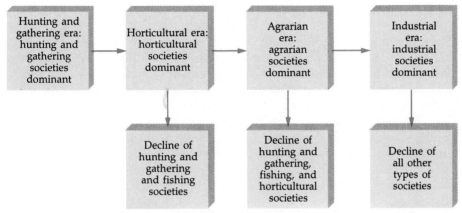

FIGURE 4.5 Model of the sequence of historical eras.

Before plunging into the detailed evidence that bears on this proposition, it may be helpful to consider a much more limited body of evidence that was assembled over a period of years by George Peter Murdock with the aid of his students and colleagues. Together they assembled and codified a tremendous amount of information on more than a thousand societies. These data enable us to classify most of these societies in terms of the taxonomy described earlier in this chapter and compare the various types of societies in a number of important ways.[15] Since the societies differ considerably in their levels of technological advance, we will be able to see whether they also differ in some of the ways that ecological–evolutionary theory says they should.

Size of Societies

One of the most important consequences of technological advance, according to ecological–evolutionary theory, is an increase in the size of societies. Table 4.2 confirms this. Technologically more advanced types of societies have, on average, much

TABLE 4.2 Median Size of Societies, by Type of Society

Type of Society	Median Size of Societies	No. of Societies
Hunting and gathering	40	46
Simple horticultural	1,500	53
Advanced horticultural	5,250	69
Agrarian	Over 100,000	38
Industrial	15,000,000	24
Fishing	90	16
Herding	5,750	19

Sources: See Appendix, pp. 441–442, and *World Development Report, 1987.*

Science and Measurement

Science requires the precise and accurate comparison of phenomena. In most cases, it is not enough simply to say, for example, that X is larger than Y, or that it is hotter, or faster, or growing more rapidly. For this reason, scientists in every field use quantitative tools to measure and describe things, and to analyze relationships among them.

Sociology is no exception. In comparing human societies, for example, it is not enough to say merely that one type of society is larger than another; this could mean that it is 1 percent larger or a thousand times larger. Such imprecise statements fail to clarify the nature of relationships that exist among phenomena and thus hamper the search for patterns and their explanation.

Sociologists and other social scientists make great use of a set of quantitative tools known as *statistics*, the most basic of which are called *summary measures*. A summary measure reduces a number of different measurements to a single measure that "summarizes" them all. The most widely used are *measures of central tendency*—or what are popularly known as "averages."

The most familiar measure of central tendency is the *arithmetic mean*. The arithmetic mean is determined by adding the measurements of the individual units and dividing the sum by the number of units. For example, if 5 hunting and gathering societies have 25, 32, 39, 48, and 56 members respectively, the sum of the individual measurements is 200; when this is divided by the number of societies—5—we obtain a mean of 40.

Another widely used measure of central tendency is the *median*. We determine the median by arranging the individual measurements in order and identifying the one that is in the middle. In the example above, the median is 39. The median is often a more meaningful measure of central tendency than the mean, because it minimizes the effect of a single, highly discrepant case. If the sizes of the 5 societies in the example above had been 25, 32, 39, 48, and 156 (instead of 56), we would have obtained a mean of 60, which would have been a poor "summary" of the situation. The median, however, would still have been 39, a truer reflection of the size of most of the societies.

larger populations. Thus, the median size (see "Science and Measurement" above) of industrial societies is larger than the median size of agrarian societies, which is larger than the median size of horticultural societies, which is larger than the median size of hunting and gathering societies. The median sizes of fishing and herding societies are also about what one would expect in view of their places in the taxonomy of societies (see Figure 4.3). Fishing societies are larger, on average, than hunting and gathering societies, but much smaller, on average, than horticultural societies. Herding societies are roughly the same size as advanced horticultural societies.

Permanence of Settlements

Ecological–evolutionary theory also predicts that technological advance leads societies to establish more permanent settlements.[16] Because the hunting of wild animals and the gathering of uncultivated vegetable products soon deplete the supply of foodstuffs in the immediate area surrounding human settlements, hunter-gatherers are forced to move about with considerable frequency. In contrast, societies that practice horticulture or agriculture should, according to our theory, be able to establish more permanent settlements.

Murdock's data confirm this. Of the 167 hunting and gathering societies for which data were available, *only 10 percent* were reported to have permanent settlements, and all of these enjoyed unusually favorable environmental conditions or partial reliance on horticulture, fishing, or other more advanced technologies. In contrast, *94 percent* of the 507 horticultural and agrarian societies had permanent settlements.

Societal Complexity

A third important prediction of ecological–evolutionary theory is that technological advance is linked to greater complexity of the social system. Murdock's data permit us to test this hypothesis in two ways. First, we can compare societies on the basis of *the amount of occupational specialization* found in them. Second, we can compare them on the basis of *the complexity of their status systems.* Thus, we can test the complexity of both the horizontal and the vertical dimensions of social organization.

Table 4.3 shows the frequency with which several kinds of occupational specialists are found in seven different types of societies. In hunting and gathering societies, technologically the least advanced, there are no specialists in the six areas indicated. Specialization in those areas occurs in a tiny minority of simple horticultural societies, but becomes considerably more common in advanced horticultural and agrarian societies. In industrial societies, there are specialists in all of these fields. In fishing societies, the level of occupational specialization is comparable to that in hunting and gathering and simple horticultural societies, while herding societies occupy an intermediate position between simple and advanced horticultural societies.

Figure 4.6 shows the relationship between subsistence technology and the complexity of status systems. Once again, as ecological–evolutionary theory would lead us to expect, there is a steady progression from hunting and gathering to industrial societies, with no complex status systems found in the former but universally present in the latter. The two environmentally specialized types of societies—fishing and herding societies—rarely had complex status systems, which is what ecological–evolutionary theory would lead us to expect. None of the fishing societies and only 3 percent of the herding societies had status systems that could be classified as complex.

TABLE 4.3 Frequency of Craft Specialization, by Type of Society (in Percentages)

Type of Society	Metal-working	Weaving	Leather Working	Pottery	Boat Building	House Building	Average
Hunting and gathering	0	0	0	0	0	0	0
Simple horticultural	0	1	1	0	8	4	2
Advanced horticultural	96	5	12	14	4	2	22
Agrarian	98	34	24	24	5	18	34
Industrial	100	100	100	100	100	100	100
Fishing	7	0	0	0	5	2	2
Herding	44	3	6	0	0	1	9

Source: See Appendix, pp. 441–442.

Ideology

Finally, ecological–evolutionary theory leads us to expect that the world views and beliefs of technologically advanced societies will differ from those of the technologically less advanced. Again, Murdock's data allow us to test this important hypothesis in at least one respect.

As Figure 4.7 indicates, belief in a God who created the world and who is concerned with the moral conduct of humans has been found in only a small minority of societies.[17] In technologically less advanced societies—hunting and gathering, simple horticultural, and advanced horticultural—this kind of belief is rare. In contrast, belief in a Supreme Creator concerned with human affairs has been observed in the majority of agrarian and industrial societies.

FIGURE 4.6 Percentage of societies having complex status systems, by type of society.

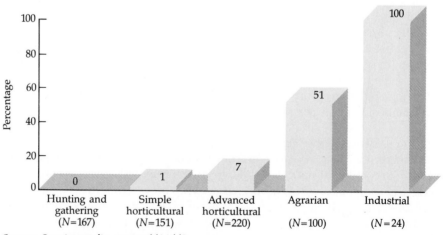

Source: See Appendix, pages 441–442.

SOCIETAL TYPES: WHAT THEY ARE AND WHAT THEY ARE NOT

By now it should be clear that the societal types with which we will be concerned throughout this volume are sets of societies in which individual societies resemble others of their type more than those of other types. The societies of one type are not identical, however. They differ from one another in many ways. Often, in fact, a number of societies of one type resemble some of the societies of another type *in certain respects* more than they resemble the majority of societies of their own type. For example, as Figure 4.7 indicates, the religious beliefs of a small minority of hunting and gathering societies (4 percent) resemble those of the majority of agrarian societies more than they resemble the beliefs of other hunting and gathering societies.

The differences between societal types are something like the differences between age categories within a population. Every society finds it useful—even necessary—to make distinctions between children and adults, and many societies go further and differentiate between infants, children, adolescents, young adults, the middle-aged, and the elderly. These distinctions reflect real and important differences within the population, but we recognize that the characteristics of all the individuals in a category are not identical. For example, a few elderly people will be in better physical condition than many middle-aged ones, and some adolescents may already be employed while some adults are still students in school. But these exceptions do not keep us from using age categories as tools that help us understand and anticipate the different ways individuals respond to various situations.

The reason we find age categories useful is because the physiological process of development and aging has such a profound impact on the daily lives of individuals. It sets limits on what is possible for individuals at various ages, and within those lim-

FIGURE 4.7 Percentage of societies with belief in a creator God concerned with the moral conduct of humans, by type of society.

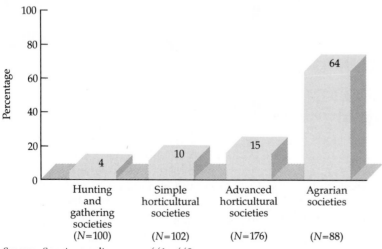

Source: See Appendix, pages 441–442.

its it makes some patterns of action more likely than others. Furthermore, the physiological process of development and aging has a similar impact on everyone who is at the same stage in the life cycle: this is why the members of a given age category resemble one another more than they resemble the members of other age categories. This is also why the members of adjacent categories resemble one another more than they resemble members of more distant categories (e.g., why adolescents resemble children or young adults more than they resemble babies or the elderly).

Obviously, however, the physiological process of development and aging is not the only force that shapes our lives and personalities. This is why all the members of a given age category are not exactly alike and why there are always differences among them.

Societal types are much like age categories in all these ways. The reason they are so valuable is because subsistence technology has such a profound impact on the life of societies. It sets limits on what is possible for individual societies at every stage of development, and within those limits it makes certain social and cultural patterns more likely than others. Furthermore, it is a force that has a similar impact on all societies that share a common mode of subsistence: this is why societies of a given type tend to resemble one another more than they resemble societies of other types. This is also why societies of adjacent types (see Figure 4.3) resemble one another more than they resemble societies of more distant types (e.g., why simple horticultural societies resemble hunting and gathering societies more than they resemble industrial societies).

But subsistence technology is not the only force that influences the nature of societies, any more than the physiological process of development and aging is the only force that influences individual personality and behavior. This is why there are differences among societies within a given societal type just as there are differences among individuals in the same age category.

In summary then, societal types are valuable analytical tools that help us to understand societies, both individually and collectively. They are sets of societies that share a single common characteristic, subsistence technology. But subsistence technology is not just any characteristic chosen at random from the almost endless list of societal characteristics. On the contrary, it appears to be *the single most powerful force responsible for the most important differences among human societies*.

Technological Determinism Rejected

Today, as in the past, efforts to understand the role of technology in human life are hindered by those who take extreme positions on the subject. Over the years, a few scholars have argued that technology explains almost every sociocultural pattern.[18] To combat this exaggerated view and to uphold the importance of ideological and organizational factors, other scholars have minimized or even denied the importance of technology.[19] Unfortunately, the unreasonableness of *both* positions has escaped many social scientists, with the result that sociology and anthropology have both been slow in coming to a realistic assessment of technology's role in the evolutionary process.

Much of the confusion results from a failure to think in *probabilistic* and *variable* terms. Few, if any, significant social patterns are determined by a single factor. Where human societies are concerned, one can rarely say that A and A alone causes B. Usually B is due to the combined effect of a number of factors, and, although A may be the most important, it is not likely to be strong enough to dictate the outcome. The most we can say, as a rule, is that if A is operative, B will occur with *some degree of probability.*

The problem is further complicated because so many of the B's we deal with are *variables*. For example, when we talk about a society's population, we are not interested in whether it exists, but in its relative size. The same is true of most of the other things we are concerned with—the *degree* of occupational specialization, the *frequency* of warfare, the *extent* of the authority exercised by leaders, and so forth. To think in categorical, either-or terms about such matters is bound to be misleading.

While ecological–evolutionary theory emphasizes the tremendous importance of technology and technological innovation in the life of human societies, it does not claim that technology can explain everything in sociocultural evolution. It recognizes that other forces have also played a part—often an important part. Its view of technology's role in human affairs can best be summarized in the following propositions:

1. Because subsistence technology sets limits on what is possible within a society, an advance in subsistence technology is a necessary precondition for any substantial growth or development in terms of size, complexity, power, and wealth; this is true both for individual societies and for the world system.
2. Because subsistence technology sets limits on what is possible within a society and greatly influences the relative cost of each of the options within those limits, it is the single most important cause of the totality of differences among societies (although not necessarily of each individual difference).
3. Because societies that have grown substantially in size, complexity, wealth, and power enjoy a great advantage in intersocietal competition and are therefore more likely to transmit their social and cultural characteristics to future generations, the nature of the world system has been increasingly shaped by the process of technological advance and increasingly reflects the characteristics of those societies that are technologically the most advanced and most innovative.

If these propositions are correct, students of human societies can ill afford to ignore or neglect subsistence technology and the role it plays in human life. In fact, these propositions indicate that the first step in analyzing any society should be to identify its primary subsistence technology. This will ensure that we take into account from the outset the most powerful of the variables affecting it.

Our basic task for the rest of this volume will be to apply these principles in a broadly comparative study of human societies. We will examine each of the major societal types that have emerged in the course of history, seeing how technological advance has influenced its social institutions and how these institutions have, in turn, reacted on technology and influenced its development. We will, for obvious reasons, give special attention to the industrial and industrializing societies of our own day. Our ultimate goal is to achieve a better understanding of the forces that influence human societies, in the hope that this will help us understand and eventually control the process of change that is such a striking, and at times threatening, feature of the contemporary world.

PART TWO

PREINDUSTRIAL SOCIETIES

5

Hunting and Gathering Societies

For the first 4 million years or more of hominid history, our ancestors all lived in hunting and gathering societies. This was the only type of society in existence throughout this period. Only in the last 10,000 to 12,000 years—the last one-fourth of 1 percent of hominid history—have other types of societies evolved.

Already, however, the end is in sight for hunting and gathering societies. They simply have not been able to compete with technologically more advanced societies for territories and other vital resources. As a result, in recent centuries hunting and gathering societies have survived only in remote and isolated regions. And now, in the twentieth century, with the aid of new technologies, members of advanced industrial societies have penetrated even those areas. Thus, few, if any, hunting and gathering societies are likely to survive into the twenty-first century.

Fortunately, during the last hundred years or more, ethnographers, missionaries, colonial administrators, and others have had opportunities to observe more than 170 of these societies and provide us with detailed reports of their way of life. For a time, some questioned the relevance of these reports for our understanding of hunting and gathering societies of the prehistoric past. Today, however, most scholars who study the prehistoric past regard modern hunters and gatherers and prehistoric hunters and gatherers of the last 20,000 years or so as "analogous peoples" with much in common.[1] The chief differences between them are the result of (1) the contacts of modern hunters and gatherers with technologically more advanced societies (e.g., the acquisition of metal knives and other things in trade), and (2) the exclusion of modern hunters and gatherers from many of the more fertile regions of the world.*

*The latter point may not be as important as it seems, since our present conception of "fertile" regions is based on their potential for farming. Yet many areas that are unsuited to farming have supported substantial populations of game animals (e.g., the Kalahari Desert, various polar regions), and thus supported populations of hunters and gatherers about as well as many areas that we think of today as much more fertile.

In our analysis in this chapter, we will not assume that prehistoric hunting and gathering societies and those of the modern era are alike, but will instead present the findings of both archaeology and ethnography (see Glossary). Only after we have done this will we explore the question of whether they provide consistent or contradictory images of hunting and gathering societies.

HUNTING AND GATHERING SOCIETIES PRIOR TO 100,000 B.C.

It is easy to speak of "the dawn of human history," but it is not so easy to assign a date to it, or even to say precisely what it means. The same evolutionary process that produced our species, Homo sapiens, first produced a number of others (e.g., Ramapithecus and Homo erectus) that were, in varying degree, "humanlike." Thus, it is impossible to say that human history began at some particular point. What *is* possible is to identify the patterns that gradually began to form during the long era of "morning twilight" that ultimately produced *fully* human creatures and *truly* human societies.

Our species, Homo sapiens, is part of the genus *Homo*, which is, in turn, part of the family *Hominidae*, better known as the hominids. This family split off from the ancestors of the modern chimpanzees and gorillas roughly 4 million years ago, according to the best available evidence,[2] and has subsequently pursued a separate and increasingly unique evolutionary course. The process of natural selection operating on a succession of hominid species gradually shaped this line in certain fundamental and important ways and culminated in Homo sapiens, the sole surviving representative of the hominid family.

FIGURE 5.1 "This could mean the end of civilization as we know it."

If we could look across the great abyss of space and time to a grass-covered plain in Africa several million years ago, we would see that early hominids were already on an evolutionary course that was distinct, in a number of important respects, from that of other primates. Fossil evidence reveals that they had abandoned their ancestors' arboreal and largely herbivorous life for a bipedal, terrestrial, and omnivorous one. In other words, our ancestors had come out of the trees; they were walking on two feet and moving about much as we do today; and they were eating fruits, vegetables, and meat obtained by hunting smaller animals or by scavenging the remains of larger ones that had died or been killed by carnivores.[3]

This drastic set of behavioral changes had involved many genetic changes, especially in the skull, mouth, hips, and limbs. The most critical of these was the new upright stance, for this meant that hominid hands were no longer needed to propel their bodies through trees or over ground, but were freed for other kinds of activity—to manipulate sticks, stones, and other objects as tools, and eventually to construct tools of their own invention.[4] This was a crucial development contributing to the evolution of our brain, for much of the development of that organ was a response to what hominids did with their hands during that long era.

Throughout hominid evolution, the attributes being selected as elements in their basic genetic heritage developed more or less in concert, not independently of one another. These included not only greater overall brain size, but an enlarging cerebral cortex (see Figure 2.3, page 25); larger physical size (the earliest hominids appear to have weighed only about fifty pounds); improvement in hand-eye coordination; a variety of other advances in the nervous system; and increased cooperation and communication.

The hominids' shift to an omnivorous diet, interestingly, seems to have led to some important new elements of social structure in hominid societies. To begin with, hunting probably played a role in the early evolution of the division of labor. Because of pregnancy, lactation, and care of the young, females were probably somewhat handicapped in hunting activities. This may have led at a fairly early date to the beginnings of a pattern found in every hunting and gathering society of modern times: males have primary responsibility for providing meat, females for vegetables, fruits, shellfish, and other materials that may be more easily "gathered." This hypothesis is supported by recently discovered evidence that, as early as 2 million years ago, hunter-scavengers in east Africa transported their meat from the place where they obtained it to an "eating-place."[5] This practice, which is so unlike that of any living species of nonhuman primate, suggests a division of labor in acquiring food, as well as the sharing of food and the organization of activities around a "home base."

The division of labor along sexual lines may well lie behind yet another development in hominid societal life that distinguished hominids from other primates: the formation of durable bonds between males and females. Most other primate societies are organized around groups of mothers and their offspring; adult males do not maintain sustained contact with the group. The sustained association between the sexes that is such a fundamental part of human life may thus have had its origin in that ancient diversification of hominid diet.

The scavenging, and later hunting, of large animals also confronted hominids with the problem of how the meat should be distributed. Recent studies of chimpanzees have shown that the time they communicate most intensely is when they are dividing up meat,[6] and it is not unreasonable to assume that our ancestors acted much the same way. Their increasing dependence on meat may thus have been an early factor in stimulating the development of symbols as a supplement to signals.

As the ages passed, hominids came to be more like modern humans in both appearance and behavior. But the rate of change was extremely slow. Archaeologists speak of the "almost unimaginable slowness of change" during this period.[7] Eventually, however, as a consequence of their increasing use of, and dependence on, tools, and as a result of the further evolution of their brains, hominids reached a point where, as the "brainiest" of the mammals, they began to make more effective use of the resources of their environment.

One manifestation of this was the beginning of big-game hunting, an activity with numerous repercussions for hominid societies. For example, the pursuit of larger animals would have required a greater capability for planning, maneuvering, remembering, communicating, and cooperating, and the males that did this best were likeliest to survive and reproduce. Thus, there appears to be an important link between this activity and the continuing evolution of the brain, especially in its development of more memory units and interconnecting nerve cells.[8]

There is also good reason to believe that the greater degree of cooperation demanded by big-game hunting strengthened the social bonds that united adults. Adult males could no longer be as independent of one another as they are in other primate societies. And the new activity probably served to reinforce the division of labor between the sexes. Females would have been even more disadvantaged in this kind of hunting, because, as the hominid brain increased in size, their hips had to become wider to enable them to accommodate the infant's head at birth; running thus became slower and more awkward for them.

The use of fire was another significant technological innovation of this period. Fire was the first important natural force to be, in any sense, brought under control. Although humans may not have been able to generate fire during this era, they could preserve it after it was started by natural causes. And fire did far more than warm these societies. It set humans apart from all other animals, giving them some control over the cycle of day and night, and giving them a little more freedom of movement. It was also important for protection, and was a powerful weapon for driving predators away from camp or out of an attractive cave that humans wanted to use. Fire was also used to harden the points of wooden spears, and possibly to kill large animals by driving them over cliffs or into swamps.

The use of fire for cooking probably affected the evolution of our teeth, and even the shape of our faces, since cooked food requires so much less chewing than raw. Fire was probably also involved in the beginnings of religious experience, as a basis of ritual, even as an object of worship. But most important, fire strengthened the network of interrelationships within societies, drawing the group together at the end of a day to communicate, to remember, and to plan.

No one can say with any certainty when Homo sapiens first appeared on the scene, but the best available evidence indicates that it was more than 100,000 years ago.[9] If we look for some dramatic change in human societies at this point, however,

FIGURE 5.2 Fire was the first great natural force to be brought under human control. Artist's conception of one of the earliest known instances of the use of fire: cave dwellers near Beijing, China, about 400,000 years ago.

we are in for a disappointment. Though the archaeological record for this period is sparse, there is nothing to suggest that there were any significant new developments until much later. Living remained precarious, and life expectancy short. An authority who analyzed the remains of forty individuals who lived as recently as 50,000 to 100,000 years ago found that only one of them apparently reached the age of fifty, and only 10 percent the age of forty. Half of them died before their twentieth year![10]

Within the last 100,000 years, hominids began to bury their dead, often placing in the grave with them artifacts that strongly suggest belief in life after death: food, flowers, implements, and red ocher, which some scholars suspect was thought to have the life-giving properties of blood.[11] At least one grave held animal bones and cinders, suggesting either burnt offerings or the remains of a funeral feast. This era also provides us with our first evidence of intraspecies violence. Several skeletons have been found with wounds that were almost certainly inflicted by other humans (e.g., a flint projectile embedded in a rib cage and a pelvis with a spear hole in it.)[12]

Although human societies were clearly becoming more dependent upon culture, cultural change was still not as important as genetic change. But the situation eventually altered. Sometime in the last 100,000 years, cultural evolution replaced biological evolution as the dominant mechanism of change.

HUNTING AND GATHERING SOCIETIES FROM 100,000 B.C. TO 7000 B.C.: SOCIOCULTURAL EVOLUTION TAKES OVER

As a result of recent (1988) discoveries in a cave near Nazareth in Israel, a number of scholars now believe that the last major step in human biological evolution occurred more than 90,000 years ago and that anatomically and genetically modern humans (Homo sapiens sapiens) were already present by that time in the Middle East.[13] Others, however, reject this. They challenge the dating of the Nazareth remains on several grounds, including the fact that no other evidence of Homo sapiens sapiens has been found anywhere that can be dated before about 40,000 B.C.

However this dispute is finally resolved, one thing is clear: *cultural evolution replaced biological evolution as the primary mechanism of adaptation and change in human societies at some point during the last 100,000 years, and perhaps only within the last 40,000 years.* The clearest indication of this is the rapid proliferation of new and improved tools and weapons in the latter period. The spear, for example, had been in use for hundreds of thousands of years, with no significant improvements except for the use of fire to harden the point. Then, in the period from 40,000 B.C. to 7000 B.C., hunters made several major improvements. First, they developed the spear-thrower, which applies the principle of the lever and doubles the distance a spear can be hurled.[14] Second, at the other end of the spear they began using sharpened bone points to increase the penetrating power. Finally, they added barbs to the spearhead to create a much more serious wound.[15]

The most important innovation in weapons, however, was the bow and arrow. Employing the principle of the concentration of energy, hunters in this period created a weapon of great usefulness and versatility. Its effective wounding range is roughly four times that of the spear and twice that of the spear thrown with the aid of a spear-

FIGURE 5.3 Two comparisons of the spear with the bow and arrow.

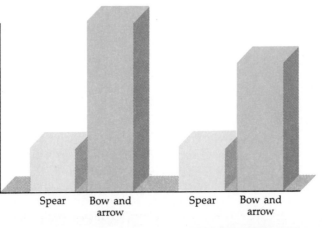

| Spear | Bow and arrow | Spear | Bow and arrow |

Effective wounding range   **Speed of missile**

FIGURE 5.4 Artist's conception of mammoth hunters' settlement in Czechoslovakia about 25,000 years ago, based on archaeological finds.

thrower.[16] Furthermore, an arrow travels two and a half to three times faster than a spear. This is important not only because of the time advantage it affords the hunter, but also because the force of the blow is a function of the missile's speed.* Finally, unlike the spear, the bow and arrow permit the hunter to sight the missile at eye level, which greatly increases the accuracy of his aim.

Other technological improvements, though less dramatic, were no less important. As one writer puts it, people of this era "began to make the tool fit the task with an altogether new precision."[17] Innovations included such diverse tools as pins or awls, needles with eyes, spoons, graving tools, axes, stone saws, antler hammers, shovels or scoops, pestles and grinding slabs (for grinding minerals to obtain coloring materials), and mattocks.

In colder regions, people usually lived in caves. This was not always possible, however, as in the case of the mammoth hunters who ranged from Czechoslovakia to Siberia and whose way of life forced them to remain in caveless country even during the winter. Figure 5.4 shows a modern reconstruction of one of their settlements. Some societies also built houses of earth and clay.[18]

The discovery of such settlements has provided us with information on the size of human societies in that era. In general, they were quite small, many with as few as six to thirty persons. The largest settlement of hunters and gatherers ever found was spread out along a two-mile stretch of river in France and may have housed as many

---

*These advantages are partly offset by the greater weight of the spear, which is why it continued to be used for some purposes.

as 400 to 600 persons,[19] but this was exceptional and may have been only a temporary gathering of a number of societies taking advantage of a salmon run or other special situation.

The best known innovation of that period is its art (see Figure 5.5). The drawings on the walls of caves in western Europe are world famous, but they are only one of the new art forms developed at that time. There was sculpture of various kinds as well as bone and ivory carvings, often on the handles of weapons and tools.[20]

It would be hard to exaggerate the importance of these artistic remains, for they provide many insights into the evolution of human thought and the rapidly growing body of nontechnological information. Drawings of men dressed to resemble animals strongly suggest magical or religious practice and a belief in sympathetic magic. This belief—that anything done to an image, or a part, of a person or animal will affect that person or animal—is further suggested by the fact that a great number of the drawings have spears or darts drawn or scratched into animals' flanks.[21] Sympathetic magic was apparently also used in an attempt to produce fertility, in both humans and animals. At least this is the most likely explanation for the numerous female figures with exaggerated evidences of pregnancy (see Figure 5.5b). Most scholars think it is no coincidence that the artist ignored the facial features and focused on the symbols of fertility.

Many examples of the art of this period indicate the development not only of new beliefs, but of ceremony and ritual. This is suggested by the drawings of men dancing and by engravings of processions of men standing before animals, heads bowed and weapons resting on their shoulders in a nonthreatening position. It has been suggested that they are asking the forgiveness of the animals they plan to kill, as some modern hunters do.[22] In summary, the art of this era reveals the growth of human consciousness and the effort of people to understand and control their environment, and it attests to the growing gulf developing between them and the rest of the animal world.

By the close of the hunting and gathering era (about 7000 B.C.), human societies possessed a far greater store of cultural information than they possessed 30,000 years before. They had, in fact, acquired more in those last 30,000 years than in all the previous millions of years of hominid history.

Table 5.1 shows how dramatic the change was in the rate of technological innovation alone. It lists all the known technological innovations of importance from the beginnings of the hominid family to the end of the hunting and gathering era. The four time intervals involved correspond to the periods which archaeologists label the Lower Paleolithic, Middle Paleolithic, Upper Paleolithic, and Mesolithic, and it should be noted that they differ tremendously in duration (from 3,000 years to 3.9 *million* years).* By dividing the number of innovations by the approximate time required to produce them, we arrive at the figures in the right-hand column, which are a rough measure of the relative *rate* of innovation during the successive periods.

---

*We have set the point of hominid origins at the latest possible date, judging from current evidence, thus making our estimates of the rise in the rate of technological innovation low and conservative.

FIGURE 5.5a The stag hunt: cave wall painting, Spain.

FIGURE 5.5b The Venus of Willendorf, Germany.

Ahh!
Art
Hist.!

FIGURE 5.5c Handle of spear-thrower, France.

TABLE 5.1 **The Rising Rate of Technological Innovation: 4,000,000 B.C. to 7,000 B.C.**

Time Periods and Their Major Technological Innovations		No. of Major Innovations	Innovations Per Thousand Years
4,000,000 to 100,000 B.C.		6	0.0015
Hand ax	Wooden spear		
Use of fire	Constructed shelters		
Fire-hardened spear point	Colored pigments		
100,000 to 40,000 B.C.		3	0.0500
Use of bone for tools	Skin clothing (probable)		
Built-in handles on tools			
40,000 to 10,000 B.C.		20	0.6667
Spear-thrower	Bow and arrow		
Lamps	Harpoon heads		
Fish gorgets	Pins or awls		
Needles with eyes	Cord		
Shovels or scoops	Antler hammers		
Stone saws	Mattocks		
Spoons	Graving tools		
Jewelry	Stone ax with hafted handle		
Separate handles	Pestles and grinding slabs		
Boats	Musical instruments		
10,000 to 7,000 B.C.		16	5.3333
Beer	Fishhooks		
Fish traps	Fishnets		
Adzes	Sickles		
Plant cultivation	Domestication of sheep		
Basketry	Domestication of dog		
Grinding equipment	Leather-working tools		
Paving	Sledge		
Ice picks	Combs		

Sources: This table is based on data in Grahame Clark and Stuart Piggott, *Prehistoric Societies* (New York: Knopf, 1965); S. A. Semenov, *Prehistoric Technology* (New York: Barnes and Noble, 1964); John Pfeiffer, *The Emergence of Man*, 3d ed. (New York: Harper & Row, 1978); Jacquetta Hawkes, *Prehistory*, UNESCO History of Mankind, vol. 1, part 1 (New York: Mentor, 1965); Alexander Marshak, *The Roots of Civilization* (New York: McGraw-Hill, 1972); P. S. Bellwood, "The Peopling of the Pacific," *Scientific American*, 243 (Nov. 1980), pp. 174–185; Bruce Bower, "When The Human Spirit Soared," *Science News, vol.* 130 (Dec. 13, 1986), pp. 376–379; Robin Dennell, "Needles and Spear Throwers," *Natural History* (Oct. 1986), pp. 70–78; John Putnam, "In Search of Modern Hunters," *National Geographic*, vol. 174, no. 4 (Oct. 1988), p. 449; and Paul Mellars, "Major Issues in the Emergence of Modern Humans," *Current Anthropology*, 30 (1989), pp. 349–385.

The rapid acceleration in the rate of change in the last 30,000 years of the hunting and gathering era cannot be explained by genetic change alone, since our species, Homo sapiens, had already evolved by 100,000 B.C. and was present for the whole of the second time period in Table 5.1. Even our *sub*species, Homo sapiens sapiens, was present for the whole of the third period.[*]

What, then, was the cause?

[*]There have been two subspecies of Homo sapiens: (1) Homo sapiens neanderthalensis (Neanderthal man), and (2) Homo sapiens sapiens (fully modern man). The two coexisted for many thousands of years, but Homo neanderthalensis died out about 35,000 years ago.

TABLE 5.2 The Growth of Human Population During the Hunting and Gathering Era

Approximate Date	Estimated Human Population	Average Percentage Increase in Human Population Worldwide Per Thousand Years*
1,800,000 B.C.	400,000	
		0.04
150,000 B.C.	800,000	
		0.40
40,000 B.C.	1,200,000	
		6.10
7,000 B.C.	8,500,000	

*These figures are our own calculations.
Source: Adapted from Fekri Hassan, *Demographic Archaeology* (New York: Academic Press, 1981), table 12.3.

In recent years, a growing number of scholars have concluded that the explosive growth in the rate of technological innovation in this period resulted from critical advances in *language*.[23] While symbol use almost certainly began much earlier than this, earlier symbol systems were probably much more primitive and much less effective as instruments for learning, remembering, and sharing information. According to proponents of this view, the relatively modest genetic changes that were involved in the transition to Homo sapiens sapiens (fully modern man) paved the way for the explosive growth of culture that occurred at the end of the Old Stone Age, and for all the revolutionary social and cultural changes that followed. In other words, there was a critical "threshold effect"* involved: until a certain point was reached in biological evolution, the development of full-fledged symbol systems was impossible. But once that point was reached, the development of language could proceed rapidly.

The striking advances in technology at the end of the hunting and gathering era coincided with, and were probably the cause of, an equally striking growth in the size of the human population. According to estimates based on recent archaeological research, the rate of growth of the human population increased substantially after 40,000 B.C. (see Table 5.2). This growth of population then would have increased the need for food and also increased the number of people looking for ways of providing it, thus contributing to the rising rate of innovation.

Despite the rapid increase in the rate of growth during this period, the human population at the end of the hunting and gathering era still numbered less than 10 million and its rate of growth was still less than 0.1 percent per year (compared with 1.7 percent per year today). The reason for this was the inability of societies to provide adequately for their members and to protect them against disease and other dangers. A recent study of more than 300 skeletons of adults from Europe and Africa during the hunting and gathering era indicates that the average age at death was just 33 years for men and 28 for women.[24] Thus, the reproductive years for women were far fewer than they are today. With the high rates of infant mortality that also prevailed,[25] it is no wonder that the rate of growth of the human population was still extremely low at the end of the hunting and gathering era.

*See footnote on page 13.

HUNTING AND GATHERING SOCIETIES
OF THE RECENT PAST

Even after the emergence of more advanced types of societies, hunting and gathering societies continued to flourish in many parts of the world. A hundred years ago there were still large numbers of them in both the New World and Australia, and smaller numbers in southwest Africa, in parts of the rain forest in central Africa, in certain remote areas in southeast Asia and neighboring islands, and in Arctic Asia.[26] As recently as 1788 there were probably 5,000 hunting and gathering societies in Australia alone[27] and almost certainly as many in North America. Although the settlement of these areas by Europeans and the spreading influence of industrialization are now destroying the last of them, we have detailed descriptions of many of these groups.

In our review, we will concentrate on hunting and gathering groups whose way of life had been least affected by contact with agrarian and industrial societies at the time they were studied. Our primary concern will be with the more remote and isolated groups and with groups that were studied before social contacts and cultural diffusion transformed or destroyed their traditional social patterns.

Even with these limitations, the societies in our sample are by no means all alike. Of the 174 hunting and gathering societies in Murdock's data set (see Appendix, page 441), 12 percent relied on hunting and gathering for their entire subsistence, while 13 percent relied on these techniques for only about half. Most groups (81 percent) depended on fishing to some extent, and a few (15 percent) obtained nearly half their food from this source. A minority (28 percent) derived part from horticulture, and a few (less than 5 percent) almost half. In short, some were pure hunting and gathering societies, but most of them incorporated limited elements of fishing or horticulture or both.

Population

Size and Density   Despite these variations in subsistence technology, modern hunting and gathering societies* have a lot in common. For example, none supports a large or dense population: nearly 80 percent have less than one person per square mile.[28] Communities, therefore, are necessarily small. And, since communities are almost always autonomous, societies are equally small. The average size of those that survived into the modern era has been approximately 40.[29] As ecological–evolutionary theory would lead us to expect, the more completely societies depend for their subsistence on hunting and gathering, the smaller they tend to be, while those that incorporate fishing, horticulture, or herding as secondary means of subsistence are larger (see Table 5.3).

*When referring to "modern" hunting and gathering societies, we mean those that survived into the modern era (i.e., the last several hundred years). In writing about these societies, the present tense is usually used for convenience even though most of the studies were conducted some years ago.

TABLE 5.3 **Average Size of Hunting and Gathering Societies, by Percentage of Food Supply Obtained through Hunting and Gathering**

Percentage of Food Supply Obtained through Hunting and Gathering	Median Size	Number of Societies
86–100*	29	34
50–85*	49	71

*These figures are estimates made by Murdock and his associates, based on nonquantitative statements in ethnographic sources.
Source: See Appendix, pages 441–442.

The rate of population growth in hunting societies is usually so low as to be virtually nonexistent.* The number of births seems to be matched by the number of deaths. In part, this is because of high death rates from natural causes, such as accidents and disease.[30] But it is also the result of biological processes which slow the birthrate: women who are nursing infants and women with little body fat are both less likely to ovulate than other women.[31]

The most important factor in producing an equilibrium between births and deaths may be cultural, however, rather than biological. Infanticide and abortion are extremely widespread in these societies. One study revealed that infanticide was practiced in 80 of 86 hunting and gathering societies examined, while another study found that abortion was practiced in 13 of 15 societies.[32] Some scholars estimate that between 15 and 50 percent of all live births end in infanticide in societies at this level of development.[33]

The members of hunting and gathering societies are not, of course, less loving than the members of other societies. Their norms and values, like those of every society, simply reflect the past experience of the group. And this has taught them that any other course of action can be disastrous. When a mother already has one child at the breast, and may have to keep it there for several years because there is no safe alternative source of nourishment,[34] another baby can mean death for both children. This is especially likely to be true if the food supply is variable, that is, if hunting and gathering provide a glut of food at some times and shortages at others. If, in addition, the mother must participate regularly in the search for food and watch over her children at the same time, and if she must carry all her possessions as well as her children to a new campsite every few weeks or months (see below), the logic of abortion and infanticide becomes obvious. They are simply measures that ensure the health and survival of mothers and children, and thus the survival of the society.

Nomadism Modern hunting and gathering societies are usually nomadic. Some groups are reported to remain in an area for periods as short as a week.[35] In contrast, a few occupy permanent settlements, but all of these either rely on fishing or horticulture as important secondary sources of subsistence or are located in areas with high concentrations of game and other food resources.[36]

---

*Rapid population growth occurs in these societies only when they are able to expand into new territories or gain access to new sources of food.

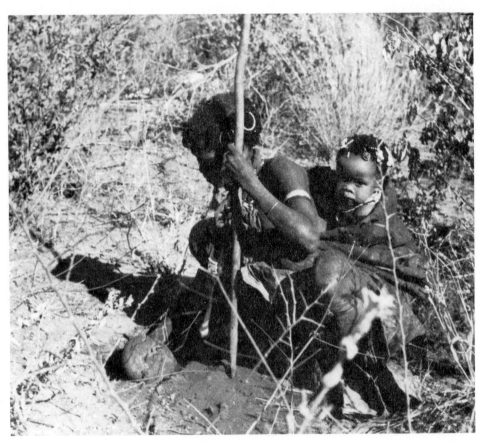

FIGURE 5.6 Bushman mother carrying infant while digging roots.

The nomadic character of most hunting and gathering groups is an inevitable result of their subsistence technology. One anthropologist described the basic problem when he said of a group of African Pygmies with whom he had lived that "after a month, as a rule, the fruits of the forest have been gathered all around the vicinity of the camp, and the game has been scared away to a greater distance than is comfortable for daily hunting."[37] He went on to say that since "the economy relies on the day-to-day quest, the simplest thing is for the camp to move."

Hunters and gatherers may also change campsites for other reasons. A recent study of the Hadza in east Africa, for example, indicates that they often move to the place where a large animal has been killed simply to avoid carrying the meat.[38] Since their possessions are few, such a move requires little effort. The Hadza also move to a new site when someone dies, or even when a member becomes sick or has a bad dream, because these are all regarded as bad omens.

Many hunting and gathering groups disperse for a part of the year, with individual families striking out on their own. This pattern has been observed in such widely scattered groups as the Bushmen of southwest Africa, the Eskimo, and the Australian aborigines. Sometimes seasonal changes in flora and fauna make it more advantageous for the group to split up and do their hunting and foraging in smaller groups. Sometimes the splitting up of the group seems to be a response to controversies and conflicts that require a cooling-off period—after which the desire for more social interaction serves to bring the group together again.[39]

Despite their nomadism, hunters and gatherers usually restrict their movements to a fairly well defined territory. When the society moves, it usually settles in or near some former campsite. There may even be a regular circuit of sites that the group uses year after year. A group is usually deterred from entering new territories because they are already occupied by others. Moreover, hunters and gatherers normally have a strong attachment to their traditional territory, which has often acquired a sacred character that is maintained through song and legend.

Kinship

Ties of kinship are vitally important in most hunting and gathering groups. It is hard for members of modern industrial societies to appreciate the tremendous significance of these ties, because so much of our own social interaction is organized independently of kinship, in terms of roles such as teacher and student, clerk and customer, or friend and friend.

In contrast, social interaction in hunting and gathering societies is usually organized around kinship roles. A student of the Australian aborigines reports that "in a typical Australian tribe it is found that a man can define his relations to every person with whom he has any social dealings whatever, whether of his own or of another tribe, by means of the terms of [kinship]."[40] Another writer says of these people that "every one with whom a person comes in contact is regarded as related to him, and the kind of relationship must be ascertained so that the two persons concerned will know what their mutual behavior should be."[41] He adds that kinship ties are the anatomy and physiology of aboriginal society and "must be understood if the behavior of the aborigines as social beings is to be understood." Though there are exceptions, *kinship is usually the basic organizing principle in hunting and gathering societies.*[42]

Viewed in evolutionary perspective, the family has often been described as the matrix, or womb, from which all other social institutions have evolved. This points to a basic truth: *in hunting and gathering societies, kin groups perform many of the functions that are performed by schools, business firms, governmental agencies, and other specialized organizations in larger, more advanced, and more differentiated societies.*

Kin groups in hunting and gathering societies are of two types, *nuclear* and *extended families*. A nuclear family includes a man, his wife or wives, and their unmarried children. Polygyny (see Glossary) is widespread; only 10 percent of the hunting and gathering groups in Murdock's data set are classified as monogamous. It does not follow, of course, that 90 percent of the *families* in this kind of society are polygynous: this is impossible, given the roughly equal numbers of men and women. Usually only one or two of the most influential men have more than one wife, and they seldom have more than two or three. This limited polygyny is possible because girls usually marry younger than boys, and some men are obliged to remain bachelors. Multiple wives appear to be an economic asset in these societies and, to some extent, a status symbol as well.

Divorce is permitted in virtually all hunting and gathering societies and is fairly common in some.[43] In others, however, it is made relatively difficult. The most we can say is that there is great variability in this matter.

The nuclear family is usually part of a larger and more inclusive kin group known as the extended family.[44] In the majority of modern hunting and gathering societies the extended family includes both maternal and paternal relatives—a pattern that is *not* found in the majority of horticultural, herding, and agrarian societies. Compared with extended family systems that emphasize ties with either maternal or paternal kin, this bilateral, or two-sided, system effectively doubles the number of people to whom an individual can turn for help in time of difficulty, an arrangement that appears to have considerable adaptive value in societies that are so small.[45]

The extended family is also important because the ties of kinship among its members encourage the practice of sharing. When the daily acquisition of food is uncertain, as it is in many hunting and gathering societies, a nuclear family could easily starve if it had to depend exclusively on its own efforts. A family might be surfeited with food for a time and then suddenly have nothing. Or all the adult members of the family could become ill or injured at the same time. In either case the family would be dependent on the generosity of others. Although sharing can, and does, take place between unrelated persons, kinship ties strengthen the tendency. In this connection it is interesting to note that many hunting and gathering peoples create what we would call fictional ties of kinship when there is no "real" relationship by blood or marriage. These ties are just as meaningful to them as "true" kinship ties and they serve to strengthen the bonds uniting the group—much like the role of godparent in some more developed societies.

Through marriages with people in nearby groups (a practice known as *exogamy*), a society gradually establishes a web of kinship ties with neighboring groups. According to one anthropologist, "One of the important functions of exogamy is that of opening up territories so that peaceful movements can take place among them, and particularly so that any large temporary variations in food resources can be taken advantage of by related groups."[46] This is also the explanation for the custom of wife lending, practiced by hunting and gathering peoples as diverse as the Eskimo and the Australian aborigines.[47] As in the case of exogamy, the purpose seems to be to strengthen, restore, or create bonds between the men involved. Thus, if two individuals or two groups have had a quarrel, they may settle it by lending one another their wives. The practice is predicated on the assumption that women are prized possessions that one does not share with everyone. It would be a mistake to suppose, however, that women are merely property in these societies; they often have considerable influence in the life of the group and are by no means mere chattels.

The Economy

Economic institutions are not highly developed in hunting and gathering societies. One reason is that the combination of a primitive technology and a nomadic way of life makes it impossible for most hunting and gathering peoples to accumulate many possessions (see Figure 5.7). In describing the Bushmen of southwest Africa, one ethnographer explains, "It is not advantageous to multiply and accumulate in this society. Any man can make what he needs when he wants to. Most of the materials he uses are abundant and free for anyone to take. Furthermore, in their nomadic lives, without beasts of burden, the fact that the people themselves must carry everything puts a sharp limit on the quantity of objects they want to possess."[48] The minority of hunting and gathering groups that are able to establish permanent settlements may

FIGURE 5.7   Home and possessions of Paiute family in southern Utah in the 1870s.

accumulate more possessions, but even they are severely limited by their primitive technology.[49]

The quest for food is obviously a crucial activity in every hunting and gathering society. Since most of these societies have no way to store food for extended periods, the food quest must be fairly continuous. Moreover, unlike the situation in more advanced societies, every adult member of the group, except some of the elderly, participates and makes a contribution in this most basic part of the economy.

Prior to the last quarter century, most studies of hunting and gathering societies emphasized the uncertainty of the food supply and the difficulty of obtaining it.[50] A number of more recent studies, however, paint a brighter picture. Reports from the Pygmies of the Congo, the aborigines of Australia, and even the Bushmen of the Kalahari Desert in southwestern Africa indicate that they all secure an ample supply of food without an undue expenditure of time or energy.[51] This has led some anthropologists to swing to the opposite extreme and refer to hunters and gatherers as "the most leisured people in the world" and to their way of life as "the original affluent society."[52]

Neither view does justice to the diversity and changeability of the situations reported by the numerous observers who have lived among these peoples. Conditions vary considerably from group to group, and within a group they may vary from season to season. For example, the Indians of northern California usually had an abundance of food, and yet even they occasionally encountered a shortage so severe that some of them starved.[53]

A very few societies do not practice hunting. For the rest, hunting usually provides less food, in terms of bulk, than gathering. According to one estimate, the gathering done by women accounts for 60 to 80 percent of the food supply of hunters and gatherers, except in arctic regions.[54] Yet hunting is valued more highly than gathering in virtually all these groups for several reasons. For one thing, meat is generally preferred to vegetables.[55] Whether this reflects a genetically based need or preference, we do not know; certainly not everyone feels this way. In some groups, preference for meat may simply reflect its scarcity. Hunting may also be valued because it requires greater skill and involves more uncertainty regarding the outcome. Added to all this is the fact that meat, unlike vegetables, is commonly shared beyond the immediate family, so success in hunting may be rewarded by widespread respect and deference. One leading anthropologist even suggests that sharing meat "is basic to the continued association of families in any human group that hunts."[56]

Because of the primitive nature of its technology, the division of labor in a hunting and gathering economy is largely limited to distinctions based on age and sex. Almost all hunting and military activities fall to the male, as do most political, religious, ceremonial, and artistic activities. The collection and preparation of vegetables and the care of children are women's responsibilities.[57] Some activities, such as constructing a shelter, may be defined as either men's or women's work, depending on the society.[58] Still other activities may be considered appropriate for both sexes. Further division of labor results because both the very young and the aged are limited in their capabilities.

There are no full-time occupational specialties in hunting and gathering societies, although there is usually some part-time specialization. For example, most groups

Why Were Women Not the Hunters?

The revival of the women's movement in recent decades and its claim that biological differences between the sexes should be irrelevant in the division of labor invites the question of why men were the hunters and women the gatherers in hunting and gathering societies. Why not the reverse, or perhaps a sharing of responsibilities?

In recent years, a number of social scientists have reexamined these questions and concluded that the biological differences between the sexes made a role reversal, or even a sharing of responsibilities, impossible in technologically limited societies such as these. Hunting with bows and spears requires speed, agility, and upper-body strength, and women, *on average*, are biologically disadvantaged in all three respects.

These disadvantages are linked to the special role of women in the reproductive process. The later stages of pregnancy, for example, reduce the speed and agility of women in obvious ways. But the requirements of reproduction have other, more subtle consequences. Because of the physiological demands of pregnancy and lactation on a mother's body, women have a higher ratio of fat to muscle than men. On average, about 21 percent of their weight consists of fatty tissue compared to 15 percent for men. This provides women with nutritional reserves on which they can draw during food shortages, both for their own sustenance and for that of a foetus or nursing infant. But less muscle tissue means reduced upperbody strength. Recent tests by the U.S. Army indicate that, on average, women have 42 percent less upper-body strength than men and that only 3 percent of women can perform "very heavy" tasks compared with 80 percent of men.

With training, women can obviously develop their muscles to a level that exceeds that of the average man. For example, when Candy Csencsits placed second in the 1983 Ms. Olympia Contest, she was down to 7 percent body fat (champion male body builders have even less, 3 to 5 percent). But when women drop below 15 percent body fat, they often cease to ovulate and become infertile. Thus, muscular development in women appears to conflict with the role of child-bearing. In other words, if there ever were societies that used women extensively in hunting, they probably did not survive because of low birth rates.

In addition to all this, women in most hunting and gathering societies must nurse their babies for at least two to four years, due to the lack of a safe and adequate substitute for mother's milk. And, since nursing infants need to be fed often, mothers are not able to roam as widely or as fast as hunting requires. Finally, in most of these societies, women are usually either pregnant or lactating and thus have little opportunity to develop and maintain the many complex skills required in hunting. The end result, therefore, has been the classic division of labor in which men hunt and women gather.

Sources: Ernestine Friedel, *Women and Men* (New York: Holt, Rinehart, and Winston, 1975); Joan Huber and Glenna Spitze, *Sex Stratification* (New York: Academic Press, 1983); Janet Saltzman Chafetz, *Sex and Advantage* (Totowa, N.J.: Rowman and Allanheld, 1984); Michael Levin, "Women as Soldiers—The Record So Far," *The Public Interest*, 76 (Summer 1984), pp. 31–44; and Blythe Hamer, "Women Body Builders," *Science 86*, 7(March 1986), pp. 74–75.

have at least a headman and a shaman or medicine man. When their services are required, they function in these specialized capacities, but, as one writer says of the
headmen of the Bergdama and the Bushmen, "when not engaged on public business
they follow the same occupations as all other people."[59] He adds that this is most of
the time.

Within hunting and gathering societies, the family or kin group is normally the
only significant form of economic organization. Sometimes, when the practice of sharing is widespread and hunting and gathering are carried on as communal activities,
even the kin group ceases to be economically important.

With respect to subsistence, each society is virtually self-sufficient. Trade between
societies often occurs, but except where contacts have been established with more
advanced societies, the bartered items tend to be nonessentials—primarily objects
with status or esthetic value. Such exchanges usually involve things that are scarce or
nonexistent in one group's territory but present in the other's (e.g., certain kinds of
shells, stones, or feathers).

Trade with advanced societies is more likely to involve economically important
items. For example, many groups obtain metal tools and weapons this way.[60] In the
past, these imports were seldom on a scale sufficient to alter the basic character of
hunting and gathering societies.[61] In the last century, however, as contacts with industrialized and industrializing societies have increased, the volume and importance
of such items have often greatly distorted traditional patterns of economic life and
done much to undermine the sociocultural system as a whole.

The Polity

The political institutions of modern hunting and gathering societies are very rudimentary. As we have seen, most local communities are autonomous and independent
entities (i.e., they are societies as well as communities) even though they have populations of fewer than fifty people. Because they are so small, hunting and gathering
societies have not developed political mechanisms of the kind required to control
and coordinate large or diverse populations.

The primitive nature of the political systems of these societies can be seen clearly
in their limited development of specialized political roles and in the equally limited
authority given to people in those roles. In most cases there is simply a headman who
provides minimal leadership for the group.[62] Allan Holmberg, who lived among the
Siriono of eastern Bolivia, wrote a description of their headmen that, except for details, is a portrait of the "typical" headman in a hunting and gathering society.

> Presiding over every band of Siriono is a headman, who is at least nominally
> the highest official of the group. Although his authority theoretically extends
> throughout the band, in actual practice its exercise depends almost entirely
> upon his personal qualities as a leader. In any case, there is no obligation to
> obey the orders of a headman, no punishment for nonfulfillment. Indeed,
> little attention is paid to what is said by a headman unless he is a member of

one's immediate family. To maintain his prestige a headman must fulfill, in a superior fashion, those obligations required of everyone else.

> The prerogatives of a headman are few.... The principal privilege ... if it could be called such, is that it is his right to occupy, with his immediate family, the center of the [communal] house. Like any other man he must make his bows and arrows, his tools; he must hunt, fish, collect, and [so forth]. He makes suggestions as to migrations, hunting trips, etc., but these are not always followed by his [people]. As a mark of status, however, a headman always possesses more than one wife.

> While headmen complain a great deal that other members of the band do not satisfy their obligations to them, little heed is paid to their requests....

> In general, however, headmen fare better than other members of the band. Their requests more frequently bear fruit than those of others because headmen are the best hunters and are thus in a better position than most to reciprocate for any favors done them.[63]

There are similar reports on headmen in most other hunting and gathering societies.[64] In a number of instances it is said that the headman "held his place only so long as he gave satisfaction."

Occasionally the headman enjoys a bit more power and privilege. Among the Bergdama of southwest Africa, for example, the headman "is treated with universal respect, being specified as a 'great man' by adults and 'grandfather' by children; he usually has the most wives (sometimes three or more); he has the pick of all wild animal skins for clothing himself and his family, and only his wives wear necklaces or girdles of ostrich eggshell beads; and he receives portions of all game killed in the chase, and tribute from men finding honey."[65]

At the opposite extreme are a number of hunting and gathering societies, including 12 percent of those in Murdock's data set, that do not even have a headman. In these societies, decisions that affect the entire group are arrived at through informal discussions among the more respected and influential members, typically the heads of families.[66]

The limited development of political institutions in hunting and gathering societies contrasts markedly with the situation in more advanced societies. The small size and relative isolation of these societies make it possible for them to handle their political problems very informally. Consensus is achieved much more readily in a small, homogeneous group of a few dozen people (of whom only the adults, and often only the adult males, have a voice) than in larger, more heterogeneous communities with thousands of members. A headman is valuable to such a small group only if he contributes special knowledge, insight, or skills.

Even if the leader of a hunting and gathering band were ambitious and eager to increase his power, he would not get very far. Unlike leaders in technologically more advanced societies, he would find it impossible to build and maintain an organization of dependent retainers to do his bidding, or to obtain a monopoly on weapons. The materials for making weapons lie ready at hand, and every man is trained to make

FIGURE 5.8 Bushman hunter, southwest Africa.

and use them. If a person becomes unhappy with the group, he or she can usually leave it and join another.[67] Thus, there are no opportunities for building political empires, even on a small scale.

Given the rudimentary nature of political institutions in hunting and gathering societies, one might suppose that there are few restrictions on people. In one sense this is true; there are few rules imposed by political authorities—no courts, no police, no prisons. Individuals are hardly free, however, to do as they wish. No society is indifferent to the actions of its members, and even in the absence of formal constraints, the group controls their conduct through informal norms and sanctions.

Though there are minor variations from one hunting and gathering society to another, similar patterns of social control have developed in groups as far apart as the Kaska Indians of the Canadian Northwest, the Andaman Islanders of southeast Asia, and the Bushmen of southwest Africa.[68] First, there is the custom of blood revenge, whereby the injured party, aided, perhaps, by his kinsmen, punishes the offender himself. As one student of the Bushmen put it, "when disputes arise between the members of the band . . . there is no appeal to any supreme authority [since] . . . there is no such authority. . . . The only remedy is self-help."[69] This mode of social control is usually invoked only when the victim of the offense is a single individual or a family. In contrast, when an entire band suffers because of a member's actions, group pressure is brought to bear on the individual. For example, if a man refuses to do his part in providing food, he is punished by losing the respect of others.[70] In the case of more serious offenses, the penalty may be ostracism or even banishment. The third method of control is a deterrent that applies primarily to violations of ritual prescriptions. In such cases, the group's fear of supernatural sanctions provides the needed restraint. Bushmen, for example, believe that girls who fail to observe the restrictions imposed on them at puberty turn into frogs.[71] All three methods of social control are very informal and would not work except in small, homogeneous groups in which ties among the members are intimate and continuous, and contradictory ideas are absent.

Stratification

The rudimentary nature of the political system and the primitive nature of the economic system contribute to yet another distinctive characteristic of modern hunting and gathering societies: *minimal inequality in power and privilege*. Differences between individuals are so slight, in fact, that a number of observers have spoken of a kind of "primitive communism." To some extent this is justified. As we have seen, political authority with the power to coerce is virtually nonexistent. Differences in *influence* exist, but only to the degree permitted by those who are influenced, and only as a result of their respect for another individual's skills or wisdom. When individuals lose this respect, they also lose their influence.

   In most hunting and gathering societies, differences in wealth are very minor. Many factors are responsible for this. For one thing, as we have seen, the nomadic way of life prevents any substantial accumulation of possessions. In addition, the ready availability of most essential resources (e.g., wood for bows, flint for stone tools) precludes the need to amass things, while technological limitations greatly restrict what can be produced. Finally, there is the widespread practice of sharing in most of these groups.

   As a general rule the concept of private property has only limited development among hunting and gathering peoples. Things that an individual uses constantly, such as tools and weapons, are always recognized as his own, but fields and forests are the common property of the entire society (see Table 5.4). These territorial rights are often taken quite seriously, and outsiders are frequently obliged to ask permission to enter another group's territory to seek food.[72] Animals and plants are normally considered common property until they are killed or gathered, at which time they be-

TABLE 5.4 Frequency of Private Ownership of Land, by Societal Type

Societal Type	Frequency of Private Ownership of Land (in Percentages)				Total	No. of Societies
	General	Frequent	Rare	Absent		
Hunting and gathering	0	0	11	89	100	9
Horticultural	36	23	23	18	100	22

Source: Derived from data in Leo Simmons, *The Role of the Aged in Primitive Society* (New Haven, Conn.: Yale, 1945).

come the property of the individual. Even then, however, use of them is hedged about by the rule of sharing.[73]

A successful hunter does not normally keep his kill for himself alone or even, in most cases, for his family.[74] The reason for this seems to be the same as that which underlies insurance systems in industrial societies: *it is an effective method of spreading risks.* As we have seen, poor hunting conditions, ill health, or just a streak of bad luck can render any individual or family incapable of providing for itself, and sharing food greatly enhances everyone's chances of survival.

Despite near equality in power and wealth, there is *inequality in prestige* in most hunting and gathering societies. The interesting thing about this, from the viewpoint of members of industrial societies, is the extent to which prestige depends on the *personal* qualities of an individual rather than on impersonal criteria, such as the offices or roles he occupies or the possessions he controls. This is, of course, a natural consequence of the limited development of specialized offices and roles and the limited opportunities for accumulating possessions and wealth. But it sharply differentiates these societies from more advanced ones.

The Andaman Islanders accord honor and respect to three kinds of people: (1) older people, (2) people endowed with supernatural powers, and (3) people with certain personal qualities, notably "skill in hunting and warfare, generosity and kindness, and freedom from bad temper."[75] Men are apparently more likely than women to become honored members of the group. Similar types of people are accorded honor and prestige in most other hunting and gathering societies, and skill in oratory is often honored as well.[76]

Because personal characteristics are so important, systems of stratification in these groups have an openness about them not often found in more advanced societies. Almost no organizational or institutional barriers block the rise of talented individuals. For example, even where the office of headman is inherited, as it is in approximately half the societies,[77] others may surpass him in achieving honor. The study of the Siriono Indians cited earlier tells of a headman who was a very poor hunter and whose status, as a result, was low. The importance attached to age also contributes to the openness of the system. Almost anyone who lives long enough usually ends up with a fair degree of honor and respect.

Religion

In almost every carefully studied hunting and gathering society of the modern era, there is evidence that its members have grappled with the problem of explaining the world around them, especially those aspects of it that influence their own lives. Up to a point, their explanations and their interpretations of reality are the same as ours: animals run when they are frightened, people become hungry when they do not have enough to eat, and serious illness can cause death.

Because their store of information is so much more limited than ours, however, members of these societies quickly reach the limits of their ability to explain things in naturalistic terms. Insufficient food causes hunger; but why is there insufficient food? Illness is the cause of a death; but what caused the illness? To answer questions such

FIGURE 5.9 Bushman shaman in trance, southwestern Africa.

as these, members of hunting and gathering societies, like people in every society confronted with what they do not fully understand, have developed their own sets of explanations. These explanations form the basis of a type of religion known as *animism*.[78]

The central element in animism is the belief that spirits inhabit virtually everything in the world of nature: rocks, trees, lakes, clouds, and other inanimate things, as well as animals and humans. These spirits are constantly intervening in human affairs, sometimes helping, sometimes harming. They cause the arrow to strike the deer, or they warn the animal so it bolts; they enter the body to heal a wound, or they settle in the intestines to twist and burn them. Furthermore, these spirits can be influenced by humans who know the proper rituals, sacrifices, and magic charms. Some humans, however, are more skillful at this than others, and when people fail in their efforts to appease a spirit, as when a sick child fails to recover, they turn to the expert in such matters, the *medicine man* or *shaman*.

Shamans are not specialists in the strict sense of the term, any more than headmen are specialists. They are individuals who spend most of their time doing the same things as others of their sex (most shamans are men, but some are women), serving in their more specialized role only when the need arises.

TABLE 5.5 Emphasis in Child-Rearing,* by Societal Type, in Percentages

Societal Type	Self-Reliance Stressed More than Obedience	Self-Reliance and Obedience Stressed Equally	Obedience Stressed More than Self-Reliance	N
Hunting and gathering	63	13	23	19
Simple horticultural	34	20	46	26
Advanced horticultural	24	13	63	39
Agrarian	12	7	82	15

*The values in this table are arithmetic averages of four separate sets of data for (1) young boys, (2) older boys, (3) young girls, and (4) older girls. Controlling for age, greater emphasis was placed on self-reliance for boys than for girls in all types of societies. Controlling for sex, greater emphasis was placed on self-reliance for older boys than for younger, but no consistent pattern was observed among girls.
Source: See Appendix, pages 441–442.

While a shaman uses his powers in various ways, one of the most common is in healing. He may also use them to ensure the success of hunting expeditions, to protect the group against evil spirits and other dangers, and generally to ensure the group's well-being. Shamans do not always use their special powers for the benefit of others, however. Sometimes they employ them to punish people who have offended them.[79]

Because of their role, shamans usually command respect and often are more influential than the headman.[80] Sometimes, as with the Northern Maidu in California, the headman "was chosen largely through the aid of the shaman, who was supposed to reveal to the older men the choice of the spirits."[81] The role of shaman also tends to be profitable, since others are usually happy to offer gifts in exchange for help or to maintain goodwill.[82]

Education

Socialization of the young in hunting and gathering societies is largely an informal process in which children learn both through their play and through observing and imitating their elders. At a relatively early age boys are allowed to join the men on the hunt, participating in any activities of which they are capable. Fathers commonly make miniature bows as soon as their sons can handle them, and encourage the boys to practice. Girls assist their mothers in their campsite duties and in gathering vegetables and fruits. Thus children prepare for their future roles.

This informal socialization is often supplemented by a formal process of initiation that marks the transition from childhood to manhood or womanhood.[83] Initiation rites vary considerably from one society to another, though girls' ceremonies are usually linked with their first menstruation. The rites for boys commonly involve painful experiences (e.g., circumcision, scarification, or knocking out a tooth), which prove their courage and thus their right to the privileges of manhood. As a rule, these rites are also the occasion for introducing young men to their group's most sacred lore, and this combination of experiences helps to impress on them its value and importance.

Compared with horticultural and agrarian societies, hunting and gathering societies put more stress on training the child to be independent and self-reliant, less on obedience (see Table 5.5). This is apparently a cultural response to a subsistence economy in which it is imperative to have venturesome, independent adults who take initiative in finding and securing food.[84] In contrast, venturesomeness and independence are less valuable and less often encouraged in technologically more advanced horticultural and agrarian societies. Rather, it is important that children in those societies learn to conform to the established norms of planting, cultivating, and harvesting, and the other proven routines of farming.

The Arts and Leisure

Modern hunting and gathering peoples have produced a variety of artistic works. Some are strikingly similar to the cave drawings and carvings of hunters and gatherers of prehistoric times. The motivation behind these efforts is not always clear, but in some cases it is plainly religious, in others, magical.[85] And sometimes it appears to be purely esthetic.

Music, too, plays a part in the lives of at least some hunters and gatherers. In Pygmy hunter festivals, songs and the music of a primitive wooden trumpet are central.[86] These festivals have great religious significance and express the people's devotion to, and trust in, the forest in which they live and on which they depend. And, as with the visual arts, music may be used purely for esthetic purposes, self-expression, and enjoyment.[87] Dancing is another valued feature of life in many of these societies, and, again, the motives for it are varied.

FIGURE 5.10 Cave art by contemporary Australian hunters and gatherers: the water snake and turtle are important figures in the religion of these people.

Another popular leisure activity is storytelling. Pygmies are said to be blessed with a lively imagination.[88] Stories range from accounts of the day's hunt (often embellished to hold the listeners' attention) to sacred myths and legends passed down over many generations. Legends commonly deal with the origins of the world and of the group. Stories about the exploits of great heroes of the past are popular and are often used to explain the group's customs. Sacred myths and legends, as we have seen, frequently enter into initiation rites, especially for boys, and they are sometimes accompanied by music and dance. This complex interweaving of art, religion, entertainment, and education provides a strong foundation for tradition and for sociocultural continuity.

Hunters and gatherers, like people everywhere, enjoy gossip, small talk, and other nonessential activities. Games are played in virtually all of these societies, but it is interesting to note that games of strategy are absent, while games of chance are more common than in other types of societies (see Table 5.6). Since a society's games, like the rest of its culture, reflect its experiences, the absence of games of strategy suggests that hunters and gatherers feel less sense of control over the events in their lives than the members of more advanced societies feel.

Tribal Ties: Links between Societies

As we have noted a number of times, each band or local group of hunters and gatherers is usually autonomous. Rarely are even two of them brought together under a single leader, and when this does happen, it usually involves groups that are no longer completely dependent on hunting and gathering.

Despite the virtual absence of formal political organizations encompassing different communities, there are often informal social and cultural ties. The most inclusive of these, and one that is nearly universal, is the *tribe*—a group of people who speak a distinctive language or dialect, share a culture that distinguishes them from other peoples, and know themselves, and are known, by a distinctive name.[89] Unlike a society, a tribe is not necessarily organized politically. On the contrary, among hunting and gathering peoples almost none are.

TABLE 5.6 **Types of Games, by Societal Type**

Type of Society	Percentage of Societies Having Games of:			No. of Societies
	Physical Skill	**Chance**	**Strategy**	
Hunting and gathering	97	81	0	129
Simple horticultural	78	34	10	67
Advanced horticultural	90	37	57	60
Agrarian	97	74	71	35
Fishing	97	61	3	33
Herding	92	39	54	13

Source: See Appendix, pages 441–442.

Most tribes appear to have been formed by the process of societal fission or division. When the population of a hunting and gathering band grows too large for the resources of the immediate area, it divides. Division may also occur because of conflict within a band.[90] In either case, although a new group is formed, its members will naturally continue to share the culture of the parent group. Normally the new group locates somewhere near the old one, if only because its technology and accumulated experience become less relevant the further it moves and the more the environment differs from the one its members have been used to. If this process of fission is repeated a number of times, a cluster of autonomous bands with the same language and similar stores of information develops, and a tribe emerges.

As this suggests, among hunters and gatherers the tribe is more important as a cultural unit than as a social unit. One writer, describing the Bushmen, reports that the tribe "has no social solidarity, and is of very little, if any, importance in regulating social life. There appears to be no tribal organization among the Bushmen, nothing in the nature of a central authority whose decisions are binding on all the members of the tribe, nor is collective action ever taken in the interests of the tribe as a whole."[91] Sometimes, as in Australia, an entire tribe assembles periodically for rituals and ceremonies, but this is not typical.

From the organizational standpoint the chief significance of these tribal groupings lies in their evolutionary potential: with technological advance, they may become political units. Even among societies still on the hunting and gathering level, there is some evidence of movement in this direction. In a few of the more favorably situated sedentary groups, for example, several villages have been brought together under the leadership of a single individual.[92] This development is greatly facilitated by their common cultural heritage.

HUNTING AND GATHERING SOCIETIES IN THEORETICAL PERSPECTIVE

Archaeological and Ethnographic Evidence Compared

Now that we have completed our review of both the archaeological and the ethnographic evidence, we can consider the relationship between prehistoric hunting and gathering groups and those of the modern era. Though indiscriminate comparisons of the two can be misleading, our evidence indicates that careful comparisons can be extremely valuable.[93] To begin with, we must recognize that we cannot equate hunters and gatherers of the modern era with early hominid hunters and gatherers of a million or more years ago—before the process of human biological evolution had produced Homo sapiens sapiens and before the basic tools and weapons of modern hunters and gatherers had been invented. We can, however, reasonably compare hunters and gatherers of the recent past with others who have lived during the last 15,000 years.

We can see why, now that we are familiar with both sets of evidence. The similarities between these two sets of hunters and gatherers are many and basic; the differences are fewer and less important. The societies of the two periods are similar in such crucial matters as subsistence technology, size, relative equality,* and minimal occupational specialization. In addition, similarities in art suggest similarities in religious belief and practice.

The differences are largely of three types. First, in many hunting and gathering societies of the modern era there are some elements that originated in more advanced societies (e.g., metal tools and some religious ideas). Second, modern hunters and gatherers have had no opportunity to move into new territories, which means that population growth has been impossible for them and the number of deaths has had to balance the number of births. Prehistoric hunters and gatherers were not always subject to this harsh restriction. Finally, technologically advanced societies have often forced modern hunters and gatherers out of territories that were suitable for farming and herding.†

As we have seen, the archaeological record is much less complete than the ethnographic, being silent on many subjects about which the latter provides a wealth of information. Therefore, when the ethnographic record shows patterns that are consistent for all or most modern groups and when these patterns do not depend on conditions peculiar to the industrial era, archaeologists now tend to regard them as applicable to most of the hunting and gathering societies of the last 15,000 years. This reflects the growing awareness of the *limiting* nature of a hunting and gathering technology,[94] and the realization that the range of variation in the basic characteristics of societies that depend on that technology will inevitably be small. In short, except where relevant conditions have changed significantly, we can probably assume substantial similarity between the advanced hunting and gathering societies of late prehistoric times and those of recent centuries.

A Model of Limited Development

In Chapter 2 we saw that human societies are systems of interrelated parts. In Chapters 3 and 4 we identified subsistence technology as the single most powerful variable influencing the other characteristics of the system. Now that we have completed our analysis of the first of the major societal types, we are in a better position to appreciate both the systemic nature of societies and the critical role of technology.

Figure 5.11 portrays the systemic qualities of a hunting and gathering society, and the relationships among its most important characteristics. The key element is the *subsistence technology* on which members of these societies depend for their survival and well-being. Because of their dependence on hunting and gathering, most of these groups are destined to be nomadic and to have a low level of productivity and a limited store of other kinds of information.

---

*This is indicated by the absence of differentiation in the burial remains of prehistoric hunters and gatherers. In contrast, in technologically more advanced societies of later eras one finds clear evidence of distinctions between rich and poor, the former having rare and costly objects buried with them.
†See footnote on page 87. Moreover, hunters and gatherers in both the New World and Australia still occupied good farming and herding lands until fairly recently, so we are not entirely without information on societies that existed under such conditions.

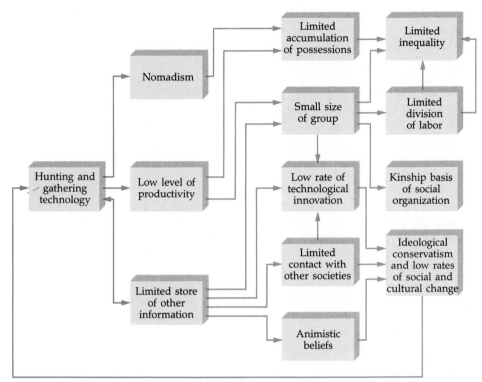

FIGURE 5.11 Model of relationships among the characteristics of hunting and gathering societies.

These characteristics lead in turn to other, second-order effects. Nomadism and the low level of productivity combine to limit possibilities for the accumulation of possessions. The low level of productivity and the limited store of other technological information, especially information relevant to transportation and communication, combine to keep hunting and gathering societies small. The limited development of these technologies also limits contacts with other societies. These characteristics combine with the small size of these societies to keep the rate of technological innovation low. The limited store of information about natural phenomena also contributes to the development of animistic beliefs.

Finally, these second-order effects, individually and collectively, produce a series of third-order effects. These include the low level of inequality that is characteristic of hunting and gathering societies, their limited division of labor, the kinship basis of social organization, and their ideological conservatism and low rates of social and cultural change. The latter, through a process of feedback, reinforces the dependence of these societies on hunting and gathering as their basic mode of subsistence. Thus, the system tends to be self-perpetuating.

The causal linkages indicated in Figure 5.11 may actually *understate* the degree to which the various characteristics of a hunting and gathering society are interrelated: some arrows that should have been included may have been omitted. The important point, however, is not the completeness of the model but the way it illustrates the systemic nature of these societies and shows the consequences of technology for every major component of the system, including basic beliefs and values.

Ecological–evolutionary theory, as we have seen, asserts that technology limits "the range of the possible" for a society, and in the case of hunting and gathering societies it is clear that *that range is remarkably narrow*. We do, of course, find differences among these societies, but not in their most basic characteristics. Many of these differences, as in modes of dress and housing, simply reflect variations in the environments to which these societies must adapt. Some differences, however, do not appear to be related to environmental conditions, and we have to assume that they reflect unknown and unknowable past experiences of the groups, experiences that led them to adopt dissimilar practices. We can see this, for example, in the case of marriage practices, which vary among societies at this level of development. It is clear that the limits set by a hunting and gathering technology are fairly broad with respect to this relationship. As a result, ideology—the information that helps people order societal life—comes into greater play.

But where the *basic* characteristics and development of hunting and gathering societies are concerned, technology sets strict and seemingly inviolable limits. These limits are less restrictive when the technology is applied to a particularly favorable environment. A society's biophysical environment, for example, may be especially rich in the resources on which the society depends, or its social environment may provide limited competition for those resources. But the only way the limits set by its technology can be *expanded* is for a hunting and gathering society to increase its store of technological information, as some of them have done by incorporating elements of fishing and horticulture.

The Last Hunting and Gathering Societies

In the summer of 1975, death came to the last full-blooded member of the Ona, a tribe of hunters and gatherers that had inhabited the southern tip of South America since at least the days of Ferdinand Magellan, the famed sixteenth-century explorer, and probably for centuries or even millennia before that.[95] It is estimated that in Magellan's day there were 2,000 Ona, divided into about thirty societies. The Ona survived the remoteness and harshness of their homeland only to be destroyed by their contacts with technologically more advanced societies. Disease, loss of territory, and loss of members to other societies all took their toll. The last Ona society died years ago; now the last Ona is also dead.

The experience of the Ona has been the experience of tens of thousands of hunting and gathering societies during the 9,000 years since hunters and gatherers first began competing for territories and other resources with technologically more advanced societies. Hunters and gatherers have had only one defense: retreat to lands that other groups regarded as worthless or inaccessible.

Today, even this defense is crumbling and the last outposts of this ancient way of life are doomed. The speed of the process is demonstrated by the experience of an

FIGURE 5.12 One of the last photographs of the Ona of Tierra del Fuego, a tribe of hunters and gatherers that is now extinct.

anthropologist who pioneered in the study of the Bushmen of the Kalahari Desert in southwest Africa. She reports that to reach them in 1951 required an arduous trip across the desert by truck, lasting eight days from the final outposts of civilization until contact with the Bushmen was made.[96] There was no road of any kind, not even a track across the sand and bush country. When she returned in 1962, only eleven years later, she reached them in one day over a well-cleared track. As Bushmen come more and more in contact with, and under the influence of, more advanced societies, their traditional way of life is doomed. Today, less than 5 percent of the 30,000 Kung Bushmen are still hunters and gatherers.[97]

By the end of this century the last hunting and gathering society will probably have vanished—and with it an irreplaceable link to our past. For thousands of years these societies maintained a remarkably stable relationship with their environments and a highly satisfying way of life. Relying entirely on cultural information that they could carry in their brains, hunters and gatherers adapted to a wide variety of bio-physical environments; and, until the advent of societies with larger populations and more sophisticated technologies, they also adapted successfully to their social environments. The process of change in each part of those sociocultural systems occurred so slowly that answering changes could occur in other parts without serious social unrest or upheaval. In short, this dying way of life served our species extremely well.

6

Horticultural Societies

Before the hunting and gathering era ended 9,000 years ago, human societies had accumulated substantial stores of information about plants and animals. People were as familiar with the behavior patterns of some animals as they were with their own, and probably understood them almost as well. They had also identified hundreds of varieties of edible plants and had become familiar with their processes of reproduction and growth. Some hunters and gatherers in the Middle East were even harvesting wild grains with stone sickles. Clearly the shift from hunting animals to herding them and from gathering fruits and vegetables to cultivating them was not as great or as difficult a step as one might imagine.[1]

But what induced societies to take that step? Why, after hundreds of thousands of years of hunting and gathering, did the members of some societies abandon that ancient, time-hallowed way of life? Above all, why did they do it when the new mode of production meant more work and less freedom?

CAUSES OF THE SHIFT FROM HUNTING AND GATHERING TO HORTICULTURE

Until recent decades, scholars tended to assume that, because of human intelligence and unsatisfied human needs, technological innovation and societal development are normal and natural and require no special explanation. By shifting from hunting and gathering to horticulture, they reasoned, societies assured themselves of a greater and more stable supply of food, and the members of any society would naturally make such a shift once the principles of plant cultivation came to be understood. Furthermore, it was generally assumed that horticulture required less labor than hunting and gathering. Thus, by adopting horticulture—that is, farming without plows—societies traded a precarious and onerous way of life for a more secure and satisfying one. Or so it seemed.

120

More recently, however, doubts have been cast on these explanations. To begin with, a growing body of archaeological research indicates that the members of many hunting and gathering societies understood and occasionally applied the basic principles of plant cultivation thousands of years before horticulture became their primary mode of subsistence. In addition, ethnographic studies of modern hunting and gathering societies have made it clear that their members place a high value on their way of life: they cherish the challenge and excitement of the hunt, and the freedom and other benefits their way of life affords. Finally, it has also become clear that most societies have not shared the positive view of innovation and change that prevails in industrial societies today. On the contrary, they place a high value on tradition and continuity.

As a result, most scholars now doubt that hunters and gatherers abandoned hunting and gathering and adopted horticulture unless they were compelled to do so by circumstances beyond their control. Instead, they have come to believe that the gradual growth of human population over millions of years (see Table 5.2, p. 97) eventually created a situation in which it became imperative to increase the supply of available food.[2] This was probably done gradually, with plant cultivation initially serving only as a minor means of supplementing the food resources obtained by hunting and gathering. But more food meant more babies surviving and still larger populations, thus necessitating still greater dependence on horticulture. Eventually, after hundreds or thousands of years the point would have been reached where horticulture replaced hunting and gathering as the dominant mode of subsistence. But the whole process would have been so gradual that the people involved would have been largely unaware of the changes that were occurring.

There is also striking evidence that the supply of large game animals was declining precipitously in many parts of the world at the very time societies were turning to horticulture as their primary means of subsistence. In North America, for example, 32 genera (i.e., *sets* of genetically related species) of large mammals became extinct between 13,000 and 7000 B.C.[3] These included horses, giant bison, oxen, elephants, camels, antelopes, pigs, ground sloths, and giant rodents. The pattern was similar in northern Europe, where the woolly mammoth, woolly rhinoceros, steppe bison, giant elk, and other large mammals vanished.[4] A study in Spain has found that in this period, people who lived on the northern coast began to eat more fish and shellfish and less meat from big-game animals and that this ultimately led to a decline in the average size of the shellfish caught, indicating overkill and depletion of that resource.[5]

The reason for the decline and eventual extinction of so many big-game animals is hotly debated.[6] Some believe that a change in climate—the end of the last Ice Age—was responsible. Others believe it was due to human activity, that improvements in weapons toward the end of the hunting and gathering era led to increasing kills, and that the larger supply of food led to larger human populations requiring even more food. Eventually the point was reached where the rate of kill exceeded the ability of slow-breeding species to maintain their numbers, and extinction resulted. It is still too early to say who is right in this debate, and time may prove that there is some truth to both views.

In summary, then, several newer lines of evidence suggest that the shift from hunting and gathering to horticulture was essentially a response forced on human societies by population growth. Overall, the shift seems to have occurred gradually, but in some areas at least, the pressures to adopt horticulture may have been intensified by advances in weapons technology that led to the rapid depletion and extinction of many species of big-game animals that previously had been important sources of food.

The shift from hunting and gathering to horticulture, though a change in only one aspect of life, was destined to have profound and far-reaching consequences for human life as a whole. We will examine the more immediate consequences in the present chapter, and the longer-term consequences in Chapters 7 through 16. Before doing this, however, we must first consider the new technology itself.

HORTICULTURE

Horticulture differs greatly from agriculture, the basic method of cultivation in Europe, North America, and much of Asia.[7] Where agriculturalists use the plow, horticulturalists use the digging stick or hoe, and where agriculturalists cultivate large fields continuously for decades or even centuries, horticulturalists cultivate a succession of small gardens, each of which is abandoned after a few years.

Sometimes the practice of horticulture is referred to as *swidden cultivation*, and sometimes it is known as *slash-and-burn cultivation*. Both of these terms refer to the widespread practice of clearing new gardens by cutting and then burning existing vegetation, especially shrubs and small trees. Larger trees are often left standing but are killed by girdling them, or cutting away a circular strip of bark all the way around the tree, thereby stopping the flow of nutrients from the roots to the branches.

After existing vegetation has been burned away, the resulting layer of ash provides fertilizer for the crops that are planted. Good yields can be expected for a year or two, but after that, as the nutrients in the ash are consumed, yields decline. Also, because there are no plows to dislodge them, weeds eventually take over. Thus, gardens must be abandoned and new plots cleared after only a few years.

The length of time a garden can be cultivated by horticulturalists varies considerably, depending on environmental conditions and on the length of time since the land was last cultivated. The longer the land remains uncultivated, the greater the amount of vegetation that grows on it and the thicker the layer of ash and nutrients when it is burned. Allowing the land to revert to jungle or forest is especially important because this destroys the weeds which spring up when land is cleared and which choke out cultivated plants.

Because of the need to allow the land periodically to revert to wilderness, horticulturalists are able to cultivate only a small fraction of the territory they occupy. Thus, horticultural societies seldom achieve the high levels of population density typical of agrarian societies. Nevertheless, their mode of subsistence is much more productive than hunting and gathering in terms of yield per acre, and their societies, as a result, almost always have larger and denser populations.

FIGURE 6.1 Women planting taro in a simple horticultural society in New Guinea. Note the tree stumps in the cultivated area: horticulturalists do not need to clear the land as thoroughly as agriculturalists, who use plows.

In the horticultural system of cultivation, men are usually responsible for clearing the land when new gardens are needed, while women are responsible for planting, tending, and harvesting the crops. This division of labor is almost certainly linked to the earlier division of labor in hunting and gathering societies, where women were responsible for providing the vegetable materials that people consumed. Men continue to hunt in many horticultural societies, but hunting is a much less productive activity since the ratio of game animals to humans is much lower (partly because of the growth of human population, partly because game animals tend to avoid areas of permanent human settlement). Overall, men's contribution to subsistence is often much less than that of women in horticultural societies and requires much less time. Thus, men in these societies often have substantial amounts of time at their disposal—a fact that has had important consequences, as we will see.

In many respects, horticulture is a more primitive form of farming than agriculture. The plow is both a more sophisticated and a more powerful tool than the digging stick or hoe, and agricultural societies are usually more productive economically than horticultural societies. It should be noted, however, that plow agriculture has not been feasible in many tropical regions and efforts to introduce it there have usually failed. Thus, while it is legitimate to say that horticulture is a more primitive form of cultivation than agriculture, there are some areas in the world where it is the only form of cultivation possible. This is why, in Figure 4.3 (page 73), one of the environmental categories was labeled "areas unsuited to plow cultivation."

In our analysis of horticultural societies, we will use the same format we used in the last chapter: we will begin with a survey of the archaeological record of the past and then turn to the evidence from horticultural societies that have survived into the nineteenth and twentieth centuries. Finally, at the end of the chapter we will return to ecological–evolutionary theory to help us formulate a coherent model of horticultural societies.

SIMPLE HORTICULTURAL SOCIETIES IN PREHISTORIC ASIA AND EUROPE

In Asia Minor, Palestine, and the hill country east of the Tigris River, archaeologists have found the remains of ancient settlements dating from about 7000 B.C., in which horticulture appears to have been the primary means of subsistence.[8] During recent years our knowledge of these early horticultural societies has been advanced substantially by developments in the field of archaeology, including the excavation of new sites and the more extensive exploration of older ones. Biologists and geologists have made important contributions to our understanding of the biophysical environment during that era. Most important of all, greatly improved techniques for dating archaeological remains have been developed since World War II. With these techniques, prehistoric materials of up to 50,000 years of age can now be dated with a substantial degree of accuracy, and many once unanswerable questions can now be answered.[9]

In traditional archaeological usage, the period in which simple horticultural societies were dominant in a region was called the Neolithic, or New Stone Age. This name was chosen because in early research in Europe and the Middle East, excavated sites often yielded stone axes, adzes, and hammers that, unlike earlier stone tools, had been smoothed by grinding or polishing. Before radiocarbon dating, these tools were the best indicators of the relative age of excavated materials and of their place in evolutionary history.

As research progressed, however, and more and more sites were excavated, it became increasingly clear that these tools were not the most distinctive feature of Neolithic societies, and certainly not their greatest technological achievement. Rather, their most important innovations were in the area of subsistence technology. For the first time in history, groups of people were primarily dependent on horticulture, and hunting and gathering was relegated to a secondary role. In this connection, it is important to recognize that these early horticultural societies had a *mixed economy*. Horticulture was their basic means of subsistence, but it was supplemented by herding, fishing, hunting, and gathering in various combinations.[10] The presence of livestock in many of these early societies was especially important, as we will soon see.

The First Great Social Revolution

Although many scholars today describe the emergence of horticultural societies as the first great social revolution in human history, it would be wrong to assume that the rate of change seemed revolutionary to those involved. As far as we can judge, the process was so gradual that the changes occurring during a lifetime were neither very numerous nor overwhelming. For example, hunters and gatherers in the Middle East had been using wild grains for a thousand years or more before the horticultural era began. Techniques of harvesting, storing, grinding, and cooking these grains were well known even before the techniques of cultivating them were adopted. Furthermore, as we have noted, hunting, and to some extent gathering, continued to play a part in the lives of early horticulturalists. There was almost certainly considerable continuity in other areas of life as well, especially in kinship, religion, and politics. The survival of fertility cults, indicated by the widespread presence of female figurines in Neolithic remains, is one evidence of this.[11] Our use of the term "revolutionary" in connection with the rise of horticultural societies, therefore, is based primarily on the *long-term consequences* of the change.

Permanence of Settlements One immediate and very important consequence of the shift to horticulture was the greater permanence of settlements. No longer did a group of people have to move about constantly in search of food; on the contrary, the practice of horticulture forced them to stay in one place for extended periods. In the Middle East and in southeastern Europe, many truly permanent settlements seem to have been established. In most areas, however, simple horticulturalists usually have had to move their settlements every few years.[12] Why this was not necessary in the Middle East and southeastern Europe is still a mystery, since only continuing fertilization (by flooding or by human activity), the use of the plow, and crop rotation permit land to be kept under continuous cultivation,[13] and so far there is no evidence of any of these practices at that time. We do know, however, that these early horticulturalists kept livestock, and so it is possible that the value of manure as fertilizer was discovered at an early date.[14] This practice may not have spread because, in other areas, there was more arable land available.

In any case, the shift from hunting and gathering to horticulture substantially increased the permanence of human settlements, thereby enabling people to accumulate many more possessions than ever before. This is evident in the archaeological remains left by horticulturalists of the Neolithic era. Tools and weapons are much more numerous and varied than in older sites, and for the first time there are large, bulky objects such as stone cups and bowls and pottery.[15] Dwellings also became more substantial. Some buildings contained several rooms and a small courtyard and were made of materials like sun-dried clay blocks, capable of lasting for as long as two generations.[16] Even more noteworthy is the appearance of such things as religious shrines or ceremonial centers, village walls, and occasional paved or timbered

FIGURE 6.2 Artist's conception of farmhouse in Denmark during the horticultural era there (about 2700 B.C.). Compare this with the dwelling of the family of the Paiute hunter on page 103.

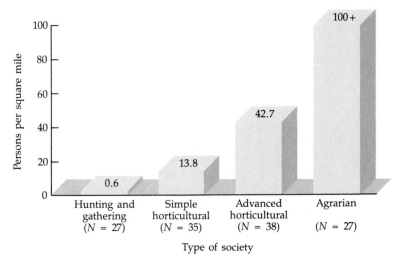

FIGURE 6.3 Median density of population, by type of society.

(corduroy style) roadways or alleys; though none of these is typical of simple horticultural communities, they are not rare.[17]

The change from hunting and gathering to horticulture also resulted in larger settlements and denser populations (see Figure 6.3). Jarmo, one of the oldest horticultural villages yet discovered, had about twenty-five houses and a population of 150,[18] nearly four times that of the average hunting and gathering band. Neolithic villages in Europe had from eight to fifty houses, suggesting populations ranging up to at least 200.[19] In several cases there were even more striking concentrations of population. One was a town located on the site of Jericho 5,000 years before the days of Joshua of Biblical fame. Excavations there have uncovered a community that apparently housed 2,000 to 3,000 inhabitants.[20] More recent excavations of Çatal Hüyük, in what is now Turkey, revealed a community occupying an even larger area with a population estimated to number at least 6,000 in 6000 B.C.[21]

Growth of Trade and Commerce These two communities, though obviously exceptional, illustrate another development associated with the rise of horticultural societies—the rapid expansion and growing importance of trade and commerce.[22] Modern scholars believe that the "great" size of Jericho and Çatal Hüyük was not due merely to the practice of horticulture. As one writer has put it, "It is . . . most unlikely that [horticulture] should have flourished more at Jericho, 200 metres below sea-level, than elsewhere in Palestine. Some other resource must have existed, and this was probably trade."[23] As he points out, Jericho, because of its location on the Dead Sea, had easy access to salt, bitumen,* and sulfur, all of which were valuable materials in

---

*Bitumen was used to fix blades in handles, mend pottery, etc.

simple horticultural societies and not available everywhere. This view of Jericho as an early center of trade is supported by the discovery there of products such as obsidian† from Asia Minor and cowrie shells from the Red Sea. In the case of Çatal Hüyük, obsidian seems to have been the key local resource responsible for its growth. Even in remote villages, there is evidence of trade. For example, shells from the Mediterranean have been found in the sites of horticultural villages and in graves in northern Europe.[24]

The growth in trade and commerce, combined with the increasing quantity of material products, may well have led to the beginnings of formal record keeping. Archaeologists have found a variety of clay tokens in horticultural sites from modern Turkey to Iran, but until recently no one could identify their use. Then it was discovered that the markings on many of the tokens were remarkably similar to symbols later used in early forms of writing for such words as "sheep," "wool," "cloth," "bread," "bed," and a variety of numerals.[25] This strongly suggests that the tokens were used to represent those same objects and numbers. Since these tokens were often stored in small clay jars, they were probably records of early business transactions, such as loans. But whatever their precise use in the societies of the time, those tokens tell us of a major breakthrough in the ability of human societies to store information.

Another probable consequence of the growth in trade and commerce was an increase in occupational specialization, at least in the chief commercial centers. Direct evidence of this has been found at several sites. For example, excavation of a community south of Jericho revealed a number of small workshops where specialized craftsmen, such as a butcher, a bead maker, and a maker of bone tools, worked.[26] This kind of specialization, however, was limited.[27] Most communities were still largely self-sufficient, and most families still produced nearly everything they used.[28] Innovations continued in the domestic arts, with the invention of pottery and weaving being especially important.[29]

Increase of Warfare There is little evidence of warfare in early horticultural societies. Graves rarely contain weapons, and most communities had no walls or other defenses.[30] Some, it is true, had ditches and fences, but these were more suitable for protection against marauding animals than against human enemies. Later in the horticultural era the picture changed drastically and warfare became increasingly common. In this period, battle-axes, daggers, and other arms are found in the graves of all adult males, reflecting the impact of technological advance, specifically metallurgy. The causes of this increase in warfare are not clear, but some scholars think it was linked with the growth of population and the resulting scarcity of new land suitable for horticulture. It may also have been related to declining opportunities for hunting, a traditional male activity. Warfare, with its demands for bravery and skill in the use of arms, would be a natural substitute, and if women were doing much of the work of tending the gardens, as is the case in most horticultural societies of the modern era, men would have had plenty of time to spend in this activity.[31] Moreover, the frictions created by growing pressure for land would provide a ready-made justification. Fi-

†Obsidian, or volcanic glass, was much sought after for use in weapons and cutting tools.

nally, some experts suspect that the increase in warfare was linked with the increase in wealth, especially in the form of cattle, which could be easily stolen.[32]

It may be no coincidence that the earliest evidence of cannibalism has been found in the archaeological remains of simple horticulturalists.[33] The bones of six people found in a cave in southern France bear cut marks similar to those on the bones of sheep, deer, and wild boar found with them. Like the animal bones, those of the humans had been broken to extract the marrow and then thrown into a refuse pit. Archaeologists speculate that these individuals (who lived about 4000 B.C.) may have been captives taken in war, since the practice of eating one's enemies has often been observed in simple horticultural societies of the modern era (see page 144).

One consequence of horticulture was that, as more and more societies adopted the new technology, it became increasingly difficult for other societies in the same area to continue hunting and gathering. As the population grew in a horticultural society, new settlements would form on the outer fringes. When they moved into territory occupied by hunters and gatherers, the horticulturalists would, by remaining in one place for a number of years, deplete the supply of game to the point that it could no longer support the hunters. If the hunters were tempted to fight for their "rights," they would usually find themselves badly outnumbered, if the population sizes of contemporary groups are any indication (see Table 4.2, page 77).[34]

The Chinese Experience   The horticultural societies of China are of special interest because the shift to the new mode of subsistence began late enough there, and writing developed early enough, that some memory of the horticultural era was preserved in legends that were eventually written down. For a long time scholars thought this material was entirely fictional, but modern archaeological research has substantiated enough of it that it is now regarded as a mingling of fact and fiction.[35]

According to the legends, China's earliest inhabitants were hunters but the growth of population eventually forced a shift to horticulture. As one source recounts, "The ancient people ate meat of animals and birds. At the time of Shen-nung [an early legendary ruler and culture hero] there were so many people that the animals and birds became inadequate for people's wants and therefore Shen-nung taught the people to cultivate."[36] Other legends relate that Shen-nung introduced pottery and describe the era as a period of peace and self-sufficiency. "During the Age of Shen-nung people rested at ease and acted with vigor. They cared for their mothers, but not for their fathers. They lived among deer. They ate what they cultivated and wore what they wove. They did not think of harming one another." This preference for mothers is especially intriguing, because it is contrary to the later Chinese tradition and yet conforms to one of the distinctive features of contemporary horticultural societies (see page 141). Finally, there is a legend that describes the Age of Shen-nung as the last era in which people were free from coercive political authority. "People were administered without a criminal law and prestige was built without the use of force. After Shen-nung, however, the strong began to rule over the weak and the few over the many."

The Ubaid Culture During the horticultural era technological progress was almost continuous, especially in the Middle East. In addition to the invention of pottery and

FIGURE 6.4 Ubaid settlement about 4000 B.C. Note the large temple in the center of the community.

weaving, metals were discovered and the basic principles of working them were developed. Thus, many of the simple horticultural societies of the latter part of the era were appreciably more advanced than their predecessors 3,000 years earlier.

The societies that flourished throughout Mesopotamia around 4000 B.C. illustrate how far these simple horticulturalists had advanced. These groups apparently shared a common culture, known today as the Ubaid culture (named after one of the archaeological sites where its remains are found). This culture was notable in many ways. To begin with, large settlements were relatively common. This is indicated by the size of cemeteries, one of which contained more than 1,000 graves, as well as by the large temples that dominated these communities.[37] A variety of technical skills were highly developed. A few copper tools and weapons were used, as well as sickles and other tools made from clay fired at high temperatures, a process that produced a remarkably efficient substitute for the stone that was lacking in that area.[38] Trade became extensive throughout Mesopotamia, facilitated by simple sailboats plying the myriad waterways.[39] This undoubtedly contributed to the wide diffusion of Ubaid culture. As one writer says, "Never before had a single culture been able to influence such a vast area, if only superficially."[40]

ADVANCED HORTICULTURAL SOCIETIES IN PREHISTORIC ASIA AND EUROPE

Each of the inventions and discoveries of the horticultural era increased to some degree the ability of societies to utilize the resources in their environments. But none had such far-reaching effects as *the use of metal in weapons and tools*. This is why metallurgy is used as the criterion for differentiating between simple and advanced horticultural societies. Societies are classified as advanced horticultural only if the use of metal weapons and tools was widespread. Societies in which this was rare, or in which metals were used only for artistic and ceremonial artifacts (as in a number of pre-Columbian South and Central American Indian societies where gold was the only metal known), are better classified as simple horticultural, since the impact of metallurgy on societal life was limited.

The Shift from Stone to Metals

To a person who is not technically inclined, the shift from stone to metal may suggest a radical break with the past and the introduction of something completely new. Actually, however, the use of metals evolved from the use of stone by a series of surprisingly small steps.

For thousands of years people had been aware of differences among rocks and stones. They knew that some were better for tools and weapons because they were harder and held a cutting edge longer. They were also aware of the colors in rocks and used the more unusual ones for beads and other ornaments, and also as a source of pigments for paint.

This interest in unusual rocks undoubtedly attracted people to copper. In its native form, copper appears as a purplish green or greenish black nugget which, when scratched or rubbed, shows a yellowish kernel of pure unoxidized copper. At first, copper was simply hammered cold into small tools and ornaments such as awls, pins, and hooks. A few articles made by this method have been found in Middle Eastern sites dating from the seventh millennium B.C.[41] Later, between 5000 and 4000 B.C., the technique of annealing was discovered.[42] By alternately heating and hammering copper, it was made less brittle and thus could be used for a wide variety of purposes. The heat from a simple wood fire was sufficient. Later still, people discovered techniques for extracting copper from ore by means of smelting, and they also found ways to melt copper and cast it in molds.[43]

These discoveries illustrate again the cumulative nature of technological progress. Since both smelting and melting copper require higher temperatures than a simple wood fire can produce, these important discoveries must have come after the invention of pottery and the pottery kiln.[44] And these inventions in turn came after the establishment of permanent communities where heavy and bulky objects could be accumulated. Figure 6.5 summarizes the complex chain of causation involved and reminds us again of the systemic nature of human societies.

As far as we can judge, the use of copper tools and weapons increased rather slowly for a variety of reasons.[45] For one thing, until smelting was discovered, the supply of copper was extremely limited; even then, the ore often had to be carried some distance by primitive and costly methods of transportation. In addition, metalworking (particularly smelting and casting) was probably mastered by only a few specialists, who may have treated their skills as a kind of magic (as smiths in contemporary horticultural societies often do) to protect a lucrative monopoly. Finally, since any man could make his own tools and weapons out of stone, people were undoubtedly reluctant to switch to the costlier product.[46] Thus, though copper was discovered as early as 6–7000 B.C., no truly advanced horticultural society (i.e., one in which

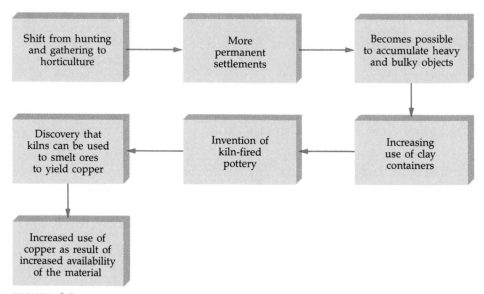

FIGURE 6.5 Model of the chain of causes leading from the adoption of horticulture to the widespread use of copper in the manufacture of tools, weapons, and other artifacts.

metal tools and weapons were widespread) seems to have developed until about 4000 B.C.[47]

To see what the widespread adoption of metal tools and weapons meant for the life of a horticultural society, we will turn to China, where the archaeological record is unusually rich and informative.

Social Consequences of Metal Tools and Weapons

Advanced horticultural societies flourished in China from the middle of the second millennium B.C. to the middle of the first.[48] The plow, for reasons that are unclear, was slow to appear in China, thus delaying the emergence of agrarian societies. This prolonged horticultural era was undoubtedly a major reason why the overall level of technological development in China's advanced horticultural societies surpassed that in most others of that type.

One indication of this is the fact that the dominant metal in China during most of this era was not copper, as in the Middle East and Europe, but bronze. This is significant because bronze,* which represents an important advance in metallurgy, is much harder than copper and can be used for many purposes for which copper is unsuitable. In the Middle East the technique of making bronze was not really mastered until some time *after* the first agrarian societies had made their appearance.[49] Variations in the sequence of such major innovations as bronze and the plow warn us

---

*Bronze involves the important technique of *alloying*, the combining of two or more metals—in this case, copper and tin.

of the inadequacy of *unilinear* theories of evolution, which assume that all societies follow exactly the same evolutionary path. Some variation is the rule, not the exception.

When the advanced horticultural era in China is compared with the simple horticultural period, the differences are striking. During the earlier era northern China was covered with many small, mostly self-sufficient, autonomous villages. But in the later period the villages were no longer autonomous and a few had become urban centers of some size and substance.

The emergence of these urban centers was largely the result of the military success of villages that had one important advantage: *bronze weapons*. As one scholar described this period, "In the course of a few centuries the villages of the plain fell under the domination of walled cities on whose rulers the possession of bronze weapons, chariots, and slaves conferred a measure of superiority to which no [simple horticultural] community could aspire."[50]

The importance of this development can hardly be exaggerated. For the first time in Chinese history people found that the conquest of other people could be a profitable alternative to the conquest of nature. Much the same thing happened in other parts of the world at this same stage of societal development. Thus, beginning in advanced horticultural societies and continuing in agrarian, we find almost as much energy expended in war as in the more basic struggle for subsistence. One might say that *bronze was to the conquest of people what plant cultivation was to the conquest of nature: both were decisive turning points in sociocultural evolution.*

From the military standpoint China's advanced horticulturalists enjoyed a great advantage over simple horticulturalists. Recently excavated burial remains show that their warriors wore elaborate armor, including helmets. They also carried shields and were equipped with spears, dagger-axes, knives, hatchets, and reflex bows capable of a pull of 160 pounds.[51] In addition, they used horse-drawn chariots carrying teams of three men(see Figure 6.6).

These societies also enjoyed substantial *numerical* superiority over simple horticultural societies and every victory brought more people under their control, enabling them to enlarge their armies still further.[52] This could not have been accomplished by a hunting and gathering society, whose primitive technology would make it impossible for conquerors to incorporate a defeated people into the group. At that level of development, the *economic surplus* (i.e., production in excess of what is needed to keep the producers healthy and productive) was small and unpredictable. But with the introduction of horticulture the situation changed dramatically. *For the first time, the conquest, control, and exploitation of other societies had become possible—and profitable.* All that was needed to transform this possibility into a reality was an advance in military technology that would give one society a definite advantage over its neighbors. That advance was bronze. It tipped the balance of military power decisively in favor of advanced horticulturalists.

The earliest advanced horticultural society in China of which we have any knowledge was established around 1600 B.C., and its structure was basically feudalistic.[53] In most regions, especially those that were some distance from the capital, power was in the hands of a warrior nobility that ruled the people in their immediate area. They

FIGURE 6.6 Chariots, together with bronze weapons, gave the advanced horticulturalists of China a great advantage over their simple horticultural neighbors. Burial remains of a warrior with his horses and chariot, eleventh century B.C.

paid tribute to the king and supported him militarily, but otherwise were essentially independent.[54] They were so independent, in fact, that they often waged war among themselves.

Marked social inequality was the rule in these societies. There were two basic classes, a small warrior nobility and the great mass of common people.[55] The warrior nobility was the governing class and lived in walled cities that served as their fortresses. It was they who enjoyed most of the benefits of the new technology and the new social system. The chief use of bronze was to manufacture weapons and ceremonial objects for the benefit of this elite class. Almost none of this scarce material was made available to the common people for farm tools.[56] The situation was much the same in the Middle East and Europe for 2,000 years or more. As one writer put it, this was a world in which metals played a major role in the military, religious, and artistic spheres, but not in subsistence activities.[57]

Kinship was extremely important in the political systems of advanced horticultural China. Membership in the governing class was largely hereditary, and as far as possible leading officials assigned the major offices under their control to kinsmen.[58] The origins of these noble families are unknown, but they were probably descendants of early conquerors and their chief officers.

The walled towns where the aristocracy lived, though small by modern standards, were nonetheless an important innovation. One recently excavated town, probably the capital of an early state, covered slightly over one square mile, or twenty times the area of Çatal Hüyük.[59] The size of the walled areas, however, does not tell the full story of these towns, especially in the earlier period, for many of the common people had their homes and workshops outside the protected area and cultivated nearby fields.

The walled area, while basically a fortress and place of residence for the governing class, was also a political and religious center. Religious activities were quite important and were so closely tied to the political system that one writer describes the state as "a kind of theocracy."[60] Though this appears to be an overstatement, ancient inscriptions prove that the ruler performed major religious functions and was what we today would call the head of both church and state.

The physical structure of those early urban centers was impressive and reflected the evolution of the state (see Glossary) and its newly acquired ability to mobilize labor on a large scale. One scholar estimates, for example, that it required the labor of 10,000 men working eighteen years to build the wall around the capital of one

FIGURE 6.7 The Great Wall of China: this 1,500-mile-long fortification, begun late in China's horticultural era, illustrates the growing power of political elites and their ability to mobilize labor on a massive scale.

early state. Such massive undertakings apparently utilized large numbers of captives taken in war, many of whom were used later as human sacrifices.[61]

Not much is known about the daily life of the common people, but their chief functions were obviously to produce the economic surplus on which the governing class depended and to provide workers and soldiers for various projects and military campaigns. Not all labor was of the brute, physical type, however. Some people were craft specialists who provided the new and unusual luxury goods that the governing class demanded for display and for ceremonial purposes; others produced military equipment.[62] Although many of these specialists were probably also part-time farmers, the increase in occupational specialization was undoubtedly accompanied by a significant growth in trade.

Despite their increasingly exploitative character, the advanced horticultural societies of China made important advances in a number of areas. The more important innovations included writing, money, the use of the horse, probably irrigation, and possibly the manufacture of iron at the very end of the horticultural era. In addition, there were lesser innovations too numerous to mention, some of them Chinese inventions or discoveries, others products of diffusion. In most cases, it is impossible to determine which were which.

HORTICULTURE IN THE NEW WORLD: TESTING GROUND FOR ECOLOGICAL–EVOLUTIONARY THEORY

No one knows for certain when humans first settled the New World. Using radiocarbon-dating techniques, archaeologists have found skeletal remains which indicate that there have been human settlements in the New World for nearly 50,000 years.[63] The original settlers appear to have been hunters and gatherers who migrated from Asia by means of the land bridge that once connected Siberia and Alaska.

When the last Ice Age ended and the waters locked in the glaciers melted, the level of the oceans rose and the land bridge was submerged. As a result, the inhabitants of the New World were cut off from the inhabitants of the Old World during the horticultural revolution. Thus, there was no way information about the techniques of plant cultivation could have spread from Asia to the Americas.[64]

Despite this, horticultural societies did develop in the New World, and some of them achieved a level of technological advance comparable to that of early agrarian Mesopotamia and Egypt. Space limitations prevent us from tracing these developments in detail, and much of the account would be repetitive if we did. But in the New World, as in the Old, the shift from hunting and gathering to horticulture was preceded by the growth of population and led to more permanent settlements, more substantial dwellings, increased wealth and possessions, greater inequality, the development of pottery and later of metallurgy, the beginnings of full-time craft specialization, the appearance of permanent markets and increased trade, the beginnings of urbanism, the establishment of permanent religious centers, the construction of massive temples and temple complexes (see Figure 6.8), and a marked increase in both militarism and imperialism.[65]

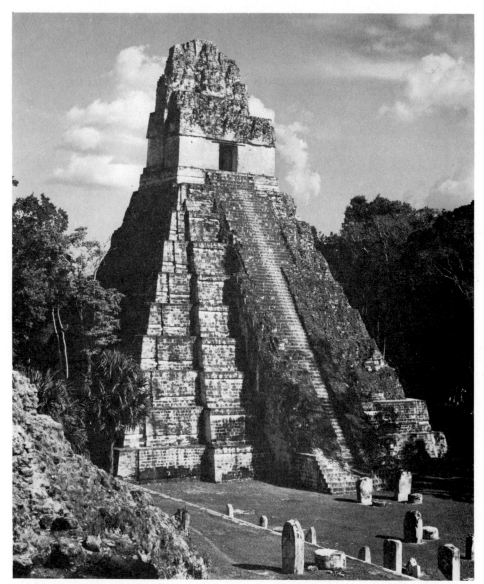

FIGURE 6.8 Mayan temple at Tikal, Guatemala. Several horticultural societies in the New World achieved a level of technological advance approaching that of ancient Egypt and Mesopotamia in the first centuries after they became agrarian societies.

There were also some differences: New World horticulturalists were not as successful in domesticating animals, for example, nor was their metallurgy as advanced. On the other hand, they developed a numerical system that included the concept of zero centuries before this was invented in the Old World. Overall, however, the similarities far outweigh the differences.

The fact that horticulture developed at all in the isolated New World is the important point, for it provides an independent test of some basic ideas. For a long time scholars debated whether the striking similarities in patterns of societal development in the Middle East, China, and Europe were due to the independent operation of the same basic laws of sociocultural evolution or were simply the result of the diffusion of ideas from a single source. The issue was impossible to resolve as long as only Old World societies were involved, because the possibility of diffusion could never be ruled out. The New World, however, is a different matter. Its contacts with the Old World ended several thousand years before horticulture began, and contact was not resumed until about 1000 A.D., when Leif Ericson briefly visited Vinland, somewhere on the northeast coast of North America.*

In short, the New World has been a kind of "Second Earth," where ideas about sociocultural evolution suggested by studies of the Old World can be put to the test.[67] The remarkable parallels between developments in the New World and the Old strongly suggest that there are limits to the amount of variation that is possible in the sequence of basic technological innovations. People must know certain things about both fire and rocks, for example, before metallurgy is possible, and a society must be familiar with the hoe before it can invent the plow. In addition, major technological innovations have fairly predictable consequences for other aspects of sociocultural systems—especially for social organization, the demographic variables, and material production.

This is not to say that sociocultural evolution compels societies to march in lockstep. But much is predictable about the critical early stages of societal development. Marvin Harris, a major contributor to ecological–evolutionary theory, put the matter as well as anyone: *"Similar technologies applied to similar environments tend to produce similar arrangements of labor in production and distribution, and these in turn call forth similar kinds of social groupings, which justify and coordinate their activities by means of similar systems of values and beliefs."*[68]

SIMPLE HORTICULTURAL SOCIETIES IN THE MODERN ERA

In recent centuries simple horticultural societies have been confined almost entirely to the New World and the islands of the Pacific. All of these societies have practiced some version of slash-and-burn horticulture. In most matters where comparisons are possible these societies are strikingly similar to simple horticultural societies of prehistoric times.[69] As with hunting and gathering societies, ethnography provides a richer source of information than archaeology. It answers many questions that would re-

---

*Though attempts have been made to prove other contacts, they have not been successful. Moreover, careful studies of the evolution of plant cultivation in the New World convince scholars that this was entirely an indigenous process. For example, the transformation of maize, or corn, from a wild plant to a cultivated plant took much longer than one would expect if the process had been guided by information on the techniques of plant cultivation brought from the Old World.[66]

main unanswered if our knowledge of horticultural societies were limited to what can be gleaned from the archaeological record.

Population and Economy

As we saw in our brief introduction to the various types of societies in Chapter 4, horticultural societies of the modern era have been substantially larger than hunting and gathering societies. Where the average hunting and gathering society of the recent past has had a population of approximately 40 people (including children), the average simple horticultural society has had about 1,500 and the average advanced horticultural society more than 5,000. Their larger numbers have given horticultural societies a substantial advantage when they have competed with hunting and gathering societies for territory, and this was almost certainly a major factor in the considerable decline in the number of hunting and gathering societies during the horticultural era (see Figure 4.4, page 75).

The larger populations of horticultural societies are due primarily to their greater economic productivity. The clearest indication of this is the greater population density that horticultural societies have been able to sustain. As Figure 6.3 indicates, simple horticultural economies have been able to support more than twenty times as many people per square mile of territory as hunting and gathering economies, and advanced horticultural economies have supported even denser populations.

Increased productivity has not been the whole story, however. The larger populations of horticultural societies also reflect the emergence of *multicommunity* societies. Among hunters and gatherers, as we have seen, each community is usually politically independent, and thus a separate society in its own right. In horticultural societies, in contrast, a number of communities are usually united under a single leader. The typical simple horticultural society consists of slightly more than ten communities, the average advanced horticultural society of seventeen.[70]

This widespread occurrence of multicommunity societies at the horticultural level and their virtual absence at the hunting and gathering level support the conclusion based on archaeological evidence (see page 133), that this shift in subsistence technology was the critical step that made possible the production of *a stable and dependable economic surplus*. Hunters and gatherers may produce surpluses for brief periods, but a complex institutional system cannot be built on such an uncertain foundation. Full-time occupational specialization involving priests, kings, craftsmen, and soldiers is possible only when an economy becomes productive enough so that some individuals regularly produce more of the necessities of life than they and their families require. In addition, they must be persuaded or forced to part with enough of this surplus to free others to perform tasks unrelated to basic subsistence. An economic surplus, therefore, is an essential precondition both for the emergence of full-time occupational specialization and for the development of complex social institutions.

One other noteworthy feature of the economies of horticultural societies is *the importance of women's productive activities*. For those whose ideas about farming are based on agricultural practices, it usually comes as a surprise to discover that in

TABLE 6.1 **The Division of Labor between the Sexes in Horticultural and Agrarian Societies**

| | Percentage Distribution | | | | |
Type of Society	Cultivation Primarily a Female Responsibility	Both Sexes Share Equally	Cultivation Primarily a Male Responsibility	Total	No. of Societies
Horticultural	39	33	28	100	389
Agrarian	8	33	59	100	100

Source: See Appendix, pages 441–442.

many horticultural societies women—not men—do most of the work of plant cultivation (see Table 6.1). As we will see shortly, the relative freedom of men from time-consuming economic responsibilities in these societies has had interesting and important consequences.

The Continuing Importance of Kinship

As with hunting and gathering societies, the ethnographic record not only supports the view provided by archaeology but broadens and extends it. For example, ethnographic studies show that kinship ties have been extremely important in simple horticultural societies of the modern era. In most instances, these ties provide the basic framework of the social system.[71] This is hardly surprising in view of the small size of these groups: almost everyone is related in some way to almost everyone else. Kinship obligations must constantly be considered in relations between individuals. The virtual absence of competing social organizations (e.g., craft guilds, political parties) further enhances the importance of kinship.

Kinship systems in these societies are sometimes very complex, with intricate systems of rules governing relations among numerous categories of kin. Extended kin groups, or *clans*, are common and usually very important, since they perform a number of essential functions for their members.[72] Above all, they function as *mutual aid associations*, providing individuals with protection against enemies and with economic support. Although both functions are important, the former is critical, for the political system is too limited in these societies to provide police services. Clans also perform important regulatory functions in the area of marriage, and they sometimes have important religious functions as well. Finally, the most powerful or respected clan often assumes leadership of an entire community, with its head serving as its headman, or even as tribal chief.

In horticultural societies, both simple and advanced, the concept of the kin group includes the dead as well as the living. This manifests itself in many ways, but especially in religious rituals designed to appease the spirits of dead ancestors. Nowhere is ancestor worship more common than in horticultural societies (see Figure 6.9).

The reason for such a high incidence of ancestor worship among horticulturalists, relative to hunters and gatherers, is probably tied to the greater permanence of their

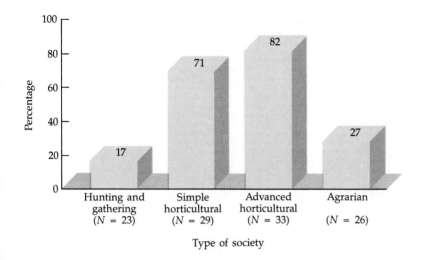

FIGURE 6.9   Incidence of ancestor worship, by societal type.
Source: Adapted from Dean Sheils, "Toward a Unified Theory of Ancestor Worship: A Cross-Cultural Study," Social Forces, 54:427-440, 1975, appendix, part B.

settlements. Because of this, the living remain in close physical proximity to their buried dead and carry on their daily activities in the very same settings in which their ancestors lived. Under such circumstances, ancestors are less easily forgotten. In agrarian societies, more awesome and more powerful polytheistic and monotheistic deities usually displaced ancestors from the central position they occupied in most horticultural societies, though ancestor worship continued to be important in many of them (e.g., China, Rome).

Another distinctive feature of kinship systems in horticultural societies is the importance many of them attach to ties with the mother's side of the family. This can be seen in Murdock's data, where the percentage of societies having *matrilineal* kin groups (i.e., descent traced through the maternal line) is as follows:[73]

Hunting and gathering societies	7%
Simple horticultural societies	24%
Advanced horticultural societies	12%
Agrarian societies	4%

This unusual pattern is apparently linked to the contribution women make to subsistence. In those horticultural societies where men also make a substantial contribution—by hunting or herding, for example—the matrilineal pattern is not as likely to develop (see Table 6.2).[74]

Developments in Polity, Stratification, and Warfare

The power of political leaders has been quite limited in nearly all simple horticultural societies. Even in the larger, multicommunity societies, local villages have vir-

TABLE 6.2 **Matrilineality among Simple Horticultural Societies, by Percentage of Subsistence Obtained from Hunting and Herding**

Percentage of Subsistence Obtained by Hunting and Herding	Percentage of Societies Matrilineal	No. of Societies
26 or more	14	29
16 to 25	24	54
15 or less	30	60

Source: See Appendix, pages 441–442.

tual autonomy except in matters of war and relations with other societies. Both the village headman and the tribal chief (i.e., leader of the multicommunity society) depend more on persuasion than on coercion to achieve their goals. This is partly because of the limited development of the governmental system; a leader has few subordinates so dependent on him that they are obliged to carry out his instructions. Also, since men still make their own weapons, no one can monopolize them and thereby dominate the others. The absence of weapons that only a few can afford limits the growth of political inequality.

In some simple horticultural societies, shamans also serve as headmen or chiefs because of the awe or respect in which they are held.[75] In others, secular leaders assume important religious functions and become quasi-religious leaders. As one writer notes, a "chief's influence is definitely enhanced when he combines religious with secular functions."[76] In short, in many simple horticultural societies of the modern era, just as in the prehistoric past, "church" and "state" are closely linked and sometimes almost become one.

The only other important basis of political power in these societies is membership in a large and prosperous kin group. As we noted earlier, the senior member and leader of the largest, most powerful, or most respected clan often becomes the village headman or tribal chief.[77] He can usually count on the support of his kinsmen, and that is a substantial political resource in this kind of society.

Social inequality is generally rather limited in most simple horticultural societies of the modern era. Although extremes of wealth and political power are absent, substantial differences in prestige are not uncommon. Political and religious leaders usually enjoy high status, but this depends far more on personal achievements than on mere occupancy of an office. Other bases of status include military prowess (which is highly honored in nearly all horticultural societies), skill in oratory, age, kinship ties, and in some cases wealth in the form of wives, pigs, and ornaments.[78] Each society has its own distinctive combination of criteria.

The more advanced the technology and economy of one of these groups, the greater social inequality tends to be. Societies that practice irrigation, own domesticated animals, or practice metallurgy for ornamental and ceremonial purposes are usually less egalitarian than groups without these characteristics. We see this clearly when we compare the villagers of eastern Brazil and the Amazon River basin with their more advanced neighbors to the north and west who, in pre-Spanish days, practiced irrigation and metallurgy. Hereditary class differences were absent in the former,

TABLE 6.3 Incidence of Warfare, by Societal Type (in Percentages)

Type of Society	Perpetual	Common	Rare or Absent	Total	No. of Societies
Hunting and gathering	0	27	73	100	22
Simple horticultural	5	55	41	100	22
Advanced horticultural	34	48	17	100	29

Source: Adapted from data in Gregory Leavitt, "The Frequency of Warfare: An Evolutionary Perspective." *Sociological Inquiry,* 14 (January 1977), appendix B.

but common in the latter, where a hereditary class of chiefs and nobles was set apart from commoners.[79]

Ethnographers have found warfare to be more common among horticulturalists than among hunters and gatherers (see Table 6.3). This finding parallels the findings of archaeology, where the evidence indicates that warfare increased substantially during the horticultural era. Now, as in the past, combat appears to serve as a psychic substitute for the excitement, challenge, and rewards which hunting previously provided and which were so important in the lives of men in hunting and gathering societies.

FIGURE 6.10 In horticultural societies, combat appears to provide a psychic substitute for the excitement, challenge, and rewards that hunting once provided. Yanamamö men intoxicated on ebene, a hallucinogenic drug, prepare for a "friendly" duel with men from a neighboring village. Such duels often turn violent and lead to war.

Warfare also functions as an important mechanism of population control in these groups. In addition to the direct loss of life in combat, warfare is a stimulus for female infanticide, which provides an even greater check on population growth.[80] In societies in which warfare is the normal state of affairs, it is imperative that the group be able to field the largest possible number of warriors, and female infanticide seems to be a common method of accomplishing this. By reducing the number of girls, the group can devote its resources to the care and nurture of its boys. A survey of studies of 609 "primitive" societies found that the sex ratio among the young was most imbalanced in those societies in which warfare was current at the time of the study and most nearly normal in those societies in which warfare had not occurred for more than twenty-five years.[81] In the former, boys outnumbered girls by a ratio of seven to five on the average, indicating that nearly 30 percent of the females born in these societies had died as a result of female infanticide or neglect.

As warfare grows in importance in a society, several new patterns tend to develop. Above all, there is the cult of the warrior, which heaps honors on successful fighters. Record keeping and publicity are as important to these warrior heroes as to modern athletes, and, in the absence of statisticians and sportswriters, they devise techniques of their own—especially trophy taking. Trophies include such things as skulls and shrunken heads, which are preserved and displayed like modern athletic trophies (see Figure 6.11).[82]

Ceremonial cannibalism, a widespread practice in simple horticultural societies, may have developed as a by-product of trophy collecting. Utilitarian cannibalism, or the eating of other humans to avoid starvation, is an ancient practice, traceable to distant prehistoric times, but ceremonial cannibalism seems to be a more recent innovation. The basic idea underlying it is that one can appropriate the valued qualities of a conquered enemy by eating his body. Ceremonial cannibalism is usually surrounded by a complex, and often prolonged, set of rituals, as the following account from South America indicates.

The prisoners taken by a Tupinamba war party were received with manifestations of anger, scorn, and derision, but after the first hostile outburst, they were not hampered in their movements nor were they unkindly treated. Their captors, whose quarters they shared, treated them as relatives. The prisoners generally married village girls, very often the sisters or daughters of their masters, or, in certain cases, the widow of a dead warrior whose hammock and ornaments they used. They received fields for their maintenance, they were free to hunt and fish, and they were reminded of their servile condition by few restrictions and humiliations.

The period of captivity lasted from a few months to several years. When, finally, the date for the execution had been set by the village council, invitations were sent to nearby villages to join in the celebration. The ritual for the slaughter of a captive was worked out to the most minute detail. The club and cord which figured prominently in the ceremony were carefully painted and decorated in accordance with strict rules. For three days before the event, the village women danced, sang, and tormented the victim with descriptions of his impending fate. On the eve of his execution a mock

FIGURE 6.11 Record keeping and symbols of success are no less important to warriors in horticultural societies than they are to modern athletes. The Jivaro Indians of South America collected heads as trophies and developed a technique for shrinking and preserving them for purposes of display.

repetition of his capture took place, during which the prisoner was allowed to escape but was immediately retaken; the man who overpowered him in a wrestling match adopted a new name, as did the ceremonial executioner.

The prisoner spent his last night dancing, pelting his tormentors, and singing songs which foretold their ruin and proclaimed his pride at dying as a warrior. In the morning he was dragged to the plaza by old women amidst shouts, songs, and music. The ceremonial rope was removed from his neck and tied around his waist, and it was held at both ends by two or more men. The victim was once more permitted to give vent to his feelings by throwing fruit or potsherds at his enemies. The executioner, who appeared painted and dressed in a long feather cloak, derided the victim, who boasted of his past deeds and predicted that his relatives would avenge him.

The actual execution was a cruel game. The prisoner was allowed sufficient freedom of movement to dodge the blows aimed at him; sometimes a club was put in his hands so that he could parry the blows without being able to strike back. When at last he fell, his skull shattered, everyone shouted and whistled. Old women rushed in to drink the warm blood, children were invited to dip their hands in it, and mothers smeared their nipples so that even infants could have a taste. While the quartered body was being roasted on a babracot the old women, who were the most eager to taste human flesh, licked the grease running from the sticks. Certain delicate or sacred portions, such as the fingers and the grease around the liver, were given to distinguished guests.[83]

The high incidence of warfare in simple horticultural societies helps to keep the channels of vertical mobility open. Almost every boy becomes a warrior and thus has a chance to win honor and influence. Nevertheless, the channels of vertical mobility are somewhat more restricted in horticultural societies than in hunting and gathering societies, because status advantages can more easily be passed from parent to child. This is partly due to the greater amount of private property in horticultural societies, and its increased importance. In addition, there are the beginnings of inequality among kin groups: it is a distinct advantage to be born into a large, powerful, and wealthy clan. Finally, the institutional structures of these societies frequently evolve to the point where they can, to some extent, supplement the personal attributes of their leaders. No longer does a headman have to be the best man in the group; he need only be competent, because he now has assistants who will support and help him. As a consequence, the headmanship is more likely to be inherited than is the case in hunting and gathering societies. This growth in the heritability of status, though modest in scope and of limited importance in simple horticultural societies, marked the beginning of a trend that was destined to become tremendously important in more advanced societies.

Intragroup Violence

For years, many anthropologists presented an idyllic view of life in simpler societies, making them seem like the last remnants of Eden.[84] A number of recent studies, however, provide a very different picture. Among one group of simple horticulturalists in New Guinea, for example, nearly a third of all deaths over a forty-year period (from 1940 to 1982) were due to homicide.[85] The rate of homicide in this society was *more than 50 times* that in the United States, which for many years has had the highest rate of any modern industrial society. Studies of other simple horticultural societies indicate that this is not an isolated instance but reflects a relatively widespread tendency in societies at this level of development.[86]

ADVANCED HORTICULTURAL SOCIETIES IN THE MODERN ERA

For several centuries advanced horticultural societies have been limited to two parts of the world, sub-Saharan Africa and southeast Asia. Until recently they occupied most of sub-Saharan Africa. In southeast Asia, on the other hand, agrarian societies have occupied most of the land, and horticulturalists have been confined to the hill country.

These advanced horticulturalists of modern times differ in one important respect from those of prehistoric times: the dominant metal in their societies has been iron rather than copper or bronze. This is important, because iron ore is so much more plentiful than copper and tin that it can be used for ordinary tools as well as weapons. However, because it is much more difficult to separate iron from the ore, the manufacture of iron was a later development.

The history of Africa proves once again that the evolutionary process does not compel all societies to follow exactly the same pattern of development. Bronze was never the dominant metal in most of Africa below the Sahara. During the period when bronze was dominant in the Middle East, cultural contacts between Egypt and the territories to the south were minimal. By the time there was sufficient contact to permit diffusion of specialized skills like metallurgy, iron had become dominant.[87] Thus, most of Africa seems to have moved directly from the Stone Age to the Iron Age.

Increased Size and Complexity

Compared with hunting and gathering or simple horticultural societies, advanced horticultural societies are usually larger and more complex. Table 4.2 (page 77) summarizes the evidence from Murdock's data set: on average, advanced horticultural societies are three and a half times the size of simple horticultural and 130 times the size of hunting and gathering societies. Table 4.3 (page 80) shows that craft specialization is much more common in advanced horticultural societies than in either simple horticultural or hunting and gathering societies. Murdock's data also show that social inequality increases markedly at this level of societal development. Slavery, for example, is found in 83 percent of advanced horticultural societies, but in only 15 percent of simple. And finally, class systems are reported in 7 percent of advanced horticultural societies and in only 1 percent of simple (see Figure 4.6, page 80).

One consequence of the more highly developed economy and stratification system in advanced horticultural societies is their increased emphasis on the economic aspect of marriage. In almost every one of these societies, marriageable daughters are viewed as a valuable property, and men who want to marry them must either pay for the privilege or render extended service to their prospective in-laws. Fortunately for young men with limited resources, extended kin groups usually view marriage as a sensible investment and are willing to loan suitors part of the bride price. This economic approach to marriage is much more common in advanced horticultural societies than in either hunting and gathering or simple horticultural societies (see Table 6.4).

Political Development

The growth in social inequality is closely linked with the growth of government. A generation ago, one of the pioneers in the study of African political systems argued that most traditional African societies fell into one of two basic categories: those "which have centralized authority, administrative machinery, and judicial institutions—in short, a government—and in which cleavages of wealth, privilege, and status correspond to the distribution of authority," and those which have none of these attributes.[88] Though recent studies suggest that this twofold division was an oversimplification, they con-

TABLE 6.4 Economic Transaction Associated with Marriage, by Societal Type

Type of Society	Percentage of Societies Requiring Purchase of Brides	Number of Societies
Hunting and gathering	36	170
Simple horticultural	37	154
Advanced horticultural	83	246

Source: See Appendix, pages 441–442.

firm that African societies differ in the ways described and that there is a strong relationship between the development of the state and the growth of social inequality.[89]

African societies afford a valuable opportunity to study the early stages of political development. A leading student of east African political systems suggests that a critical step in the process occurs when the head of a strong clan begins to take on, as retainers, men who are not related to him, thereby overcoming one of the traditional constraints on power and its expansion.[90] These retainers are usually individuals who have been expelled from their own kin group for misconduct or whose group has been destroyed in war or by some natural disaster, and they offer their allegiance and service in exchange for protection and a livelihood.

FIGURE 6.12 Trade and commerce are much more important in horticultural societies than in hunting and gathering societies: the marketplace in Ouagadougou, Burkina Faso.

Since there is a natural tendency for men in this position to turn to the strongest extended family in their society, power begins to accumulate. This is reinforced by the wealth of such a family, which permits it to buy more wives to produce more sons and warriors, and by the development of myths that attribute the group's success to the magical powers of its leader. The final link in this chain of *state building* is forged when less powerful families, and even whole communities, are brought under the control of the head of a strong kin group—either by conquest or by the decision of weaker groups to put themselves under the strong group's protection. When this happens, each of the subordinate groups is usually allowed to retain its land, and its leader his authority within his own group, but the group is compelled to pay tribute. The leader of the dominant group then uses these revenues to support his kinsmen and retainers, thereby increasing their dependence on him and, he hopes, their loyalty as well.

Sometimes this state-building process is stimulated by feuds that get out of hand. Where strong political authority is lacking, feuds can be a serious matter. Individuals and families are forced to settle their own grievances, which often sets off a deadly cycle of action and reaction. More than one east African group has voluntarily put itself under the authority of a strong neighboring leader just to break such a cycle and reestablish peace among its members.

One might imagine that these processes, once set in motion, would continue until eventually all Africa came under a single authority. But powerful countervailing forces have prevented this. Technological limitations, especially in transportation and communication, were most important. Advanced horticulturalists in Africa, as in the New World, had no knowledge of the wheel and did not have draft animals until contact with Europeans. As a result, the farther a ruler's power was extended into outlying areas, the weaker it became. Not only were these areas vulnerable to attack by other societies, but even more serious, they were likely to revolt. From the territorial standpoint, Songhay was probably the largest kingdom that ever developed in sub-Saharan Africa. In the early fourteenth century it controlled approximately 500,000 square miles in the western Sudan (i.e., twice the size of present-day France).[91] Most African kingdoms, however, were much smaller.

By the standards of modern industrial societies, the governments of Africa's advanced horticultural societies were extremely unstable. Revolts were a common occurrence, not only in outlying provinces but even in the capitals. These were seldom, if ever, popular risings. Rather, they were instigated by powerful members of the nobility, often the king's own brothers. This pattern was so common that the Zulus had a proverb that "the king should not eat with his brothers lest they poison him."[92]

In virtually every politically developed society of horticultural Africa there was a sharply defined cleavage between a hereditary nobility and the mass of commoners. Historically, this distinction grew out of the state-building process.[93] Nobles were usually descendants of past rulers and their chief officers, or hereditary leaders of subordinated groups. They comprised a warrior aristocracy supported by the labor of the common people. Below the commoners there was often a class of slaves, many of them captives taken in war and, as in other horticultural societies, they were frequently slaughtered as human sacrifices (see Figures 6.14 and 6.17).

FIGURE 6.13 In almost every politically advanced society of horticultural Africa there was a sharp cleavage between nobles and commoners: early bronze casting of Dahomean chief and his entourage of relatives and retainers. Note the fine workmanship.

In horticultural Africa, as in the New World and elsewhere, religion and politics were intimately related. In many instances the king was viewed as divine or as having access to divine powers.[94] This served to make tyrannical and exploitative practices legitimate. It also helps explain why no efforts were made to establish other kinds of political systems: given their ideological heritage, any alternative was inconceivable. These beliefs did not protect a ruler against attacks from his kinsmen, however, because they shared his special religious status and thus were qualified to assume the duties and privileges of the royal office—if they could seize it.

A comparison of the politically complex societies of horticultural Africa with those which remained autonomous villages shows that the former were more developed in other ways as well. They were far more likely to have full-time craft specialization, for example, and they were also more likely to have urban or semiurban settlements—a few with populations of 20,000 or more.[95]

Horticultural Societies in Southeast Asia

Before concluding this discussion of advanced horticultural societies in the modern era, a brief comment on those in southeast Asia is necessary. The striking feature of these societies is their organizational backwardness, especially in terms of their political development. In most instances, villages have been autonomous, and when

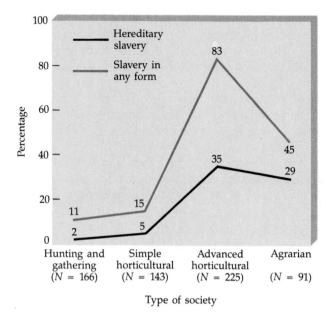

FIGURE 6.14 Percentage of societies with slavery, by type of society.

multicommunity societies have developed, they have invariably been small.[96] Urban or semiurban settlements have been absent.

The reason appears to be ecological. Centuries ago, after this region came under the domination of more powerful agrarian societies, horticultural societies survived only in hill country where transportation was difficult and the land unsuited to the plow and permanent cultivation. This combination of more powerful neighbors and the deficiencies of their own territories apparently prevented all but the most limited development and caused these groups to be looked down upon, and often exploited, by their agrarian neighbors. Ecological factors of a different type had a similar effect in certain parts of Africa: political development was quite limited in the tropical rain forests. Apparently the dense vegetation and other hindrances to the movement of armies and goods made it impossible to build and maintain extensive kingdoms.[97]

HORTICULTURAL SOCIETIES IN THEORETICAL PERSPECTIVE

Few events in human history have been as important as the shift from hunting and gathering to horticulture. It is no exaggeration to say that *the adoption of horticulture in the realm of technology was comparable to the adoption of symbol use in the realm of communication: each was a decisive break with the animal world.* Hunting and gathering, like the use of signals, are adaptations our species inherited from its prehuman ancestors. In contrast, horticulture and symbols are uniquely human.

Of all the changes in human life that resulted from the horticultural revolution, the most fundamental—the one with the most profound consequences—was the creation of a *stable economic surplus*. Hunting and gathering societies were rarely able to create such a surplus: food producers and their dependents usually consumed within days all they were able to provide. With nothing left over to support *non*producers of food, except children and the aged, only the most limited occupational specialization was possible. There could be no governmental or religious institutions staffed by full-time officials and priests, nor could there be full-time artisans and merchants. And this, in turn, ruled out the development of towns and cities, since these are based on populations that are freed from the necessity of producing their own food.

The shift from hunting and gathering to plant cultivation provided societies with the means of establishing an economic surplus, but only if the benefits of the growth in productivity were not wiped out by a corresponding growth in population. To translate the potential for a stable surplus into a *reality*, a society needed an ideology that

FIGURE 6.15 Kano, a city in northern Nigeria, has been an important commercial and political center for more than 500 years. The style of architecture remains much as it was centuries ago.

would motivate the producers of food to turn over part of their harvest to an individual in authority who could dispense it as he saw fit.

Traditional religious beliefs often answered this need. In a number of societies people were already accustomed to offering sacrifices, and nothing was more natural than that they should continue this practice as they shifted to plant cultivation, giving part of their yield to priests. With greater productivity, rituals became more elaborate and more frequent and priestly activities became full-time, for one man at first and eventually for others. In this way, small proto-urban communities began to develop around important shrines—communities that could exist only if a stable economic surplus was maintained.

In other societies the development of a stable surplus appears to have evolved out of a tradition of turning over to the headman part of the fruits of the hunt to distribute to the families of unsuccessful hunters. Here too the increase in productivity that resulted from the shift to plant cultivation made full-time employment possible, first for a headman, later for his aides. Thus, the foundation was laid for the emergence of the state as a specialized entity, distinct from the rest of society.

In either case, the outcome was the same: the potential for a stable, dependable economic surplus became a reality, opening up important new possibilities for the organization of societal life. The possibilities would not all be realized in horticultural societies, however. The most dramatic and the most revolutionary would be realized only in agrarian and industrial societies, where the size of the economic surplus would be many times larger.

It is important to note that in horticultural societies we see, for the first time, ideology playing a role in societal development. In hunting and gathering societies, the limits set by technology are so narrow that ideology's role in the developmental process is negligible. But the picture changes with the shift to horticulture, where ideological differences sometimes give rise to significant differences in development.

Figure 6.16 summarizes the effects of the shift from hunting and gathering to horticulture. Not all of these consequences occurred in every horticultural society, but the model indicates *the possibilities* inherent in the new subsistence technology.

At a minimum, the shift to horticulture meant more food and more permanent settlements, and frequently more free time for men. More food meant population growth and, when combined with certain traditional beliefs concerning the role of headmen and shamans, created the possibility of a stable economic surplus. The increase in free time for men often led to increased warfare and the emergence of the cult of the warrior. More permanent settlements made it feasible for people to accumulate far more possessions than was possible when frequent moves were necessary. Also, more permanent settlements, in combination with the emergence of the cult of the warrior, frequently led to the practice of ancestor worship, and the greater frequency of warfare contributed to the practice of female infanticide.

The development of a stable economic surplus was especially important since it paved the way for growth in the size of societies, the formation of multicommunity societies, an increased division of labor, urban communities, increased trade and commerce, the formation of the state, and greatly increased inequality. Several of these developments, especially the formation of multicommunity societies, the formation

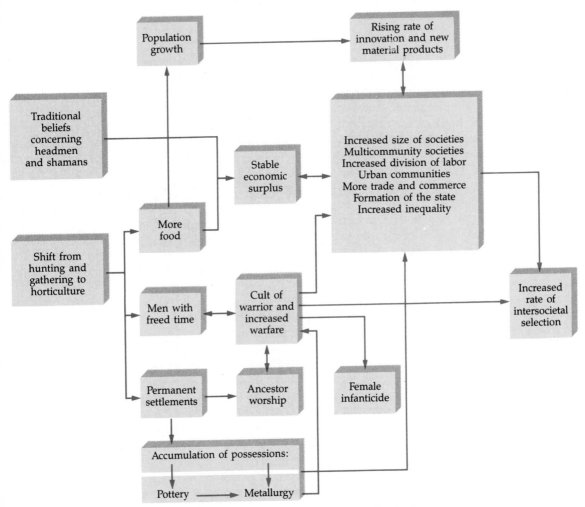

FIGURE 6.16 Model of the potential effects of the shift from hunting and gathering to horticulture.

of the state, and increased inequality, were also stimulated by the increase in warfare, the increasing accumulation of possessions, and the production of new material products of many kinds. Finally, all of these developments, but especially the increase in warfare and the increasing differences in the military might of societies (many of which remained at the hunting and gathering level) contributed to a substantial rise in the rate of intersocietal selection.

In several instances boxes in Figure 6.16 are connected by two-headed arrows. These indicate that a process of feedback was operating, with the paired developments mutually stimulating one another. The most important of these is the two-headed arrow linking a stable economic surplus with the important set of changes in social organization in the large box to the right. In other words, once the creation of a stable economic surplus had given rise to an increased division of labor, urban communities, multicommunity societies, the formation of the state, and so forth, these developments in social organization tended to stabilize and ensure the continued production of an economic surplus. New institutional arrangements ensured that priests, political and military leaders, merchants, craftsmen, and other specialists would get a share—and usually a disproportionate share—of the goods and services produced in the society. These specialists would have the first claim on food and other essentials. Thus, in order to survive, farmers were obliged to produce more than they and their families required.

The rise in the rate of intersocietal selection is another feature of Figure 6.16 that merits attention. It is a reminder that the horticultural revolution meant dramatic change not only for individual societies but also for the world system of societies. If Figure 6.16 is compared with Figure 3.8 (page 65), the similarity in trends is striking. This is no coincidence, since the shift from hunting and gathering to horticulture was the first major step along the road that has led to the modern world system.

Before concluding this summary, a brief comment on the ethical consequences of the horticultural revolution is needed, lest anyone still suppose that the technological and organizational advances of horticultural societies implied ethical progress. As numerous scholars have noted, it is one of the great ironies of evolution that progress in technology and social organization is often linked with ethical *regress*. Horticultural societies provide several striking examples. Some of the most shocking, by the standards of modern western culture, are the increases in head-hunting, cannibalism, human sacrifice, and slavery, all more common in technologically progressive horticultural societies than in the more primitive societies of hunters and gatherers.

Another development many would regard as ethical regression is the decline in the practice of sharing and the growing acceptance of economic and other kinds of inequality. This is not as simple a matter as it seems on the surface, however. Although inequality is an inevitable accompaniment of an economic surplus, the establishment of that surplus seems to have been a prerequisite for the development of civilization—with all that implies—and for subsequent improvements in the standard of living. In other words, without an economic surplus, all the benefits of technological advance would have been consumed by population growth, and there would simply have been more people living at the subsistence level. Our judgment concerning the growth in inequality, therefore, depends largely on whether we take a short-term or a long-term view.

FIGURE 6.17 Human sacrifice, from carving on Mayan temple, Chichen Itza, Mexico.

Excursus: Race and Societal Development

After the first explorers returned to Europe from Africa, the Americas, and Asia, Europeans were intrigued by differences in the level of development of societies in various parts of the world. Interest in these differences led quite naturally to efforts to explain them.

Over the years the most popular explanation has been the racialist. Racialist theories assert that societies differ in their level of development and in other ways because the members differ in their culture-building abilities.[98] Translated into modern scientific terminology, these theories assert that societies differ in their levels of development because of differences in the genetic heritages of their populations.

These theories have had great appeal because they seem to fit the evidence rather well. During the last several hundred years, societies dominated by Europeans have been technologically the most advanced and organizationally the most complex and powerful. Societies dominated by Asians have ranked next, while societies dominated by Africans have been the least developed technologically and organizationally. Since the level of societal development is obviously not responsible for the race of a population, racialist theorists have argued that the race must be responsible for the level of development.

Racialist theories can be quite compelling if one does not have an ecological and evolutionary perspective. If one adopts such a perspective, however, those theories prove to have a number of weaknesses. To begin with, we find that the recent ranking of societies in terms of development has not always prevailed. For thousands of years Middle Eastern societies—not European societies—were the most highly developed.[99] Also, for many centuries China equaled or surpassed northwestern Europe. Finally, for several centuries before and after the start of the Christian era, the center of civilization was in the Mediterranean basin, and North African societies, such as Carthage and Egypt, were much more advanced than the barbarian societies of northwest Europe. While there have been some changes in the racial composition of some populations during this period (e.g., in ancient times the proportion of fair-haired and fair-skinned individuals in Greek and Roman societies seems to have been appreciably higher than today), they do not appear to have been great enough to cause the substantial changes that have occurred in the relative level of societal development.

If, then, the evolutionary record undermines the credibility of racialist theories, where do we look for an explanation? Here the ecological perspective comes to our aid. It suggests that environmental differences offer a promising alternative. Recent research has shown that many tropical and semitropical regions are poorly suited to plow agriculture.[100] Although the lushness of tropical rain forests suggests rich and fertile soils, modern research has found the opposite: the soils of tropical rain forests are among the poorest in the world. While it is possible to clear small and temporary gardens in these forests, as horticulturalists have done for centuries, it is not possible to clear permanent fields and cultivate them continuously as agriculturalists do. The fertility of these soils is quickly exhausted and, worse yet, some of the soils harden and become compacted to the point where cultivation of any kind is impossible. In addition, large-scale clearing of the rain forest appears to break the hydrological cycle and rainfall declines. In short, *indigenous* development beyond the level of horticultural societies seems to have been impossible in much of sub-Saharan Africa and much of Latin America (see Figure 4.3, page 73).

In addition, recent research has shown that human populations in tropical regions are exposed to many more tiny predators than are populations in temperate regions.[101] In fact, the number, variety, and seriousness of the parasites (bacteria, viruses, worms, etc.) that prey on human populations seem to increase steadily as one moves from polar regions to the tropics. In the tropics, the problems created by these micropredators have often been overwhelming. Large portions of the population have been affected by debilitating diseases of one kind or another—diseases such as malaria, onchocerciasis (which causes blindness), and schistosomiasis (which causes people to become listless and lacking in energy).

Prior to the invention of the microscope, the causes of such diseases were not only unknown, but *unknowable*. Societies afflicted by them were badly handicapped, but they had no method of overcoming their handicap. Thus, the most serious challenges that confronted horticulturalists in the tropics were profoundly different from those that confronted horticulturalists in temperate areas such as Europe. In the latter, the basic challenge was to increase the food supply, and this could be achieved through the gradual improvement of tools of various

Thus, the adoption of an ecological and evolutionary perspective provides quite a different explanation of the relationship of race and societal development than that provided by earlier racialist theories. Moreover, because this explanation fits more of the facts than the latter, it has greater scientific credibility. Although it would be premature to suggest that we now fully understand the causes of the complex relationship between race and societal development, it appears that ecological–evolutionary theory substantially advances our understanding of it.

7

Agrarian Societies

"The thousand years or so immediately preceding 3000 B.C. were perhaps more fertile in fruitful inventions and discoveries than any period in human history prior to the sixteenth century, A.D."[1] So wrote V. Gordon Childe, the most influential archaeologist of the twentieth century. The innovations of that period included the invention of the wheel and its application both to wagons and to the manufacture of pottery, the invention of the plow, the harnessing of animals to pull wagons and plows and their use as pack animals, the harnessing of wind power for sailboats, the invention of writing and numerical notation, and the invention of the calendar.[2]

Collectively, these innovations transformed the conditions of life for societies in the Middle East, and eventually for societies throughout the world. With these new cultural resources, societies expanded their populations, increased their material wealth, and developed social organizations far more complex than anything known before.

SIMPLE AGRARIAN SOCIETIES

Technology

Although all of the innovations mentioned above were important, the *plow* had the greatest potential for social and cultural change. To a modern city dweller, the plow may not sound very exciting, yet without it we would still be back in the horticultural era. To appreciate its importance, we need to recognize two basic problems that confront farmers everywhere: controlling weeds and maintaining the fertility of the soil.[3] With traditional horticultural tools and techniques, both problems become more severe the longer a plot of ground is cultivated. Weeds multiply faster than horticulturalists with hoes can root them out, while the soil's nutrients seep deeper into the ground, below the reach of plants and too deep to be brought back to the surface with hoes

158

and other simple tools. Within a few years the yield from a garden usually becomes so small that the farmer is forced to abandon it and clear a new one.

The plow, if it did not eliminate these problems, at least reduced them to manageable proportions. Because it turns the soil over to a greater depth than the hoe, the plow buries weeds, not only killing them but adding humus to the soil. Deeper cultivation also brings back to the surface the nutrients that have seeped below root level. Thus, the plow made permanent cultivation of fields a common practice for the first time in history and led to the replacement of horticulture (from the Latin *horti cultura*, or the cultivation of a garden) by agriculture (from *agri cultura*, the cultivation of a field).

The invention of the plow also paved the way for the harnessing of animal energy.[4] As long as the digging stick and hoe were the basic tools of cultivation, men and women had to supply the energy. But a plow could be pulled, and it did not take long for people to discover that oxen could do the job. The importance of this discovery can hardly be exaggerated, since it established a principle with broad applicability. In Childe's words, "The ox was the first step to the steam engine and the [gasoline] motor."[5]

More immediately, however, the harnessing of animal energy led to greatly increased productivity. With a plow and a pair of oxen, a farmer could cultivate a far larger area than was possible with a hoe.[6] In addition, the use of oxen led, in many societies, to feeding them in stalls, and this in turn led to the use of manure as fertilizer.[7] In short, the shift from hoe to plow not only meant permanently cultivated fields and larger crops; it also meant the potential for a larger economic surplus and new and more complex forms of social organization.

The earliest evidence of the plow comes from Mesopotamian cylinder seals and Egyptian paintings dating from a little before 3000 B.C.[8] Modern research indicates that the plow, like so many other innovations in the last 10,000 years, presupposed certain earlier inventions and discoveries—underlining again the cumulative nature of technological change. The first plows of the Mesopotamians and the Egyptians were, in fact, simply modified versions of the hoe, the basic farm implement of all advanced

FIGURE 7.1 Early Egyptian ox-drawn plow (about 2700 B.C.). Note the primitive and inefficient method of harnessing the animals—a simple bar attached to the horns.

horticultural societies. In the earliest period, the plow was probably pulled by men, but before long cattle and oxen were used. These plows, like all plows in simple agrarian societies, were made of wood, though sometimes the plowshare was made of bronze for greater strength.

The plow and related techniques of agriculture apparently spread by diffusion until agrarian societies were eventually established throughout most of Europe and much of North Africa and Asia. The plow did not spread to sub-Saharan Africa until the period of European colonialism, and in the New World, too, it was unknown until introduced by Europeans.

The full impact of the new technology was not felt immediately in either Mesopotamia or Egypt. Even so, the shift to agriculture was followed quickly by several important developments, notably the invention of writing, the rise of urban communities, and empire building on a greatly expanded scale (which in Egypt led to the unification of the entire country under a single ruler for the first time in history). This was the period that historians refer to as "the dawn of civilization."

Similar developments occurred (though at later dates) in *horticultural* societies in China and Mexico, proving that an agrarian technology is not a necessary precondition for literacy, urbanism, and imperialism. But the rarity of these developments in horticultural societies and their frequency in agrarian societies shows that the shift to agriculture, by increasing productivity, greatly increased the probability of their occurrence.

Religion and the Growth of the Economic Surplus

In the earliest agrarian societies, religion was an extremely powerful force. Mesopotamian societies believed that "man was . . . created for one purpose only: to serve the gods by supplying them with food, drink, and shelter so that they might have full leisure for their divine activities."[9] Each temple was believed to be, quite literally, the house of a particular god, and each community had its own special deity. Priests and other attendants constituted the god's court or household, and their chief task was to minister to his needs. Another responsibility was to mediate between the god and the community, trying to discover his will and appease his anger. In order to perform these tasks, temples and their staffs had to be supported by a steady flow of goods. Over the years the temples were continually enlarged and became increasingly costly. In fact, they became, in many respects, substantial business enterprises, a development that apparently provided the stimulus for the *invention of true writing*, which was originally a means of recording the business activities of temples.[10] Many scholars have described the early Mesopotamian city-states as theocracies, since the local deity was regarded as the real ruler and the king merely as his "tenant farmer."[11]

Egypt was also a theocracy, but of a different type. The ruler was himself believed to be a god.[12] To his subjects he "was the incarnation, the living embodiment, of the god of any district he happened to be visiting; he was their actual God in living form, whom they could see, speak to, and adore."[13] Like the gods of the Mesopotamian city-states, he was the owner of all the land and entitled to a portion of all that was

FIGURE 7.2 The temple of Luxor, Egypt, built about 1400 B.C.

produced; as in Mesopotamia, these revenues supported a small army of specialists (e.g., officials, craftsmen, soldiers).

In later years there was a secularizing trend, especially in Mesopotamia.[14] By then, however, these societies had developed other institutional arrangements—notably political ones—to ensure the continued transfer of the economic surplus from the peasant producers to the governing class. Nevertheless, religion continued to play an important role as a legitimizing agency. It provided a rationale to justify the operation of the political system and its often harsh economic consequences.

The experience of Mesopotamia and Egypt thus supports the impression gained from horticultural societies concerning the importance of religion in the formation of an economic surplus. *Technological advance created the possibility of a surplus, but to transform that possibility into a reality required an ideology that motivated farmers to produce more than they needed to stay alive and productive, and persuaded them to turn that surplus over to someone else.* Although this has sometimes been accomplished by means of secular and political ideologies, a system of beliefs that defined people's obligations with reference to the supernatural worked best in most societies of the past.

Population: Growth in Size of Communities and Societies

In the first few centuries after the shift to agriculture, there was striking growth in the size of a number of communities, especially in Mesopotamian societies.[15] These became *the first full-fledged cities in history.* The largest of them were the capitals of the largest and most prosperous societies. Although it is impossible to determine exactly the size of the cities and towns of the third and second millennia B.C., scholars believe that one or more of them had a population of at least 100,000.[16]

Egypt was the largest of the simple agrarian societies of ancient times and politically the most stable. It enjoyed the unique distinction of being a united and independent nation throughout most of the time it was a simple agrarian society. This achievement was due to its unique environmental situation: no other society had such excellent natural defenses (i.e., the surrounding desert) and was so little threatened by other societies.

In the second half of the second millennium, Egypt embarked on a program of expansion that extended its boundaries to Syria and the Sudan. There were also other important empires in this era, especially those established by the Babylonians in the eighteenth century B.C. and the Hittites in the thirteenth century B.C. Babylonia succeeded briefly in uniting most of Mesopotamia, while the Hittites conquered much of what is now Turkey and Syria.

FIGURE 7.3 Egyptian painting of soldiers attacking a fortress (about 1940 B.C.).

The Polity: Growth of the State

These conquests posed serious organizational problems for the rulers of early agrarian societies. Traditional modes of government based on kinship ties were no longer adequate for administering the affairs of societies whose populations now sometimes numbered in the millions. Though rulers continued to rely on relatives to help them govern, they were forced to turn increasingly to others. One solution was to incorporate a conquered group as a subdivision of the conquering society, leaving its former ruler in charge but in a subordinate capacity. Eventually all of the more successful rulers found it necessary to create new kinds of governmental structures that were no longer based on kinship ties alone.

We can see these newer patterns evolving in both military and civil affairs. For example, the first armies in agrarian societies, like those in horticultural, were simply militia made up of all the able-bodied men in the society.[17] During this period, wars did not last long and were fought only after the harvest was in. In fact, the period following the harvest came to be known as the "season when kings go forth to war." These limitations were necessary because, with the shift to agriculture, men's responsibilities in farming were much greater than they had been in horticultural societies.

As long as wars were brief and limited to skirmishes with neighboring peoples, militias were adequate. But once rulers became interested in empire building, a new system was necessary. As early as the middle of the third millennium, would-be empire builders in Mesopotamia established small but highly trained *professional armies*. For example, Sargon, the famous Akkadian king, had a standing army of 5,400 men.[18] As far as possible, recruits were sons of old soldiers, and thus a military caste was gradually created. The Egyptians followed a similar policy except that they relied chiefly on foreign mercenaries. These new armies were *royal*, rather than national, armies. Their expenses were paid by the king out of his enormous revenues, and the profits resulting from their activities were his also. Not only were these armies useful in dealing with foreign enemies, they also served as a defense against internal threats.[19]

In civil affairs, too, the casual and informal practices of simpler societies proved inadequate. As states expanded and the problems of administration multiplied, new kinds of governmental positions were created and *governmental bureaucracies* began to take shape.[20] In addition to the many officials who comprised the royal court and were responsible for administering the king's complex household affairs, there were officials scattered throughout the countryside to administer the affairs of units ranging from small districts to provinces with hundreds of villages and towns. Each official had a staff of scribes and other lesser officials to assist him, and written records became increasingly important as administrative problems grew more complex.[21]

Throughout most of the history of the simple agrarian societies of antiquity, writing was a complex craft mastered by only a few individuals after long apprenticeships.[22] This is not surprising, considering the complex systems of writing then in use. Even after a 2,000-year process of simplification, Mesopotamian cuneiform script still had between 600 and 1,000 distinct characters. Before a person could learn to read or write, he had to memorize this formidable array of symbols and learn the complex rules for combining them. The Egyptian hieroglyphic and hieratic scripts were equally complicated. Thus, those who could write formed a specialized occupational group in society—the scribes—and their services were much in demand. For the most part, this occupation was filled by the sons of the rich and powerful, since only they could afford the necessary education.[23] Because of the political importance of their skill and the limited supply of qualified personnel, most scribes were at least members of the middle class.

One consequence of the growth of empires and the development of bureaucracy was the establishment of the first formal legal systems. Over the centuries every society had developed certain concepts of justice, as well as informal techniques for implementing them. The most common solution, as we saw in our survey of hunting and gathering societies, was to rely on blood revenge by the injured party and his relatives. Because of the anarchic tendencies in such a system, people began to seek settlement by arbitration, and to help them in this they would turn to the most respected and powerful members of the community. In this way, headmen and other political leaders gradually acquired judicial powers (i.e., the power to administer justice). Later, as empires grew, peoples of diverse cultures were brought within the

FIGURE 7.4 Model of a royal granary, found in an Egyptian tomb (about 2000 B.C.). Note the scribes sitting by the door recording the deliveries of grain.

framework of a single political system. In many instances the official appointed to rule over an area was not a native and was therefore unfamiliar with local conceptions of justice (which varied considerably from place to place). This generated pressure to clarify and standardize judicial practice, which eventually led to the *first formal codes of law*. The most famous of these was the Code of Hammurabi, the great Babylonian empire builder of the early second millennium.

The Economy: The First Monetary Systems and the Growth of Trade

Money as we know it was absent in the first simple agrarian societies. There were, nevertheless, certain standardized media of exchange. Barley served this function in ancient Mesopotamia, wheat in Egypt. Wages, rents, taxes, and various other obligations were paid in specified quantities of these grains.[24]

As media of exchange, grains were less than ideal because they were both perishable and bulky. So, from a fairly early date, various metals, particularly silver and copper, were adopted as alternatives.[25] Initially, they were circulated in the form of crude bars of irregular size and weight, and their use was restricted to major transactions, since metal was still scarce. Later, as the production of metals increased, smaller units were introduced in local trade and sizes and weights were gradually standardized. As a final stage in the process, governments assumed the responsibility for manufacturing metallic currencies and full-fledged monetary systems took shape. This did not occur, however, until the very end of the simple agrarian era.

The growth of monetary systems had enormous implications for societal development. *Money has always facilitated the movement, the exchange, and ultimately the production of goods and services of every kind*. The establishment of a monetary system greatly expands the market for the things each individual produces, because products can then be sold even to people who produce nothing the producer wants in exchange. Thus the demand for goods and services is increased.

One immediate consequence of the emergence of a monetary system is the growth of opportunities for *merchants*, or middlemen, who purchase goods which they do not want for themselves but which they know are in demand by others. Once a class of merchants has come into being, it serves not only to satisfy existing demands but to create new ones. By displaying new and unusual articles, merchants generate new needs and desires and thereby stimulate economic activity.

In the long run, a money economy subverts many of the values of simpler societies, especially the cooperative tendencies of extended kin systems. It fosters instead a more individualistic, rationalistic, and competitive approach to life, and lays a foundation for many of the attitudes and values that characterize modern industrial societies.

All of these tendencies were still quite limited, however, in the simple agrarian societies of the ancient Middle East. The newly emerging money economies barely penetrated the rural villages, where most people lived. Even in the cities and towns, the role of money was quite limited compared with what we are accustomed to. Fully developed cash economies still lay far in the future.

Stratification: Increasing Inequality

In most simple agrarian societies of the ancient world, newly emerging or expanding social and cultural differences created internal divisions within society, and sometimes conflict as well. Three cleavages were especially serious. First, there was one between the small governing class and the much larger mass of people who had no voice in political decisions and who had to hand over all or most of the surplus they produced to the governing class. Second, there was a division between the urban minority and the far more numerous rural population. Finally, there was a cleavage between the small literate minority and the illiterate masses.

Because these three lines of cleavage tended to converge, their impact was greatly magnified. The small and often literate urban governing class lived in a strikingly different world from that of the illiterate, rural, peasant majority—despite the fact that they were members of the same society. Each group had its own distinct subculture.[26]

The subculture of the common people was a mixture of primitive superstition and the practical information they needed in their daily lives. It was extremely parochial in outlook and knew little of the world beyond the village. The subculture of the governing class, in contrast, incorporated the refinements we identify with "civilization," such as philosophy, art, literature, history, and science. It also included a contempt for physical labor of any kind, and for those who engaged in it.

In many respects the differences within simple agrarian societies were greater than those between them. Apart from the problems of language, an Egyptian peasant could have adapted far more easily to the life of a Babylonian peasant than to the life of a member of the governing class of his own society. As this gulf widened, members of the governing class found it increasingly difficult to recognize the ignorant, downtrodden peasants as fellow human beings. The scribes of ancient Egypt were fond of saying that the lower classes lacked intelligence and had to be driven like cattle, with a stick.[27]

Slowdown in the Rate of Technological Innovation

Another significant development in these societies was a marked slowdown in the rate of technological innovation and progress, beginning within a few centuries after the shift from horticulture to agriculture. V. Gordon Childe described the change this way:

> Before the [agrarian] revolution comparatively poor and illiterate communities had made an impressive series of contributions to man's progress. The two millennia immediately preceding 3,000 B.C. had witnessed discoveries in applied science that directly or indirectly affected the prosperity of millions of [people] and demonstrably furthered the biological welfare of our species by facilitating its multiplication. We have mentioned the following applications of science: artificial irrigation using canals and ditches; the plow; the harnessing of animal motive-power; the sailboat; wheeled vehicles; orchard husbandry; fermentation; the production and use of copper; bricks; the arch;

glazing; the seal; and—in the earliest stages of the revolution—a solar calendar, writing, numerical notation, and bronze.

The two thousand years after the revolution—say from 2,600 to 600 B.C.—produced few contributions of anything like comparable importance to human progress. Perhaps only four achievements deserve to be put in the same category as the fifteen just enumerated. They are: the "decimal notation" of Babylonia (about 2,000 B.C.); an economical method for smelting iron on an industrial scale (1,400 B.C.); a truly alphabetic script (1,300 B.C.); aqueducts for supplying water to cities (700 B.C.).[28]

Childe went on to note that two of these four innovations, the smelting of iron and the development of the alphabet, "cannot be credited to the societies that had initiated and reaped the fruits of the [agrarian] revolution" but rather were the products of somewhat less advanced neighboring societies.[29]

At first glance this slowing of the rate of cultural innovation seems an unlikely development. Larger populations, increased intersocietal contacts, and the greater store of information available to potential innovators should have produced *higher* rates of innovation, especially in technology. The fact that they did not poses an interesting problem.

To explain this unusual development, we need to return to the concept of feedback. This, as we have seen, is the effect produced when the impact of an initial force reverts back to, and influences, the initial force itself. Until now, however, we have only seen examples of *positive* feedback, in which the secondary effect enhances or strengthens the original force. This is the type of feedback that has been involved in all of the major social and cultural changes we have examined so far. Now we are seeing one of the rare instances in sociocultural evolution in which major technological advances generated *negative* feedback. In other words, this is a case in which the secondary effect diminished or weakened the original force.

As Figure 7.5 indicates, changes in social organization and ideology that were themselves consequences of technological advance had the effect of *slowing* the rate of technological innovation and advance. As the older system of a militia that included all of a society's able-bodied men was replaced by a professional army, there was a substantial increase in the power of the governing class, which controlled the new army. New beliefs and values emerged that justified and legitimized the new system and thereby reinforced it and made it even worse. Thus, the governing class found it increasingly easy to extract most of the economic surplus from the peasants, so that peasants were left with little more than the bare necessities of life.[30]

As a result, the peasants lost all incentive for creativity, knowing that any benefits that resulted from their inventions and discoveries would simply be appropriated by the governing class.* At the same time, the governing class, though it had a vested

---

*It is possible that the process was even more complicated and that the mental capacities of many peasants may have been impaired by protein-deficient diets and by environments not conducive to learning in early childhood. In short, the basic intelligence and creative potential of many peasants may have been permanently impaired.

FIGURE 7.5 Model of the causes of the decline in the rate of technological innovation during the first two millennia of the agrarian era.

interest in a more productive economy, no longer had the necessary knowledge of and experience with subsistence technology and thus was in no position to make creative innovations. In short, *expertise and incentive were inadvertently divorced*, with disastrous results for technological progress.

Under the circumstances it is hardly surprising that members of the governing class turned increasingly to warfare and conquest as the best way to increase their wealth. Warfare was something they understood; moreover, in their system of values, waging war was one of the few occupations considered appropriate for members of their class. More than ever before, the resources of societies were turned from the conquest of nature to *the conquest of people*.[31] And this, due to the new, more productive technology, could be a highly profitable enterprise. With vast numbers of peasants producing more than they needed to survive and remain productive, there was a large economic surplus that could be extracted by means of taxes, tribute, tithes, and rents and used to support the host of servants and artisans who catered to the whims of the governing class and the army of soldiers and officials who ensured the flow of revenues.

These developments help to explain the growing complexity of social organization during this period. Having cut themselves off from the sweaty world of work and having turned their efforts instead to conquest, members of the governing class found new challenges for their creative talents in the field of social organization. The exercise of power and the manipulation of others were activities in keeping with their dignity. Moreover, they were rewarding: the better organized an army or government, the greater its chances of success in struggles with other groups.[32]

By the end of the period when simple agrarian societies were dominant, substantial changes had occurred in societies that had adopted the new technology. The largest of them were substantially larger than any horticultural society had ever been, and substantially more complex. There was a much greater division of labor within them, and social inequality had also increased. But as impressive as they were, these changes were only a prelude to what was to come in the remainder of the agrarian era.

FIGURE 7.6 One consequence of the growth of empires was an increase in the economic surplus extracted from conquered peoples in the form of tribute: Egyptian carving showing tribute bearers (about 2000 B.C.).

ADVANCED AGRARIAN SOCIETIES

Technology

During the period in which simple agrarian societies dominated the Middle East, the most important technological advance was the discovery of the technique of smelting iron. Prior to this, bronze had been the most important metal. But since the supply was limited* and the demands of the governing class always took precedence over the needs of peasants, bronze was used primarily for military, ornamental, and ceremonial purposes. It never really replaced stone and wood in ordinary tools, certainly not in agricultural tools, and so its impact on the economy was limited.

People knew of iron at least as early as the first half of the third millennium B.C.,

---

*This was because of the scarcity of tin, an essential component of bronze.

but apparently only in its meteoric form, which is very scarce.[33] Sometime during the second millennium, the Hittites of Asia Minor discovered iron ore and invented a technique for smelting it. For centuries they kept this a closely guarded secret, which gave them a monopoly on a highly valued commodity. Then, about 1200 B.C., their nation was destroyed. This led to the rapid dispersal of both the Hittite people and the technology of smelting iron.

As one would expect, in view of the class structure of simple agrarian societies, the initial use of iron was limited largely to the governing class. Some of the earliest iron objects recovered from Egypt were a dagger, a bracelet, and a headrest found in the tomb of the pharaoh Tutankhamen. Prior to the military collapse of the Hittite empire, iron was five times more expensive than gold, forty times more than silver. It was not until about the eighth century B.C. that iron came into general use for *ordinary tools*. Thus, it is not until this period that we can speak of true advanced agrarian societies, although many Middle Eastern societies of the previous three or four centuries were certainly transitional types.

During this transitional period two further discoveries greatly enhanced the value of iron. First it was found that if the outer layers of the iron absorbed some carbon from the fire during the forging process, the metal became somewhat harder. Later it was discovered that this carburized iron could be hardened still further by quenching the hot metal in water, thus producing steel. With these developments, iron became not only more common than bronze but also more useful for both military and economic purposes. As one writer has said, "After the discovery of quench-hardening, iron gradually passed into the position from which it has never subsequently been ousted; it became the supremely useful material for making all the tools and weapons that are intended for cutting, chopping, piercing, or slashing."[34]

From its point of origin in the Middle East, iron-making spread until eventually it was practiced in nearly all of the Old World, even in many horticultural societies. By the time of Christ, advanced agrarian societies were firmly established in the Middle East, throughout most of the Mediterranean world, and in much of India and China. Within the next thousand years, the advanced agrarian pattern spread over most of Europe and much of Southeast Asia, and expanded further in India and China. Still later it was transplanted to the European colonies in the New World.

Compared with simpler societies, advanced agrarian societies enjoyed a very productive technology. Unfortunately, the same conditions that slowed the rate of technological advance in simple agrarian societies continued to prevail. As a result, their progress was not nearly what one would expect on the basis of their size, the degree of contact among them, and, above all, their store of accumulated information.[35]

Nevertheless, over the centuries quite a number of important innovations were made. A partial list would include the catapult, the crossbow, gunpowder, horseshoes, a workable harness for horses, stirrups, the wood-turning lathe, the auger, the screw, the wheelbarrow, the rotary fan for ventilation, the clock, the spinning wheel, porcelain, printing, iron casting, the magnet, water-powered mills, windmills, and, in the period just preceding the emergence of the first industrial societies, the workable steam engine, the fly shuttle, the spinning jenny, the spinning machine, and various other power-driven tools. Because of these and other innovations, the most advanced

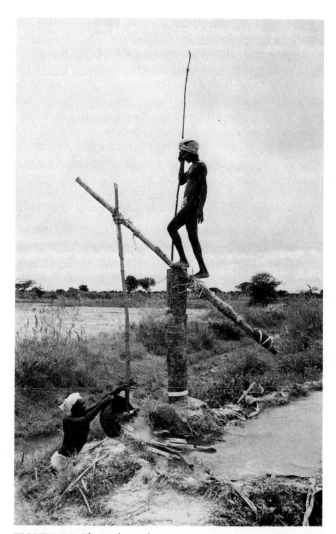

FIGURE 7.7 Throughout the agrarian era societies depended
on humans and animals as their chief sources of energy:
Indian peasants raising water from ditch to irrigate field. The
man on the post moves back and forth on the crossbeam to
raise the water and to lower the bucket again to the ditch
below, where the other man refills it.

agrarian societies of the eighteenth century A.D. were far superior, from the technological standpoint, to their predecessors of 2,500 years earlier.

The level of technological development was not uniform throughout the agrarian world, despite diffusion. Information spread slowly in most cases, and some areas
were considerably ahead of others. During much of the advanced agrarian era, espe-

cially from 500 to 1500 A.D., the Middle East, China, and parts of India were technologically superior to Europe.[36] In part, this was simply a continuation of older patterns: the Middle East had been the center of innovation for more than 5,000 years
following its shift to horticulture. An even more important factor in Europe's relative
backwardness, however, was the collapse of the Roman Empire. For centuries afterward, Europe was divided into scores of petty kingdoms and principalities that had
only enough resources to maintain the smallest urban settlements and the most limited occupational specialization. Therefore, Europeans were inactive on many of the
most promising and challenging technological frontiers of the time. Though they made
relative gains during the later Middle Ages—thanks largely to the diffusion of knowledge from the East—they did not really catch up until the sixteenth century and did
not take the lead until even later.

Population: Continuing Trends

Size of Societies and Communities The populations of advanced agrarian societies were substantially larger than those of any societies that preceded them. This was
due partly to advances in agricultural technology that permitted greater population
densities, and partly to advances in military technology that aided the process of empire building. The largest simple agrarian society, Egypt, probably had fewer than 15
million members.[37] In contrast, the largest advanced agrarian society, mid-nineteenth-
century China, had approximately 400 million.[38]* While that was exceptional, India
reached 175 million in the middle of the nineteenth century, and the Roman and the
Russian empires each had at least 70 million people.[39]

Similar differences are found in communities. The largest cities in simple agrarian societies had populations of about 100,000. By comparison, the upper limit for
cities in advanced agrarian societies was about a million.[40] Only the capitals of major
empires ever attained this size, however, and they maintained it but briefly. Cities of
100,000, while much more numerous than in simple agrarian societies, were still quite
rare by modern standards.

Fertility and Mortality Birthrates in both simple and advanced agrarian societies
have averaged 40 or more births per 1,000 population per year, triple that of most
modern industrial societies.[41] In general, there seems to have been little interest in
limiting the size of families, since large families, particularly ones with many sons,
were valued for both economic and religious reasons. From the economic standpoint,
children were viewed by peasants as an important asset, a valuable source of cheap
labor.[42] Children were also important as the only form of "old-age insurance" available to peasants. Religion added yet another incentive for large families, either by
encouraging ancestor worship, for which perpetuation of the family line was essential, or simply by declaring large families to be a sign of God's favor.[43]

One of the few constraints on the growth of families was the threat of severe

*Growth in China's population *after* the middle of the nineteenth century was due increasingly to the beginnings of industrialization. The same was true in India.

deprivation. When crops failed and famine was imminent, families often resorted to infanticide, abandoning their newborn by the roadside or leaving them at the door of a church or monastery in the hope that someone who was able to provide for the baby might take pity and raise it.[44] If conditions became bad enough, even older children would be abandoned by their parents (see "Mother Goose Revisited," page 180).

There is also evidence that many women would have liked to avoid the burdens and risks of repeated pregnancies. Unfortunately for them, in societies in which men were dominant and in which an effective contraceptive technology did not yet exist, their wishes had little effect.

Despite their high birthrates, advanced agrarian societies grew slowly. Sometimes they failed to grow at all or even declined in size. The reason was that death rates were almost as high as birthrates, and sometimes higher. Wars, disease, accidents, and famine all took their toll. Infant mortality was especially high before the development of modern sanitation and medicine. Recent studies show that children born in Rome 2,000 years ago lived only 20 years on average.[45] Even as recently as the seventeenth century, the children of British queens and duchesses had a life expectancy of only 30 years, and nearly a third died before their fifth birthday.[46] For the common people, conditions were even worse. With death rates averaging nearly 40 per 1,000 per year, life expectancy at birth was barely 25 years, and even those who reached adulthood usually died young. (See Table 7.1)

Large cities were notoriously unhealthy places, especially for the common people. The citizens of Rome, for example, had a shorter life expectancy than those in the provinces.[47] England in the early eighteenth century presented a similar situation. During the first half of that century, there were an estimated 500,000 more deaths than births in London.[48] The reasons for this become clear when we read descriptions of sanitary conditions in medieval cities:

> The streets of medieval towns were generally little more than narrow alleys,
> the overhanging upper stories of the houses nearly meeting, and thus
> effectually excluding all but a minimum of light and air.... In most
> continental towns and some English ones, a high city wall further impeded

TABLE 7.1 Average Age at Death of Those Who Reached Adulthood During Agrarian Era

	Males	Females
Early Bronze Age, 3000 B.C.	33.7	29.5
Middle Bronze Age, 2000 B.C.		
Commoners	36.3	30.8
Royalty	35.9	36.1
Late Bronze Age, 1500 B.C.	39.5	32.1
Early Iron Age, 1150 B.C.	38.6	31.3
Imperial Rome, 120 A.D.	40.2	34.6
Medieval Byzantium, 1400 A.D.	37.7	31.1

Sources: J. L. Angel, "Ecology and Population in the Eastern Mediterranean," *World Archaeology*, 4 (1972), pp. 88–105; and J. L. Angel, "Paleoecology, Paleodemography, and Health," in Steven Polgar, *Population, Ecology, and Social Evolution* (The Hague: Mouton, 1975), pp. 167–190.

FIGURE 7.8 Sanitary standards were low in most agrarian societies: open-air butcher shop in the Middle East.

the free circulation of air.... Rich citizens might possess a courtyard in which garbage was collected and occasionally removed to the suburbs, but the usual practice was to throw everything into the streets including the garbage of slaughter houses and other offensive trades.... Filth of every imaginable description accumulated indefinitely in the unpaved streets and in all available space and was trodden into the ground. The water supply would be obtained either from wells or springs, polluted by the gradual percolation through the soil of the accumulated filth, or else from an equally polluted river. In some towns, notably London, small streams running down a central gutter served at once as sewers and as water supply.... In seventeenth century London, which before the Fire largely remained a medieval city, the poorer class house had only a covering of weatherboards, a little black pitch forming the only waterproofing, and these houses were generally built back to back. Thousands of Londoners dwelt in cellars or horribly overcrowded tenements. A small house in Dowgate accommodated 11 married couples and 15 single persons.... Another source of unhealthiness were the church vaults and graveyards, so filled with corpses that the level of the latter was generally raised above that of the surrounding ground. In years of pestilence, recourse had to be made to plague pits in order to dispose of the harvest of death.[49]

This account calls attention to one of the striking demographic characteristics of advanced agrarian societies: the disasters that periodically overtook them and produced sharp increases in the death rate.[50] The most devastating of all, the Black Plague that hit Europe in the middle of the fourteenth century, is said to have killed between a quarter and a half of the population in a four-year period.[51]

Crop failures and famines seldom affected such large areas, but they were more frequent and could be just as deadly. One Finnish province lost a third of its population during the famine of 1696–1697, and many parts of France suffered comparable losses a few years earlier.[52] Even allowing for a considerable margin of error in the reports of such disasters, it is clear from other kinds of evidence—for example, the severe labor shortages and the abandonment of farms that followed plagues and famines—that the number of deaths was huge. For these reasons, the growth of advanced agrarian populations was anything but continuous.

The Economy: Increasing Differentiation

Division of Labor The growth in both territorial and population size that came with the shift from the simple to the advanced agrarian level brought with it an increase in the division of labor. For the first time, there was significant economic specialization both by regions and by communities, and this was accompanied by increased occupational specialization.

The Roman Empire provides a good illustration of both regional and local specialization. North Africa and Spain were noted as suppliers of dried figs and olive oil; Gaul, Dalmatia, Asia Minor, and Syria for their wine; Spain and Egypt for salted meats; Egypt, North Africa, Sicily, and the Black Sea region for grain; and the latter for salted fish as well.[53] The tendency toward specialization at the community level is illustrated by a passage from a manual for wealthy farmers, written in the second century B.C., which advised:

> Tunics, togas, blankets, smocks and shoes should be bought at Rome; caps, iron tools, scythes, spades, mattocks, axes, harnesses, ornaments and small chains at Cales and Minturnae; spades at Venafrum, carts and sledges at Suessa and in Lucania, jars and pots at Alba and at Rome; tiles at Venafrum, oil mills at Pompeii and at Rufrius's yard at Nola, nails and bars at Rome; pails, oil urns, water pitchers, wine urns, other copper vessels at Capua and at Nola; Campanian baskets, pulley-ropes and all sorts of cordage at Capua; Roman baskets at Suessa and Casium.[54]

Similar patterns are reported in other agrarian societies.[55] Even at the village level a measure of specialization was not uncommon. In the agricultural off-season, peasants often turned to handicrafts to make ends meet, and villages often developed a reputation for a particular commodity.

In the larger urban centers occupational specialization reached a level that surpassed anything achieved in simpler societies. For example, a tax roll for Paris from the year 1313 lists 157 different trades, and tax records from two sections of Barcelona in 1385 indicate a hundred occupations (see Table 7.2).[56] The clothing industry alone contained such specialized occupations as wool comber, wool spinner, silk spinner (two kinds), girdle maker, and headdress maker (seven kinds, including specialists in felt, fur, wool and cotton, flowers, peacock feathers, gold embroidery and pearls, and silk). Though such specialization was found only in the largest cities, smaller cities often had forty or fifty different kinds of craftsmen, and even small towns had ten or twenty.[57] In addition to craft specialists, urban centers also had specialists in government, commerce, religion, education, the armed forces, and domestic service. There were also specialists in illegal occupations (e.g., thieves, prostitutes), which were a normal part of urban life in advanced agrarian societies.

Command Economies   Because politics and economics were always highly interdependent in advanced agrarian societies, the people who dominated the political system also dominated the economic system. The leading officeholders in government were usually the chief landholders as well, and in these societies land and control of those who worked it was the most important economic resource. As one economic historian has written, this was a time in which "true wealth consisted in being master."[58]

In these societies, the answers to basic economic questions—how resources should be used, what should be produced and in what quantities, and how those products should be distributed—were determined less by the forces of supply and demand than by arbitrary decisions of the political elite. These were *command economies*, not market economies.[59]

The economy of an advanced agrarian society consisted of two distinct parts: a rural agricultural sector and an urban commercial and productive sector. These were not of equal economic importance, however. One historian has estimated that the Roman state derived approximately twenty times more tax revenue from agriculture than from trade and handicrafts. He went on to say that "this apportionment of the burden of taxation probably corresponded roughly to the economic structure of the empire. All the evidence goes to show that its wealth was derived almost entirely from agriculture, and to a very small extent from industry and trade."[60] The same could be

TABLE 7.2 Occupations of Householders in Two Sections of Barcelona in 1385 A.D.

Sailors	227	Longshoremen	50	Silversmiths	29
Merchants	151	Innkeepers	49	Curriers	29
Shoemakers	108	Brokers	45	Notaries	28
Tailors	96	Carpenters	43	Tavern-keepers	27
Fishermen	94	Bakers	40	Spicers	26
Seamen	73	Janitors	39	Bargemen	25
Wooldressers	70	Hucksters	36	76 other occupations	525
Weavers	63	Butchers	34		
Tanners	61	Scriveners	32	Total	2000

Source: Adapted from Josiah Cox Russell, *Medieval Regions and Their Cities* (Bloomington: Indiana University Press, 1972), p. 170.

said of every agrarian society. This does not mean, however, that the urban economy was of little interest to members of the governing class. On the contrary, it was of great interest because it provided the luxury goods they valued so highly. The urban economy, however, depended on the ability of the rural economy to produce a surplus that could support the urban population.

In many respects the economy of the typical agrarian society resembled a tree with roots spreading in every direction, constantly drawing in new resources. The pattern was similar to that shown in Figure 7.9. At the economic center of the society was the national capital, controlled by the king or emperor and the leading members of the governing class. Surrounding it were various provincial or regional capitals controlled by royal governors and other members of the governing class. Each of these in turn was surrounded by smaller county seats and market towns controlled by lesser members of the governing class. Finally, each of these towns was surrounded by scores of small villages.

In this system, there was a steady flow of goods from smaller units to larger, or from villages to county seats, and then on to regional and national capitals. Basically this flow was achieved by means of taxation, but it was supplemented by rents, interest on debts, tithes and other religious offerings, and profits, all of which helped to transfer the economic surplus from the peasant producers to the urban-based governing class, its allies, and their dependents.

Some scholars have argued that this was a symbiotic relationship in which the villagers freely exchanged the goods they produced for goods and services produced in the urban centers. Although there is an element of truth in this, the historical record shows that the relationship was largely one-sided and that the peasants were forced

FIGURE 7.9 In agrarian societies there was a steady flow of goods from villages to county seats and from there to regional and national capitals: model of the flow of goods in these societies and of the movement of the economic surplus to the society's capital.

to give far more than they received. The peasants obviously resented this, as indicated by the frequency of their protests and revolts.[61]

With what they retained of their surplus after paying taxes, rents, interest, and other obligations, peasants could go to the urban centers and trade for commodities that were not available in their villages (e.g., metal tools, salt, etc.). Many towns and cities were also religious centers, and the peasants often used these facilities. Finally, the peasants did benefit to some degree from the maintenance of law and order provided by urban-based governments, even though the law was used disproportionately to protect the rights of the governing class and keep the peasants in a subordinate position. The maintenance of order was extremely important in an agrarian society because so much depended on the success of each harvest, and each harvest depended on months of prior effort. Disruption at any point in the agricultural cycle could be disastrous for everyone.

The Rural Economy   In most advanced agrarian societies, the governing elite (which included religious leaders) owned a grossly disproportionate share of the land. Although there are no precise figures for earlier times, the traditional pattern could still be seen recently in many parts of Latin America, the Middle East, and Southeast Asia. Typically, a minority of 1 to 3 percent of the population has owned from one-third to two-thirds of the arable land in these societies.[62]

Not only did the governing class usually own most of the land, but it often owned most of the peasants who worked it. Slavery and serfdom were common in agrarian societies, with large landholdings and large numbers of slaves or serfs normally going hand in hand. Thus, one nineteenth-century Russian nobleman who owned 2 million acres of land also owned nearly 300,000 serfs. Rulers always had the largest holdings. Prior to the emancipation of the serfs in Russia, the czar owned 27.4 million of them.[63]

Even when the peasant owned his own land and was legally free, he usually found it difficult to make ends meet. A bad crop one year, and he had to borrow money at rates as high as 120 percent a year.[64] In any event, there were always taxes, and these usually fell more heavily on the peasant landowner than on his wealthier neighbor, either because of special exemptions granted the latter or simply because of his greater ability to evade such obligations.[65] If a peasant did not own his land, he had to pay rent, which was always high. In addition, he was often subject to compulsory labor service, tithes, fines, and obligatory "gifts" to the governing class.[66]

Because the number and variety of obligations were so great, it is difficult to determine just how large the total was, but in most societies it appears to have been at least half the total value of the goods the peasants produced.[67] The basic philosophy of the governing class seems to have been to tax peasants to the limit of their ability to pay.[68] A story is told of a leading Japanese official of the seventeenth century who, returning to one of his estates after an absence of ten years and finding the villagers in well-built houses instead of the hovels he remembered, exclaimed, "These people are too comfortable. They must be more heavily taxed."[69]

Living conditions for most peasants were primitive, and many were worse off than most hunters and gatherers had been thousands of years earlier. For example,

FIGURE 7.10 Peasant using traditional plow, Iran.

the diet of the average peasant in medieval England consisted of little more than a hunk of bread and a mug of ale in the morning; a lump of cheese and bread with perhaps an onion or two to flavor it and more ale at noon; and a thick soup or pottage with bread and cheese in the evening. Meat was rare and the ale thin. Household furniture consisted of a few stools, a table, and a chest to hold the best clothes and any other treasured possessions.[70] Beds were uncommon; most peasants simply slept on earthen floors covered with straw.

Even later in France, toward the end of the agrarian era,

> Great masses of the people lived in a state of chronic malnutrition,
> subsisting mainly on porridge made of bread and water with some
> occasional, home-grown vegetables thrown in. They ate meat only a few
> times a year, on feast days or after autumn slaughtering if they did not have
> enough silage to feed the livestock over the winter . . . For most peasants
> village life was a struggle for survival, and survival meant keeping above the
> line that divided the poor from the indigent.[71]

But many did not survive and lost their farms. "Then they took to the road for good, drifting about with the flotsam and jetsam of France's *population flottante* ('floating population'), which included several million desperate souls by the 1780s." The same author concludes by saying that "The human condition has changed so much since then that we can hardly imagine the way it appeared to people whose lives really were nasty, brutish, and short."[72]

In China, conditions were so wretched that female infanticide was widely practiced. One nineteenth-century scholar indicated that in some districts as many as a quarter of the female infants were killed at birth.[73] Sometimes signs were posted near ponds, reading, "Girls may not be drowned here." In rural areas, the traditional greeting when peasants met was "Have you eaten today?" (the equivalent of "How are you today?").

To compound the misery created by their economic situation, peasants were often subjected to further cruelties. Families were sometimes split up if it served their master's economic interests.[74] Peasants often found it difficult to defend their wives and daughters from the amorous attentions of the governing class, and in some areas the lord of the manor maintained the notorious *jus primae noctis* (i.e., literally, the right of the first night, meaning the right to initial sexual relations with all brides on their wedding nights).[75] Finally, peasants were subject at all times to the whims and

---

Mother Goose Revisited

Most of us think of Mother Goose rhymes and stories as charming survivals from a simpler, happier world of the past. Yet if we look at them closely, and at other older folk tales, a very different picture emerges. It is a picture of widespread poverty and despair, except for the fortunate few who lived in palaces.

Recall for a moment old Mother Hubbard who went to the cupboard to fetch her poor dog a bone, or the old woman who lived in a shoe and had so many children she didn't know what to do. We also learn something of life in agrarian societies from the story of Tom Thumb. In a late seventeenth-century French version, the story begins, "Once upon a time there was a woodsman and his wife, who had seven children, all boys. . . . They were very poor, and their seven children were a great inconvenience, because none was old enough to support himself. . . . A very difficult year came, and the famine was so great that these poor folk resolved to get rid of their children." Shades of Hansel and Gretel! And in the French version of "The Sorcerer's Apprentice," a poor father sells his son to the devil in exchange for an ample supply of food for twelve years.

Though fairy tales often had happy endings, these endings usually depended on magic, trickery, or uncommon luck—not ordinary hard work. Cinderella had her fairy godmother; Jack (of beanstalk fame) combined a generous mix of magic, trickery, daring, and luck to win his fortune; and the miller's son in Puss 'n Boots, who inherited only a cat, inherited a most remarkable cat.

If Mother Goose has powers to charm, it is because we overlook the poverty and despair that are portrayed, or we imagine that they are just part of the world of make-believe, like the fairy godmothers who provided the happy endings. But if we look closely at the conditions of life of ordinary people in agrarian societies, we find that there is at least as much truth as fiction in these old rhymes and tales.

tempers of their superiors, who could invoke severe punishments even for minor offenses. Even petty thievery could be punished by death, often by cruel and frightful means.[76]

To the governing class, all this seemed only fitting and proper, since most of them, like their predecessors in simple agrarian societies, viewed peasants as subhuman. In legal documents in medieval England, a peasant's children were listed not as his *familia*, but as his *sequela*, meaning "brood" or "litter."[77] Estate records in Europe, Asia, and the Americas often listed peasants with the livestock.[78] Even so civilized a Roman as Cato the Elder argued that slaves, like livestock, should be disposed of when no longer productive.[79]

As shocking as these views seem today, they were not illogical, but simply one facet of the belief systems that emerged in this kind of society. These new beliefs and values reflected the cleavages within societies and the increasingly diverse experiences of their members. So divergent were the ways of life of the governing class and the peasantry, and so limited their contacts (normally a class of supervisory officials and retainers stood between them[80]), that it may be more surprising that some members of the privileged class recognized their common humanity than that the majority did not.

Despite the heavy burdens laid on them, not all peasants were reduced to the subsistence level. By various means, many contrived to hide part of their harvest and otherwise evade their obligations.[81] A small minority even managed, by rendering special services to the governing class or by other means, to rise a bit above their fellows, operating larger farms and generally living a bit more comfortably.[82]

For the majority, however, the one real hope for a substantial improvement in their lot lay, ironically, in the devastation wrought by plagues, famines, and wars. Only when death reduced their numbers to the point where good workers were scarce was the governing class forced to bid competitively for their services, thus raising incomes above the subsistence level.[83] Usually, however, high birthrates kept this from occurring, or, when it did, soon brought about a return to the former situation.

The Urban Economy When we think of famous agrarian societies of the past, most of us conjure up images of cities: Rome, Constantinople, Alexandria, Jerusalem, Baghdad, Babylon, and others that loom large in the historical record. Thus it is with a sense of shock that we discover that rarely if ever did all of the urban communities of an advanced agrarian society contain as much as 10 percent of its total population, and in most cases they held even less.[84]

How can this be? Why are our impressions of these ancient societies wrong? The reason is that their histories were recorded by a literate minority—people who themselves usually lived in cities and towns and who regarded the life of the rural villages as unimportant and unworthy of their attention. Thus, the historical record is largely a record of city life, particularly the life of the governing class.

The most striking feature of the cities and towns of these societies was the great diversity of people who lived in them. City residents ranged from the most illustrious members of the governing class to beggars and other destitute people who barely managed to stay alive. Unlike most of the cities and towns in modern industrial societies, these were not primarily centers of production. Though some industrial activity was carried on in them, their political and commercial functions, and frequently their religious ones as well, were much more important.

Since cities and towns were the centers of government, and social and cultural centers as well, most members of the governing class preferred to live in them.[85] As a result, urban populations included not only civil and military officials, but the extensive households of the governing class as well. Servants were far more numerous in these societies than in ours, both because of the absence of laborsaving devices and because the governing class viewed manual work of any kind as degrading. Furthermore, one of their chief forms of status competition was to see who could maintain the most luxurious household. The household staff of the head of one small kingdom, Edward IV of England, numbered 400.[86] A more important ruler, such as the Roman emperor at the height of empire, had thousands. As one historian put it, one "is dumbfounded by the extraordinary degree of specialization [and] the insensate luxury" of the imperial household.[87] One group of servants was responsible for the emperor's palace clothes, another for his city clothes, another for those he wore to the theater, yet another for his military uniforms. Other servants attended to eating vessels, a different group to those used for drinking, another to silver vessels, and still others to gold vessels and those set with jewels. For entertainment, the emperor had his own choristers, an orchestra, dancing women, clowns, and dwarfs. Lesser mem-

FIGURE 7.11 Servants were far more numerous in advanced agrarian societies than in modern industrial societies, both because of the lack of labor-saving devices in homes and because the governing class considered it degrading to do any kind of manual work: slaves transporting a wealthy Roman matron.

bers of the Roman governing class obviously could not maintain household staffs as elaborate as this, but many had staffs of hundreds, and some had a thousand or more. *All this was made possible by the labors of the peasantry.*

Part of the peasants' surplus also went to support two important groups that were allied with the governing class yet separate from it. The first of these was the clergy, of whom more will be said shortly. The second was the merchant class. Merchants were a peculiar group in the structure of agrarian societies. Although some of them were extremely wealthy, they were rarely accepted as equals by members of the governing class—even by those who were much less wealthy. For merchants worked to obtain their wealth, and this, by the values of the governing class, was demeaning.[88] Nevertheless, the latter avidly sought the goods that merchants sold and coveted their wealth, acquiring it whenever they could by taxes, marriage, or outright confiscation.[89] The attitude of the merchants toward the governing class was equally ambivalent: they both feared and envied them, but, given the chance, they emulated their way of life and sought to be accepted by them.

Like modern merchants, the merchants of agrarian societies often created the demand for their goods, thereby spurring productivity. And like modern advertisers, they were primarily interested in creating a demand for luxuries. One reason for this was the high cost of moving goods from town to town. With the primitive transportation available,[90] only lightweight luxury items such as silks, spices, and fine swords could be moved far without costs becoming prohibitive.

A report on China shortly after World War II indicates what an enormous difference modern methods of transportation have made in the cost of moving goods. To ship a ton of goods one mile at that time, the costs were as follows (measured in United States cents at that time).[91]

Steamboat	2.4	Pack mule	17.0
Railroad	2.7	Wheelbarrow	20.0
Junk	12.0	Pack donkey	24.0
Animal-drawn cart	13.0	Carrying by pole	48.0

Figures from Europe are strikingly similar: in 1900, for example, it cost ten times more to move goods by horse-drawn wagon than by rail.[92] In short, modern methods of transportation have slashed this cost by 80 to 95 percent.

The prosperity of the merchant class was due in no small measure to the labors of another, humbler class with which merchants were closely affiliated—the artisans, who numbered approximately 3 to 5 percent of the total population.[93] Except for the peasantry, this class was the most productive element in the economy. Most artisans lived in urban centers and, like the rest of the urban population, were ultimately dependent on the surplus produced by the peasants. Craft specialization was rather highly developed in the larger urban centers, as we have seen.

The shops where artisans worked were small by modern standards and bore little resemblance to modern factories. In Rome in the first century B.C., a shop employing fifty men was considered very large.[94] A pewter business employing eighteen men was the largest mentioned in any of London's medieval craft records, and even this modest size was not attained until the middle of the fifteenth century.[95] Typically,

FIGURE 7.12 The souk, or market, Fez, Morocco: compare with the market in Ouagadougou, page 148.

the shop was also the residence of both the merchant and his workmen, and work was carried on either in the living quarters or in an adjoining room.[96]

The economic situation of the artisans, like that of the merchants, was variable. In Beijing at the time of World War I, wages ranged from $2.50 a month for members of the Incense and Cosmetic Workers Guild to $36 a month for members of the Gold Foil Beaters Guild.[97] Those in highly skilled trades and some of the self-employed fared moderately well by agrarian standards. Apprentices and journeymen in less skilled trades, however, worked long hours for bare subsistence wages. In Beijing, for example, a seven-day workweek and ten-hour workday were typical, and many artisans remained too poor ever to marry.

Merchants and artisans in the same trade were commonly organized into *guilds*. These organizations were an attempt to create, in an urban setting, a functional approximation of the extended kin groups of horticultural societies. Many guilds spoke of their members as brothers, for example, and functioned as mutual aid associations, restricting entry into the field, forbidding price cutting, and otherwise trying to protect the interests of their members.[98] But a guild included merchant employers as well as artisan employees, and the employers were naturally dominant, controlling key offices and formulating policies that benefited themselves more than the artisans.[99]

Beneath the artisans in the class structure of the cities were a variety of other kinds of people, including unskilled laborers who supplied much of the animal energy required by the system. The working conditions of these men were usually terrible, and accidents and injuries were common. As a result, their work life was short. For example, early in the present century, the average Beijing rickshaw man was able to work only five years, after which he was good for little except begging.[100]

The class of unskilled laborers shaded off into still more deprived groups—the unemployed, the beggars, and the criminals. The high birthrates of agrarian societies ensured a perennial oversupply of unskilled labor, and such people usually migrated to the cities, hoping to find some kind of employment. As long as men were young and healthy, they could usually get work as day laborers. But after they were injured or lost their youth and strength, they were quickly replaced by fresh labor and left to fend for themselves, usually as beggars or thieves. No agrarian society ever found a solution to this problem. But then, the leading classes were not especially interested in finding one. The system served their needs quite well just as it was.

Many of the sisters of the men who made up the urban lower classes earned their livelihood as prostitutes. Moralists have often condemned these women as though they elected this career in preference to a more honorable one. The record indicates, however, that most of them had little choice: their only alternative was a life of unrelieved drudgery and poverty as servants or unskilled laborers, and many could not even hope for that.[101] The men they might have married were too poor to afford wives, and the system of prostitution was often, in effect, a substitute for marriage that was forced on these people by society. To be sure, the poor were not the only ones to avail themselves of the services of prostitutes, nor were all girls in that "profession" because of poverty. But economic factors were clearly the chief cause of its high incidence in agrarian societies.

The number of profitable working years for prostitutes was hardly longer than that for the rickshaw boys, porters, and others who sold their physical assets for a meager livelihood. As a result, the cities and towns in agrarian societies often swarmed with beggars of both sexes. Estimates by observers suggest that beggars comprised from a tenth to as high as a third of the total population of urban communities.[102] The proportion was not nearly so high for society as a whole, of course, since many of the rural poor migrated to the cities and towns in the hope of finding greater opportunities.

The Polity: Continuing Development of the State

In nearly all advanced agrarian societies, government was the basic integrating force. In any society created by conquest and run for the benefit of a tiny elite, coercion was necessary to hold things together. Not only did the natural antagonisms of the peasant masses have to be kept in check, but diverse groups of conquered people often had to be welded together politically. The scope of this problem is suggested by the size of some of these societies. Whereas the largest simple agrarian society, Egypt, controlled roughly 800,000 square miles (much of it desert and uninhabited), several advanced agrarian societies covered between 2 and 8 million square miles.

Nearly every advanced agrarian society was a monarchy headed by a king or emperor whose position was usually hereditary. Republican government, in which power was divided among a small ruling elite, was an infrequent exception limited

FIGURE 7.13 Working equipment for member of the governing class in sixteenth-century Europe.

almost entirely to the least powerful and least developed agrarian societies.[103] The prevalence of monarchical government seems to have been the result of the militaristic and exploitative character of societies at this level. Governments were constantly threatening, or being threatened by, their neighbors. At the same time, they were in danger from internal enemies—dissatisfied and ambitious members of the governing class, eager to seize control for themselves, and restless, hostile members of the far larger lower classes. Under such conditions republican government was nearly impossible.[104]

Because of the tendency to romanticize the past, many today are unaware of the frequency of both internal and external conflict in the great agrarian empires. In Rome, for example, 31 of the 79 emperors were murdered, 6 were driven to suicide, 4 were forcibly deposed, and several more met unknown fates at the hands of internal enemies.[105] Though Rome's record may have been worse than most, struggles for control were common in all advanced agrarian societies.[106]

Peasant uprisings were another form of internal conflict. One expert states that "there were peasant rebellions almost every year in China," and an authority on Russia reports that in the short period from 1801 to 1861, there were no less than 1,467 peasant uprisings in various parts of that country.[107] Most of these disturbances were confined to a limited area only because authorities acted swiftly and ruthlessly. Had they not, many would have spread as widely as the famous English revolt of 1381 or the German Peasants' War of 1524–1525.

External threats were no less frequent or serious, and warfare was a chronic condition. A survey of eleven European countries of the agrarian era found that, on average, these countries were involved in some kind of conflict with neighboring societies nearly every second year.[108] Such conditions encouraged the rise of authoritarian governments.

Most members of the governing class considered political power a prize to be sought for the rewards it offered rather than an opportunity for public service, and the office of king or emperor was *the supreme prize*. Efforts to raise the living standards of the common people were rare, efforts at self-aggrandizement commonplace.[109] In many societies, government offices were bought and sold like pieces of property, which the purchasers then used to obtain the greatest possible profit. Officeholders demanded payment before they would act, and justice was typically sold to the highest bidder. No wonder the common people of China developed the saying "To enter a court of justice is to enter a tiger's mouth."[110]

These practices reflected what is known as *the proprietary theory of the state*, which defines the state as a piece of property that its owners may use, within broad and ill-defined limits, for their personal advantage.[111] Guided by this theory, agrarian rulers and governing classes saw nothing immoral in the use of what we (not they) would call "public office" for private gain. To them, it was simply the legitimate use of what they regarded as their "patrimony." It is said of the Ptolemies of Egypt, for example, that they showed the first emperors of Rome "how a country might be run on the lines of a profitable estate."[112] In the case of medieval Europe, we read:

> The proprietary conception of rulership created an inextricable confusion of public and private affairs. Rights of government were a form of private ownership. "Crown lands" and "the king's estate" were synonymous. There was no differentiation between the king in his private and public capacities. A kingdom, like any estate endowed with elements of governmental authority, was the private concern of its owner. Since *"state" and "estate" were identical*, "the State" was indistinguishable from the prince and his personal "patrimony."[113]

The proprietary theory of the state can be traced back to horticultural societies and, in a sense, even to hunting and gathering bands. In those simpler societies, no

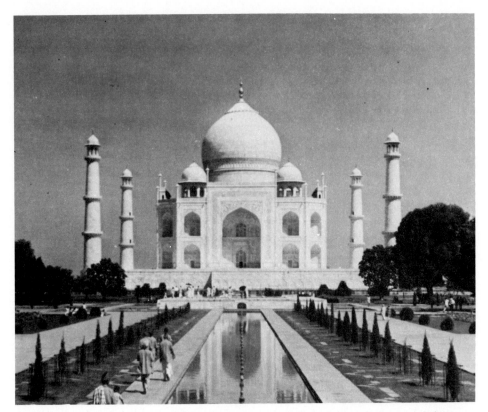

FIGURE 7.14 One use of the economic surplus in an agrarian society: the Taj Mahal, a tomb erected by the Mogul emperor Shah Jahan in memory of his favorite wife.

distinction was made between the private and public aspects of the lives and activities of rulers. When a surplus first began to be produced, at least part of it was turned over to the leader, who held it as trustee for the group. As long as the surplus was small and consisted of perishable commodities, there was little the leader could do with it except redistribute it, thereby winning respect for his generosity. Eventually, however, as we saw in Chapter 6, it grew large enough to permit him to create a staff of dependent retainers who could be used to enforce his wishes. At this point, the proprietary theory of the state was born. Later rulers merely applied it on an ever-expanding scale, as productivity and the economic surplus steadily increased.

Recent research provides a good picture of the extremes to which rulers and governing classes have carried the proprietary principle. In late nineteenth-century China, for example, the average income for families not in the governing class was approximately 20 to 25 taels per year. By contrast, the governing class averaged 450 taels per year, with some receiving as much as 200,000.[114] The emperor's income, of course, was considerably larger even than this. To cite another example, the English nobility at the end of the twelfth century and early in the thirteenth had an average income roughly 200 times that of ordinary field hands, and the king's equaled that of 24,000 field hands.[115] Putting together the evidence from many sources, it appears that the combined income of the ruler and the governing class in most advanced agrarian societies equaled *not less than half of the total national income*, even though they numbered 2 percent or less of the population.[116]

Despite their many similarities, the polities of advanced agrarian societies varied in a number of ways, the most important being the *degree of political centralization*. In some societies the central government was very strong; in others its powers were severely limited. In the main, these differences reflected the current state of the perennial struggle between the ruler and the other members of the governing class. The king or emperor naturally wanted the greatest possible control over his subordinates, and the subordinates just as naturally wanted to minimize his control. Since land (including the peasants who worked it) and political office were the most valuable resources in agrarian systems of stratification, most of the struggles between rulers and the governing class were over them. In a few instances, very powerful rulers gained such great power that both land and political offices were held solely at their pleasure and were subject to instant confiscation if an individual's services were judged unsatisfactory.[117] A Dutch traveler of the early seventeenth century left a vivid picture of the situation in the Mogul empire in India:

> Immediately on the death of a lord who has enjoyed the King's [favor], be he great or small, without any exception—sometimes even before the breath is out of the body—the King's officers are ready on the spot and make an inventory of the entire estate, recording everything down to the value of a single piece, even to the dresses and jewels of the ladies, provided they have not concealed them. The King takes back the whole estate absolutely for himself, except in a case where the deceased has done good service in his lifetime, when the women and children are given enough to live on, but no more.[118]

In Turkey, specially trained slaves became high-ranking officials over whom the sultan held life-and-death power.[119] At the other extreme, during much of the medieval period in Europe, the governing classes were very independent. Though their lands were typically royal grants given in exchange for pledges of service, their monarchs usually lacked the power to enforce these pledges.[120] Although examples of both extremes can be found, the usual pattern was something in between, and in most cases the powers of the ruler and the governing class were fairly evenly balanced.

Religion: The Emergence of Universal Faiths

During the era in which advanced agrarian societies were dominant, there were a number of important developments in the religious sphere. The most important by far was the emergence and spread of three new religions, Buddhism, Christianity, and Islam. Each proclaimed a *universal faith*, and each succeeded in creating a community of believers that transcended societal boundaries. In contrast, in older religions, people's beliefs and loyalties were determined solely by the accident of birth. Where one lived determined the god or gods one worshiped, for the prevailing view was that there were many gods and that, like kings, each had his or her own people and territory.

The ancient Israelites were some of the first to reject this view and move toward a more universalistic outlook. Centuries before the birth of Christ, the prophets proclaimed that there was only one God and that He ruled over the entire world. For a time, Judaism was a missionary religion and won converts in many parts of the Roman world.[121] This ended, however, when early Christian missionaries won most of these Gentile converts to the new faith. From then on, implementation of the universalistic vision became the mission of Christians and Muslims, who eventually converted, at least nominally, most of the population of Europe, North Africa, and the Middle East, and some of the people of India, Central Asia, China, and Southeast Asia.

Buddhism, the other major universal faith, began in India as an offshoot of Hinduism and spread through most of Southeast Asia, China, Korea, and Japan, though it later died out in the land of its origin. Older ethnic faiths, such as Hinduism, Confucianism, and Shintoism, still survived in much of Asia, but even they eventually incorporated some elements of universalism in their thought.

FIGURE 7.15 Islam is one of the universal faiths that emerged in the agrarian era: interior of mosque in Baghdad, Iraq.

The emergence and spread of universal faiths reflected the broader social and intellectual horizons that resulted from advances in transportation technology and the spreading web of trade relations. Empire building, by bringing diverse populations under a single government, also helped to weaken parochial or "tribal" views. As people's knowledge of other societies increased, and with it their awareness of the essential unity of all humanity, the basic postulate of the older ethnic faiths (i.e., the belief in tribal deities) was gradually undermined.

Another important development was the growing separation of religious and political institutions.[122] Compared with the situation in advanced horticultural and simple agrarian societies, the governments of advanced agrarian societies were much more secular. Kings and emperors were, it is true, still said to rule "by the grace of God"; the divine right of kings was still generally accepted; and occasionally a ruler even claimed to be a god. But few rulers functioned as high priests, and theocracies (i.e., states in which a priesthood rules in the name of a god) were almost unknown. This separation of church and state was part of the more general trend toward institutional specialization that has been so basic in the evolutionary process since the start of the horticultural era.

Despite the growing separation of politics and religion, leaders in the two spheres continued to work closely together. This was especially evident in struggles between the governing class and the common people. When rebellious voices challenged the right of the governing class to control the economic surplus, the clergy usually defended the elite, asserting that their power had been given them by God and any challenge to it was a challenge to His authority.[123] By legitimizing the actions of the governing class in this way, the clergy reduced the need for costly coercive measures against the lower classes.

In appreciation for this, and also because of their own religious beliefs, agrarian rulers were often extremely generous with religious groups, giving them large grants of land and special tax exemptions. In effect, a symbiotic relationship was established, with a religious organization legitimizing the actions of the governing class in return for generous financial support. Modern research indicates that religious groups frequently owned as much as a quarter or a third of a nation's land.[124]

Despite such profitable alliances, most religions of the agrarian era fostered some concern for distributive justice. This is especially evident in Judaism and Christianity.[125] One historian captured the contradictory nature of medieval Christianity in this discerning characterization: "Democratic, yet aristocratic; charitable, yet exploitative; generous, yet mercenary; humanitarian, yet cruel; indulgent, yet severely repressive of some things; progressive, yet reactionary; radical, yet conservative—all these are qualities of the Church in the Middle Ages."[126]

Magic and Fatalism   Two other aspects of the beliefs of agrarian societies deserve comment: (1) the widespread belief in magic and (2) the equally widespread attitude of fatalism.[127] Logically, these are contradictory. If magic really works, people do not need to be fatalistic, and if they are true fatalists, they should have no confidence in magic. But people are not always logical: they often hope for things they know are impossible. Considering the tremendous pressures operating on the common people in agrarian societies, and their limited sources of information, it is hardly surprising that many of them held these mutually contradictory views.

Fatalism and belief in magic both contributed to the slowdown in the rate of technological advance in agrarian societies. Magic encouraged people to depend on supernatural forces for the answers to their problems. Fatalism convinced them that control was out of their hands. Neither attitude motivated people to try to improve conditions themselves by building better tools or devising better techniques for satisfying their needs.

Kinship: Declining Importance in Society

For individuals, kinship ties remained of great importance throughout the agrarian era. For societies, however, they ceased to be the chief integrating force. In most horticultural societies, the largest and most powerful clan in a society, aided perhaps by dependent retainers, could still provide enough people to staff important political offices. But in advanced agrarian societies, this was no longer possible. Civil and military offices were so numerous that not even the largest of extended families could fill them all.

The fact that kinship ties were no longer the chief integrating force in societies did not mean, however, that they were no longer politically important. The royal office itself was inherited in most societies, as were numerous other political offices. Many of these, civil and military offices alike, were a family's patrimony, handed down like any other family possession from father to son (or, sometimes, daughter). Offices that were not actually owned might still be closed to anyone who was not a member of the nobility or who did not qualify as coming from one of the "right families."

Even in the allocation of offices to which such restrictions did not apply, families continued to play an important role. Family funds might be used to purchase an office, for example. And those who had it in their power to assign an office were naturally influenced by their own family's interests. Although nepotism still occurs in modern industrial societies, it is usually a violation of the law and lacks public approval. In advanced agrarian societies, however, it was an accepted part of life, and there was little criticism, and still less punishment, of those who practiced it.

During the agrarian era, the family remained very important in the economic sphere as well. In fact, it was usually *the basic unit of economic organization*. Businesses were almost always family enterprises; the corporate form of enterprise, owned jointly by unrelated persons, was virtually unheard of, even in the largest cities. And in rural areas the peasant family was the basic work unit.

The family's economic significance is evident in many ways. For instance, because of its economic implications, marriage was considered much too important to be decided by young people; even among the peasantry, marriages were usually arranged by parents, often with the aid of marriage brokers.[128] Sometimes the young couple did not even meet until the ceremony itself. In selecting spouses for their children, parents were primarily concerned with the economic and status implications of the match and only secondarily with other matters. Marriage arrangements often involved an outright economic transaction. The husband might make a payment for the bride, or her parents would provide her with a dowry.[129]

As one would suppose, marriages contracted in this way did not necessarily produce sexual or psychological compatibility between the spouses, but this was not seen as the primary purpose of marriage. Ties between man and wife usually endured because of the value that was placed on the relationship by society, and because the economic arrangement was usually of critical importance to the individuals involved. Within these families, male dominance was the rule and obedience was generally held to be the prime virtue in women and children.[130] In this, the family reflected the general authoritarian pattern of life in agrarian societies.

Leisure and the Arts

Although the life of the peasant was hard, even harsh, there were occasional opportunities for leisure and recreation.[131] Weddings and religious festivals, for example, were important occasions for people to get together for a good time. Singing and dancing were the chief forms of entertainment at such festivies and, in most societies, alcoholic beverages added to the merriment. People also amused themselves with games and contests, courtship and lovemaking, gossiping and storytelling, and a host of other activities.

Class distinctions were as evident in leisure activity as in any other, with falconry, jousting, and chess among the activities favored by the governing class. But some forms of entertainment, such as archery and dice, had a universal appeal. Gambling in particular was popular with every class.

The rise of professional entertainers was part of the general trend toward occupational specialization. Actors, minstrels, jesters, clowns, acrobats, jugglers, and geishas are some of the more familiar. In general, the status of such people was extremely low, probably because of their economic insecurity and their excessive dependence on the favor of others. Yet entertainers who had a powerful patron often found their work quite lucrative.

Recreation was frequently raucous and crude. It could also be brutal and violent, and in this the Romans were probably unsurpassed. In their so-called games, first in the Circus Maximus, later in the Colosseum, tens of thousands came to watch wild animals devour helpless victims, and armed gladiators maim and kill one another. When the Colosseum was first opened in 80 A.D., the Emperor Titus promised the people of Rome 100 consecutive days of such games, with fights to the death between more than 10,000 prisoners and 5,000 wild animals (including lions, tigers, and elephants), and a naval battle between 3,000 men in an arena especially flooded for the occasion.[132]

In agrarian Europe, cockfights and dogfights were very popular, and public hangings often drew large and exuberant crowds. Wedding parties and other festivities frequently ended in drunken brawls. In fact, violence typically followed drinking. From what we know of life in agrarian societies, it would appear that alcohol simply removed a fragile overlay of inhibitions, revealing people's frustrations and bitterness.

But if the agrarian world at play was often unattractive, its artistic accomplish-

FIGURE 7.16 Recreation was frequently violent and brutal in agrarian societies, and the Romans were probably unsurpassed. In their so-called games, tens of thousands came to watch wild animals devour helpless victims, and armed gladiators maim and kill one another.

ments were quite the opposite. In their sculpture, their painting, and their architecture, these societies left monuments of lasting beauty. Thousands of cathedrals, churches, mosques, pagodas, temples, and palaces, and the treasures within them, testify to an impressive development of the arts during that era. Achievements in literature were probably no less impressive, though language barriers make it difficult for us to appreciate them as fully.* Developments in music during most of the agrarian era seem to have been less spectacular than in the other arts. Toward the end of the era, however, the invention of new instruments and the genius of composers like Bach, Handel, Mozart, and Beethoven combined to produce an outburst of magnificent music that has transcended societal boundaries in unprecedented fashion.

Most artists were subsidized by the governing class or by the religious elite, drawing on the economic surplus extracted from the peasant masses. Thus, the remarkable artistic achievements of agrarian societies were a product of their harshly exploitative social system. Yet, if the peasants had been allowed to keep the surplus, the result would simply have been more poor people. Again, as with horticultural societies, this link between an exploitative class system and impressive cultural achieve-

*Robert Frost once said that "poetry is what gets lost in translation," and anyone who has ever seriously tried to translate a poem understands the complexity of the language problem.

ments reminds us of the difficulty we face in passing ethical judgments on complex sociocultural systems.

Stratification: Increasing Complexity

The basic cleavages in advanced agrarian societies were much the same as they had been in simple agrarian societies and, as a consequence, so were the basic patterns of inequality. The principal division in society was still the one between the governing class and the great mass of peasants and others over whom it exercised control both politically and economically. But the system of stratification had altered in one respect from that of simpler societal types: it had become more complex.

This growing complexity can be seen in two areas. First, in advanced agrarian societies there were more people in occupations whose status fell somewhere between the extremes. These people were either directly employed by the governing class (e.g., household servants, stewards, men-at-arms) or served them indirectly (e.g., merchants, artisans).

Second, advanced agrarian societies experienced a growing overlap in the statuses of different categories of people, especially in terms of wealth and property. Some merchants, for example, now had more wealth than some members of the governing class, and a tiny minority of peasants, by luck and hard work, actually amassed greater wealth than some impoverished members of the nobility. Although members of the governing class still had greater wealth, *on average*, than merchants or any other group, this was no longer true of every member of the class. Similarly, although merchants were, *on average*, wealthier than peasants, there were exceptions.

Figure 7.17 depicts the status system of advanced agrarian societies. The ruler was invariably the most powerful, prestigious, and wealthy individual in society: he was, in fact, literally in a class by himself. For example, the English kings Richard I and John, who ruled in the last decade of the twelfth century and the first decade of the thirteenth, had incomes thirty times that of the wealthiest nobleman of the day.[133] By the reign of Richard II, at the end of the fourteenth century, the king's income had risen to forty times that of the wealthiest member of the governing class. In late fifteenth- and early sixteenth-century Spain, the king was reputed to enjoy one-third of all the revenues of the land (meaning, apparently, one-third of the economic surplus). Similar patterns are reported in virtually every advanced agrarian society.

At the opposite extreme in the system of stratification was a wretched class of individuals for whose labor the society had no need. These were mostly peasant sons and daughters who were unable to inherit land or to marry someone who did, and thus were forced out on their own in a society that suffered a chronic labor surplus. As we have seen, these individuals could usually eke out a living while they were young and healthy, but most of them soon drifted into the ranks of the expendables (see Figure 7.17) and died at an early age.[134]

On the whole, the class divisions within advanced agrarian societies were more serious than those within simple agrarian societies. In particular, they were more likely to lead to violence. Earlier, we noted the frequency of peasant risings. Though most of these were local incidents involving small numbers of people, some spread to be-

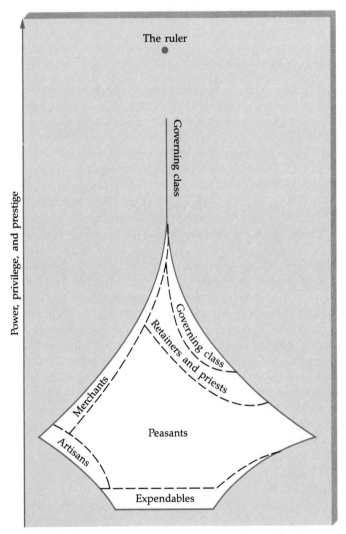

FIGURE 7.17 Model of the class structure of advanced agrarian societies.

come large-scale insurrections. In either case, they were something new in history and foreshadowed revolutions to come. Nor was it only the peasants who revolted against the governing class. The artisans and even the merchants followed suit on a number of occasions,[135] and these groups, unlike the peasants, sometimes emerged victorious. In Europe, the merchants were so successful in their challenges to the governing class that eventually *they* became the governing class in many cities and towns. From an evolutionary perspective, this proved to be a very important development indeed, as we will see.

VARIATIONS ON AGRARIAN THEMES

In surveying societies at the same level of development, it is natural to emphasize those characteristics which are found in all or most of them, and to slight the differences. This may give an impression of greater uniformity than really exists. Obviously there were variations in every area of life in advanced agrarian societies, and we have noted many of them, or at least hinted at them in qualifying phrases, saying that a particular pattern was found in "most" or "many" of these societies.

To begin with, advanced agrarian societies varied technologically. The first to emerge resembled their simple agrarian predecessors more than they resembled the advanced agrarian societies of northwest Europe on the eve of the Industrial Revolution. Furthermore, the size of advanced agrarian societies ranged all the way from tiny principalities to giant empires. Most were monarchies, but a few were republics. Some were governed by enormously powerful autocratic rulers; in others, power was diffused more widely among members of the governing class. Similar variations occurred in almost every area of life.

Clearly, then, there has been variation among societies at the advanced agrarian level—indeed, at *every* level of societal development. There is, however, one important difference. In the less advanced societal types (i.e., hunting and gathering, fishing, and simple horticultural), intratype variation is due primarily to differences in the *biophysical environment*. We see this clearly when we compare the Eskimo with the Australian aborigines, for example, or the Bushmen of the Kalahari Desert with the Pygmies of the rain forest. In advanced agrarian societies, on the other hand, differences in the biophysical environment have not been as important a cause of intratype variation. This is exactly what ecological–evolutionary theory would lead us to expect, since the further a society advances on the evolutionary scale, the greater is its ability to overcome the limitations imposed by the biotic and physical world and the more likely it is, because of geographical expansion, to include within its borders a variety of environments, thus making its overall environment less distinctive.

In studying advanced agrarian societies, historians have often focused attention on religion as the chief source of the differences among them. Thus, they have contrasted Christian societies with Islamic societies, for example, or Buddhist societies with Hindu societies.

There is, of course, no doubt that each of these religions was responsible for social and cultural variations among advanced agrarian societies. Christianity and Islam, like Judaism, had a special day of worship and rest each week, while the Oriental religions did not. Most of the religions encouraged monasticism, but Protestantism and Islam did not. Islam sanctioned the practice of polygyny, which Christianity forbade; Confucianism encouraged ancestor worship; Buddhism encouraged families to send their sons to live in monasteries for a year or two before assuming adult responsibilities; and Hinduism had a hereditary priestly caste. Theologically, there were tremendous differences among the various religions, and members of advanced agrarian societies often fought and died in order to extend or defend their faith.

Without denying the importance of these and other religious influences, we cannot fail to note that no faith was able to break the "agrarian mold" that shaped the basic patterns of life in these societies.* For regardless of its dominant religion, every advanced agrarian society was much like the rest with respect to its fundamental characteristics. Class structure, social inequality, the division of labor, the distinctive role of urban populations in the larger society, the cleavage between urban and rural subcultures, the disdain of the governing class for both work and workers, the widespread belief in magic and fatalism, the use of the economic surplus for the benefit of the governing class and for the construction of monumental edifices, high birth and death rates—all these and more were present in all advanced agrarian societies.

The greatest variations among advanced agrarian societies stemmed not from ideological differences but from differences in their *social environments*. These differences were of two kinds. One involved proximity to trade routes and the other the influence of frontier territories.

From the standpoint of trade, the most advantageous location for a society was at the point where several important trade routes intersected.[136] Having such a location ensured continuing contact with a large number of other societies and increased opportunities for acquiring useful information through diffusion. It also provided a valuable source of income and fostered economic growth and development. Societies that were not so well situated were handicapped and tended to be less developed, unless some compensating factor offset this handicap. Because of the importance of trade routes, societies in the Middle East, where routes from Europe, Asia, and Africa converged, remained at the forefront of social and cultural development for most of the agrarian era. Toward the end, however, as trade with the New World became important, the advantage shifted to western European societies.

A very different kind of environmental influence made itself felt when agrarian populations expanded into territories that previously were uninhabited or were inhabited by smaller, less advanced societies. Under the radically altered conditions that were encountered, traditional patterns of life often broke down and a new and different kind of society—*a frontier society*—emerged briefly.

The first known instance of this was the establishment of the new nation of Israel in the largely uninhabited hill country in the eastern part of Palestine in the thirteenth century B.C.[137] More recently, the process was repeated in the Norwegian-Irish settlement of Iceland; in the settlement of North America by migrants from Britain, France, and other parts of northwest Europe; in the British settlements of Australia and New Zealand; in the Boer settlement of South Africa; and in the Cossack settlement of the Russian steppes.[138] In each instance the frontier region escaped for a time from the control of traditional authorities and land became available for settlement by lower-status members of agrarian societies who were willing to assume the risks and hardships of frontier life.

Frontier societies are of special interest from the standpoint of ecological–evolutionary theory because they show the extent to which the agrarian way of life was shaped by an oversupply of labor and an undersupply of land. When these conditions were eliminated even temporarily, as happened in frontier regions, striking deviations from the usual patterns of agrarian life developed.

---

*For a discussion of religion's role in the rise of industrial societies, see Chapter 9, pages 222ff.

To begin with, the settlers themselves tended to be the poor, the dispossessed, the noninheriting sons and daughters, troublemakers, misfits, and even criminals deported by the parent society. Frontier regions held little attraction for the rich and powerful, who preferred to remain close to the traditional centers of power and influence. Thus, in frontier regions established authority was usually weak or absent, and because societal life was not under the control of the governing class, traditional agrarian patterns tended to break down and new patterns emerged.[139]

One of the most significant changes that occurred was the breakdown of the traditional class system. Except when elites created a plantation system and the native population was enslaved or enserfed (as in much of Latin America) or when slaves were imported (as in the Caribbean and the southern United States), a highly egalitarian system of family farms and ranches was likely to develop.[140] This is what happened in Canada, the United States (except in the South) Australia, New Zealand, and South Africa. In these areas there was a chronic shortage of labor; workers were more highly valued than in the older, settled areas, where there was usually a surplus of labor. On the frontier, there were neither enough farmers to cultivate the newly opened land nor enough fighters to defend it. It is not surprising, then, that frontier life generated a striking independence of spirit and a stubborn resistance to authority. Having risked their lives to establish themselves in a new land, frontier settlers were not prepared to hand over their surplus to anyone. Thus, frontier conditions usually broke down the sharp inequalities and exploitative patterns that characterized traditional agrarian societies.

This condition was usually temporary, however. As resistance from the native population came to an end and the population of settlers grew in number and density, as roads were built and governmental authority was established, there was a waning of the spirit of independence and individualism and the traditional system began to reassert itself. To be sure, this did not happen overnight. On the contrary, it usually took a century or more. But in the end, the typical agrarian pattern usually prevailed.

Only one thing ever prevented this from happening—the onset of industrialization. In a number of instances during the last century and a half, the Industrial Revolution generated a new demand for labor before the frontier was fully absorbed into the old system. This happened in the United States, Canada, Australia, and New Zealand. These societies were thus spared the agony of slowly sliding back into the classic agrarian pattern in which a massive, impoverished peasantry is dominated and exploited by a small, hereditary aristocracy.

In the United States this process had actually gotten well under way in much of the South with its system of slavery. But the Confederacy's defeat in the Civil War and the South's eventual industrialization halted the restoration of the old agrarian system. In other parts of the country, the process had barely begun before the forces of industrialization intervened.

Looking back, it seems clear that the frontier experience was excellent preparation for the Industrial Revolution. Above all, it established a tradition of individual initiative, innovation, and receptivity to change that were lacking in other agrarian societies. Also, by creating a more egalitarian class system, the frontier prepared the way for the more open and fluid class systems of modern industrial societies. These developments help explain the relative ease with which the overseas English-speaking democracies (i.e., the United States, Australia, Canada, and New Zealand) made the transition to the industrial era, and why they have so long been in the forefront with respect to productivity, standard of living, and political stability. It is interesting to speculate on what the situation in these societies might be today if they had been settled a thousand years earlier and a more typical agrarian social system had had time to take root.

AGRARIAN SOCIETIES IN THEORETICAL PERSPECTIVE

The initial effect of the shift from horticulture to agriculture, as we saw at the beginning of this chapter, was an increase in food production. Societies that adopted the plow were able to produce substantially more food in a given territory than those that relied on the hoe and digging stick.

This increase in productivity could be used, as Figure 7.18 indicates, either to expand the economic surplus of the society or to expand its population. Actually, the historical record shows that in most agrarian societies *both* of these things happened to some degree. The expansion of the economic surplus was more significant than population growth, however, since it was a necessary precondition for so many social and cultural changes. Figure 7.18 makes no attempt to portray all of them, or all of their interrelationships, since that would require an impossibly complex diagram. Instead, the figure focuses only on the most critical developments.

The single most important consequence of the greater economic surplus was further *growth of the state and in the power of the governing class* that controlled it. This contributed, directly or indirectly, to most of the other important social and cultural changes of the agrarian era. It lay behind the shift from militias to professional armies; the increase in inequality, and the development of ideologies justifying inequality and the power of elites; the rise of the merchant class and the increase in trade and commerce; the growth of urban populations; the increase in the division of labor; and the slowing of the rate of innovation.

Many of the changes in agrarian societies were a continuation of trends that began in horticultural societies. But the shift to agriculture magnified those trends dramatically. To cite a single example, the largest society ever constructed on a horticultural foundation appears to have been the Aztec empire in the years immediately preceding the Spanish conquest of Mexico. At the peak of its power it is estimated to have controlled a population of 5 to 6 million people.[141] In contrast, mid-nineteenth-century China, before it began to industrialize, had a population of approximately 400 million, and the Roman and Russian empires each had at least 70 million.[142]

As great as they are, these differences in population size are probably no greater in degree than differences in many other basic features of these two types of societies. Their numbers, in other words, are but a reflection of the vastly different potentials inherent in the subsistence technologies on which horticultural societies and agrarian societies were built.

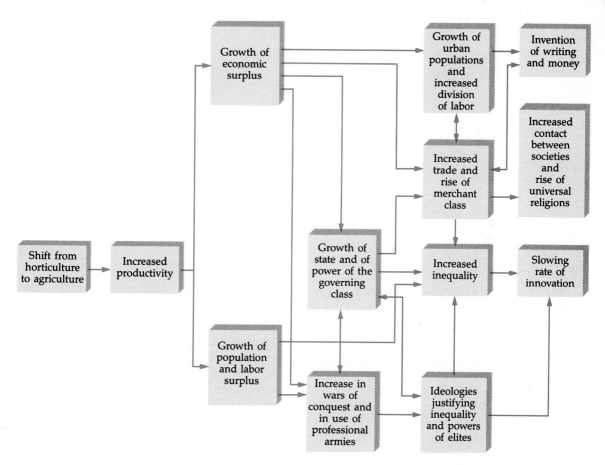

FIGURE 7.18 Model of the effects of the shift from horticulture to agriculture.

8

Some Evolutionary Bypaths
and a Brief Review

ENVIRONMENTALLY SPECIALIZED SOCIETAL TYPES

Up to this point in our survey of human societies, we have concentrated on those types which have been in the mainstream of evolutionary history, the ones that developed their technologies around the resources of fields and forests. The types of societies to which we now turn have adapted to *less common environments*—two to aquatic environments and one to grasslands and arid environments. Though these specialized kinds of societies have contributed to sociocultural evolution in many important ways, their contributions have been more limited than those of the mainstream societies. This is because of the specialized nature of the problems with which they have dealt in their subsistence activities. For these reasons, we will not examine them in the same detail as the others.

Fishing Societies

To call any group a "fishing" society is something of a misnomer, for no society ever depended exclusively on fishing for its food supply.[1] Except in the Arctic, nearly all fishing peoples obtain fruits and vegetables by foraging or cultivation. Many of them also supplement their diet by hunting, and occasionally by raising livestock. To call a society a fishing society, then, merely indicates that fishing is its most important subsistence activity.

In recent centuries fishing societies have been found in many parts of the world, but the majority have been in the northwestern part of North America—Oregon, Washington, British Columbia, Alaska, and the arctic regions of Canada. There have also been some in northeastern Asia, among the islands of the Pacific (though most of the Pacific peoples have been simple horticulturalists), in scattered parts of Africa and South America, and elsewhere.

Historically, fishing societies are probably the second oldest type, emerging about

202

FIGURE 8.1 African fishing village, Benin.

a thousand years before the first horticultural societies. The practice of fishing is, of course, even older and more widespread and has provided a supplementary source of subsistence in many societies for thousands of years.

In some ways fishing societies might be regarded as hunting and gathering societies that have adapted to aquatic environments rather than terrestrial. One might argue that the chief difference is simply that fish rather than land animals are the object of the hunt and that the technology of the group is modified accordingly. But there is a reason why fishing societies should be considered a separate societal type: *a fishing economy has the potential for supporting a larger, more sedentary population than a hunting and gathering economy.*

This is because fishing peoples are much less likely to deplete the food resources of their environment than are hunters and gatherers. Fish have much higher reproductive rates than most land animals. In addition, fishing peoples usually work only a small part of their food-producing territory. Even if they catch all the fish in their immediate area, the supply is quickly replenished by the great surplus spawned in adjacent areas. This could not happen with land animals, at least not after hunting and gathering bands occupied most of the habitable territory.

Thus, although fishing societies are only a bit more advanced technologically

FIGURE 8.2 The Shui-jen, or water people, of southern China are descended from fishing peoples of an earlier time. They still depend on fishing for their livelihood and remain largely separate from the mainland population.

than hunting and gathering societies, we would expect them to be somewhat larger, more sedentary, and more complex.[2] This is, in fact, precisely what we find. With respect to size, they are more than twice as large. Murdock's data set shows that the average size of modern fishing communities is approximately 90, the average size of hunting and gathering groups only 40.[3] With respect to settlement patterns, only 10 percent of the hunting and gathering societies live in permanent settlements, compared to 55 percent of the fishing societies.

Social inequality, too, is both more common and more pronounced. A system of hereditary nobility is found in 28 percent of fishing societies but in only 2 percent of hunting and gathering societies, while slavery occurs in slightly over 50 percent of fishing societies, but in only 11 percent of hunting and gathering.

Unlike hunting and gathering societies, fishing societies seldom evolved into a more advanced type.* There are several reasons for this. To begin with, territories

---

*It is possible that some evolved directly into maritime societies, but there is no real evidence of this. Maritime societies seem, instead, usually to have evolved out of advanced horticultural or agrarian societies.

suited to a predominantly fishing economy are strung out along thin coastal strips, so that it has been virtually impossible to create large, defensible political entities.[4] Instead, when neighboring horticultural societies became powerful enough, fishing societies have usually been conquered and absorbed by them. Even though fishing continued in the area, it became only a minor part of the economy of the larger society, and the leaders of the fishing groups were reduced to the status of minor officials, too weak to defend the local surplus. As a result, fishing communities in *agrarian* societies have often been socially and culturally less advanced (except in subsistence technology) than the fishing communities of more primitive *fishing* societies. Typically, their situation was no better than that of peasant villages, and for the same reason—their surplus was confiscated by more powerful elements in the society.[5]

Herding Societies

Herding societies, like fishing societies, represent an adaptation to specialized environmental conditions. Other than that, the two have little in common. Their environments are radically different, and the technology of herding societies is usually more advanced.

Herding societies cover approximately the same range of technological development as horticultural and agrarian societies. Animals were first domesticated about the same time plants were first cultivated, and the two practices typically went hand in hand in the horticultural and agrarian societies of the Old World.* In some areas, however, crop cultivation was severely limited because of insufficient rainfall, too short a growing season (in northern latitudes), or mountainous terrain. This was true of much of central Asia, the Arabian peninsula, and North Africa, and also parts of Europe and sub-Saharan Africa. Because it was possible to raise livestock in many of these areas, however, a new and different type of society emerged.†

A pastoral economy usually necessitates a nomadic or seminomadic way of life.[6] In fact, "nomad" comes from an early Greek word meaning a "herder of cattle."[7] In the sample of herding societies in Murdock's data set, nearly 90 percent are wholly or partially nomadic. In this respect they closely resemble hunters and gatherers.

Herders are also like hunters and gatherers in the size of their communities. On average, their communities are a bit smaller than fishing communities and much smaller than simple horticultural, as the following figures show:

Hunting and gathering communities	40
Herding communities	72
Fishing communities	90
Simple horticultural communities	138

The explanation for this is primarily environmental. Given the sparse resources of their territories, large and dense settlements are impossible.[8]

---

*This was not true in most of the New World, where there were almost no large animals suitable for domestication.

†Most of these societies have also had some secondary means of subsistence, usually horticulture or agriculture on a small scale.

Despite the small size of their communities, herding *societies* are usually fairly large. Whereas the typical hunting and gathering or fishing society contains only a single community, and the typical simple horticultural society less than a dozen, the average herding society contains several dozen. Thus, the median population of herding societies far surpasses those of the other three types:

Hunting and gathering societies	40
Fishing societies	90
Simple horticultural societies	1,500
Herding societies	5,750

The greater size of herding societies reflects the combined influence of environment and technology. Open grasslands, where the majority of herders live, present few natural barriers to movement and, therefore, to political expansion. Furthermore, since early in the second millennium B.C. many herding peoples have ridden horses or camels, which made them a potent military force and greatly facilitated political expansion.

The basic resource in these societies is livestock, and the size of the herd is the measure of a man. Large herds signify not only wealth but power, for only a strong man or the head of a strong family can defend such vulnerable property against rivals and enemies. Thus, in most of these societies, and especially in the more advanced (i.e., those with horses or camels and herds of larger animals such as cattle), marked social inequality is the rule. Hereditary slavery, for example, is far more common in herding societies than in any other type.[9]

With respect to kinship, herding societies are noteworthy on at least two counts. First, they are more likely than any other type of society to require the payment of a bride price or bride service.[10] Second, they are the most likely to require newly married couples to live with the husband's kinsmen.[11]

These strong patriarchal tendencies have several sources. Above all, they reflect the often militant nature of pastoral life. Raiding and warfare are frequent activities, and as we have noted before, these activities stimulate the growth of political authority. In addition, the basic economic activity in these societies is men's work. In this respect they stand in sharp contrast to horticultural societies, where women often play the dominant role in subsistence activities.

One of the most important technological advances made by herding peoples was the utilization of horses, and later camels, for transportation. This practice originated in the eighteenth century B.C., when certain herding groups in the Middle East began harnessing horses to chariots.[12] This gave them an important military advantage over their less mobile agrarian neighbors and enabled them to win control of much of the Middle East—at least until the new technology was adopted by the more numerous agrarian peoples. Herders later learned to *ride* their horses, which led to a new wave of conquests, beginning in the ninth century B.C.[13]

During the next 2,500 years, a succession of herding groups attacked agrarian societies from China to Europe, frequently conquering them. The empires and dynasties they established include some of the largest and most famous in history—the

FIGURE 8.3 Livestock is the basic resource in herding societies, and the size of his herd is the measure of a man. Large herds signify not only wealth but power, for only a strong man or the head of a strong family can defend such vulnerable property: roundup time in Mongolia.

great Mongol empire, for example, founded by Genghis Khan early in the thirteenth century A.D. and expanded by his successors. At the peak of its power, the Mongol empire stretched from eastern Europe to the shores of the Pacific and launched attacks in places as distant as Austria and Japan. Other famous empires and dynasties founded by herding peoples include the Mogul empire, established in India by a branch of the Mongols; the Manchu dynasty in China; the Ottoman empire in the Middle East; and the early Islamic states established by followers of the prophet Muhammad.

Despite their many military victories, herding peoples were never able to destroy the agrarian social order. In the end, it was always they, not agrarian peoples, who changed their mode of life. There were a number of reasons for this, but it was primarily because the economic surplus that could be produced by agricultural activities was so much greater than what could be produced by converting the land to herding activities. After a few early conquerors tried to turn fields into pastures, they realized they were, in effect, killing the goose that laid the golden eggs, and abandoned their preferred way of life for economic reasons. Thus, despite impressive military victories, the limits of the herding world were never extended.

Although herding continued to be an important secondary source of subsistence in the agrarian world, it was the primary source only in areas not suited to plant cultivation. In recent centuries, even these areas have, in most cases, been brought under the control of agrarian or industrial societies, and herding societies, like other preindustrial types, are vanishing.

Maritime Societies

Maritime societies have been the rarest of all the major societal types. Never have there been more than a few at any one time. Yet once they played a very important role in the civilized world.

Technologically, maritime societies were much like agrarian societies. What set them apart was the way they used this technology to take advantage of the special opportunities afforded by their environmental situation. Located on large bodies of water in an era when it was cheaper to move goods by water than by land (see page 183), these peoples found trade and commerce far more profitable than either fishing or the cultivation of their limited land resources and gradually created societies in which overseas trade was the chief economic activity.

The first maritime society in history may have been that developed by the Minoans on the island of Crete, late in the third millennium B.C. We are told that the wealth and power of the Minoan rulers "depended more upon foreign trade and religious prerogative than upon the land rents and forced services."[14] The island location of Minoan society was important not only because it afforded ready access to the sea, but also because it provided protection against more powerful agrarian societies. In fact, most maritime societies developed on islands or peninsulas that were difficult to attack by land (see Figure 8.4). Their only military advantage was in naval warfare.

During the next 1,500 years a number of other maritime societies were established in the Mediterranean world. These included the Mycenaeans, or pre-Hellenic Greeks of the second millennium B.C.; the Phoenicians; the Carthaginians; and possibly some of the later Greek city-states. The spread of the maritime pattern in this period was largely, perhaps wholly, the result of diffusion and the migration of maritime peoples. Eventually all of these societies were conquered by agrarian societies and either destroyed or absorbed as subunits. This was not the end of overseas trade and commerce, of course, since these were important activities in most advanced agrarian societies. It was, however, a temporary end to societies in which this was the *dominant* form of economic activity.

Then, more than a thousand years later, there was a revival of maritime societies during the Middle Ages. Venice and Genoa are the best known, but there were others (e.g., Danzig and Lübeck in northern Europe). Later, the Netherlands became an important maritime society and during the seventeenth and eighteenth centuries apparently derived the major part of its income from overseas trade.[15] Britain moved far in this direction in the seventeenth, eighteenth, nineteenth, and early twentieth centuries but probably never quite reached the point where it depended more on overseas commerce than on, first, agriculture and, later, industry. Nevertheless, because of the great growth of overseas commerce, Britain acquired a number of the characteristics of maritime societies. Finally, in the twentieth century, Danzig for a time and, more recently, Singapore, have emerged as maritime societies.

In many ways maritime societies resembled advanced agrarian societies, particularly their urban centers. But there were also important differences. To begin with, most maritime societies were much smaller, often containing only a single city and the area immediately around it. Only two maritime societies, Carthage and the Neth-

FIGURE 8.4 Maritime societies usually developed on islands or peninsulas that were difficult to attack by land: aerial view of the Lebanese city of Tyre, once an important maritime society. When Tyre was a Phoenician city-state, no land bridge connected it to the mainland.

erlands, ever developed empires worthy of the name and, significantly, both of these were *overseas* empires.[16] In each case the empire was created more as an adjunct of commercial activity than as a political venture.

This curious feature is linked with another, more basic peculiarity of maritime societies. In a largely agrarian world in which monarchy was the normal—almost universal—form of government, maritime societies were usually republics. There were some monarchies among them, but this pattern was most likely to occur early in a maritime society's history, suggesting a carryover from a premaritime past.[17]

The explanation for the republican tendency in maritime societies seems to be that commerce, rather than warfare and the exploitation of peasant masses, was the chief interest of the governing class. Being less concerned than the typical agrarian state with conquest and the control of large peasant populations, these nations had less need for a strong, centralized, hierarchical government. An oligarchy of wealthy merchants could do the job, since their primary responsibilities would be to regulate commercial competition and to provide naval forces to defend their access to foreign ports.

Another peculiarity of maritime societies was their unusual system of values and incentives. As we saw in the last chapter, the governing class in agrarian societies typically viewed work of any kind as degrading. Since this was the class that all others

FIGURE 8.5 A Venetian merchant's bedroom reveals the wealth that commercial activities brought to leading citizens of most maritime societies.

looked up to and emulated, its view of economic activity rubbed off on the rest. This was especially evident in the case of merchants, who, when they became wealthy, usually gave up their commercial activities. As we noted, this antiwork ethic undoubtedly contributed to the slowdown in the rate of technological innovation and progress.

In maritime societies, in contrast, merchants were the dominant class, and a very different view of economic activity prevailed. Though more research is needed on the subject, there is reason to believe that maritime societies made disproportionate technological and economic contributions to the emergence of modern industrial societies. It is also significant that the rate of technological advance in *agrarian* societies appears to have been correlated with the social and political strength of their merchant class.[18] In other words, *the greater the social status and political influence of its merchants, the higher the rate of technological and economic innovation in preindustrial societies tended to be*. This suggests one possible explanation of the striking differences in levels of development of societies in our own era.

A BRIEF REVIEW: SOCIOCULTURAL EVOLUTION TO THE EVE OF THE INDUSTRIAL REVOLUTION

Now that we have completed our survey of the various types of preindustrial societies, we need to pause and briefly review the ground we have covered. In particular, we should consider how well the evidence we have examined conforms to ecological–evolutionary theory.

As we saw in Chapter 3, the central thesis of this theory is that subsistence technology is the key to societal growth and development, both for individual societies and for the world system of societies. Technological advance expands the limits of what is possible for a society and thereby improves its chances in the process of intersocietal selection. As a consequence, technological advance has also been the basic determinant of the patterns of sociocultural evolution in the world system.

Figure 3.8 on page 65 suggests that this evolutionary process has generated a number of fundamental trends in the world system. These trends provide us with an excellent test of the validity of ecological–evolutionary theory as it applies to the experience of human societies through the first 99.9 percent of human history.

What exactly *had* happened with respect to each of those trends by the time the agrarian era was coming to a close?

Growth of Human Population   In the opinion of the experts, there were between 3 and 10 million people at the end of the hunting and gathering era (7000 B.C.). By the end of the agrarian era (1800 A.D.), there were more than 700 million.

Growth in Average Size of Societies and Communities   At the end of the hunting and gathering era, the average size of both societies and communities appears to have been somewhere between 25 and 50. Although it is impossible to obtain reliable estimates of the average size of communities and societies for the entire world system at the end of the agrarian era, there is no doubt that both were substantially larger because by then there were so many horticultural, herding, maritime, and agrarian societies. We also know that, whereas the largest society prior to the horticultural era had no more than a few hundred members at most, by the end of the agrarian era there was one with 400 million, and a number with over 10 million.

Increased Permanence of Communities   Before the first fishing and horticultural societies appeared, nearly all human communities were nomadic. By the end of the agrarian era, only a small minority were nomadic.

Expansion of Societies into New Environments   Most of this trend occurred either before the end of the hunting and gathering era or during the industrial era. The horticultural and agrarian eras, however, did see greatly heightened activity in marine environments. By the end of the agrarian era, oceans, lakes, and rivers had become important both as sources of food and as trade routes.

Increasing Impact of Societies on the Biophysical Environment Prior to the horticultural era, the most notable impact of human societies on the biophysical environment seems to have been their apparent extermination of numerous species of large mammals. Societies of the horticultural and agrarian eras had a far more profound effect on the physical landscape, clearing vast forests, damming rivers, irrigating arid areas, and mining an increasing variety of minerals.

Invention of New Symbol Systems During the horticultural era, the first primitive record-keeping systems were invented. These were followed, during the agrarian era, by prealphabetic and eventually alphabetic systems of writing, numeral systems, measurement systems, systems of musical notation, and monetary systems.

Increasing Store of Technological Information During the horticultural and agrarian eras, the store of technological information increased enormously, a fact amply attested to by the great growth of human population. Striking technological advances occurred in plant cultivation, animal domestication, metallurgy, construction, transportation, and communication. By the end of the agrarian era, societies knew how to produce enormous quantities of foods, fibers, and other things; move people and products over great distances; build monumental edifices of great durability; and inflict tremendous damage on one another, to cite but four of the more significant consequences of the expanded store of technological information.

Increasing Store of Other Kinds of Information During the horticultural and agrarian eras, the store of nontechnological information increased dramatically. By the close of the agrarian era, many societies had amassed great amounts of political, economic, philosophical, ideological, historical, esthetic, scientific, and other kinds of information. Much of this new information emerged as a by-product of the growing size and complexity of societies, a process that created new problems requiring new solutions and new information and that led to the emergence of new norms, beliefs, and values.

Growth in the Quantity, Diversity, and Complexity of Material Products No brief summary can do justice to this trend, though there are many comparisons that provide dramatic illustrations. Compare, for example, the greatest structures created by advanced agrarian societies—cathedrals, temples, palaces—with the greatest created by the members of hunting and gathering societies—shelters made from rocks and branches as temporary protection for one or more families. More important, by the end of the agrarian era, human societies were providing the material necessities required to sustain 100 times more people than they had provided for at the end of the hunting and gathering era.

Increasing Complexity of Social Organization In hunting and gathering societies, full-time occupational specialization was extremely rare, possibly nonexistent. The usual pattern was a division of labor by age and sex, with part-time specialization by a headman and/or a shaman. In agrarian and maritime societies, in contrast, occupational specialties numbered in the hundreds, and there was a complex division of labor that often involved specialization by communities and even regions. In hunting and gathering societies the only organized groups were families, whereas in agrarian societies there were separate communities, often organized into provinces, plus numerous specialized associations, especially religious, political, economic, and educational. Political and religious associations, in particular, were often extremely complex.

Increasing Inequality within and among Societies In hunting and gathering societies, there were only minor status distinctions among individuals. The members of agrarian and maritime societies, however, were usually born into classes, which profoundly influenced their opportunities in life. Similarly, prior to the horticultural era, differences among societies were minimal; but by the end of the agrarian era, advanced agrarian and maritime societies were far wealthier and far more powerful than other societies in the world system.

Accelerating Rate of Social and Cultural Change During the last 9,000 years of the hunting and gathering era, the rate of social and cultural change was greater than it had been prior to that time. But that could not compare with the increase in the rate of change in the next 9,000 years. Although there was a temporary slowing of the rate of technological innovation during the first part of the agrarian era, it accelerated again well before the end of the agrarian era, as shown in Figure 3.4 (page 57).

By 1800 A.D., near the close of the agrarian era, the patterns of human life had been dramatically altered for all but the few who still lived in hunting and gathering societies in remote areas. The vast majority of people were now living in either agrarian or advanced horticultural societies, with smaller numbers in simple horticultural, herding, maritime, and fishing societies. This was not, of course, a stable world system. The deadly process of intersocietal selection that had begun thousands of years earlier was still working to the disadvantage of the technologically less advanced. And every time advanced agrarian societies took another step forward, they tilted the balance a bit more in their favor and against the rest.

This was the human situation on the eve of the Industrial Revolution.

PART THREE

INDUSTRIAL SOCIETIES
AND
INDUSTRIALIZING SOCIETIES

9

The Industrial Revolution

Throughout much of the agrarian era, the rate of technological innovation was less than one would expect in view of the size of agrarian societies, the amount of information available to them, and the extent of contact among them. As we have seen, the cause of this lay in their highly exploitative social systems and in the ideologies that shaped their members' economic attitudes and activities. Not surprisingly, these had *negative feedback effects* on both technological innovation and economic development.

Late in the agrarian era, however, the rate of innovation in western Europe increased substantially within a relatively short period of time, and by the latter part of the eighteenth century the Industrial Revolution was well under way. Not long thereafter, England became the first truly industrial society—that is, the first society to derive more than half of its income from productive activities involving machines powered by inanimate energy sources. With this, a new era of far more rapid and pervasive social and cultural change was launched.

What was responsible for this important development? What happened to break the agrarian mold and produce this burst of technological innovation in societies that had been so resistant to change? What happened, in other words, to turn the system of negative feedback into a system of *positive* feedback?

CAUSES OF THE INDUSTRIAL REVOLUTION

The Accumulation of Information in the Agrarian Era

Probably the least heralded of the major causes of the Industrial Revolution was the gradual accumulation of technological information throughout the agrarian era. For despite the slowdown in the *rate* of innovation, discoveries and inventions did not

217

cease. Evidence of significant advances can be found in agriculture, mining, metal-lurgy, transportation, construction, and various other fields.[1] Advances in construction and engineering, for example, can still be traced if one compares the churches and cathedrals built in western Europe in successive centuries. As a result of many such advances, the store of technological information available in the eighteenth century was far greater than in the thirteenth, just as it had been far greater in the thirteenth century than in the eighth. This enormous store of information held obvious potential for an increase in the rate of technological innovation when other conditions within societies became favorable.

Late in the sixteenth century, during the reign of Queen Elizabeth I, the noted English philosopher and statesman Francis Bacon wrote that three inventions "had changed the whole face and state of things throughout the world"—the mariner's compass, the printing press, and gunpowder.[2] He was right: the world, especially his part of it, had already changed significantly because of these inventions, and the pace of change in western Europe was quickening. Bacon was more insightful than most of his contemporaries in recognizing the importance of technological innovation. But even someone as observant as he could not conceive of the vastly greater changes yet to come, since the first modest stirrings of the Industrial Revolution still lay more than a century in the future.

Advances in Water Transportation and the Conquest of the New World

As Bacon perceived, some innovations of the late agrarian era were more important for societal change than others. Those with a potential for altering agrarian social structure and ideology were most important of all, and in this respect, improvements in ships and navigation proved to be some of the most critical.

Prior to the introduction of the compass in Europe, late in the twelfth century, navigation beyond the sight of land was so hazardous that it was undertaken only for short distances or in familiar areas, as in crossing the English Channel or the Mediterranean Sea. Acquisition of the compass was followed over the next several centuries by a series of important advances in the technology of shipbuilding. These included the invention of the stern rudder (which replaced steering oars attached to the sides of ships), the construction of larger ships with multiple masts, the substitution of several smaller sails for a single large sail on each mast, and a reduction in the width of ships relative to their length.[3] All of these innovations made ships more responsive and more manageable, and therefore safer on stormy seas.

With such ships at their command, and with the compass to guide them, western European sailors increasingly ventured out into open seas for extended periods. During the fifteenth century they began a series of voyages intended to find new trade routes to India and China that would enable Europeans to bypass the merchants of the Middle East. Instead, of course, they discovered the New World and quickly subdued it. Less than fifty years after Columbus first set foot in America, Spain had con-

FIGURE 9.1 Recent reconstruction of the Santa Maria, flagship of Christopher Columbus's fleet on the first voyage to the New World, illustrates advances in shipbuilding in the late medieval period. Note the multiple masts and sails, the stern rudder, and the relatively narrow beam.

quered the two most powerful societies in the New World, the Incan empire in Peru and the Aztec empire in Mexico.*

Almost immediately the conquerors began to ship vast quantities of gold and silver back to Europe. This had a number of consequences, one of which was a tremendous growth in the money economy and a decline in the older barter system.[4] Although money had been used for more than 2,000 years, the supply of precious metals remained so limited that many payments were still made in goods rather than in cash—especially in rural areas, but by no means only there. This situation seriously hindered economic and technological advance, because an economy that operates on the basis of barter is not flexible and the flow of resources from areas of oversupply to areas of short supply is sluggish. Furthermore, it is difficult to determine what is economically most advantageous in a barter system. When money is used, it is much

---

*Despite the undeniable impact of gunpowder on world history, that invention, unlike the compass and printing press, was not a significant cause of the Industrial Revolution. In fact, in the conquest of the New World, the decimation of native populations by diseases brought from Europe (e.g., smallpox, measles), and to which these populations had no immunity, appears to have been of much greater importance than European arms.

easier for people to calculate their costs and incomes and thus determine which of the alternatives open to them is likely to yield the greatest profit.

Money is extremely important in breaking down barriers to technological innovation. In societies where technological progress has been halting and uncertain for centuries and where there is no efficient accounting system, people with money are reluctant to invest in new and unproven enterprises. Also, where money is scarce, people tend to state obligations (e.g., wages, rents, debts) in relatively inflexible and traditional terms, which makes the economy unresponsive to changing conditions and new opportunities. But all of this began to change in western Europe during the sixteenth and seventeenth centuries in response to the flow of precious metals from the New World.

This influx of gold and silver had a second important effect: it produced inflation.[5] This was a natural consequence of the greatly increased supply of money combined with a much more limited increase in the supply of goods. Prices doubled, tripled, even quadrupled within a century. As is always the case when this happens, some people prospered and some were hurt. In general, those with fixed incomes, especially the landed aristocracy, were hurt, while merchants and entrepreneurs tended to benefit. This meant a marked improvement in the position of merchants relative to the governing class. More of the economic resources of European societies wound up in the hands of people who were interested in, and knew something about, both economics and technology. More than that, *these were people oriented to rational profit making (not a typical orientation in agrarian societies) and therefore motivated to provide financial support for technological innovations that would increase the efficiency of people and machines*. The rise in prices in the sixteenth century was simultaneously a stimulant to feverish enterprise and an acid dissolving traditional relationships.[6]

The benefits to Europe from the discovery of the New World were even greater in the eighteenth and nineteenth centuries than they had been earlier. As the population of European colonists increased, so did opportunities for trade. The colonists provided a growing market for Europe's manufactured goods and paid for them with a swelling flood of cheap and abundant raw materials.[7] Between 1698 and 1775, Britain's trade with its colonies increased more than fivefold,[8] and that was only the beginning. As a result, *the center of world trade shifted for the first time in more than 5,000 years, as western Europe replaced the Middle East in the favored position*.

Looking backward, it is difficult to exaggerate the importance of the discovery and conquest of the New World, with respect both to the rise of European power in the world system of societies and to the subsequent occurrence of the Industrial Revolution. Suddenly, a handful of relatively small societies had access to an enormous treasure house of resources. In addition to the gold and silver, western European societies quickly gained control over vast territories whose forests were a source of great quantities of cheap lumber and, when cleared, provided seemingly endless acres of rich farmland. Contact with the native peoples of the Americas also provided Europeans with information about new plants—especially corn and potatoes—that became valuable new food resources. Never before in history had technologically advanced societies enjoyed such a favorable ratio of resources to population. It was almost as though a new Garden of Eden had been created, but for the benefit of a favored few.

The Printing Press and the Spread of Information

The printing press was another technological innovation that played an important role in helping western European societies break the traditional agrarian mold. Printing sped the dissemination of both new technological and new ideological information, and thus was a major factor in overcoming resistance to innovation and change.[9]

Printing apparently originated in China about the fifth century A.D.[10] This early method of printing was extremely expensive, however, because it required a highly skilled craftsman to engrave the contents of every page on a separate block of wood. As a result, printed materials remained a luxury until Johann Gutenberg, a goldsmith and engraver, invented a system of movable type in the middle of the fifteenth century.[11] Thus, the expense of skilled engraving was eliminated from printing, except in the manufacture of the type (i.e., letters and other symbols), which could be combined in various ways and used over and over again.

Gutenberg's invention resulted in a tremendous increase in the quantity of printed materials in western Europe. In medieval monasteries, it took ten to fifteen years to produce a single copy of the Bible using traditional methods. One historian has concluded that more books were printed in the first fifty years after the invention of the printing press than all the scribes of Europe had produced in the previous thousand years.[12] Among the materials that achieved wider circulation were treatises on the new scientific theories of men like Copernicus and Galileo in the sixteenth and seventeenth centuries and books on farming that revolutionized English agriculture in the eighteenth. One of the most significant applications of the printing press, however, occurred less than a century after its invention, when it was used to spread the

FIGURE 9.2 The earliest known picture of a printing press, dating from 1499. The typesetter is reading copy on the left, the press and the pressman are on the right. The large figures in the rear symbolize the presence of death, a recurring theme in medieval art.

teachings of the Protestant reformers. Historians today regard the printing press as a major factor in the success of the Protestant movement.[13]

As many scholars have observed, a number of the new Protestant doctrines substantially altered the thinking of many members of agrarian societies in ways that were conducive to economic and other kinds of change.[14] In the first place, the reformers taught that work is an important form of service to God. Martin Luther, for example, insisted that all honest forms of work are as truly Christian callings as the ministry or priesthood. This challenged both the medieval Catholic view of work as a punishment for sin and the traditional aristocratic view of work as degrading and beneath the dignity of a gentleman. At the same time, it supported the efforts of merchants and craftsmen to upgrade their status. Second, the new Protestant faiths undermined fatalism and trust in magic and, in the long run, stimulated the spread of rationalism. Though the reformers dealt with these things only in the area of religion—and even there imperfectly—they strengthened a trend that ultimately had far-reaching consequences.[15] Some branches of Protestantism, for example, encouraged their adherents to plan their lives rather than merely live from day to day, as the name "Methodism" reminds us. Third, many of the newer Protestant faiths emphasized the value of denying the pleasures of this world and living frugally, a practice that enabled those who became economically successful to accumulate capital.

To the extent that people followed these teachings, they developed a new outlook on life: they worked harder, acted more rationally, and lived more thriftily. In short, the Reformation remolded the attitudes, beliefs, and values of countless people in ways that undermined the traditional agrarian economy and stimulated economic and technological innovation. Related to this, certain branches of Protestantism, notably Calvinism, elevated the activities of merchants and businessmen to a status they had not previously enjoyed in any agrarian society. As one scholar has noted, this was not surprising in a faith which had its headquarters in Geneva and its most influential adherents in other leading business centers, such as London, Antwerp, and Amsterdam.[16]

Protestantism was also important to economic development because of the insistence of the reformers that people should be able to read the Bible for themselves and thus have direct access to God's Word. This meant that literacy assumed a new significance in societies that became Protestant: it became a religious obligation for the masses rather than an option for elites. But while the initial motivation for the spread of literacy among the masses was religious, its most important long-term effects were broader. More literate populations proved to be more innovative and creative than their less literate competitors, and societies that encouraged literacy at an early date gained an important advantage over other societies in the developmental process.[17]

In summary, it seems more than coincidence that the Industrial Revolution had its beginnings in predominantly Protestant nations. The new Protestant ideology, like the conquest of the New World, undermined belief systems and social structures that had been formidable barriers to innovation and change. Above all, it encouraged a new respect for work and rational planning and discouraged both fatalism and reliance on magic. But it is important to recognize that the success of the Reformation movement and its influence on the subsequent course of European history were due in no small measure to prior changes in technology and economics and to the discovery and conquest of the New World with its vast treasure of natural resources. The latter development was especially important because it enabled many of those who adopted the Protestant work ethic to prosper to a degree that otherwise would not have been possible, thereby confirming the validity of the new ethic and reinforcing it. In short, the Protestant Reformation was an important link in the chain of causation that led to the Industrial Revolution, even if it was not the critical link that some have suggested.

Advances in Agriculture

Throughout the agrarian era, the chief restraint on societal growth and development was the state of agricultural technology. The rural elite, so long as it managed to extract a surplus sufficient to maintain its customary lifestyle, was content to preserve the status quo. And the peasants, so long as they managed simply to survive, were content to follow the practices inherited from their forebears—or if not content, at least not motivated to change them. Thus agriculture, which was the basis of the economic surplus, remained largely the same from one century to the next.

In the sixteenth century, however, the situation began to change in much of western Europe.[18] The growth of trade, the increased use of money, and, above all, inflation began to undermine the traditional system. On the one hand, a growing number of large landowners found that, as transportation costs declined in the wake of advances in shipping, markets for certain farm commodities (e.g., wool, grain) expanded. On the other hand, the effects of inflation were threatening the profitability of their farms, which depended on rents and other obligations that had been established long before the rise in prices. Many landowners realized that if they hoped to maintain their traditional standard of living under the new economic conditions, they had to try something new. Some of them therefore brought new land under cultivation by draining swamps, or by enclosing for their own private use what had previously been "common land," pastures available to both peasants and elites. Other landowners turned to raising sheep in an effort to benefit from the growing trade in wool. Still others eliminated traditional modes of payment by which tenants paid their landlords through customary services or with goods or produce, and began to require instead payments of money, which had become more important in economic relationships and which could more easily be adjusted to take account of inflation. Thus, during the sixteenth and seventeenth centuries, agriculture in Europe, and particularly in England, gradually became more profit-oriented and capitalistic and less governed by tradition and custom.

Then, in the eighteenth century, a new wave of inflation hit western Europe, and landowners were again faced with a choice between innovation and a declining standard of living.[19] In England, where the traditional system of agriculture had already been seriously weakened, a number of other important innovations were adopted. Early in the century, for example, one landowner devised a system of crop rotation that enabled farmers to keep all of their land continuously under cultivation;

previously, farmers had to leave land fallow, or uncultivated, one year in four in order to restore its fertility. A little later another landowner discovered the principle of selective breeding, simultaneously making a fortune for himself from his stud farm and greatly improving the quality of British livestock. Other members of the rural elite invented a variety of simple machines that increased the efficiency of farm labor, while still others published books expounding the new techniques. The practice of enclosing common lands, meanwhile, continued.

By the end of the eighteenth century, the traditional system of agriculture had been replaced in most of England by a new system of larger, more efficient farms operated on rational and capitalistic principles. But the adoption of this new system meant the massive displacement of many poor rural families whose labor was no longer needed and whose right to common lands was no longer protected by tradition. Some of these people migrated to the new frontier societies overseas. Many others, however, migrated to the cities and towns, where they became a source of cheap labor in the mills and factories that were beginning to appear.

A Model of the Causes of the Industrial Revolution

Figure 9.3 summarizes the principal causes of the Industrial Revolution. As the model indicates, *the basic cause was the growing store of technological information in the latter part of the agrarian era*. Advances in navigation and shipbuilding were espe-

FIGURE 9.3 Model of the causes of the Industrial Revolution in western Europe.

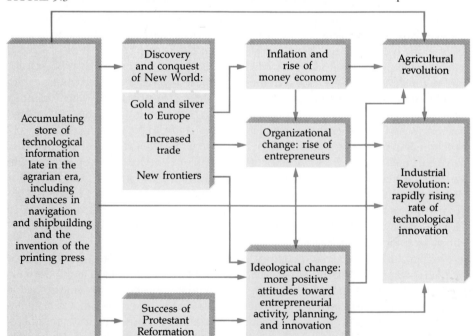

cially important because, without them, the societies of western Europe could not have won control of the resources of two vast continents. This revolutionary development, abetted by the success of the Protestant Reformation, led to changes in economics, social organization, and ideology which made it possible for these societies to break the historic agrarian mold. Because of this, the long-time agrarian pattern of negative feedback from social organization and ideology to technology was transformed into a positive one, thereby freeing creative forces that had been curbed for centuries.

It is interesting to note that England, the first society to become industrialized, experienced significant change in several of the factors that are primarily responsible for shaping a society's development. Its environment was drastically altered through the discovery and conquest of the New World, and its store of both technological and ideological information underwent substantial change in the sixteenth, seventeenth, and eighteenth centuries. These developments combined to produce major changes in the processes of innovation and selection. These developments will also provide us with useful clues when, in a later chapter, we ponder the question of why societies trying to industrialize today find it so much more difficult than did the societies that industrialized a hundred years or more earlier.

A BRIEF HISTORY OF THE INDUSTRIAL REVOLUTION

Before the end of the nineteenth century, economic historians were already beginning to use the term "Industrial Revolution" to refer to the series of dramatic technological and economic innovations that occurred in England during the period from about 1760 to 1830. In their view, the mechanization of the textile industry, the technical advances in, and expansion of, the iron industry, the harnessing of steam power, the establishment of the factory system, and other, related developments of that period had transformed English society. What was still essentially an agrarian society in the middle of the eighteenth century had become an industrial society by the middle of the nineteenth.

The time limits that early writers assigned to the Industrial Revolution are now widely questioned. Most scholars today believe it is a mistake to put a terminal date on a revolution that is still continuing.[20] Others argue that 1760 is too late a starting date, since the acceleration in industrial activity began not in the middle of the eighteenth century but in the middle of the sixteenth or earlier.[21]

There is some merit in both criticisms. The rate of technological advance did, in fact, begin to accelerate long before 1760, as we have seen. But it does not follow that we should treat those earlier developments as part of the Industrial Revolution. To be meaningful, this term should be limited to *the period during which the productive activities of societies were rapidly transformed by the invention of a succession of machines powered by newer, inanimate sources of energy, such as coal, electricity, petroleum, and natural gas*. Using this criterion, we cannot put the start of the Industrial Revolution much, if any, before the middle of the eighteenth century.

The other criticism of the dates is sounder: the Industrial Revolution definitely was *not* over by 1830. Only its first phase ended at that time. Subsequently, there have been three other phases, and each has contributed substantially to the importance of industrial activity in the societies involved, and to their transformation.

We cannot assign precise dates to these phases, since they are all rather arbitrary divisions in what has been essentially a continuous process of development. However, by organizing our review in terms of phases, we can see more clearly the progression of events. In the first phase, which began in mid-eighteenth-century England, the revolution was concentrated in the textile, iron, and coal industries, and the invention of the first true steam engine was the most important innovation. The second phase got its start in the middle of the nineteenth century and involved rapid growth in the railroad industry, the mass production of steel, the replacement of sailing ships by steamships, and use of the new technology in agriculture. Around the turn of the century, the Industrial Revolution entered a third phase, with rapid growth in the automobile, electrical, telephone, and petroleum industries. World War II marked the beginning of the fourth phase, distinguished by remarkable developments in aviation, aluminum, electronics, plastics, nuclear power, computers, and automation.

These four phases should not be thought of as stages that each society must pass through to become industrialized. On the contrary, many societies in recent decades have skipped over certain phases, or at least parts of them, and combined elements from different phases. For example, a Third World nation today often develops its railway, highway, and air transportation systems simultaneously. But a review of the way things happened *initially* enables us to see how one innovation often makes further innovations possible, even imperative.

First Phase

The first phase of the Industrial Revolution, as we noted, began in the middle of the eighteenth century and lasted about a hundred years. Geographically, it was centered in England. Many of the best known innovations occurred in the textile industry and were of two kinds: machines that increased the efficiency of human labor, and machines that harnessed new sources of energy. The flying shuttle is a good example of the first—and a good example, too, of the way one invention stimulated others. Because it enabled one weaver to do the work formerly done by two, spinners could no longer keep up with the demand for yarn. This disruption of the traditional balance between spinning and weaving triggered a succession of further inventions. First, the traditional spinning wheel was replaced by the spinning jenny, which enabled a worker to spin 4 threads simultaneously and, after a number of modifications, 120 threads. But although the spinning jenny was a tremendous improvement from the standpoint of speed, its yarn was so coarse and loose that flax had to be mixed in with the cotton to produce a satisfactory fiber. This was remedied with the water frame, a machine that could satisfactorily spin pure cotton, and later with the spinning mule, whose cotton threads were stronger and finer. All of these advances in spinning reversed the earlier situation: now weaving was the bottleneck in the industry—until a new series of innovations in weaving machines helped restore the balance once again.

By the end of the eighteenth century, the new looms had become so large and heavy that they were almost impossible to operate. To work the treadle even at a slow

FIGURE 9.4 James Hargreave's spinning jenny.

speed required two powerful men—and they had to be relieved after a short time.[22] This led to a search for alternative sources of power. One possibility was waterpower, which had already been used for a variety of purposes for centuries.[23] But England was poorly supplied with suitable streams and rivers, and the wheels and troughs used in water systems were extremely inefficient.[24] Eventually, James Watt developed the first true steam engine,[25] a source of power that could be employed anywhere, and by the end of the century it had been adapted for use in the textile industry.

The net effect of these innovations was such a rapid expansion of the British textile industry that between 1770 and 1845 its contribution to the national income increased more than fivefold.[26] This was an extraordinary rate of growth by the standards of traditional agrarian societies. The actual increase in production was even larger, since per unit costs of production dropped considerably during this period.

One of the immediate consequences of advances in textile production was *the creation of the factory system*. Prior to the Industrial Revolution, and even during its early years, spinning and weaving were cottage industries. Entrepreneurs provided the raw materials, and poor families, working in their own homes and using their own spinning wheels and looms, provided the labor. But after heavier and more expensive machines came to be used, this arrangement was impossible: families could neither afford the new equipment nor power it. Businessmen were forced to buy their own machines, construct buildings to house them, and provide engines to run them, thereby creating the factory system that has become such a prominent feature of modern industrial societies.

Iron was another industry that expanded greatly during the first phase of the Industrial Revolution. Despite increasing demand for iron by both the textile industry and the military, technical difficulties greatly restricted its manufacture until late in the eighteenth century. One problem was England's growing shortage of wood, which

FIGURE 9.5 Prior to the Industrial Revolution, and even during its early years, entrepreneurs provided poor families with raw materials for spinning, weaving, and garment making in their own homes: early nineteenth-century print of English family sewing uniforms for the army under the domestic, or putting-out, system that preceded the factory system.

was used to make charcoal for smelting and refining. This problem had been partially solved earlier in the century, when it was found that coke (derived from coal) could be substituted for charcoal, at least in the smelting process. But a serious bottleneck remained. Because it is hard and brittle, pig iron must be converted into wrought, or malleable, iron before it can be used for most purposes. This process required charcoal and was very time-consuming until the traditional forge was replaced by the newly invented coal-fired blast furnace. These innovations opened the way for rapid expansion: in 1788, England produced only 68,000 tons of iron; by 1845, it produced twenty-four times that.[27] The new blast furnaces also made it possible to perform all the processes of iron making in a single establishment. Thus, the factory system spread from the textile industry to the iron industry.

Between them, the iron industry and the steam engine substantially increased the demand for coal. At the same time, the steam engine helped alleviate the ancient problem of flooding in coal mines by providing power to pump out the water that constantly seeped into shafts and tunnels. The growth of the coal industry, though not quite so dramatic as that of the iron industry, was still impressive: in 1760, Britain produced barely 5 million tons; by 1845, the figure had risen over ninefold.[28]

No discussion of developments in this period would be complete without mention of the machine-tool industry. Although never as large or financially important as the textile, iron, and coal industries, it was crucial for technological progress because it produced the increasingly complex industrial machinery. This industry, which began undramatically with the invention of the first practical lathe, was soon producing machines capable of precision work to the thousandth of an inch.[29] For many years a single tool was used for drilling, boring, grinding, and milling; but special tools were gradually designed for each operation.

Another striking advance in the eighteenth century was the production of machines with interchangeable parts. This greatly facilitated industrial growth, since damage to one part of a complex machine no longer meant that the entire machine had to be discarded or a new part specially made. Spare parts could now be kept on hand and replacements made on the spot by mechanics with limited skills and equipment.

During this initial phase of the Industrial Revolution, shortly after 1800, Britain became the first nation in which machine-based industry replaced agriculture as the most important economic activity, and thus the first industrial society.[30] The United States would not reach this point until 1870.[31]

Second Phase

The second phase of the Industrial Revolution began in the middle decades of the nineteenth century. Expansion continued at a rapid pace in the textile, iron, and coal industries, but now there were breakthroughs in a number of others as well. By the end of the century industrialization had occurred in most segments of the British economy. Meanwhile, the Industrial Revolution began to make significant headway in several other countries of northwestern Europe and in the United States.

One of the most important developments during this phase was the application of the steam engine to transportation, something inventors had been trying to accomplish for decades. By 1850 most of England was linked together by a network of railroads.[32] The results were tremendous: the greatly reduced cost of moving goods by rail led to a significant reduction in the price of most heavy bulk commodities, and this in turn led to greater demand. In addition, railroads helped break down local monopolies and oligopolies (i.e., markets with only a few sellers), and this increased competition and further lowered prices. Thus, England gradually became a single giant market for a growing number of commodities, a development destined to have far-reaching consequences.

Even before the steam engine was adapted to land transportation, it had been used on water. For many years, however, steamships were limited to coastal and river shipping, both because inefficient engines made it impossible to bunker enough wood or coal for long voyages and because paddle wheels worked poorly in high seas. Then, in only a few decades, several things happened. More efficient compound engines substantially reduced the amount of fuel required; iron and steel began to replace wood in ship construction, permitting longer and larger vessels with greater carrying capacity (the upper limit in length for wooden ships was only about 300 feet); and the screw propeller replaced the cumbersome and easily damaged paddle wheel.[33] After this, steamships increased so rapidly that by 1893 steam tonnage exceeded sailing tonnage worldwide.

In the iron industry, meanwhile, a way was finally found to produce steel cheaply and in large quantities, making it available for many new purposes.[34] Between 1845

FIGURE 9.6 Model of the DeWitt Clinton, built in New York in 1831. On its first run between Albany and Schenectady, it traveled twelve miles in less than an hour. Note the similarity of the coaches to stagecoaches and the similarity of the engine to an ordinary steam engine of the kind already in use in factories and mines.

and the early 1880s, Britain's production of iron and steel increased more than five-fold.[35] This meant that in less than a century, from 1788 to the early 1880s, the increase was 100-fold, and the quality of the product was vastly improved.

The tremendous growth in railroads and steamships and the expansion of the iron industry all combined to increase the demand for coal. Though there were no spectacular breakthroughs in mining techniques, improvements in engines and in the quality of steel tools pushed production up fivefold.[36]

A number of new industries emerged in addition to the railroads, none as important at the time, but some destined to surpass them later on. The rubber industry developed after Charles Goodyear discovered the technique of vulcanization, which prevented rubber goods from becoming sticky in hot weather, stiff and brittle in cold. About the same time, Samuel Morse and several others invented the telegraph, and this quickly became the basis of another new industry. Then, in the 1860s, the electric dynamo was invented, and the door was opened to the use of electricity in industry. A second critical development in this field, the invention of the transformer, helped alleviate one of the greatest impediments to the use of electricity: the loss of energy during long-distance transmission. The petroleum industry also got its start in these years, chiefly by providing a substitute for whale oil in lighting homes.

The Industrial Revolution began to have an impact even on agriculture, through improved equipment (e.g., sturdier steel plows), new kinds of machines (e.g., threshing machines, mowers, reapers, steam plows), and synthetic fertilizers from the growing chemical industry. The result was a substantial increase in productivity. In Germany, for example, production per acre rose 50 percent in only twenty-five years. In the United States, the number of hours required to produce a given amount of corn and wheat was cut in half between 1840 and 1900.[37]

An important organizational innovation in this second phase of the Industrial Revolution was the *multidivisional enterprise with a hierarchy of salaried managers*.[38] This occurred first in the new railroad, steamship, and telegraph industries, all of which required workers in widely scattered locations. No longer was it possible for a single family to fill all or even most of the managerial positions needed to supervise employees and coordinate their activities: hired personnel had to assume this responsibility. This was an important step in the development of the modern *corporation*.

Another spur in this direction was the great quantity of new material products that had become available to the members of society. As further advances in production and transportation continued to lower the cost of goods and increase the demand for them, the sheer volume of sales made it impossible for the owners of some businesses to oversee all of the transactions. For example, around the turn of the century, Sears, Roebuck was processing 100,000 orders a day, more than any merchant of an earlier generation would have handled in a lifetime.[39] As sales increased, so did the number of retail outlets in a wide variety of businesses, each requiring a local manager at first, and eventually intermediate layers of management.

Throughout this period, industrialization was spreading rapidly in northwest Europe and North America. Before the century closed, Britain had lost its position of economic and technological dominance. The iron and steel industry illustrates the trend: although Britain nearly doubled its production of pig iron between 1865 and 1900, its share of the world market dropped from 54 to 23 percent.[40] Its chief rivals were the United States and Germany, whose respective shares rose from 9 to 35 percent and from 10 to 19 percent.

As these figures indicate, though industrialization was spreading, it was still largely limited to a few countries. The United States, Britain, Germany, and France, for example, produced 84 percent of the world's iron in 1900. A similar picture emerges when we look at national shares of *all* manufacturing activity. In 1888, the percentages are estimated to have been as follows:[41]

United States	32%
Britain	18%
Germany	13%
France	11%
All other countries	26%

The fact that "all other countries" contributed more to *all* types of manufacturing than to iron production indicates that the new technology spread faster in light industries, such as textiles, than in heavy industries. This was because light industries required less capital and because the rate of innovation in them had slowed considerably, thus reducing the need for highly skilled and innovative personnel.

The last factor points to a final characteristic of this phase of the Industrial Revolution: a growing dependence on science and engineering. Before 1850 most of the major advances were made by simple craftsmen or gentlemen amateurs. After that date, key inventions came primarily from people with formal technical or scientific training. This was especially true in the chemical industry, but it was evident in others as well.

Finally, near the end of the nineteenth century, the innovative process began to be institutionalized, and laboratories were built to enable teams of trained people to work together to solve technical problems.[42] The laboratories established by Thomas Edison exemplified the new trend, and the successes he and others achieved led many to emulate them, especially in Germany and the United States. These developments also contributed to the growth of scientific study in universities, to the training of engineers, and to increasing cooperation between innovative industries and institutions of higher education. Most of these developments did not come to full flower, however, until the third and fourth phases of the Industrial Revolution.

Third Phase

Around the turn of the century, the Industrial Revolution entered a phase that lasted until the beginning of World War II and was characterized by major advances in *energy technology*. The foundation for some of the twentieth century's most distinctive innovations had been laid in the late nineteenth century with the invention of the internal combustion engine and of machines capable of generating and transmitting electricity in quantities great enough, and at prices cheap enough, to be industrially useful and commercially profitable.

One of the most dramatic developments was the tremendous expansion of the automobile industry. In 1900 no more than 20,000 cars were produced in the entire world, most of them in France.[43] By 1929 the total was over 6 million, 85 percent of them made in the United States.[44]

Just as remarkable as the automobile industry's rate of growth was its impact on other industries. In 1937, for example, the manufacture of cars in the United States consumed 20 percent of the nation's steel, 54 percent of its malleable iron, 73 percent of its plate glass, and 80 percent of its rubber.[45] More striking yet, 90 percent of its gasoline went to run those vehicles.

FIGURE 9.7 Early automobile assembly line: dropping the engine into the Model T chassis, Highland Park, Michigan.

TABLE 9.1 **Percentage Distribution of World Industrial Output (Excluding Handicrafts), in 1888 and 1937, by Society**

Society	1888	1937
United States	32	34
United Kingdom	18	10
Germany	13	11
France	11	5
Russia	8	10
Japan	No data	4
All others	17	26

Source: Calculated from W. S. Woytinsky and E. S. Woytinsky, *World Population and Production: Trends and Outlook* (New York: Twentieth Century Fund, 1953), pp. 1003–1004.

The electrical industry was another that mushroomed during the third phase as electricity came to be used widely for industrial purposes. This was also the period in which small electric motors began to be used widely to power household appliances. Between 1900 and 1940 the capacity of all the generating plants in the world increased 200-fold.[46] Again the United States led the way, producing 40 to 45 percent of the world's electric power.

The proportional growth of the petroleum industry was less dramatic, because it had already grown substantially before 1900. Even so, production in 1940 was thirteen times greater than it was in 1900.[47]

The telephone industry also grew rapidly in this period. The number of telephones in the United States increased from 1.4 million in 1900 to 20.8 million in 1940, by which time the industry had investments valued at $5 billion.[48]

During this phase, as during the second, the Industrial Revolution was felt not only in new sectors of the economy but in new parts of the world as well, which meant some change in the relative ranking of nations. While the United States continued to lead, Britain, Germany, and France all lost ground relatively (see Table 9.1) despite substantial growth in absolute terms. The chief gains were registered by nations that were just beginning to industrialize, especially Russia and Japan.

Fourth Phase

No previous war was as dependent on industrial activity as World War II, as every major nation made tremendous efforts to increase its output of military supplies. One of the long-term consequences was the great stimulus this gave the aviation industry. In the United States, the production of aircraft rose from 3,600 in 1938 to more than 96,000 in 1944.[49] Though the manufacture of new aircraft declined substantially at the end of the war, the air transportation industry expanded rapidly. Since 1940, the number of passenger-miles flown by scheduled airlines has risen from 1.2 billion to nearly 500 billion, and the number of ton-miles flown in hauling freight and mail from 14 million to 10 billion.[50] The year 1958 marked a significant shift in transportation patterns: for the first time, planes moved more passengers more miles in the United States than trains, and they also replaced steamships as the chief carriers of trans-Atlantic passengers.

Just as automobiles spurred the petroleum industry, so aviation spurred alumi-num. Though it was first manufactured in the nineteenth century, its production was quite limited until Germany and Italy began building their air forces in the 1930s. In just four decades (from 1938 to 1978), world production increased twenty-five times, and it is still increasing, though less rapidly, as new uses continue to be found.[51]

The plastics industry is another that came into its own during this fourth phase. Its origins go back to 1861, when nitrocellulose was plasticized with camphor to pro-duce artificial ivory and used in eyeglass frames. Thanks to many subsequent devel-opments, plastics have become the most versatile of modern materials: they can now be manufactured to almost any set of specifications. Not surprisingly, the industry has mushroomed: as recently as the late 1930s, world output was under 200,000 tons; today, it is nearly 50 million and growing, with American production a quarter of the total.[52]

The nuclear power industry has also grown tremendously since World War II. Although the atomic age began with Hiroshima in 1945, the world's first nuclear power facility did not begin operating until 1955, when the Soviet Union opened a small installation with a 5,000-kilowatt capacity.[53] Today, there are nearly 400 reactors op-erating in 26 nations with a capacity of nearly 2 trillion kilowatts.[54] In recent years, however, the rate of growth of the industry has slowed substantially in many coun-tries because of concerns for safety and the costs of both plant construction and the disposal of radioactive waste.

Electronics is another industry with a spectacular rate of expansion, and its im-pact on daily life has been as dramatic as its growth. Its products include audio and video equipment of many kinds, computers, calculators, testing and measuring equip-ment, industrial control equipment, and microwave communications systems, to name but a few. With the development of servomotors—small power units that respond instantly to signals of various kinds (e.g., a temperature change)—machines that not only act but *react* became possible, and the foundation was laid for automation and robotics.

The most revolutionary innovation of the fourth phase, however, has been the computer, which is the functional equivalent of a radical advance in certain capabil-ities of our species' most valuable tool, the human brain. The first electronic digital computer was built in 1946, less than fifty years ago. A massive piece of equipment weighing thirty tons and occupying an entire room, it required 140,000 watts of elec-tricity and had a memory of only 20 ten-digit numbers. Today, a vastly greater information-handling capacity resides in the circuits of a tiny quarter-inch silicon chip, and the newest computers can perform as many as 20 billion information-processing operations per second.[55]

Such leaps in capability dwarf the other technological advances of the fourth phase,* and carry with them a great potential for change in human societies. One indication of this is the use of computerized robots in the automobile industry, first in Japan and more recently in the United States. Although early reports greatly exag-

---

*It is reported that if the automobile industry had made comparable advances, a Rolls-Royce would now cost only $70.

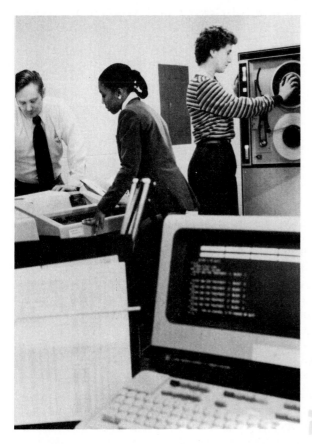

FIGURE 9.8 The most revolutionary innovation of the fourth phase of the Industrial Revolution has been the computer, which is the functional equivalent of a radical advance in certain of the capabilities of our species' most valuable genetic resource, the brain.

gerated the impact of this particular application, there have been substantial changes in other areas where labor consists of routine and repetitive operations. Meanwhile, computers are integral components in everything from children's toys to military weapons systems.

Several of the rapid-growth industries of the third phase maintained their high rate of growth in the fourth. Since 1940, world output of electricity has increased twentyfold, world production of motor vehicles and petroleum tenfold.[56] The United States is still a major producer, but its contribution to total world production in these industries has declined considerably. For example, its share of world automobile production dropped from 85 percent in 1929 to less than 20 percent in recent years.

A comparison of Tables 9.1 and 9.2 shows some of the important changes that have occurred in the last hundred years with respect to industrial development in the world system. The most striking fact revealed by this comparison is the precipitous decline of Britain, which in 1888 still ranked as the second leading industrial power. Japan, on the other hand, has made impressive advances. The dynamic nature of modern industrial technology means that no society is assured of continuing leadership

TABLE 9.2 **Percentage Distribution of Gross World Product, by Society, in 1986**

Society	Percentage Share of Gross World Product
United States	26
Japan	13
Union of Soviet Socialist Republics	8
West Germany	6
France	4
China	3
United Kingdom	3
All others	37

Source: Adapted from *Statistical Abstract of the United States,* 1988, tables 1387 and 1388; the Soviet figure has been adjusted downward to take account of recent evidence provided by leading Soviet economists, *New York Times,* Apr. 24, 1990.

simply because it enjoys that status during a particular phase of the continuing Industrial Revolution. It means, too, that it has become increasingly difficult for any nation or set of nations to dominate the industrial scene. In 1888, the five most highly industrialized societies were responsible for 83 percent of the world's industrial output. A century later, the output of the top five was only 57 percent, reflecting the diffusion of industrial technology throughout the world as a whole (see Table 9.2).

The fourth phase of the Industrial Revolution has been a period of extraordinary economic growth in the vast majority of societies. Gross domestic product, or GDP, is a measure of the value of all the goods and services produced by a society. Since 1950, the combined GDPs of the industrialized societies of western Europe, North America, Japan, Australia, and New Zealand have increased nearly 300 percent, while the combined GDPs of the developing nations of the Third World have increased more than 500 percent![57] Such growth *on a global scale* is without precedent.*

New Energy, New Machines, New Materials: The Key Innovations

In studying the Industrial Revolution, it is easy to become so immersed in the details of individual inventions and discoveries that we fail to see the larger picture. When we look for basic patterns, however, we find that the revolution in technology has involved three kinds of critical innovations.

First, the Industrial Revolution has greatly increased the amount of *energy* available to societies. New technologies have made accessible for the first time vast quantities of energy stored in coal, petroleum, natural gas, and certain radioactive materials. The importance of this development is difficult to exaggerate.

---

*Although some argue that the gains in GDP have not benefited the majority of people in Third World societies, this view is challenged by data on trends in infant mortality, life expectancy, literacy, school enrollments, and other basic indicators of quality of life. While millions in the Third World are still mired in poverty, millions of others have experienced significant improvements in living standards. To appreciate the magnitude of the change, one need only compare current conditions in those societies with those of the agrarian era.

Second, the Industrial Revolution has produced thousands of *new machines* which use this energy to perform an enormous variety of tasks. These machines provide billions of people with countless goods and services—many of which were previously unavailable to even the most powerful kings and emperors.

Third, the Industrial Revolution has made available many *new materials* to use in the construction of new machines and new products. Plastic has probably been the most useful new material to date, for it is easily the most versatile material that humans have ever had to work with.

Collectively, these three sets of innovations—the vast new stores of energy, the new machines, and the new materials—have transformed the world. As we will see in the next several chapters, these advances in our species' ability to take resources from the biophysical environment and convert them into things we need or want have given rise to a social and cultural revolution unequaled in history, not only in its scope and speed, but in the enormity of its impact on human life.

CAUSES OF THE CONTINUING INDUSTRIAL REVOLUTION

As the twentieth century draws to a close, the technological revolution that began in the eighteenth century shows no signs of abating. On the contrary, the rate of innovation continues to accelerate. Thus, to understand the Industrial Revolution it is not enough merely to understand the forces that gave it its start several centuries ago. We also need to understand the forces that are responsible for its continuation today.

Greater Informational Resources and a Larger Population

Several of these forces are ones that we first identified in Chapter 3. For example, the existing store of useful information about the material world is far greater today than ever before. This means that the informational resources available to would-be innovators today are vastly greater than in the past (see Table 3.2 and the related discussion, page 55). In addition, the human population is substantially larger today than it was two centuries ago, and this means more minds at work on the problems confronting human societies.

Changing Attitudes toward Innovation

In preindustrial societies, traditions have always been held in high esteem and change has generally been viewed as undesirable, even dangerous. Innovators, far from being praised or admired for their efforts, have commonly been accused of abandoning the hallowed ways of the past and of their forebears. Because of this strong attachment to the past, social scientists often refer to preindustrial societies as "traditional" societies.

In contemporary industrial societies, in contrast, the attitude toward innovation and change is largely positive. Members of these societies are not just tolerant of innovation: *they actively promote and encourage it*. Many, in fact, are *neophiles*, people who love novelty for its own sake. In the arts, for example, innovation is often praised merely because of its novelty and without regard to esthetic criteria (see "Neophilic Art"), with the result that on a number of occasions entries submitted to art exhibits as hoaxes have actually won prizes.

In the educational world, a strongly positive attitude toward innovation is also much in evidence. In preindustrial societies, the basic function of education was to transmit the cultural heritage of the past to successive generations, and great emphasis was placed on rote learning of materials. Today, most educators scorn memorization and argue that the chief aim of schools should be to train young people to think creatively. Universities, in turn, have increasingly become centers of research and innovation. Faculty members are often expected to devote more time and energy to research than to teaching.

The institutionalization of innovation is also evident in industry and government. Industrial enterprises and governmental agencies have created countless research centers within their own organizations, and they often subsidize research in universities as well. As a result, expenditures for research and development have risen enormously. In the United States, for example, even after adjustments for inflation, these expenditures have increased sixtyfold since 1953.[58] Industrial societies are the first in history to search systematically and continuously for new technological answers to human problems.

The reasons for the modern attitude toward innovation and change are not hard to find. For the most part, the changes that have already occurred have meant im-

---

Neophilic Art

Not long ago, the Associated Press reported that two pieces of sculpture by abstract expressionist John Chamberlain had been mistaken for junk and carted away by trash collectors. Walter Kelly, owner of the art gallery, valued them at $20,000. "I had them at the side of my warehouse to clean them up a little for a prospective buyer."

The pieces of art were the usual tangles of metal that have made Chamberlain famous. They were fashioned from car bumpers, sheet metal from old washing machines, and similar materials.

"I'm certain it wasn't a theft," Kelly said, "and that makes it worse, because whoever took them might destroy them. These are important works by a great artist. One of Chamberlain's works is on permanent display at the Art Institute of Chicago."

The Associated Press reported that it was difficult to describe the sculptures, but quoted Kelly as saying, "They are very powerful, dynamic, forceful and . . . you have to form your own opinion of what is represented."

provements in the quality of life for the vast majority of people in industrial societies—greatly improved standards of living, improved health, and greater longevity. Under the circumstances, it would be much more surprising if people's attitudes toward change had *not* changed.

The Rise of Modern Science

The emergence of science as a major new institutional system is another development that has contributed greatly to the continuing revolution in technology. Although science is sometimes confused with technology, the two are not the same. Science is the search for general and abstract principles that explain the workings of the world we live in. Technology, in contrast, is information about specific ways in which the material world can be manipulated to satisfy human needs and desires. It is a much more practical and "down-to-earth" body of information.

Science and technology today are obviously interdependent. Almost all of modern science presupposes an advanced technology. Modern science is possible only because of technological advances which have enhanced the powers of our senses and of our brains, thus enabling us to learn things which would otherwise remain forever unknown. For example, modern molecular biology and modern medical science are possible only because of the invention of the microscope and the electron microscope, which revealed for the first time the previously invisible and unknowable world of cells and molecules, bacteria and viruses. Similarly, modern astronomy is possible only because of the invention of the telescope, the radio telescope, and space probes, which extend the range of our vision far beyond what was previously possible.

But if modern science is a product of the Industrial Revolution, it is also an important cause of its continuation. Today, technological advance depends increasingly upon the kind of abstract, theoretical knowledge that is the special concern of the sciences. More and more, fundamental discoveries and major inventions are the work of men and women with advanced scientific training, and less and less the work of untrained mechanics. Without the contributions of modern science, it is highly unlikely that the rate of technological innovation would still be accelerating.

The Threat of War

Prior to the Industrial Revolution, military technology changed slowly. As a result, military success among societies at the same level of development depended largely on the size of armies and the organizational and tactical skills of their commanders.

Today, in contrast, military technology becomes obsolete in a very short time and the size of armies and their commanders' skills are often less important than the productive capacity of a nation's economy and the skills of its engineers and scientists. To maintain their relative military preeminence, the leading military powers are obliged to invest substantial sums in technological research of many kinds.[59] Although the aim of this research is to create new and improved weapons systems, the new technologies that result often have significant nonmilitary applications. A classic example of this is the silicon chip, which was developed in response to the need to reduce the size and weight of materials used in the space program, a program whose funding has depended greatly on its military relevance.

Environmental Feedback

For the first time in history, the most significant changes in the biophysical environments of most societies are not the result of spontaneous natural forces but, rather, of human actions. The global ecosystem now has to support a much larger human population than ever before, and the standards of living for much of this population are steadily rising. As a result, natural resources of every kind are being consumed far more rapidly than in the past, and supplies of many of them are threatened with depletion. In addition, many new technologies have had unanticipated side effects, such as acid rain. The need to solve such problems leads to further research and the development of still newer technologies. Thus, technological advance has itself become one of the most important causes of the need for continued technological advance.

The Desire for Ever Higher Standards of Living

Finally, it is clear that one of the most important factors responsible for the continuing Industrial Revolution is the desire of most people for ever higher standards of living. One might suppose that the tremendous improvements in living standards in industrial societies during the last two hundred years would satisfy their members, but this has not been the case. The desire for goods and services seems insatiable: the more people have, the more they want.

This appears to be part of our genetic heritage—an element of human nature that results from our enormous capacity for learning, and especially from our powers of imagination. No matter what we have, or what we are able to do, we can always dream of more. And having dreamed, some are driven to make the dream a reality. Where this process will end—or if it will end—no one can say. For the present, however, it is a powerful force contributing to the continuing revolution in technology.

LEVELS OF INDUSTRIALIZATION IN THE WORLD SYSTEM OF SOCIETIES

Societies today differ enormously in the degree to which they have industrialized. Some rely almost entirely on the newer energy sources, such as coal, oil, natural gas, and nuclear energy, while others still depend primarily on human and animal power, wind, water, and wood. Some have become almost totally dependent on machine technology while others still rely primarily on hand tools. And some are now heavily dependent on new kinds of materials, while others still depend largely on traditional ones.

Unfortunately, there is no single measure of industrialization that enables us to gauge perfectly the degree to which contemporary societies have adopted the new industrial technology. Different measures reflect different aspects of industrialization and thus yield somewhat different rankings of societies. Whatever measure is used, however, it must be a *per capita* (i.e., per person) measure, to take account of differences in the population size of societies. For example, if we simply took the total production of societies as a measure, as in Table 9.2 (page 236), China would appear to be one of the most industrialized societies in the world system. But this is a distortion caused by China's huge size: its level of industrialization is actually very low by contemporary standards.

TABLE 9.3 Gross Domestic Product per Capita, Excluding Extractive Industries and Farming: A Sample of Contemporary Societies

Society	GDP/Capita Excluding Extractive Industries and Farming	Society	GDP/Capita Excluding Extractive Industries and Farming
West Germany	$16,986	Ecuador	$772
Japan	16,738	Colombia	704
United States	16,232	Congo, People's Republic	677
Norway	15,231	Cameroon	674
Denmark	14,414	Thailand	656
Sweden	14,094	Honduras	526
France	13,823	Dominican Republic	506
Austria	13,314	Morocco	489
Finland	13,036	Egypt	468
Belgium	12,793	Zimbabwe	448
Netherlands	12,398	Bolivia	440
Canada	11,687	Philippines	403
Italy	10,955	Indonesia	224
Australia	9,051	Zambia	211
United Kingdom	8,601	Pakistan	204
New Zealand	7,914	Central African Republic	202
Spain	6,234	Kenya	191
Greece	3,436	Rwanda	184
Saudi Arabia	3,120	Liberia	172
South Korea	2,190	India	166
Venezuela	2,115	Niger	162
Peru	1,766	Ghana	161
Argentina	1,725	China	148
Brazil	1,672	Somalia	103
South Africa	1,638	Nigeria	80
Algeria	1,594	Bangladesh	76
Mexico	1,421	Ethiopia	56
Jamaica	894	Uganda	54
Turkey	833	Nepal	49
El Salvador	785	Tanzania	46

Source: Our calculations based on World Bank, *World Development Report 1989* (New York: Oxford University Press, 1989), tables 1 and 3.

One of the best measures currently available is closely related to GDP or gross domestic product. It is the *per capita* value of all the goods and services produced within a society *except* the products of its farms and extractive industries. By excluding the products of extractive industries, this measure avoids exaggerating the level of industrialization attained by a number of oil- and mineral-rich nations that have relatively high GDPs primarily because of that wealth, yet are still so little industrialized that they must depend heavily on more advanced societies for the technology and expertise needed to extract and process those resources.

Using this measure, West Germany and Japan are the most industrialized societies in the world system, at least among those that have provided the World Bank with the relevant data. Table 9.3 reveals several important patterns. First, there are enormous differences in the levels of industrialization of contemporary societies. Second, only a small minority of them can be considered full-fledged industrial societies. Third, with the exception of Japan, all of these are either in Europe or were settled primarily by European peoples. Fourth, most of the least industrialized societies are in Africa and Asia, while most of the intermediate cases are found in Latin America, the Middle East, and along the Pacific rim of Asia.

When we consider the distribution of these societies on a map of the world (see Figure 9.9), it becomes clear that all of the technologically most advanced societies are in temperate regions, while nearly all of the least advanced are located in tropical or semitropical regions. This is no coincidence. Rather, it is an indication of the tremendous importance of the *biophysical environment*. As we have noted before, en-

FIGURE 9.9 Industrial societies in the late twentieth century are shown in dark blue.

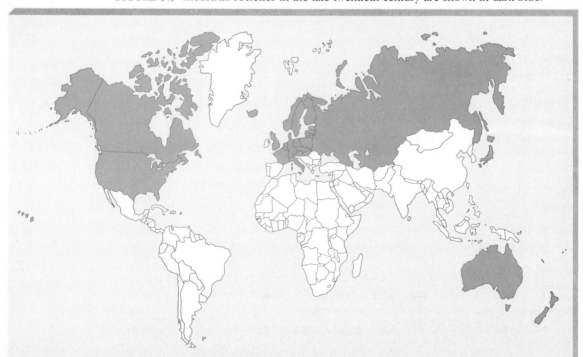

vironmental variables, such as climate, the quality of soils, and the prevalence of disease, have had an enormous impact on societal development, not only in the distant past but also in the modern era. Although little attention has been paid these variables by even the most eminent of scholars,[60] they have been a kind of "hidden" factor in the developmental process, greatly favoring some societies and badly handicapping others.[61]

In the remainder of this chapter and in those that immediately follow, we will be concerned with the small minority of societies that are highly industrialized. Our goal will be to see how the new technology they have created has transformed the conditions of life for the hundreds of millions of people living in them. Then, in Chapters 15 and 16, we will turn to the societies of the Third World, which retain far more of the elements of their preindustrial past.

CONSEQUENCES OF THE INDUSTRIAL REVOLUTION

From an early date it was clear that the Industrial Revolution involved more than just a change in the techniques of production: it was also producing far-reaching changes in virtually every aspect of human life. Though our chief concern in this volume is with the long-run consequences of the revolution, we cannot ignore its impact on the lives of those who were first exposed to it and the new social order to which it gave rise.

Initial Consequences

The first indication of serious change came with the invention of the new spinning and weaving machines in the late eighteenth century. Because of their greatly increased size and weight, they required specially constructed buildings and either steam engines or waterfalls to power them. In short, the new technology necessitated the creation of factories.

Factories, however, required a concentrated supply of dependable labor. A few of the early ones were built in open countryside, but their owners quickly found they could not hire enough workers unless they built adjoining tenements and thus, in effect, created new urban settlements. Most factories were built in or near existing towns, and the cry that went out from them for workers coincided with the declining need for labor on the farms.

Although the ensuing migration to urban areas was not new, its *magnitude* was, and most communities were unable to cope with the sudden influx. The migrants themselves were badly prepared for their new way of life. Sanitary practices that had been tolerable in sparsely settled rural areas, for example, became a threat to health, even to life itself, in crowded urban communities.

Equally serious problems resulted from the abrupt disruption of social relationships. Long-standing ties of kinship and friendship were severed and could not easily be replaced, while local customs and institutions that had provided rural villagers with some measure of protection and support were lost for good. Thus, it was an uprooted, vulnerable mass of people who streamed into towns and cities and were thrown into situations utterly foreign to them, and into a way of life that often culminated in injury, illness, or unemployment. A multitude of social ills—poverty, alcoholism, crime, vice, mental and physical illness, personal demoralization—were endemic.

Local officials had neither the means nor the will to cope with rampant problems in housing, health, education, and crime. Cities and towns became more crowded, open space disappeared, and people accustomed to fields and woodlands found themselves trapped in a deteriorating environment of filthy, crowded streets and tenements, polluted air, and long workdays rarely relieved by experiences of either beauty or hope.[62]

The misery of the new urban dwellers was compounded by the harshness of the factory system, which often operated along quasi-penal lines.[63] Regardless of how hard life had been before, country folk had at least had some control over their own hour-to-hour movements; but now work was, if anything, longer, more arduous, and more restrictive. Women and children, though they had always worked extremely hard in homes and fields, now worked in factories with dangerous, noisy machinery and in

FIGURE 9.10 During the early stages of the Industrial Revolution, large numbers of children were employed in factories in both the United States and Britain: textile mill employees in North Carolina, 1908.

dark and dangerous mines. Minor infractions of complex rules, such as whistling on the job or leaving a lamp lit a few minutes too long after sunrise, led to fines, more serious infractions to floggings. One observer of the period wrote poignantly of hearing children, whose families could not afford clocks, running through the streets in the dark, long before the mills opened, so fearful were they of being late.[64]

The immediate effects of industrialization have been traumatic for vast numbers of people in virtually every society that has made the transition from agrarianism. The

---

Children and the Factory System

The following testimony was given by Peter Smart to a Parliamentary committee investigating working conditions in 1832. Similar testimony was provided by numerous others.

Q. Where do you reside?
A. At Dundee.
Q. Have you worked in a mill from your youth?
A. Yes, since I was 5 years of age.
Q. Had you a father and mother in the country at the time?
A. My mother stopped in Perth, about eleven miles from the mill, and my father was in the army.
Q. Were you hired for any length of time when you went?
A. Yes, my mother got 15 shillings for six years, I having my meat and clothes.
Q. What were your hours of labor, as you recollect, in the mill?
A. We began at 4 o'clock in the morning and worked till 10 or 11 at night; as long as we could stand on our feet.
Q. Were you kept on the premises constantly?
A. Constantly.
Q. Locked up?
A. Yes, locked up.
Q. Night and day?
A. Night and day; I never went home while I was at the mill.
Q. Do the children ever attempt to run away?
A. Very often.
Q. Were they pursued and brought back again?
A. Yes, the overseer pursued them and brought them back.
Q. Did you ever attempt to run away?
A. Yes, I ran away twice.
Q. And you were brought back?
A. Yes; and I was sent up to the master's loft, and thrashed with a whip for running away.
Q. Do you know whether the children were, in point of fact, compelled to stop during the whole time for which they were engaged?
A. Yes, they were.
Q. By law?
A. I cannot say by law; but they were compelled by the master; I never saw any law used there but the law of their own hands.

Source: *Parliamentary Papers*, 1831–32, vol. XV.

details have varied, but the suffering has been no less acute in socialist societies than in capitalist. Whether life for the new urban working class was better or worse than it had been for the peasants and the urban lower classes of the old agrarian societies is still a matter of debate.[65] But one point is not debatable: the transition to an industrial economy has exacted a cruel price in terms of human suffering and demoralization for countless millions of people.

Long-Run Consequences: An Overview

In subsequent chapters we will examine in detail the new societies and the distinctive life patterns that have resulted from two centuries of industrialization. For the moment, however, we will note just a few of the most important and most striking consequences. Collectively, these changes in population, social organization, ideology, and language add up to a revolution without parallel in human history, from the standpoint of scope as well as speed.

1. World population has multiplied sevenfold (from 725 million to more than 5 billion) just since 1750, a rate of growth more than fifteen times higher than the rate between the time of Christ and 1750.
2. The rural–urban balance within societies has been reversed: agrarian societies were approximately 90 percent rural, whereas several advanced industrial societies are more than 90 percent urban and most more than 70 percent.
3. The largest urban communities of the industrial era are nearly twenty times the size of the largest of the agrarian era.
4. Women in industrial societies give birth to only about a third as many children as women in preindustrial societies.
5. Life expectancy at birth is almost three times greater in advanced industrial societies than it was in agrarian.
6. The family, for the first time in history, is no longer a significant productive unit in the economy.
7. The role and status of women in the economy and in society at large has changed substantially.
8. The role and status of youth has also changed, and youth cultures have become a significant factor in the life of industrial societies.
9. The average per capita production and consumption of goods and services in advanced industrial societies is at least ten times greater than in traditional agrarian societies.
10. The division of labor is vastly more complex.
11. Hereditary monarchical government has disappeared in industrial societies, except as a ceremonial and symbolic survival, and the proprietary theory of the state has vanished entirely.
12. The functions and powers of government have been vastly enlarged.
13. Free public educational systems have been established and illiteracy has been largely eliminated in industrial societies.

14. New ideologies have spread widely (notably socialism, capitalism, national-ism, and pragmatism), while older ones inherited from the agrarian era have been substantially altered or have declined in influence.
15. The speed of travel has increased a hundred times and the speed of com-munication 10 million times, rendering the entire planet, in effect, smaller than England in the agrarian era.
16. A global culture has begun to emerge, as evidenced in styles of dress, mu-sic, language, technology, and organizational patterns (e.g., factories, public schools).
17. Global political institutions (e.g., the United Nations, the World Court) have been established for the first time.
18. Several societies have acquired the capacity to obliterate the entire human population.

All this in only 200 years!

Amazing!

10

Industrial Societies: Information and Population

There is no sharp line of demarcation that separates industrial societies from other societies in the modern world system. Instead, the level of industrialization varies by degree, ranging from very high levels in societies such as West Germany and Japan to very low levels in those like Tanzania and Nepal (see Table 9.3, page 241).

Based on the best available indicators of industrialization, about two dozen societies are generally recognized as full-fledged industrial societies:

Australia	France	Norway
Austria	Hungary	Poland
Belgium	Iceland	Soviet Union
Canada	Italy	Sweden
Czechoslovakia	Japan	Switzerland
Denmark	Luxembourg	United Kingdom
East Germany	Netherlands	United States
Finland	New Zealand	West Germany

Although some might add Bulgaria, Ireland, Israel, Romania, or Spain to this list, our concern will be with the twenty-four most fully industrialized societies, since they provide us with the best picture of what industrialization means.

THE INFORMATIONAL BASE: TECHNOLOGY AND IDEOLOGY

The same kinds of cultural information that are most important in shaping the patterns of life in other human societies are most important in industrial societies as well. First, there is *technological information*, which defines the "limits of the possible" and the costs of the various alternatives within those limits. Because the tech-

248

TABLE 10.1 **Productivity of American Agriculture, 1800–1986**

Activity	Number of Worker-Hours Required			Percentage Reduction in Worker-Hour Requirements
	1800	1910–1917	1982–1986	
Production of 100 bushels of wheat	373	106	7	98.1
Production of 100 bushels of corn	344	135	3	99.1
Production of a bale of cotton	601	276	5	99.2
Production of 1,000 pounds of milk	n.a.*	38	2	94.7
Production of 1,000 pounds of beef	n.a.*	46	9	81.4
Production of 1,000 pounds of chicken	n.a.*	95	1	98.9

*Not ascertained.

Sources: U.S. Department of Commerce, *Historical Statistics of the United States: Colonial Times to 1970*, pp. 500–501, and U.S. Department of Commerce, *Statistical Abstract of the United States*, 1989, table 1110.

nological bases of all advanced industrial societies are fairly similar, these limits and cost calculations are much the same in all of them, and this, not surprisingly, leads to many other important similarities. Second, there is *ideological information*, the basic beliefs and values that guide a society or its leaders in selecting from among the alternatives made possible by its technology. The ideological differences between societies are often greater than the similarities and can lead to important institutional and organizational differences, as we shall see.

Technology

The best way to appreciate the dramatic difference between an agrarian society and an industrial one is to look at the measurable changes that have occurred as a result of the shift from the older technology to the new, and *agricultural productivity* is a good place to begin. As Table 10.1 shows, the application of industrial technology to agriculture has had a revolutionary impact on production, making it possible to produce a given quantity of grain, fiber, milk, or meat with only a tiny fraction of the labor required with the older agrarian technology.* The labor used to produce a given quantity of wheat, corn, cotton, and chicken has been cut more than 98 percent. In the case of milk and beef, the reductions have been somewhat less, but still dramatic. Because of these advances in agricultural technology, tens of millions of people who would otherwise be required on farms are free to engage in other kinds of economic activities. As a result, the percentage of farmers and farm workers in the American labor force dropped from 72 percent in 1820 to only 2 percent today.[1]

The basic factor responsible for this remarkable trend has been the harnessing of new energy sources. In agrarian societies, people and animals were the chief sources of the energy used in most work activity, such as pushing, pulling, digging, lifting, and cutting. Their efforts were supplemented to some extent by wind power and water-

*In this discussion, we draw heavily on data from the United States because excellent statistical materials make it possible to trace trends well back into the nineteenth century.

power. As recently as 1850 these four sources still supplied over 87 percent of the energy used in work activities in the United States. Today, they account for less than 1 percent.[2] In their stead, industrial societies use coal, petroleum, natural gas, hydroelectric power, and nuclear power. Except for coal, these sources were still untapped in 1850, and even coal had not been used as a substitute for human and animal energy until the invention of the steam engine in the eighteenth century.

Not only have energy sources changed, but the quantities used have multiplied enormously. In 1850, all the prime movers in the United States (human bodies, work animals, steam engines in factories, sailing ships, etc.) had a capacity of less than 10 million horsepower; today, it is more than 35 *billion*—a 3500-fold increase in only a little more than a century, and a 350-fold increase in *per capita* terms.[3]

This remarkable jump in the production and consumption of energy has been closely linked to enormous increases in the production and consumption of a wide variety of other things. In the case of iron and steel, for example, British production multiplied nearly 7,000-fold between 1750 and 1970,[4] while production in the United States increased 12,000-fold from 1820 to the present.[5]

The production and consumption of raw materials in modern industrial societies are tremendous. In the most recent year for which figures are available, the United States produced 4.2 tons of stone for every man, woman, and child in the population; 3.7 tons of sand and gravel; 3.6 tons of coal; 640 pounds of cement; 360 pounds of phosphate rock; 360 pounds of iron ore; 360 pounds of clay; and 300 pounds of salt, to cite but a few items.[6] Altogether, mineral production totaled about 14 tons per person per year.

FIGURE 10.1 The application of industrial technology in farming has had a revolutionary impact on production, making it possible to reduce the labor required in wheat production by more than 98 percent: combines and trucks returning from wheat fields in the American midwest.

FIGURE 10.2 The ability to harness enormous amounts of relatively cheap energy has been one of the basic factors responsible for the great productivity and high standard of living of modern industrial societies: offshore oil rig.

Change in a society's gross national product (GNP), corrected for the effects of inflation, is one of the best ways to measure the magnitude of the technological advance brought about by industrialization.* It tells us the extent to which the changes in technology have enhanced the society's ability to produce goods and services. When we compare British society's GNP in 1830 with current figures, we find that there has been a fifteenfold increase.[7] As striking as this figure is, it is considerably smaller than the American figure, which shows a *50-fold* increase since 1870.[8] As these figures indicate, the technologies of industrial societies are much more powerful than the technologies of even the most advanced agrarian societies of the past. Small wonder that the advances in technology have been accompanied by revolutionary changes throughout society!

Ideology

During the last five centuries the bounds of human knowledge have expanded enormously. The voyages of exploration that began in the fifteenth century gave humans

---

*A society's GNP is simply its GDP *plus* net income from other societies. Although it is important to use *per capita* measures when comparing two or more societies of very different sizes (as in Table 9.3, page 241), when we compare the same society at two different times, *total* GNP or *total* GDP is the preferred measure, since our goal is to identify the magnitude of the change that has occurred in a society's productive capacity.

their first accurate picture of the earth as a whole. Astronomers of the sixteenth and seventeenth centuries did the same for the solar system. More recently, the natural sciences have given us a vision of a universe of incredible complexity, whose age is measured in billions of years and whose size must be expressed in billions of light-years. And, finally, in the last hundred years, the social sciences have begun the task of demythologizing the social order, challenging ancient beliefs about the nature of man and subjecting virtually every aspect of human life to systematic scrutiny.

Theistic Religions Not surprisingly, this flood of new information about ourselves and the world we live in has shaken and unsettled many traditional beliefs, and the institutional systems based on them. This is especially evident in the case of theistic religions. The thought forms of the great historic faiths—Judaism, Christianity, Islam, Hinduism, and Buddhism—bear the imprint of the agrarian era during which they evolved. But beliefs about the natural world and the social order that were "self-evident" during the agrarian era often appear alien and antiquated to members of industrial societies. This has created an acute crisis for theistic faiths in industrial societies. Religious leaders have tried, in many cases, to translate the most important elements of their traditions into modern terms, while steering a course between irrelevant orthodoxy and heretical innovation. The turmoil and controversy within the Roman Catholic Church created by Vatican Council II was but the most recent in a series of intellectual crises that began at the time of Copernicus and Galileo.

Although the majority of people in most industrial societies still profess a belief in God when questioned, a growing number say they are agnostics or atheists. In a recent international survey of religious beliefs, those identifying themselves as such ranged from 16 percent in Italy to 61 percent in Japan, with an average of 33 percent for the eight industrial societies in the survey.[9] Even "believers" often indicate that they doubt many basic historic beliefs. In most of western Europe, for example, barely half of the population say they believe in a life after death, and fewer still believe in hell or the devil.[10] Even bishops and theologians are sometimes quoted as questioning or reinterpreting historic doctrines.

These trends are less pronounced in Canada and the United States than in western Europe, but even in these societies change is clearly evident. In Canada, for example, people reporting church or synagogue attendance in the previous week dropped from 60 percent in 1957 to 32 percent in 1988.[11] In the United States, the number of people who say that religion is very important in their lives dropped from 75 percent in 1952 to 53 percent in recent surveys, while the number who believe that religion can answer today's problems dropped from 81 to 57 percent.[12] The latter is especially important, since it suggests that the members of industrial societies are placing increasing faith in new secular ideologies in their efforts to solve their own and their societies' problems.

The New Secular Ideologies Beginning in seventeenth- and eighteenth-century Europe, a number of new ideologies appeared in which the role of supernatural beliefs was substantially reduced or totally eliminated. While some of these new ideologies quickly died out, a number of them not only survived but have prospered in the industrial era. The most important of these new faiths are democratic republicanism, capitalism, democratic socialism, revolutionary socialism (or communism), nationalism, and pragmatism. It is these ideologies that guide the members of industrial societies in shaping their economies and polities.

Democratic republicanism, as its name suggests, is a special form of the more general ideology known as republicanism. The basic doctrine of republicanism is its repudiation of hereditary monarchy—the type of government that prevailed in most agrarian societies of the past—and the proprietary theory of the state (see page 186).

Although republicanism has existed as an ideology for thousands of years, republican governments were rare in the agrarian era, except in maritime societies. Prior to the nineteenth century, most republicans rejected democratic republicanism, preferring instead *oligarchical* republicanism. In other words, they advocated a form of government in which power was concentrated in the hands of a few wealthy individuals, as it was in maritime societies. Oligarchical republicans have generally been distrustful of the masses of common people, afraid that they would misuse the powers of government if they ever gained political control.

The government of the United States in the first fifty years following the American Revolution provides a good example of oligarchical republicanism. Most members of the new political elite thought it wise to limit political power to a small minority of the population—men of property who, in their view, had the greatest stake in the welfare of society and also the greatest capacity to govern. In the new constitution adopted by the state of North Carolina in 1776, for example, the right to vote was limited to landowners, and the right to sit in the state senate was limited even more—to those who owned 300 acres. To be eligible to be governor of the state, a man had to have a net worth of £1,000, eight times the net worth of the average white adult male in the South at the time.[13] Similar provisions were present in the constitutions of virtually all of the other states in postrevolutionary America.

Not everyone in early America was satisfied with oligarchical republicanism, and even in the eighteenth century there were some who advocated *democratic* republicanism, or what Abraham Lincoln would later describe as "government of the people, by the people, and for the people." Not surprisingly, many of the most ardent advocates of democratic republicanism were people who lived on what was then the western frontier. As we saw in Chapter 7 (pages 198–200), frontier regions have long been noted for their egalitarianism and their resistance to established systems of authority. With strong support from this increasingly important part of the population, democratic republicanism won growing support in the early decades of the nineteenth century. With the election of Andrew Jackson in 1828, the fate of oligarchical republicanism in the United States was sealed. Property requirements for voting were gradually reduced, and soon eliminated altogether. By the late 1850s, nearly all white males were eligible to vote.

Since that time, democratic republicanism has been the dominant political ideology in American society and has won the support of hundreds of millions of other people throughout the world. Nevertheless, only a small minority of societies are as yet governed by democratic principles, and these are largely confined to the industrial societies of Western Europe, North America, Oceania, and Japan. One reason for

FIGURE 10.3 Adam Smith.

this has been the rise of a new, competing ideology, revolutionary socialism (see be-low, pages 256–258).

Capitalism is another important new ideology of the industrial era. Its intellec-tual father was Adam Smith, a Scottish professor of moral philosophy who combined an analytical mind with a crusading nature.[14] In his most influential work, *An Inquiry into the Nature and Causes of the Wealth of Nations*, published in 1776, Smith made a powerful case for the thesis that the intervention of government into the economic life of a society retards growth and development. The only useful function govern-ment can perform in the economic sphere, according to Smith, is to enforce contracts that individuals enter into freely. To do more than this is harmful. Smith backed up his argument with an impressive analysis designed to show that the law of supply and demand, operating in a truly free market,* would ensure that "the private interests and passions of men" are led in the direction "most agreeable to the interest of the whole society."[15] It would be a self-regulating system, but it would function, said Smith, as though an "invisible hand" were at work, ensuring the best possible outcome.

Smith's work laid the foundation for the emerging academic discipline of mod-ern economics. More important, his basic beliefs about the harm done by govern-mental intervention in the economy became the basis of a powerful new ideology that for 200 years has exercised a profound influence on societies around the globe. This ideology has provided moral justification for policies that minimize governmen-

---

*See Glossary and discussion of market economies, page 279.

tal control of businessmen and business enterprises. In societies where capitalism is the dominant ideology, the term "free enterprise" has become a symbol that is often invoked with considerable success to influence public opinion. As we will see shortly, the realities of contemporary capitalism are strikingly different from its ideals, as has been true, of course, of every ideology from Christianity to socialism.

Another important new ideology of the industrial era is *socialism*. While its underlying principle has been applied in hunting and gathering societies for thousands of years, the modern concept dates from the nineteenth century and was an explicit response to, and reaction against, the realities of early capitalism. Socialists argued that the basic economic resources of a society should be the common property of all its members, and used for the benefit of all. Where proponents of capitalism praised free enterprise for the growth in productivity it generated, socialists attacked it for its harsh working conditions, its low wages and economic inequality, its unemployment, its child labor, its boom and bust cycles, and its alienating and exploitative character. Where capitalists advocated the private ownership of the means of production (i.e., mines, factories, railroads, utilities), socialists favored public ownership. Where capitalists argued that economic inequality is necessary to provide incentives for people to work productively, socialists insisted that a more egalitarian distribution would achieve a better result.

Since early in its history, the socialist movement has been split into a variety of warring sects that have often fought more with one another than with the advocates of capitalism and other ideologies.[16] In the long run, however, the most important split has been between *democratic socialism* and *revolutionary socialism.*

Democratic socialism assumes that socialist principles have an inherent appeal to most people. Its proponents therefore maintain that, in democratic societies, socialists should seek power by democratic means, and that, after coming to power, they should let other political parties compete freely for the support of the electorate and return to power any time they can win a majority of the vote. Democratic socialists believe that any other policy defeats one of socialism's basic aims: to maximize the freedom of individuals. They argue that political democracy is as essential to socialism as public ownership of the means of production, and that failure to practice political democracy subverts the very nature of socialism.

During the twentieth century, parties adhering to these principles (e.g., the New Democratic Party in Canada, the Labour Party in Britain, the Social Democratic Party in Germany, the Socialist Party in France) have developed large followings and won many elections. Because of the continuing appeal of capitalist principles in these societies, however, none of these parties has tried to abolish entirely private ownership of the means of production. Although they have taken some steps in that direction (i.e., they have nationalized some industries), the major thrust of their policies has been the creation of a *welfare state*. In other words, they have used the powers of government to tax the profits of privately owned enterprises in order to fund health, educational, and social service programs that benefit ordinary citizens who do not own any significant amount of property. This allows everyone to share in the benefits of the productive system without totally abolishing private ownership and control.

In contrast, the other major faction within the socialist movement has doubted the possibility of achieving socialism through peaceful, democratic means. In the view of revolutionary socialists, this can be achieved only by force and by the expropriation of private property. The spiritual father of revolutionary socialism is Karl Marx, whose writings and political activities in the nineteenth century laid the foundation for the Communist parties of the twentieth century. In societies controlled by his followers, he has occupied an honored status not unlike that accorded great religious figures of the past. His doctrines have been taught to children in all the schools, his writings have been cited by the party elite to justify their policies, and pictures and statues of him have been placed in prominent locations.

Marx believed that the evils found in societies can all be traced to the influence of the institution of private property. This institution stimulates greed and selfishness, exploitation, injustice, and oppression. By destroying it, humans can free themselves forever from these evils and set human societies on a new course that will lead in time to the development of a world in which freedom, justice, and equality prevail and in which everyone's material and spiritual needs are met.

Marx based these beliefs on a complex and interesting theory of history in which

FIGURE 10.4 Karl Marx.

he argued that capitalism contains the seeds of its own destruction and that socialist revolutions, led by members of the then-new and growing army of industrial workers, are not only inevitable but will ultimately prevail. In short, after a brief but bloody period of revolution, human societies will advance to a stage of societal development in which everyone's legitimate needs and desires will be fulfilled. In an initial phase of this new stage of development, people will be rewarded according to the socialist principle, "to each according to his *work*." In a later, higher phase of development, people will be rewarded according to the communist principle, "to each according to his *need*."

Marxist socialism is a far more comprehensive ideology than either capitalism or democratic socialism. Where these other ideologies allow people to make their own choices in most aspects of their lives, Marxism has traditionally imposed its own standards on everything from politics and economics to art and religion. In this respect, Marxism resembles traditional religions more than it does other modern ideologies.[17]

Revolutionary socialism makes broad claims on the lives not only of its adherents but of all who come under its power. Despite its professed aim of maximizing human freedom, it has become the most totalitarian and repressive of all the major new ideologies. This seeming paradox reflects to a great degree the influence of Vladimir Ilich Lenin, Marx's foremost disciple. Lenin extended and modified some of Marx's key ideas in ways that profoundly influenced the subsequent course of revolutionary socialism. It is no mere coincidence that in revolutionary socialist societies, Lenin has usually been honored and revered even more highly than Marx himself.[18]

Lenin's chief contribution to revolutionary socialism was to define the role of the Communist Party in *post*revolutionary societies. Not surprisingly, since Marx died in 1883, thirty-four years before the first successful socialist revolution, his writings dealt primarily with prerevolutionary conditions. He had relatively little to say about postrevolutionary societies and was generally vague and unspecific in what he did say. Lenin, in contrast, wrote extensively on the subject. In his writings he gave an important new meaning to a concept that Marx had mentioned only briefly and in an ambiguous manner: *the dictatorship of the proletariat*, or working class.

Marx had written that such a dictatorship would probably be necessary for a brief period after a socialist revolution in order to effect the transition from capitalism to socialism.[19] Lenin took this concept and gave it a striking new meaning: for him, the "dictatorship of the proletariat" became the justification for seemingly permanent dictatorship by the leaders of the Communist Party.[20] Lenin justified this on the elitist principle that ordinary workers are not qualified to govern and must be controlled by the Party's leaders, since only they understand the principles of "scientific" socialism.

Because of Lenin, modern revolutionary socialism became a curious combination of radical goals and reactionary means. Marxism-Leninism, as the dominant version of modern revolutionary socialism has come to be known, still claims its goal is to establish freedom, justice, and equality throughout the world, but it proposes to achieve this by the dictatorial rule of tiny elites. Unfortunately, when Leninist means (i.e., the rule of these elites) and Marxist ends (i.e., freedom, justice, equality) come into conflict, as they often do, Party leaders have, until recently, invariably given priority to the means.* For them, the preservation of Party power, which also meant their own power, became the highest priority.[22] As a result, Marxism-Leninism has provided a remarkably effective ideological justification for establishing elite rule and preserving the political status quo. Thus, ironically, an ideology that began as a radical, idealistic, even utopian faith was transformed into a remarkably reactionary and elitist political doctrine wherever its adherents came to power.†

The fifth of the major new secular ideologies is *nationalism*.[23] As with other ideologies, some of its elements have existed for thousands of years: group loyalty and tribalism, for example, are hardly new. During the agrarian era, however, the peasant masses, who made up 80 percent or more of the population, had little interest in politics beyond the village level.[24] The rise and fall of empires were of no concern to them—unless, of course, they were drawn into these struggles against their will. This lack of interest in politics at the national level was only natural in societies in which the dominant ideology defined the state as the private property of the ruler.

With industrialization, the situation began to change. Expanded educational systems, increasing urbanization, shorter workweeks, an improved standard of living, and the new mass media all combined to bring politics within the sphere of concern of the average individual. With this came a heightened sense of personal identification with the nation-state, especially in times of international tension and conflict. Nationalism has been a potent ideology in colonial territories ever since the American Revolution, and it is important today in many societies of the Third World that have recently become free of colonial control. It has also become a potent force among ethnic and religious minorities in industrial societies, such as the French in Canada, Catholics in Ulster, Basques in Spain, blacks and Hispanics in the United States, and a variety of ethnic minorities in the Soviet Union.

In many societies in recent decades, nationalism has been combined with other ideologies. The Nazi (literally, National Socialist) regime in Germany prior to World War II is one example. In American society, nationalism of a far milder variety is often linked to Christianity and capitalism to form what some have called the nation's "civil religion."[25]

The last of the major new ideologies, *pragmatism*, differs from all the others in one essential respect: it offers no preconceived ideas as to how societies should be organized. Rather, it asserts that social institutions should be judged by their conse-

---

*The elitist character of modern Communist parties cannot be attributed entirely to Lenin, since Marx himself provided a strong initial impetus in this direction.[21] In his own participation in the revolutionary socialist movement of his day, Marx was extremely autocratic and unwilling to share power with those who disagreed with him. Nevertheless, Lenin seems to have been primarily responsible for institutionalizing elitist rule under postrevolutionary conditions. His doctrine of "democratic centralism," which places all power within the Party in the hands of a tiny elite of self-chosen leaders, made efforts to democratize the Party all but impossible. Similarly, his doctrine of the "leading role" of the Party made it extraordinarily difficult to have political pluralism and democratic elections in societies controlled by Leninists.

†In societies in which they are *not* in power, Marxist-Leninists are more easily able to project an image of idealism, since their primary role in these societies is that of critic of the existing elite, and every elite is vulnerable to criticism.

quences and those that prove beneficial should be strengthened and preserved while those that are not should be eliminated.

The spiritual father of modern pragmatism was the American philosopher William James. Like Adam Smith and Karl Marx, he developed, expanded, and systematized certain ideas that had existed for centuries. But, unlike the teachings of Smith and Marx, his have not given rise to any organized group of disciples. Yet the basic principles of pragmatism have been adopted widely in the modern world. In fact, it would be no exaggeration to say that many contemporary world leaders who profess to believe in other ideologies are also, to greater or lesser degree, pragmatists. (Deng Xiaoping, China's recent Communist leader, once said, regarding his un-Marxist economic innovations, that he did not care if a cat was black or white as long as it caught the mouse.) Such leaders have discovered that no ideology provides a completely satisfactory blueprint for organizing and governing society. If they hope to be successful, or merely retain power, they have to improvise, and this means they have to adopt the pragmatic principle of judging policies and programs by their consequences.

The extent to which they do this varies considerably: Hungarian Marxists, for example, have been much more pragmatic than Czech Marxists, just as some of Adam Smith's followers have been much more pragmatic and flexible than others. The important point is that the principle of judging social arrangements by their results has become characteristic of an ever-increasing number of the leaders of modern societies.

FIGURE 10.5 William James.

Surprising as it may seem, despite their many differences, the new secular ideologies all have one thing in common: *they are all based on the belief that human destiny is largely subject to human control.* This is in sharp contrast to ideologies that originated in the preindustrial past. Those ideologies asserted that events depended on forces beyond human control—fate, God, the gods—and taught that the way to appease those forces was through magic, ritual, and adherence to tradition.

Members of modern societies are not nearly so passive. New information in areas ranging from science to history has improved their understanding of human nature and of the world they inhabit, while new technological information has increased their capacity to alter and adapt to that world. The result has been a growing awareness of humanity's potential for shaping its own future. This awareness underlies all of the new secular ideologies of the industrial era, and the members of contemporary societies have come to rely increasingly on these ideologies, and less and less on traditional ones, in their efforts to control their lives and shape the life of society as a whole.

DIFFERENCES AMONG INDUSTRIAL SOCIETIES

Because of their similar technologies and their increasingly pragmatic ideologies, industrial societies are similar to one another in many ways, as is apparent to anyone who has traveled among them. There are also, of course, important differences, and these reflect differences in their biophysical environments, in their social environments, and in numerous features of the cultures they have inherited from the past (see Figure 1.4, page 18). The effects of such differences can be clearly seen when we compare traditionally Protestant Sweden in northern Europe with traditionally Catholic Italy in southern Europe, for example, or former frontier societies, such as Australia and the United States, with their motherland, England.

The most significant differences among industrial societies in the twentieth century, however, have been consequences of the new *secular* ideologies. As technology has expanded the limits of the possible for these societies and increased the range of their alternatives, *the ideologies that guide them in choosing among the alternatives and in using their enormous economic surpluses have become an important source of societal variation.* Industrial societies have many potentially significant options available to them that were not available to any society in the past, and they are guided in making their choices among these options by the beliefs and values contained in their ideologies.

The importance of ideology was never more evident than in the revolutionary socialist societies of eastern Europe—the Soviet Union, East Germany, Czechoslovakia, Poland, and Hungary*—and in comparisons of these societies with the much more pragmatic democracies of western Europe, North America (Canada and the United States), Oceania (Australia and New Zealand), and Japan. Prior to the 1990s, differences between these two sets of societies were strikingly evident in their polities,

---

*Although Albania, Bulgaria, Romania, and Yugoslavia have also been revolutionary socialist societies, we will not include them in our discussions in Chapters 10 to 14, since none of them is fully industrialized.

economies, education, mass media, stratification, religion, and even art. Although many of these differences have sharply declined or even disappeared (see "The Autumn of 1989: A Special Note"), others are likely to remain for some time to come. Thus, in discussing industrial societies, we will often differentiate between the patterns and practices that have prevailed in the revolutionary socialist societies of eastern Europe and those in the western democracies.

The Autumn of 1989: A Special Note

Twenty years ago, in the first edition of *Human Societies*, we discussed the important differences between the western industrial democracies and the revolutionary socialist societies of eastern Europe. We also drew attention, however, to a number of often overlooked changes that were even then occurring in eastern Europe (e.g., greater pragmatism of leaders, gradual changes in some of their economies and polities)—changes that were causing those societies to become more like other industrial societies.[26] At that time, we predicted, on the basis of ecological–evolutionary theory, that these trends would almost certainly continue and would lead to a gradual convergence of the two sets of industrial societies.[27] We repeated this prediction in each subsequent edition.

As we prepare this, the sixth edition of *Human Societies*, the process of change in eastern Europe has accelerated enormously, surprising everyone, ourselves included. Each day brings dramatic changes. We naturally rejoice in the changes occurring at this time, primarily because they appear to mark the close of a long, dark night of oppression for hundreds of millions of people and because they lessen the threat of a nuclear holocaust.

But we are also happy in our role as sociologists. For one thing, *glasnost* and the dramatic political changes of recent months have unleashed a flood of new information about life in revolutionary socialist societies, facts that were once closely guarded secrets (e.g., homelessness, crime, the privileged lifestyle of political elites). And we are equally pleased that events have so stunningly confirmed the basic premise of ecological–evolutionary theory, that technology has been the most potent force in societal development. Indeed, *when the demands of industrialization collided with the requirements of ideology in the societies of eastern Europe, it was the latter that were forced to yield*.

We do not pretend to foresee what will happen in eastern Europe in the immediate future: after all, the "limits of the possible" for those societies are broad, and short-run reversals of recent trends would not be surprising. But we continue to predict that, *in the long run*, there will be a further reduction in the differences among industrial societies.

The Authors

Even if all of the differences between these two sets of industrial societies were to disappear tomorrow, it would still be important to know what the revolutionary socialist societies of eastern Europe were like. The rulers of those societies, guided by Marxist ideology, conducted some of the most important social experiments in human history, testing the "limits of the possible" in new and important ways. Students of human societies need to study these efforts and learn why and how they failed, since we can often learn as much from experiments that fail as from those that succeed.

Societies *within* each of the two basic sets of industrial societies also differ, of course. In the east bloc, the Soviet Union has long been politically dominant, but East Germany and Czechoslovakia have been technologically more advanced and their citizens have enjoyed a higher standard of living, while Hungary and Poland have been the most innovative politically and economically. Again, such differences reflect the diverse past experiences, environments, and cultural heritages of these societies.

Among the western democracies, the United States enjoyed political and economic preeminence for several decades following World War II, but more recently it has been challenged economically by Japan. In matters of ideology, the democracies differ considerably in the degree to which they have adopted and institutionalized the principles of socialism or, conversely, of capitalism. Since the primary difference between socialists and capitalists concerns the issue of *how and by whom* basic economic decisions are made, the relative strength of the two ideologies in a society is reflected in *the extent to which its economy is controlled by government.*

One measure of this control is how much of a society's GDP (gross domestic product) or national income the government controls through taxes (see Table 11.4, page 285). Taxation rates are highest in the Scandinavian democracies—nearly twice as high, in fact, as in Japan and the United States. This reflects the popularity of democratic socialism in Scandinavia and the success of its Social Democratic parties in creating and expanding what has come to be called "the welfare state" or "welfare capitalism." In contrast, the much lower levels of taxation in Japan and the United States reflect the preference of a majority of their citizens for individual, as opposed to governmental, decision making in economic matters.

As we will soon see, *when members of industrial societies are given a choice, most of them choose a mixture of socialism and capitalism in preference to either pure socialism or pure capitalism.* To a great extent, this preference is the result of painful experiences with the more extreme versions of these two ideologies. In recent years, this has been especially evident in eastern Europe, where even Communist Party leaders have tried to reintroduce into their economies some of the elements of capitalism that would encourage individual initiative and decision making.

POPULATION

Growth in Size of Societies

Industrialization has led to a substantial increase in the size of most human societies since the beginning of the industrial era. Population growth in the most fully industrialized societies, however, has not been nearly as great as their technological advances and gains in productivity would lead one to expect. For example, England and Wales had a population of approximately 9 million at the start of the nineteenth century, and their current population is about 50 million.[28] While this five- to sixfold increase is impressive when compared to rates of population growth in the preindustrial past, it falls far short of the hundredfold increase in Britain's gross national product during that same period. The same thing is true of other societies that have industrialized, with the exception of the United States, Canada, Australia, and other former frontier societies that entered the industrial era with abnormally small populations for their geographical size.

Trends in Health and Longevity

Throughout the agrarian era, sickness and disease were a pervasive feature of human life. Prior to the invention of the microscope, it was impossible for anyone even to know of the existence of bacteria or viruses, much less to devise effective means of combating them. Medical knowledge was not advanced much beyond what had existed at the end of the hunting and gathering era and, for most illnesses, people were forced to rely on faith healing, magic, or medical practices of dubious value (e.g., the use of leeches and bloodletting) when they became ill. As we have seen (page 173), average life expectancy at birth in even the most advanced societies ranged from 20 to 25 years, and even the children of royalty and the upper classes did not have a much greater life expectancy.

During the industrial era, however, there has been an explosive growth in the store of information concerning the prevention and cure of disease—especially communicable diseases, such as influenza, tuberculosis, diphtheria, and smallpox, that once killed large numbers of people and afflicted many more. As a result, the death rate from communicable diseases has dropped tremendously (see Table 10.2) and life ex-

TABLE 10.2 Death Rates for Communicable Diseases, 1860–1986

Cause of Death	Deaths per 100,000 Population per Year		
	Mass., 1860*	U.S., 1900	U.S., 1986
Influenza and pneumonia	†	202	14
Tuberculosis	365	194	1
Gastritis, enteritis, etc.	†	143	0
Typhoid fever	76	31	0
Diphtheria	68	40	0
Smallpox	27	†	0
Measles	18	13	0
Scarlet fever	†	10	0

*Massachusetts was the first state to keep reliable statewide records on the causes of death; reliable national data are not available until 1900.

†Not reported.

Source: Historical Statistics of the United States: Colonial Times to 1970, pp. 58 and 63; *Statistical Abstract of the United States, 1989*, table 117.

pectancy at birth has tripled in industrial societies. Today, newborns in most of these societies can expect to live 70 years or more, on average. Equally important, they will live far healthier lives than was possible in most preindustrial societies.

In recent decades, however, there have been disturbing reversals in these long-term trends in several of the revolutionary socialist societies. In Hungary, for example, life expectancy at birth for males has declined from 68.1 years in 1966 to 65.6 years.[29] There have been similar reversals in other eastern European societies. In the Soviet Union, the downward trend became so embarrassing that the government has not published statistics on deaths since 1976.[30]

The reasons for these reversals in longevity are not entirely clear, but the political and economic problems of these societies appear to play the major role. In Hungary, for example, despite relaxed political controls and relative affluence by Soviet-bloc standards, alcoholism, industrial accidents, and suicide have all increased. Deaths from cirrhosis of the liver (due to excessive use of alcohol) have risen more than 350 percent since 1966, and deaths from industrial accidents and suicide more than 50 percent.[31]

Patterns in the Soviet Union are similar to those in Hungary. Twice in the last decade, Soviet leaders felt compelled to launch nationwide campaigns to reduce alcohol consumption,[32] and Soviet sociologists have found that the suicide rate is rising.[33] Western observers report that industrial accidents take a heavy toll, and identify several other factors as sources of recent trends in health and longevity: increasing environmental pollution, rising infant mortality, declining standards of health care, and apparent reductions in governmental expenditures on health care.[34]

Declining Birthrates and Increasing Immigration

As health conditions improved and death rates declined, industrial societies experienced a period of rapid population growth. This was because birthrates remained at traditional levels, which created a widening gap between birthrates and death rates.

Within a few decades, however, birthrates also began to decline. During the last 150 years, technological advances on various fronts (e.g., the vulcanization of rubber, the development of the contraceptive pill, safe methods of abortion and sterilization) have made it possible for members of industrial societies to control the number of their offspring by safe and effective means. At the same time, technological advances in other areas, together with various social changes (e.g., the creation of social security programs, prohibitions against child labor), have virtually eliminated the historic *economic* incentive for having children. In addition, the increasing employment of women outside the home has made child-rearing more difficult and more expensive. As a result, birthrates have dropped greatly in all industrial societies.

In most industrial societies, in fact, birthrates have dropped substantially below the level required to keep populations at their present size. To maintain stable populations, women in industrial societies today must have, on average, about 2.15 children each.* As Table 10.3 makes clear, the fertility rate in almost every industrial society is well below this figure. Should Italy's birthrate continue at its present level, for

*To achieve this, 15 percent would have to produce three offspring, and the rest two. Since about 10 percent of couples are infertile, however, nearly 40 percent of women would have to have three children.

TABLE 10.3 **Total Fertility Rates in Industrial Societies**

Society	TFR	Society	TFR
Italy	1.3	France	1.8
West Germany	1.4	Norway	1.8
Austria	1.5	United Kingdom	1.8
Denmark	1.5	Australia	1.9
Belgium	1.6	New Zealand	1.9
Finland	1.6	Sweden	1.9
Netherlands	1.6	United States	1.9
Canada	1.7	Czechoslovakia	2.1[*]
East Germany	1.7[*]	Poland	2.3[*]
Japan	1.7	Soviet Union	2.4[*]

[*]TFR from 1988 report; all others from 1989 report.

Sources: World Bank, *World Development Report 1989* (New York: Oxford University Press, 1989), table 27; and *World Development Report 1988*, Table 28.

example, that nation could experience as much as a 40 percent decline in population size in the next seventy or seventy-five years, while Austria, West Germany, Denmark, Belgium, the Netherlands, Finland, and Switzerland face possible declines ranging from 25 to 35 percent.

Declines of these magnitudes are unlikely, however, because of the great influx of immigrants from the Third World. The economic opportunities and high standards of living in the industrial democracies, together with the growth of the welfare state and its many benefits, are a powerful magnet for people whose own societies are suffering the throes of early industrialization. According to one recent report, there are now more than 13 million *legal* immigrants in western Europe, and an unknown number of illegal ones.[35] Currently, about 40 percent of schoolchildren in the small industrial society of Luxembourg, on the border between France and Germany, are children of Portuguese immigrants.[36] In New York City, more than 40 percent of the children entering kindergarten are from homes in which some language other than English is used.[37] In West Berlin, one of every four schoolchildren is non-German.[38] Twenty percent of Australia's population is foreign-born, 16 percent of Canada's, 11 percent of France's.[39] And in England, there are some schools in which not a single English child is enrolled.[40] (This has not been a problem in the revolutionary social-ist societies of eastern Europe, since migrants from the Third World have shown little inclination to settle in any of those societies.)

Changes of this magnitude create problems in any society and are especially serious when substantial cultural differences are introduced into populations that have been culturally homogeneous for centuries. It is difficult to exaggerate, for example, the cultural gulf that separates devout Muslims from Pakistan, Turkey, and Algeria from the nominally Christian but largely secularist native populations of England, Germany, and France.[*] Even when the migrants are Christians from southern Europe, as with

---

[*]One indication of the magnitude of this gulf emerged in the late 1980s when Muslim immigrants in England—a nation that prides itself on freedom of expression—threatened to assassinate the author of a book they found offensive, while burning his book in public rallies and threatening stores that sold it. More recently, problems have emerged in France, where Muslim immigrants have challenged traditional dress codes in the schools.

FIGURE 10.6 Immigration from the Third World to advanced industrial societies has become so great that immigrants often outnumber the native population in large sections of major cities: Turkish shops in the Kreuzberg district of West Berlin.

Yugoslav immigrants in Germany or the Portuguese in Luxembourg, the effect can be unsettling.

In addition to the strains imposed by the relatively rapid introduction of a new and vastly different culture into a society, the situation calls for exceptional responses from a variety of institutions. No industrial society, for example, could possibly create enough jobs for all the would-be immigrants from the Third World: many of them already find it difficult to create and maintain sufficient jobs to satisfy their own citizens. And competition for jobs and welfare benefits is an almost certain formula for ethnic and racial strife.

It is not surprising, therefore, that several new political parties have emerged in the western democracies with the aim of restricting immigration. While supporters of these parties have been accused of bigotry and prejudice, it is clear that important issues and interests are involved. The twentieth century has shown that ethnic and religious conflicts are among the most intractable of all intrasocietal conflicts. Unfortunately, though the danger signals are increasingly evident, political leaders of the major parties, except in Japan, seem determined to ignore the problem as long as possible.[41]

Population Distribution: The Growth of Urban Populations

Another revolutionary demographic change has been the massive shift of population from rural areas to cities and towns. Even in the most advanced agrarian societies, the limitations of agricultural technology required that 90 to 95 percent of the population live in rural areas, where the basic raw materials were produced. Since urban com-

FIGURE 10.7   Cities in industrial societies are much larger than cities in agrarian societies. The population of greater New York now numbers about 16 million.

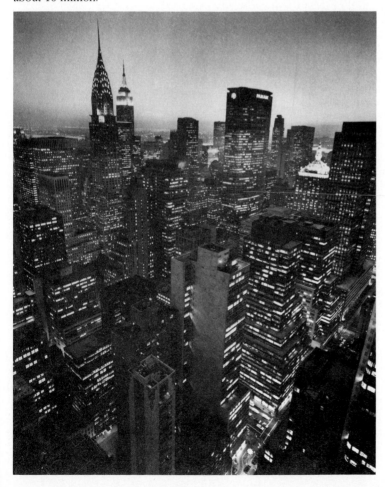

munities were largely dependent on the surplus that could be extracted from the peasantry, they could never grow beyond 5 to 10 percent of the population.

Advances in agriculture in the last two hundred years removed this constraint on urban growth. Thanks to the new technology, farms required fewer workers (see Table 10.1, page 249). Simultaneously, the new system of factory production, with its need for large concentrations of workers, stimulated the growth of cities and towns. As a result, three-quarters or more of the populations of industrial societies now live in urban areas.

Nowhere are the consequences of the Industrial Revolution more clearly evident than in the major cities of the industrial world. Vast concentrations of people live and work in organizational systems of extraordinary complexity. Most of the time these systems function so smoothly that we forget the complex infrastructure of water and sewer systems, power systems, communications systems, and transportation systems on which they depend. It is only when we encounter such disasters as earthquakes, hurricanes, or war, and these systems begin to unravel, that we are reminded of the technological foundation on which industrial societies are built and on which they depend.

11

Industrial Societies: Their Economies

The economy of a society is, in effect, an institutionalized set of answers to the basic questions of production and distribution: What kinds of goods and services will be produced? In what quantities? At what prices? And by what means will they be allocated to the various members of society?

The way in which these questions are answered reflects, to a large degree, constraints imposed by the environment, by the technology on which a society depends, and by the necessity of keeping the productive system functioning. But it also reflects the beliefs and values—the ideology—of those who control the society. Thus, as we have noted, there have been fundamental differences between the economies of the revolutionary socialist societies of eastern Europe and the western industrial democracies, as well as less profound differences within both sets of societies.

Before we consider these differences further, we need to consider a number of characteristics that are common to the economies of *all* industrial societies. These shared characteristics, too, are important. They are due chiefly to constraints imposed by the new technology on which each of these societies depends.

CHARACTERISTICS COMMON TO ALL INDUSTRIAL ECONOMIES

The Urbanization of Production

Prior to the Industrial Revolution, agriculture was the chief form of economic activity, production was centered in rural areas, and farmers were a substantial majority of the labor force. In addition to farming, the rural population often engaged in a variety of crafts during the winter months, using this less demanding period as a time to earn additional income. Urban populations were small, and many urban residents were members of the governing class and not actively involved in the labor force. Moreover, many of the urban dwellers who were employed produced nonessential goods and services for the enjoyment of the upper class.

The Industrial Revolution changed all this. As we saw in Chapter 9, the new machines required the development of factories and large concentrations of industrial workers. At the same time that new urban industries were generating a growing demand for workers in cities and towns, technological advances in agriculture were reducing the need for workers on farms. As a result, industrialization led to a massive migration of people from rural areas to urban—a migration that only now seems to be nearing its end in the most advanced industrial societies.

The effect of these changes has been to shift the locus of production in societies from rural areas to urban. In advanced industrial societies today, less than 15 percent of gross domestic product (GDP) comes from agricultural activity, and in most cases it is less than 5 percent.[1] Equally important, the rural economy of industrial societies has been completely transformed. Many of the people who live in rural areas today commute to work in urban communities. In much of eastern Europe, for example, there is a segment of the population that has come to be known as worker-peasants: the men commute to cities and towns where they work in factories during the week, and on weekends they help the women on the farms. (Women generally continue to work on the farms during the week.) Similar patterns have also developed in western societies: by 1970 the majority of American "farmers" were already earning more from nonfarm activities (e.g., work in factories) than from the sale of farm products.[2]

Rise in Productivity and in the Standard of Living

The most striking characteristic of the economies of industrial societies is their remarkable productivity. As we noted earlier, Britain's gross national product has grown approximately a hundredfold since 1801, and that of the United States about fiftyfold just since 1878. Most other industrialized societies have experienced comparable growth. Because most of this increase in productivity has not been consumed by population growth, there has been an enormous increase in the size of the economic surplus in every industrial society.

In agrarian societies, any new surplus would have been taken almost entirely by a small minority of the population. In industrial societies, the surplus is spread far more widely among the members.[3] In other words, the growth of the economic surplus has greatly improved the standard of living for the vast majority of people in most of these societies (the improvement has not been nearly as great in the Soviet Union and Poland). Per capita income in Britain today is about *twenty* times what it was in 1801, early in the Industrial Revolution, and in the United States it is *eleven* times greater than in 1878, the first year for which such data are available.

That these figures reflect real gains in the living standards of the masses is evident when we consider the lifestyle of the average member of most industrial societies today—keeping in mind the situation of the typical peasant in agrarian societies of the past and of workers during the early phases of the Industrial Revolution. Most members of industrial societies today enjoy a food supply that is larger, more dependable (i.e., less subject to acute shortages), and of higher quality and greater va-

FIGURE 11.1 The most striking characteristic of the economies of industrial societies is their remarkable productivity: Saks Fifth Avenue, a New York department store.

riety than was available in any agrarian society of the past. Most live in superior housing, with an indoor water supply, plumbing, electricity, usually central heating, and sometimes even air conditioning in warmer climates. The majority of their homes and apartments are equipped with furnishings and appliances that are more than adequate for health and comfort, and some of them would have aroused envy in the elites of agrarian societies of the past. Widespread educational opportunities are available, and so is vastly improved health care. Modern transportation and communication systems broaden and enrich their lives and provide them with varied forms of entertainment. And countless other goods and services too numerous to catalog, and unheard of in agrarian societies, are also available to the majority of people in most industrial societies, and to a large minority in the rest.

This is not to suggest that life in industrial societies is free of problems: obviously, it is not. But it is clear that industrialization has meant a remarkable improvement in the standard of living for the average individual compared with the average individual in preindustrial or early industrial societies. Relative to the peasant masses of the agrarian era, most members of industrial societies live lives of unbelievable affluence and abundance. And there are very few people in these societies whose standard of living approaches the degradation of the expendables of agrarian societies. Even those dependent on public welfare are much better off than that.

The Shift from Labor-Intensive to Capital-Intensive Industries

The basis of the enormous productivity and affluence of modern industrial societies is their fantastic store of technological information. But most of this information would be useless unless it were *converted into capital goods*. Without the complex machines, factories, transportation facilities, power plants, and other capital goods essential to production in an industrial society, the output of its workers would not be much greater than that of workers in agrarian societies.

We can see the importance of capital goods when we compare two contemporary industries, one capital-intensive and the other labor-intensive. The petroleum industry is a good example of the former: it has expensive, highly automated machinery and a small labor force. The fast-food industry, utilizing simpler and less expensive machines, is far more labor-intensive. Exxon, for example, recently reported average annual sales of more than $850,000 *per employee*, while the sales of McDonald's hamburger chain amounted to only $40,000 per employee per year.[4]

One of the chief reasons for the tremendous growth in per capita GNP in industrial societies has been the massive movement of workers away from small, capital-poor family farms and into capital-intensive industries during the last 150 years. As

FIGURE 11.2 The petroleum industry is a capital-intensive industry requiring heavy investment in machines but minimal investment in human labor: Soviet oil refinery in Kazakhstan.

these farmers joined the urban labor force, their economic contribution increased substantially. Since about 80 percent of the population of the typical agrarian society were food producers, in contrast to a tiny minority—in some cases less than 5 percent—in industrial societies, the impact of that shift has been tremendous.

Today, however, that flow has largely ended, and with it a major boost to economic growth. The small, traditional family farm has been largely replaced by huge agribusinesses, state farms, and collective farms that are as capital-intensive as some urban-based industries. To appreciate the changes that have occurred in farming, one need only consider First Colony Farms, a 375,000-acre, $700 million enterprise in northeastern North Carolina.[5] This highly mechanized, capital-intensive agribusiness employs fewer than 1,000 workers and operates on the same basis as any other large corporation. Its products are sold in national and international markets.

Cows and Computers

Ron Van Zee and his brother, Bill, still like to think of their dairy farm as a "family farm," but a visit to the barn suggests otherwise. All of their 200 cows are now linked to computers that provide the Van Zees with a detailed set of records on each cow, and the computer is hooked to a radio transmitter that controls each animal's allotment of feed.

As the cows are milked mechanically, Ron Van Zee punches their ID numbers into the computer. If one light goes on, it means that the cow's milk is fit to drink, but if another light goes on it means that the cow is medicated and her milk must be discarded. Stored in the computer is a file on every cow in the herd, with eighty statistics on each, such as her milk production, milk-fat content, and the number of calves she has produced. There is even a measure of her disposition, on a scale from 1 to 9.

The Van Zees lease their computer system for $900 a month and believe their investment has been well worth the expense. Since introducing the computer, they have been able to reduce the feed their cows consume by 1,650 pounds per day by adjusting the amount each receives to take account of where she is in the calving cycle. Research has shown that there are times in the cycle when extra feed only produces useless fat, not more milk. When a cow sticks her head into a computerized feed trough, her four-digit ID number is transmitted to the computer, which scans the relevant data and determines whether more food is indicated. If she has not yet eaten her allotted amount, the feeder is instructed to crank out another serving. As a minor incidental benefit of the new system, the Van Zees have the computer programmed to alert them if the door to the feeding parlor has been left open by accident.

Source: Wall Street Journal.

Although agricultural operations on this scale are still unusual, small-scale farming with minimal capitalization is becoming a thing of the past. According to the most recent U.S. census of agriculture, the average value of the land, equipment, buildings, and other resources of full-time farmers in Iowa is approximately $500,000, and in California it is more than $1,000,000.[6]

Changes in the Labor Force

The Shift from Primary Industries From the onset of industrialization there has been a movement of workers out of primary industries, the ones that produce raw materials (i.e., farming, fishing, mining. and forestry). In traditional agrarian societies these industries provided a livelihood for 80 percent or more of the labor force. With industrialization, most of these people, or their children, gradually moved either into secondary industries, the mills and factories that process the raw materials and turn them into finished products, or into tertiary industries, which provide the great variety of services found in industrial societies—education, health care, police and fire protection, social services, government, retail trade, and so on. As industrialization proceeds, the initial rapid growth in secondary industries slows down considerably, and tertiary industries become the chief area of growth in the economy.

Table 11.1 shows how striking this process has been in the United States, completely transforming the labor force in the last 140 years. From a 70 percent concentration of workers in primary industries, there are now 70 percent in tertiary industries, and growth in these industries continues at the expense of the other two. Similar trends are found in every industrial society, although growth in the tertiary industries has been much less pronounced in the societies of eastern Europe.

Growth of White-Collar Jobs Another striking change in the labor force has been the rapid expansion of white-collar, or nonmanual, jobs. This trend is especially evident in the United States. At the beginning of the present century, only 17 percent of American workers were employed in white-collar jobs; today, 60 percent are in such jobs.[7]

The rapid growth of white-collar jobs has been associated with the growth of the tertiary, or service, industries. As opportunities for farm employment have de-

TABLE 11.1 Changing Patterns of Employment in the American Labor Force, 1840 to 1987: Percentages Employed in Primary, Secondary, and Tertiary Industries

Year	Primary Industries	Secondary Industries	Tertiary Industries	Total
1840	69	15	16	100
1870	55	21	24	100
1900	40	28	32	100
1930	23	29	48	100
1960	8	30	62	100
1987	4	25	71	100

Sources: Calculations based on *Historical Statistics of the United States: Colonial Times to 1970,* series D152–166; and *Statistical Abstract of the United States, 1989,* table 645.

clined, opportunities for employment in clerical and sales work, the professions, and management have increased. More recently, jobs in the secondary industries (i.e., manufacturing, construction) have also begun to decline, both in absolute and in relative terms, and this has meant a decline in blue-collar jobs. In 1960, for example, 30 percent of American workers were employed in secondary industries. Today, that figure is only 25 percent (see Table 11.1).[8]

Increased Employment of Women Outside of Households   Until the twentieth century, most women worked only within households—as wives, mothers, sisters, or daughters in their own family's household, or as servants in someone else's. The Industrial Revolution and the new technology have changed all this. Today, the majority of women in industrial societies are also employed outside households, working for corporations, state enterprises, and other kinds of work organizations.

In many work organizations, especially in the service sector, a majority of the workers are women. This is particularly true of a number of white-collar jobs that have come to be identified as women's jobs (e.g., nursing, social work, elementary school teaching, secretarial work, clerical work, retail sales work of most kinds). Despite efforts by feminists to discourage the sexual division of labor, it is remarkably persistent, at least partly because of the preference of many women, but also because of the demands of marriage and family life.

Growth in the Size of Work Organizations   Workers today find themselves increasingly in the employ of organizations of enormous size. Governments have become the largest employers of all, even in nonsocialist societies. The federal government of the United States, for example, currently employs 5.2 million people,[9] while the governments of eleven states and municipalities employ more than 100,000 each (the largest, New York City, employs 395,000).[10] Many private corporations also employ large numbers of workers: General Motors has 766,000; Sears Roebuck, 520,000; and IBM, 387,000, to name three of the largest.[11]

Increase in Occupational Specialization   Growth in the size of work organizations along with advances in technology have been responsible for yet another important trend: the substantial increase in the level of occupational specialization. Contemporary industrial societies have an astonishing number of highly specialized occupations. The United States Department of Labor lists more than 20,000 different kinds of jobs that are found in American society today.[12] The meat-packing industry illustrates the extremes to which occupational specialization is often carried. Forty-hour-a-week jobs in that industry include:

belly opener	gut sorter	rump sawyer
bladder trimmer	head splitter	side splitter
brain picker	jowl trimmer	skull grinder
gland man	leg skinner	snout puller
gut puller	lung splitter	toe puller

Further increases in specialization seem unlikely in most blue-collar occupations, since extreme specialization appears to be counterproductive: workers quickly

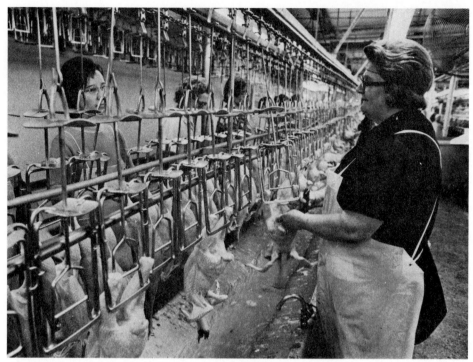

FIGURE 11.3 Extreme occupational specialization has been characteristic of industrial societies: women processing poultry.

become bored and this often leads to carelessness, hostility, and even sabotage. In many industries, management has responded by diversifying work activities, thus reversing the historic trend toward greater specialization. Indiana Bell Telephone, for example, used to assemble its telephone books in twenty-one steps, each performed by a different clerk. Now, each clerk has responsibility for assembling an entire book, with the result that labor turnover (a sensitive measure of worker morale) was reduced as much as 50 percent.[13] Volvo, the Swedish automobile manufacturer, developed two experiments to reduce boredom and improve morale. One is a system of job rotation involving work at a variety of highly specialized tasks; the other is a system of teamwork involving groups of three to nine workers who share a common set of responsibilities, choose their own leader, and are paid on the basis of group output.[14] These changes reduced Volvo's annual worker turnover from 40 to 10 percent. Other industries are responding to the problem of boredom by replacing workers with robots and other automated machines.

While the trend toward greater occupational specialization is apparently waning in blue-collar occupations, it is still growing in many kinds of white-collar jobs. This is especially evident in professional and managerial occupations, where many people seem to derive greater satisfaction from their work when their areas of responsibility and expertise are more narrowly defined. This is because professional and managerial occupations usually involve such complex bodies of information that no one can master them entirely; as a result, frustration is more likely to come from too little specialization than from too much. Thus, general practitioners in medicine have been largely replaced by a variety of medical specialists, just as general historians in the academic world have been replaced by specialists in such fields as medieval English history and nineteenth-century German history. In addition, some of the traditional components of professional and managerial jobs are now being performed by machines, and more efficiently. This is true, for example, of some kinds of teaching (e.g., foreign-language instruction, elementary math) and medical diagnosis (e.g., CAT scans, computerized laboratory tests).

Unemployment   As we saw in Chapter 7, widespread unemployment was a chronic problem in agrarian societies of the past. Except in the aftermath of plagues and famines, those societies always had a large class of expendables, people for whom there were no jobs and who were obliged to beg for a living or turn to criminal activities.

Despite the extraordinary economic successes of industrial societies in most respects, none has found a satisfactory solution to this problem. There is unemployment in all of them, even in the revolutionary socialist societies of eastern Europe.

As in agrarian societies of the past, the magnitude of the problem fluctuates, though no longer in response to plagues and famines. In western industrial societies, the rate of unemployment fluctuates in response both to business cycles and to the impact of major technological innovations that from time to time eliminate the need for large numbers of workers (e.g., the introduction of automation and robotics into the automobile and telephone industries).

At one time, revolutionary socialist societies seemed to have solved the problem by simply guaranteeing everyone a job. Eventually, however, the costs of this in terms of inadequate worker motivation, economic inefficiency, and low standards of living caused most of these societies to abandon this approach, and some of them now have rates of unemployment that equal or exceed those in the west; in the Soviet Union, unemployment rates are over 20 percent in several of the larger republics, according to *Pravda*.[15] Rates this high have not been seen in western industrial societies since the Great Depression of the 1930s.

While millions are unemployed in industrial societies today, work that would benefit society as a whole either is left undone or is addressed inadequately, from caring for the young, the aged, and others with special needs, to caring for urban and other environments. At the same time, these societies are forced to subsidize or support most of the individuals and families that lack jobs or unemployment benefits, but they do so in a variety of unsatisfactory and often demeaning ways that range from soup kitchens for the homeless to public housing and confinement in correctional institutions. These "solutions" often have a shockingly high price tag (in the United States, for example, it costs more to incarcerate the average prisoner than it would to send him or her to Harvard University for the same period of time). It is hard to believe that societies with so many options available to them will not soon devise better responses to this problem.

Formation of Labor Unions   Since the beginnings of the Industrial Revolution, large numbers of workers have found themselves confronted with similar problems and grievances, including long working hours (70-hour workweeks were not uncommon in the past), inadequate pay, dangerous working conditions, abusive supervisors, and lack of job security. These conditions have led to the formation of labor unions designed to protect and promote the common interests of workers.

In some instances, unions have been organized along craft or trade lines, such as bricklayers and carpenters unions. Others have been organized on an industry-wide basis, as in steel workers and auto workers unions. In several instances, unions have been organized on a national basis, with every worker in the entire nation eligible to join, as in the case of Solidarity in Poland.

The history of the labor union movement is a history of alternating periods of success and failure. In recent decades union membership in most western industrial societies has declined even as the labor force has been growing, and the influence of unions in collective bargaining and on legislation has fallen off appreciably.[16] Ironically, in the revolutionary socialist societies of eastern Europe, where independent labor unions were illegal, the trend has been different. During the 1980s Solidarity became a major force in Polish society, and workers elsewhere have begun to organize and act independently of the unions established and controlled by the Communist Party and the government. In 1989, seventy years after the Revolution that was supposedly for their benefit, Soviet workers finally won the right to strike (although they still could not organize independent labor unions and strikes are still illegal in a number of basic industries).[17]

THE ECONOMIES OF WESTERN INDUSTRIAL SOCIETIES

In the prehistoric past, before societies were able to produce a sustained economic surplus, all economies were essentially *subsistence* economies in which each community provided for its own members' needs, and trade and exchange were limited to nonessentials (e.g., feathers, amber, and other objects valued for ceremonial and esthetic reasons). With the shift from hunting and gathering to farming, conditions changed in a number of important ways. No longer was it necessary for all adults to be food producers. New and more specialized kinds of occupations developed, trade and commerce increased, and political systems developed that were able to impose the will of small political elites on the other members of society.

With these developments, subsistence economies came to be supplemented either by command economies or by market economies. A *command economy* is elitist: basic choices among economic alternatives are made by a tiny political elite. Sometimes these decision makers claim to act on behalf of the population as a whole, but they are not willing to transfer their enormous decision-making power to the larger population on whose behalf they claim to act.

In a *market economy*, in contrast, producers freely exchange what they produce for goods and services produced by others. Prices are set by the forces of supply and demand, that is, by the relative quantity and quality of the various things that are

FIGURE 11.4 Despite the Communist Party's claim to govern in the interest of the working class, Soviet workers were denied the right to strike until 1989, when this right was granted, but only in nonessential industries: Soviet miners striking illegally in July, 1989, for better food, a ban on special privileges for Party officials, and a new national constitution.

available and by the relative eagerness of would-be consumers. As this suggests, decision making in a market system is considerably more democratic than in a command economy.*

The Rise of Market Economies

The origins of modern market systems can be traced back to the simple barter systems of prehistoric societies. But a full-fledged market economy (i.e., one in which market forces shape the majority of major economic decisions) was not possible until the use of money became widespread and most of the goods and services people valued had acquired a monetary value. In addition, the basic economic resources of land, labor, and capital had to be freed from traditional constraints on their use and transfer. People had to be free to sell ancestral lands when that was profitable; workers had to be free to leave their jobs and take new ones when they could get higher

---

*Market economies, in contrast to command economies, resemble democratic systems of government in which everyone has a vote. The comparison is imperfect, however, because a market system allows wealthy individuals with their greater purchasing power to "vote" more often than poorer individuals, and therefore have a greater impact on the economy.

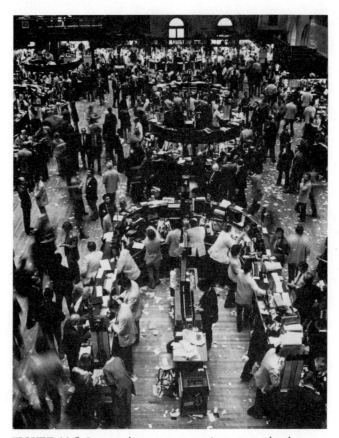

FIGURE 11.5 In a market economy, prices are set by the forces of supply and demand: floor of the New York Stock Exchange.

wages or better working conditions; and owners of businesses had to be free to use their capital however they wished. Restraints on economic activity based on family sentiments, religious taboos, social customs, or organizational restrictions (guild restrictions on output, for example, or legal restrictions on the movement of serfs and slaves) had to be substantially reduced or eliminated. In short, individual economic advantage, as measured in monetary terms, had to become the decisive determinant of economic action.

As we saw in Chapter 9, the discovery of the New World gave a powerful impetus to the first requirement: the great flow of gold and silver led to the emergence of a money economy in western Europe. At the same time, a series of ideological changes weakened traditional social bonds that had previously immobilized both people and property. These same factors also sparked the Industrial Revolution, and once that was under way and the economy had changed further, the effect became cumulative. Each change stimulated further change; the more resources that came under the control of western Europe's entrepreneurial class, the better able they were to promote other changes.

By the end of the nineteenth century it looked as if every industrial society would soon have a market economy. Industrial societies were coming increasingly under the control of political parties that were dominated by businessmen committed to the philosophy of laissez-faire capitalism, or free enterprise. Following the teachings of Adam Smith, this new governing class argued that the most productive economy, and the most beneficial, was one in which governmental restrictions were held to a minimum.

Moves toward Mixed Economies

It was not long, however, before it became evident that the new market economy was not the unmixed blessing its enthusiasts made it out to be. In their pursuit of profits, businessmen often adopted practices that were harmful to others. In an attempt to cut labor costs, many employers fired adult workers and replaced them with children, simultaneously creating adult unemployment and endangering the health and welfare of children. Efforts to reduce costs also led to dangerous working conditions and the production of shoddy, even unsafe, merchandise.

Protests soon began to be raised, sometimes by social reformers like Robert Owen, sometimes by poets and novelists like Thomas Hood and Upton Sinclair. Even before the middle of the last century, the British Parliament began enacting legislation to protect society against the extremes of free enterprise. The Factory Acts of 1833 and 1844, the Mines Act of 1842, and the Ten Hour Law of 1847 prohibited the employment of children under the age of 9 in textile factories, restricted children under 13 to six-and-a-half hours of work per day in factories, forbade the employment of women or of boys under 10 in the mines, limited women and young people aged 13 to 18 to ten working hours per day, and provided for inspectors to enforce these laws.[18] By 1901 the minimum age for child labor in England was raised to 12, and in 1908 limitations were finally imposed on the working hours of men. Other

FIGURE 11.6 Boys working in a British mine in the nineteenth century: after the Mines Act of 1842, boys under the age of 10 could no longer be employed in mines.

legislation forced employers to provide for the safety of their employees in dangerous industries and established the first minimum wage.

None of these reforms would have come about, however, without the efforts of workers themselves. By the latter part of the eighteenth century, small groups of workers had already begun banding together to negotiate with their employers on wages, hours, and working conditions. During the nineteenth century, the labor movement had many ups and downs, but by 1900 there were 2 million members of labor unions in Britain and nearly a million each in the United States and Germany.[19]

Before that date, however, another major defect in the market system had become evident. There was a tendency for it to lose its competitive character and evolve in the direction of monopolies. This danger was greatest in industries in which *fixed costs* were a significant part of total costs. Fixed costs are costs of production that do not increase in proportion to the quantity of goods produced. The costs of designing, tooling, and advertising a new model car, for example, are all fixed costs: they remain essentially the same whether 5 million cars of that model are produced or only 1 million. As a result, the company that sells 5 million cars can either price its cars less than its competitors or offer a better car for the same money. Either way, the larger company tends to win its rivals' customers, which increases its advantage even more.

Table 11.2 illustrates how, in an industry in which fixed costs are relatively great compared to variable costs, the company that has the highest volume of sales has *a growing competitive advantage*. Note that the amount that the three companies in the example spend on variable costs varies directly with the number of units each produces—one dollar per unit. But fixed costs are the same for each company—$5,000—regardless of how many units it produces. Thus, the differences in "cost per unit" are due entirely to the influence of fixed costs. Note also that the initial pricing advantage enjoyed by Company A because of its initial high volume of sales enables that com-

TABLE 11.2 Illustration of How Fixed Costs Contribute to the Growth of Monopoly in a Free Enterprise System

Time Period and Firm	Number of Units Sold	Variable Costs*	Fixed Costs*	Total Costs	Cost per Unit†
Time I:					
Company A	10,000	$10,000	$5,000	$15,000	$1.50
Company B	9,000	9,000	5,000	14,000	1.56
Company C	8,000	8,000	5,000	13,000	1.63
Time II:					
Company A	11,500	11,500	5,000	16,500	1.43
Company B	8,500	8,500	5,000	13,500	1.59
Company C	7,000	7,000	5,000	12,000	1.71
Time III:					
Company A	13,000	13,000	5,000	18,000	1.38
Company B	8,000	8,000	5,000	13,000	1.63
Company C	6,000	6,000	5,000	11,000	1.83

*Variable costs need not be exactly proportional to sales volume, and fixed costs need not be exactly identical for all firms, but they are shown this way to make the essential principles clearer.
†Cost per unit equals total cost divided by number of units sold.

pany to gain a growing share of the market, and, with it, an increasing ability to undersell its competitors. As this example illustrates, if pure market forces were allowed to operate with no restrictions, smaller competitors would eventually be forced out of business in any industry in which fixed costs are a significant part of total costs.

In an effort to prevent the growth of monopolies, the United States passed the Sherman Antitrust Act in 1890. Although it has not been vigorously enforced, this act has served as a deterrent. A number of industries might now be dominated by a single company had not the managers of the leading firms been fearful of the legal consequences. For example, economists and even industry leaders have testified before Congress that economies of scale made it possible for General Motors to undersell its American competitors by a substantial margin for years. But rather than face antitrust action, GM's managers chose to price their cars competitively, thereby increasing their profits while perhaps offering their customers a bit more car for the money.[20]

The situation in which an industry is dominated not by a single firm but by a very few of them is known as *oligopoly*. This has become common in capitalist societies. Table 11.3 gives some idea of the current situation in the United States. As a rough rule of thumb, economists consider an industry oligopolistic when as few as four companies control 50 percent or more of production.[21] This standard can be deceptive, however, because the degree of national concentration means different things in different industries, depending chiefly on whether the market is local, regional, or national. The newspaper industry in the United States, for example, might appear highly competitive since, according to government statistics, the four largest companies produce only 22 percent of the papers. But a moment's reflection reminds us that most newspapers produce for a local market, and in most communities the paper or papers are owned by a single person or firm.[22] Since the same is true of a number of other industries as well, Table 11.3 actually *understates* the extent of oligopoly.

Where oligopoly prevails, the law of supply and demand often stops functioning, primarily because collusion between firms is so easy. Collusion can take various forms. A fairly common practice in the construction industry is *bid-rigging*, whereby

TABLE 11.3 Percentage of Production by the Four Largest Companies in Selected Industries in the United States

Industry	Percentage	Industry	Percentage
Home refrigerators	94	Steel mills	42
Motor vehicles	92	Meat packing	29
Washing machines	91	Petroleum refining	28
Breakfast cereals	86	Pharmaceuticals	26
Turbines	84	Paints	24
Tires	66	Newspapers	22
Roasted coffee	65	Poultry dressing	22
Aircraft	64	Fluid milk	16
Radios and TVs	49	Fur goods	12
Distilled liquor	46	Women's dresses	6

Source: Adapted from U.S. Department of Commerce, Bureau of the Census, *Census of Manufacturing, 1982, Subject Series, Concentration Ratios in Manufacturing* (Washington, 1986), table 5.

firms get together and decide among themselves who will take which job and then bid accordingly, with the "low" bid set as high as they dare. *Price leading*, a perfectly legal practice, appears to be standard procedure in several major industries: one firm, usually the largest, sets its prices at a level that ensures profits for all and maximizes profits for itself. In this situation, competition is largely restricted to secondary matters, such as design and advertising.

Another development which has weakened the role of market forces has been the increase in what is known as *vertical integration*, the process by which a company gains control of companies in other industries that either supply it with materials or buy its products.[23] A furniture manufacturer, for example, buys up a number of lumber companies and sawmills to provide its raw materials and then buys into retail establishments that sell the furniture it produces. In this way, it eliminates many of the uncertainties of the market situation. Another device with a similar purpose is to establish *interlocking directorates*, which bring the top officials or directors of a company on which one depends for some essential commodity onto the controlling board of one's own company. This device is widely used to bring officers of major banks onto the boards of firms that require ready access to large amounts of capital.[24]

Finally, the market system has been weakened by the nature of military technology. Modern warfare requires the mobilization of all of a nation's economic resources. Obviously this effort must be planned and implemented far in advance of the outbreak of hostilities. In societies that wish to maintain a strong military position, this inevitably leads to the development of a military-industrial complex from which most elements of the market system are eliminated. For one thing, there is only one buyer for the product, the government. In addition, there is frequently only one producer, and seldom more than a handful, for a particular weapons system. The situation is prejudicial to an open market in yet another way: the military is not inclined to shop around for bargains, because this increases security risks, and truly competitive bidding encourages companies to cut corners and turn out defective products. So long as the military has the taxing power of the government behind it, it has little motivation to economize. Thus, there is a natural tendency for market forces to be replaced by the principles of command in the vast and important area of military procurement, even in societies whose leaders are committed to the principles of free enterprise.

We can summarize most of the foregoing by saying that the experience of the last two hundred years has revealed *three basic flaws in market systems.* First, not only do they fail to protect the weaker and more vulnerable members of society, such as workers and consumers; they compel the strong to act ruthlessly if they wish to remain strong. Second, the market system has what might be called a built-in tendency to self-destruct, which causes most free competitive markets to evolve into oligopolistic or monopolistic markets unless checked by governmental intervention. Finally, the market system cannot respond adequately to many or most of the needs of society as a whole, as contrasted with the needs and desires of individuals.

This final flaw is particularly evident during societal crises, such as wars, depressions, or environmental crises. As long as individuals and organizations are free to act according to what they perceive as their own best interests, the more selfish ones tend to win out. A corporation that responds voluntarily to environmental problems by installing expensive anti-pollution devices, for example, may well find itself at a competitive disadvantage with firms that do not.

For a variety of reasons, then, even those societies that have remained ideologically most committed to the market system and to the principle of free enterprise now have what can only be described as *mixed market-command economies.* The role of government in the economic life of these societies is enormous. Privately owned businesses are obliged to operate within well-defined limits set by an increasingly complex system of governmental regulations. Minimum wage laws must be observed, governmentally prescribed safety standards maintained, and compulsory social insurance payments for workers made, to name but three of the many controls that governments now exercise.

A good measure of the greatly increased power of government in the economic life of all western industrial societies is the growth in the percentage of national income that their governments control through taxes and use to support various activities. As Table 11.4 indicates, this figure has, on average, *doubled* since 1950 in the eleven societies for which data are available. And if the experience of the United States is at all typical, the percentage of the GNP spent by governments has been increasing since the beginning of the century.[25]

Finally, it should be noted that in most of the non-Marxist industrial societies of Europe, major industries, such as steel, telecommunications, auto making, airlines, and utilities, are often operated as state enterprises. In a survey conducted a decade ago, it was found that the majority of the most basic industries in all but one of those societies were state owned.[26]

Thus, while the socialist revolution that Marx predicted has never occurred in any of the historic centers of modern capitalism, capitalism of the kind advocated by Adam Smith has all but disappeared. What passes for capitalism today is really a mixed

TABLE 11.4 Governmental Expenditures as a Percentage of National Income in 1950 and of Gross Domestic Product in 1986, in Western Industrial Democracies

Society	1950	1986
Sweden	19.9	53.5
Denmark	16.6	50.6
Netherlands	30.3	45.5
France	34.6	44.2
United Kingdom	34.9	39.0
Finland	31.2	38.4
West Germany	17.1	37.5
Canada	16.8	33.2
Switzerland	9.6	32.6
United States	18.8	28.9
Japan	5.0	28.8
Median	18.8	38.4

Sources: Adapted from United Nations, *Statistical Yearbook, 1955,* tables 156 and 166; and *Statistical Abstract of the U.S., 1989,* table 1421.

market-command economy that combines in a complex way elements of both capitalism and socialism. In fact, it even incorporates elements of communism (i.e., rewards allocated on the basis of need) in such areas as education, health, and welfare. The nature of the economic mix varies considerably from society to society, with governmental intervention in, and control of, the economy being greater in western Europe and less in Japan, the United States, and Canada.

Viewed from a sociological perspective, the mixed economies that have evolved in western industrial societies during the last hundred years reflect an effort by the members of these societies to achieve two goals that seem, to some degree at least, mutually contradictory. On the one hand, they want the economic growth and higher standard of living that market systems and capitalism seem better able to provide. On the other hand, they also want the economic security and attention to the needs of society as a whole that command economies and socialism seem better able to provide.

Small groups of ideologues continue to argue for a purer type of economic system, but the majority of citizens in the western industrial democracies seem to prefer the more pragmatic approach represented by a mixed market-command economy. While people argue endlessly over details of the mix, there seems to be little popular support for abandoning or substantially reducing either of the two basic components of the mixed economy.

Evolution of the Modern Corporation

Before turning to the command economies of the industrial societies of eastern Europe, we need to consider briefly the nature of the modern corporation, a strikingly new and important kind of organization that has evolved in recent centuries in the western world. During the last hundred years, this new kind of organization has become the dominant form of private enterprise in western Europe, North America, Oceania, and Japan. Its only serious rival in modern industrial societies is the state-owned enterprise.

The origins of the modern corporation lie in the sixteenth century, when English and Dutch merchants, trading in remote areas, banded together in what came to be known as joint stock companies.[27] This form of organization had several advantages over family enterprises and partnerships. Above all, it permitted people to pool capital and thereby spread their risks. This was extremely important in ventures where risks were great and large investments essential. In addition, a joint stock company, unlike a family enterprise or a partnership, was not disrupted by the death of one of the owners.*

During the next several centuries, the joint stock company, or corporation, gradually spread to new fields of enterprise, and a series of changes made it safer and more attractive to investors. The most important change was the adoption of the principle of *limited liability*. Prior to the nineteenth century, stockholders in most corpo-

---

*The law requires, for example, that a partnership be dissolved on the death of any of the partners. This was not required of joint stock companies.

rations had unlimited liability: in case of bankruptcy they could lose not only their investment in the company but all their personal property as well. This naturally made investors extremely cautious; unless they had intimate knowledge of a business and those running it, they were taking an enormous risk. The passage of laws limiting the liability of stockholders to the investment itself greatly stimulated the flow of capital into this new form of enterprise.

In non-Marxist societies today, nearly all of the largest and most powerful private enterprises are corporations. In the United States in recent years, for example, nearly 90 percent of all business was done by corporations, and among larger concerns (i.e., those with annual receipts of $1 million or more), they accounted for 96 percent of the total.[28] And the very largest concerns, those with annual profits in the hundreds of millions or billions of dollars, are all corporations.[29]

As corporations have grown, there has been a tremendous change in their character, especially with respect to their control. The largest ones are rarely controlled by the people who own them (i.e., the stockholders); they are controlled by employees who have been hired to manage them.[30] This shift is a consequence of the fragmentation of stock ownership which has accompanied the enormous growth in size of these organizations. In some corporations, no one owns even as much as 1 percent of the stock, and most stockholders own only a minute fraction of 1 percent. Furthermore, the stockholders are scattered around the world. Mobilizing a majority of the voting stock to wrest control from the managers is extraordinarily difficult and expensive.

The character of the corporation has also been altered during the twentieth century by increasing government control. As we have seen, this intervention of government into the economy has been a response to the inherent defects of an unregulated market system. Over the years, the scope of government involvement in corporations has steadily increased, creating some problems while alleviating others. Many economic questions that were once resolved by the forces of supply and demand are now decided by government officials, much as they are in socialist societies. As a result of such changes, the owners of the largest corporations have become, in most cases, merely investors: *real control of these organizations now lies in the hands of management and government*.

THE COMMAND ECONOMIES OF REVOLUTIONARY SOCIALIST SOCIETIES

Whenever revolutionary socialists have seized control of a society, one of their primary goals has been to destroy the institution of private property and the market economy associated with it. Private businesses and farms, large and small, have been confiscated and the entire economy brought as quickly as possible under governmental control. Centralized planning replaces the market system of supply and demand as the mechanism for answering basic economic questions, with bureaucrats in governmental ministries determining wages, prices, production quotas, and other vital matters.

FIGURE 11.7 Shortages of consumer goods have been a characteristic feature of stores in many revolutionary socialist societies: empty shelves in yard-goods store in Katowice, Poland.

Most of the goods and services in revolutionary socialist societies are produced by *state-owned* enterprises. Other state-owned enterprises distribute and sell these goods to consumers. All of the schools, hospitals, theatres, newspapers, other media, and most other service enterprises are also owned and operated by the state.

Most exceptions to state production and distribution of goods and services are found in farming and the service sector. Workers on state farms are usually allocated small plots of land on which they are allowed to raise food for their families and sell the surplus directly to consumers in what are known as farmers' markets. In the service sector, the pattern varies somewhat from society to society. In the Soviet Union, for example, individuals and families are permitted, after registering with the authorities, to operate restaurants, make and sell toys and handicrafts, and provide such services as tutoring, auto repair, plumbing, carpentry, dress making, key cutting, hairdressing, taxi service, and medical services.

These activities are hedged about with all kinds of restrictions, however.[31] For example, except for pensioners, housewives, and invalids, private entrepreneurial activity in Soviet society is supposed to be a part-time activity that is performed only after individuals have completed their regular jobs in state enterprises. Able-bodied people of working age who live exclusively on private incomes can be jailed for a year for the crime of "parasitism," and pensioners automatically lose their pensions if they register as private workers. In addition, would-be entrepreneurs often find that

FIGURE 11.8 Waiting in line for scarce commodities has been a daily experience in revolutionary socialist societies: Muscovites waiting at a store selling fruit.

authorities are unwilling to make supplies and facilities (e.g., space for a restaurant) available to them. Sometimes small businesses are shut down merely because the authorities think they are too profitable.[32] Finally, since it is illegal to hire anyone to work in a private business, unrelated people can work together only by forming a cooperative, and the size of cooperatives is severely limited.

Not surprisingly, despite Mikhail Gorbachev's program of restructuring Soviet society, the private sector remains tiny. In a nation with a labor force of well over 100 million people, less than half a million are officially registered for "individual labor activity" or employed in one of the 14,000 small cooperatives, and in 1987 *Pravda* reported that they provided less than one-twenty-fifth of 1 percent of the nation's GDP.[33]

A much larger number of people, however, are *unofficially* and *illegally* engaged in private business activities. Some of these are people who fail to register their activities in order to avoid governmental regulations and oversight. But in many instances, the activities themselves are illegal, as with workers who steal materials from their workplace or leave their jobs during working hours to pursue private business interests. Tax avoidance is another reason for failure to register. *Izvestia*, the official government newspaper, estimates that 17 to 20 million people are involved in what is called "the second economy" and that collectively these people provide goods and services representing about 1 percent of the nation's GDP.[34] Although these numbers are much larger than those officially recognized as composing the private sector, they are still a tiny part of the total Soviet economy.

In Poland and Hungary, resistance to Marxist orthodoxy has been far greater than in the Soviet Union, with the result that, for years, Communist Party leaders have had to be more tolerant of private enterprise. In Poland, for example, it is estimated that 75 percent of all farmland is privately cultivated and that private businesses provide about 10 percent of nonfarm goods and services.[35] People are also allowed to hire others to work for them: one unusually successful businessman, an ex-Communist Party member, has 240 employees.[36] In Hungary, an estimated 75 percent of families are involved in the private sector (mostly on a part-time basis) and people devote about 25 percent of their working hours to this type of activity.[37] Private enterprise now accounts for about a third of Hungary's GDP,[38] though in some areas of economic activity it is much higher: 70 percent of homes are constructed privately, for example, and private enterprise provides 74 percent of the nation's poultry.[39]

State Enterprises and Central Planning

In some respects, the state enterprises of the socialist societies of eastern Europe are similar to the large corporations of other industrial societies. Both are administered by complex hierarchies of managers whose powers, responsibilities, and rewards vary according to their rank in the organization. Both have a complex division of labor in which the duties of every individual are carefully defined, and both require individuals in subordinate positions to obey the orders of their superiors.[40] As one Polish sociologist describes the situation,

> ... the workers are still hired labor. The socialist revolution does not change the relation of the worker to the machine, nor does it change his position within the factory.... His relation to the machine and to the organizational system of work requires his subordination to the foreman and to the management of the factory.[41]

In other ways, however, the differences between state enterprises and private corporations are tremendous. For example, the top managers of most western corporations enjoy almost complete autonomy and can run the organization as they deem best, provided they produce a profit and do not violate the law. In contrast, top managers in the state enterprises of eastern Europe have had, until recently, very little autonomy. All of the most important decisions were made for them by central planners located in the nation's capital: where raw materials would be obtained, and at what price and in what quantities; what commodities would be produced, and how many; to whom they would be sold, and at what price; and what wages and other benefits would be given workers.[42] The principal responsibility of the managers was to see that assigned production quotas were met. If they were, no one ever asked if the enterprise was operated efficiently or was profitable, since authorities were not interested in such capitalist concerns. Similarly, officials never inquired into the quality of the products produced; planners were concerned only with quantity.

Because of such flaws in the system, resources were often used unwisely, and products—especially consumer goods—were generally shoddy. Enterprise managers stockpiled both raw materials and workers to protect themselves against the possibility of future shortages or increased production quotas. Unlike businesses operating in a competitive market, there was no penalty for inefficient use of resources. On the contrary, managers were rewarded for it, because it helped them to exceed their production quotas and thus earn hefty bonuses. Moreover, since every enterprise had a guaranteed market for whatever it produced, there was no reason to be concerned with the quality of either goods or services. If consumers did not like what was offered them, there was nothing they could do about it.[43]

The economic consequences of centralized planning have been vividly demonstrated recently as private enterprises in Poland and Hungary have begun competing with state enterprises. For example, in Poland, a new, privately owned company, which buys waste products from meat packing plants and converts them into animal feed and base material for cosmetics, boasts worker productivity *six* times greater than that in state enterprises doing the same thing, thus enabling the owner to pay his employees two-and-a-half times the wages offered by state enterprises.[44] A major reason for this high rate of productivity is the relatively small number of people in managerial positions: only five people in a work force of 240 are engaged in administrative activities. In contrast, state enterprises, like most other governmental organizations, are greatly overstaffed at the top.

Similar problems plague most state enterprises in eastern Europe. The giant Lenin Steelworks in southern Poland, for example, uses 30,000 workers to produce the same quantity of steel that modern western plants produce with only 7,000 workers.[45] This is partly due to outdated equipment, but it is also a consequence of an economic system which, for ideological reasons, has been unwilling to reward superior performance or penalize carelessness and incompetence. According to one local Communist union leader, only three or four of the eight men in a typical steel mill crew really work; the rest are "lazy, alcoholic, aging, or ill."

Not surprisingly, worker morale is quite poor in most of the state enterprises of eastern Europe. Workers quickly learn that their bosses' chief concern is to meet quotas and earn bonuses. Furthermore, until recently, workers had no fear of being fired—both because managers "stockpiled" workers (like other resources) and because of the government's guarantee of a job for everyone who avoided political trouble. As a result, carelessness, indifference, and irresponsibility became widespread and work was viewed by many as a form of welfare. East European workers came to say, "They pretend to pay us, and we pretend to work."

The position of workers in the revolutionary socialist societies of eastern Europe has been distinctive in another way. These societies have been controlled for decades by Marxist elites that claim to govern on behalf of, and in the interest of, workers; yet workers have had no voice in the selection of their leaders, nor have they been allowed to organize independent labor unions or to strike.

Until recently, the only unions in eastern Europe were organized and controlled by the political elite and they functioned much like the "company unions" that once flourished in capitalist societies. Their primary responsibility has been to control workers by offering such benefits as apartments and health and recreational facilities to docile conformists while withholding them from trouble-makers. No truly independent union was tolerated or granted legal status until 1989, when Solidarity was recognized by the Polish government. That same year Soviet workers in certain industries were, for the first time, granted a severely limited right to strike.

Prior to the Russian Revolution of 1917, many critics of socialism argued that it would be impossible to operate an industrial economy without private ownership of property and the free play of market forces. Later, this argument was heard less frequently as glowing reports of economic successes poured out of the USSR and were widely accepted by influential well-wishers in other societies.[46] By the late 1980s, however, the economies of most socialist societies were in such disarray that even top Communist Party leaders felt compelled to call for radical change, including the reintroduction of private enterprise and the market system.

Moves toward Mixed Economies

Among revolutionary socialist states, Yugoslavia—not yet a fully industrialized society—was the first to acknowledge the flaws inherent in a purely socialist economy and move away from central planning. Some years later Hungary followed suit, then Poland. During those years, some Soviet economists began to advocate a form of mixed economy that they called "market socialism," but it was not until the mid-1980s, when Mikhail Gorbachev came to power and called for a radical restructuring (*perestroika*) of Soviet society and its economy, that there was evidence of any real change. Change in the Soviet economy has been painfully slow, however, and it is far from certain that Gorbachev will succeed in his efforts to restructure it,.

In contrast, economic change and movement toward a mixed economy have been far more rapid in several other eastern European societies. Hungary, for example, now has a small stock exchange in which individuals can buy or sell shares in private businesses.[47] Far more important, however, the leaders of most eastern European societies now acknowledge that central planning stifles initiative, promotes inefficient use of resources, and leads ultimately to economic stagnation.

The failures of the older system have become increasingly apparent as Gor-

FIGURE 11.9 Capitalism in eastern Europe: traders on the new Budapest stock exchange.

bachev's policy of *glasnost*, or openness, has brought to light information concerning the actual performance of the Soviet economy. One striking example involves a process known as continuous casting, a critical improvement in the manufacture of steel that the Soviets themselves invented in the 1950s. More than a quarter of a century later this process had been adopted by 62 percent of the steel industry in West Germany and by 79 percent in Japan, but by only 12 percent of the Soviet Union's own steel industry.[48] That this is not an isolated example is indicated by a recent study showing that within the first two years after patents are issued for Soviet inventions, only 23 percent have been put into production, whereas in West Germany the comparable figure is 64 percent and in the United States, 66 percent.[49] Illustrative of another kind of failure is the fact that while the Soviet Union produces twice as much steel as the United States, the industries that *use* this steel are able to produce only three-quarters as much as their American counterparts because so much of the Soviet product is defective.[50] As the respected British journal, *The Economist*, put it recently, "Shoddiness had become Russia's trademark."[51]

As the failure of central planning and command economies has become increasingly apparent, movement toward some form of mixed economy has become imperative. In the future there will probably be considerably less variation in the economies of industrial societies than there has been in the last half-century. The leaders of most industrial societies now seem to accept the necessity of a mixed type of economy in which the forces of both market and command play important roles, with market forces being used to achieve greater efficiency and governmental controls used to protect the corporate interests of society and to limit the amount of economic inequality. This is not to suggest, of course, that differences between economic systems will be eliminated. But differences among industrial societies will probably be greatly reduced as economic pragmatism replaces the older and more doctrinaire ideologies of both socialism and capitalism.

INCREASING ECONOMIC INTEGRATION OF THE WORLD SYSTEM

To be complete, our survey of the economies of modern industrial societies must take note of one further development: the growing web of economic ties among societies, industrial and nonindustrial, throughout the world.

Human societies have exchanged goods with one another since prehistoric times, but the volume of trade was always small because of the limitations of technology. Since the cost of transporting goods was often greater than the cost of producing them, intersocietal trade was largely restricted, for thousands of years, to small items of substantial value, especially luxury goods produced for elites.

With advances in ship construction and navigational technology in the thirteenth, fourteenth, and fifteenth centuries, the volume of international trade began to increase. By 1850, the volume of goods exchanged was six times what it had been in 1750, and in 1950, it was twenty times what it was in 1850.[52] More recently, during the last forty years, the dollar value of international trade (corrected for inflation) has been grow-ing at a rate that would be equivalent to a 400-fold increase if it lasted a century.[53]

The result of this trend has been a substantial increase in the division of labor among societies, and a growing economic integration of the world system. The other side of the coin, of course, is that societies are steadily declining in economic self-sufficiency. As Table 11.5 shows, the value of foreign trade now equals 20 percent or more of the gross national product in most industrial societies.

The societies of western Europe have moved further in this direction than other industrial societies and have formed the European Economic Community, whose goal is the complete integration of the economies of the member societies. This develop-ment could be the prelude to political unification and the formation of a new mul-tinational society embracing much of western Europe.

In the world system as a whole, movement toward economic and political uni-fication is far less advanced, but a number of international organizations—economic and political—have emerged, most of them in the last half-century. These include the International Monetary Fund, the Food and Agriculture Organization, the World Bank, the International Labor Organization, the World Health Organization, the International Court of Justice, and the United Nations.

One of the striking developments of the last century has been the transforma-tion of an ever-growing number of businesses into multinational corporations. Some now have a greater volume of sales outside their home countries than within them. Fifty-six percent of Coca-Cola's sales, for example, are now outside the United States, and 58 percent of IBM's. Sony and Canon, two leading Japanese corporations, have 66 and 68 percent of their sales abroad, while Glaxo, a British drug manufacturer, has a remarkable 87 percent.

Corporations not only increasingly sell their products or services abroad, but produce abroad as well. The opening of German and Japanese automobile plants in the United States is only one instance of what has become a common practice. In

TABLE 11.5 Imports as a Percentage of GNP in Selected Industrial Societies

Society	Imports as Percentage of Gross National Product
Belgium	60
Netherlands	43
Switzerland	28
Austria	28
Sweden	26
United Kingdom	23
Canada	22
Italy	20
West Germany	20
France	19
Japan	16
Australia	13
United States	9

Source: Adapted from *Statistical Abstract of the United States, 1989,* tables 1412 and 1440.

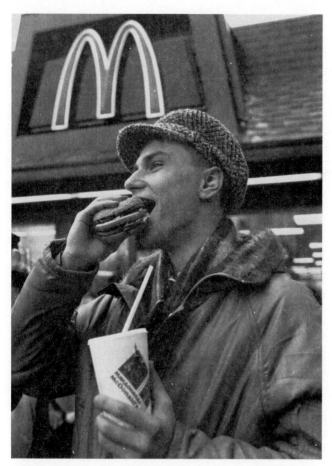

FIGURE 11.10 The web of economic ties among societies is expanding: the first McDonalds in Moscow opened in 1990.

many instances, corporations based in industrial societies manufacture products in Third World societies to take advantage of cheaper labor.

Economic integration is further heightened through foreign aid programs and foreign loans, the latter provided by private corporations as well as by governments and intergovernmental bodies like the World Bank. Banks in Europe, Japan, and North America have extended tens of billions of dollars of loans to Third World societies. Nor is borrowing limited to the Third World: the United States has become the world's largest debtor nation.

The future is not likely to see any significant reversal of the trend toward greater economic integration within the world system of societies. The technologies of communication and transportation have advanced to the point where economic ties between societies are almost as easy to create and sustain as ties within societies. Today, no nation—and few large corporations—can afford to be isolated from the expanding economic network of the world system.

12

Industrial Societies: Their Polities

A society's *polity* is an institutionalized set of answers to questions about how it should be governed. Who will have power to make what decisions, and under what conditions? How will those decision makers be chosen, and when and how will they be replaced? Above all, what limits or checks, if any, will there be on their powers?

The answers to these questions obviously reflect a society's dominant ideology, whether it involves belief in the divine right of kings, belief in democracy, or belief in the doctrines of Marx and Lenin. The answers also say something about a society's level of technological development. For it is no coincidence that multiparty democracy is a product of the industrial era and is found most often in industrial societies. In fact, we cannot understand the polities of industrial societies unless we recognize the remarkable political transformation that has occurred in them as a by-product of industrialization.

THE DEMOCRATIC TREND

Prior to the Industrial Revolution, nearly all large and powerful nations were monarchies governed by hereditary kings and emperors. The power to govern was believed to be a God-given right and the state was viewed as the private property of the ruling family. The state and the ruler's estate were one and the same—and the heads of states were "rulers," not merely "leaders." In 1750, the republican idea that the powers of government are derived from the consent of the governed was still only a thesis for philosophers to debate, not a political reality.

Today, the older view of government has all but disappeared, especially in industrial societies. While a few of them still retain some of the trappings of monarchy, as in Britain, Sweden, and Japan, the western industrial societies are all democratic republics. Even in eastern Europe, where oligarchical republicanism recently held sway, the democratic form of republicanism appears to be taking hold.

People who are sensitive to the undemocratic elements that still exist in western industrial societies sometimes have difficulty appreciating the enormity of the changes that have occurred in almost all industrial societies. These include not just the introduction of contested elections and the formation of political parties that mobilize the masses of people in support of particular leaders and policies, but—most important of all—*the exercise of the powers of government to benefit the masses of ordinary people in countless ways*. This was unheard of in agrarian societies of the past, where the powers of government were used almost entirely for the benefit of the governing class.

The nature of the change may best be symbolized by the way ordinary people are referred to in legal codes. In agrarian societies of the recent past, they were called "subjects"; in industrial societies today, they are "citizens."

Democracy as a Variable

In discussing political systems, we should resist the temptation to think in categorical, either-or terms. To divide governments into those that are democratic and those that are not is to oversimplify. In the real world, governments differ by degree in their practice of democracy, and the degree of democracy in a given society often changes over time. Thus, we need to think of democracy as a variable like other societal characteristics, such as population size or economic productivity. Thinking of democracy in this way helps us recognize why large and complex societies can never be completely democratic. Full and equal participation by everyone in all political decisions would require that people abandon most of their other activities. This would be difficult even in a small horticultural society, and to attempt it in an industrial society would require a reversal of one of the most basic and rewarding trends in societal evolution—increasing specialization and division of labor in virtually every area of life. Thus, not surprisingly, even the most democratic industrial society has never achieved more than a representative form of democracy.

Causes of the Democratic Trend

The tremendous strength and appeal of democratic ideology has been one of the more remarkable characteristics of the industrial era. In the history of industrial societies, there has been only a single instance in which members of a democratic nation abandoned democracy in favor of another form of government, and that happened in a society (Germany in the 1930s) that was confronted by an exceptional set of circumstances, both economic and political. Thus, the record suggests that the democratic trend has been no accident but rather a response to a powerful set of forces.

For the most part, these seem to be the same forces that gave rise to *all* the major new ideologies of the industrial era—the Protestant Reformation, the conquest of the New World, and, most important of all, the Industrial Revolution. Protestantism appears to have been especially significant in the early rise and spread of democratic beliefs and values.[1] If it did nothing else, the Protestant Reformation proved that established authority *could* be challenged and overthrown. But even more important,

FIGURE 12.1 Luther nailing his famous 95 theses to door of the castle church, Wittenberg, Germany, 1517. Luther's doctrine of the priesthood of all believers had revolutionary social implications; though Luther was slow to see this, others soon did.

the Protestant doctrine of the priesthood of all believers—the doctrine that all believers are equal in God's sight and can relate directly to him without the mediation of the clergy—had *political implications of a revolutionary nature*. Though the Reformers, Luther and Calvin, did not recognize this, others soon did, and the bitter German Peasants' Revolt of 1524–1525 and the Leveler movement a century later in England were both stimulated by it.

This new doctrine also led to the adoption of democratic or semidemocratic forms of church government by the more radical Protestant groups, such as the Ana-

FIGURE 12.2 The Founding Fathers of the United States created an oligarchical republic, not a democratic republic: the Constitutional Convention, Philadelphia, 1787.

baptists, Mennonites, Baptists, Quakers, Puritans, and Presbyterians. It is no coincidence that democratization began in church governments some generations before it began in civil governments. Nor is it coincidence that when it did begin in civil government, its early successes were chiefly in countries where the democratization of church governments had already made considerable headway. The first major and enduring victory of the democratic movement was in the United States, a country which since colonial days had been a refuge for the more radical and more democratic Protestant groups.

The conquest of the New World was another important factor in the spread of democratic government. Conditions in the frontier regions of the United States, Canada, Australia, and New Zealand were far more favorable to democracy than conditions in the older, heavily settled societies of Europe. In fact, the Jacksonian movement, which did so much to broaden the base of political participation in American society, had its greatest strength in what was then the western frontier. The conquest of the New World was also important because, as we noted in Chapter 9 (see page 218), it weakened the power of the traditional governing classes in European societies and strengthened the influence of the merchant class, which had long been noted for its republican tendencies.

As important as these influences were, however, the democratic movement could not have succeeded without the Industrial Revolution. Industrialization eliminated the need for large numbers of unskilled and uneducated workers living at or near the subsistence level, and as new sources of energy were tapped and new machines invented, societies had to produce more skilled and educated workers. But people with skills and education are much less likely to be politically apathetic and servile. On the contrary, they tend to be self-assertive, jealous of their rights, and politically demanding.[2] Such characteristics are essential in a democracy, for they hold in check the powerful oligarchical tendencies that are present in any large and complex social system.

Industrialization also made possible the remarkable development of the *mass media*. To a great extent this has been a response to the spread of literacy and to the increased demand for information generated by the rising level of education. Through newspapers, magazines, radio, and television, the average citizen of a modern industrial society is vastly more aware of political events than his or her counterpart in agrarian societies. Although much of the information received is superficial and distorted, it nevertheless generates interest and concern. Thus the media not only satisfy a need, they also help to create it.[3]

Finally, industrialization, by stimulating the growth of urban communities, further strengthened democratic tendencies. Isolated rural communities have long been noted for their lack of political sophistication and for their paternalistic political patterns. Urban populations, in contrast, have always been better informed and more apt to challenge established authority without waiting for conditions to become desperate. Thus, merely by increasing the size of urban populations, industrialization contributed to the democratic trend.

THE POLITIES OF WESTERN INDUSTRIAL SOCIETIES

Once we recognize the variable nature of democracy, we can better appreciate the magnitude of the change that has occurred in the polities of western industrial societies during the last hundred and fifty years. As recently as 1865, 76 percent of the members of the British Parliament were members of the aristocracy and gentry (i.e., the old governing class of preindustrial Britain) and nearly half of the seats were filled in uncontested elections.[4] One-quarter of the members of Parliament belonged to just thirty-one families, a fact that led one writer of the period to refer to Parliament as "one vast cousinhood."[5]

In the United States, as we saw in Chapter 10, the government was originally an oligarchical republic. The right to vote was limited to men of property, as in Britain, and the great majority of people were denied this right. This was still true even half a century after the republic was established. In the presidential election of 1824, only 350,000 votes were cast, indicating that less than 10 percent of the adult population was entitled to vote.[6] Since then, the elimination of property requirements for the right to vote and to hold office, the abolition of slavery and the extension of the franchise (i.e., the right to vote) to blacks, women, and eighteen-year-olds, the passage of the civil rights acts, the direct election of senators, and the "one person, one vote" decision of the Supreme Court have greatly increased not only the percentage of Americans who are eligible to vote but, equally important, the effectiveness and importance of their votes. As a result, nearly half of all governmental expenditures in the United States today are for social programs that benefit the masses of ordinary people.[7]

TABLE 12.1 Percentage of the British Population Age Twenty-one and Over Eligible to Vote

Before First Reform Act, 1831	5.0
After First Reform Act, 1832	7.1
After Second Reform Act, 1867	16.4
After Third Reform Act, 1884	28.5
After World War I, 1919	74.0
After Equal Franchise Act, 1928	96.9

Source: Judith Ryder and Harold Silver, *Modern English Society: History and Structure, 1850–1970* (London: Methuen, 1970), p. 74.

This is a tremendous change from the practices of governments during the agrarian era.

Similar trends can be observed in the recent history of the other western democratic societies, although nearly all of them lagged behind the United States in removing property requirements for the right to vote. In Sweden and Britain, for example, these requirements were not finally removed until after World War I (see Table 12.1).[8] On the other hand, the democracies of western Europe now spend a higher percentage of their total income on social programs than the U.S. does.

Mass Political Parties

The growth of democracy and the rise of industrial societies have produced a totally new kind of political organization, the mass political party, which serves to mobilize public opinion in support of political programs and candidates. Wherever there are more candidates than offices, there is a process of selection, and the candidates that are supported by parties usually win.

Party organizations differ in several respects. Some, such as the Republican and Democratic parties in the United States, are largely pragmatic, *brokerage-type parties*. They have no strong ideological commitments and no well-defined political programs. Their chief goal is to gain control of public offices in order to trade favors with special interest groups, offering preferential legislative treatment in exchange for electoral and financial support. In this type of party, discipline is weak, since each elected official is free to work out his or her own "deals." Some degree of party unity is maintained, however, because once an interest group establishes close ties with the officials of a certain party, it usually continues working with them. This is reinforced by the tendency of the more ideologically inclined to separate into opposing camps, liberals gravitating toward one party, conservatives toward the other. Sometimes the more ideologically inclined win control of the party machinery, but this is usually short-lived.

In contrast to brokerage-type parties, many of which were formed in the nineteenth century, political parties formed in the twentieth century have often had strong ideological commitments. Such parties, including both fascist parties of the right and socialist parties of the left, traditionally had well-developed programs designed to transform society, and their leaders were willing to be defeated again and again rather

FIGURE 12.3 Mass political parties are a totally new kind of organization: the 1988 Republican Party convention that nominated George Bush for president.

than compromise principles they held sacred. Since World War II, however, many of these parties have become less ideological and more pragmatic.

Nationalist ideologies have given rise to political parties in several industrial societies. The most famous was the German National Socialist (Nazi) Party organized by Adolf Hitler following Germany's defeat in World War I. Usually, however, nationalist ideologies are simply one element in the overall program of the major conservative parties in democratic societies. Thus, the Republicans in the United States, the Conservatives in Britain and Canada, and the conservatives in France usually place more emphasis on national defense and other policies relevant to nationalist ideals than their opponents do.

In ethnically divided societies, minorities sometimes form nationalist parties to protect or promote their own group's special interests. This has happened among the French in Canada, the Scottish and Welsh in Britain, and the Basques in Spain.

Finally, religious groups in western Europe and Japan have formed a number of political parties. The most successful of these have been the Christian-Democratic parties formed by Catholics in Italy, Germany, Austria, and several other countries. While the original aim of these parties was to defend the church's position on such issues as birth control, abortion, and tax support for church schools, they have often become the chief conservative opposition to social democratic and Communist parties.

Experience has taught professional politicians that parties which remain ideologically pure are likely to remain numerically small and politically weak, except in times of crisis. Thus, the more successful Communist parties in the democracies of western Europe have softened their stance on a number of issues in recent years. The Italian Communist Party, in fact, came to support the participation of Italy in the NATO alliance and pledged itself to support the principles of western-style democracy long before Gorbachev.

The most recent development in party organization in industrial societies has been the formation of so-called "Green" parties by environmentally concerned groups. Concerns with environmental issues have grown considerably in much of Europe in recent years in response to fear of nuclear war, the Chernobyl nuclear accident in the Soviet Union, and Europe's dying forests and polluted air and bodies of water.

In elections to the European Parliament in 1989, Green parties won 39 of the 518 seats, double their representation following the last election in 1984.[9] Green candidates were successful in West Germany, Belgium, France, Italy, and Spain; and although they won no seats in Britain, they attracted 14 percent of the vote.

The future of these parties is uncertain because they are still small and there are increasing signs that the established parties are adopting stronger policies on environmental issues to regain the support of voters who have shifted to the Green parties.[10] Modern technology could, of course, change things overnight: another Chernobyl ex-

FIGURE 12.4 The explosion at the nuclear power plant at Chernobyl, which spread radioactive materials over much of Europe and rendered the surrounding area uninhabitable for years to come, gave powerful impetus to Green parties in western Europe.

plosion or comparable environmental disaster, especially one in western Europe it-self, and the Green parties could become a major force.

Special Interest Groups

The industrial democracies are made up of a great variety of groups, each with its own special interests. Labor and management are two of the more familiar, but there are many others. In American society, for example, blacks, Hispanics, Catholics, Prot-estants, Jews, welfare mothers, veterans, professional groups, retired people, women, men, pro-choice groups, pro-life groups, environmentalists, pro-handgun advocates, anti-handgun advocates, groups representing individual industries, and dozens more are organized to promote their own interests. What is more, all of them have interests that conflict, to greater or lesser degree, with the interests of other groups, and often with the interests of society as a whole.

One of the more difficult problems facing democratic societies today is that of protecting the interests of society as a whole against the claims and demands of these special interests. Paradoxically, it is far easier for politicians to rally support for pro-grams that offer special favors to limited interest groups than for programs designed to promote the common good.* The reason is simple: since political success in a dem-ocratic society depends on voter support, politicians tend to respond most readily to the appeals of groups that are able to mobilize large numbers of voters. Some rationalize their actions by arguing that the interests of society are simply the sum of the interests of its parts, but that argument ignores the systemic nature of human societies.

Interest groups vary greatly in their ability to influence public policy, and their success is largely a function of their political and economic resources. The most im-portant resource is the active support of large numbers of voters. Money is also es-sential in many societies, especially in those where the allegiance of voters to political parties is weak and where large campaign contributions can be used to influence vot-ers through the mass media—especially television.

Political Conflict and Stability

Every social system generates internal conflict, and industrial societies are no excep-tion. Nevertheless, their success in channeling such conflict into nonviolent forms is remarkable. Compared with agrarian societies in particular, they are much less prone to revolutions, coups, and other serious political upheavals. This is especially true of the democracies and other societies that are past the transitional or early phase of industrialization. One study of sixty-two societies found an extremely strong statistical correlation between their levels of political stability and their levels of economic development.[11]

---

*The construction of the interstate highway system in the United States, for example, was primarily a re-sponse to a massive lobbying effort by the trucking industry, the highway construction industry, the cement industry, and the automobile industry, and only secondarily a response to the public's desire for safer and faster highways.

There are a number of reasons for the political stability of the western industrial democracies. First, their greater productivity and their higher standards of living give the majority of the population a vested interest in political stability. Revolution and anarchy would be very costly for most members of advanced industrial societies. Second, a democratic ideology strengthens the allegiance of most segments of the population to their government and weakens support for revolutionary movements. Especially noteworthy in this connection is the loyalty shown by the military and the absence of military coups in advanced industrial societies. Finally, the very complexity of the structure of industrial societies seems to generate a readiness to compromise on most controversial issues. This is partly because *there are so many people in intermediate positions between the contending groups.* Most of the population, for example, has modest property holdings. Such people are likely to benefit from peaceful compromise and therefore reject extreme or violent proposals. Contrary to Marx's expectations, this is true of the great majority of blue-collar workers. Moreover, since the complexity of industrial societies means that each individual simultaneously fills a number of different roles and often belongs to a variety of groups, people who are opponents in one controversy are often allies in another. For example, middle-class whites and blacks who may be divided over racial issues often find themselves allied on economic issues. This, too, has a moderating effect.

Although political conflicts are restrained in industrial societies, they are still present in various forms and involve a wide range of issues. The most common type of conflict is between economic classes and, in most democratic nations, this has become the basic framework for partisan politics. Typically, some parties appeal primarily to the working class and other less advantaged elements in the population, promising improved conditions if they are elected. Opposing parties rely for support on the more privileged elements in the population and campaign for office on a platform promising economic growth.

Sweden provides a good example of a strong relationship between economic class and party preference. As Table 12.2 shows, support for the Socialist and Communist parties is more than twice as strong in the working class as in the middle and upper classes. The strength of the relationship between party preference and economic class varies greatly in industrial societies, however, being strongest in Scandinavian societies and weakest in North American, as Table 12.3 shows. The limited relation between class and party preference in the United States and Canada is due in part to the absence of major working-class parties with strong ideological commit-

TABLE 12.2   **Party Preferences of the Swedish Population in Elections by Occupational Class, in Percentages**

	Socialist and Communist	Other Parties	Total
Upper and middle classes	30	70	100
Working class	74	26	100

Source: Adapted from Walter Korpi, *The Democratic Class Struggle* (London: Routledge & Kegan Paul, 1983), figure 5.3.

TABLE 12.3 Strength of Relationship between Occupational Class and Party Preference in Eleven Industrial Societies

Society	Percentage Point Difference*
Finland (average of 3 surveys)	50
Norway (average of 3 surveys)	46
Denmark (1 survey)	44
Sweden (average of 8 surveys)	44
Italy (1 survey)	37
Britain (average of 14 surveys)	37
Australia (average of 7 surveys)	35
West Germany (average of 9 surveys)	22
France (average of 2 surveys)	22
United States (average of 10 surveys)	16
Canada (average of 10 surveys)	7

Specifically, the figures are the difference between the percentage of urban upper- and middle-class people who support Labor, Socialist, Green, and Communist parties and the percentage of urban working-class people who do so. Canada's Liberal Party and the Democratic Party in the United States are also included, since there are no mass socialist parties in those societies.

Sources: See note 12, page 470.

ments. In both countries, the two major parties are pragmatic, brokerage types that tend to downplay class-related issues.

Another factor that influences the relation between economic class and party preference is the presence of serious ethnic and religious divisions within a population. It is probably no coincidence that the countries in Table 12.3 with the strongest relation between class and party preference are generally the most homogeneous both ethnically and religiously. In contrast, Canada has for years been divided by struggles between an English-speaking majority and a large French-speaking minority. In both Canada and the United States, religion and ethnicity have been important determinants of party preference.

Modern industrial democracies differ dramatically from traditional agrarian societies by virtue of their inclusion of ethnic and religious minorities and the economically disadvantaged in the political process. In agrarian societies, such groups had little or no political power. In industrial societies, in contrast, these groups have sometimes won control of the machinery of government, or at least a share in it, as the working class has done in Scandinavia, the French in Canada, and the Catholics in the Netherlands.

THE POLITIES OF REVOLUTIONARY SOCIALIST SOCIETIES

The revolutionary socialist societies of eastern Europe have been by far the least democratic of modern industrial societies. Lenin, the founder of modern Soviet society, was contemptuous of western-style democracy, which he was sure would always be controlled by a few wealthy capitalists.

In its stead he advocated a new kind of "democracy" that he maintained would benefit the new industrial working class. Two critical features of this new form of government were (1) the "leading role of the Communist Party" within society, and (2) "democratic centralism" within the Party itself. In practice, the first of these principles meant that no opposition to the Communist Party was tolerated, and the second, that the Party functioned like an army, with orders flowing from the top down and the leadership answerable to no one but itself. In short, Lenin created a new and extraordinarily repressive kind of oligarchical republicanism—one in which almost total power was concentrated in the hands of a tiny elite that ruled by virtue of its control of the Communist Party organization, the police, the army, and the other agencies of government.

As one would expect, the practice of Leninism quickly led to *totalitarianism*: Party leaders claimed control of virtually every aspect of human life. Under Stalin in the Soviet Union, and under the men he placed in power in other eastern European societies, Party leaders executed or imprisoned millions of people who challenged or even dared question the ideas of Party leaders. Those who suffered included not only political opponents (both inside and outside the Party) and small businessmen and farmers, but artists, writers, and scientists who failed to follow the Party line, and simple believers who sought to practice their faith. To ensure adherence to the Party line, Stalin and his successors created a massive system of spies and informers within every organization to report on what people were saying and thinking. And until the mid-1980s, children were taught in school and in youth organizations to report on their parents, as in Hitler's Germany (see Figure 12.5).

Communist Party leaders adopted some of the trappings of democracy, but stripped them of their substance. For example, periodic elections were held, but voters were offered only a single candidate chosen by Party leaders. If a person wished to vote against this candidate, he or she had to place the ballot in a separate box in full view of local Party officials. Not surprisingly, Party leaders often received 99.95 percent of the vote.

Not all Marxists have been happy with this state of affairs. Even in Lenin's own lifetime, the famous Polish Marxist, Rosa Luxembourg, criticized his elitist policies and practices. She wrote at one point that while democratic institutions have their shortcomings,

> ...the remedy Lenin [has] found, the elimination of democracy, is worse than the disease it is supposed to cure; for it stops up the very living source from which alone can come the correction of all the innate shortcomings of social institutions.[13]

She also wrote that unless all of the people were involved in building socialist societies, these societies would be controlled by a handful of elitist intellectuals and bureaucrats.[14] Despite such criticisms, Lenin and his followers throughout eastern Europe ruthlessly suppressed efforts to open up the system and make it more demo-

FIGURE 12.5 Until the mid-1980s, Soviet children were taught to admire Pavlik Morozov, a boy who denounced his father to the authorities and later was killed by outraged neighbors because of this: adult leader of the Young Pioneers recounting the story of Morozov's "heroism" to children soon to be inducted into this children's affiliate of the Communist Party, Moscow, 1985.

cratic, using every means at their disposal to indoctrinate people in the view that their monopoly of power was justified.

The Democratic Trend in Revolutionary Socialist Societies

Ultimately, however, these efforts appear to have failed. There have been massive public protests against the system on numerous occasions: in East Germany in 1953, in Hungary and Poland in 1956, in Czechoslovakia in 1968, in Poland again in 1970 and 1980, and in the late 1980s in Poland, Hungary, East Germany, Czechoslovakia, and the Soviet Union itself, as well as in the industrializing societies of Romania, Bulgaria, and China. The most dramatic Soviet protests have been in various non-Russian republics (e.g., Estonia, Latvia, Lithuania, Georgia, Azerbaijan, and Armenia), but there have also been large public demonstrations in Moscow itself.

These developments, together with others in these societies (see "Causes of the Democratic Trend" on page 297), have resulted in dramatic changes in the polities of several eastern European societies. In 1989 the Hungarian Communist Party, for example, changed its name and repudiated its revolutionary socialist heritage. New leaders identified the party and themselves with democratic socialist principles and gave the country a new constitution that endorses "the values of both bourgeois democ-

FIGURE 12.6 In 1989, peaceful democratic revolutions swept eastern Europe: thousands of demonstrators gathered in Moscow's Red Square to demand elimination of Article 6 of the Soviet constitution, which gave the Communist Party a political monopoly and total control of the government.

racy and democratic socialism."*[15] It allows Hungarians to organize other political parties and to compete freely for political power. Most important of all, the new leadership promised to yield control of the government if it were defeated in a free and open election, something never before agreed to by a Marxist Party in power.

In Poland, things have moved even more rapidly in some respects. That country now has a non-Communist prime minister, and a Senate (a body with only limited powers) made up entirely of non-Communists who defeated Communist candidates in elections in 1989. Unlike Hungary, however, Poland's Communist Party continues to be a Marxist-Leninist, or revolutionary socialist, party and has used its control of the police and army to maintain control of the presidency and the powerful lower house of Parliament.

*"Bourgeois democracy" has long been a term of opprobrium in revolutionary socialist societies. In China, for example, one of the most serious charges leveled by Party leaders against the students and others involved in the dramatic events at Tiananmen Square in 1989 was that they were advocating "bourgeois democracy."

FIGURE 12.7 In 1989, the first contested elections since the Russian Revolution were held in the Soviet Union: the newly elected Congress of People's Deputies being addressed by the late Andrei Sakharov, long-time advocate of western-style liberal democracy and critic of Leninism, who was elected to the Congress despite vigorous opposition by the Communist Party.

In Czechoslovakia, the Communist president was forced to resign as a result of massive public protests, and one of the nation's leading dissidents (a playwright who had spent five years in prison for his political activities) was elected to take his place by a still Communist-dominated parliament. This same parliament also voted to abolish the Communist Party's constitutionally based monopoly of power.

In East Germany, the man who headed the Party for nearly two decades was forced to resign and was then arrested. Although currently free, he is under investigation by the new government on charges of corruption involving tens of millions of dollars reportedly hidden in Swiss bank accounts. When elections were held early in 1990, the Communist Party was swept from power and a coalition of non-Communist parties took office.

Even the Soviet Union has adopted a number of important democratic innovations. In 1989, under the leadership of Mikhail Gorbachev, contested elections were held for the majority of seats in the Congress of People's Deputies and several hundred people opposed by Party candidates were elected. Equally striking, a number of important Party officials who had run for office without opposition were defeated when more than half of the voters scratched their names from the ballot—a practice long allowed under Soviet law but considered too dangerous to use. When the newly elected Congress was convened, 360 of the 2,250 members immediately formed an opposition group whose leaders spoke out on a variety of controversial issues and had their speeches broadcast on national television.[16] More recently, 40 percent of the members of the new Soviet Congress of People's Deputies either voted against Mikhail Gorbachev or abstained in the vote by which he was elected to the office of president, a remarkable show of independence and a striking change from the past.

At this point, it is still impossible to say whether or not current efforts to achieve greater democracy in eastern Europe will ultimately prevail. One thing is clear, however: all of the efforts of Communist Party elites have failed to kill the yearning for democracy in the industrial societies of eastern Europe, just as efforts to maintain oligarchical republicanism and monarchical rule failed earlier in other industrial societies. One has to believe that there is a fundamental incompatibility between industrialization and nondemocratic government.

CHARACTERISTICS OF ALL INDUSTRIAL POLITIES

The Growth of Government

Apart from the rise of democracy, the most important political change associated with industrialization has been the growth of government. The range of activities and the diversity of functions performed by government are far greater in modern industrial societies than in any other type of society. In a traditional agrarian society, the government's chief functions were defense, taxation, the maintenance of law and order, and the support of religion. In modern industrial societies, the last of these has usually been dropped, but dozens of new functions have been added.

Many of the new functions of government arise because they are required by an industrial system. For example, with industrialization, machines increasingly do the work that was once done by illiterate, unskilled workers, but the economy requires more educated workers. To ensure continuing economic growth, public educational systems must be created, first at the elementary level, then at the secondary, and finally at the university level. Only governments have the power to raise the money needed to finance such expensive systems.

A better educated populace quickly becomes a more demanding populace. Educated people want or require things that uneducated peasants in agrarian societies of the past never dreamed of: health care, pensions for their later years, dependable systems of transportation and communication, adequate housing, and much more.[17] While private businesses can supply many of these things, there are some they cannot supply and others they cannot supply *profitably* for the entire population.

Highways are an example of the former, housing of the latter. A modern highway system is both too complex (requiring land condemnation powers, for example) and too unprofitable to be constructed with private resources. Housing, on the other hand, can be profitably supplied by private businesses for most of the population in most industrial societies, but governments must step in to provide housing for those who cannot afford what is offered by private enterprise.

In the western industrial democracies, much of the growth of government reflects the influence of two important developments we noted earlier: (1) the rise of democracy and (2) the movement away from pure laissez-faire capitalism toward a mixed economy. In the first instance, a democratic system of government provides the masses of ordinary citizens with a powerful instrument for pressuring elites to satisfy their needs and desires. In the second, a mixed economy is, by definition, one in which government plays a greatly expanded role.

In the revolutionary socialist societies of eastern Europe, the absence, until recently, of a democratic system of government made it far more difficult for ordinary citizens to express their wishes and to pressure political elites into using the society's resources for things they wanted. Despite this, a vast expansion of the scope of governmental activity occurred, simply because socialism led to the virtual abolition of private enterprise. Thus, while the mechanisms involved in eastern Europe and in the western democracies have been different, the end result in both cases has been a vast expansion in the scope and power of government.

Governmental Bureaucracies: Their Expansion and Transformation

One of the best measures of the growth of government is the size of the governmental bureaucracy. In the United States, for example, the number of civilian employees of the federal government has risen steadily for more than a century and a half:[18]

1821	7,000
1861	37,000
1901	239,000
1941	1,438,000
1986	3,019,000

This increase far outdistanced the growth of the population as a whole. While the latter increased twentyfold, the number of federal employees shot up 400-fold. Contrary to what many people think, it is not only the federal bureaucracy that has been growing: since 1929 (the earliest year for which national totals are available), the number of employees in state and local governments has increased more than fivefold, while the general population has only doubled.[19]

The great growth in the powers of governments and in the size of their bureaucracies has made top administrative officials extremely powerful figures in industrial societies. Although this might be interpreted as simply a perpetuation of the old agrarian pattern with its dominance by a hereditary governing class, it is not. Government offices are no longer private property to be bought and sold and inherited by one's children. Rather, they tend to be assigned competitively on the basis of education and experience. Furthermore, in the exercise of the office, officials are expected to act on the basis of the public interest rather than of private advantage. Although reality falls far short of these ideals, there is a marked contrast between the practices of officials in most modern industrial societies and the practices of those in traditional agrarian societies. Members of industrial societies have discovered this repeatedly in their dealings with the officials of many of the governments of less industrialized societies of the Third World, where bureaucratic corruption is a customary way of life.

FIGURE 12.8 "Now that elections are over we can get back to the real business of government . . . Growing bigger!"

In large measure, the explanation for the change lies in the newer ideologies, which assert that the powers of government are derived from the people and should therefore be used for their benefit. This is in sharp contrast to the traditional ideology of agrarian societies, which defined the state as the property of the ruler. When modern officials use public office for private advantage, they are subject to a variety of official sanctions, including criminal prosecution. Such constraints were rare in agrarian societies of the past.

Despite the less venal behavior of public officials in industrial societies, the growing size and power of government bureaucracies has become a matter of concern. A series of Gallup polls taken since 1967 shows that far more Americans fear big government than fear big business or big labor. In a recent poll, 51 percent saw big government as a threat to the nation compared with 19 percent who saw big business and 18 percent who saw big labor as threats.[20] In the industrial societies of eastern Europe, scholars and ordinary citizens alike consider the unsatisfactory performance of their entrenched bureaucracies to be one of their most serious defects.[21]

One of the chief problems of bureaucracies everywhere is to maintain a sense of public responsibility in their personnel. Officials in welfare agencies, for example, often become more concerned with enlarging their staffs, and hence raising their own rank and salary, than with delivering services to those whom the agency was created to serve. In most governmental bureaucracies it is also difficult to get individuals to accept responsibility for decisions. Buck-passing, paper-shuffling, and endless delays become standard operating procedures. Because of the tremendous division of labor, and hence of responsibility, within these organizations, it is frequently impossible to establish accountability, and as a result these patterns persist year after year, and generation after generation. These problems have been especially serious in the socialist societies of eastern Europe, where command economies put enormous power in the hands of a greatly expanded and extremely complex set of bureaucracies.[22]

So far, critics of bureaucratic power have not come up with any workable alternative. The sheer size and complexity of government in a modern industrial society make mass participation in decision making impossible. A substantial delegation of power, therefore, is inevitable, and those to whom the power is delegated generally do what they deem appropriate. This is one of the most serious limitations to the application of democratic principles in any large-scale organization.

WARFARE

Compared to some of the wars of the agrarian era (e.g., the Thirty Years' War), wars among industrial societies have been of shorter duration. This is not an indication of the spread of pacifism. Rather, it reflects the awesome power of industrial technology. World Wars I and II caused over 23 million military deaths, maimed and killed many millions of civilians, and destroyed so much property that a reliable estimate is virtually impossible.[23]

Since the Second World War, weapons technology has advanced at a startling pace. The atomic bomb that fell on Hiroshima was the equivalent of 13,000 tons of TNT, while a single hydrogen bomb today may be the equivalent of 59 *million* tons.[24] Any future conflagration involving the major military powers would cause vastly more

FIGURE 12.9   The city of Hiroshima shortly after the explosion of the first atomic bomb used in warfare, 1945. Advances in weapons technology since then have led to bombs that have 4,000 times the explosive force of the Hiroshima bomb.

suffering and devastation than wars of the past. In fact, some experts believe that full-scale war between the United States and the Soviet Union would, at a *minimum*, cause industrial societies to regress permanently to a preindustrial state.[25]

The tremendous destructive power of the modern military machine is simply a corollary of the tremendous power of modern industrial technology. The invention of the automobile gave rise to the tank, the invention of the airplane to fighter planes and bombers. While the relationship is often reversed, with advances in weapons technology leading to important civilian applications (radar, for example), the point is the same: industrial societies, like societies before them, do not segregate or separate the military and nonmilitary components of technology. As a consequence, technological advance carries with it the potential for ever greater destruction.

Unfortunately, industrial societies, like their predecessors, have failed to develop nonmilitary means of settling serious disputes. Some kind of world government would seem the logical solution, but this raises difficult problems of its own, as we will see in Chapter 17. For the present, the major industrial societies seem content to rely on treaties between nations, and occasionally on the United Nations, in their efforts to control the arms race and avoid catastrophe.

13

Industrial Societies: Social Stratification

Prior to the Industrial Revolution, every major technological advance led to an increase in social inequality within societies. This was true of the horticultural revolution, and it was true of the agrarian. During the early stages of the Industrial Revolution, it seemed that the pattern would be repeated and that industrial societies would become the least egalitarian of all.

More recently, however, as a number of societies have reached a more advanced stage of industrialization, this 9,000-year trend of increasing inequality has begun to falter and even show signs of a reversal. This has not meant a return to the highly egalitarian pattern of hunting and gathering societies. Far from it. But it has meant a less unequal distribution of power, privilege, and prestige within advanced industrial societies than in many technologically less advanced societies, especially agrarian societies.

POLITICAL STRATIFICATION

Despite the great differences in the political systems of western democratic societies and those of eastern Europe, one thing is true of them all: their political elites have the greatest influence in choosing among the wide range of options available to industrial societies and in determining how their huge economic surpluses will be apportioned. Therefore, in examining the patterns of inequality in industrial societies, we begin with these elites and with the system of political stratification.

Revolutionary Socialist Societies

For decades, the system of political stratification in the revolutionary socialist societies of eastern Europe had a structure both simpler and more sharply defined than

316

FIGURE 13.1 Members of the Politburo of the Soviet Union review Red Army honor guard after ceremonial wreath laying at the tomb of the unknown soldier.

that of the other industrial societies. In effect, the Communist Party controlled society and top Party leaders controlled the Party.

This leadership consisted of a small number of individuals (sometimes only a single person) within the Politburo, the highest authority. These people not only decided Party policy, they controlled promotion within the Party and appointments to all important offices throughout society. When vacancies occurred within the Politburo itself, the leading member or members of that body chose replacements. Although such decisions had to be ratified by a somewhat larger group of Party leaders known as the Central Committee, ratification was almost always assured because appointments to the Central Committee itself were controlled by the same members of the Politburo.

One of the most striking features of these societies has been their use of a system of social control known as the *nomenklatura*, a list of important positions that could be filled only by individuals approved by Party leaders. These were the most powerful and important positions in the government, the economy, the military, the police, the mass media, education, and science, and control of appointments to these positions ensured control of society as a whole. In effect, the individuals who occupied *nomenklatura* positions, together with their families, constituted the governing class in these societies.[1]

Decisions concerning appointments to *nomenklatura* positions were made at varying levels within the Party. The most important positions were controlled by members of the Politburo and Central Committee and less important ones by Party leaders at regional and local levels. Political criteria were decisive in appointments to *nomenklatura* positions. Most of the people who were appointed were already trusted Party members, though occasional exceptions were made for appointments to administrative posts in research institutes, universities, or health centers. In these kinds of organizations, non-Party people with outstanding technical qualifications were sometimes chosen if they were believed to be politically dependable.

Although the *nomenklatura* system existed for decades, details concerning its size and operation have been difficult to obtain. According to one recent estimate, approximately 750,000 positions in Soviet society have been subject to *nomenklatura* control.[2] Reports from Poland indicate that there have been approximately 100,000 *nomenklatura* positions in that country.[3] These figures indicate that the governing class (including family members) in Marxist societies has comprised a little less than 1 percent of the population. Despite their limited numbers, the members of this class have, until recently, effectively controlled virtually all of the organizational structures and institutional resources of these societies.

Those who were part of this class enjoyed many special privileges denied to the rest of the population. Although their official salaries have not been unusually high compared to others, they have been able to obtain, at public expense or at bargain prices, superior living quarters, second homes, special schools for their children, vacations at the best resorts, automobiles, servants, and many consumer goods available only at special stores closed to the general public.[4] Because the many perquisites and privileges enjoyed by this elite were never openly acknowledged, others could only guess at their nature and extent. As one delegate to the 1988 Communist Party Conference in Moscow observed, "We know more about [President] Reagan's income and the British Royal Family's budget." His remark was received with laughter and applause by other delegates.*[5]

Beneath this small governing class there has been a much larger class of lesser officials who have also enjoyed special privileges, but on a more modest scale, including better living quarters and the right to purchase goods not generally available. This class has included, among others, members of the police, lesser party and government officials, journalists and writers, and prominent scientists, artists, and athletes. The basic function of this class, which in Poland has numbered about 20 percent of the population, has been to help preserve the Party's control of society.

Immediately below the politically advantaged classes in revolutionary socialist societies has been the much larger class of ordinary Party members. In Soviet society this has comprised about 8 percent of the population, in Hungary about 6 percent. The chief attraction of Party membership for these people has been the opportunity it provided for advancement into the ranks of the *nomenklatura*. Ordinary Party mem-

---

*Since then, however, we have learned of the luxurious lifestyle of former top East German Communist Party leaders and of their multimillion-dollar Swiss bank accounts funded from profits from the sale of arms to Third World countries. Even more startling reports emerged from Romania after the overthrow of the Communist Party there, when it was reported that the Party's leader had taken over for his personal use more than 20 palaces and 40 villas in various parts of the country.

bers have also enjoyed other benefits, such as preference in obtaining apartments and other goods and services in short supply.

Lower still in the system of political stratification have been those who, though outside the Party, have not been regarded as a particular threat to the Party and its policies. Until recently this included the vast majority of the population. Within this class, incomes and other benefits have varied considerably from group to group depending on their potential for disruptive activity.[6] Thus, coal miners—who have demonstrated their ability to disrupt the entire economy by striking or by slowing production—have received far higher wages than most other workers, while occupational groups dominated by women have generally received the lowest wages.

Finally, at the bottom of the political class system have been those whom the authorities viewed as a threat. The size of this class has varied from time to time and from society to society. In Stalin's day, millions were imprisoned, tortured, and executed in the Soviet Union and other east European societies; by the mid-1980s executions were rare and the numbers imprisoned in labor camps and psychiatric hospitals greatly reduced.[7] Except for the Soviet Union, this class has disappeared entirely from the industrial societies of eastern Europe, and there is good reason to hope that the few remaining political prisoners in that country will soon be freed.

Overall, the distribution of the economic surplus in the revolutionary socialist societies of eastern Europe has been guided less by the classical socialist principle "To each according to his work" than by the older Machiavellian principle "To each according to his contribution to the preservation of the political status quo."[8] This is one reason why the stratification systems in these societies have resembled those in agrarian societies in so many ways.

Thanks to the recent democratic revolutions, the revolutionary socialist system of political stratification appears to be dead or dying in industrial societies (though not in some *industrializing* societies, such as Cuba, China, and North Korea). Communist elites have lost their monopoly of power and are being forced to compete with others for popular support. As this happens, the *nomenklatura* system will almost certainly be dismantled, though most of the individuals who rose through this system appear to be retaining their positions of authority because of the difficulty of quickly finding qualified replacements.* In the long run, however, political stratification in these societies appears destined to become more like that in the western democracies, but the process will take time.

The Industrial Democracies

In some respects, the system of political stratification in the industrial democracies is simpler than that in socialist societies; in others, however, it is more complex. Its complexity is especially evident in the nature of its political elites. In the socialist societies of eastern Europe, these elites have always been a small, homogeneous, and well-defined group. In democratic societies, in contrast, the openness of the system

* A similar problem developed after the Russian Revolution, when Lenin was unable to replace many of the officials of the old czarist regime.

FIGURE 13.2 Nine of the most powerful individuals in American society: members of the Supreme Court of the United States.

allows people to enter the ranks of the political elite through multiple channels, while the multiparty system produces competing groups of elites. To complicate matters further, constitutional principles in the democracies often provide a variety of checks on executive authority, while federal systems divide political power between national officials and regional officials.

In the United States, for example, political power is divided among officials at federal, state, and local levels, and among executive, legislative, and judicial branches of government. Moreover, these people have achieved office in a variety of ways. Some have been appointed, others elected. Of the latter, some have been elected as Republicans, others as Democrats, and still others have run as third-party candidates or in nonpartisan elections. Political power also lies in the hands of many people who hold no governmental office and exercise no governmental responsibilities. These are people who command substantial economic resources (e.g., heads of large corporations, heads of large private foundations, wealthy individuals) or who are able to deliver large blocs of votes (e.g., heads of labor unions, leaders of some ethnic and religious groups). Last, but hardly least, those who control the flow of information in American society—newspaper editors, television newscasters, and others—help define the nation's political agenda and influence the decision-making process (see "The Mass Media," page 350).

The mix of elements in the political elites of other industrial democracies varies somewhat from society to society, depending on the relative strength of the various ideologies and interest groups within them. Also, the nature of the mix tends to change over time in response to technological advances, international developments, and other events. But most of the groups mentioned above are influential in most of the western democracies and compete with one another for control of the economic surplus and for a voice in shaping the policies of their societies on a plethora of issues.

In a number of western democratic societies, there is a strong symbiotic relation between politicians and economic elites. This is especially evident in societies with brokerage-type political parties. In these societies, politicians constantly need money to finance expensive election campaigns, while economic elites seek legislative favors (e.g., lower taxes, larger governmental subsidies, less restrictive regulation) that only politicians can provide. Although this kind of symbiotic relationship is strongest where brokerage-type parties are dominant, leaders of some of the more ideologically oriented parties (e.g., the French Socialists) have discovered that electoral success can depend on economic conditions, and this often forces them to work more closely with economic elites than they might otherwise choose to do.

Control of the economic surplus in western societies is not simply a matter of elites versus the masses, as it is sometimes made to appear. Different sets of elites often come into conflict with one another. For example, President Reagan's tax proposals in 1985 led to conflicts between the heads of older "rust-belt" industries of the midwest and executives in the newer high-tech industries in other parts of the United States.

Another significant feature of the relation between elites and the masses in western industrial democracies is the amount of power that has been acquired by organizations representing large blocs of ordinary citizens. The growth in power of labor organizations earlier in the century is a good example of this. By organizing politically and economically, union members were able to share significantly in the benefits of the rapidly expanding economic surplus. Traditional elites resisted less vigorously than they might have been expected to, because the rapid expansion of the surplus made it possible for them to avoid costly conflicts while still obtaining greater benefits for themselves. In other words, the great expansion of the economic surplus changed the nature of the conflict from the near zero-sum game (see Glossary) it had been throughout most of the agrarian era to a strongly positive-sum game from which almost everyone could benefit.

More recently, organizations have been formed to promote a variety of different viewpoints (e.g., antiwar groups, pro- and anti-abortion groups) and the interests of a variety of nonelite groups (e.g., racial minorities, women, retired people, the handicapped). While such groups have never gotten all they wanted, they have often won important concessions, including a larger share of the economic surplus.

Today, because of the enormous productivity of western industrial societies and because of their democratic polities, *almost all parts of the population share to some degree both in the control of the economic surplus and in its benefits*. To be sure, they do not share equally in either, but they do share in them. As a result, the vast majority of the members of these societies enjoy a standard of living far above the subsistence level. Even people who are classified as living in poverty in these societies usually live considerably above the subsistence level—which is why so many people in Third World societies are eager to migrate to the western democracies (see "Prison Proves 'Best Home'," page 322).

Because so many different groups have a voice in modern democratic societies, no year passes without efforts to redistribute wealth and income or effect other changes.

Prison Proves "Best Home"

Ramchandra Gnanu Malekar, Maryland Correctional Training Center inmate 130755, leaned back in his chair and raised both feet to display his shoes. "Look here," he said in wonder. "I have never seen shoes like this kind."

They were fairly ordinary two-tone shoes, but Malekar, who grew up in a village outside Bombay where sandals were considered something of a luxury, found them astonishing. "And I have undershirts," he said, unbuttoning far enough to show off a small patch of silky blue material. "Nylon, poplin, cotton. I have never in my whole life had such clothes in my house."

For Malekar, "my house" is now a large Maryland jail facility, where the young Indian citizen is serving a six-year sentence for manslaughter. He was convicted of strangling Lalita Khambadkone, the woman who brought him from Bombay to Maryland to work as a servant.

Last Friday, almost two years to the day after the slaying, Malekar sat in the brightly lit visiting center of the jail and described it as the finest home he has ever known. He has a bed for the first time in his life, he said, and eats off plates. Though he had been "so emaciated that a child could have pushed him," he has now developed into a robust young man with muscular upper arms that he boasts are 13 inches around.

"Fried chicken," he said delightedly, when asked what foods were new to him. "French toast, scrambled egg, pancake, Spanish rice, Chinese rice, chicken stew, macaroni, sweet potato, mashed potato."

It is all very different from the poverty-ridden village where Malekar grew up. Prison in the United States is far better than the life he knew in India.

Source: The Washington Post

Although elected officials make most of the final decisions, they know that they can be replaced if a majority of the electorate becomes dissatisfied with their actions—or inaction. This makes it impossible for them to ignore the more pressing concerns of the masses of ordinary citizens.

THE DISTRIBUTION OF INCOME

One of the best measures of the level of social inequality in a society is the distribution of income among its members. This is especially true in western industrial societies, where money can be used to purchase almost anything. The more money individuals have, the more easily they are able to satisfy their needs and desires.

TABLE 13.1 Distribution of Household Income in Western Industrial Societies

Society	Percentage of Total Household Income Received By Top 10 and Bottom 20 Percent of Households		Ratio of Top to Bottom
	Top 10 Percent	Bottom 20 Percent	
Japan	22.4	8.7	2.6
West Germany	24.0	7.9	3.0
United Kingdom	23.4	7.0	3.3
Finland	21.7	6.3	3.4
Norway	22.8	6.0	3.8
Denmark	22.3	5.4	4.1
United States	23.3	5.3	4.4
Canada	23.8	5.3	4.5
France	26.4	5.5	4.8
Australia	30.5	5.4	5.6

Source: World Bank, *World Development Report, 1989*, table 30.

In revolutionary socialist societies, the distribution of income is not nearly as good an indicator of inequality, since political power is much more valuable than money as a means of obtaining the good things of life, and the uses to which money can be put are far more limited than in other industrial societies. In the Soviet Union, as we have seen, many goods and services are simply not available in stores open to the public and can be purchased only at special stores that are closed to everyone except members of the governing class. They are not available to anyone else except at black market prices, if at all. Many other things, such as housing, are generally not for sale but are allocated by the authorities, and allocations are based largely on an individual's political clout.[9] Thus, the value of money is much more limited than in other industrial societies. Yet even in revolutionary socialist societies, income distribution data provide some insights into the level of inequality, as we will see.

In the western industrial democracies, incomes vary enormously. In the United States, for example, there are many families whose annual incomes total less than $10,000 per year, even when the value of welfare payments, food stamps, housing subsidies, medical aid, unemployment compensation, social security, and other benefits is included. At the other end of the income scale, there are some athletes, entertainers, and business executives with incomes of $1 million or more per year. Beyond them, there is a tiny group of entrepreneurs who have made $10 million or more in a single year, and there are several families with enormous fortunes that should, at normal interest rates, provide them with incomes in excess of $100 million per year. Thus, the range of family income in the United States appears to be more than 10,000 to 1.

As large as this difference is, income inequality in industrial societies is not as great as in agrarian societies of the not-so-distant past. As we saw in Chapter 7, the top 1 or 2 percent of the families in those societies received not less than half of the total income. In contrast, the top 1.2 percent of the American population currently receives less than 10 percent of the total income and even the top 10 percent receives less than a quarter of the total.[10] As Table 13.1 indicates, the figures for other western industrial democracies are fairly similar.

It is also interesting to note that the distribution of income in the socialist societies of eastern Europe is surprisingly like that in the nonsocialist societies of the West, despite the egalitarian ideals of the former. According to a recent estimate by a French scholar, there is a ratio of 10 to 1 between the combined incomes of the highest-paid 10 percent of the Soviet population and the lowest-paid 10 percent; by comparison, the ratio for Britain is just 8 to 1, and for West Germany, 15 to 1.[11] If one could make an adjustment for the value of the nonmonetary benefits that members of the Soviet governing class enjoy, the Soviet ratio would almost certainly be as high as the ratio for West Germany, and probably higher.[12]

One of the significant developments of the 1980s was the acknowledgment by leaders of several eastern European societies of the extent of poverty in their countries. Soviet authorities, who had long insisted that poverty was an evil due entirely to capitalism, now report that nearly 30 percent of Soviet citizens live in poverty.[13] Studies in Hungary have indicated that a quarter of its population lived in poverty, while Polish economists estimated that the number there has been as high as a third.[14] In the United States, by comparison, less than 14 percent of the population lives in poverty,[15] and many who are classified as poor by the American government would not have been so classified by eastern European standards.

An interesting discovery concerning income distribution in the United States is that relatively few individuals remain persistently below the poverty level year after year. In fact, a major study found that only a little over half of the individuals living in poverty in one year were still living at the poverty level a year later, and less than 1 percent of the American population remained at the poverty level for an entire decade.[16] This is quite a change from the situation in agrarian and early industrial societies.

THE DISTRIBUTION OF WEALTH

One of the important differences between the societies of eastern Europe and the industrial democracies is that the former have numerous constraints on the private ownership of wealth. Private ownership of land and capital goods has usually been forbidden by law.[17] Citizens have been allowed, however, to own their homes and furnishings—even second homes or vacation cottages. If they have good political connections or substantial financial resources, they have also been permitted to own automobiles. Finally, they have been allowed to have savings accounts in state banks, and there has been no legal limit on the size of these accounts.

Unfortunately, revolutionary socialist societies have not published data on the distribution of wealth. The Soviet Union once published data on funds held in savings accounts, but discontinued the practice many years ago—perhaps because the data proved embarrassing. In the last year for which data were published, 3 percent of the depositors owned 43 percent of the money on deposit.[18]

TABLE 13.2 **Distribution of Wealth in Britain**

	Percentage of Wealth Owned	
Percentage of Population	Excluding Pension Rights	Including Pension Rights
Top 1 percent	28	17
Top 5 percent	54	35
Top 10 percent	67	46
Top 20 percent	82	59
Bottom 80 percent	18	41

Source: Royal Commission on the Distribution of Income and Wealth. Report No. 1. *Initial Report on the Standing Reference* (London: H.M. Stationery Office, 1975), tables 36 and 39.

More important, however, is the fact that a tiny minority of the population has *controlled* virtually all of the wealth of revolutionary socialist societies.[19] As we have seen, decisions concerning the use of the wealth of these societies, and how the benefits of its use are distributed, have been made by the 1 percent or less of the population in *nomenklatura* positions. While this governing class does not legally "own" the property, its members have enjoyed all of the powers and most of the privileges associated with ownership in nonsocialist societies. Ironically, the very ideology that developed as a reaction against what was felt to be excessive power and control by the *propertied* elite in capitalist societies has led to an even greater concentration of power and control by a new *political* elite in socialist societies.

In western industrial societies there are, of course, great differences in wealth. A small number of individuals have assets worth several billion dollars. In the United States the wealthiest 1 percent of the population own approximately 21 percent of all private assets.[20] Although this is substantial, it is significantly less than half a century earlier, when the figure was 32 percent.[21]

Research by the Royal Commission on the Distribution of Income and Wealth yields a similar picture for Britain, though their analysis calls attention to one feature that is often ignored: *workers' equity in governmental and private pension systems.* As Table 13.2 indicates, when the wealth accumulated in these pension systems is taken into account, the assets of the great majority of British citizens more than doubles. A similar situation appears to exist in other western industrial societies. In the United States, for example, public and private pension funds now own nearly half the stock of the 500 largest companies in the country.[22]

OCCUPATIONAL STRATIFICATION

Despite the differences in the ideologies of eastern and western industrial societies, there are important similarities in their systems of stratification, especially occupational. The similar organizational constraints imposed both by size and by similar technologies have resulted in an essentially similar division of labor.

In addition, industrial societies all appear to be similarly constrained in the way they reward people in various occupations. If elites want to attract capable people to the more demanding and responsible professional and managerial roles, they have to provide material incentives. When such incentives have been withdrawn for ideological reasons and income differences between occupational strata have been minimized (as happened in the Soviet Union in the early 1920s and again in the late 1920s, and in Czechoslovakia in the early 1960s), the flow of qualified individuals into these positions declined and serious problems developed.

For most members of industrial societies, their occupations are the chief determinant of their income and wealth. More than 70 percent of the national income of the United States today, for example, is distributed in the form of wages, salaries, and fringe benefits of employment, such as health insurance and employers' contributions to social security.[23]

The range of benefits received by people in different kinds of occupations varies greatly in the United States, with the top 10 percent enjoying incomes that are 10, 15, or more times larger on average than the incomes of those in the bottom 10 percent—the unemployed, part-time workers, and the unskilled. A handful of people at the *very top* of the occupational ladder in the western democracies—business leaders, entertainers, and athletes—are paid about 1,000 times more than full-time workers who receive the minimum wage. In Soviet society, this ratio was reported to be about 50 to 1 in the early 1980s,[24] but individuals holding *nomenklatura* positions enjoy many special benefits apart from their incomes, as we have seen.

In both the societies of eastern Europe and the western democracies, managerial and professional occupations are the most highly rewarded, followed by manual workers in skilled occupations or heavy industries (e.g., tool and die makers, electricians, steelworkers, miners). These are followed by lower white-collar employees engaged in clerical and sales work, while unskilled manual workers are at the bottom of the occupational hierarchy.

As Table 13.3 indicates, the rank order of these major occupational groups is basically the same in both the United States and the four socialist societies of eastern Europe for which comparable data are available. The resemblance between the two sets of societies even includes a similar reversal in the relative ranking of the two

TABLE 13.3 Relative Earnings of Four Major Occupational Groups in Five Industrial Societies

Society	Unskilled Manual Workers*	Lower White-Collar*	Skilled Manual Workers*	Professionals and Managers*
United States	100	108	146	169
Czechoslovakia	100	133	136	164
East Germany	100	95	120	140
Hungary	100	114	123	156
Poland	100	113	110	144

*To facilitate comparisons among the six societies, the earnings of unskilled manual workers for all societies have been standardized at 100.

Sources: *Statistical Abstract of the United States, 1985*, table 699; and Gyorgy Akszentievics, "International Comparative Survey on the Situation of Industrial Workers," in Antal Boehm and Tomás Kolosi (eds.), *Structure and Stratification in Hungary* (Budapest: Institute for Social Sciences, 1982), p. 420.

middle occupational classes. Prior to World War II, lower white-collar workers enjoyed, on average, higher incomes than skilled blue-collar workers in both the Soviet Union and the United States.[25] Since then, however, the relative rankings of these two classes have gradually been reversed, creating the present pattern, which favors skilled manual workers in most countries.

An even more important change in the occupational system in industrial societies has been the substantial growth in the relative number of high- and middle-status occupations. As Table 13.4 indicates, the percentage of upper white-collar jobs in the American labor force has more than doubled since the beginning of the century. There has also been relative growth in the two intermediate occupational classes—skilled manual workers and lower white-collar workers, especially the latter. These developments have brought about an important change in the class structure of American society and, to a lesser extent, other industrial societies. No longer are the majority of people concentrated in the lower class, as in agrarian societies of the past (see Figure 7.17, page 196). Today, most of the people in most industrial societies are members of the middle class. This is yet another consequence of the technological innovations that have so transformed the conditions of life for members of these societies since the beginnings of industrialization.

EDUCATIONAL STRATIFICATION

One of the great achievements of industrial societies has been the tremendous expansion of educational opportunities. Formal education is no longer a privilege limited to children of a small affluent minority. Today, all children are allowed to attend school for ten years or more at public expense.

Despite the great increase in educational opportunities, inequalities in their utilization persist. Some young people drop out of school as soon as possible, while others go on to receive advanced degrees. The amount of education an individual receives is a function of many things—intelligence, motivation, health, peer influence, family tradition, family resources.[26]

Differences in educational achievement, whatever the cause, have substantial consequences for subsequent achievement in the occupational system of stratification.

Table 13.4 Distribution of Adult Population among Occupational Classes in the United States, 1900 and 1987 (in Percentages)

Occupational Class	1900	1987
Upper white-collar	10	25
Upper blue-collar	11	12
Lower white-collar	7	31
Lower blue-collar	34	29
Farmer and farm laborer	38	3
	100	100

Sources: Figures based on data in U.S. Bureau of the Census, *Historical Statistics of the United States: Colonial Times to 1970,* series D182-232, and *U.S. Bureau of the Census, Statistical Abstract of the United States, 1989,* table 642.

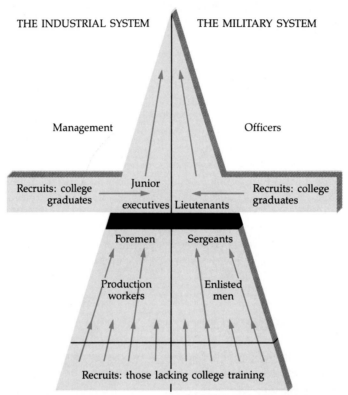

FIGURE 13.3 Model of recruitment and promotion in modern industry compared with recruitment and promotion in the military.

Most jobs in modern industrial societies have educational prerequisites, and insufficient years of education or lack of an appropriate diploma can bar otherwise qualified individuals from careers in many fields. In effect, modern personnel practices have created a civilian counterpart to the traditional military caste system, with its sharp distinction between officers and enlisted men. Just as the ceiling on promotion for enlisted men is normally the rank of sergeant, so the ceiling on promotion for less educated workers in industry tends to be the rank of foreman, or possibly plant superintendent. Higher positions in industry and government are usually reserved for people with a college or university degree who are recruited directly from outside the organization. Figure 13.3 illustrates the pattern.

The importance of educational stratification today is clearly evident in data on the relationship between education and income. The most highly educated young Americans, for example, receive almost three times more income than their least educated counterparts.[27] Available evidence indicates that the impact of education on income and occupation in eastern Europe is at least as great as in the western industrial societies. Because of the great economic value of education in modern industrial societies, many economists and sociologists have begun to refer to it as "cultural capital." Like the more traditional forms of capital, it has the power to produce income.

RACIAL AND ETHNIC STRATIFICATION

Many industrial societies have racial or ethnic divisions within them. Canada, for example, has a serious cleavage between its French- and English-speaking populations, Belgium between Flemings and Walloons, and the United States between blacks and whites—to cite but three of the more serious instances. When membership in an ethnic or racial group has an appreciable influence on an individual's access to the benefits a society offers, the group has become, in effect, a class.

Classes of this kind, however, are different from most others in several respects. For one thing, the resource that is involved in ethnic and racial systems of stratification is an *ascribed characteristic*: racial or ethnic background, unlike occupation and education, cannot be altered by individual effort. In addition, racial and ethnic classes usually have a greater degree of class consciousness than most others, more, say, than people with high school diplomas, more even than manual workers. Finally, because physical traits (i.e., appearance) and primary relationships (i.e., ties with family and

FIGURE 13.4 Much basic learning occurs while a child is small: learning opportunities in Spanish Harlem.

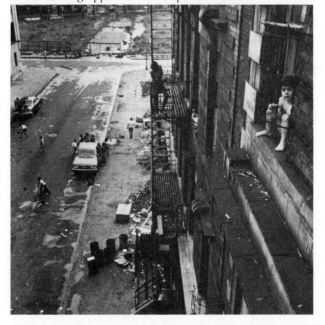

close friends) are often involved, it is more difficult for an individual to move into or out of an ethnic or racial class.

The most striking example of this type of stratification in the United States involves the two major racial groups. Since colonial times, blacks have been a subordinate group. Before the Civil War, the majority of blacks were slaves and the property of members of the white group. Even before the Emancipation Proclamation in 1862, a few blacks had established businesses and become wealthy (some even became slave owners themselves); but despite their achievements, they continued to suffer from handicaps imposed because of race. Their access to clubs, churches, housing, and services of almost every kind was much more limited than that of whites with comparable income and wealth.

Today, most of these limitations have been removed. Civil rights legislation ensures blacks equal treatment in stores, hotels, restaurants, and other business establishments, and affirmative action legislation even provides preferential treatment in college admissions, hiring, and promotions. But discrimination often continues in housing, club membership, and some other areas. Even more important, the general cultural and economic deprivation of the past has left many blacks unable to take full advantage of the new opportunities. So much basic learning occurs while a child is small that large numbers of black children with poorly educated, low-income parents are already badly handicapped when they begin school. Many of these youngsters leave school poorly equipped to compete in the demanding occupational system of a modern industrial society.

These problems are frequently aggravated by family situations in which the father is absent because of divorce, desertion, illegitimacy, or other reasons. More than half of all black children in the United States today live in households where the father is absent, compared to 16 percent of white children.[28] Children in these families are deprived not only of a father's contribution to socialization but of an important source of income as well. The average income of these families is $9,710 compared with $27,182 for black families in which both parents are present.[29] Whatever the underlying causes of the high proportion of broken families among blacks (the subject of a lively controversy), its impact on children is undeniable.

Although the white population is sometimes thought of as a unit, it is, of course, divided along ethnic lines. People of British extraction enjoy the highest status, then those of other northwestern European ancestry, followed by those of southern and eastern European ancestry.[30] This reflects the historic dominance of those who first settled this country. Until about 1830, most of the white population was of British extraction and occupied most of the dominant positions in the major institutions. Since most of the later immigrants were poor, had little education, and were unable to speak English, they tended to fill the more menial positions at first. The more they had in common with the older stock, the more readily they were accepted in marriage and in the better jobs, clubs, and neighborhoods. Northwestern European Protestants were thus accepted more readily than southern and eastern European Catholics and Jews.

In Canada, the most serious cleavage is along ethnic lines and divides French-speaking Canadians from English-speaking ones. Although the French settled the country first, they were later conquered by the British, who dominated the political system from the eighteenth century on. The problem was further aggravated because the English industrialized while the French clung to an agrarian way of life. As a result, the English also dominated the economy, even in Quebec, the home province of the French.[31] In recent years the French have succeeded in eliminating most discriminatory practices through political action, but a substantial minority desires political independence.[32]

AGE AND SEX STRATIFICATION

Inequalities based on age and sex have been a part of every human society, past as well as present. To some extent, these inequalities reflect genetic differences among the members. On average, men have been stronger than women, and they have not been burdened biologically by the responsibility for bearing and nursing children. Adults have been larger, stronger, and more knowledgeable than children, though aged adults have become disadvantaged whenever their health, vitality, and mental abilities have declined.

These biologically based differences have been reenforced and extended in most societies by cultural norms. Thus, the fact that the average woman is not as strong as the average man has often led to norms that exclude *all* women from activities for which a minority of women would be physically qualified.

With respect to age and sex stratification, modern industrial societies resemble preindustrial societies in many ways. Continuity can be seen most clearly in the frequency with which older men still control the more powerful organizations. Most members of the United States Senate, for example, are men, and their average age in recent years has been 56 (the more powerful members of the Senate have been even older because of the seniority system that is used to select committee chairmen).[33] Most business leaders are also men, and a recent listing of the chief executive officers of 818 of the largest American companies indicated an average age of 57 years.[34] Finally, a study of American military leaders, all of whom were male, found that their average age was 54.[35]

In most revolutionary socialist societies, the dominance of older males has been even more pronounced, especially at the pinnacles of power. This is because of the many barriers these leaders have erected to protect themselves against potential challengers. As a result, the average age of the all-male Soviet Politburo in 1984 was nearly 70 (in China in 1985, Politburo members averaged an astonishing 75 years of age).[36]

In all the years of Soviet rule, only one woman has ever become a member of that select group. Even in the less exclusive Central Committee of the Party, less than 3 percent of the members are women.[37] As one observer has stated, "The position of Soviet women does not differ in principle from that of their counterparts in capitalist society."[38]

In nearly all of the industrial societies for which data are available, the income of women is substantially lower than that of men. As Table 13.5 shows, women usu-

FIGURE 13.5 Women can vote today in every industrial
society and have served as prime ministers in Britain and
Norway: Margaret Thatcher, prime minister of Britain, with
Soviet President Mikhail Gorbachev, outside Number 10
Downing Street.

ally earn about three-fourths as much as men. There are a variety of reasons for this,
but the most important appears to be the persistence of the division of labor between
the sexes. In all industrial societies there are certain occupations that are filled primarily by men and others that are filled primarily by women (in addition, there are
some in which there is a more balanced representation of the sexes). The occupations filled primarily by women usually have lower wages or salaries than those filled
primarily by men. They also tend to be occupations that offer fewer opportunities for
promotion to more responsible positions.

The concentration of women in these lower-paying jobs is partly a heritage of
the past when women seldom worked for long outside the home (see Figure 14.2,
page 345) and when those who did were assumed (sometimes incorrectly) to be sup-

TABLE 13.5 Women's Earnings as a Percentage of Men's Earnings in Sixteen Industrial Societies

Society	Percentage	Society	Percentage
Sweden	90	Netherlands	74
Denmark	85	West Germany	73
Australia	83	Canada	71
Norway	83	United States	71
France	78	United Kingdom	69
New Zealand	78	Switzerland	68
Finland	77	Soviet Union	65
Belgium	74	Japan	58

Sources: Francine Blau and Marianne Ferber, *The Economics of Women, Men, and Work* (Englewood Cliffs, N.J.: Prentice-Hall, 1986), table 10.2; Michael Swafford, "Sex Differences in Soviet Earnings," *American Sociological Review*, 43 (1978), p. 661; Mary Brinton, lecture, University of North Carolina, Jan. 24, 1985.

plementing their husband's or father's income and, therefore, less in need of high wages than men, who were expected to be the primary providers for families. Once established, this pattern has persisted because it tends to shape the expectations and aspirations of many women. Thus, the pattern of women's employment has become, in part, a matter of choice, with many women viewing marriage as a more attractive alternative than the job market and a commitment to family as more rewarding and more important than a commitment to career.[39]

Change is occurring, but it has been slow. In the United States, for example, women's earnings have risen from a little less than 60 percent of men's earnings in 1939, the first year for which data are available, to 71 percent in recent years.[40] In Soviet society the situation of women appears to have regressed somewhat, since the percentage employed in lower-paying, predominantly women's occupations has risen from one-fifth to one-third in recent years.[41]

Overall, however, the situation of women has greatly improved as a result of industrialization. Laws that once restricted their right to own property have been eliminated, and women now own much of the wealth in all western societies.[42] Barriers to higher education have also been largely eliminated. Even in the political arena, women have made substantial gains. As recently as 1900, women were permitted to vote only in New Zealand and in four American states.[43] Today, they enjoy this right in every industrial society, and women have served as prime ministers in both Britain and Norway.

VERTICAL MOBILITY

Compared with agrarian societies, industrial societies offer many more opportunities for individuals to improve their status. In agrarian societies, high birthrates ensured an oversupply of labor in almost every generation. At every level in society, a substantial percentage of the children were obliged to work in occupations of lower status than their parents or to join the ranks of beggars, outlaws, prostitutes, and vagabonds. Although a few improved their situation, far more were downwardly mobile.

Organizational Discrimination or Individual Preference?

Not long ago, a large American corporation was sued by several of its female employees for discriminating against women in promotions. In support of their claim they showed that while 82 percent of the entry-level clerical jobs in the company were filled by women, only 74 percent of the promotions had gone to women. This, they charged, was clear evidence of discrimination.

Management in this company had long prided itself on its policy of promoting on the basis of merit and was greatly distressed by the suit and by the allegation that it had failed in this regard. To find out whether it had, in fact, failed and, if so, how, the company hired sociologists to study the matter.

Interviews with 850 employees of the firm demonstrated that women in entry-level clerical positions were much less likely than their male counterparts to seek, or even to desire, promotions (e.g., 39 percent of the women reported that they had no desire for a higher-level position compared to 21 percent of the men). Also, male employees in these positions were twice as likely as female employees to have requested promotion during the previous year (28 percent versus 14 percent). Females, however, were more likely to report that they had received encouragement from management when they sought promotion (70 percent versus 55 percent). These and other findings indicated that the lower rate of promotion for women in this company was the result of choices made by the women themselves rather than sex discrimination by the company.

These findings raised the obvious question of why women were less inclined to seek promotion than men. Further research indicated that both men and women saw promotions as requiring longer working hours and a greater burden of responsibility. This was a price that fewer women were willing or able to pay, especially married women. Whether by choice or necessity, they and their spouses had apparently developed a division of labor within the family that assigned primary responsibility for providing income to the husband and primary responsibility for child care and care of the home to the wife. Thus, the job was a secondary responsibility for the majority of married women in these entry-level positions and this led, not surprisingly, to lower rates of promotion.

This study also found, however, that among individuals already in supervisory positions, the rates of promotion were the same for both sexes. The authors of this study concluded that this was because the selective process operating in the entry-level positions weeded out those individuals of both sexes who were unwilling or unable to make the sacrifices required by supervisory responsibilities. This further supported the conclusion that it was a mistake to infer from the simple statistics on rates of promotion that the company was guilty of sex discrimination.

One cannot infer from this one study that *all* differences in rank and income between the sexes in industrial societies are the result of women's preferences, but it serves as a caution against the common assumption that sex discrimination is the sole explanation, or even the chief explanation, for the underrepresentation of women in managerial positions.

Source: Adapted from Carl Hoffman and John Shelton Reed, "Sex Discrimination?—The XYZ Affair," *The Public Interest*, no. 62, Winter, 1981, pp. 21–39.

In industrial societies, conditions are strikingly different. Falling birthrates have reduced the oversupply of labor, while technological advances have greatly increased the proportion of high-status, high-income jobs. Furthermore, because the upper classes have smaller families than the lower classes, opportunities are created for many children of the latter to become upwardly mobile. Finally, flawed though they are, the systems of free public education in industrial societies give talented and disciplined children from the lower classes an opportunity to acquire skills that can help them move up the social ladder.

As a result of these developments, there is no industrial society in which the rate of downward mobility greatly exceeds the rate of upward mobility. At worst, downward mobility may be slightly greater in a few of them.[44] In most industrial societies, however, there appears to be more upward mobility than downward, a remarkable change from the recent preindustrial past.

This development has undoubtedly been a factor in reducing the threat of working-class revolution predicted by Marx and his followers. If, in every generation, a quarter or more of the children of workers are able to rise into the ranks of the middle class, resentment against the system is almost certain to be less than if only a few move up the ladder, the pattern Marx expected. Furthermore, since those who rise tend to be the more talented and ambitious members of the working class, much of its potential leadership for protest movements is lost.

SOCIAL INEQUALITY: TWO BASIC TRENDS

When we began our examination of stratification in industrial societies, we noted the trend toward greater social inequality that began with the horticultural revolution 10,000 years ago and continued into the early stages of the Industrial Revolution. We also noted that with continuing industrialization this trend was halted, and then reversed. Before concluding our review of stratification, we need to take a closer look at this important development, and at another important trend as well.

In agrarian societies of the past, systems of inequality were often built into the *legal codes*. There was no pretense that people were equal. Some were legally classified as members of a privileged nobility, some as commoners, others as slaves or serfs, and their legal rights and privileges varied accordingly. Democracy as we understand it was unknown in these societies. Political decisions were the God-given prerogative of a tiny elite; the rest of the population had no voice in decision making. The only thing that limited the power of the governing elite was the knowledge that if conditions became too oppressive the masses might revolt. Because of their enormous power, the ruler and the rest of the governing class together usually enjoyed not less than half of the national income and sometimes as much as two-thirds.[45]

In advanced industrial societies, legally based hereditary status has been virtually eliminated. In Britain and a few other societies, titles of nobility remain, but nearly all of the special rights and privileges that were once attached to them no longer exist. Equally important, the disadvantaged legal statuses of serf and slave have been completely abolished. Although social inequalities remain, they are no longer based solely on the accident of birth.

FIGURE 13.6 The relation of the level of income inequality to the level of economic development in the modern world system of societies.

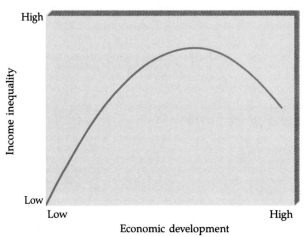

Source: Based on World Bank, *World Development Report 1989,* tables 1, 3, and 30. Income is measured by the log of the income of the highest 10 percent of households; economic development is measured by the log of GDP per capita excluding extractive industries and farming.

In addition, opportunities for participation in *political* decision making have substantially increased in industrial societies. The franchise has been extended ever more widely until virtually the entire adult population is now able to vote in all of them. Although the system falls far short of equal influence for all, it is, by democratic standards, a tremendous advance over the situation that prevailed in agrarian societies not long ago.

Finally, *economic* inequality has been greatly reduced in industrial societies. Though substantial inequalities still exist, the change has been tremendous. As we have seen (Table 13.1; page 323), the top 10 percent of the population in the western democracies appears to receive only 20 to 30 percent of the national income, compared to the 50 percent or more that was received by the top 1 or 2 percent of the population in agrarian societies. While truly comparable data on income distribution in the industrial societies of eastern Europe are not available, the evidence we do have indicates that the situation in those societies is roughly the same as in the western democracies.

Thus, *the overall level of inequality in industrial societies is considerably less than that in agrarian societies of the past, or in most nonindustrial societies in the world today* (see Figure 13.6). The best explanation for this egalitarian trend seems to be the enormous growth in productivity unleashed by the Industrial Revolution.[46] With national incomes increasing rapidly, the dominant classes found it was no longer in their interest to fight all the claims of other classes to a larger share of the economic surplus. Periodic concessions to the lower and middle classes could help elites preserve much of their power and privilege. By giving ground in *relative* terms (i.e., by conceding a larger share of total income to nonelites), they could even improve their economic position in *absolute* terms (i.e., their total income and wealth actually increased). This was possible because technological advances had transformed the old zero-sum game that prevailed in most preindustrial societies into a positive-sum game. Elites apparently concluded that it was better to settle for a smaller share of a much larger pie than to fight to preserve their historic share and, in the process, risk an end to economic growth and the loss of all the benefits it afforded.

But while the new technology has helped reduce the level of inequality within industrial societies, it has had the opposite effect on the world system. *The gap between rich and poor societies has been widening ever since the start of the industrial era.* Between 1860 and 1980, the wealthiest quarter of the world's population increased its share of world income from 58 to 74 percent, while the share of the bottom quarter fell from 12.5 to 2.3 percent.[47] With the new technology gradually eroding the barriers between societies, the social impact of this trend is bound to increase. We will return to this subject in Chapters 15 and 16, when we examine the complex problems of the Third World as it struggles to industrialize in the shadow of far wealthier and more powerful societies.

14

Industrial Societies:
The Family, the Media,
and More

THE FAMILY

The impact of industrialization on kinship has been no less dramatic than its impact on population, the economy, the polity, and stratification. The consequences for kinship, the oldest institutional system in human societies, can be seen in its declining functions, in the smaller size and altered composition of nuclear families, and in the changing roles of women and young people.

Declining Functions of the Family

In the simplest human societies, the basic integrative force in societal life was the kin group, an all-purpose organization that provided for the physical, political, economic, educational, religious, and psychic needs of all its members. As societies grew in size and complexity, this had to change. No longer could an individual's relationships with other people always be defined in terms of kinship. New roles and organizations began to take shape and, in the process, the functions of the kin group were gradually eroded.

Although this process began thousands of years ago, kin groups remained of great importance throughout the entire agrarian era. Above all, the nuclear family (i.e., mother, father, and children) was still the basic productive unit in the economy. The peasant family was almost invariably a work unit, and this was also true of many other families. Place of work and place of residence were normally the same, and all of the members of a family, including the children, shared in the work.

Government, too, was still a family affair. Members of the political elite usually inherited their status, while the royal family considered the state its personal property. Education remained primarily a family responsibility: boys usually learned the male role and productive skills from their fathers; girls learned theirs from mothers and aunts. With the growth of urban communities, the kinship system was not always as strong or pervasive as it had been in simpler societies. But family ties remained central in the lives of most people and provided the basic framework for societal life.

In industrial societies, many of the family's traditional functions have been eliminated or greatly altered. The family is an economic unit only in terms of *consumption*, not of production. Families no longer control the political system; nepotism (preferential treatment of relatives in the work place) may still occur, but it is not accepted as normal or legitimate. Schools, religious groups, and other organizations have assumed much of the responsibility for the education, socialization, and supervision of children, and a wide variety of organizations, from youth groups to summer camps and from beauty colleges to universities, have taken over the task of providing young people with the skills they will need in their adult lives.

But the family has not been stripped of all its historic functions. Some of the most critical ones, including reproduction and the early socialization of children, still fall to the nuclear family. And as the larger kin system, or extended family, has diminished in importance, and as societal life has become increasingly complex and depersonalized, the nuclear family's responsibilities have in some ways become more important. For example, it usually bears the primary responsibility for fulfilling the psychic and emotional needs of its members. With respect to children, the nuclear family is still expected to be the major factor in personality development, instilling basic values, providing affection, providing guidance and encouragement in school and career decisions, training in the use of money, and much more. And all of this must be accomplished in a social environment that is culturally far less homogeneous, and therefore far more difficult, than the one in which most agrarian families raised their children.

Marriage today is undertaken for more personal reasons than in the past. Because most horticultural and agrarian societies viewed marriage largely in economic terms, marriages were usually arranged by parents with economic considerations in mind. The individuals most intimately involved were often denied even veto power. Sexual attraction and affection were not considered of primary importance: everyone knew that these might grow or wane, but the family's need for a firm economic base would persist.

In industrial societies, in contrast, marriage has become an arrangement that is undertaken primarily to enhance personal happiness and to permit individuals to fulfill personal goals, such as establishing a home or having children. Most people today view marriage as the union of a man and a woman who are attracted to one another both physically and emotionally and who hope to find pleasure, comfort, convenience, and companionship by sharing their lives. In short, *marriage and the family are becoming more a matter of choice than of necessity*. One indication of this is the growing number of people who live apart from any family group. Currently, more than 11 percent of American adults live this way.[1]

Causes of Change in the Family

Change in the family is essentially the result of technological advance and the organizational and ideological changes that accompanied it. One of the most important of these changes has been the enormous increase in specialization. As a result, special-ized organizations of various kinds have steadily removed from home and family much of the responsibility for a wide range of services. These include not only educating and caring for the young, but caring for the ill and the aged, processing food and preparing meals, making and caring for wearing apparel, and much more. As a result, the nuclear family itself has become a more specialized institution.

Specific elements of the new technology have also had a great impact on the nuclear family, especially those that have given people control over fertility. Because of advances in methods of limiting family size, couples today have a much wider range of options available to them in almost every area of their lives than couples had in societies of the past. Nothing better illustrates how technological advance expands the "limits of the possible," for individuals and families as well as for societies, than these advances.

Industrialization has also served to undermine the traditional structure of the family with respect to authority. The father is no longer the head of the family in the way he was in agrarian societies, and parents do not have nearly as much control over their children's conduct as they had in agrarian societies or earlier in the indus-trial era. Peer group influence and the mass media have become much more pow-erful than family influences for many teenagers, and serious family conflict often results.

In large measure, the drastic decline in parental authority is an inevitable result of the technological and other changes that have destroyed the family's role as a pro-ductive unit that had to work together for the mutual benefit, even the survival, of its members. Related to this, industrialization has had the effect of drawing families apart both physically and psychologically. Most fathers and many mothers are away from home all day because of work, while schools and other organizations draw children out of the family for other purposes. Today, children in the lower grades may spend more time with their teachers than with their mothers, and teenagers often spend more time with friends than with parents or siblings. Similarly, husbands and wives see less of one another or of their children than of their co-workers. One study of the fathers of 1-year-olds in the United States found that they spent an average of only 20 minutes a day with their infants.[2]

Another important cause of the decline of authority within the home has been the new democratic ideology which has permeated industrial societies, and which carries with it an individualistic bias that puts more emphasis on the rights of indi-viduals than on their responsibilities to the groups to which they belong. Just as the democratic trend has altered roles within political, economic, and educational insti-tutions, so it has altered roles within the family.

A final factor contributing to the weakening of family ties is the greater number of options available to individuals who wish to sever those ties. Divorce is easier, and so is economic independence for women, even women with children (see below). As a result of all of these factors—increased specialization, new ideologies, and new technologies—the nuclear family today is far less cohesive than its agrarian prede-cessor.

Finally, the *extended* family has been substantially weakened by technological advances that make the populations of industrial societies highly mobile. Although the lower cost and greater ease of transportation and communication make it possible for individuals to stay in contact with relatives across greater distances, the relationships are not as intimate as when relatives live within the same community.

The Nuclear Family in Industrial Societies

One of the most drastic changes in the nuclear family is in the number of children, as Table 14.1 indicates. British marriages contracted around 1860 produced a median of six children. Barely two generations later, the median had dropped to two. Families with eight or more children declined from 33 percent of the total to only 2 percent. Although the decline was more rapid in Britain than in most industrial societies, the general pattern has been quite similar.[3]

    Comparisons like the one in Table 14.1 are somewhat misleading if we assume that they also reflect the degree of change in the number of children actually living within a family at the same time. In the earlier period, the death rate among children was so much higher than it is today that there were often considerably fewer children living in an agrarian family than were born into it. Another factor that reduced the number of children living with their parents at any given time was the long duration of the childbearing period. Women who had eight, ten, or more children often bore them over a period of twenty years or more. Typically, by the time the youngest children were five or ten, many of their older siblings would have left home or died. Thus, although the nuclear family was larger in agrarian societies, the number of its members who actually lived together at any one time was not as different as the change in birthrates suggests.

    Perhaps more significant than the shrinking size of the nuclear family is the change that has occurred in its composition due to increases in divorce and in the

TABLE 14.1 Number of Children Born to British Couples Married around 1860 and around 1925

Number of Children Born	Percentage of Marriages	
	Marriages around 1860	Marriages around 1925
None	9	17
One	5	24
Two	6	25
Three	8	14
Four	9	8
Five	10	5
Six	10	3
Seven	10	2
Eight	9	1
Nine	8	0.6
Ten	6	0.4
Over ten	10	0.3
Total	100	100

Source: Royal Commission on Population, *Report* (London: H. M. Stationery Office, 1949), p. 26.

FIGURE 14.1 During the nineteenth and early twentieth centuries, large families were the rule: the Dudleys of Richmond, Virginia, 1903.

number of people raising children outside of marriage. During the last hundred years, the divorce rate in virtually every industrial society has risen substantially. In the United States in 1890 it was only 0.5 per 1,000 population; today it is 4.8.[4] In large measure, this trend is a result of the altered functions of the family, the changed perception of marriage which has accompanied it, the new options available to women, and the newer attitudes of society toward divorce. Half or more of all divorced people eventually remarry, however, which indicates that marriage is still considered a meaningful and valuable institution.[5]

Despite the great increase in divorce, its impact on the nuclear family has not been as dramatic as one might suppose. This is because marriages during the agrarian era, and early in the industrial era, were disrupted about as often as they are today, though for a different reason: *the death of one or both parents*. In eighteenth-century Sweden, approximately 50 percent of nuclear families were broken by parental death before all the children had reached adulthood; in late eighteenth-century France, the figure was 60 percent; and in early twentieth-century India it was 70 percent.[6] Thus, despite the rising divorce rate, the percentage of ever-married women between the ages of 45 and 64 who were still living with their first husband has remained virtually unchanged in the United States during most of the twentieth century.

More recently, however, as the divorce rate has continued to rise, and as more women have opted to raise children outside of marriage, there has been a rapid increase in one-parent families. This trend has been particularly pronounced in the United States, where 27 percent of all children under the age of eighteen live in single-parent homes.[7] Eighty-seven percent of these families are headed by women.[8] During the 1980s, the number of single-parent families increased 20 percent, and at a time when the number of two-parent families was actually declining slightly.

This kind of family arrangement has not worked out at all well for large numbers of the people involved. Nearly half of all female-headed families in the United States have incomes below the poverty level, compared with only 7 percent of families with both parents present.[9] In addition, many of the children in these families do poorly in school and become involved in crime or drugs. In short, these families contribute disproportionately to several of the major problems confronting modern industrial societies.

The nuclear family today also has fewer extended kin living with it. Its household less frequently accommodates aged grandparents or unmarried aunts and uncles. This is no longer necessary in most cases because modern urban communities provide so many alternative facilities for single individuals—apartments, nursing homes, restaurants, laundries, and so on. Moreover, as these facilities have developed, changes have occurred in societal values: most members of industrial societies are jealous of their privacy and value it more highly than the benefits they might enjoy as members of larger and more inclusive households.

The Changing Role of Women

Nowhere are the effects of industrialization on society's norms, values, and sanctions seen more clearly than in the changing role of women.[10] Throughout history most women spent their prime years bearing children, nursing them, caring for them when they were sick or dying, and rearing them when they survived; doing domestic chores; tending gardens; and often helping in the fields. It is hardly surprising, therefore, that women seldom played significant roles outside the home or made outstanding contributions to the arts.

The first signs of change came in the nineteenth century, when the economic benefits of large families began to be outweighed by their costs. Efforts to limit fertility were soon aided by innovations in the area of birth control. During the nineteenth and early twentieth centuries, however, the average woman still produced a large family, still had babies for whom there was no alternative but prolonged breast feeding, still carried the full burden of child care and housework, and sometimes was also obliged to work outside the home.

Because women were usually supplementary wage earners for their families, they were not trained for skilled jobs and were relegated to those that paid the least. Their availability for work at low wages posed a threat to the emerging labor movement and, as a consequence, women were virtually excluded from it. It was, in effect, a working*men's* movement, and its goal was to wrest a greater share of the growing economic surplus from the upper classes.

In contrast, the early women's movements in western societies were dominated by the better educated, more leisured, and economically secure women of the upper classes, and their goals were primarily to obtain for women some of the legal and civil rights that already belonged to upper- and middle-class men: the right to vote, to hold public office, to own property, and to attend universities. Late in the nineteenth

The Young Housekeeper's Friend

Women's liberation owes more to technological advance than many people realize. Cookbooks and other guides for nineteenth-century housewives are interesting reminders of the revolutionary changes that have occurred in the care of a home and family.

Baking, for example, was a very time-consuming job in a day when homes had either a reflecting oven beside an open fire or a brick oven built into a chimney. Books written for young housewives often advised them to set aside a day or two each week for baking, and *The Young Housekeeper's Friend*, published in 1859, stressed the importance of careful planning. As Mrs. Cornelius, the author, advised, "The bread first—then the puddings—afterward pastry—then cake and gingerbread—lastly, custards." With respect to bread, Mrs. Cornelius wrote that "A half hour is the least time to be given to kneading the bread . . . and an hour's kneading is not too much."

Laundry was another time-consuming task, and an exhausting one as well. Water had to be carried from the well or cistern to the stove to be heated, and then carried to the washtubs. White items required boiling. Most items required scrubbing by hand while bending over a washboard. After washing, rinsing, boiling, blueing, and starching, everything had to be carried outside and spread on bushes or hung on a line to dry, and collected later. Ironing for a large family could easily consume most of a day. And from time to time the housewife had to prepare her own soap from wood ashes, fat, and grease.

Today, with a single twist of the dial on a modern gas or electric oven, a person accomplishes the equivalent of cutting and splitting the firewood, hauling it in from the yard, and building and maintaining the fires, while "brown and serve" rolls are more likely to go into the oven than dough that has been kneaded for half an hour. Similarly, automatic washers and dryers and no-iron fabrics have reduced by 95 percent the expenditure of time and energy required by a family's laundry, even as standards of personal care and cleanliness have risen.

century, they also became concerned with the situation of working mothers and sought to have their hours of employment shortened and night work eliminated entirely.

By the 1920s, the original goals of the women's movements in western industrial societies had been largely achieved and these movements declined. Changes continued to occur in the role of women, but chiefly as a result of technological innovations—not because of organized political efforts. These innovations included many laborsaving devices for the home, such as refrigerators, freezers, automatic washing machines and dryers, vacuum cleaners, electric irons, and frozen foods, all of which, taken together, greatly reduced the time and energy consumed by housekeeping (see

"The Young Housekeeper's Friend"). The development of a safe alternative to breast-feeding and more effective methods of birth control were especially important in freeing married women from historic constraints on their lives and in enabling substantial numbers of them to seek employment and engage in other activities outside the home for the first time.

During the twentieth century, there has been a rapid increase in women's participation in the labor force in most industrial societies. Figure 14.2 shows the trend for the United States. Today more than half of all American women are employed outside the home, including more than 70 percent of those between the ages of 20 and 45.[11] In eastern Europe, the rates of female employment are even higher. In the Soviet Union, 82 percent of women between the ages of 15 and 55 are employed outside the home, in Czechoslovakia, 87 percent.[12]

The tremendous increase in women's participation in the labor force in recent decades has been the foundation for the new women's movement that began in the 1960s. This newer movement has had a diversity of goals, but one underlying objective: to break the restrictive molds in which societies have cast women. This is based on the premise that with a single exception—women's capacity for childbearing—the differences between the sexes no longer provide a valid basis for the division of labor. Modern technology is able to compensate to a large degree for differences that are purely physical (e.g., strength, lactation), while differences with psychological components (e.g., emotional responses, competitiveness) are to some undetermined degree the result of socialization rather than genetics and therefore modifiable.

The women's movement also emphasizes that power and prestige in modern societies derive from activities *outside* the family and that if women are to have equal access to these rewards and share equally in shaping society's institutions, they must

FIGURE 14.2 Female labor force participation in the United States by age, 1900–1980.

Sources: V. K. Oppenheimer, "Demographic Influence on the Employment and Status of Women," *American Journal of Sociology,* 78 (Jan. 1973), p. 948, and *Statistical Abstract if the U.S., 1985,* table 669.

participate fully in both the economy and the polity. But women cannot have equal access to the more interesting and demanding jobs and to promotions, higher pay, political offices, and other opportunities outside the home unless the burden of responsibilities *within* the home is divided more evenly. Thus, the women's movement seeks both to increase men's participation in household responsibilities and child care and to spread the burden of child care by tax rebates for working parents and by the creation of tax-supported child care centers.

As Table 14.2 indicates, married men and women in the United States who are employed spend approximately equal amounts of time working (57 hours per week for men, 55 hours per week for women), but men spend a much higher percentage of their time working for pay, while women spend proportionately more on family responsibilities. Similar patterns are reported in the Soviet Union and elsewhere.[13] This is, of course, one reason for both the differences in earnings between the sexes and the lower proportion of women who rise to supervisory and managerial positions (see "Organizational Discrimination or Individual Preference?" page 334). One response to this problem has been the decision by an increasing number of employers to provide paternity leave for fathers. In the United States today, more than a third of employers are reported to provide such leave—usually unpaid and for a period of up to three months.[14] In Sweden, the parents of a newborn child are given nine months paid leave, and they decide how to divide the leave between them.[15]

Despite efforts such as these to deal with the changing role of women, numerous problems remain. Many individuals find it difficult to combine the role of employee with the roles of parent and spouse and to meet all of their responsibilities. More often than not, the demands of the job take precedence and marital and parental obligations are sacrificed (e.g., many children are left alone and unsupervised).

Efforts to expand nursery schools and other child care facilities have only partly met the need, even in eastern Europe, where women's involvement in the labor force is greatest. East Germany, for example, was reputed to have the most extensive and the best child care system of any industrial society, but even it provided for only 60 percent of children under three years of age.[16]

For women themselves, the consequences of changes in their role are becoming increasingly evident. Not surprisingly, there has been considerable erosion of many traditional differences between the sexes in areas beyond employment and family life. It is evident in everything from clothing to mental and physical health, and from

TABLE 14.2 Average Hours Urban Americans Devoted Each Week to Work for Pay and to Care of Home and Family, by Employment Status, Marital Status, and Sex

Employment Status, Marital Status, and Sex	Work for Pay	Home and Family Care	Total
Employed married men	47.4	9.7	57.1
Employed married women	30.1	24.9	55.0
Full-time housewives	1.1	44.3	45.4

Source: U.S. Department of Commerce, Bureau of the Census, *Social Indicators, 1976,* table 10/1.

tobacco and alcohol consumption to frequency of crime, automobile accidents, and suicide.[17] Betty Friedan has argued that middle-aged women suffer less from depression and insomnia today than they did fifteen or twenty years ago, and others report a decline in the use of tranquilizers by women. On the other hand, the once-large differences between the sexes in smoking habits has all but vanished, and among teenagers, more girls than boys now smoke. Similarly, differences in the incidence of heart disease between men and women are declining, and one recent study found that heart disease among middle-aged mothers employed in clerical and sales jobs was twice as common as among housewives.[18] And, finally, in the last half century, the percentage of arrests involving women has more than doubled.[19]

The Changing Role of Youth

In preindustrial societies, children were typically given chores to do while they were still quite young, and their responsibilities increased with every year. By their middle teens, sometimes earlier, they were doing much the same work as their parents and other adults. Reminders of this older pattern still survive in the rites of passage of some religious groups (e.g., confirmation rites and bar mitzvahs), which occur around the age of thirteen. In an earlier era, these signaled the end of childhood and the beginning of adulthood, a period in which the individual was obliged to earn his or her own way and contribute to the support of others.

With the rise of industrialization, the need for human labor was reduced to such an extent that children came to be viewed as a threat to adults in the job market, and labor unions fought to make child labor illegal. Their efforts were reinforced by the passage of legislation to make school attendance compulsory. Young people were thus gradually edged out of the labor force or into marginal, part-time jobs. In the home, there were fewer siblings for older children to care for, and fewer chores to perform. As opportunities for participation in the adult world were curtailed, a new age role gradually emerged. Whereas most people in their teens, and certainly those in their early twenties, had previously been viewed as young adults, they came increasingly to be seen as occupying an intermediate role, a role that of neither adult nor child.

Most individuals in this new age role are students. Table 14.3 shows how rapidly the school population in the United States increased during the last hundred years. Today, 95 percent of Americans aged 14 to 17 are enrolled in school, and 32 percent

TABLE 14.3 **Growth of High School and College Student Populations in the United States, 1880–1980**

Date	Enrollment in Public Schools, Grades 9–12	Enrollment in Colleges and Universities	Total	Percentage of American Population Enrolled
1880	100,000	100,000	200,000	0.4
1930	4,400,000	1,100,000	5,500,000	4.4
1980	14,700,000	12,100,000	26,800,000	11.8

Sources: U.S. Department of Commerce, Bureau of the Census, *Historical Statistics of the United States: Colonial Times to 1970* (1975), series H–424 and H–706; and *Statistical Abstract of the United States, 1984,* table 214.

of those aged 18 to 24.[20] As this suggests, some industrial societies may have expanded their educational institutions beyond what is actually needed to equip people for their roles in the economy, or even for their roles as citizens in a democratic society.[21] In addition, these societies have failed to take account of the fact that some individuals are not disposed to be students for such a long period. Many young people have little interest in the intellectual aspect of education, or even in its vocational relevance, but would rather move quickly into adult roles. They frequently discover, however, that there are no viable alternatives. Many of those who drop out of the educational system have trouble finding employment and getting established in the world of work.

As always happens when one segment of a population is cut off for an extended period from full participation in the life of the larger society, young people in industrial societies have developed their own subculture. Many of its more distinctive features (e.g., music, sports, experimentation with sex and drugs) are a natural consequence of the distinctive attributes of youth, such as vitality, curiosity, the desire for fun and excitement, and resistance to adult authority. The innovative nature of youth culture in areas such as music, language, and dance is at least partly the result of deliberate efforts to establish a barrier between youth and adults. The faster youth culture changes, the harder it is for adults to keep up with it, thereby keeping them at a distance and preventing them from moving in and dominating the youth scene.

At a more fundamental level, however, youth culture simply reflects many of the distinctive characteristics of industrial societies themselves: their high rate of innovation, their affluence, their leisure, their emphasis on individuality, and their tendency to specialize. The preoccupation of young people with changing fads and fashions, for example, can be viewed as simply another expression of their society's enormous economic surplus and its love of novelty.

The differences between the norms and values of the youth culture and those of the larger society can cause serious problems, however, especially when they involve decisions with long-term implications. Teenaged pregnancy is a compelling example of this. Every year in the United States alone, more than 700,000 unmarried girls in their teens become pregnant,[22] usually because they begin sexual activity while they are still emotionally immature and have inadequate information on reproduction and contraception. These individuals are thus forced to make decisions that neither their own experience nor the norms and values of the youth culture have equipped them to make. Should the girl have an abortion or have the child? Marry the father or remain single? Put the child up for adoption or struggle to raise it alone?

Even when the decision to marry is made without the complications of an unplanned pregnancy, teenaged marriages are high-risk ventures, largely because the qualities that the youth culture values most highly in the opposite sex have little to do with the qualities that adults value in a marriage partner. Similarly, because their peer group values success in sports more highly than success in academics, many boys make a heavy investment in athletics at the expense of their studies, only to find their skills no longer in demand once they are through high school or college. As Table 14.4 shows, barely one high school varsity athlete in a thousand makes it into the ranks of the professionals.

In most industrial societies, great numbers of specialized youth groups have developed, each with its own distinct subculture. In the democracies these have included

FIGURE 14.3 The heavy investment in athletics that many boys make in high school rarely pays off in their adult years: only one high school player in eight hundred makes it to the National Football League and one in seventeen hundred to the National Basketball Association.

religious cults, counterculture groups, ghetto gangs, motorcycle gangs, homosexual groups, communes, and political groups of various persuasions. And youth culture became as much a part of the socialist societies of eastern Europe as of other industrial societies. After trying for years to prevent the intrusion of what were viewed as degenerate products of decaying capitalist societies, Communist Party officials adopted the philosophy that "if you can't beat them, join them." Thus, the Komsomol (the party youth organization) now operates, in Moscow alone, more than 260 clubs featuring disco dancing and punk rock.[23] State factories, meanwhile, produce great quantities of blue jeans. Despite this, a growing number of Soviet and other eastern European youth continue to flout authority, engaging in such deviant activities as church attendance and crime.

Crimes of violence are associated with youth in all industrial societies. In Soviet society, for example, 80 percent of those convicted for assault with intent to rob are under 25 years of age.[24] In the United States, 66 percent of those arrested for robbery, the legal definition of which involves the threat or use of violence, are under 25, as are 53 percent of those arrested for all crimes.[25] Political violence is also largely the work of younger people, though older adults often guide such activity.

TABLE 14.4 Number of Men and Boys Playing Basketball and Football in High School, College, and Professional Sports

Level of Competition	Basketball	Football
High School	513,000	930,000
College	13,000	75,000
Professional	304	1,232

Source: 1989–1990 Handbook of the National Federation of High School Associations, p. 71; National Collegiate Athletic Association; and our calculation of professional athletes based on roster size multiplied by number of teams in the NBA and NFL.

Many attempts have been made to explain the tendency toward violence among younger people, especially younger males, in industrial societies. In American society, scholarly explanations usually place the blame on society (e.g., widespread unemployment among youth, racism).[26] In Soviet society, in contrast, blame is usually placed on individuals (e.g., the parents of the criminal, the criminal himself).[27] Soviet scholars also explain the problem as an inevitable by-product of the difficult transition from the submissiveness and obedience of childhood to the self-assertiveness and relative autonomy of adulthood.[28]

In trying to understand this phenomenon, it is important to keep in mind what many experts seem not to realize: young men were often involved in crimes of violence in agrarian societies, and most hunting and gathering and horticultural societies provided *frequent, socially approved* opportunities for violence in hunting or warfare. While there is yet no definitive explanation of violence in younger men, it is certain that the causes are complex and probably include the biological influences of age and sex as well as distinctive characteristics of the individual, his family and friends, and the larger society. Without waiting for more explicit explanations, however, industrial societies would do well to provide more socially acceptable (even socially useful) activities and programs that offer the kind of emotional and physical outlets large numbers of young men clearly require.

THE MASS MEDIA

Some of the most striking technological advances of the industrial era have been in the field of communications. First the telegraph and later the telephone made it possible for individuals in widely separated places to communicate with one another almost as easily as though they were face to face.

Meanwhile, another set of inventions made *mass* communications a potent force in daily life for the first time. The printing press, which was invented late in the agrarian era, was a step in that direction, enabling writers to reach many more people than they ever had before. But books and pamphlets were still a limited mode of communication, because the majority of people were still illiterate and books were quite expensive.

The first of the true mass media was the penny newspaper, which got its start in New York in the 1830s. Published daily, these papers enabled a small group of journalists and advertisers to transmit ideas and information on a regular basis to a relatively large audience. The invention of the telegraph at about the same time made newspapers much more attractive than they would otherwise have been, since it enabled them to report events in distant places much more quickly than had previously been possible.

Later in the nineteenth century other inventions paved the way for new and psychologically more powerful means of communication that utilized visual images and sound. The first of these was motion pictures, which became technologically and commercially feasible shortly before 1900. Movies were followed by radio a quarter of a century later, and after another quarter of a century by television—the most powerful of all the instruments of mass communication.

It is hard to exaggerate the impact of the mass media on industrial societies (and increasingly on other societies as well). Most adult members of industrial societies read a newspaper, and many also read a weekly news magazine, while specialized magazines of other kinds have wide circulation. Radio and movies are popular modes of entertainment, and sometimes sources of news and other information as well.

But it is television that has most altered modern life. "By the time the average American youngster graduates from high school," according to one authority, "he has spent more hours watching the television screen than he has spent in school, or in any other activity except sleeping."[29] For adults, too, television viewing is a major activity. In Japan, the average family spends more than 57 hours a week in front of the tube, while in the United States the average is 53 hours.[30]

There are a number of reasons for television's great appeal. It combines the most attractive features of the other media: like printed matter and the radio, it can be enjoyed in the comfort of one's home, and, like movies, it presents things vividly. In addition, it informs and entertains while requiring little or no mental or physical effort on the viewer's part. This makes it especially attractive for people who are tired at the end of a day's work or who are simply unwilling or unable to engage in more demanding activities.

Because the images created by television are so vivid, they impress themselves on our consciousness in ways not unlike personal experience. Celebrities seen repeatedly on the screen become to many people a very real part of their lives; countless viewers have written expressions of love, even proposals of marriage, to actors and actresses whom they have never seen in person. More important, events witnessed on television have the power to unite millions of people emotionally. This happened in the United States, for example, when President Kennedy was shot, when the first men landed on the moon, and when earthquakes and hurricanes have caused wide-

FIGURE 14.4 "Notice how much less violent the news seems on radio?"

spread devastation. And the same thing can happen when events *divide* a society, as in demonstrations and other activities relating to abortion, environmental pollution, and other issues.

Television's impact becomes particularly important if it is the major source from which people derive their images of social reality. Newscasts, "soaps," and network prime time shows bombard viewers with images that distort reality to varying degrees. One month-long analysis of network prime time shows, for example, found a grossly distorted image of the American labor force: there were twelve prostitutes shown for every machinist, two butlers for every government worker, and twelve times more detectives than production workers.[31]

Not only can the media distort people's perceptions of reality, they can influence events themselves. A study of the 1976 presidential election in the United States found that the media, by biases in their coverage, create a bandwagon effect that tends to throw elections to candidates who win the earliest primaries.[32] That year Jimmy Carter won a very modest plurality in the first primary, receiving only 28 percent of the vote compared to 23 percent for the candidate who ran second and 49 percent for other candidates. But his victory in the media was overwhelming. Both *Time* and *Newsweek* featured him on their covers and devoted 90 percent of their reports on the primary to him, dividing the remaining 10 percent among all of the other Democratic candidates! During the week that followed, both television and the daily press gave Carter four times the coverage of all his rivals combined. This proved to be decisive, because, as the study found, 95 percent of the voters in subsequent primaries voted for the candidate they felt they knew best—and that, thanks to the media, was Carter.

Because television has enormous potential for fostering beneficial change in human societies, it has proved a vast disappointment to many. Perhaps the basic reason for its deficiencies, at least in the United States, lies in its commercial character. As some have observed, commercial television is in the business of selling audiences to advertisers. Since the value of advertising carried in any time slot depends on the size of the audience, television producers and market researchers have worked diligently to identify the ingredients that maximize audience size and industry profits. These include sex, violence, youth, and settings suggestive of wealth, glamour, and "the good life."

News departments in commercial television have a similar approach. To maximize audiences and hence their own salaries, they emphasize visually dramatic and exciting stories, often at the expense of events that are far more important to the viewing public.[33] Thus, a large fire or violent crime may be covered while an unexciting but important debate in Congress is ignored. It is not surprising that a recent *Washington Post* poll found that 54 percent of Americans could identify Joseph Wapner, the judge in a popular but trivial television show, while only 9 percent could identify William Rehnquist, Chief Justice of the United States Supreme Court and one of the nation's most powerful individuals.[34]

In eastern Europe prior to Gorbachev and his reforms, writers, movie makers, and television producers were all compelled to use their talents to indoctrinate the masses in the virtues of Marxism-Leninism, the wisdom and benevolence of the Party's leaders, the correctness of their policies, and the inevitable success of the Party and its program. From the standpoint of Party leaders, this was the chief justification for both the arts and the media in a socialist society.

Although western observers often maintained that most east Europeans did not really believe what the media told them or accept the views they presented, recent developments have made it clear that much of the population was profoundly influenced. One indication of this is the surprise with which most east Europeans have responded to recent revelations on subjects that were long taboo, such as the extent of poverty and industrial pollution in their societies and the frequency of airline and other accidents.

While none of the western industrial democracies has ever experienced anything like the propaganda fed the revolutionary socialist societies of eastern Europe (and those of the Third World as well), the western media are certainly not innocent of bias, distortion, and even propaganda. The saving grace in the democracies has been the pluralistic nature of media control: no single party and no single group of individuals is able to control all of the mass media. Thus, the media speak with many voices and people have access to multiple sources of information.

In conclusion, it should be stressed that the mass media have become an integral part of industrial societies. They are an essential source of many kinds of infor-

FIGURE 14.5 Soviet television was transformed after Gorbachev introduced his policy of *glasnost*, or openness: election campaign debate televised in Moscow, 1989.

mation that the members of these societies require in their daily lives, especially the members of democratic societies. And, at their best, the media are a rich and rewarding cultural resource that greatly enhances the quality of life for hundreds of millions of people.

At the same time, it is important to remember that while informing and entertaining us, the media also mold our ideas about the world and influence our beliefs about good and evil, right and wrong. For a growing number of younger people, the media have replaced schools and churches, and sometimes even family and friends, as primary agents of socialization after the early years. This lifelong process occurs not only in informational programming, but in programs that seem intended merely to entertain. (We may, in fact, be more susceptible when viewing the latter, for then our mental defenses are usually down.) By presenting in a positive light lifestyles and beliefs that the majority has traditionally rejected, or by holding up to ridicule lifestyles and beliefs that have been traditionally honored, *those who control the media can change a society's standards without public awareness until after the fact*. For unless people have been trained to recognize the media's subtle biases and distortions—both intentional and unintentional—they are vulnerable to manipulation. Small wonder the editors of *Webster's Third New International Dictionary* define the mass media as communications *"that tend to set the standards, ideals, and aims of the masses."*

LEISURE AND THE ARTS

No preindustrial society ever offered such rich and varied opportunities for recreation as modern industrial societies provide. With the aid of electronic devices, one can now "command" performances by the world's greatest symphony orchestras, artists, and actors (even some now dead), all in the comfort of one's own home. With other elements of modern technology, individuals can travel quickly and comfortably to distant lands or, alternatively, bring the sights and sounds of those places into their own living rooms via television or video recorders. For those who prefer physical activity, there are scores of opportunities, from miniature golf to hang gliding.

Industrial societies are also unique in the extent to which they have commercialized recreation. Entertainment and the manufacture of equipment for leisure activities are important industries. Ironically, even when members of industrial societies go camping to get "back to nature," they usually take numerous products of modern technology with them.

One of the attractive features of leisure in industrial societies is its relative democracy. Most members of these societies enjoy substantial amounts of leisure (see Table 14.5) and most can afford a wide variety of recreational activities. Members of

Richard Salant, a former president of CBS News, acknowledged the presence of intentional biases in television journalism when he stated that "our job is to give people not what they want but what we decide they ought to have." Roone Arledge, president of ABC News, is a bit more cautious and says that the media elite "can't decide *everything* that people should be allowed to see" (emphasis in original), but he asserts that they have the right and responsibility to impose their own judgments in presenting the news.[35]

TABLE 14.5 **Average Hours Urban Americans Spend per Week on Leisure Activities and Personal Care, by Marital Status, Employment Status, and Sex**

Marital Status, Employment Status, and Sex	Hours per Week of Leisure and Personal Care
Single individuals:	
Employed men	64.0
Employed women	58.3
Married individuals:	
Employed men	57.5
Employed women	57.9
Housewives	65.8

Source: Adapted from U.S. Department of Commerce, Bureau of the Census, *Social Indicators, 1976,* table 10/1.

agrarian societies of the recent past would find the opportunities available to the average member of modern industrial societies unbelievable.

Although technology's influence on the growth of leisure and on the creation of new recreational activities is obvious, its impact on the fine arts may not be. Yet the modern symphony orchestra is a triumph of modern technology, while recent trends in sculpture and painting reflect at least in part the influence of new materials and new processes that were not available to artists of an earlier era. It is also significant to note that modern art, with its movement away from realism and toward impressionism, expressionism, and abstractionism, began in the latter half of the nineteenth century as the new technology of photography was coming into its own. One cannot help but wonder if the new approach to painting and sculpture would have evolved if technology had not provided the camera as a substitute means of depicting reality and capturing images of people, places, and events for posterity. In any event, one of the most important consequences of the new technology for the arts has been an indirect one: traditional standards have given way to the belief that "newer is better" (see "Neophilic Art," page 238). This could not occur except in societies that have benefited greatly from change in other areas.

PROBLEMS AND PROGRESS

The members of contemporary industrial societies are in a paradoxical situation. They are, on average, far healthier, wealthier, and freer to choose among alternative lifestyles than were the vast majority of their ancestors of the last 5,000 years, and they are probably happier as well (see pages 408–410). Yet they are far more vocal concerning the shortcomings and problems of their societies.

Like so many other changes, this is basically a consequence of industrialization. The mass media and, in most industrial societies, multiparty political systems serve to keep social problems before the attention of the general public. Better education and new ideologies, meanwhile, provide people with an enhanced capacity for envision-

FIGURE 14.6 The modern symphony orchestra is a triumph of technology as well as of art: the New York Philharmonic at Avery Fisher Hall.

ing and expecting improvements in their living conditions and in other areas, and if improvements do not occur, they often become critical of both their leaders and the social system. Finally, affluence gives people the means and leisure to voice their opinions, and democratic polities give them the opportunity. As a result, social problems receive far more attention and are far more salient in democratic industrial societies than in any other kind of society.

There are, of course, good grounds for the concerns expressed by members of industrial societies. Their new high-information, high-energy technologies have a potential for creating problems more serious than those which confronted societies of the past. The threat of nuclear war and the deterioration of the environment are the most obvious, but they are not the only ones. Others include the rapid consumption of nonrenewable resources, the weakening of family ties, drug and alcohol abuse, rising crime rates, urban decay, the use of terrorist tactics as a means of achieving political goals, and more. In addition, many older problems persist, even though progress has been made in dealing with some of them.

Although there is considerable controversy concerning the amount of progress industrial societies have actually achieved in dealing with humanity's problems, there is general agreement on several points. First, despite the presence of many continuing problems from the past, the most serious problems facing industrial societies today are either new problems, or old problems with major new dimensions. Second, these problems are largely by-products, or consequences, of technological advance. Third, although many of these problems are distressingly complex, most of them could be alleviated by rational human effort—though in many cases not without great cost to many people. Finally, a completely problem-free society is not likely ever to be achieved, partly because of our species' genetic heritage, partly because of the constraints of the environment, partly because of the extraordinary complexity of modern social systems, and partly because the very process of problem solving itself so often creates new needs and new problems.

Because the problems that remain unsolved by one generation define the agenda for the next generation, we will postpone our analysis of them until the final chapter. In that chapter we will be concerned primarily with the future and what can, and cannot, be said about it.

INDUSTRIAL SOCIETIES IN THEORETICAL PERSPECTIVE

When we compare modern industrial societies with societies of the past, it is clear that they are a radically new type of sociocultural system. This is evident in everything from the family to the polity, and from ideology to technology. The foundation for these societies is, of course, their rich store of information, especially the technological information that enables them to harness vast amounts of energy to drive enormously productive machines.

If human societies had never created this technology, we would all still be in the agrarian era. The vast majority of people would still be illiterate peasant farmers eking out a marginal existence, women's lives would still be dominated by the cycle of reproduction and child care, and authoritarian elites that knew little and cared less about the lives of the masses would still regard the economic surplus as their rightful property. If we imagine a different sequence of events—one in which industrial societies had evolved, but were subsequently forced, in the early 1990s, to return to the technology of the agrarian era—*75 percent or more of the world's current population would die.* For an agrarian technology could sustain no more than a fourth or a fifth of the world's present population.

We will not try to trace here all of the consequences of the shift from an agrarian to an industrial technology or detail all of the causal linkages, as we did at the end of earlier chapters. These consequences are so numerous, and the linkages so complex, that a single diagram could not do justice to them. Instead, we will simply restate some of the basic points that have emerged from our analysis.

First, in industrial societies as in their predecessors, *technological innovation continues to be the most basic underlying force responsible for societal change and development.* Although other kinds of innovations also influence the course of social and cultural change, they tend to be dependent on prior technological change. We have seen numerous examples of this, especially in the new beliefs and values which shape these societies' institutions—beliefs and values which had little or no impact prior to industrialization.

Second, *many of the trends of the industrial era are continuations of trends that began in earlier eras*. Although industrialization intensified them, each of the following was initiated by technological advance in the more distant past:

The growing store of information

The increasing ability to produce and harness energy

The growing productivity of societies

The expanding economic surplus

The growth of world population

The growth in size of societies and communities

The increasing diversity of material products

The growth of capital goods

The increasing division of labor *within* societies

The increasing division of labor *among* societies

The increasing economic interdependence of societies

The growing complexity of associations and communities

The relative decline in importance of kinship systems

The increasing number and variety of symbol systems

The increasing impact of human activities on the biophysical environment

The increasingly destructive potential of military technology

Third, *some of the trends in industrial societies are new and represent a break with trends of the past*. The most significant of these involves inequality. During the long period between the close of the hunting and gathering era and the early stages of the industrial, technological advance was accompanied by a steady decline in both political and economic equality. As a result, either advanced agrarian or early industrial societies achieved the dubious distinction of having the greatest degree of inequality of any type of society in history. Advanced industrial societies have appreciably reversed this trend. Other new trends include democratization, greatly improved opportunities for education, more upward mobility, declining birth and death rates, the institutionalization of science, of research, and of innovation, and changes in the family and related roles, especially in those of women and youth.

Fourth, *industrial societies are the first in human history in which the greatest threats posed by the biophysical environment are products of prior human activity*. Before the Industrial Revolution, famine and disease were two of the greatest threats to a society. Technology and science have succeeded in eliminating the first of these scourges in industrial societies, and they have brought the second largely under control: the members of industrial societies now die primarily from degenerative diseases that reflect the natural limits of our species' life span. Now, however, societies are threatened by *feedback effects of their own technology* on the biophysical environment.

Fifth, and finally, thanks to the many advances in technology and the enormous growth in the economic surplus that these advances have made possible, the leaders of industrial societies today have far more policy options available to them than the leaders of preindustrial societies would have imagined possible. As a result, *the differentiating influence of ideology on industrial societies has been far greater than on any other type of society*. One indication of this is the frequency with which it has been necessary to differentiate between the western democracies with their mixed economies and the revolutionary socialist societies of eastern Europe with their elitist polities and command economies. With preindustrial societies, ideologically based intratype distinctions were unnecessary because the differentiating impact of ideology on the political and economic systems of those societies was not nearly so great.

Excursus: Testing the Limits of the Possible

From a theoretical standpoint, the revolutionary socialist societies of eastern Europe have been extraordinarily important. The aim of their founders was to create a radically new kind of society—one in which all of the ills and evils of capitalism would be eliminated while the many benefits of modern industrial technology would be preserved and used for the benefit of the masses of working people.

In their efforts to achieve this, revolutionary socialists challenged a number of important assumptions about human nature and society. For example, they argued that selfishness and greed are not normal human traits: rather, these are patterns of behavior that people acquire when they live in societies that allow the private ownership of the means of production. By abolishing the institution of private property, one could eliminate greed and selfishness and all of the other evils that flow from them: exploitation, inequality, oppression, poverty, crime, alcoholism, alienation. In effect, revolutionary socialism proposed to test the limits of the possible.

Sociologists are especially interested in revolutionary socialist societies because of their potential for providing valuable information on several fundamental questions. For by their actions the leaders of revolutionary socialist societies have carried out a series of massive social experiments in which important ideas concerning human nature and society were put to the test.

The task of evaluating these experiments has barely begun.[36] For decades, the leaders of these societies kept much of the life of their societies wrapped in secrecy. To confuse matters further, they issued a constant stream of glowing reports, many of which were naively accepted at face value by western visitors and observers who were swayed by wishful thinking. Now, however, thanks to the radical political changes of recent years, more facts are coming to light—facts that enable us to arrive at a far more accurate view of the results of the experiments carried out in response to revolutionary socialist beliefs.

Today, it is clear that it is far easier to conceive of a utopia than to create one.[37] In fact, the very effort to create an ideal society—no matter how noble the intent—can have disastrous consequences. Noble ends can easily be used to justify ignoble means, and brutal tyrannies can be established in the name of freedom and justice. We have also learned once again the truth of the assertion that "Power corrupts, and absolute power corrupts absolutely."

The experience of the revolutionary socialist societies of eastern Europe has also proved that the elimination of private ownership of the means of production does not mean the elimination of unequal control, nor does it ensure an equitable distribution of benefits among the members of a society. On the contrary, public ownership in the revolutionary socialist societies of eastern Europe led to a system in which people were rewarded far more for their contribution to the preservation of the political status quo than for their contributions to society and its welfare.[38]

We have learned, too, that eliminating private ownership of the means of production does not eliminate selfishness and greed. If anything, the tremendous concentration of power that is placed in the hands of a small political elite when private ownership is abolished promotes an extremely selfish and ruthless struggle for power within a society.[39] And, finally, we have learned that it is exceedingly difficult to make a command economy function efficiently. As a member of the Soviet Congress of People's Deputies expressed it recently, his society has taught the world a valuable lesson by testing, at great cost, what has proven to be *"an impossible system of economic development."* He added, "An experiment with a negative outcome enriches science no less than a successful one."[40]

Thus, while Marx's goals of freedom, justice, and equality still have great appeal, the means that he and his followers have proposed for achieving those goals have been largely discredited. Even the goals themselves, when viewed in light of the experience of revolutionary socialist societies, appear unrealistic and utopian: they ignore the limits of what is possible even in highly productive modern industrial societies. For they ignore the constraints that are imposed on societies by our species' genetic heritage, by the biophysical and sociocultural environments to which societies must adapt, and by the limitations of existing technology.

This does not mean, of course, that human societies cannot be improved or that people must accept the world as they find it. The experience of modern industrial societies as a whole proves that this is not true. But the massive social experiments conducted by the Marxist-Leninist elites of eastern Europe demonstrate that *we are still a very long way from being able to create the ideal society of which we sometimes dream, and that attempts to do so may cause vastly more harm than good.*

Ironically, then, despite the enormous efforts of Marxist-Leninist elites to create a radically new and better type of society, we are forced to conclude that the revolutionary socialist societies of eastern Europe have really been just a variant form of industrial society. Although there have always been important differences between these societies and the western democracies, the two types have had even more in common, and the similarities are growing while the differences are declining. The extent of these similarities becomes fully evident, however, only when industrial societies are compared with the preindustrial societies of the past and with the still industrializing societies of the Third World today.

15

Industrializing
Agrarian Societies

Despite the rapid spread of industrialization during the last two centuries, less than a quarter of the world's population lives in societies that can be considered highly industrialized. The great majority, however, do live in societies that have been substantially altered as a consequence of the diffusion of modern industrial technology. These hybrid societies are best described as *industrializing* societies—the ones commonly referred to as the developing nations of the Third World.

These nations are in a transitional phase, moving from an older agrarian or horticultural way of life to the modern industrial. Social scientists often refer to this as the *modernization* process, a process that involves all aspects of the life of society, not just the technological. Unfortunately, the transition period is proving to be longer and much more difficult than most scholars had expected. Thus, for both theoretical and practical reasons these societies merit careful study.

Although it is customary to think of all nonindustrial societies today as "developing nations" or simply as "the Third World," this practice obscures many important differences among them. Some, such as South Korea and Taiwan, are enjoying extremely rapid economic growth and rising standards of living, while others, such as Liberia and Haiti, are experiencing the opposite. Some, such as Iraq, Iran, and Vietnam, have fought long and costly wars with other nations; some, such as Afghanistan and Kampuchea, have been convulsed by bloody civil wars; and others, such as Mexico and Botswana, have managed to avoid both kinds of conflicts.

Much of the diversity among these societies results from circumstances that are unique to individual societies. But some of their most important differences reflect a single underlying variable: *their traditional subsistence technology*. For some of them were agrarian societies while others were horticultural. This fundamental distinction has had enormous consequences, for both the current situation and the future prospects of societies hoping to industrialize today.[1] This is, of course, what ecological–evolutionary theory leads us to expect, since the social and cultural characteristics of a society in one period are major determinants of its characteristics in a later period (see Figure 1.4, page 18). For these reasons, we will examine industrializing agrarian and industrializing horticultural societies separately.

First, however, we should note that, although quite a number of hunting and gathering and fishing societies also survived into the modern era in remote and isolated areas, advances in transportation and communication have opened up their territories to members of more advanced societies and thus destroyed their only real defense. As a result, most of these groups have either been destroyed or herded onto reservations where they live as wards of their conquerors, usually under conditions that make the preservation of their traditional ways of life virtually impossible. Even the few groups that still enjoy some degree of autonomy have usually adopted cultural elements from more advanced societies and thus are no longer pure types. But this does not make them *industrializing* societies; that implies something utterly beyond their adaptive capacities. Groups with such limited social and cultural resources cannot possibly evolve into anything so advanced in the little time available to them. Unhappily, they are simply unusual hybrids with a very limited future.

Apart from agrarian and advanced horticultural societies, the only types of preindustrial societies that have a chance of surviving into the twenty-first century and successfully industrializing are maritime and herding societies. Because of limitations of space, however, we will not examine these two sets of societies. Instead, we will concentrate on the more numerous, and therefore more important, industrializing agrarian and industrializing horticultural societies, examining the former in this chapter and the latter in Chapter 16.

Industrializing agrarian societies comprise most of Latin America, southern and eastern Asia, the Middle East, and North Africa, and are also found in parts of southern and eastern Europe (see Figure 15.1). When we discuss industrializing agrarian societies, we are talking about China, India, the Philippines, Egypt, Yugoslavia, Portugal, Brazil, Cuba, Mexico, and several dozen other societies.

Naturally, these societies differ from one another in many ways, reflecting differences in their histories, in the social and biophysical environments to which they must adapt today, and in their levels of technological advance. Yet despite their differences, they share a number of important characteristics because they all combine elements of both the agrarian past and the industrial present. Recognition of this fact can be enormously helpful as we try to understand them and their problems.

By at least one criterion, industrializing agrarian societies are the most important type in the world today: approximately 70 percent of the world's population lives in these societies. But this is not the only reason for us to be concerned with them. These societies have, for decades, been struggling with problems that often threaten to overwhelm them. Despite partial industrialization, many of their citizens are as poor as the common people ever were in traditional agrarian societies (see Table 15.1, page 364). At the same time, improved education and the mass media have raised their hopes and expectations and given them an awareness of the possibility of a better life. This contradiction has created a situation that affects not only those societies but the entire world.

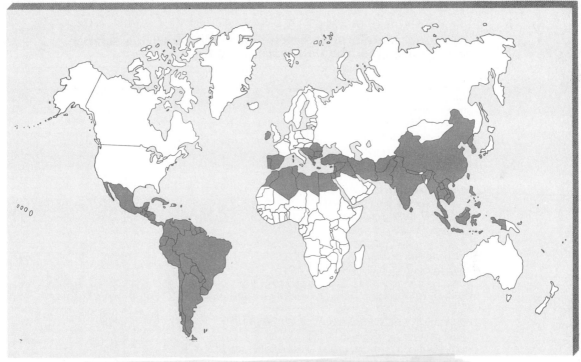

FIGURE 15.1 Industrializing agrarian societies in the world today are shown in dark blue.

Sometimes it is suggested that the problem of the less developed countries is simply their technological and economic backwardness. The problem is much more complex than that, however, for it involves all of their social institutions—polity, economy, family, religion, education—as well as the attitudes and values of their people. In addition, their position in the world system creates further problems, as will soon become clear.

TECHNOLOGY AND PRODUCTIVITY

Technologically, an industrializing agrarian society is a bewildering mixture of the ancient and the modern. Peasant farmers using techniques and tools much like those their forefathers used 2,000 years ago work in sight of such marvels of modern technology as the Aswan Dam in Egypt or the Tata Iron and Steel Works in India.

Preindustrial technology is still widespread in the agricultural sector of these societies, resulting in low levels of productivity. In China, for example, farmers make up 74 percent of the labor force but produce only 31 percent of the nation's gross domestic product; in India, farmers are 70 percent of the labor force but produce only 32 percent of GDP; and in Mexico, farmers are 37 percent of the labor force and produce only 9 percent of GDP.[2] In contrast, workers in the industrial sector comprise only 13 percent of the Chinese labor force but they produce 46 percent of GDP; in India, industrial workers are 13 percent of the labor force and produce 29 percent

TABLE 15.1 An Industrial Society and an Industrializing Agrarian Society Compared: The United States and India

	U.S.	India
Population (in millions)	246	817
Area (in millions of square miles)	3.6	1.2
Population density (population per square mile)	68	681
Birthrate per 1,000 population	15	31
Death rate per 1,000 population	9	11
Rate of natural increase (percent per year)	0.6	2.0
Infant mortality per 1,000 live births	11	94
Life expectancy at birth (in years)	75	57
Doctors per 10,000 population	21	4
Nurses per 10,000 population	143	6
GNP per capita, in dollars	18,530	300
Percentage growth in real GNP, 1975–1985	34	55
Percentage growth in real GNP per capita, 1975–1985	21	25
Hundreds of kilograms of energy consumed per capita per year	95	3
Petroleum production per capita, in pounds annually	3,829	84
Coal production per capita, in pounds annually	6,608	447
Steel consumption per capita, in pounds annually	986	37
Wheat, rice, and corn production in pounds per capita per year	2,437	390
Daily calorie consumption per capita	3,645	2,238
Passenger cars per 1,000 population	556	2
Telephones per 1,000 population	760	5
Newspaper circulation per 1,000 population	268	21
Radios per 1,000 population	2,126	78
Televisions per 1,000 population	813	7

Sources: Calculations based on data in *Statistical Abstract of the United States, 1989,* sec. 31, and World Bank, *World Development Report, 1989,* tables 1, 2, and 28.

of GDP; and in Mexico they are 29 percent of the labor force and produce 39 percent of GDP. The pattern is similar in virtually all industrializing agrarian societies.

There is great variation in the level of technological and economic development found in industrializing agrarian societies. Per capita GNPs range from less than $200 per year in Ethiopia, Nepal, and Bangladesh, for example, to more than $6,000 per year in Spain and Ireland.[3] These differences are closely linked to the extent of industrial development: in Nepal, industrial workers constitute only 1 percent of the labor force; in Spain, they are 37 percent of the labor force; and in Ireland, 34 percent.

Many discussions of the less developed countries give the impression that most of them are technologically and economically stagnant or regressing, but this is not the case. Over nearly a quarter of a century, from 1965 to 1987, all forty-one of the industrializing agrarian societies from which the World Bank was able to obtain data reported at least some net growth in GDP. Growth rates ranged from 1.0 percent per

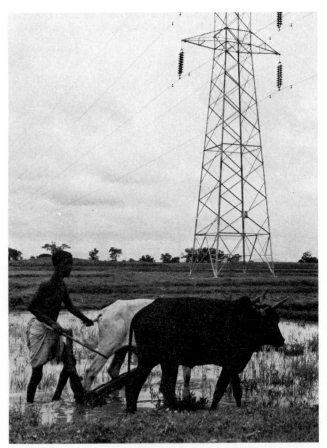

FIGURE 15.2 The old and the new: Indian farmer plowing with oxen under high-power electrical transmission lines.

year in Jamaica to 9.2 percent in South Korea. The median for all forty-one societies was 4.5 percent.[4] (By comparison, the median for seventeen industrial societies in the same period was only 3.1 percent, or nearly one-third less.) Unfortunately, these gains in productivity have not benefited living standards as much as one might expect, because of rapid population growth in most of these societies.

POPULATION GROWTH AND ITS CONSEQUENCES

With the introduction of modern medicine and sanitation, death rates have declined sharply in almost every industrializing agrarian society. Birthrates, however, have declined much more slowly. As a result, the rate of natural increase in these societies is high—2 percent or more per year in most of them, and over 3 percent in some (see

TABLE 15.2 Crude Birthrates, Death Rates, and Rates of Natural Increase for Some Industrializing Agrarian Societies in Most Recent Year Reported

Society	Crude Birthrate*	Crude Death Rate†	Rate of Natural Increase‡
Pakistan	47	12	3.5
Nicaragua	41	8	3.3
Iran	41	9	3.2
Bangladesh	41	15	2.6
Egypt	36	10	2.6
Mexico	29	6	2.3
Peru	31	9	2.2
Philippines	30	8	2.2
India	32	11	2.1
Turkey	30	9	2.1
Brazil	28	8	2.0
Indonesia	29	9	2.0
Colombia	26	7	1.9
Thailand	25	7	1.8
Sri Lanka	23	6	1.7
China	21	7	1.4
Argentina	21	9	1.2
Ireland	17	9	0.8
Yugoslavia	15	9	0.6
Spain	12	9	0.3
Portugal	12	10	0.2

*Live births per 1,000 population per year.
†Deaths per 1,000 population per year.
‡Percentage growth of population due to excess of births over deaths per year.
Source: World Bank, *World Development Report, 1989,* table 27.

Table 15.2). While growth rates of 2 or 3 percent per year may not sound high, they are *twenty to thirty times higher than the average rate of growth of world population during the agrarian era.* A society growing at a rate of 2 percent a year will double in size in just 35 years, and one growing at a rate of 3 percent will double in less than 24 years!

When societies grow this fast, it is extraordinarily difficult for them to find the resources needed to satisfy even the most basic needs of all their members or create enough new jobs to provide employment for the growing numbers of people looking for work.* Table 15.3 shows the cost of rapid population growth for some of the industrializing agrarian societies of Asia and Latin America. As the right-hand column shows, more than half of the economic gains they achieved in recent decades was

*Some Americans have used the history of their own country during the eighteenth and nineteenth centuries to argue that rapid population growth actually speeds economic growth and raises the standard of living in societies. They forget, however, that prior to the twentieth century the United States had a very small population in relation to its size and the wealth of its resources, and because of this the country suffered from labor *shortages.* This is not the situation in which Third World nations find themselves today. On the contrary, most of them suffer from a *surplus* of labor.

TABLE 15.3 The Effect of Population Growth on the Growth of Per Capita GDP for Various Industrializing Agrarian and Industrial Societies, 1965–1987

	Average Annual Percent Increase in GDP 1965–1987	Average Annual Percent Increase in Population 1965–1987	Percentage of Gain in GDP Consumed by Population Growth*
Industrializing Agrarian Societies			
Nicaragua	1.6	3.2	200
Bangladesh	2.9	2.8	97
El Salvador	2.7	2.2	81
Philippines	3.8	2.8	74
Mexico	4.5	2.8	62
Pakistan	5.6	3.1	55
India	4.0	2.2	55
Industrial Societies			
United States	2.8	1.0	36
Canada	4.3	1.2	28
Japan	5.5	1.0	18
Sweden	2.4	0.4	17
Italy	3.2	0.5	16
West Germany	2.7	0.2	7

*The figures in this column were arrived at by dividing the rate of growth of population by the rate of growth of GDP.
Source: Adapted from World Bank, *World Development Report, 1989,* tables 2 and 26.

wiped out by the effects of population growth—much more than was lost to population growth in industrial societies.

Population growth is a serious problem for industrializing societies, not only because it means so many more mouths to feed, but because of its implications for the entire process of development. For example, high birthrates make universal public education prohibitively expensive in these nations, and yet without it the population is not equipped for most jobs in modern industry. This forces large numbers of people to find employment in traditional occupations, especially farming, and this in turn leads to the subdividing of already small farms to the point where they become hopelessly inefficient and the introduction of modern machinery is impossible. For example, in Egypt in 1950, 70 percent of farm owners were already trying to make a living with less than half an acre.[5] As one observer remarked, "Most of those who are working the land work not because the land requires their labor but because they require the work."[6] As early as 1939, it was estimated that 10 percent of Egypt's farmers could have supplied all the necessary labor if Egypt's farms had been even half as mechanized as America's. The story is much the same in other industrializing agrarian societies.

Another factor retarding economic development is the poverty of the excess population. Because these people cannot afford to buy anything but the basic necessities, they fail to generate a demand for the kinds of products that are essential components of the economy of every industrial society. Finally, this surplus population compounds all the other problems by its own productive achievements: an abundance of children. The society is thus trapped in a vicious circle.

In recent years, the leaders of a number of industrializing agrarian societies have finally begun to grasp the seriousness of the population problem and its relation to economic growth and have encouraged the use of modern methods of birth control. In many cases, however, their efforts have not been very successful, largely because children are still perceived as an economic asset by the average peasant farmer. While they are growing up, they are cheap labor, and when their parents become too old to work, the children can support them. If too many children survive to adulthood, they can be sent to the cities to look for work. Unfortunately, a growing number of them will be looking for jobs that do not exist, or jobs they can fill only while they are young and strong. After that they will drift into the ranks of the underemployed and the unemployed and become a further drain on the economy. People like these occupy the squatter settlements and shantytowns that contain from one-fourth to two-thirds of the populations of most Third World metropolises.[7] These settlements are growing at an annual rate of 12 percent a year, which means *they double in size in about six years*.

By the middle 1970s, there began to be increasing concern in a number of industrializing agrarian societies for the problems caused by unchecked population

FIGURE 15.3 According to a United Nations' study, one-fourth to two-thirds of the populations of most Third World cities live in squatter settlements and shantytowns, such as this one in Lima, Peru.

growth. In 1976, the Indian state of Maharashtra, which has a population as large as that of France, adopted a law that provided jail sentences and fines for couples of childbearing age who had three or more children and refused sterilization.[8] Introducing the legislation, the state's minister of health said, "If the alarming rate of growth is not checked it will be impossible to remove poverty and realize the fruits of economic development." India's Minister of Health and Family Planning announced that this law was soon to be adopted nationwide, but plans for this were shelved because of widespread reaction against the government's quota system for male sterilization. This public outcry soon led to the downfall of the government. Under the new government, the number of sterilizations performed annually dropped by 90 percent, and the birthrate edged up from 33 per 1,000 population per year to 35.[9] Since then, the Indian government has been reluctant to act in this sensitive area.

In contrast, the People's Republic of China under Deng Xiaoping's leadership moved vigorously to check population growth. The government announced that if every woman of childbearing age had only three children, by the year 2080 China's population would rise to 4.3 billion, nearly the equivalent of the present *world* population![10] To avert this, the government created a system of sanctions that encouraged small families and discouraged large ones. Contraceptives, abortions, and sterilizations were made available at no cost. Women could not register to marry until age twenty-three, and men until age twenty-five in rural areas and twenty-six in urban.[11] When women checked into hospitals to have their first child, they were offered bo-

FIGURE 15.4 In recent years, the People's Republic of China has moved vigorously to check population growth: billboard promoting the one-child family, Chengdu.

nuses if they permitted postnatal sterilization, and there has been a national campaign to pressure young couples into signing a "one family, one child" pledge. Couples who marry late and those who have only one child have been given top priority in housing assignments, while physicians, nurseries, and schools are instructed to give preference to children who have no siblings. There are punishments as well as rewards. Couples who have three children, for example, are fined 10 percent of their pay for fourteen years, the time it takes for most children to join the labor force.

Taiwan is another industrializing society whose leaders have recognized the need for vigorous action. They have created a system whereby couples with two children receive a credit of $25 a year for a period of ten years, with the accumulated funds plus interest later made available for the children's education. If a third child is born, the annual payments are cut in half, and a fourth child disqualifies the family.[12] The most recent figures from Taiwan indicate striking success: its birthrate has dropped to less than 17 per 1,000 population per year, a figure that is not much above that of most advanced industrial societies. If other Third World nations are willing to initiate measures comparable to China's and Taiwan's, there is reason to hope that the era of runaway population growth will draw to a close and that standards of living in these nations will improve more rapidly.

THE ECONOMY

The economies of industrializing societies consist of two basic components. The traditional component is very similar to the economy of the typical agrarian society of the last 2,000 years. The tools and techniques are much the same, and so is the level of productivity. The modern—or at least modernizing—component has tools, techniques, and patterns of economic organization that have, for the most part, been borrowed from industrial societies.

Obviously, such a division results in tremendous internal differences within a society. The people in some areas are living much the way their forebears did centuries ago, while in other parts of the same society, many people are living very much like the residents of Washington, London, or Tokyo. Table 15.4 illustrates the kinds and degrees of differences that can separate the members of industrializing agrarian societies. A similar cleavage exists in most industrializing societies.

TABLE 15.4 **Some Indicators of Regional Differences in Greece**

Indicators	Greater Athens	Thrace
Per capita consumption of electric energy in kilowatt-hours	833	34
Private cars per 10,000 inhabitants	168	8
Percentage of households with inside baths or showers	30	2
Percentage of households with running water	72	21
Number of doctors per 10,000 inhabitants	33	3
Number of hospital beds per 10,000 inhabitants	142	17

Source: Nikos Mouzelis and Michael Attalides, "Greece," in Margaret Archer and Salvador Giner (eds.), *Contemporary Europe* (New York: St. Martin's, 1972), p. 187.

The industrial sector of the economy of these societies is not simply a scaled-down version of the economy of a typical industrial society, however. In other words, it is not likely to contain a representative sample of industries—some small steel mills, a small automobile plant or two, some textile mills, a variety of wholesale and retail distributors, and so on. Instead, this sector of the economy is often rather one-sided in its development, with one or two key industries heavily overrepresented.

To understand why this is so, we have to bear in mind the tremendous difference in the circumstances under which these nations are industrializing and those under which the fully industrial societies industrialized. Today's developing societies are industrializing in a world that is dominated politically and economically by *already industrialized* societies with which they are interdependent. Producers in the already industrialized societies have easy access to their own large and affluent home markets and thus are now able to spread their fixed costs (see page 282) over a large volume of goods. This gives them a great competitive advantage in many industries. Add to this the low cost of moving goods today, thanks to advances in transportation technology (see page 183), and it is easy to see why producers in industrializing societies are often in a poor competitive position *even in their own home markets*. Thus, European, American, and Japanese firms have come to dominate world markets for most manufactured products.

As a result, many of the industrializing societies have been forced into a distinctive ecological niche: they have become the producers of raw materials for the world economy. Furthermore, because of pressures generated by world markets and by their own desire to maximize income, they often become dangerously specialized (see Table 15.5).

A society that depends so heavily on just one commodity is highly vulnerable to any shift in the world economy that affects its specialty. Technological innovations (e.g., synthetic fibers, coffee or sugar substitutes) may permanently reduce, or even wipe out, demand for the product. This sensitivity to change often creates an unstable

TABLE 15.5 Leading Exports of Ten Industrializing Agrarian Societies and Their Percentage Dependence on These Commodities for Foreign Exchange

Society	Commodity	Percentage Dependence
Venezuela	Petroleum	95
Cuba	Sugar	75
Algeria	Petroleum	63
Indonesia	Petroleum	44
Bangladesh	Textiles	38
Pakistan	Textiles	37
Honduras	Bananas	33
Guatemala	Coffee	32
Bolivia	Tin	25
Thailand	Rice	17

Source: Adapted from United Nations, *Yearbook of International Trade Statistics, 1986,* vol. 1, table 5.

FIGURE 15.5 The economies of industrializing societies consist of two distinctive sectors, a rural sector which has changed little from the preindustrial past and an urban sector where the impact of industrialization is clearly evident. Two views of Yugoslavia: peasants plowing with oxen and city scene in Belgrade.

"boom or bust" atmosphere that is not conducive to rational economic planning and development by either business or government. Instead, it encourages a speculative approach with the goal of making a quick profit and then transferring capital to safer investments elsewhere.

Despite such drawbacks, these specialized industries can help developing societies industrialize more rapidly. For one thing, they move people out of traditional subsistence agriculture and into jobs in the modern sector. These people are thus introduced to the new world of machine technology, to new skills, and to new attitudes and values.[13] Equally important, these industries serve as a source of capital to finance further industrial development. Some of the Middle Eastern oil states have used part of their income for this purpose, creating their own steel mills, petrochemical plants, aluminum smelters, fertilizer plants, and other industrial establishments.[14] One result is that, whereas industrializing societies had to import 30 percent of their steel as recently as 1970, they are now *net exporters* by a small margin.

It is still too early to say whether the benefits of specialized export industries will, in the long run, outweigh their costs. This will probably depend on the product involved. In the case of societies that export petroleum and natural gas, for which there is great demand, a finite supply, and low costs of production, the long-term prospects seem reasonably good. With adequate political leadership, these societies should be able to industrialize eventually.

In contrast, societies that produce commodities which are not essential or for which substitutes can easily be found, or commodities whose prices are highly unstable, will find industrialization much more difficult. The experience of Cuba under Castro is a classic case (see Table 15.5): despite the shift from capitalism to socialism, Cuba is still largely dependent on its sugar crop (and on the large Soviet subsidy it receives in exchange for military services provided to Soviet allies in various parts of the Third World).[15]

As Cuba reminds us, a number of industrializing agrarian societies are now controlled by Marxist-Leninist elites. They include Yugoslavia, Bulgaria, Romania, Albania, China, North Korea, Vietnam, Kampuchea, Laos, Afghanistan, and Ethiopia. At present, these societies have a variety of economies. Yugoslavia has developed a type of economy that it calls "market socialism," and China, too, has moved in the direction of a mixed economy. Cuba, Albania, North Korea, and Vietnam, meanwhile, have classical command economies, while in Kampuchea, Afghanistan, and Ethiopia conditions are in such turmoil that neither a true market nor a command economy can function properly.

A number of non-Marxist industrializing agrarian societies have also adopted command economies to a greater or lesser degree in recent decades. India and Mexico are examples, but they are not the only ones.

Based on the experience of societies such as China, Cuba, India, and Mexico—all of which have maintained command economies for a quarter of a century or more—it is clear that such an economy works no better in industrializing societies than in industrial. Compared with industrializing agrarian societies that have relied much more on market mechanisms (e.g., Taiwan and South Korea), the records of China, Cuba, India, and Mexico are very disappointing. In fact, China's performance has been so disappointing that its leaders have felt compelled to reintroduce market mechanisms

FIGURE 15.6 Between 1980 and 1985, the number of private businesses in China increased from 660,000 to 10.6 million: small entrepreneur, Beijing.

of various kinds. Between 1980 and 1985, the number of private businesses in that country increased from 660,000 to 10.6 million, and 14 percent of all retail sales now occur in the private sector.[16] Furthermore, at least one large Chinese-owned private corporation has been reestablished and several small stock exchanges have opened.[17]

Underlining the importance of these developments, the Chinese Communist Party newspaper, *People's Daily*, declared in a major editorial that the Chinese people can no longer rely on the writings of Marx and Lenin for answers to their problems, since these men never encountered or wrote about the kinds of problems that China faces today.[18] According to Party leaders, the Chinese people must become pragmatic and learn from experience. If these policies prove successful in China, which has long been noted for its recalcitrant economic problems, other industrializing societies may well follow its example and rely more on market mechanisms and pragmatism and less on centralized economic planning and doctrinaire ideologies.

THE POLITY

In industrializing agrarian societies, one of the greatest hindrances to development has been the kind of governing class they inherited from the past. This class enjoyed a privileged status for centuries, and its members have seldom shown any desire to change things in the twentieth century. Their ideal has been the kind of society that flourished before intellectuals, students, and the common people ever heard of liberty, equality, democracy, socialism, or communism. From their perspective, change is something to be resisted or, when possible, exploited for their personal benefit.

In the last hundred years, a growing number of voices have been raised against this backward-looking, exploitative class. In some societies, proponents of development have seized control of the government, hoping they could use the power of the state as a force for political, economic, and social change. These modernizers have been a mixed lot. Some have been military men with a strong spirit of nationalism; some have been civilians and democratic socialists. A number have been Marxists, and in at least one case—Iran—the monarch himself played this role.

Would-be modernizers have usually found, however, that it is not enough simply to win control of the government. To implement their plans, they need the support of thousands of lower- and middle-level officials who are both efficient and honest. Unfortunately, such people are hard to find in societies that for centuries provided education for only a few and viewed government office as a means for self-aggrandizement. The problem is further compounded by the political need to provide public-sector employment for large numbers of graduates of high schools and universities who might otherwise be unemployed and attracted to revolutionary movements, and by the inability of governments to pay them an adequate wage. Thus, older patterns of corruption and inefficiency are frequently perpetuated and the plans of would-be modernizers frustrated.

One of the most important issues facing the leaders of industrializing societies today concerns the role of government in the developmental process. In recent decades there have been two contrasting models to choose from, one provided by the western industrial democracies, especially Britain, France, and the United States, the other by revolutionary socialist societies, especially the Soviet Union.

Prior to World War II and for some time thereafter, most would-be modernizers in the Third World chose the western democracies as their model. A democratic government with limited powers working in combination with a market economy seemed to them to offer the best hope for societal development. But the adoption of these institutions seldom produced the results they expected. Industrializing societies that adopted this model often became bogged down in divisive party rivalries, corruption of officials frequently undermined public support, economic growth was generally slower than had been anticipated, and persisting economic inequalities led to social unrest. As a result, democratic governments in the Third World were toppled with increasing frequency by authoritarian elites of one kind or another.

In many societies, the new elites were army officers who had become disgusted with the corruption and incompetence of democratic politicians. Some of these officers saw their task simply as one of removing corrupt and incompetent leaders and quickly restoring democratic government. Others, however, lost faith in the democratic process and came to see themselves as their nation's rightful leaders.

Following World War II, an increasing number of modernizers, both military and civilian, adopted Soviet society as the model to emulate. They were attracted both by the ideals of Marx and by the authoritarianism of Lenin, a combination that promised to eliminate the kinds of political conflicts that are inevitable in democratic societies. Instead, it concentrated political power in the hands of a tiny group of individuals who shared a common vision of the future and were prepared to use all the powers of the state to implement that vision. Under the leadership of dedicated Marxist-Leninists, revolutionary socialist regimes were established in Yugoslavia, Albania, China, North Vietnam, North Korea, and Cuba.

For a number of years it seemed as if the Soviet model was providing effective solutions to the problems of industrializing societies. By carefully controlling the flow of information out of their societies, the new elites were able to project an image of great success.[19] More recently, however, as the facts have become better known, a very different picture has emerged. In China, Mao's successors openly acknowledged the failure of the Soviet model and began making drastic changes.[20] In Vietnam, where the leadership continued to adhere to the Soviet model, the economic situation deteriorated so badly that visitors to Hanoi report being stunned by the "grinding poverty." Especially disturbing is the fact that conditions are not improving; on the contrary, the standard of living seems lower today than at the end of the war. Similarly, in Cuba, where Castro has also been unwilling to make changes, large numbers of people seem eager to leave, and there is little evidence of economic progress.

In some industrializing agrarian societies, meanwhile, the failure of both the western and Soviet models of development has produced movements that advocate a return to the past. This tendency has been especially evident in Islamic societies, with Iran being the most striking example. While the negative aspects of this movement (e.g., animosity toward non-Muslims) have an obvious appeal for the masses of peasants and others who are frustrated by the slowness of progress and angered by their continued poverty, it is hard to see how backward-looking movements will improve their standard of living or solve their other problems. Disillusionment has, in fact, already set in in Iran, and one suspects that the same will happen in other societies after traditionalist regimes have been in power long enough for their own shortcomings to become obvious.

Based on the experience of most industrializing agrarian societies to date, it seems that there is no simple political solution to their many problems. No form of government can solve all of them, and every form of government is vulnerable to criticism and perhaps even to revolution. Thus, continued political instability may prove to be the unhappy fate of many of these societies—at least until they are able to provide a higher standard of living for more of their people.

SOCIAL STRATIFICATION

Systems of stratification in industrializing agrarian societies are as varied as the polities and economies to which they are linked. In a number of them, the class structure is still much as it was in agrarian societies of the past, though modified to some degree by industrialization. In others, the traditional class structure has been modified not only by industrialization but by revolutionary socialism as well.

In societies of the first variety, the upper class is still basically an aristocracy of long-established, wealthy, landowning families that dominate the government, the army, the religious establishment, and other social institutions. The middle class is small and made up of merchants, lesser officials, lesser members of the clergy, and a few prosperous peasants. In addition, it includes a growing number of business and professional people with modern education and skills, members of the civil service with modern educational qualifications, and teachers trained in such new disciplines as science and engineering. As industrialization and modernization progress, some members of the new middle class may penetrate into the upper class by virtue of their wealth or political success. In effect, however, there tend to be two separate systems of stratification in these societies. One is dominant in rural areas and reflects the old order; the other is dominant in urban areas and reflects the new. With the passage of time, the newer system of stratification, which is based on the industrial economy, tends to become dominant throughout the country as a whole.

In societies with revolutionary socialist regimes, the transformation of the system of stratification has been quicker and more ruthless. Many members of the old upper class were killed and the rest have had their property taken from them. They have been replaced by a new elite made up of leading Party cadres. Merchants and private entrepreneurs were also eliminated from the ranks of the elite and replaced by the managers of state enterprises, who now make up a significant portion of the middle and upper classes. Overall, the system of stratification in these societies closely

FIGURE 15.7 As the experience of China, Cuba, Vietnam, and Russia have shown, revolutions led by young people often become gerontocracies: Deng Xiaoping, once a youthful revolutionary, clung to power until well into the ninth decade of his life.

resembles that of the former revolutionary socialist societies of eastern Europe, except that the proportion of peasants is much greater.

Modern education, especially training in engineering and science, is valuable in every industrializing society. It places many of the younger generation in a relatively advantageous position, since they tend to be better educated. This advantage is often reinforced by the effects of political revolutions. Because revolutions are usually the work of young people, they are usually followed by a period in which youth is an asset and young people are promoted much faster than they would be otherwise. As the Chinese, Vietnamese, Russian, and Cuban revolutions have demonstrated, however, this is a temporary phenomenon, and revolutionary elites often become gerontocracies.

The major variations in the composition of the lower classes in industrializing agrarian societies are the result of differences in levels of economic development. The less developed the society, the larger the peasant class and the smaller the urban class, especially people who work in factories and other modern industries. At one extreme, 80 to 95 percent of the labor force in Nepal, Kampuchea, and Ethiopia are still in agriculture and only a small percentage in industry. At the opposite extreme, countries like Mexico, Argentina, and Portugal have less than half of their workers in agriculture and 25 to 40 percent in manufacturing.[21]

Life is grim for large numbers of the lower classes in most industrializing agrar-

Satahu Sahni: Rickshaw Man

Satahu Sahni, one of Calcutta's poorer citizens, pulls a rickshaw for a living. He works from 6 *a.m.* to midnight, earning $3 a day. He lives in a one-room hut with his wife and two children. They spend about $2.50 a day for food alone, which provides tea and cookies for breakfast, a wheat cake for lunch, and rice and dried peas for supper. Satahu says of his work, "This job shouldn't be done by any human being, but I couldn't find any other thing to do."

Up and down hills, through broiling molten tar, across rough cobblestones, hauling heavy carts often loaded with more than one passenger as well as freight, Satahu and his fellow rickshaw men run day after day. In high humidity and with summer temperatures often above 100, a few of these men simply slip from between the shafts of their carts and drop dead every day. "It's really quite awful lately," said a British-educated Calcuttan, who has his own air-conditioned Mercedes and never rides in a rickshaw. "Not only do the poor runners die, but many passengers are injured when the rickshaws tip over backwards. Quite awful." But Satahu is fortunate compared to the hundreds of thousands of jobless persons and beggars in Calcutta who have no home at all and are forced to sleep on the open sidewalks at night and beg their food.

Source: Adapted from a copyrighted story by Myron Belkind of the Associated Press, by permission.

ian societies. High birthrates, low death rates, and inadequate educational systems combine to ensure an oversupply of unskilled labor, a situation that is aggravated by the economy's shift from human labor to machines. The excess population typically migrates from rural areas to the cities, where there are at least some employment opportunities for the young and able-bodied. But as in agrarian societies of the past, aging, accidents, and illness soon deprive these people of their economic value, especially when there is a steady stream of fresh labor continually moving into the cities.

CLEAVAGES AND CONFLICTS

Few societies in history have had such serious internal divisions as the majority of those now undergoing industrialization. Most of them are torn not only by ancient cleavages inherited from the preindustrial past, but also by some that are peculiar to societies trying to industrialize today.

The most basic of the older cleavages in industrializing agrarian societies is the one that separates the few who control the nation's resources from the vast majority who supply the labor and get little more than the barest necessities in return. The traditional antagonisms between urban and rural populations, and between the literate minority and the illiterate majority, are also present, though they tend to become less pronounced as advances in transportation and communication reduce the isolation, and hence the ignorance, of the rural and the illiterate.

As we have already seen, the struggle to industrialize and modernize creates its own animosities and conflicts. There is a split within the more favored classes, for example, between those educated along traditional lines and those with modern scientific and technical training. These groups often have difficulty understanding one another and tend to be mutually prejudiced against one another. Another new cleavage separates the powerful old landowning aristocracy and the new industrial entrepreneurs, who often have greater wealth.

As the monarchical political system found in agrarian societies has broken down, many new groups have become politically active and many new issues have become politically relevant. For example, the political unrest and other changes associated with industrialization often intensify old tensions between religious and ethnic groups. This has occurred in such widely scattered countries as Vietnam, Indonesia, Sri Lanka, India, Lebanon, Iraq, Iran, Egypt, Guyana, and others. In addition, the breakdown of the older political system and efforts to establish a modern regime can produce serious tensions between civilian leaders and the military. Struggles between these groups have caused countless crises in Latin American, Middle Eastern, and Asian nations. In democratic countries, mass political parties have introduced yet another cleavage. Although support for the various parties tends to follow other lines of cleavage, it is seldom a perfect reflection of them. Thus, it creates further divisions within already badly divided populations.[22]

Finally, the rapid rate of change characteristic of industrializing societies invariably creates a cleavage between the generations. This appears to be more serious than the generation gap in societies that have already industrialized, as indicated by the frequency and the bitterness of conflicts between students and political authori-

FIGURE 15.8 Few societies in history have had such serious internal divisions as the majority of those now undergoing industrialization: hundreds of thousands of Chinese students and workers gathered in Tiananmen Square in Beijing in 1989 to protest their society's lack of democracy.

ties in these nations and by the frequency of revolutionary activity in the younger generation. This is hardly surprising, of course, in societies that are changing so rapidly. The experiences of the different generations are so dissimilar that conflict is almost inevitable. Universities are often the centers of discontent, because they bring together large numbers of people who have maximum exposure to new ideas but little power to implement them. The result is often explosive.

Authoritarian governments of both the right and the left often manage to suppress their internal conflicts, so they are not always visible to the outside world. Yet as the Chinese experience indicates, suppressing them is not the same as eliminating them: any relaxation of control by the authorities results in new struggles for power. The fact of the matter is that industrialization and modernization are extremely stressful processes, and when the cleavages they generate are added to the historic cleavages inherent in an agrarian social order, the choice is often between harsh repression and chronic conflict.

EDUCATION

The importance of education for economic growth is abundantly clear: the most prosperous nations are those that have invested heavily in education. In the United States and Japan—two of the more striking examples of economic growth—high levels of national expenditure on education *preceded* industrialization.[23] In Japan, half the male population was literate by the 1870s, and in the United States, 90 percent of white adults were literate as early as 1840.

The relation between education and economic growth is borne out by studies that indicate that expansion of primary and secondary school enrollments, especially the latter, has been linked to increases in per capita GNP since World War II.[24] However, these same studies found that this relation did not exist in the case of expanded enrollments in *higher* education. The reasons for this are not clear, but it may reflect the fact that many industrializing societies have overemphasized training in the humanities and neglected training in fields required by industrialization. In both eastern and western Europe, for example, from one-third to one-half of university students study science or engineering, compared to only 23 percent of those in Asia and 16 percent in Latin America.[25]

These figures are important not only because industrializing societies so urgently need technical and engineering skills, but because those societies have so much trouble absorbing the nontechnical professionals their universities turn out. In India, for example, 58 percent of the students were recently enrolled in the humanities, fine arts, and law.[26] Most graduates simply cannot find jobs that utilize these skills. Unwilling to accept lesser employment, they become a kind of intellectual proletariat with deep-seated hostilities toward the existing social order. Because such people are easily attracted to revolutionary movements, this leads to more political instability, and this, in turn, hampers economic progress. In short, far from aiding economic growth, an oversupply of nontechnically trained students in a society actually hinders it.*

IDEOLOGIES OLD AND NEW

Most leaders of modernizing movements are aware that social and economic progress requires more than increased capital and improved techniques of production. New creeds and new gods are needed to arouse and mobilize the common people who, after centuries of frustration, are often apathetic and fatalistic. Ironically, even a dedicated Marxist like Mao Zedong came to place the struggle for people's hearts and minds ahead of the struggle to transform the economy.

Today, in all but the most backward parts of the industrializing agrarian world, there is an intellectual ferment and a clash of ideas between the advocates of traditional belief systems and the proponents of newer ones. The situation is often extremely complicated, because both traditionalists and modernizers differ among themselves on many points, while others favor various blends of the old and the new.

A lot of the intellectual and ideological resistance to modernization has come from leaders of the traditional faiths. In southern and eastern Asia, these have been

*One may ask why the leaders of these societies allow this kind of educational imbalance to develop. There are two main reasons. First, in allowing the humanities to dominate their educational systems, they are following the example of the oldest and most prestigious educational institutions in the world—Oxford, Cambridge, and the famous continental universities—as well as their own native traditions. Second, it costs much more to provide technical education, and these nations have very limited resources.

Buddhism, Hinduism, and Islam; in the Middle East, Islam.* In all these areas, religious leaders have often been the leaders of conservative and traditionalist movements. This is hardly surprising considering the historic role of these ideologies in agrarian societies and the nature of their beliefs. In general, they believe that the quest for truth is essentially complete: what people need to know has already been revealed— in the Vedas, or in the Koran, or to the Sangha. True wisdom, in their opinion, lies in turning to religious authorities for guidance and following their directions. In describing the traditionalist approach to education in the Middle East, one writer has said, "Education, as far as it is under the control of the ulema [the spiritual leaders of the Muslim community], is still bound up with authoritarianism, rote learning, and a rigid devotion to ancient authorities—providing only already known solutions to already formulated problems."[27] This approach sees little need for change, unless it is to root out whatever modernizing influences have crept in.

In the late nineteenth and early twentieth centuries, many western intellectuals thought these older faiths would simply die out as their adherents came to recognize the "obvious" superiority of western creeds such as Protestantism, humanism, and socialism. These newer faiths were then winning converts, especially among the better educated, and it looked as if it were only a matter of time until the older faiths would vanish altogether.

Since World War I, however, and even more since World War II, the situation has changed drastically in many areas. With the development of nationalist movements and a growing resistance to western ideas and influences, some of the traditional faiths have experienced a remarkable reinvigoration. After Sri Lanka won its independence, for example, a significant number of Christian converts there reconverted to Buddhism. In India, Hindu traditionalist forces became strong enough to pass laws forbidding the entry of foreign missionaries. In Egypt, most of the leaders of the Communist Party were imprisoned or executed. In Iran, the Ayatollah Khomeini led an Islamic revolution that overthrew the Shah and ended his program of modernization.

Although religious leaders have often been among the most conspicuous proponents of traditionalism, they have usually had strong support from the old governing class, especially the large landowners.[28] In fact, the rural population as a whole, emotionally involved in its traditional religion and unfamiliar with alternatives, has generally supported them. Members of such old "professions" as herbalists and practitioners of traditional medicine have also been strong supporters of traditionalist ideologies and belief systems, because they recognize that their skills would become obsolete in a modern industrial society.

Ranged against the traditionalists are individuals and groups who, by virtue of educational, occupational, or other experience, have been converted to the newer faiths. Early in a modernization movement, a disproportionate number of the leaders are people who were won over to the new outlook during visits to industrial societies, either as students or as workers. This was true, for example, of India's Nehru and of Vietnam's Ho Chi Minh.[29] Later, however, most of the leaders are people who were

---

* Roman Catholicism plays a similar role in Latin America in one respect: its opposition to all forms of birth control. Until a decade or so ago, the Catholic Church was also a very conservative force politically and economically, but that has changed considerably in more recent years.

FIGURE 15.9 Much of the intellectual and ideological resistance to modernization has come from the leaders of traditional faiths: the late Ayatollah Khomeini, a leading opponent of modernization in the Islamic world, addressing a group of his followers.

converted by experiences in their own countries. Frequently they are children of members of the old governing class who rise to positions of leadership because of their superior training and other resources.

As we have noted earlier, there are usually competing groups of modernizers, some advocating western-style democracy, others Marxism-Leninism, still others some kind of hybrid system. The liberal democratic model was the first to be tried in most industrializing agrarian nations, as we also noted. It has had its greatest support from the more prosperous segments of the new middle class—professional people, managers in new industries, and others with modern education. Socialism was usually tried next. Its support has been greatest among intellectuals, students, and the economically insecure—landless peasants and unemployed urban workers.

A more recent approach to modernization is nationalism, which reflects the dissatisfaction of many of the current generation of leaders with both of the models. Nationalists often advocate a synthesis not only of capitalism and socialism but of modernism and traditionalism as well. Nationalism has often been a reaction against colonialism, especially in countries that were under foreign control until recently. It is also a reaction against the continued technological and economic dependence of industrializing societies on the more advanced industrial societies.

There is more to modern nationalism than this, however. It is also an effort to reaffirm the importance of a society's own cultural traditions. Sometimes this helps to heal the breach between traditionalists and modernists by providing a position that is acceptable to both. Moreover, it gives dignity to a nation's leaders in their relations with technologically more advanced societies.

Unfortunately, the cultivation of nationalist sentiments can easily lead to hatred of other nations. If this does not happen spontaneously, leaders may even encourage it to divert criticism from themselves and their policies. It can be very useful to blame foreigners for all the defects and shortcomings, inevitable and otherwise, of one's own policies.

Before attempting to draw conclusions about the experience of industrializing agrarian societies, however, we need to consider industrializing horticultural societies. A comparison of the two types will help us understand both of them better.

16

Industrializing
Horticultural Societies

Approximately 10 percent of the world's population live in industrializing horticultural societies. These societies are found in only three places: Africa south of the Sahara, Papua New Guinea in the South Pacific, and Haiti in the Caribbean. Horticultural societies also flourished until recently in some of the less accessible parts of southeast Asia and Latin America, but all of them have been either conquered or peacefully assimilated by larger and more powerful industrializing agrarian societies.[1] In sub-Saharan Africa, New Guinea, and Haiti, however, things are different: horticulture, rather than agriculture, remains the dominant mode of subsistence, and many social and cultural patterns from the preindustrial past survive and even flourish.

Industrializing horticultural societies, like industrializing agrarian societies, are confronted by a rapidly changing social environment dominated by industrial societies. They, too, are forced to adapt to the new industrial technology and to all of the changes and challenges that follow in its wake. And they, too, find many of the new cultural elements disruptive of their social institutions and traditional way of life.

There are, however, important differences between these two kinds of industrializing societies that stem from their dissimilar histories. Compared to societies with an agrarian heritage, those with a horticultural heritage are badly handicapped in the industrial era.[2] Their social and cultural experiences have not equipped them and their people to cope with the modern world as effectively as the heritages of agrarian societies. For many of the cultural elements that are essential in the industrial era—such as urbanism, governmental bureaucracy, standardized monetary systems, and literacy—were either absent in horticultural societies or were far less developed than in agrarian societies. Thus, horticultural societies have been poorly prepared for the highly complex and highly competitive world system created by the Industrial Revolution, and for its formidable challenges.

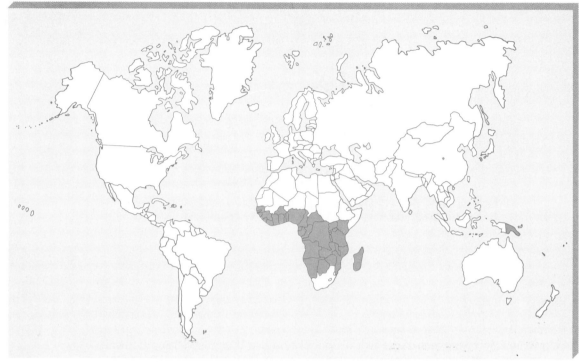

FIGURE 16.1 Industrializing horticultural societies in the world today are shown in dark blue.

TECHNOLOGY AND PRODUCTIVITY

Technologically, industrializing horticultural societies are much less advanced than industrializing agrarian societies, especially in their indigenous, or native, technology. This is revealed in a number of ways. For one thing, they are far less urbanized: industrializing agrarian societies have on average 48 percent of their populations living in urban communities, while industrializing horticultural societies have only 26 percent on average.[3] This difference is important, because the size of the urban population is a good indicator both of the size of the economic surplus and of the growth of specialized crafts and trade and commerce.

Per capita GNP is a useful summary measure of the level of both technological advance and productivity in the two types of industrializing societies. In the late 1980s, the median per capita GNP for 26 industrializing horticultural societies was $320; for 44 industrializing agrarian societies, it was $1,100.[4]

One of the most disturbing features of industrializing horticultural societies has been the limited success most of them have had in raising the standards of living of their people. In fact, in the quarter of a century since 1965, the standard of living has declined in more than a third of them. And in some—Ghana, Liberia, Madagascar, Uganda, Zaire, and Zambia—per capita income dropped more than 20 percent![5]

This is in sharp contrast to the situation in industrializing agrarian societies, of which only 12 percent experienced any decline in living standards during that period and only Nicaragua suffered more than a 20 percent decline. The differences are even greater when we look at the other end of the scale: per capita GNP has grown 2.0

percent or more annually in over half of industrializing agrarian societies but in only 14 percent of industrializing horticultural societies. And, finally, when *median* rates of growth in per capita income for the two sets of societies are compared, industrializing agrarian societies lead by a margin of almost five to one (2.4 percent per year to 0.5 percent).

The reasons for the economic difficulties of industrializing horticultural societies are not hard to find. First and foremost, there is the runaway rate of population growth (see Table 16.1). Second, many of them are controlled by leaders who are corrupt or repressive or both.[6] Third, there are the environmental problems described in the Excursus following Chapter 6—especially the problems caused by diseases and poor soils. Finally, as we noted above, the social and cultural heritages of these societies put them at a severe disadvantage in the modern world system. This handicaps them badly as they struggle to compete in a world dominated by societies whose social and cultural heritages include much that they lack.

POPULATION GROWTH AND ITS CONSEQUENCES

Industrializing horticultural societies appear to have the highest rates of population growth of any major set of societies in human history. Collectively, they are growing

TABLE 16.1 Crude Birthrates, Death Rates, and Rates of Natural Increase for Eighteen Industrializing Horticultural Societies

Society	Crude Birthrate*	Crude Death Rate†	Rate of Natural Increase‡
Kenya	52	11	4.1
Zambia	50	13	3.7
Ivory Coast	51	15	3.6
Tanzania	50	14	3.6
Rwanda	52	18	3.4
Uganda	50	17	3.3
Zimbabwe	44	11	3.3
Ghana	46	13	3.3
Nigeria	47	15	3.2
Liberia	45	13	3.2
Zaire	45	14	3.1
Mozambique	45	17	2.8
Papua New Guinea	39	12	2.7
Gabon	42	16	2.6
Sierra Leone	48	23	2.5
Guinea	47	23	2.4
Chad	44	20	2.4
Haiti	34	13	2.1

*Live births per 1,000 population per year.
†Deaths per 1,000 population per year.
‡Percentage growth of population due to excess of births over deaths per year.
Source: World Development Report, 1989, table 27.

3 percent or more a year. At that rate, their populations would multiply at least 16 times in less than a century! Small wonder that their economies are unable to keep pace and their standards of living are declining.

What is most disturbing about the current situation is the unwillingness of their governments to acknowledge the problem and adopt programs that would slow this runaway growth.[7] Western governments are not blameless in this matter either, since they have encouraged the idea that economic development alone can solve the problems of industrializing horticultural societies. Furthermore, western medical missionaries and others have worked to bring down the death rates in those societies without concerning themselves with the need to balance those changes with corresponding changes in birthrates. The result, as Table 16.1 shows, is that death rates have been drastically reduced while birthrates have remained at preindustrial levels (in fact, there are a number of indications that birthrates in Africa are now even higher than in the preindustrial past).

FIGURE 16.2 Western medical missionaries have worked to reduce death rates in industrializing societies without concerning themselves with the need to balance change with a corresponding reduction in birthrates. European nutritionist examining child in Zaire.

TABLE 16.2 Average Annual Growth Rates for Food Production and for Food Production Per Capita in Sub-Saharan Africa, 1970–1987, in Percentages

	1970–75	1976–79	1980–87
Food production	1.6	1.1	1.2
Food production per capita	−1.2	−1.5	−2.0

Source: Adapted from United Nations, *World Economic Survey, 1984: Current Trends and Policies*, table 1–6; and World Bank, *World Development Report, 1989*, tables 2 and 26.

Because of the extraordinarily rapid growth of population in industrializing horticultural societies, it has been impossible for economic growth to keep pace. In fact, as Table 16.2 indicates, the growth of population has run well ahead of the growth of food production since at least 1970, with the result that the amount of food available to the average individual has steadily declined. The economic problems that the societies of sub-Saharan Africa have faced in recent years cannot be explained away by droughts and natural disasters (though these have played an important part in some of them, at least since the middle 1970s). As Table 16.2 makes clear, the overall production of food has actually increased in those societies as a whole despite such events. Hunger has become a major problem because population has increased *even faster*.

THE ECONOMY

In some ways, the economies of industrializing horticultural societies resemble those of industrializing agrarian societies. For one thing, they, too, are a mixture of traditional and modern elements, with the result that there is often little resemblance between the economic patterns found in a nation's outlying villages and those in its largest cities. In addition, like many industrializing agrarian societies, the societies of

TABLE 16.3 Leading Exports of Nine Industrializing Horticultural Societies and Their Percentage Dependence on These Commodities for Foreign Exchange

Society	Commodity	Percentage Dependence
Nigeria	Petroleum	95
Zambia	Copper	90
Burundi	Coffee	88
Angola	Petroleum	82
Kenya	Coffee	58
Burkina Faso	Cotton	55
Ghana	Cocoa	55
Malawi	Tobacco	50
Togo	Phosphate	49

Source: Adapted from United Nations, *Yearbook of International Trade Statistics, 1989*, vol. 1, table 5.

FIGURE 16.3 Many industrializing societies have been forced into a specialized ecological niche as producers of raw materials for industrial societies. For years, more than half of Ghana's foreign exchange has come from the sale of cocoa, which is shown being collected at a cooperative marketing society.

sub-Saharan Africa are unable to compete in world markets with industrial societies in the production of most manufactured goods. Thus, they, too, tend to become highly specialized and to be suppliers of raw materials in these markets. In fact, their economies tend to be even more specialized than the economies of industrializing agrarian societies (compare Table 15.5, page 371, and Table 16.3).[8]

Since independence, many of the industrializing horticultural societies of Africa have proclaimed themselves socialist, or even Marxist-Leninist, societies. But African socialism is very different from European or Asian socialism. It is, in fact, as varied as the societies that have adopted it. Former President Senghor of Senegal, in a book entitled *African Socialism*, wrote, "We have rejected prefabricated models," and the economy of Senegal combines a communal system of agriculture with mixed public-private utilities and private ownership of banks, commerce, and industry.[9] Although the details vary from society to society, this blending of public and private ownership of the means of production is widespread. There are a few societies, such as Kenya and Ivory Coast, that lean heavily toward private ownership, and a larger number, such as Tanzania, Angola, and Mozambique, that lean heavily toward state ownership. But the majority mix capitalist and socialist principles, together with a generous component of subsistence farming and other traditional African economic practices.

The economic development programs of the more idealistic African leaders, such as former President Julius Nyerere of Tanzania, emphasized the need to improve the conditions of life for the common people and minimize economic inequalities. According to western experts on whom Nyerere relied, this would lead to a burst of economic growth and prosperity. This did not happen, however. Despite the creation of an extensive educational system and greatly improved health and sanitary facilities in 8,000 villages, the production of cash crops for export (which is essential to the economy) declined steadily. Were it not for the continuing infusion of foreign aid amounting to more than a quarter of Tanzania's GNP, the economy would be in desperate shape.[10]

Because the urban sector of the economy in horticultural societies has historically been so much less developed than in agrarian societies, urban populations in industrializing horticultural societies have had less experience with such fundamentals of modern life as money, occupational specialization, literacy, and bureaucracy. This makes it very difficult for modernizing governments and businesses to find skilled personnel to staff their organizations. The problem is especially serious in societies in which national pride often demands that businesses and government be staffed with native personnel, regardless of the cost in organizational efficiency.[11]

Data on education provide some idea of the relative magnitude of this problem for the two types of industrializing societies. The most recent data available show that, on average, 46 percent of young people in industrializing agrarian societies attend secondary schools, while in industrializing horticultural societies the comparable figure was only 16 percent.[12] As a secondary education increasingly becomes a minimum requirement for effective participation in modern economic life, it is clear that it will be many years before industrializing horticultural societies develop a fully qualified labor force.

Horticultural societies face still other problems in economic development. We can see why when we consider the traditional values and norms relating to work in these societies. Some years ago, the Inter-African Labour Institute characterized the work traditions of horticultural Africa this way:

1. Work is viewed in its relation to the basic institution of family or clan; within the family, it is divided on the basis of age and sex.
2. Work is linked with religious rites.
3. Work activities are evaluated in the light of a subsistence economy rather than a profit economy (i.e., they are oriented more to the production of the necessities of life than to the production of an economic surplus).
4. Work requires neither foresight nor planning.
5. Time is largely irrelevant in work activities; no time limits are set for most tasks.
6. There is little specialization.
7. For men, work is episodic; when a task has to be done, men often do it without a break, but intervals of inactivity are long and frequent.
8. Men hardly ever work alone; work activities (e.g., hunting parties and work parties) often resemble a collective leisure activity in modern industrial society.[13]

These traditions did little to prepare the members of these societies, especially the men, for work in a modern industrial economy. A parallel list of the characteristics of work in industrial societies would, in fact, be almost the opposite.

One of the biggest problems is suggested by item 7. In analyzing horticultural societies in Chapter 6, we saw that farming is often primarily women's work. Men's responsibilities tend to be limited to the occasional clearing of new gardens. While women do the sustained, tedious chores—planting, cultivating, and harvesting crops—men are free to do more interesting and exciting things—hunting, fighting, politicking, socializing, and participating in ceremonial activities. The disciplined, routinized patterns of work that are typical of an industrial economy are seldom experienced by men in these societies. In this respect, the peasant farmers of agrarian societies are far better prepared for industrialization. Yet even they find the transition difficult.[14]

There is tremendous economic and social variation within every industrializing horticultural society. A few villages are still largely untouched by the influences of industrialization, while in some cities the older patterns have been largely destroyed.[15] In addition, there is every conceivable combination of the old and the new—such as the woman in Nairobi who practiced witchcraft in order to earn the down payment on a truck so she could go into the trucking business.[16] A much more common practice is for men to work for extended periods in factories in the cities, while their wives continue to practice traditional horticulture in the villages.

One observer reports that there have been four basic economic patterns in Africa in the twentieth century.[17] The first, which has become extremely rare, is a pure subsistence economy in which the local village consumes only what it produces or obtains through barter with its neighbors. The second pattern is "taxed subsistence," in which a village also raises a cash crop or sends its young men out to work for cash so it can pay the taxes levied by the government. The third is a mixed economy: villagers still rely on subsistence farming for their basic necessities, but they also work for cash—not only because of taxes but so they can buy modern consumer goods. The fourth pattern is a predominantly cash economy in which even food is purchased and laborers are hired to work on farms.

These patterns, which usually follow one another in sequence in a particular area, show how internal and external forces combine to transform a society's economy. On one side there are the values and preferences of the villagers themselves; on the other are the demands made, and the attractions offered, by alien groups and institutions. It is easy to underestimate the power of the internal forces and to think of economic development as a process that is forced on reluctant villagers who would rather be left alone to live as their forebears did. But the problem is more complex than this. Given a choice, most of the members of horticultural societies choose the industrial way of life—not knowing, it is true, all the implications and ramifications of their choice. Sometimes they adopt it *in toto*, like the family that migrates to the city. In other cases, they adopt only part of it, like the family that stays in the village but earns all the cash it can to buy modern tools, cloth, soap, a sewing machine, a radio, a bicycle, and other products of an industrial economy; or the family in which the husband and father migrates to the city to earn money to buy such goods, which he brings back with him on periodic visits.

THE POLITY

One of the striking features of industrializing horticultural societies is how new most of them are: almost without exception, they were established in the late nineteenth or the twentieth century. Most of them are products of European colonialism, and their boundaries are largely the result of the rivalries of colonial governments or missions, the outcomes of battles, the location of rivers, and other things that had little to do with the boundaries of the older societies they replaced. Actually, the process was not too different from the one that produced most other contemporary societies.

Because of their newness, however, and because of their recent horticultural past, most industrializing horticultural societies suffer from serious internal divisions rooted in traditional tribal loyalties. Colonial powers seldom destroyed the older tribal groups. On the contrary, they usually preserved these groups in order to use them as instruments of administrative control, allowing tribal rulers to serve as lower-echelon officials. Colonial governments often pretended that these tribal groups were autonomous, because this enabled them to put the burden, and the onus, of political control on their leaders. They even encouraged tribal rivalries, applying the ancient principle "Divide and rule." As a result, after independence was won, there was a fundamental tension between tribal loyalties and national loyalties in most industrializing horticultural societies. This is a problem that few industrializing agrarian societies have had to contend with.

The consequences of tribalism have been serious for industrializing horticultural societies. Civil wars based on tribal divisions nearly destroyed Zaire in the early days of its independence. In Angola, Nigeria, Uganda, Zimbabwe, and others, the fuse

FIGURE 16.4 Frequency of multiparty democratic government, by societal type.

Source: Adapted from John Paxton (ed.), *The Statesman's Year-book, 1988–1989* (New York: St. Martin's Press, 1988), updated to take account of changes since publication.

burned more slowly but the results were even worse. In most African countries, tribalism remains a divisive force, often with the potential for civil war. When they were fighting for independence, many African leaders (as well as their friends in industrial societies) ignored or minimized the importance of these tribal loyalties, believing that their compatriots valued them as little as they did and that the old ties were rapidly losing their vitality. Although this may have been true in a few countries, it proved a serious misjudgment in most.[18] Even in cities and towns, tribal loyalties are still meaningful.[19] In view of the ethnic and linguistic diversity in these societies (Cameroon's 10 million citizens belong to 200 tribes and speak 24 languages; Zaire and Papua New Guinea each have 700 languages and dialects[20]), and considering the virtual absence of any national institutions in these societies until recently, this is hardly surprising. With increasing urbanization, with the establishment of schools that cultivate national loyalties, and with the growth of the mass media to reinforce these early lessons, tribal loyalties will probably disappear in time. But this will take decades or even generations, and in the meantime these allegiances often produce bitter and costly conflicts. The industrializing horticultural societies of Africa are currently spending $12 billion a year for armies and weapons—nearly twice the amount they receive in foreign aid.[21]

Compared to industrial and industrializing agrarian societies, industrializing horticultural societies are much less likely to have democratic governments (see Figure 16.4). Prior to independence, most of the leaders of these countries professed to be democrats and to believe in the multiparty system and free elections. Subsequently, however, when their policies were challenged and opposition forces threatened to turn them out of office, the leaders of most of these societies became advocates of a one-party government, with control in the hands of a single "strong man"—themselves. Only three industrializing horticultural societies—Botswana, Gambia, and Papua New Guinea—have maintained democratic governments. Former Tanzanian president Nyerere observed not long ago, "We spoke and acted as if, given the opportunity for self-government, we would quickly create utopias. Instead, injustice, even tyranny, is rampant."[22]

Related to this, the governments of many industrializing horticultural societies have had a major problem with corruption. In Zaire, for example, an international grant of $1.8 million to repair Kinshasa's broken-down city buses was reportedly "swindled down" to $200,000 by the time it reached the Transportation Ministry, while in Gabon the president built himself a $650 million marble palace with revolving rooms and walls that disappear at the touch of a button. For a number of years, oil-producing Arab nations were generous providers of foreign aid to sub-Saharan African societies, but they soon cut back on it after a series of bad experiences. A leading Arab publication reported, "In some cases now coming to light, for every $1 million of aid, less than $100,000 finds effective applications in African countries like Zambia and Zaire."[23]

SOCIAL STRATIFICATION

Although most industrializing horticultural societies profess to be socialist, the level of inequality in them tends to be higher than in the nonsocialist industrial democracies of Europe and America. In Kenya and Zambia, for example, government figures indicate that 46 percent of the national income goes to the top 10 percent of households, compared with 23 percent, or half as large a share, for the top 10 percent of American households.[24] In Zaire and in other societies where corruption has been widespread, the level of inequality may be even greater, though no statistics are available.

Since independence from colonial rule was achieved, the composition of the upper class has been substantially altered in most industrializing horticultural societies. The upper class is now composed mainly of new political elites whose control of the government is the basis of their wealth and power. Sometimes these elites are primarily military leaders, sometimes they are mainly civilians. Because of the continuing importance of kinship in these societies, the upper class includes many members of the extended families of these leaders. In addition, the upper class may include some intellectuals and some wealthy businessmen.

Beneath this politically and economically dominant class, there are two fairly distinct systems of stratification. In the rural areas, where traditional patterns still prevail, an individual's status is largely a function of his own and his family's relation to traditional authorities (especially the village headman and the tribal chief). In urban areas, where industrialization has had a far greater impact, the crucial criteria of status are education, occupation, income, and connections with the new political elite.

FIGURE 16.5 Even today, tribal leaders in industrializing horticultural societies often remain powerful and wealthy, especially in rural areas: the "king" of Akure in western Nigeria with a few of his 156 wives, a servant, and two of his late father's wives.

IDEOLOGIES OLD AND NEW

The traditional religions of horticultural societies were relatively undeveloped, both organizationally and intellectually, compared to those of agrarian Europe and Asia. There were no complex organizations of priests or monks, no body of sacred writings to serve as the core of a common faith, no tradition of philosophical speculation, and, most important of all, no universal faith to provide a bond between members of different societies. As a result, these faiths could not easily defend themselves against the inroads of Islam and Christianity, especially when the latter were introduced by peoples who were politically and economically dominant and whose way of life, therefore, seemed so obviously worthy of emulation.

People who still cling to the older tribal faiths are usually residents of the more isolated rural areas or the less educated residents of the towns. Since this describes the majority of people in these societies, adherents of the older faiths are obviously still numerous. In Benin and Togo, for example, only 30 percent of the people are even nominally Christian or Muslim; in Gabon and Zaire, less than 40 percent.[25] In the cities, however, the picture is very different. In Dar es Salaam, the capital of Tanzania, 99.8 percent of the population claimed to be either Muslim or Christian twenty-five years ago, at a time when 40 percent of the society as a whole were non-Muslim and non-Christian.[26] Similarly, in Monrovia, Liberia's capital, 72 percent were either Christian or Muslim at a time when only 25 percent of the nation as a whole were Christian or Muslim.[27]

Conversion to Islam and Christianity is often for nonreligious reasons. For many people it is a status symbol, an effort to identify with modern ways and avoid being regarded as ignorant, backward country folk. In Dar es Salaam, for example, many pagan tribesmen "on arrival in town call themselves Muslims—some few call themselves Christians—in order to conform, not to be conspicuous in a [community] where Islam is supreme and where to 'have no religion,' as people put it, is the mark of the uncivilized. Some go so far as to be circumcised and to be formally admitted to Islam: most merely use a Muslim name instead of a tribal one; some have two names, a Christian and a Muslim, to cover all eventualities."[28] Under the circumstances, it is hardly surprising to find that "the outward observances of religion are strikingly absent in Dar es Salaam: it is rare to see an African Muslim praying his daily prayers [and] in Ramadhan [the Muslim month of fasting] people may be seen anywhere eating and drinking publicly during the daily hours [a forbidden practice]," and the consumption of alcohol, also forbidden, is almost universal.[29] In Monrovia, where Christianity is dominant, the pattern is not quite so pronounced, but even here "the professing of Christianity remains a basic requirement of 'civilized' status," and "for a great many of the civilized, church membership has become largely a question of social status."[30] In many areas, both urban and rural, those who have adopted Christianity or Islam often continue to practice traditional tribal religions as well.[31]

In the early years of colonial rule, Christian missions were an important force for modernization. This was primarily due to the mission schools, which introduced literacy and elements of western culture and, most important of all, opened up channels of communication with the larger world. As a result, the areas that came under

Christian influence advanced more rapidly than those where paganism or Islam prevailed. In discussing Tanzania, one writer asserts:

> Mission schools and mission hospitals have been very important factors in
> changing tribal society, although their influence has been felt much more
> strongly in some areas than others. Very nearly a one-to-one correlation
> exists between mission influence, the cash-crop economy, fertile land, education, and the general desire for progress.[32]

Similarly, many people have commented on the singular economic success of the Christian Ibo of southeastern Nigeria compared with the Muslim and pagan tribes to the north.

With the rise of the independence movement after World War II, identification with Christianity became a somewhat ambiguous social attribute. Christianity was linked with colonialism, and colonialism was considered detrimental. Missionaries came under heavy attack for dominating the churches and refusing to let native Christians assume positions of leadership. Furthermore, in an era of great social change and uncertainty, mission-brand Christianity often seemed too tame and too western. In many areas, new sects were founded, some basically Christian, others largely pagan, many a mixture of both.[33] These sects have their greatest appeal for individuals who are in mid-passage in the difficult transition from traditional culture to modern. Such people are subject to great insecurity, both economically and intellectually, and the sects often provide a link to the past. They also are popular because they permit polygyny and other traditional practices condemned by the missionaries.

There are also new nontheistic ideologies in industrializing horticultural societies, the most important of which is nationalism. In many cases, nationalism functions simply as a secular ideology. But sometimes, when it demands supreme loyalty, it assumes a truly religious character. In Ghana, for example, President Nkrumah assumed messianic titles, and his political party took on quasi-religious functions.[34] Whether nationalism will survive in such an extreme form no one can say. This will probably depend on the experience these new societies have with the modernization process. The quicker and easier that is, the poorer the chances for the more extreme forms of nationalism.

KINSHIP

In horticultural societies of the past, kin groups were extremely important. As one writer put it, "the [kin group] was the basic building block of [horticultural] society."[35] More than that, it was psychologically the center of the individual's world, establishing a person's identity and defining most of his or her basic rights and responsibilities.

Now the historic bases of power of the kin group are being undermined in these societies. In the modern sector of the economy, the kin group no longer controls its members' access to the means of livelihood, which it traditionally did through its control of the land. Similarly, the family plays a smaller role in the political system. And the once-important cult of the ancestors, centered in the kin group, has declined in importance as Christianity and Islam have expanded.

In the past, most of the advantages of the kin group were enjoyed by the older generation, while the disadvantages fell disproportionately on the younger. Before the growth of cities and towns, young people had no choice but to accept the burdens and patiently await the day when they would become the privileged elders. The growth of cities and towns has changed all this: by migrating to these urban centers, young people can largely escape the control of their elders.[36] Although ties to the extended family are not entirely eliminated, they are greatly weakened, and this has become a cause of social instability in most industrializing horticultural societies.[37]

These changes in the kinship system also appear to have contributed to the runaway growth of population in these societies.[38] For example, the traditional stigma attached to unmarried mothers is no longer as powerful as it used to be when family controls over young people were stronger. In addition, the decline of polygynous households (a result of the influence of Christian missions) has apparently contributed to higher birthrates. As some Africans point out, although a few older, wealthy men could afford many wives and have large numbers of children, the wives in polygynous households usually had fewer children than women in monogamous households. Thus, a pattern of marriage that might seem to increase the birthrate actually had the opposite effect.

INDUSTRIALIZING SOCIETIES IN THEORETICAL PERSPECTIVE

Not many years ago, the prospects for industrializing societies looked bright. All they had to do, it appeared, was to follow the path blazed by the societies that had already industrialized. In fact, some people believed that because developing societies had the experience of others to go on, they would be able to avoid many of the problems of modernization and speed up the process.

Today, that prediction seems hopelessly naive. In most of the Third World, development has been distressingly slow. Improvements in the standard of living for the masses of their citizens have been especially disappointing. Hundreds of millions of people continue to live in poverty, with little prospect of any significant improvement in their situation.

Why were earlier predictions so wrong? Why have the majority of societies of the Third World been unable to take greater advantage of the vastly expanded store of technological information that is now available?

One answer, originally developed by a group of Latin American scholars in the 1960s and known as *dependency theory*, is that the difficulties of the less developed societies are due to their social environment, specifically to the actions of industrial societies.[39] The backwardness and problems of the less developed societies, they argue, are the result of exploitation and oppression by the more developed societies. Dependency theory is, in effect, an extension to the *global* level of Marx's theory that the growth of an increasingly impoverished proletariat is an inevitable consequence of the growing wealth of the bourgeoisie, or capitalist class.

There are currently a number of versions of dependency theory, each providing a somewhat different explanation of the Third World's problems. But all of them locate the source outside the industrializing societies themselves.[40] Some blame multinational corporations, some blame the governments of industrial societies, and others blame the capitalist world economy that has caused so many developing nations to concentrate on the production of raw materials and on low-technology industries. Whatever the cause, dependency theorists blame the difficulties of the Third World on western industrial societies.

Another group of scholars, mostly American, has developed a very different explanation of the Third World's problems. *Modernization theory* finds the source of these problems within the industrializing societies themselves.[41] As with dependency theory, there are a number of versions of modernization theory, but most of them focus on the attitudes and values of the members of Third World societies as the chief deterrent to industrialization. The difficulties of these societies, in their view, are due to the persistence of ideologies and institutional systems which were inherited from the preindustrial past and are incompatible with the needs and requirements of industrialization. They point out, for example, the persistence of fatalism, trust in magic, resistance to innovation and change, and the conflict between traditional patterns of work (see page 391) and the requirements of modern industrial enterprises. They emphasize the consequences of illiteracy and the lack of the information, training, and skills that are essential in the modern world. In short, modernization theory locates the causes of lagging development within the less developed societies themselves, rather than in their social environments.

In any attempt to evaluate the relative merits of dependency theory and modernization theory, it is important to keep two things in mind. First, there is little evidence to support the claim of some dependency theorists that life was better in most Third World societies before the industrial era. Such a view cannot be supported by the historical record of the last 5,000 years. It is a mistake, therefore, to ask, What has caused these societies to regress? Rather, the question must be, Why have the conditions in so many of them improved so slowly?

The second point to remember is that there is no reason to assume that the source of problems in the Third World is primarily internal *or* primarily external. On the contrary, ecological–evolutionary theory asserts that the characteristics of human societies—including the degree of their development—are the product of both internal *and* external forces (see Figure 1.4, page 18). To ignore or neglect either is to misunderstand and misinterpret the complex process of societal development.

One indication of the danger of neglecting either set of forces is provided by the results of the foreign aid programs created by western industrial societies in recent decades. Because of the tremendous success of the Marshall Plan in rebuilding West Germany following the massive destruction of World War II, many western leaders assumed that large transfers of capital to the less developed societies of Asia, Africa, and Latin America would produce similar results. Unfortunately, however, the results of aid to most of these societies have been extremely disappointing. As noted earlier, much of the money was wasted on ill-conceived projects or simply vanished into the pockets of corrupt officials. It has gradually become clear that the success of foreign aid programs depends as much on the characteristics of the recipient society as on the generosity of the donors. Effective use of large amounts of capital presupposes supportive institutions and ideologies in the recipient society, plus large numbers of people with administrative and technical skills and honest elites capable of organizing vast and complex programs.

The greatest deficiency of both modernization theory and dependency theory, however, is their failure to focus more closely on the distinctive demographic features of Third World societies. For the fact is that *no society has ever successfully industrialized while burdened with anything approaching the rate of population growth existing in most of these societies today*. Even impressive economic gains can be completely consumed by runaway population growth.

From the perspective of ecological–evolutionary theory, it is clear that the demographic peculiarities of Third World societies, as well as those characteristics of ideology and social structure that work against the resolution of their problems, all stem from a more basic underlying source. In most societies throughout human history, all of the basic components of their sociocultural systems—population, technology, ideology, social structure, and material products—evolved more or less in concert with one another. *In contrast, in societies industrializing today, selected elements of an enormously powerful industrial technology have been introduced into sociocultural systems that are still geared to much less potent agrarian or advanced horticultural technologies*.

Not surprisingly, these societies have had enormous difficulty in coordinating technological advance with changes in other areas of life. Even the western industrial democracies, in which the new technology evolved largely *in concert with* changes in population, ideology, social structure, and material products, have encountered difficulties in adjusting to the new industrial technology. In fact, most of their major problems reflect the failure of political ideologies, religious beliefs and values, legal norms, organization principles, and other cultural and structural elements to respond quickly enough to the new conditions created by ongoing changes in their technology.

Considering the problems an industrial technology can create *even in those societies in which it evolved*, it is hardly surprising that an industrial technology creates far greater ones when it is introduced as an alien force in societies still geared to simpler technologies. And when only selected elements of the new technology are introduced, the results can be disastrous.

India provides an excellent example of this. Over the last hundred years, improvements in transportation (especially railroads) and food production steadily reduced the number of deaths from famine, and programs of mass immunization and other health measures reduced deaths from disease. While this drastic reduction in the death rate was occurring, the vast majority of Indians, unlike the members of earlier industrializing societies, were not really involved in the industrialization process as a whole. Most of them continued to live as peasant farmers in relatively isolated villages, eking out a marginal existence on tiny farms, using traditional tools and techniques. As a result, their beliefs, values, and customs remained much as they had been for centuries, with large families highly valued and change viewed with profound skepticism. Not only the family but all of India's institutions (e.g., its educational system and its polity) were little altered by this *partial and selective diffusion* of industrial technology. The experience of most Third World societies, especially those with the greatest problems, has been similar to India's.

In the past, such imbalances in a sociocultural system would have been corrected through the play of natural forces. We saw earlier (page 121) how population pressures during the late hunting and gathering era led to the overkill of large game animals and, eventually, to the emergence of a more advanced technology and a new way of life. And we have seen how plagues and famines of the past periodically decimated the populations of agrarian societies, restoring their demographic equilibrium. In the case of India and other societies industrializing today, however, more advanced societies have repeatedly averted this resolution of the problem by shipping in large amounts of food. In doing so, they have created the likelihood of more serious crises and greater problems in the future.

It is clear from this that the solution to the major problems of the Third World lies in correcting this basic imbalance as quickly as possible. If new cultural mechanisms in the form of new beliefs, values, and sanctions to implement birth control technology fail to alleviate this problem, such forces as war, civil strife, famine, and disease will increase. And the longer it takes for the leaders of Third World societies to devise the necessary cultural solutions, the greater the chance that these forces will be activated. They are, in fact, already playing a significant role in much of the Third World.

Thus, from both selfish and altruistic points of view it would appear that industrial societies should begin shifting the focus of their efforts to help the Third World. Instead of trying primarily to alleviate symptoms, such as hunger, malnutrition, and disease, they should be directing their efforts toward eliminating the underlying causes of those symptoms. They will have to recognize that it is irresponsible to provide aid programs that seek to increase food production or improve infant health without simultaneously helping societies to lower their birthrates. Aid programs, in short, must become far more selective than they have been in the past, focusing always on underlying problems, not only in the area of population but also in such areas as education and energy.

The importance of both education and energy are fairly obvious. In the case of energy, however, the members of industrial societies have a special responsibility toward societies that are currently trying to industrialize. Not because of evil motives, but simply because they were the first to industrialize, advanced societies have been a major cause of high energy prices. Yet the availability of cheap and plentiful energy was an essential ingredient in their own industrialization and a major factor in their rapid climb to affluence. Without assistance, either in the form of financial subsidies to reduce the cost of energy in key industries or in the form of new and inexpensive energy technologies, Third World societies could well be condemned to a kind of global ghetto. In this area too, however, industrial societies would be well advised to make rigorous population policies a precondition for aid.

Of one thing we can be sure: the problems of the Third World are not going to be solved quickly. Because of the failure of most of these societies to control population growth in the past, they have large numbers of young people who are only

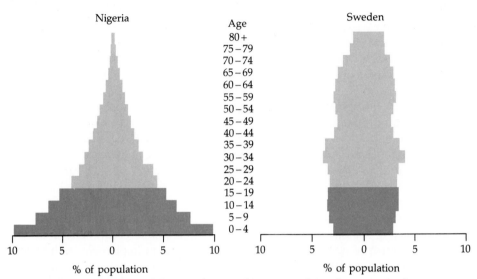

FIGURE 16.6 Age profiles of the populations of Nigeria and Sweden: note the large proportion of the Nigerian population that is less than 20 years of age and has only just entered the reproductive years.

now entering the reproductive years. As Figure 16.6 indicates, the age distribution of the population in an industrializing society such as Nigeria is vastly different from the age distribution in an advanced industrial society such as Sweden. Of every hundred Africans alive today, 55 are under twenty years of age; in contrast, of every hundred Europeans, only 30 are that young.[42] Because of the disproportionately large number of children and teen-agers in Third World societies, most of their populations will increase 50 percent in the next several decades even if every couple from now on were to limit itself to only two children. Under those unlikely circumstances, these societies would still have a heavily mortgaged future: a 50 percent increase in GNP would translate into no gain at all in *per capita* GNP.

In summary, industrializing societies provide a fascinating means of testing ecological–evolutionary theory, and other sociological theories as well. Their problems are so complex that they compel us to consider all of the components of sociocultural systems—population, culture, material products, social organization, and social institutions—as well as the relations among them. They also compel us to consider the relation of these sociocultural systems to the larger world system—which is good preparation for an analysis of the future, our primary concern in the final chapter.

17

Retrospect and Prospect

When we study something as complex as the evolution of human societies, it is easy to become so immersed in details that we lose sight of the larger picture. For this reason, we begin this final chapter with a brief look back over the long sweep of human history. Then we go on to consider an important question that we could not address until this point: What has sociocultural evolution really meant for humanity? More specifically, how has technological advance affected the quality of human life? Has it brought greater freedom, justice, and happiness? Or has the quality of life declined?

After considering these questions, we will turn our attention to *the future*. What lies ahead for human societies? Can ecological–evolutionary theory help us anticipate the problems and prospects of the next few decades? This is an important question, and a practical one as well. For most of us will live in that world, and it could be very different from the world we live in today.

LOOKING BACK

When we look back over the long course of hominid history, we see that we and our societies are an integral part of the global ecosystem and that our species' development has always been part of the same grand process of biological evolution that shapes all life on this planet. Yet it is equally clear that our species' development has been different from that of the rest of the biological world in some fundamental ways. If we understand where and how our path diverged, we can better understand our problems and those of our societies, and perhaps be able to create a better, happier future.

The Divergent Path

For millions of years there was little to suggest that our early ancestors were destined to become anything more than just another variety of primate. But genetic changes

403

gradually provided our ancestors with the ability to create symbol systems, a trait that is as much a product of natural selection as wings, gills, social instincts, and the other adaptive mechanisms of the biotic world.

With the aid of symbol systems, hominids were able to use their primate capacity for learning to far greater advantage. They could now create and share vast amounts of information that had been gleaned from individual experience. Eventually, hominid societies came to depend far more on new cultural information than on new genetic information in their adaptive efforts, and *human evolution came to be shaped primarily by the processes of cultural innovation and selection*, rather than by the processes of biological evolution.

The explanation of the tremendous adaptive capacity of cultural information is its potential for creating diversity. In this respect, it is like genetic information, which is responsible for the striking diversity in the biotic world. In the case of cultural information, however, *all of the diversity is concentrated within a single species*. As a result, despite a common genetic heritage, human individuals become, with culture, far more varied than the members of any other species. Human societies are also extremely varied—again, unlike the situation in other social species. Though such diversity enhances our species' survival potential, it is a major source of problems, both within and among societies.

Another manifestation of culture's capacity for creating diversity is the great variety of needs and desires that humans have developed, *needs and desires not even remotely related to our survival as individuals or as a species*. To satisfy these culturally triggered or intensified needs, societies have depended primarily on the kind of information—technological—that helps people utilize environmental resources in new ways and for new purposes. As technology advanced, however, it altered the conditions of life, and as that happened, further needs emerged. Efforts to satisfy these needs created further change, which led in turn to new needs, a process of positive feedback that has continued at an accelerating pace for at least 10,000 years.

Through this process, *humans established a new and unique relationship with the biophysical environment*. Since every other species of plant or animal uses the resources of its environment to satisfy only a limited set of genetically programmed needs, this characteristic is perhaps the most fundamental divergence of all.

The Question of Progress

Despite the problems that have attended our species' reliance on culture, one thing is clear: *culture has been a highly successful adaptive mechanism*. Humanity has not only survived, it has flourished by biological standards: there are far more of us alive today than at any time in the past, and our numbers are growing rapidly. Moreover, humans have spread into an enormous variety of environments—another important measure of biological success.

But numbers and dispersion are not enough on which to base an assessment of *human* evolution. We must also ask whether the process of sociocultural evolution has meant progress in terms of more uniquely human criteria and goals, such as freedom, justice, and happiness.

It is not easy to assess progress in terms such as these. For one thing, these concepts are so broad that they apply to countless aspects of human life. For another, the way we define such terms is the product of past experience, and this, as we have seen, varies greatly among individuals, groups, and societies. Nevertheless, because the subject is too important to ignore, we must at least make the effort to evaluate human progress in terms of these goals and try to determine whether our species' growing store of cultural information has had the effect of advancing or hindering them.

Freedom The high value that the members of modern industrial societies attach to freedom is revealed in the growing challenge to all forms of authority, not only in the liberal democracies of the West but in the authoritarian nations of eastern Europe as well. Even those who are not in the forefront of the libertarian movement are likely to consider the degree of freedom accorded individuals one of the basic measures of the attractiveness, and hence the progress, of a society, and they would deny that a technologically advanced, politically repressive society is truly progressive.

But human freedom is more than the absence of repressive social controls; it is also freedom from restraints imposed by nature. People who must spend most of their waking hours in an exhausting struggle to produce the necessities of life are not truly "free"—even if there are few social restraints on their actions. A woman whose life is a long succession of unwanted pregnancies is not "free"—regardless of the kind of society she lives in. Disease, physical and mental handicaps, geographical barriers, and all the laws of nature restrict people and deny them freedom. For freedom does not exist where there are no alternatives; and freedom can be measured only by the range of choices that are available. The fewer the viable choices, the less freedom there is—and it matters little whether the constraints are imposed by nature or by other people.

Once we recognize this, it becomes clear that humanity's long struggle to advance technologically is not irrelevant to the desire for freedom. Every technological innovation reflects the desire to overcome natural limitations on human action. Thanks to this struggle, some of us are now free to talk across oceans, free to travel faster than sound, free to live longer lives in better health while enjoying a range of experiences that far surpass in richness and variety what was available to the greatest kings and emperors of the past.

There has been a price to pay, of course: technological progress has necessitated larger and more complex social systems. If we want the option of flying to another part of the country instead of walking there, or of watching the day's events on a screen in our home instead of hearing about them weeks later, we have to accept certain social controls. The goods and services essential for those options can be produced only where there are organizations with rules and with sanctions to enforce the rules, and individuals with authority to exercise the sanctions. And these organizations can function efficiently only within a society that has rules to govern the relationships among them, and an authority system to enforce those rules. The only alternative is anarchy—and the loss of all the freedoms that modern technology affords.

Critics of modern society often say that the price has been too high, that the increased social restrictions outweigh the gains in freedom we derive from modern technology.[1] This is a matter each of us must decide for himself or herself. In doing so, however, we need to beware of romanticizing the past. Before deciding that people are less free than they used to be, we must read accounts of peasant life in agrarian societies and of the life of horticultural and hunting and gathering peoples. In doing this, we must resist the temptation to abstract the attractive features and ignore the appalling ones. We must remember that slavery and serfdom were not accidental characteristics of agrarian societies, but reflections of basic, inescapable conditions of that way of life, as were the high mortality rate and short life span of many hunting and gathering peoples.

Once we recognize the danger of comparing some rosy version of life in less advanced societies with the negative side of life in industrial societies, we are in a better position to consider whether freedom is a correlate of technological advance. We can say, first of all, that technological progress has clearly raised the *upper* limit of freedom in human societies. Individuals with the greatest measure of freedom in contemporary societies—that is, members of the upper classes—enjoy a far wider range of choice than individuals with the greatest measure of freedom in agrarian societies, and the elites of agrarian societies had far more freedom than the elites of less advanced societies. This has been true with respect to everything from the use of a leisure hour to the use of a lifetime. In this sense, then, there is a high positive correlation between technological advance and gains in human freedom.

The relation between technological advance and freedom for the *average* member of society is more complicated. If we compare the typical peasant in an agrarian society with a typical hunter and gatherer, it is not at all clear that there were gains. In fact, the peasant had to live with a lot of new social controls while gaining very little freedom from natural controls. Thus, during much of the course of history—especially after the formation of the state—the average individual probably experienced a *decline* in freedom. With industrialization, however, the pattern changes. Once the difficult period of transition is past, technological progress and freedom for the average person are positively related, as Figure 17.1 illustrates. Whether people in industrial societies have more freedom than hunters and gatherers is less certain. Clearly they have more social restraints, but far fewer physical and biological ones.

Before leaving the subject of freedom, we should take note of the popular misconception that governmental activity necessarily results in a loss of freedom for the members of society. This is at best a half-truth. Laws do, of course, place restrictions on people, but in democratic societies this is often done in order to increase freedom, not reduce it. The Pure Food and Drug Act in the United States, for example, was designed to restrict the freedom of businessmen who were willing to sell spoiled food and dangerous drugs for profit, but it increased the freedom of the millions of people who used their products. Sometimes, of course, laws restrict everyone's freedom in one area—the freedom to proceed at will through a busy intersection, for example—in order to preserve it in others. In short, most legal norms *redistribute* freedom.

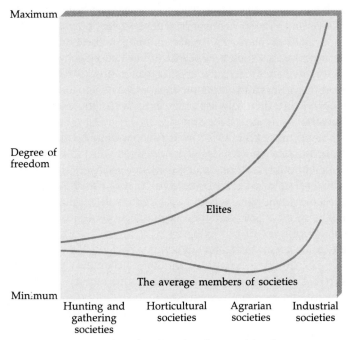

FIGURE 17.1 Trends in freedom for elites and for the average members of societies.

Justice Justice has to do with the *fairness* of a society in its treatment of its members. Although no one would quarrel with the idea that a society should be "fair," we run into trouble when we try to define what this means. Is a society fair when it rewards people on the basis of their contributions to the common good, or is it more equitable to allocate rewards on the basis of individual needs? Should handicapped individuals, for example, be paid the same as those who are able to outproduce them with less effort? And how does one arrive at a fair evaluation of the relative contributions of people in dissimilar activities—a symphony conductor, a bricklayer, a housewife, a garbage collector, a student?

And what about punishments? Does a "fair" society punish its members strictly in accordance with the letter of the law, or is it fairer to take circumstances and intent into account? What of a parent's theft to feed a hungry child, for example, or a mercy killing? And should a society deal less severely with those in positions of power than with lesser members of society when they commit crimes, or should everyone be treated equally? Questions like these point up the difficulty of measuring progress with respect to justice. Since an adequate treatment of the subject would require volumes, all we can do here is call attention to basic trends and offer tentative conclusions.

To begin with, as we observed in earlier chapters, social inequality became more pronounced as societies advanced technologically and status became increasingly dependent on the family into which one was born. The result was a weakening of the link between a person's *efforts* and a person's rewards. Whereas every normal, healthy boy in a hunting and gathering group had a chance of becoming the best hunter (and hence the most important man) in his society, a peasant's son had little hope of advancing even a notch above his father's social level, no matter how hard he tried. Increasingly rigid stratification systems locked people into roles and situations where they could neither develop nor use their talents, while those with little talent might occupy positions for which they were grossly unsuited.

The trend in punishment, meanwhile, was toward increasingly harsh and discriminatory treatment. In most agrarian societies, the privileged were free to abuse members of the lower class without fear of reproof; if the latter retaliated they would be punished swiftly and severely. A master involved in a conflict with his slaves or serfs was often both prosecutor and judge; he could beat them with impunity and, in many societies, kill them if he wished. Nor were there legal sanctions against the beating of children by parents, employers, or schoolmasters.

Courts of law were equally harsh. In eighteenth-century England, the death penalty could be invoked for 222 different offenses, including such minor infractions as the theft of a handkerchief, the shooting of a rabbit, or the forgery of a birth certificate.[2] Nor was execution always a humane process: we are told that the hangman in Elizabethan England was "an artist, and the knife was his chief instrument; the art consisting in tossing his man off the ladder, hanging him, but cutting him down before he breaks his neck, so that he may be dismembered and disemboweled while still alive."[3]

In general, societies seem to have become less fair and less just as they advanced technologically. With industrialization, however, there are clear signs of a reversal. With respect to material rewards, industrialization has resulted in some decline in the level of social inequality among the members of a society. Public education now provides at least some chance for almost all children to develop their abilities, and women and minorities have gained numerous legal and economic opportunities long denied them. Industrial societies are also more solicitous of their poor and their handicapped, and provide a far broader range of legal rights and protections for their members, whatever their social status. Criminal justice is far less harsh. Industrial societies today rarely execute their members, and never for minor infractions, nor do they maim them, as was common in the agrarian era. In short, after a long period of declining justice with respect to both rewards and punishments, there is finally movement in the other direction.

Happiness Of all the possible measures of progress, happiness is the most elusive, for it depends so much—perhaps primarily—on the quality of interpersonal relations: whether there is love, mutual respect, cooperation, and so forth. And these things do not depend on the level of technological development. Studies of modern hunting and gathering groups indicate that the most primitive peoples develop these qualities as surely as members of modern industrial societies do.[4]

There are several ways, however, in which technological progress is relevant to this kind of happiness. To begin with, some of life's greatest tragedies involve the premature death of a loved one—a cherished child, a parent, or a partner in a happy marriage. We saw how common this was in most societies prior to the Industrial Revolution and can therefore appreciate how the recently increased life span has contributed to human happiness.

Health, too, contributes to happiness. When we are seriously ill, life may not seem worth living. Disease was very poorly understood through most of human history, and technological advance prior to the Industrial Revolution had minimal impact in this area. More recently, however, advances in sanitation and medicine have dramatically improved the physical well-being of the members of many societies. Unfortunately, modern medical technology has also had a negative effect: it has been used to keep alive individuals who, in simpler societies, would mercifully be allowed to die. In balance, however, the result has undeniably been positive.

Hunger, another cause of enormous human misery over the centuries, has been drastically reduced in many societies as a result of industrialization. As recently as the eighteenth century, local crop failures in much of Europe could still result in starvation because of an inadequate transportation network. Today, thanks to advances in technology, food supplies can be safely stored for long periods, and moved to areas of scarcity, in every industrial society and in an increasing number of industrializing ones.

The industrialization of agriculture has also meant a substantially improved food supply, with respect to quality, quantity, and diversity, for most members of industrial societies. During the winter, for example, people can now enjoy fresh fruits and vegetables shipped in from areas with different growing seasons. Nor do the members of industrial societies have to subsist on short rations in the months prior to harvest, as members of traditional agrarian societies had to do. As with improvements in health, it is easy to take such benefits for granted and to lose sight of the numerous links between technological advance and human happiness.

The increased production of other kinds of goods and services, especially nonessential ones, has probably had much less effect on happiness. The absolute quantity of luxuries we enjoy is often not as important in this regard as how they compare with what people around us have. Thus the headman in a simple horticultural society may be quite content with his few special possessions, because they are more than his neighbors own and as good as anything he knows about, while middle-class Americans, surrounded with goods and services the headman never dreamed of, may feel terribly deprived when they compare themselves with more prosperous neighbors. In other words, insofar as happiness depends on material possessions, *the degree of inequality* may be more important than anything else.

When we take into account the advances in health, the greater abundance and improved quality of food, and the drastic reduction in premature deaths, to say nothing of the improvements in freedom and justice, it is clear that industrialization has eliminated the source of much of the misery of earlier eras. Putting it all together, we are again led to the tentative conclusion that the long-term trend for the average individual has been curvilinear, as shown in Figure 17.1 (page 407). Conditions seem to have been more conducive to human happiness for the average individual in hunting and gathering societies than in horticultural societies, and better in horticultural than

TABLE 17.1 Degree of Happiness and Satisfaction with Life Expressed by Members of Societies around the World

	Percentage Very Happy or Fairly Happy	Percentage Highly Satisfied with Their Lives*
North America	91	50
Western Europe	80	41
Latin America	70	40
Africa	68	15
Far East†	48	11

*The values shown in this column are the arithmetic means of responses to questions about satisfaction with ten specific areas of life (see table 6 of Gallup's article).

†The Far East includes both Japan and India, and Gallup notes that "the differences between Japan [an advanced industrial society] and India [an industrializing agrarian society] with respect to personal happiness are very large."

Source: Adapted from George H. Gallup, "Human Needs and Satisfactions: A Global Survey," *Public Opinion Quarterly*, 40 (Winter, 1976–1977), tables 2 and 6, pp. 465 and 467.

in agrarian or even early industrial. But with further advances in industrialization, the situation of the average individual seems to have improved considerably, reversing the long-term trend.

Recent evidence, the first of its kind, tends to support this conclusion. In a study of almost seventy nations containing two-thirds of the world's population, the Gallup Poll and its associates abroad found a striking relation between the level of happiness expressed by the people they interviewed and the level of technological advance of the societies in which they lived (see Table 17.1). The same relation was found between societal development and people's satisfaction with specific aspects of their lives (e.g., family life, health, housing, work). The results of this survey led George Gallup to comment: "For centuries, romantics and philosophers have beguiled us with tales of societies that were 'poor but happy.' If any such exist, the survey failed to discover them."

Concluding Thoughts It should be clear by now that there is no simple one-to-one correspondence between technological advance and progress in terms of freedom, justice, and happiness. In fact, one may well ask whether technological advance has not proven to be a "bitch goddess" who lures societies into evolutionary paths where the costs often outweigh the benefits.

Had human history come to an end several hundred years ago, one would have been forced to answer affirmatively. During the last hundred years, however, technological advance has begun to make a positive contribution to the attainment of humanity's higher goals. Whether or not this will continue in the future is another question. We can say this, however: technology has at last brought into the realm of *the possible* a social order with greater freedom, justice, and happiness than any society has yet known.

Whatever our judgment about the wisdom of our species' pursuit of technological advance, one thing is clear: *for the evolution of human societies as a whole, technological advance can be equated with progress only in the limited sense of growth in the store of cultural information, and the consequences of its use.*

LOOKING AHEAD

A noted scholar once wrote, "The past is not dead history; it is living material out of which man makes the present and builds the future."[5] Humanity has indeed created the present world from materials of the past and just as surely is now laying the foundation for the future. But what kind of future will it be? And what kinds of changes are we likely to encounter in the next several decades?

Trying to foresee the future has always been a risky business. A hundred years ago, for example, some very knowledgeable people proclaimed that warfare had developed to the point where no further advances in weaponry could be expected![6] Despite the difficulties, it is important to try to anticipate what lies ahead because the sooner we recognize problems and begin to address them, the better our chances of finding solutions.

There are several things to keep in mind as we try to see across the years. First, we need to be aware that there are some potential developments which *cannot* be anticipated but which could alter the picture substantially—the emergence of some new and virulent pestilence or plague, for example, or a shift in climate that is unrelated to human activity. Second, the subject we can speak about with the greatest confidence when discussing the future, especially the next quarter of a century or so, concerns the *problems* societies will face. For the serious, unresolved problems of societies today will almost surely continue to be problems in the years ahead.

Third, and finally, the more thoroughly a prediction is *grounded in a tested analysis of the past and present*, the better its chances of success. Our predictions will thus be based on our analysis of societal evolution up to the present, with special attention to anticipated changes in population, the biophysical environment, technology, ideology, political and economic institutions, the world system of societies, and the higher human goals.

We will not attempt to make flat, unqualified predictions, but rather frame statements which say that certain outcomes are likely under given circumstances. This puts the assumptions on which our predictions are based out in the open where others can examine them, and challenge or modify them as new information or insights become available. In time, this should lead to more useful and more accurate predictions.

Prospects: Population

Population growth during the decades ahead poses an ominous threat to the entire world system of societies. If our numbers continue to swell at the current rate, 1.7 percent per year, there will be 8 billion people by the year 2015 and 10 billion by the year 2030. Since 2030 is well within the expected life span of today's young people, they should be aware that a report by the National Academy of Science in the United States warns that a population of 10 billion would be "close to (if not above) the maximum that an *intensively* managed world might hope to support with some degree of comfort and individual choice."[7]

What will it mean to see the population climb from 5.3 to 8 billion or more in barely 25 years? For one thing, it will mean that world population will increase by about 100 million *every year*. It will mean that the world system will have to find enough new resources to support the equivalent of *two more Chinas* in only a few decades. Since these additional people must all be fed with little or no increase in the amount of arable land available, it will mean far greater use of fertilizers, pesticides, and water.[8] In addition to the added strain this will place on the environment, it will almost certainly increase the cost of food worldwide. It will probably also mean an enormous increase in the number of hungry and malnourished individuals, because there is little reason to expect that food will be more equally distributed than it is today. The World Bank predicts the number of malnourished people in the Third World (where 95 percent of population growth will occur) could reach 1.3 billion as early as 2000.[9]

Because of advances in agricultural technology, and because of rural overcrowding in Third World societies, most of the population growth will be concentrated in cities. Overcrowding in urban areas, which is already a serious problem, will thus become far worse during the years ahead, and so will the attendant problems of poverty, disease, crime, and social unrest. Calcutta's population, for example, is expected to increase from 10 million to 20 or 30 million by 2025, and Mexico City's from 16 million to more than 30 million.[10] The combined urban populations of Third World societies was only one billion in the mid-1980s, but it will be almost 4 billion by 2025, and most of that growth will occur in their already enormous and overcrowded slums.

It is obvious that our species' population growth must be halted at some point, and it is equally obvious that the consequences will grow more serious with every year that passes. As demographers remind us, rapid population growth is like a heavily loaded freight train on a downhill grade: it takes considerable time to bring it to a complete halt. In the case of population growth, the difficulty is due to the fact that most Third World nations today have large numbers of young people who have not yet reached the reproductive years. Even if these young people were to limit their families to two children apiece, far more babies would be born than older people would die. In fact, *even if small, two-child families became the rule tomorrow, world population would double before the present cycle of growth came to an end.* And since two-child families are not likely to become the worldwide norm any time soon, growth will be far greater—unless wars, famines, plagues, and other disasters take a heavier toll than they have taken in the recent past.

FIGURE 17.2

The most critical question confronting human societies today may well be, *When will the nations of the world take steps to bring population growth under control?* Although this is impossible to predict, there are indications that a growing number of them will take serious steps to that end during the next quarter century. For one thing, there has been a significant shift in the attitudes of leaders of industrializing societies on the subject of family planning and population control, from nearly universal indifference or condemnation only twenty-five years ago to widespread approval today. Many of them now recognize the futility of trying to improve living standards when population is increasing so rapidly.

Recognition of the problem has done little to halt population growth thus far, however, because few Third World leaders have yet taken the kind of action that is necessary. Some are apparently reluctant for ideological reasons to intrude in this traditionally private area of life and place sanctions on their people's reproductive activities. They hope that increased education and gradually changing beliefs and values will be enough to halt growth before the consequences become disastrous. Others are more realistic—and pessimistic—in their assessment of the situation, but avoid imposing sanctions because they fear the consequences for themselves. They have not forgotten that after India's government mandated forcible sterilization on a limited scale, it was swept from office. So far, only a handful of Third World nations have developed the kind of rigorous programs of population control that are needed if growth is to be halted within the next several decades.

It is difficult to believe that other Third World governments will not also begin to instigate more rigorous—even coercive—programs in the next decade, but how many will do so, and how effective their efforts will be, will depend on a variety of factors whose relative strength it is difficult to assess. They include ideological factors, such as the extent to which the elite is influenced by either Islam or Catholicism (both of which oppose population control), and the extent of the elite's commitment to planning. They also include such factors as the extent of hunger and poverty within the society, the degree of political unrest and the strength of the elite, and the amount of pressure applied by outside forces. The latter might be in the form of offers of economic aid made conditional on the development of an effective program of population control. Until now, most aid has been given with the sole purpose of keeping people alive—and able to reproduce. It is difficult to believe that well-intentioned donors in industrial societies will not soon perceive that such aid does no lasting good unless it is linked to a program designed to check runaway population growth.

Another demographic trend we can anticipate is continuing migration from the Third World to industrial societies. This trend is already well under way, as we have seen, and it is likely to accelerate in coming years. It is even possible to envision the day when the indigenous populations of some industrial societies will become minorities in their own homelands, a development that would almost certainly have explosive political consequences.*

---

*This has already happened in the Soviet republic of Latvia, once an independent nation, where Russian migrants now outnumber native Latvians.

Prospects: Biophysical Environment

During the next few decades, there will certainly be important changes in the bio-physical environment. Some will be the result of natural catastrophes, such as earth-quakes, volcanic eruptions, and major storms. But some will be the result of the use of modern industrial technology, and it is these that are likely to have the greatest impact on human societies.

Such a possibility did not exist throughout most of human history. For the first several million years, human societies simply adjusted to environmental conditions as they found them; they could do little or nothing to alter them. Then, late in the hunt-ing and gathering era, advances in weapons technology enabled societies to make their first irreversible alteration in the biophysical environment, as hunters apparently destroyed a considerable number of species of large animals.

Following the horticultural revolution, societies gradually began changing the landscape, clearing forests and planting gardens in their place. Although the balance of nature was affected wherever this happened, the impact was not great, because horticulturalists usually had to relocate every few years and their abandoned gardens gradually reverted to wilderness. The agrarian revolution, however, changed this. Fields became permanent and cultivated land no longer reverted to wilderness, while larger populations took increasing amounts of minerals and other natural resources from the earth. Even so, the impact of human societies on the environment was still rela-tively limited.

Industrial technology, in contrast, has enabled human societies to change the biophysical environment in unprecedented ways. The landscape has been so drasti-cally rearranged that large areas that once teemed with plant and animal life have been virtually destroyed. Complex ecosystems that required millions of years to evolve have been damaged beyond repair in a matter of decades. The earth has been plun-dered of many of its resources, some of them seriously depleted. Vast quantities of toxic matter have been poured into the earth's atmosphere and into its rivers, lakes, and oceans. Some experts now predict that as many as a fifth of all the species of plants and animals alive in 1980—some 500,000 to 2 million of them—may be extinct by the year 2000 as a consequence of pollution and loss of habitat.[11]

Environmentalists have been warning for years that our biophysical environment is vulnerable, that it does not have an unlimited capacity for renewing itself. Yet even as we have heard the warnings, our demands on the environment have risen at a fantastic rate. Since 1950, an infinitesimal period of time by geological standards, the gross world product has risen from approximately $1.5 trillion to $12 trillion. If we consider what this means in terms of our impact on the environment, no future crises will surprise us. For the simple fact is that *the biophysical environment can sustain neither an infinite growth of the human population nor the endless demands of an advancing technology.*

This is why it is difficult to be optimistic about the state of the environment during the decades immediately ahead. The human population will almost certainly increase by at least 2 billion during the next quarter century, while simultaneously the technology of the world system becomes increasingly industrialized. Merely providing for the basic subsistence needs of that many more people will put a formidable strain on an already overworked environment. At the same time, the factories of industrializing societies will be demanding ever greater quantities of raw materials, and their members ever more material products as they struggle to raise their standards of living. Nor is it reasonable to expect that the governments of those hard-pressed societies will rank environmental protection as a high priority.

What we *can* expect during the next quarter century, therefore, is greater abuse of the environment by societies whose impact in the past has been relatively minor, with these abuses aggravating an already serious problem. We can see how this will happen by considering a problem that is already of concern to many scientists: the buildup of carbon dioxide and other gases in the earth's atmosphere.[12] Too great a concentration of these gases would trap so much of the sun's heat that a "greenhouse effect" would result, causing a warming trend on the earth's surface. Some predict an increase in average global temperature of 3 to 8 degrees Fahrenheit in the next century. This would have devastating consequences for agriculture in some regions and would probably melt glaciers and the polar icecaps, causing the flooding of many major cities and coastal regions.

The reason for the growing amount of carbon dioxide in the atmosphere is that more of it is being released than can be handled by natural mechanisms—the leaves of green plants and the oceans and lakes that absorb it. Societies are currently producing 5 billion tons of carbon dioxide every year, and, as they turn to greater use of coal, the problem can only grow worse.[13] What is more, lakes, oceans, and forests are themselves vulnerable and will apparently be able to handle less carbon dioxide in the future than they do now. Although forests have been leveled in the past, it is now happening at an unprecedented rate. In their search for an affordable source of energy (i.e., firewood) and new acreage for farming, many Third World societies are destroying vast forests, leaving the land unfit either for cultivation or for reforestation.

The loss of these forests will have consequences that go well beyond the greater pollution of the atmosphere and the loss of species noted earlier. It will also accelerate the deterioration and destruction of resources that developing societies so desperately need, both for agriculture and for industrialization. The depletion of forests will aggravate problems of flooding, cause siltation in streams and rivers, deplete groundwater, and create water shortages. To make matters worse, the world's need for fresh (i.e., not sea) water is rapidly increasing, with much of the increase being used for irrigation.[14] Meanwhile, an area the size of Maine becomes desert, and unsuitable for agriculture, every year. If this trend continues only until the year 2000, there will be almost 20 percent more desert on our planet than there was as recently as 1975!

Growing world population, increasing industrialization, and rising energy needs are not the only reasons for predicting growing problems with the environment. Another cause for concern is that many elements of industrial technology are adopted before their full potential for harm can be determined. Just as societies of the recent past could not predict that the burning of fossil fuels would lead to a potentially dangerous buildup of carbon dioxide in the atmosphere, so contemporary societies are

FIGURE 17.3 Destruction of tropical rain forests is occurring at an unprecedented rate, leaving vast areas unfit for cultivation or reforestation.

adopting practices that could produce serious, but still largely unsuspected, problems. Toxic chemicals, for example, are a largely unknown quantity. Because they are of such diverse kinds, have been so widely used, and are often so poorly stored or disposed of, chemical pollution could do far greater environmental and ecological damage in the near future than it has in the past. Among those substances, for example, are vast quantities of lethal nerve gases that are stored in containers vulnerable to decay, earth tremors, and accidents. In short, a big question mark must be inserted into any predictions about the biophysical environment, since it could already contain the seeds of a major disaster.

Another thing that makes it difficult to be optimistic about the state of the environment during the next twenty-five years is the response of advanced societies during the last twenty-five. Industrial societies are the ones that can best afford to develop and apply new technologies to protect the soil, water, and air and help safeguard the finite store of resources on which we all depend. Yet their responses have been fairly limited, and often dictated by short-term economic considerations.

Industrial societies will almost certainly become more active in this area in the years ahead, however. As the full impact of modern technology on the environment and the dynamics of the process become increasingly clear, so will the costs of continued neglect of problems. Thus, we can predict that these societies will begin to weigh more carefully the hidden, longer term costs (e.g., illness, genetic damage) and that they will also come to recognize that it is usually far more costly to rectify environmental damage than to prevent it in the first place.

Another reason industrial societies will become more environmentally concerned in the next quarter century is that the growing scarcity of a number of natural resources will increase their value. This should lead to greater conservation efforts—not only of energy and minerals but of wood and water as well. Conservation will involve far greater emphasis on *recycling*—of heat, of water, of wood, of minerals, and of paper, glass, and plastic products. Recycling often produces multiple benefits. Not only does it reduce the quantity of materials that must be taken from the environment, it often saves energy as well (e.g., it takes only 4 percent as much energy to produce recycled aluminum as to produce "new" aluminum from bauxite ore) and reduces air and water pollution (e.g., the recycling of steel is estimated to cut air pollution 86 percent, and water pollution 76 percent).[15]

Recycling and other techniques for reducing the harmful impact of human societies on the environment will require substantial capital expenditures, and therefore it is unlikely that they will be widely adopted in the Third World until they become economically attractive. Although there have been some encouraging signs (China, for example, closed several plants causing pollution, and heavily fined another[16]), pollution and a host of other environmental problems are certain to become far worse in the Third World during the years ahead. With respect to industrial societies, there is no reason to believe that they, even with their new technologies, will *remove* more pollutants, contaminants, and hazardous materials from the biophysical environment during the next quarter century than they put into it. Thus, we can predict that the environment will deteriorate further before societies effect a reversal of that trend.

Prospects: Technology

Technological advance has been the most important factor in shaping the evolution of the world system in the past, and there is little reason to doubt that it will continue to be of major, perhaps paramount, importance in coming decades. Many of the most pressing problems of societies today are stimulating searches for technological solutions, and the new technologies that result will almost certainly give rise to social and cultural changes of many kinds.

Rate of Change Benjamin Franklin once said that nothing is certain in this world but death and taxes. Were he alive today, he might add technological advance. A prediction of continuing advance at an accelerating rate does not depend simply on an extrapolation of the current trend. The basic factors responsible for the trend—the magnitude of the existing store of information, the great size of societal populations, and the amount of communication between societies (see pages 54–56)—are still operative and give every indication of providing even stronger impetus to innovation in the future than they do today. Furthermore, for the first time in history advanced industrial societies are engaging in a systematic, large-scale pursuit of new information. Investments in scientific and technological research and development have grown tremendously, while computers and other devices that increase our ability to acquire, analyze, and process data add their own impetus to the rate of change.

The only things that might slow the rate of technological innovation in the next several decades are nuclear war, collapse of the world economy, or an environmental catastrophe. Fortunately, none of these appears likely in that time frame.

Content of Change   The development of new sources of energy is one area in which industrial societies have an enormous stake. Their way of life depends on the consumption of vast and ever-increasing amounts of energy, and many of these societies are poorly endowed with energy resources of their own. Japan, for example, imports 83 percent of its energy, and France 59 percent.[17]

More important yet, the supply of two vital energy resources—petroleum and natural gas—is limited. Although we do not know precisely how much more petroleum and natural gas exist, we have a rough idea. Proven reserves of petroleum, for example, will be exhausted in thirty-five years at current rates of consumption.[18] And while discoveries of new fields, the development of more efficient techniques of extraction, and conservation efforts will increase the period in which petroleum remains available, much of those gains will undoubtedly be offset by increasing demands for energy. Although small pools of petroleum may still be available a century or more from now, the price will probably be too high for most of the uses to which petroleum is put today.

In the case of natural gas, proven reserves are larger relative to current consumption, and prospects for the discovery of new reserves are much better. But again, the supply is finite while the demand is infinite. Sooner or later, therefore, prices will rise and other forms of energy will have to be found to replace petroleum and natural gas, the resources that have fueled much of the growth of the world's economies in the last half-century.

Coal is the one alternative source of energy that not only exists in great abundance but for which the relevant technology is already available. Proven reserves are so vast that they will last for at least several centuries. Unfortunately, most of the coal that is available gives off large amounts of sulfur dioxide, nitrogen oxide, and carbon dioxide when it is burned. These chemicals have already caused serious damage to forests and to buildings, bridges, and other structures. More serious still is the potential for a "greenhouse effect," which we discussed earlier. Since coal emits 25 percent more carbon dioxide (CO_2) per unit of energy produced than oil does, few see it as a long-term solution to the world's energy needs. At best, it may prove a resource that societies can fall back on if shortages of petroleum and natural gas develop before new energy sources become available to take their place.

In recent years, scientists and engineers have conducted a wide-ranging search for new energy sources that would reduce societies' dependence on fossil fuels. Among the possibilities that have been, or are being, explored are nuclear fission, nuclear fusion, solar energy, geothermal energy (i.e., energy derived from heat deep beneath the earth's surface), wind power, ocean wave power, shale oil, coal gasification, liquid hydrogen derived from water, methane gas derived from manure and garbage, and just plain trash. Except for nuclear fission, none of these technologies is yet available at competitive costs for mass use, though some, such as solar energy, geothermal energy, liquid hydrogen, wind and wave power, and methane gas from garbage, are in use on a limited basis. Although some of these possibilities will eventually prove impractical or uneconomical, it will be surprising if one or more of them does not contribute significantly to the energy needs of societies in the twenty-first century.

Another major effort that will continue in the years ahead is the development of machines that use energy more efficiently. At present, the average *energy end-use efficiency* of the various technologies in use in industrial societies is estimated to be only 10 percent.[19] In other words, 90 percent of the energy is wasted (e.g., by the generation of heat by equipment intended to provide light) or consumed in the production and transmission of energy to the ultimate consumer. While anything approaching 100 percent efficiency is impossible, even small improvements would be significant. If the efficiency of energy-using machines in the United States could be raised from the current 10 percent to just 11 percent, for example, this would free almost the amount of energy required today to power all American automobiles.[20] And if such improvements were adopted by other societies throughout the world, it would be the equivalent of the discovery of a major new energy source.

A recent study of energy use concluded that one-fourth of the energy currently consumed in manufacturing processes in the United States, or one-tenth of the nation's total energy consumption, could be saved merely by applying technologies that are already available, and at costs no greater than would be offset by the energy savings. For example, many of the heating processes required for the manufacture of metals, ceramics, glass, and cement are carried out in furnaces at very high temperatures. Exhaust gases from these furnaces, which currently go unused, could be used to generate electricity. The history of modern technology provides ample grounds for optimism about the prospect for increasing the energy efficiency of many existing technologies. Figure 17.4 (page 420) shows the steady improvement that has been achieved in the efficiency of both steam engines and forms of lighting, and the same could be demonstrated for other technologies as well.

Pollution of the environment, like the depletion of resources, will also provide a spur for technological innovation during the next quarter century. Some of these efforts will be directed toward further development of devices that reduce or eliminate undesirable emissions from industry and other sources into the air, water, and soil. One of the more likely innovations will be electric vehicles. In the early days of automobiles, electrically powered cars competed with gasoline-powered cars. When the discovery of vast new fields of petroleum made gasoline extremely cheap, electric cars could not compete and vanished from the scene. Today, with the era of cheap gasoline drawing to an end and with air pollution a growing problem in cities around the world, there is new interest in electric vehicles, especially for use in urban areas, and several major automobile companies are investing in research designed to lower their costs. Efforts are also under way to utilize natural gas and hydrogen as fuels for vehicles, since they, too, are less polluting than gasoline.

On another front, numerous organizations are trying to develop more economical ways of recycling the refuse of societies. Industrial societies in particular produce enormous quantities of solid waste. The United States alone creates more than 150

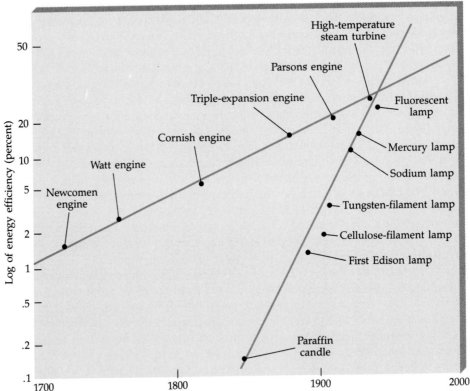

FIGURE 17.4 Increasing energy efficiency in two areas of modern technology: steam engines and illumination. Note the logarithmic scale that is used to plot energy efficiency; if an ordinary linear scale had been used, the trend lines would be even steeper.

million tons of it a year, nearly twice the amount it produced just a quarter of a century ago.[21] Disposal of these mountains of refuse has become an increasingly expensive problem, and recycling is the obvious solution, since it converts some of the waste into useful materials. Unfortunately, there is still no technology for converting most of it; and even where appropriate technology exists, the costs of conversion are often greater than the market value of the recycled materials. With the seriousness of the waste disposal problem increasingly obvious, however, investment in research is growing and prospects are good for advances in recycling technology in the decades just ahead.[22]

Safer disposal of toxic substances will be another focus of research. Untold millions of containers of radioactive water, nerve gas, and other lethal materials are currently buried or stored in unsafe containers. Scientists have recently made a breakthrough with respect to one of these problems: the disposal of plutonium, an extremely hazardous waste product of nuclear reactors that remains radioactive for thousands of years.[23] By slightly altering a molecule that occurs naturally in living organisms, they have devised a chemical means for removing plutonium from the wastewater in which it is stored, rendering it far more compact and thus much easier to dispose of. Similar techniques can probably be devised to aid in the safer handling of other hazardous wastes.

Another area in which there will probably be technological innovations in the next quarter century is *population control*. Although technologies for limiting population growth already exist, many Third World societies have been slow to accept them, as we have seen. Ideological and economic changes will have to occur before this problem is overcome, but the development of cheaper, safer, simpler, and more reliable methods of contraception, sterilization, and abortion will speed the process. For example, one new technique currently being tested is the administration of ovulation-controlling hormones by injection. Some women in Third World nations appear to be much more receptive to shots administered by medical personnel than to pills or devices they use at home. The "morning after" pill is another innovation that will almost surely be adopted widely in the next several decades.

The current effort to find technological solutions for *hunger*, which is so widespread in the Third World, will certainly continue in the years ahead. Although this problem is, as we have seen, primarily the result of uncontrolled population growth in these societies, it is aggravated by dietary patterns in industrial societies. The heavy consumption of meat by members of advanced societies necessitates increased production of grain for livestock feed. Since 1 calorie of food energy derived from meat requires approximately 7 calories of grain to produce,[24] the average American today effectively consumes nearly 2,000 pounds of grain per year, compared to the 400 pounds consumed by the average person in a society with a predominantly cereal diet.[25] There may well be increased moderation of meat consumption in some industrial societies, though this may be primarily for reasons of their members' health.

At the present time there are a number of new technologies at various stages of development that promise to increase the world's food supply. One of these, fish farming, is already in operation in a number of societies and promises to provide an increased supply of high-quality protein at relatively low cost.[26] Another promising innovation is soilless cultivation, which involves a recycled mixture of water and nutrients that is sprayed on the roots of plants suspended in frames. Developed in Israel, this technique should greatly increase food production in arid and semiarid areas. In addition, the new technology of recombinant DNA (see page 422) will probably provide new and improved strains of plants and animals.

As important as such advances may be, most agricultural experts believe that increases in the world's food supply during the next quarter century will come primarily from the diffusion of technologies already available. During one recent decade, 40 percent of the increase in food production in 90 industrializing societies came solely from the increased use of fertilizers, and much of the rest came from the diffusion of other well-established technologies.[27] This pattern seems likely to continue during the next quarter century.

Another area in which we can expect technological innovations of major significance is *the application of the computer and microcircuitry (i.e., the silicon chip) to new industrial tasks*. Computers have already been devised to guide "smart robots" in spot-welding and other tasks in automobile assembly plants, and this, like other fundamental innovations, will undoubtedly be adapted for use in similar operations in a variety of industries, although the heavy capital costs involved will slow the process. In addition, the time frame for the adoption of a technology which replaces human labor will be affected by such factors as the amount of unemployment in a society, the cost of labor, and the attitudes of labor leaders and other elites. Microcircuitry's potential is clear. By substituting microcircuitry for mechanical parts, a manufacturer of cash registers reduced the number of parts in its product from about 5,000 to several hundred. This, in turn, led to a reduction in the number of workers on its assembly line from about 400 to 15 or 20—an even more drastic reduction in labor than that achieved by the automobile industry's use of "smart robots."[28]

Yet another fundamental innovation with revolutionary potential for human societies in the next quarter century is the new technology of *recombinant DNA*. In recent years geneticists have learned how to remove a bit of genetic material from the cell of one kind of organism and implant it in the cell of another species. This new technology is particularly fascinating from the perspective of ecological–evolutionary theory, for it marks *a new stage in our species' capacity for handling information*. Until recently, the only information we could manipulate and recombine was cultural information. Now we can use the genetic alphabet in the same way (but only to a very limited extent so far) to create combinations of genetic information which do not exist in nature and which can serve as tools for accomplishing human purposes.

So far, most applications of recombinant DNA technology involve the transplantation of genes that govern the production of rare proteins from the cells of slower-breeding animals, including humans, into the cells of plants and bacteria. Bacteria grow and divide so rapidly that a single one can produce 100 trillion identical cells in 24 hours, each one containing at least 100 molecules of the desired protein.[29] In this way, large quantities of rare and valuable chemicals (e.g., insulin) can be produced at minimal cost.

By inserting human genes into plants, scientists have created tobacco plants that produce antibodies, potatoes that produce serum albumin, and rape plants that produce enkephalin, a painkiller normally produced in the human brain.[30] A biotechnology company in California is planning to market a new protective sun screen containing human skin pigment (melanin) grown in tobacco. These are just the beginning of what promises to become a flood of important innovations employing recombinant DNA.

Many other kinds of technological innovations can also be expected during the next few decades. Substantial resources are being invested in medical research of various kinds, including organ transplants and genetic diseases. Striking advances have recently been made in communications, data processing, and office automation, and further advances in these areas should be only a matter of time. In addition, it is very possible that some unanticipated breakthrough or breakthroughs, comparable to the silicon chip or recombinant DNA, will lay the foundation, as all fundamental innovations do, for a host of new applications.

One area in which the rate of innovation is likely to *decline* sharply in the years ahead is the area of weapons technology. For the last half-century, war and the threat of war forced many industrial societies to invest heavily in armaments and in weapons research. If, however, the Cold War continues to wind down and the threat of war recedes, budgetary priorities will change, especially in the United States and the Soviet Union, the two societies that have spent the most on weapons research for several decades.

Prospects: Ideology

If, as it appears, human societies are nearing a critical, or at least dangerous, point with respect to their impact on the biophysical environment, it seems safe to predict that ideology will play an even larger role in shaping societal change and development than it has played in the past. The beliefs, values, norms, and hence the institutions of a number of societies are certain to alter in some important ways. It will be surprising, for example, if industrial societies do not begin to perceive themselves less as rivals or even potential enemies, and see themselves instead as allies that must join forces to confront the "real" enemy—much as, in science fiction, the nations of planet Earth forget their quarrels and band together to defeat the "aliens from outer space." In this case, of course, the threats they must confront will be overpopulation and environmental deterioration.

During the next several decades, the most advanced and wealthy nations will almost surely begin to try to persuade some of the less developed to alter the norms of their members with respect to family size. This may be done through the offer of incentives, such as loans and aid programs that are linked to population control, or by introducing new technologies. Industrial societies will also begin to provide their own populations with greater incentives and stronger sanctions aimed at protecting the environment (e.g., incentives to encourage recycling and taxes on unnecessary waste products). And one can also be fairly certain that the next quarter century will find growing numbers of scientists and others uniting in international efforts to devise ways of alleviating these increasingly urgent problems.

With respect to the dominant political and economic ideologies of societies, there will certainly be continuing change there as well. The most striking change of this kind for many decades has been the apparent collapse of Marxism-Leninism in most of eastern Europe, and its decline in China and some other nations. While these developments have been accompanied by some increase in support for democratic socialism and capitalism, it is *pragmatism* which has made the greatest gains, and will probably continue to do so. Deng Xiaoping, the recent Chinese leader, said it best: when some complained that his program of economic reform was a reintroduction of capitalism, he responded that it does not matter whether a cat is black or white as long as it catches mice.

The chief exceptions to the trend toward increasing pragmatism will probably be found in parts of the Third World. In societies where Muslims are numerous, Islamic fundamentalism is spreading. This ideology is essentially a rejection of most of the social and cultural changes that have developed in response to industrialization. The goal of Islamic fundamentalists is to return to life as it was in the past, before industrialization and modernization began to make themselves felt. Because of the great numbers of Muslims in the Middle East, where so much of the world's oil reserves are located, the probable spread of this anti-modern ideology during the coming decades cannot be lightly dismissed.

In Latin America, revolutionary socialism still has great appeal, especially for students, intellectuals, and many members of the Catholic clergy. For the latter, the appeal is based on a modified version of Marxism known as "liberation theology," a new ideology that emphasizes the similarities in some of the ideals of Marxism and Christianity while ignoring or minimizing the many differences in both ideals and methods. Like orthodox Marxism, liberation theology combines a harsh critique of the existing social order with an idealized vision of a new socialist society created by revolutionary means. Unfortunately, this vision ignores the lessons learned at such great cost by the peoples of eastern Europe, China, and elsewhere. In addition, it is certain that the process of industrialization in any society will only be made more difficult by an ideology that ignores the imperative of population control.

In politically stable, fully industrialized societies, the ideologies most likely to create problems during the coming decades are hedonistic philosophies, encouraged by excessive affluence, that lead people to focus on their personal concerns to the neglect of societal problems. If, however, an industrial society should become destabilized by some economic, political, or environmental crisis, then the greatest ideological threat will probably lie in nationalistic or other emotionally charged ideologies that promise simple solutions to complex societal problems.

Prospects: Polity

The most important political trend in the twentieth century has been the spread of democracy. This has involved both the increasing democratization of societies in which the process began prior to the start of the century and the beginnings of democracy in others.

The year 1989 saw the beginning of a remarkable series of political changes in most of the revolutionary socialist societies of eastern Europe, when the Communist Party was forced to renounce its monopoly of power and compete with other parties in free elections. Although the process is still in its early stages as these words are written, a return to the old Leninist system seems unlikely. Even many of the leaders of the Communist Party in these societies lost faith in the old system, and disillusionment was greatest among younger members, on whom the future of the Party depended. Thus, we are likely to see further democratization in all of the more fully industrialized of these societies during the next quarter century, though occasional pauses and even short-term reversals would not be surprising.

In the Third World, prospects for increasing democracy are mixed. They appear to be good in those societies that are industrializing most rapidly and whose better-educated populations will insist on a greater voice in the formulation of governmental policies that affect their daily lives. In much of the Third World, however, especially in industrializing horticultural societies, prospects for greater democracy look slim. Faced with the staggering problems created by runaway population growth, and with a social and cultural heritage that equips them poorly for competition in the modern world economy, most of these societies will probably find democratic government a luxury they cannot afford.

A second important political trend that appears likely in the decades just ahead is the growth of nationalist movements. This trend is already strikingly evident in the Soviet Union and Yugoslavia, as the power of the Communist Party declines. But the trend is not limited to those societies. Nationalist movements by ethnic minorities are also active in Canada, Northern Ireland, Spain, Bulgaria, Romania, Turkey, Iraq, Israel, India, Sri Lanka, Indonesia, Sudan, Ethiopia, Somalia, and much of sub-Saharan Africa, and there is the potential for such movements in a number of other societies as well.

Intrasocietal violence organized by revolutionary socialist parties appears likely to decline in the decades ahead. In the recent past, much of this depended on the economic and military support of the Soviet Union, East Germany, Czechoslovakia, and China. With support from these sources diminished or eliminated, revolutionary socialist movements will find it much more difficult to mount serious challenges to established governments.

Prospects: Economy

Barring a collapse of the world economy, there will probably be continuing economic growth for the world system as a whole during the next quarter century. The wider application of techniques that are already known should so improve energy efficiency that increased productivity will be ensured, even when energy costs increase. In addition, there will almost certainly be advances in energy technology that boost world production higher still.

Whether living standards also rise will depend on the number of people who must share the fruits of the increased productivity. The projected rates of population growth combined with rising energy costs could well offset the effects of the rise in GWP (i.e., gross world product), and thus prevent improvement in living standards for the world as a whole. And even if per capita GWP rises, it does not necessarily follow that per capita GNPs (gross national products) will rise in every society. Improvements are unlikely in most African societies, where runaway population growth threatens economic disaster and widespread starvation. Although the situation may be alleviated temporarily by international aid programs, the basic problems in these societies will persist until their leaders face up to the problems confronting them. Unfortunately, there are few signs of this so far.

In contrast, a number of industrializing agrarian societies will almost certainly become fully industrialized in the next quarter century. Based on their current levels of development and current rates of economic growth, South Korea, Taiwan, Spain, and Ireland are the most likely candidates. Other possibilities include Israel, South Africa, Yugoslavia, Romania, Bulgaria, and Chile, though each of these societies has serious political problems that must be overcome before substantial economic development can be achieved. Saudi Arabia, Portugal, Venezuela, Uruguay, and Brazil may also become industrialized, but they, too, are confronted by a variety of problems that promise to delay the process.

During the 1980s, capitalism gained substantially at the expense of socialism, not only in eastern Europe but in western Europe and much of the Third World as well. This gain was the result of a desire for more rapid economic growth, and a growing recognition that market economies and private enterprise are more conducive to such growth than planned economies and state enterprises. In western Europe, this trend may not continue much longer and may even be reversed, since those societies already have economies that are complex and varied mixtures of both capitalism and socialism. Future changes in their economies will probably be more a matter of "fine-tuning" than of major overhauling.

In eastern Europe and much of the Third World, on the other hand, private enterprise was almost nonexistent until recently, and their command economies were dominated by bloated, inefficient, and often corrupt governmental bureaucracies and state enterprises. Movement toward mixed economies has barely begun in most of these societies and will have to continue for years if a balance between market forces and governmental control is to be achieved. In view of the tremendous pressures for better living standards in those societies, it seems likely that the trend will persist for some years.

In Japan, the United States, and Canada, in contrast, the economies, though mixed, are even more market-oriented than those of western Europe. Changes in these societies, therefore, are likely to be in the direction of greater governmental control of the economy. But as in western Europe, the change is not likely to be drastic.

Another economic trend that is almost certain to continue is the increasing division of labor in the world system. Since 1750, the volume of international trade has increased more than 1,000-fold, which is, in part, a reflection of the growth of economic specialization during that time. This trend, a consequence of technological advances that have drastically reduced the cost of moving goods, has been highly beneficial for the most part. Societies now export things that they can produce more cheaply than other societies and import what they find more costly to produce.

The world economy, which is essentially a *capitalist* economy, has not been without its disadvantages, especially for societies that specialize in products whose value on the world market fluctuates sharply. Yet even these societies have found this system more rewarding than trying to produce for themselves everything they need. For a few of these societies, the oil producers in particular, the system has worked enormously to their advantage, greatly enhancing their position in the world system of societies. In the long run, however, they will not be able to rely exclusively on this one highly profitable product, and their future in the world economy will come to depend on the extent to which they use their oil profits to build more diversified modern economies.

During the next quarter century, economic ties among societies will probably grow even stronger than they are today. As this happens, societies will gradually lose more and more of their economic independence. At some point many societies, perhaps most, will find that these economic ties have become so vital that they cannot be left vulnerable to disruption by international disputes or war. When this point is reached, it will provide an enormous boost to proposals for the creation of a single world government. Although there is little likelihood that a true world government will be established in the next several decades, it could occur later in the twenty-first century (see "Prospects: The World System" below).

Finally, there is one glaring defect in the economies of virtually every contemporary society that will almost surely become more apparent during coming decades. This is the failure to attach realistic "price tags" to things. The cost of "storing" unrecycled waste materials in trash dumps for decades, for example, is a cost not currently included in the price of most discardable items. When those charges are routinely added to the price of plastic, glass, and aluminum containers, packaging materials, disposable diapers, and other materials accumulating today, buying patterns will alter, recycling will gain impetus, and new materials will be developed. Similarly, societies must eventually begin to assess the true—but usually delayed—costs of such things as inadequate systems of health care, child care, and education. A more realistic approach to assessing costs is long overdue and, when it is adopted, will be accompanied by widespread change in virtually every area of societal life. But the next few decades will probably see only the beginnings of such change.

Prospects: The World System

As the world system of societies becomes increasingly integrated economically and in other ways, societies will become more dependent on one another. The striking changes in the European Economic Organization scheduled for 1992 will be one of the most important developments in this process of increasing interdependency, but almost certainly not the last. As the volume and importance of international trade increases, and provided the changes in the European Economic Organization prove successful, other societies may well initiate similar programs.

With increasing economic integration, individual societies will be ever more vulnerable to anything that threatens the functioning of the system as a whole. Above all, they will be vulnerable to nuclear war, regardless of where it occurs or which nations are involved.

There is no need to recount here estimates of the number of deaths and the magnitude of destruction that a nuclear war would produce. Suffice it to say that virtually all those who have studied the matter carefully, including people of very different ideological persuasions, agree that such a war would be unwinnable. For not only would the combatants be damaged beyond imagination, but neutral societies and noncombatants would also suffer enormously, from radioactive fallout and from the disruption of the world economy that would inevitably follow such a war.

During the next quarter century, the threat of nuclear war will no longer lie primarily with the NATO powers and the Soviet Union, as it has in the past. The technology of nuclear weapons is now widespread, and several Third World nations already have small nuclear arsenals. The greatest danger, therefore, is likely to come from the use of these weapon systems by irrational or fanatical leaders (e.g., an Idi Amin or an Ayatollah Khomeini) or from a process in which some more limited conflict escalates out of control.

The potential for such conflicts in the next several decades is great. Even if relations among the major powers continue to improve, resource shortages and population pressures will lead to deteriorating relations among many other societies. For example, in an era of growing water shortages, 200 of the world's major river basins are shared by at least two different societies.

Another cause for concern at the present time is the possible disintegration of the Soviet Union's multinational empire. Struggles between its constituent groups (e.g., between Azerbaijanis and Armenians or even between Ukrainians and Russians) could easily come to involve other societies in an escalating process similar to that in which the struggles within the multinational Austro-Hungarian Empire earlier in the century contributed to the outbreak of World War I.

Faced with such threats, the obvious solution would seem to be the formation of a world government that would not interfere with the internal affairs of societies, but which would have the authority, the mechanisms, and the sanctions necessary to monitor the production of weapons and control their use. Although it would be exceedingly difficult to develop such a polity, it would be possible if the leaders of most societies wanted it badly enough.

One of the most difficult problems in such an endeavor stems from the great discrepancies in economic development and in standards of living between industrial and Third World societies. A number of industrial societies, for example, currently have per capita GNPs of $15,000 or more per year, while the average in Third World societies is less than $1,000.[31] Inclusion of Third World societies in a world polity would almost certainly lead to demands for a substantial redistribution of world wealth and income. In exchange for permission to monitor their military installations, industrializing societies would probably insist upon major economic concessions. But this could easily kill enthusiasm for world government by members of industrial societies. For if world income were distributed equally among the world's societies, per capita income would be reduced by nearly 80 percent in many industrial societies, causing a decline in living standards to *one-fifth* their current level.

Although this is hardly an attractive prospect, some less extreme version of income redistribution may eventually be agreed on. Even if it still seemed harsh to advanced societies, they might consider it preferable to the continuing threat of war and disruption of the world economy. If there is to be a viable compromise in the next century, however, governments should begin soon to narrow the economic gap between societies. Incentives should be provided to industrializing societies to bring population growth to an end, so that their standards of living can be improved, and industrial societies should be prepared to sacrifice some of their own potential growth to provide these incentives and to reduce the gap between haves and have-nots. At present, however, the prospects for such action by the governments of industrial societies seem little better than the prospects for an end to population growth in the Third World.

Somewhat more likely in the next few decades is a gradual strengthening of the United Nations, the closest thing to a world polity that now exists. The greatest obstacle to the effectiveness of that organization is probably the system of representation in the General Assembly, which provides an equal vote for the People's Republic of China, with its population of more than a billion people, and for the Democratic Republic of São Tomé and Principe, which has only 90,000. The special powers vested in the Security Council, the veto power in particular, partly compensate for this, but the present organizational structure of the United Nations as a whole does not generate much confidence on the part of larger and more powerful nations.

Substantial changes will be needed if the United Nations is to become the basis of a future world polity. Until such a polity is established, the world system will remain vulnerable to massive disruption of the increasingly important and valuable network of ties among societies.

FIGURE 17.5 The General Assembly of the United Nations: every nation, regardless of size, has an equal vote.

Prospects: The Higher Goals

Early in this chapter we reached the conclusion that sociocultural evolution has, more often than not, been accompanied by declining levels of freedom, justice, and happiness for the majority of people, but that technological advances in the last 150 years have reversed this trend, at least for the vast majority of members of industrial societies. It would be gratifying to be able to predict that the increasing industrialization of the world system during the next quarter century will have a similar impact on the world as a whole. As our examination of population trends, the environment, and other matters has made clear, however, the prospects for greater attainment of humanity's higher goals in the decades immediately ahead are uncertain.

In the Third World, we can probably expect a decline in individual freedom to accompany an increase in the number of authoritarian regimes. This could have the effect of alleviating some human misery, however, since such regimes would be better able to control birthrates and thus perhaps lower the number of severely malnourished individuals in these societies. But even if this happens, there is not likely to be any great gain in either happiness or justice, since so many people will still be doomed to lives of abject poverty in crowded slums and shantytowns. What is more, population growth and shortages of vital resources will probably retard the pace of industrialization in many societies during the next few decades, greatly delaying the day when advances in productivity begin to provide appreciable benefits for most of their members.

Whatever difficulties human societies experience during the next few decades, however, they may suffer even more later in the next century. Levels of freedom, justice, and happiness are almost certain to decline seriously for the world system as a whole during that period—unless humanity begins *soon* to address its most basic problems. Our potential for shaping a better world is still, at this point, excellent—far greater, in fact, than it has ever been before. But this situation will not last: *the range of attractive options will decline with every year we fail to act.* Thus, the larger the human population becomes before growth is halted, the more likely it is that future political regimes will be harshly authoritarian and individual freedoms severely limited. The further the biophysical environment deteriorates before that trend is reversed, the less likely it is that the human population as a whole will ever enjoy the enormous potential benefits of an industrial economy. And the longer sociocultural evolution continues to be shaped primarily by the blind forces of conflict and intersocietal selection, the more likely it is that our future will be shaped by convulsive changes that are forced upon us by developments beyond our control.

The latter is, in fact, precisely the outcome predicted for human societies by some who have considered the problem. For example, Robert Heilbroner, an economic historian long noted for his insightful analyses, has written a book entitled *An Inquiry into the Human Prospect* in which he forecasts such events as nuclear wars among societies that are experiencing severe population and environmental crises.[32] He predicts, in effect, a future in which the forces of nature—including the irrational forces that are part of our own genetic heritage—provide the answers to problems that *humanity failed to resolve with social and cultural resources.*

Heilbroner is not unaware of our species' remarkable adaptive capabilities. In fact, he believes that, in principle, we are capable of solving our problems through social and cultural mechanisms. What he doubts is our ability to do it *in time to avoid catastrophe.* He feels that it will require too long to alter certain dangerous behavior patterns—patterns that reflect our genetically based tendencies toward individualism, self-centeredness, and expansiveness of needs, and which are reflected in our lack of cooperation, our lack of concern for future generations and for members of other societies, and our disinclination to deny ourselves. Heilbroner points out the futility of pinning our hopes on what we believe it is possible for humanity eventually to *become.* Rather, he says, we must consider what people are likely *to be* during the period in question, and he notes that the socialization process tends to produce individuals who are a generation or more behind the times, people who, tomorrow, will finally be prepared to respond to yesterday's problems.[33]

Even if one does not entirely agree with Heilbroner's pessimistic assessment, it is impossible to deny that certain aspects of our genetic heritage seriously handicap us in our efforts to solve our most urgent problems, or that the socialization process and other social and cultural mechanisms are often inadequate in helping societies adapt to the conditions created by a rapidly changing technology. But while there is nothing we can do to alter our genetic mechanisms, at least in the immediate future, *we can alter our social and cultural mechanisms.*

If we hope that humanity will be capable of handling the problems that confront it tomorrow, we must act *today* toward that end. Our decisions cannot be based on wishful thinking about the future; they must be based on cold, hard facts. We must recognize, for example, that the kinds of culturally derived needs and desires that develop in our children and grandchildren will have to differ in some ways from those that motivated our parents or that are central in our own lives. We cannot rely solely on traditional solutions in shaping our actions: if we are to be responsible, we must be innovative; if we are to be compassionate, we must be rational and analytical. In short, our values, ideals, and goals must become less and less unthinking responses to technological advance and more and more the product of deliberate and rational choices made with full awareness of all the alternatives.

Of all the species on this planet, ours is the only one not doomed to have its evolutionary course shaped entirely by forces beyond its control. Thanks to symbol systems and culture, we can not only comprehend the evolutionary process, *we can chart for ourselves an evolutionary course within the limits set by our genetic heritage on the one hand and the constraints of the biophysical environment on the other*—a course that can provide for most people a high degree of freedom, justice, and happiness.

We also have the option to ignore this possibility until it is too late.

Glossary

Adaptation   The process of adjusting to, or changing, environmental conditions; hence, broadly, problem solving.

Agrarian era   The period in history when there were no societies technologically more advanced than agrarian societies (about 3000 B.C. to 1800 A.D.).

Agrarian society   A society that depends primarily on agriculture for subsistence. *Advanced* agrarian societies have iron tools and weapons; *simple* agrarian societies do not.

Agriculture   The cultivation of fields using the plow.

Anthropoid   Resembling humans; a suborder of primates that includes monkeys, apes, and humans.

Archaeology   The study of cultures of the past, based on analysis of their physical remains.

Arithmetic mean   The value that results when the sum of a set of items is divided by the number of items; a measure of central tendency.

Artisan   A craftsman. The term is usually applied to a worker who, unlike a modern factory worker, uses hand tools and produces a complete product.

Autocracy   Rule by one person (compare with *Democracy, Oligarchy*, and *Theocracy*).

Autonomous   Free from outside political control.

Band   A nomadic community at the hunting and gathering level; most bands are also societies.

Biological evolution   The process of genetic change by which existing species of plants and animals have developed out of preexisting species.

Biophysical environment   The biological and physical aspects of the environment.

Bureaucracy   (1) The administrative component of a government or formal organization; (2) an administrative system that is characterized by a highly formalized division of labor, a hierarchical system of authority, and action guided by a complex and formalized system of rules.

Capital goods   The goods in a society that are devoted to the production of other goods. Capital goods include factories, machinery, tools, and livestock.

Capital-intensive industry   An industry in which the ratio of capital costs to other costs is high.

Capitalism   An economic system in which the means of production are privately owned and the basic problems of production and distribution are settled within a market system, with minimal governmental regulation or control (see *Market economy,* and contrast with *Socialism*).

Civilization   An advanced sociocultural system. The term is usually reserved for the cultures of societies with urban communities and writing.

Clan   A kin group whose members claim descent from a common ancestor.

Class   (1) An aggregation or group of people whose *overall* status is similar; (2) an aggregation or group of people who share some important resource that affects their access to power, privilege, or prestige.

Command economy   An economy in which the basic questions of production and distribution are decided by political elites (contrast with *Market economy*).

Communication   The exchange of information by means of signals or symbols.

Communism   A future state of society hypothesized by Marx in which the distribution of goods and services would be based on individual need; a society in which there is no inequality.

Community   An informally organized secondary group whose members are united by a common place of residence or by a common subculture.

Continuity   The persistence of cultural elements in a society.

Cooperation   Interaction by two or more individuals for their mutual benefit.

Culture   Symbol systems and the information they convey.

Customs   Informal norms that define acceptable behavior in a society or in a subgroup within a society.

Democracy   A political system in which sovereignty is vested in the people (contrast with *Autocracy, Oligarchy*, and *Theocracy*).

Demography   The study of populations, especially their size, composition, and change.

Determinism   The belief that a specific set of identifiable factors is sufficient to explain completely a given phenomenon.

Development, societal   A process of change in which technological advance causes greater organizational complexity within a society or set of societies (compare with *Growth*).

Diffusion   Transmission of cultural elements from one society to another, or from one group to another within a society.

Discovery   New cultural information acquired by means other than diffusion (compare with *Invention*).

DNA   Deoxyribonucleic acid; the chemical molecule that embodies genetic information.

Ecological–evolutionary theory   Theory concerning (1) the relationships within and among human societies, (2) the relationships between societies and their biophysical environments, and (3) the processes of sociocultural change and development.

Ecology   The science of the interrelationships of living things to one another and to their environments.

Economic surplus   Production that exceeds what is needed to keep the producers of essential goods and services alive and productive.

Economy   The economic system of a group, especially a society; in effect, an institutionalized set of answers to basic questions concerning the production and distribution of goods and services.

Egalitarian   Characterized by relative equality.

Elites   The most powerful and privileged members of a society or institutional system.

Energy   The capacity for performing work.

Environment   Everything external to an entity (organism, population, society, etc.) that affects it, or is affected by it, in any way.

Era   A period of time during which a particular type of society is the most advanced in existence (e.g., the agrarian era).

Ethnography   The description of sociocultural systems based on direct observation.

Evolution   In general, a process of long-term, cumulative change in which later stages develop out of earlier stages (see *Biological evolution* and *Sociocultural evolution*).

Extended family   A group of related individuals that is more inclusive than the nuclear family and less inclusive than the clan.

Family   A group organized around ties of kinship (see also *Nuclear family* and *Extended family*).

Feedback   A special type of causal relationship in which part of the effect produced by an initial cause or event reverts back to its source, modifying or reinforcing it (i.e., the influence that B exerts on A as a result of A's earlier influence on B).

Feudalism   A decentralized type of polity found in some agrarian societies, in which many powers of government are exercised by local and regional elites rather than by the king or central bureaucracy.

Fishing society   A society dependent primarily on fishing, or fishing and gathering, for subsistence.

Fixed costs   Costs of production that remain more or less constant regardless of the number of units produced (contrast with *Variable costs*).

Freedom   The absence of constraints imposed by society or nature.

Frontier society   An agrarian society that is expanding into territories which are uninhabited, or inhabited by less advanced societies.

Function   (1) A characteristic activity of a person, thing, or institution; or (2) a consequence of, or purpose served by, that activity.

Fundamental innovation   An invention or discovery that either (1) opens the way for many other innovations or (2) alters the conditions of human life so that many other changes become either possible or necessary.

Gathering   Foraging for wild fruits and vegetables.

Gene   The basic unit of heredity; a conveyer of genetic information.

Genetic constants   Genetic attributes that are the same in every population of a species.

Genetic variables   Genetic attributes that vary among the populations within a species.

Governing class   A largely hereditary class from which the political leaders of a society are recruited.

Gross domestic product (GDP)   The monetary value of the goods and services produced within a society during a specified period (usually a year).

Gross national product (GNP)   Gross domestic product plus net income from other nations.

Group   An aggregation whose members (1) cooperate to satisfy common, or complementary, needs; (2) have shared norms; and (3) have a sense of common identity. The term is applicable to a society and also to intersocietal and intrasocietal aggregations.

Growth   An increase in size. For societies, the term may refer either to population size or to territorial size (compare with *Development, societal*).

Guild   A mutual aid association of merchants and artisans in the same trade (found in agrarian and maritime societies).

Headman   The leader of a local community in a preliterate society.

Herding society   A society dependent primarily on herding for subsistence.

Hominid   A member of the genus *Homo*, which includes our own species as well as an undetermined number of humanlike species that preceded us but are now extinct.

Homo sapiens   Our species.

Homo sapiens sapiens   Our subspecies; genetically modern humans.

Horticultural era   The period in history when there were no societies technologically more advanced than horticultural societies (about 7000 to 3000 B.C.).

Horticultural society   A society that depends primarily on horticulture for subsistence. *Advanced* horticultural societies are differentiated from *simple* by the manufacture of metal tools and weapons.

Horticulture   The cultivation of small gardens using a hoe or digging stick as the chief tool. Horticulture is differentiated from agriculture by the absence of the plow.

Hunting and gathering era   The period in history when there were no societies more advanced than hunting and gathering (to about 7000 B.C.).

Hunting and gathering society   A society that depends primarily on hunting and gathering for subsistence.

Hybrid society   A society that relies about equally on two or more of the basic modes of subsistence.

Hypothesis   A proposition tentatively assumed to be valid until disproven.

Ideology   Cultural information used to interpret human experience and order societal life. An ideology consists of a system of beliefs and related norms and values.

Industrial era   The period in history when industrial societies have been dominant (from about 1800 A.D. to the present).

Industrialization   A process of increasing reliance on inanimate sources of energy and the machines powered by them (compare with *Modernization*).

Industrial Revolution   The revolution in technology that began in England in the eighteenth century and has since spread through most of the world system.

Industrial society   A society that derives most of its wealth and income from productive activities dependent on machines powered by inanimate energy sources (i.e., coal, petroleum, natural gas, hydroelectric power, nuclear power).

Information   A record of experience that is stored in the memory system of a plant, animal, or machine.

Innovation   The process of introducing new cultural elements into a society; the new cultural element itself (see *Variations*).

Institution   A system of social relationships and cultural elements that develops in a society in response to some set of basic and persistent needs.

Institutional system   A system of interrelated institutions.

Intelligentsia   Well-educated persons; the upper part of the nonmanual occupational class in eastern European societies.

Intersocietal selection   The process of selection *among* societies, whereby some survive while others become extinct.

Intrasocietal selection   The process of selection *within* a society, whereby some of its cultural elements survive while others are eliminated.

Invention   An innovation that results from a useful new combination of information already possessed by a society (compare with *Discovery*).

Labor-intensive industry   An industry in which the ratio of labor costs to other costs is high.

Language   A system of symbols.

Laws   Norms sanctioned by government.

Learning   The process by which an organism acquires, through experience, information with the potential for changing its behavior.

Legitimate   That which is morally or legally justified by the norms or laws of a group.

Legitimize   To make legitimate; to provide an ideological or moral justification for a practice that might otherwise be regarded as objectionable.

Macrosociology   The branch of sociology that studies large social systems, especially human societies and the world system of societies.

Maritime society   A society in which overseas commercial activity is the primary source of wealth and income.

Market economy   An economy in which the basic problems of production and distribution are resolved by the forces of supply and demand (see *Capitalism*, and contrast with *Command economy*).

Mass media   Communications media that influence the masses (i.e., TV, radio, newspapers, magazines, and movies).

Mean, arithmetic   See *Arithmetic mean*.

Median   The middle number in a series of numbers arranged in order from highest to lowest; a measure of central tendency.

Mixed economy   An economy that combines two or more basic principles of economic decision making, especially one that combines market and command principles.

Mobility, vertical   See *Vertical mobility*.

Modernization   All of the long-term social and cultural changes associated with industrialization (compare with *Industrialization*).

Monogamy   Marriage with but one person at a time (compare with *Polygamy* and *Polygyny*).

Monopoly   A commodity market with only a single seller.

Nation   A society governed by full-time officials (see *State*).

Nationalism   An ideology that emphasizes the importance of a nation or an ethnic group.

Neophilia   The love of novelty or change for its own sake.

Nomad   A member of a group that has no permanent settlement and moves about periodically (usually in a well-defined territory) to obtain food and other necessities.

Nomenklatura   (1) A list of positions in revolutionary socialist societies that can be filled only by Party approval; (2) the governing class in revolutionary socialist societies.

Norms   Definitions of acceptable behavior for the members of a society in their various roles; norms may be formal (e.g., laws) or informal (e.g., customs).

Nuclear family   A man, his wife or wives, and their unmarried children living with them.

Oligarchy   The rule of the few (contrast with *Autocracy, Democracy*, and *Theocracy*).

Oligopoly   A commodity market dominated by a few sellers.

Organism   A living entity; a plant or animal.

Peasant   An agricultural worker in an agrarian society.

Per capita income   National income divided by population size.

Polity   The political system of a group, especially of a society; in effect, an institutionalized set of answers to basic questions concerning the governance of a society.

Polygamy   A form of marriage in which an individual of either sex has two or more spouses at the same time (compare with *Polygyny*).

Polygyny   A form of marriage in which a man has two or more wives at the same time (compare with *Polygamy*).

Population   (1) Organisms of the same species that tend to interbreed because of geographical proximity; (2) the members of a society, or a subgroup within a society, considered collectively.

Positive-sum game   A contest in which the gains of one participant are not necessarily at the expense of others (contrast with *Zero-sum game*).

Pragmatism   The belief that social arrangements should be judged on the basis of their consequences rather than on the basis of preconceived ideas.

Primary group   A small group in which face-to-face relations of at least a fairly intimate and personal nature are maintained; a family or clique.

Primary industries   Industries that produce or extract raw materials (especially farming, mining, forestry, and fishing).

Primates   An order of mammals that includes the anthropoids and prosimians.

Process   A series of related events with a definable outcome.

Race   A breeding population in which certain traits occur with a frequency that is appreciably different from that of other breeding populations within the same species; among humans, races are differentiated on the basis of skin, hair and eye color, hair type, body build, and shape of face and head.

Religion   The basic beliefs of a group of people and the practices associated with those beliefs. The term can refer to nontheistic ideologies, such as communism and humanism, but is more often applied to ideologies that involve theistic beliefs.

Republic   A nonmonarchical government.

Revolution   Change that is unusually sudden, rapid, violent, or far-reaching.

Revolutionary socialism   A socialist ideology developed by Marx and extended by Lenin that advocates the seizure of power by adherents and denial of power to others; a totalitarian or semitotalitarian system of government.

Role   A position that can be filled by an individual and that has distinctive norms attached to it. The term may also be used to refer to the part a group, institution, or other social unit plays in the life of a society.

Sanction   A reward or punishment; also, the act of rewarding or punishing.

Secondary group   Any group that is larger and more impersonal than a primary group.

Secondary industries   Industries that process raw materials and turn out finished products.

Selection   The process that determines the fate of the variations (1) in a gene pool, (2) in a sociocultural system, or (3) in the world system of societies (see *Intersocietal selection*, *Intrasocietal selection*, and *Variations*).

Serf   A peasant farmer who is bound to the land and subject to the owner of the land.

Shaman   A person believed to enjoy special powers because of a relationship he or she has established with the spirit world; a medicine man.

Signal   An information conveyer whose form and related meaning are both determined genetically (contrast with *Symbol*).

Social   Having to do with relationships among the members of societies.

Social controls   Mechanisms that order societal life by regulating people's actions and relationships; norms and their related sanctions.

Social environment   The other social systems with which a given social system has contact.

Social institution   See *Institution*.

Socialism   An economic system in which there is little or no private ownership of the means of production (compare with *Capitalism*).

Socialization   The process through which individuals learn to become functional members of their society.

Social movement   A loose-knit group that seeks to change society.

Social organization   The network of relationships among the members of a society or group.

Social structure   See *Social organization* and *Structure*.

Social system   A generic term that may be applied to all kinds of human groups, from primary groups to the world system of societies.

Societal   Of or pertaining to a society or societies.

Society, human   A politically autonomous group of people engaged in a broad range of cooperative activities.

Sociocultural   A combination of *social* and *cultural* elements.

Sociocultural evolution   The process of change and development in human societies that results from cumulative change in the store of cultural information available to them.

Sociocultural system   A system composed of a human population and its social organization, culture, material products, and social institutions; a human society.

Sociology   The branch of science that specializes in the study of human societies.

State   The government of a society governed by full-time officials (see *Nation*).

Status   The relative rank of a person, role, or group, according to culturally defined standards.

Stratification   Class or status differentiation within a population; hence, inequality.

Structure   The organization of the parts of a system.

Subculture   The distinctive culture of a group within a society.

Subsistence   The material necessities of life; also, the process by which they are obtained.

Subsistence technology   The technology that is used by the members of a society to obtain the basic necessities of life.

Surplus   See *Economic surplus*.

Symbol   An information conveyer whose form and meaning are determined by those who use it (contrast with *Signal*).

System   An entity made up of interrelated parts.

Systemic   Having the qualities of a system.

Technology   Cultural information about the ways in which the material resources of the environment may be used to satisfy human needs and desires.

Tertiary industries   Industries that perform services (e.g., retail trade, government, the professions).

Theocracy A society ruled by a priesthood in the name of some deity, or by a ruler believed to be divine.

Theory An explanation of some aspect of the natural world; a coherent set of principles that form the basic frame of reference for a field of inquiry.

Third World Industrializing societies of the contemporary world; hence, less developed societies.

Tribe A preliterate group whose members speak a common language or dialect, possess a common culture that distinguishes them from other peoples, and know themselves, or are known, by a distinctive name.

Urban community A community whose inhabitants are wholly or largely freed from the necessity of producing their own food, fibers, and other raw materials.

Values Moral beliefs to which the members of a group subscribe.

Variable Any property of an entity that can vary in degree.

Variable costs Costs of production that tend to vary in proportion to the number of units produced (contrast with *Fixed costs*).

Variations Products of the process of innovation; new or alternative elements in a sociocultural system (see *Innovation* and *Selection*).

Vertical mobility Change of status, either upward or downward.

Working class Members of modern industrial societies belonging to families headed by manual workers.

World system The totality of human societies and their interrelationships.

Zero-sum game A contest in which the gains of any participant are necessarily at the expense of other participants. This concept is applicable to societies in which economic growth is absent and contrasts with the positive-sum game concept, which assumes economic growth.

Appendix

Many of the figures and tables for preindustrial societies are either new or have been substantially revised for the 6th edition of *Human Societies*. This task was greatly facilitated by publication of Douglas White's "electronic journal," *World Cultures*, which makes George Peter Murdock's complete *Ethnographic Atlas* (1267 cases) and a number of additional data sets for a "standard sample" of societies (186 cases) available to subscribers in computer-readable ("floppy disk") form.

We report results from analyses of the *Ethnographic Atlas* data in most of the tables and figures because they depict the experience and characteristics of the largest, most extensive "sample" of human societies. To guard against the possibility that the total data set gives a distorted or lopsided picture of human societies, however, all the analyses were recomputed for a subset (734 cases) of the *Ethnographic Atlas* argued to be more "representative" of human societies. In all instances results for this "world sample" were substantially the same as those for the complete *Atlas*.

In those cases where the "standard sample" data sets contain information not available in the *Atlas*, we report results using them. The "standard sample" was carefully constructed to "represent" the regional, cultural, and developmental diversity of human societies, and as new variables are added, the volume and diversity of data on it continue to grow. This growing body of data greatly extends cross-cultural research possibilities, and strongly complements the *Atlas*. The variables we used are identified below.

Dominant mode of subsistence was coded according to information on the society's percent dependence on each of five basic modes of subsistence (v1–v5 in the *Atlas*, v203–v207 in the *Sample*): (1) hunting, (2) gathering, (3) fishing, (4) animal husbandry, and (5) agriculture; together with information on the presence or absence of metals (v44, v55 in the *Atlas*; v248, v249 in the *Sample*), and the presence or absence of the plow (v39 in the *Atlas*, v243 in the *Sample*).

After summing the scores for hunting and gathering to produce a composite measure of societal dependence on these two modes of subsistence, we classified societies on the basis of the following criteria:

1. If dependence on hunting and gathering, fishing, or animal husbandry was 6 or greater (more than 56% reliance), that mode was coded as dominant (i.e., the society was coded "hunting and gathering," "fishing," or "herding," respectively).
2. If agriculture was 6 or greater, the plow ABSENT, and metals ABSENT, the society was coded "simple horticultural."
3. If agriculture was 6 or greater, the plow ABSENT, and metals PRESENT, the society was coded "advanced horticultural."

4. If agriculture was 6 or greater, and the plow PRESENT, the society was coded "agrarian."
5. If a dependence score was 4 (36–45%), or 5 (46–55%), and NO OTHER MODE WAS SCORED AS HIGH OR HIGHER, that mode was classified dominant.
6. If no score was 4 or greater, two modes were scored equally high, or relevant data were missing, the society was coded "other."
7. Also, because of their anomalous and hybrid nature, "mounted hunters" (those in which hunting and gathering was dominant, and in which v40 in the *Atlas* or v244 in the *Sample* indicated horses were present) were coded "other."

These coding rules produced the following distributions of societal types:

Distribution of Societal Types in Different Data Sets

Societal Type	Ethnographic Atlas		World Sample		Standard Sample	
	N	%	N	%	N	%
Hunting and gathering	174	21	84	16	27	17
Simple horticultural	155	19	146	27	35	22
Advanced horticultural	246	30	140	26	38	24
Agrarian	103	13	90	17	32	20
Fishing	60	7	38	7	11	7
Herding	78	10	37	7	16	10
Totals	816	100	535	100	159	100

Note: A total of 451 cases from the *Ethnographic Atlas*, 199 from the *World Sample*, and 27 from the *Standard Sample* were missing relevant data, or were otherwise not classifiable according to the criteria. It should also be noted that the numerical base for particular tables and figures in the text varies because of missing data on the traits in question.

Data Sources for New and Revised Tables and Figures

Table 4.2 Median Size: *Atlas,* V89, Political Integration.
Table 4.3 Craft Specialization: *Atlas,* V55-V60, Craft Specialization.
Figure 4.6 Complex Status Systems: *Atlas,* V65, Class Stratification.
Figure 4.7 Belief in a Supreme Creator: *Atlas,* V34, High Gods.
Table 5.3 Community Size: *Atlas,* V31, Mean Size of Local Communities.
Table 5.5 Emphases in Child-Rearing: *Standard Sample,* V306-V309, V322-V325.
Table 5.6 Types of Games: *Atlas,* V35, Games.
Figure 6.3 Population Density: *Standard Sample,* V156, Density of Population.
Table 6.1 Division of Labor: *Atlas,* V54, Sex Differences in Agriculture.
Table 6.2 Matrilineality: *Atlas,* V43, Descent.
Table 6.4 Economic Transaction: *Atlas,* V6, Mode of Marriage.
Figure 6.14 Slavery: *Atlas,* V69, Type of Slavery.

Further information on tables and analyses are available from the authors.

Notes

Chapter 1

1 William R. Catton, Jr., *From Animistic to Naturalistic Sociology* (New York: McGraw-Hill, 1966).

2 Kingsley Davis, *Human Society* (New York: Macmillan, 1949), p. 27. See also Alfred E. Emerson, "Human Cultural Evolution and Its Relation to Organic Evolution of Insect Societies," in Herbert Barringer et al. (eds.), *Social Change in Developing Areas: A Reinterpretation of Evolutionary Theory* (Cambridge, Mass.: Schenkman, 1965), pp. 50–51.

3 Edward O. Wilson, *Sociobiology: The New Synthesis* (Cambridge, Mass.: Belknap, 1975), part III.

4 This definition is a slightly modified version of that provided by W. H. Thorpe, *Learning and Instinct in Animals*, 2d ed. (Cambridge, Mass.: Harvard, 1963), p. 55.

5 Wilson, pp. 151–152.

6 Sherwood L. Washburn and David A. Hamburg, "The Implications of Primate Research," in Irven DeVore (ed.), *Primate Behavior: Field Studies of Monkeys and Apes* (New York: Holt, 1965), p. 613.

7 Sherwood Washburn, "The Evolution of Man," *Scientific American*, 239 (September 1978), p. 204; Dorothy Miller, "Evolution of the Primate Chromosomes," *Science*, 198 (Dec. 16, 1977), pp. 1116–1124. See also Mary-Claire King and A. C. Wilson, "Evolution at Two Levels in Humans and Chimpanzees," *Science*, 188 (Apr. 11, 1975), pp. 107–116.

8 This paragraph is based on Wilson, pp. 176–185.

9 Karl von Frisch, "Dialect in the Language of the Bees," *Scientific American*, 167 (Aug. 1962), pp. 3–7.

10 Masukazu Konishi, "The Role of Auditory Feedback in the Control of Vocalization in the White-Crowned Sparrow," *Journal of Comparative Ethology*, 22 (1965), pp. 770–783.

11 See, for example, Francine Patterson, "Conversations with a Gorilla," *National Geographic*, 154 (October 1978), pp. 438–466. For a more skeptical view of the ability of apes to use symbols, see Roger Brown, "Why Are Signal Languages Easier to Learn than Spoken Languages? Part Two," *Bulletin of the American Academy of Arts and Sciences*, 32 (December 1978), pp. 38–39.

12 John E. Pfeiffer, *The Emergence of Man*, 2d ed. (New York: Harper & Row, 1972), p. 381, citing Jane van Lawick-Goodall as authority.

13 Helen Keller, *The Story of My Life* (New York: Doubleday, 1903).

14 Robert Lord, *Comparative Linguistics*, 2d ed. (London: English Universities Press, Ltd., 1974), pp. 288–289.

Chapter 2

1 Anatol Rapaport, "Systems Analysis: General Systems Theory," *International Encyclopedia of the Social Sciences* (New York: Macmillan and Free Press, 1968), vol. 15, p. 454.

2 Francis Thompson, "The Mistress of Vision."

3 John Locke, *An Essay Concerning Human Understanding* (New York: Dover, 1959, first published 1690).

4 Reinhold Niebuhr, *The Nature and Destiny of Man* (New York: Scribner, 1943), vol. 1; Robert Heilbroner, *An Inquiry into the Human Prospect* (New York: Norton, 1974), chap.

4; and Jan Szczepański, *Polish Society* (New York: Random House, 1970), p. 100 and chap. 9.

5 Theodosius Dobzhansky, *Mankind Evolving* (New York: Bantam, 1962), pp. 224–225, and John E. Pfeiffer, *The Emergence of Man,* 2d ed. (New York: Harper & Row, 1972), chap. 18.

6 Rene A. Spitz, "Hospitalism," *The Psychoanalytic Study of the Child*, 1 (1945), pp. 53–72, and "Hospitalism: A Follow-up Report," ibid., 2 (1946), pp. 113–117.

7 Pfeiffer, pp. 429–430, and Carl Sagan, *The Dragons of Eden* (New York: Ballantine Books, 1977), pp. 47–48.

8 Stephen Jay Gould, "Human Babies as Embryos," *Natural History*, 85 (February 1976), p. 22ff.

9 Curtis, pp. 717–720.

10 Noam Chomsky, *Syntactic Structures* (The Hague: Mouton, 1957); *Aspects of the Theory of Syntax* (Cambridge, Mass.: MIT Press, 1965); and *Cartesian Linguistics* (New York: Harper & Row, 1966).

11 Dobzhansky, p. 354. See also Pierre van den Berghe, "Evolution and Creativity," unpublished paper, University of Washington.

12 For a more detailed discussion of this subject, see Gerhard Lenski, *Power and Privilege* (New York: McGraw-Hill, 1966), pp. 25–32.

13 A. H. Maslow, *Motivation and Personality* (New York: Harper & Row, 1954), especially chap. 5. See also Edward O. Wilson, *Sociobiology: The New Synthesis* (Cambridge, Mass.: Belknap, 1975), p. 143.

14 William Graham Sumner, *Folkways* (New York: Mentor, 1960, first published 1906), p. 32.

15 J. S. Weiner, *The Natural History of Man* (Garden City, N.Y.: Doubleday Anchor, 1973), p. 170.

16 Theodosius Dobzhansky, Francisco Ayala, G. Ledyard Stebbins, and James Valentine, *Evolution* (San Francisco: Freeman, 1977), chap. 5.

17 For brief but fascinating discussions of the relation between human physique and climate, see Theodosius Dobzhansky, *Mankind Evolving* (New York: Bantam, 1962), p. 287ff; Weiner, p. 160ff.; and E. Adamson Hoebel, *Anthropology: The Study of Man*, 3d ed. (New York: McGraw-Hill, 1966), p. 214ff.

18 Weiner, pp. 153 and 167.

19 Dobzhansky, Ayala, et al., p. 148.

20 Dobzhansky, p. 158ff.

21 Paul R. Ehrlich and Richard W. Holm, *The Process of Evolution* (New York: McGraw-Hill, 1963), fig. 11.1, p. 253.

22 Fred Blumenthal, "The Man in the Middle of the Peace Talks," *Washington Post*, July 14, 1968.

23 Helene Curtis, *Biology*, 2d ed. (New York: Worth, 1975), p. 159.

24 Hoebel, p. 35.

25 Karl G. Heider, *The Dugum Dani: A Papuan Culture in the Highlands of West New Guinea* (New York: Wenner-Gren Foundation, 1970) pp. 32–33.

26 Hoebel, p. 35.

27 Robert Lord, *Comparative Linguistics*, 2d ed. (London: English Universities Press, 1974), p. 316. For other interesting examples of changes in the meanings of words, see Charlton Laird, *The Miracle of Language* (Greenwich, Conn.: Premier Books, 1953), p. 54ff.

28 Edward Sapir, *Selected Writings in Language, Culture, and Personality*, David Mandelbaum (ed.) (Berkeley: University of California Press, 1949), p. 162.

29 See, for example, Dell Hymes, "Linguistics: The Field," *International Encyclopedia of the Social Sciences*, vol. 9., p. 22.

30 V. Gordon Childe, *Man Makes Himself* (New York: Mentor, 1951), p. 144ff.

31 This view of ideology borrows from Talcott Parsons's thesis that the prime function of religion is making sense out of the totality of human experience. If the term "religion" is defined to include nontheistic faiths (as we do in this volume), religion in the historic western sense becomes one form of ideology. See Parsons, *The Structure of Social Action* (New York: Free Press, 1968), vol. II, pp. 566–567, 667–668, and 717.

32 See, for example, Robert S. Merrill, "Technology: The Study of Technology," *International Encyclopedia of the Social Sciences*, vol. 15, p. 576.

33 Ralph H. Turner, "Role: Sociological Analysis," ibid., vol. 13, pp. 552–557.

34 For a more extended discussion of strata and classes, see Lenski, pp. 73–82.

35 James K. Feibleman, *The Institutions of Society* (London: G. Allen, 1956), p. 52.

Chapter 3

1 See, for example, Fekri Hassan, *Demographic Archaeology* (New York: Academic Press, 1981); and Don E. Dumond, "The Limitation of Human Population," *Science*, 187 (Feb. 28, 1975), p. 717.

2 For an early statement of this distinction, see F. Stuart Chapin, *Cultural Change* (New York: Century, 1928), p. 345.

3 A. L. Kroeber, *Anthropology* (New York: Harcourt, Brace, 1948), pp. 353–355. For other examples, see Howard A. Rush, "Right Time and Place: Many Medical Discoveries Found to Result from Series of Accidents," *New York Times*, June 8, 1969; Irving Page, "A Sense of the History of Discovery," *Science*, Dec. 27, 1974, p. 1161; and Vern Riportella, "Fifty Years of Radio Astronomy," *Science News*, 123 (Apr. 30, 1983), p. 283.

4 William F. Ogburn and Dorothy S. Thomas, "Are Inventions Inevitable? A Note on Social Evolution," *Political Science Quarterly*, 37 (1922), pp. 93–98.

5 Glynn Isaac, "The Food-Sharing Behavior of Protohuman Hominids," *Scientific American*, 238 (April 1978), pp. 90–108.

6 For an early statement of this principle, see William F. Ogburn, *Social Change* (New York: Viking, 1922), chap. 6.

7 Ogburn mentioned this factor briefly, but did not stress it. (Ibid., 1950, p. 110).

8 Ralph Linton, *The Study of Man* (New York: Appleton-Century, 1936), pp. 326–327. Reprinted by permission of Prentice-Hall, Inc.

9 Basil Davidson with F. K. Buah, *A History of West Africa* (Garden City, N.Y.: Doubleday Anchor, 1966), pp. 8–9; William H. McNeill, *Plagues and Peoples* (Garden City, N.Y.: Doubleday Anchor, 1976).

10 Ogburn, 1950, p. 107.

11 Rudolf Braun, "Zur Einwirkung soziokulturelle Umweltbedingungen auf das Unternehmverhalten," in Wolfram Fischer (ed.), *Wirtschafts und sozialgeschichtliche Probleme der frühen Industrialisierung* (Berlin: Colloquium, 1968), p. 257.

12 O. D. Duncan, "Social Organization and the Ecosystem," in R. E. L. Faris (ed.), *Handbook of Modern Sociology* (Chicago: Rand McNally, 1964), pp. 37–39. See also Leslie White, *The Science of Culture* (New York: Grove, 1949), pp. 363–393.

13 See William F. Cottrell, *Energy and Society* (New York: McGraw-Hill, 1955), p. 2, for a somewhat similar assertion concerning energy's impact on human life.

14 Robert Carneiro, "On the Relationship between Size of Population and Complexity of Social Organization," *Southwestern Journal of Anthropology*, 23 (1967), pp. 234–243.

15 Ernest Gellner, *Plow, Sword and Book: The Structure of Human History* (Chicago: University of Chicago Press, 1989).

16 Robert Carneiro, "Political Expansion as an Expression of the Principle of Competitive Exclusion," in Ronald Cohen and Elman Service (eds.), *Origins of the State* (Philadelphia: Institute for the Study of Human Issues, 1978), pp. 205–223.

17 F. G. Bailey, *Tribe, Caste, and Nation* (Manchester: Manchester University Press, 1960).

18 See, for example, Ernst Mayr, *The Growth of Biological Thought: Diversity, Evolution, and Inheritance* (Cambridge, Mass.: Belknap, 1982), chap. 8.

19 Thorstein Veblen, *Imperial Germany and the Industrial Revolution* (New York: Macmillan, 1915). See also Elman Service, "The Law of Evolutionary Potential," in Marshall Sahlins and Elman Service (eds.), *Evolution and Culture* (Ann Arbor: University of Michigan Press, 1960), pp. 93–122.

Chapter 4

1 See Marvin Harris, *The Rise of Anthropological Theory* (New York: Thomas Y. Crowell, 1968), chap. 2; and Robert Nisbet, *Social Change and History* (New York: Oxford, 1969), chap. 4.

2 This method of classification is an expansion and modification of one developed earlier by Walter Goldschmidt in *Man's Way: A Preface to the Understanding of Human Society* (New York: Holt, 1959), chap. 6, and also reflects the influence of V. Gordon Childe, *Man Makes Himself* (New York: Mentor Books, 1951).

3 See, for example, R. F. Watters, "The Nature of Shifting Cultivation: A Review of Recent Research," *Pacific Viewpoint*, 1 (1960), pp. 59–99.

4 Goldschmidt, p. 194.

5 See, for example, Frederic Pryor, "The Invention of the Plow," *Comparative Studies in Society and History*, 27 (1985), pp. 727–743.

6 Goldschmidt, p. 210.

7 See Jacquetta Hawkes, *Prehistory* (New York: Mentor Books, 1965), chap. 6, for a good summary of archaeological finds relating to fishing. See also Grahame Clark and Stuart Piggott, *Prehistoric Societies* (New York: Knopf, 1965), chap. 7.

8 Robert Braidwood, "The Earliest Village Communities of Southwest Asia Reconsidered," and Karl Butzer, "Agricultural Origins in the Near East as a Geographical Problem," in Stuart Struever (ed.), *Prehistoric Agriculture* (Garden City, N.Y.: Natural History Press, 1971), pp. 222 and 249.

9 James Mellaart, *Earliest Civilizations in the Near East* (London: Thames and Hudson, 1965), p. 105; and R. J. Forbes, *Studies in Ancient Technology* (Leiden: Brill, 1971–1972), vols. 8 and 9.

10 See, for example, Leslie Aitchison, *A History of Metals* (London: MacDonald, 1960), vol. 1, p. 41, and Forbes, op. cit.

11 E. Cecil Curwen and Gudmund Hatt, *Plough and Pasture: The Early History of Farming* (New York: Collier Books, 1961), p. 64.

12 Aitchison, pp. 102 and 111–113; and Forbes, vol. 9, chap. 3.

13 Mellaart, p. 20.

14 William H. McNeill, *The Rise of the West: A History of the Human Community* (New York: Mentor Books, 1965), p. 150.

15 See Appendix, pages 441 to 442, for details concerning our use of these data.

16 Goldschmidt, p. 115.

17 This method of classifying religious beliefs is based on work by G. E. Swanson in *The Birth of the Gods: The Origin of Primitive Beliefs* (Ann Arbor: University of Michigan Press, 1960), chap. 3.

18 Leslie White was the leading proponent of this point of view for many years. See, for example, his stimulating but extreme essay, "Energy and the Evolution of Culture," in *The Science of Culture* (New York: Grove Press, Inc., 1949), pp. 363–393.

19 Talcott Parsons is one of many who have consistently minimized the role of technology in the process of social change. Though not as extreme as some in his views, he has been very influential. See *Societies: Evolutionary and Comparative Perspectives* (Englewood Cliffs, N.J.: Prentice-Hall, 1966), especially pp. 113–114, for his views.

Chapter 5

1 For an example of the use of the term "analogous peoples," see Grahame Clark and Stuart Piggott, *Prehistoric Societies* (New York: Knopf, 1965), p. 133. On the value of inferences from ethnography, see Frank Hole and Robert Heizer, *An Introduction to Prehistoric Archeology* (New York: Holt, 1965), especially pp. 211–214 and chap. 16; or Grahame Clark, *Archeology and Society: Reconstructing the Historic Past*, 3d ed. (London: Methuen, 1957), pp. 172–174. In several instances, contemporary hunters and gatherers have provided explanations for previously unexplained archaeological findings. See, for example, John E. Pfeiffer, *The Emergence of Man*, 4th ed. (New York: Harper & Row, 1985) p. 289ff. See also Colin Renfrew, *Before Civilization* (Cambridge: Cambridge University Press, 1979), p. 254.

2 For more conservative estimates based on recent work in immunology, see Vincent Sarich and Joseph Cronin, "Molecular Systematics of the Primates," in Morris Goodman et al. (eds.), *Molecular Anthropology* (New York: Plenum, 1976), pp. 141–170; or Allan Wilson et al. "Biochemical Evolution," in Esmond Snell et al. (eds.), *Annual Review of Biochemistry*, 46 (1977), pp. 573–640. For estimates of earlier dates of speciation based on evidence from archaeology and paleontology, see Pfeiffer, prologue and chap. 2; and Richard E. Leakey and Roger Lewin, *Origins* (New York: Dutton, 1977), p. 56.

3 Roger Lewin, "Man the Scavenger," *Science*, 224 (May 25, 1984), pp. 861–862, and Bruce Bower, "Hunting Ancient Scavengers," *Science News*, 127 (Mar. 9, 1985), pp. 155–157.

4 J. S. Weiner, *The Natural History of Man* (Garden City, N.Y.: Doubleday Anchor, 1973), p. 50ff; and C. Owen Lovejoy, "The Natural Detective," *Natural History* (Oct., 1984), pp. 24–28.

5 Glynn Isaac, "The Food-Sharing Behavior of Protohuman Hominids," *Scientific American*, 238 (April 1978), pp. 90–108.

6 Geza Teleki, *The Predatory Behavior of Wild Chimpanzees* (Lewisburg, Pa.: Bucknell University Press, 1973).

7 Jacquetta Hawkes, *Prehistory: UNESCO History of Mankind*, vol. 1, part 1 (New York: Mentor Books, 1965), p. 172. See also Clark and Piggott, p. 45, or Grahame Clark, *The Stone Age Hunters* (London: Thames and Hudson, 1967), p. 25.

8 William Laughlin, "Hunting: An Integrating Biobehavior System and Its Evolutionary Importance," in Richard Lee and Irven DeVore (eds.), *Man the Hunter* (Chicago: Aldine, 1968).

9 Pfeiffer, chap. 8, and Leakey and Lewin, p. 122. See also the comments by Carleton S. Coon, Dean Falk, W. W. Howells, and others following Grover Krantz's paper, "Sapienization and Speech," *Current Anthropology*, 21 (1980), p. 780ff.

10 H. V. Vallois, "The Social Life of Early Man: The Evidence of Skeletons," in Sherwood Washburn (ed.), *Social Life of Early Man* (Chicago: Aldine, 1961), pp. 214–235.

11 Marvin Harris, *Culture, People, Nature*, 3d. ed. (New York: Harper & Row, 1980), p. 128; and Pfeiffer, p. 150ff.

12 Pfeiffer, pp. 154–155.

13 H. Valladus et al., "Thermoluminescence Dating of Mousterian 'Proto-Cro-Magnon' Remains from Israel and the Origin of Modern Man," *Nature*, 331 (Feb. 18, 1988), pp. 614–616.

14 S. A. Semenov, *Prehistoric Technology*, trans. M. W. Thompson (New York: Barnes & Noble, 1964), pp. 202–203.

15 E. Adamson Hoebel, *Anthropology*, 3d ed. (New York: McGraw-Hill, 1966), pp. 176–177; and Hawkes, pp. 212–213.

16 This and the following statements concerning the bow and arrow are based on Semenov, pp. 202–204.

17 Hawkes, p. 212.

18 J. G. D. Clark, *Prehistoric Europe: The Economic Basis* (London: Methuen, 1952), pp. 132–133.

19 Hawkes, pp. 184–188; and Pfeiffer, p. 192.

20 Peter Ucko and Andreé Rosenfeld, *Paleolithic Cave Art* (New York: McGraw-Hill, 1967); or Grahame Clark, *The Stone Age Hunters*, chap. 4.

21 Clark and Piggott, pp. 93–95.

22 Hawkes, pp. 293–294, including fig. 35b.

23 Sherwood Washburn, "The Evolution of Man," *Scientific American*, 239 (Sept., 1978), p. 206.

24 L. J. Angel, "Paleoecology, Paleodemography and Health," in Steven Polgar (ed.), *Population, Ecology and Social Evolution* (The Hague: Mouton, 1975), table 1, pp. 182–183.

25 Fekri Hassan, *Demographic Archaeology* (New York: Academic Press, 1981), chap. 12.

26 For summaries of work on hunters and gatherers, see Richard Lee and Irven DeVore (eds.), *Man The Hunter* (Chicago: Aldine, 1968); Carleton S. Coon, *The Hunting Peoples* (Boston: Little, Brown, 1971); and Elman Service, *The Hunters* (Englewood Cliffs, N.J.: Prentice-Hall, 1966).

27 This figure is based on Elkin's estimate that there were approximately 300,000 aborigines in Australia at the time of the first white settlement. This estimate was divided by 60, a very generous estimate for the average size of these societies. See A. P. Elkin, *The Australian Aborigines*, 3d ed. (Sydney: Angus and Robertson, 1954), p. 10.

28 Our calculations based on 27 societies in Murdock's data set.

29 See Table 4.2 of this volume.

30 Gertrude E. Dole, *The Development of Patterns of Kinship Nomenclature* (unpublished Ph.D. dissertation, University of Michigan, 1957), p. 26, found an average life expectancy at birth in very primitive societies of only 22 years and also found that individuals who live to age 50 are rare. Allan Holmberg, *Nomads of the Long Bow: The Siriono of Eastern Bolivia*, Smithsonian Institution, Institute of Social Anthropology, 10 (Washington, 1950), p. 85, reported that the average life span among the Siriono was only 35 to 40 years *even among those who survived infancy*.

31 Gini Bara Kolata, "!Kung Hunter-Gatherers: Feminism, Diet, and Birth Control," *Science*, 185 (Sept. 13, 1974), p. 934.

32 William Divale, "Systemic Population Control in the Middle and Upper Paleolithic: Inferences Based on Contemporary Hunters and Gatherers," *World Archaeology*, 4 (1972), fig. 11, p. 230; and John Whiting, "Effects of Climate on Certain Cultural Practices," in Ward Goodenough (ed.), *Explorations in Cultural Anthropology: Essays in Honor of George Peter Murdock* (New York: McGraw-Hill, 1964), table 9, pp. 528–533.

33 Don Dumond, "The Limitations of Human Population: A Natural History," *Science*, 187 (Feb. 28, 1975), p. 715.

34 Kolata, op. cit.

35 See, for example, John Garvan, *The Negritos of the Philippines* (Vienna: Ferdinand Berger, 1964), p. 27; or Edwin Loeb, *Sumatra: Its History and People* (Vienna: Institut für Volkerkunde, 1935), p. 283, on the Kubu.

36 Only one of the seventeen nonnomadic hunting and gathering societies in Murdock's data set depended on hunting and gathering for more than three-quarters of its subsistence, whereas three-quarters of the 150 nomadic hunting and gathering societies were in this category. The one exception among the nonnomadic societies (the Nomlaki) was located

in the Sacramento Valley of northern California, a territory as favorable for a hunting and gathering people as any in the world (see Baumhoff, pp. 205–231).

37 Colin Turnbull, "The Mbuti Pygmies of the Congo," in James Gibbs (ed.), *Peoples of Africa* (New York: Holt, 1965), pp. 286–287.

38 James Woodburn, "Ecology, Nomadic Movement and the Composition of the Local Group among Hunters and Gatherers: An East African Example and Its Implications," in Peter J. Ucko, Ruth Tringham, and G. W. Dimbleby (eds.), *Man, Settlement and Urbanism* (London: Duckworth, 1972), p. 201ff.

39 Richard B. Lee, "Work Effort, Group Structure and Land-Use in Contemporary Hunter-Gatherers," in Ucko et al., pp. 181–184.

40 A. R. Radcliffe-Brown, "The Social Organization of Australian Tribes," *Oceania*, 1 (1930), pp. 44–46.

41 Elkin, p. 56 (Doubleday Anchor edition).

42 Service, *The Hunters*, p. 32ff. For some exceptions, see Colin Turnbull, *Wayward Servants, The Two Worlds of the African Pygmies* (Garden City, N.Y.: Natural History Press, 1965), pp. 109–112.

43 See, for example, Elkin, p. 50; Ivor Evans, *The Negritos of Malaya* (London: Cambridge, 1937), p. 254; and Garvan, p. 82.

44 Service, p. 42.

45 David Aberle, "Matrilineal Descent in Cross-Cultural Perspective," in D. Schneider and K. Gough (eds.), *Matrilineal Kinship* (Berkeley: University of California Press, 1961), p. 677; or Burton Pasternak, *Introduction to Kinship and Social Organization* (Englewood Cliffs, N.J.: Prentice-Hall, 1976), pp. 111–112.

46 Elman Service, *Primitive Social Organization: An Evolutionary Perspective* (New York: Random House, 1962), chap. 3, especially p. 61.

47 See, for example, Elkin, pp. 134–137.

48 Lorna Marshall, "The !Kung Bushmen of the Kalahari Desert," in Gibbs, pp. 257–258. Quoted by permission of Holt, Rinehart and Winston, Inc. See also Charles Hose and William McDougall, *The Pagan Tribes of Borneo* (London: Macmillan, 1912), pp. 190–191; Holmberg, p. 11; or Loeb, p. 300.

49 See, for example, Walter Goldschmidt, *Nomlaki Ethnography*, University of California *Publications in American Archaeology and Ethnology*, 42 (Berkeley, 1951), pp. 333–335 and 417–428.

50 See, for example, Loeb, p. 294, or Holmberg, pp. 30 and 91.

51 Turnbull, pp. 287 and 297; Frederick McCarthy and Margaret McArthur, "The Food Quest and the Time Factor in Aboriginal Economic Life," in Charles Mountford (ed.), *Records of the American-Australian Expedition to Arnhem Land* (Melbourne: Melbourne University Press, 1960), pp. 190–191; Kenneth MacLeish, "The Tasadays: Stone Age Cavemen of Mindanao," *National Geographic*, 142 (August 1972), pp. 243–245; Richard B. Lee, "What Hunters Do for a Living, or How to Make Out on Scarce Resources," in Lee and DeVore, pp. 36–37.

52 See Marshall Sahlins, "Notes on the Original Affluent Society," in Lee and DeVore, pp. 85–89.

53 Goldschmidt, p. 417. See also Asen Balicki, "The Netsilik Eskimos: Adaptive Responses" and the comments of Lorna Marshall and Colin Turnbull, in Lee and DeVore, pp. 78–82, 94, and 341, for challenges to the effort to portray life in hunting and gathering societies as idyllic and trouble-free.

54 Lee and DeVore, op. cit.

55 See, for example, Lee, p. 40.

56 Coon, *The Hunting Peoples*, p. 176.

57 In the hunting and gathering societies in Murdock's data set, hunting was entirely a male activity in 96 percent of the cases and predominantly a male activity in the rest. On the other hand, gathering was wholly or largely a female activity in 87 percent of the societies and predominantly a male activity in only 4 percent (in the remainder the activity was shared by both sexes).

58 Of the hunting and gathering societies in Murdock's data set, 53 percent defined this as a male responsibility, 26 percent as a female, and 21 percent regarded it as appropriate to both sexes.

59 I. Schapera, *Government and Politics in Tribal Societies* (London: Watts, 1956), p. 93. See also Holmberg's description of the Siriono headman quoted on p. 106 of this volume, and Hose and McDougall, p. 190, on the Punan shaman. Other specialists, much less common, may include part-time workers in certain arts and crafts and occasionally an assistant to the headman. Such individuals are most likely to be found in settled communities that depend less than totally on hunting and gathering or in those with especially favorable environments. See, for example, Goldschmidt, pp. 331–332, and Elkin, p. 254ff.

60 See, for example, Turnbull, pp. 287–288; Evans, pp. 57 and 112–113; Garvan, p. 66; or Hose and McDougall, p. 191. Turnbull warns, however, that many scholars exaggerate the dependence of the Pygmies on the neighboring horticultural villagers. He maintains that they turn to the villagers only for luxuries and diversion. See *Wayward Servants*, pp. 33–37.

61 Gerhard Lenski, *Power and Privilege* (New York: McGraw-Hill, 1966), pp. 95–96.

62 Occasionally there might be a second official. See, for example, Kaj Birket-Smith, *The Eskimos*, rev. ed. (London: Methuen, 1959), p. 145; Goldschmidt, pp. 324–325; and Frank Speck, *Penobscot Man* (Philadelphia: University of Pennsylvania Press, 1940), pp. 239–240.

63 Holmberg, pp. 59–60. Quoted by permission of the Smithsonian Institution Press. Following an older usage, Holmberg referred to the leaders of Siriono bands as "chiefs." In current usage, such persons are usually referred to as "headmen," and the term "chief" is reserved for the leaders of multicommunity societies. For this reason, the term "headman" has been substituted.

64 See, for example, John Cooper, "The Ona," in Julian Steward (ed.), *Handbook of South American Indians*, Smithsonian Institution, Bureau of American Ethnology, Bulletin 143 (Washington, 1946), vol. 1, p. 117; A. R. Radcliffe-Brown, *The Andaman Islanders* (Glencoe, Ill.: Free Press, 1948), p. 47; Hose and McDougall, p. 182, on the Punan of Borneo; Speck, p. 239, on the Penobscot of Maine; I. Schapera, *The Khoisan Peoples of South Africa* (London: Routledge, 1930), p. 151; and Roland Dixon, "The Northern Maidu," in Carleton S. Coon (ed.), *A Reader in General Anthropology* (New York: Holt, 1948), p. 272.

65 Schapera, *Government and Politics*, p. 117. Quoted by permission of C. A. Watts & Co., Ltd. See also A. H. Gayton, *Yokuts-Mono Chiefs and Shamans*, University of California *Publications in American Archaeology and Ethnology*, 24 (Berkeley, 1930), pp. 374–376.

66 See, for example, Colin Turnbull, *Wayward Servants*, chaps. 11 and 12, or *The Forest People* (New York: Simon & Schuster, 1961), on the Mbuti Pygmies. As he indicates, the office of headman is sometimes found among these people, but it has been more or less forced on them by the Bantu villagers and is of little significance except in their contacts with these villagers.

67 See, for example, Schapera, *Government and Politics*, p. 193, or Turnbull, *Wayward Servants*, pp. 100–109.

68 See John Honigmann, *The Kaska Indians: An Ethnographic Reconstruction*, Yale University *Publications in Anthropology*, 51 (1954), pp. 90–92 and 96–97; Radcliffe-Brown, *The Andaman Islanders*, pp. 48–52; and Schapera, *The Khoisan Peoples*, pp. 151–155.

69 Schapera, *The Khoisan Peoples*, p. 152.

70 Radcliffe-Brown, *The Andaman Islanders*, p. 50.

71 Schapera, *The Khoisan Peoples*, p. 152.

72 See, for example, Evans, p. 21; Marshall, "!Kung Bushmen," p. 248; or Radcliffe-Brown, p. 29. For an exception, see Birket-Smith, pp. 145–146. For intermediate cases, see Honigmann, pp. 84, 88, and 96; Elkin, p. 45; and H. Ling Roth, *The Aborigines of Tasmania* (London: Kegan, Paul, Trench, Trubner, 1890), p. 71.

73 Sometimes certain trees become the private property of an individual who stakes a special claim to them, but this is uncommon and the number of trees involved is generally small. See, for example, Radcliffe-Brown, *The Andaman Islanders*, p. 41, or Goldschmidt, p. 333.

74 See, for example, McCarthy and McArthur, "Aboriginal Economic Life," pp. 179–180; Schapera, *The Khoisan Peoples*, pp. 100–101; Radcliffe-Brown, *The Andaman Islanders*, p. 43; Hose and McDougall, p. 187; or Speck, p. 47.

75 Radcliffe-Brown, *The Andaman Islanders*, pp. 44–48.

76 See, for example, Goldschmidt, pp. 324–326.

77 Among the sample of hunting and gathering societies in Murdock's data set, 53 percent had provision for the hereditary transmission of the office, usually to a son of the previous headman.

78 William D. Davis, *Societal Complexity and the Sources of Primitive Man's Conception of the Supernatural* (unpublished Ph.D. dissertation, University of North Carolina, Chapel Hill, 1971), chap. 5. Davis reports such beliefs in all but one of the eleven hunting and gathering societies he studied. See also Service, *The Hunters*, pp. 68–70.

79 For descriptions of shamans and their practices, see Evans, chaps. 19–20; Coon, *The Hunting Peoples*, chap. 16; Honigmann, pp. 104–108; Schapera, *The Khoisan Peoples*, pp. 195–201; Radcliffe-Brown, *The Andaman Islanders*, pp. 175–179; Elkin, chap. 11; or Gayton, pp. 392–398.

80 See, for example, Dixon, p. 282.

81 Ibid., p. 272.

82 Jacob Baegert, S.J., *Account of the Aboriginal Inhabitants of the California Peninsula*, in Coon, *A Reader in General Anthropology*, p. 79. See also Radcliffe-Brown, *The Andaman Islanders*, p. 177.

83 See, for example, Elkin, chap. 7; Marshall, "!Kung Bushmen," pp. 264–267; Turnbull, "The Mbuti Pygmies," pp. 306–307; or Coon, *The Hunting Peoples*, chap. 14.

84 Herbert Barry III, Irving L. Child, and Margaret K. Bacon, "Relation of Child Training to Subsistence Economy," *American Anthropologist*, 61 (1959), p. 263. See also Michael R. Welch, *Subsistence Economy and Sociological Patterns: An Examination of Selected Aspects of Child-Training Processes in Preindustrial Societies* (unpublished Ph.D. dissertation, University of North Carolina, 1980).

85 Some of the best evidence of religious motivation comes from Australia (see Elkin, pp. 191–192, or 232–234). For an example of art employed as an instrument of sympathetic magic, see Evans, p. 130ff.

86 Turnbull, "The Mbuti Pygmies," pp. 308–312, *The Forest People*, chap. 4, and *Wayward Servants*, pp. 259–267.

87 See, for example, Hose and McDougall, p. 192, and Speck, p. 270ff.

88 Turnbull, *The Forest People*, p. 135.

89 This definition is based on Hoebel, *Anthropology*, p. 572; and Elkin, *The Australian Aborigines*, p. 25.

90 Examples are provided by the Punan of Borneo (Hose and McDougall, p. 183) or the Mbuti Pygmies of Africa (Turnbull, *Wayward Servants*, pp. 100–109).

91 Schapera, *The Khoisan Peoples*, p. 76. Quoted by permission of Routledge & Kegan Paul, Ltd.

92 See, for example, Goldschmidt, p. 324.

93 For similar comparisons, see Grahame Clark, *The Stone Age Hunters*, op. cit., and Pfeiffer, op. cit.

94 See, for example, Clark and Piggott, *Prehistoric Societies*, p. 130ff; or Hole and Heizer, *Introduction to Prehistoric Archeology*, pp. 225–226.

95 Orlando Lizama, "Death of Woman Marked Tribe's End: First Seen by Magellan," *Washington Post*, Aug. 17, 1975.

96 Marshall, p. 273.

97 Kolata, p. 932.

Chapter 6

1 Jack Harlan, "The Plants and Animals That Nourish Man," *Scientific American*, 235 (September 1976), pp. 89–97; Jack Harlan, *Crops and Man* (Madison, Wis.: American Society of Agronomy, 1975); or Stuart Streuver (ed.), *Prehistoric Agriculture* (Garden City, N.Y.: Natural History Press, 1971), parts II and IV.

2 Mark Cohen, *The Food Crisis in Prehistory* (New Haven: Yale University Press, 1977); and Michael J. Harner, "Population Pressure and the Social Evolution of Agriculturalists," *Southwestern Journal of Anthropology*, 26 (1970), pp. 67–86.

3 Marvin Harris, *Cannibals and Kings: The Origins of Cultures* (New York: Vintage Books, Inc., 1978), p. 31.

4 Ibid., p. 30.

5 Lawrence Guy Straus et al., "Ice-Age Subsistence in Northern Spain," *Scientific American*, 242 (June 1980), pp. 142–152.

6 Bruce Bower, "Extinctions on Ice," *Science News*, 132 (Oct. 31, 1987), pp. 284–285; and Donald Grayson, "Death by Natural Causes," *Natural History* (May, 1987), pp. 8–13.

7 See, for example, R. F. Watters, "The Nature of Shifting Cultivation," *Pacific Viewpoint*, 1 (1960), pp. 59–99; or B. H. Farmer, "Agriculture: Comparative Technology," in *International Encyclopedia of the Social Sciences*, vol. 1, pp. 202–208.

8 See, for example, Robert Braidwood and Bruce Howe, "Southwestern Asia beyond the Lands of the Mediterranean Littoral," in Robert Braidwood and Gordon Willey (eds.), *Courses toward Urban Life: Archeological Considerations of Some Cultural Alternatives* (Chicago: Aldine, 1962), pp. 137, 152–153, and 346; James Mellaart, *Earliest Civilizations of the Near East* (London: Thames and Hudson, 1965), pp. 12, 32–38, 47–50, and 81; or Barbara Bender, *Farming in Prehistory* (London: John Baker, 1975), chap. 6.

9 For a good description of the radiocarbon technique, see Frank Hole and Robert Heizer, *An Introduction to Prehistoric Archeology* (New York: Holt, 1965), pp. 145–150.

10 Braidwood and Howe, p. 140; Mellaart, chap. 3ff.; V. Gordon Childe, "The New Stone Age," in Harry Shapiro (ed.), *Man, Culture, and Society* (New York: Oxford Galaxy, 1960), p. 103; E. Cecil Curwen and Gudmund Hatt, *Plough and Pasture: The Early History of Farming* (New York: Collier Books, 1961), p. 33.

11 Jacquetta Hawkes, *Prehistory, UNESCO History of Mankind*, vol. 1, part 1 (New York: Mentor Books, 1965), pp. 442–452; Mellaart, p. 42; Childe, "The New Stone Age," p. 107.

12 Childe, "The New Stone Age," pp. 100–101.

13 See, for example, Farmer, pp. 204–205; or Curwen and Hatt, p. 68 and chap. 16.

14 V. Gordon Childe, *What Happened in History*, rev. ed. (Baltimore: Penguin, 1964), pp. 64–65.

15 Mellaart, pp. 50–51, or Jean Perrot, "Palestine-Syria-Cilicia," in Braidwood and Willey, pp. 156–157.

16 Hawkes, pp. 384–395; Childe, "The New Stone Age," pp. 104–105; or Perrot, pp. 154–155.

17 Hawkes, pp. 395–401; and Mellaart, pp. 40–42.

18 Mellaart, p. 47; and Bender, pp. 148–149.

19 Childe, "The New Stone Age," p. 105. Elsewhere Childe speaks of twenty-five to thirty-five households as "a not uncommon number" in central Europe and southern Russia. See *What Happened in History*, p. 66.

20 Mellaart, p. 36; or Hawkes, p. 310.

21 Mellaart, pp. 81–101; W. K. Stevens, "Prehistoric Society: A New Picture Emerges," *New York Times*, Dec. 16, 1986.

22 See, for example, Childe, "The New Stone Age," p. 106, or *What Happened in History*, pp. 67–68. See also Braidwood and Howe, p. 138.

23 Mellaart, p. 36. See also p. 84 for his views on Çatal Hüyük.

24 Childe, "The New Stone Age," p. 106.

25 Denise Schmandt-Bessert, "The Earliest Precursor of Writing," *Scientific American*, 238 (January, 1978), pp. 50–59.

26 Mellaart, pp. 43–44.

27 See Childe, *What Happened in History*, p. 67.

28 Childe, "The New Stone Age," p. 106, and *What Happened in History*, p. 67.

29 For a good review of these developments, see Hawkes, pp. 401–410 and 414–417; or V. Gordon Childe, *Man Makes Himself* (New York: Mentor, 1953), pp. 76–80.

30 Childe, "The New Stone Age," p. 107, or *What Happened in History*, p. 74.

31 Karl Heider, *The Dugum Dani: A Papuan Culture in the Highlands of West New Guinea* (New York: Wenner-Gren Foundation, 1970). See also the film "Dead Birds," based on the same society.

32 Childe, "The New Stone Age," p. 107.

33 "Cannibalism in France," *Archaeology* (Jan./Feb., 1987), p. 85.

34 For the ethnographic evidence, see Table 4.2, p. 77.

35 See Kwang-chih Chang, *The Archaeology of Ancient China* (New Haven, Conn.: Yale, 1963), pp. 130–131. See also Curwen and Hatt, pp. 16–18, on truths contained in ancient traditions.

36 The quotations in this paragraph are all from Chang, pp. 131–133, and are used by permission of the Yale University Press.

37 Mellaart, pp. 130–131; and V. Gordon Childe, *New Light on the Most Ancient East* (London: Routledge, 1952), p. 118ff.

38 Childe, *New Light*, p. 115; and Hawkes, p. 425.

39 Childe, *New Light*, p. 115.

40 Mellaart, p. 130.

41 Colin Renfrew, *Before Civilization* (Cambridge: Cambridge University Press, 1979), p. 167.

42 R. J. Forbes, *Studies in Ancient Technology*, 2d ed. (Leiden, Netherlands: Brill, 1972), vol. 9, p. 30; or Leslie Aitchison, *A History of Metals* (London: MacDonald, 1960), vol. 1, p. 21.

43 Forbes, pp. 32–34; or Aitchison, p. 40.

44 Aitchison, ibid.; Forbes, vol. 8, p. 26; or Ronald Wallace, *Those Who Vanished* (Homewood, Ill.: Dorsey, 1983), pp. 294–295.

45 Childe, *Man Makes Himself*, p. 99.

46 V. Gordon Childe, *The Bronze Age* (London: Cambridge, 1930), p. 11.

47 See, for example, Childe, *New Light*, p. 116. There is still some uncertainty about this point.

48 William Watson, *The Chinese Exhibition* (a guide to the exhibition of archaeological finds of the People's Republic, exhibited in Toronto, 1974), p. 14.

49 Some bronze seems to have been manufactured accidentally a few centuries earlier as a result of using copper derived from ores containing tin, but the deliberate and conscious

alloying of metals did not begin in the Middle East until after 3000 B.C. See Forbes, vol. 9, pp. 151–152. Recent research by scholars at the University of Pennsylvania suggests that the invention of bronze may have occurred in Thailand prior to 3600 B.C., which would explain why bronze was an integral part of advanced horticultural societies in China, but not in the Middle East.

50 William Watson, *China: Before the Han Dynasty* (New York: Praeger, 1961), p. 57.
51 Te-k'un Cheng, *Archaeology in China: Shang China* (Cambridge, England: Heffer, 1960), pp. 206–207.
52 Shang kings, for example, mounted "many military expeditions with an army of between 3,000 and 5,000 men." Ibid., p. 210; and Cho-yun Hsu, *Ancient China in Transition* (Stanford, Calif.: Stanford, 1965), p. 67.
53 See note 48 above.
54 Cheng, pp. 200–206.
55 Ibid., pp. 200–215 and 248. For a more detailed picture of the system of stratification in the Chou era, see Hsu, op. cit. In reading this book one must keep in mind that the Chan Kuo period, the "period of the warring states," is included, and by then, north-central China seems to have reached the agrarian level of development.
56 Watson, *China: Before the Han Dynasty*, p. 141, and Chang, p. 195ff.
57 Aitchison, p. 97.
58 Hsu, pp. 3–7 and chap. 4.
59 Chang, p. 150.
60 Watson, *China: Before the Han Dynasty*, p. 106. See also Hsu, p. 15ff., on the interrelations between religion and politics in Chou China.
61 Chang, pp. 150 and 159.
62 Ibid., p. 171.
63 Jesse D. Jennings, "Origins," in Jesse D. Jennings (ed.), *Ancient Native Americans* (San Francisco: Freeman, 1978), pp. 1–41.
64 This view is reinforced by recent archaeological finds revealing the progressive evolution of maize, beans, and other crops from wild, uncultivated forms to the cultivated forms found today. See Marvin Harris, *People, Culture, Nature*, 3d. ed. (New York: Harper & Row, 1980), p. 165; or Wallace, p. 218ff.
65 For a valuable survey of these developments, see Harris, chap. 10; for an extended survey of the three most highly developed cultures of the New World, the Aztecs, Mayas, and Incas, see Victor von Hagen, *The Ancient Sun Kingdoms of the Americas* (Cleveland: World, 1961). See also William Sanders and David Webster, "The Mesoamerican Urban Tradition," *American Anthropologist*, 90 (1988), pp. 521–546; and Norman Hammond, *Ancient Maya Civilization* (New Brunswick, N.J.: Rutgers Press, 1982).
66 For an alternative view, see Stephen C. Jett, "Precolumbian Transoceanic Contact," in Jennings, pp. 593–650.
67 Marvin Harris, *The Rise of Anthropological Theory* (New York: Crowell, 1968), p. 4.
68 Harris, ibid., p. 4. Emphasis added.
69 A careful comparison of societies in the two eras suggests that modern simple horticulturalists may be a bit less advanced than their prehistoric predecessors. For example, 40 percent of those in Murdock's sample did not make pottery and 60 percent did not engage in weaving, both common practices in simple horticultural societies of prehistoric times.
70 Our calculation based on Murdock's data set.
71 See, for example, Steward and Faron's statement, p. 300, with reference to villagers who occupied most of the northern half of South America, that "kinship was the basis of society throughout most of this area." Many similar statements could be cited.

72 See E. Adamson Hoebel, *Anthropology*, 3d ed. (New York: McGraw-Hill, 1966), pp. 374–376, for a good, brief summary of these functions.

73 For similar findings based on Murdock's earlier sample of 565 societies, see David Aberle, "Matrilineal Descent in Cross-cultural Perspective," in David Schneider and Kathleen Gough (eds.), *Matrilineal Kinship* (Berkeley: University of California Press, 1961), table 17.4, p. 677.

74 Aberle reached a similar conclusion, p. 725. He states that "in general, matriliny is associated with horticulture, in the absence of major activities carried on and coordinated by males. ... " See also Janet Saltzman Chafetz, *Sex and Advantage* (Totowa, N.J.: Rowman & Allenheld, 1984), pp. 42–43.

75 This dual role seems to have been quite common in South America. See Julian Steward and Louis Faron, *Native Peoples of South America* (New York: McGraw-Hill, 1959), p. 301, on the Indians of eastern Brazil and the Amazon Basin; or Julian Steward, "The Tribes of the Montaña and Bolivian East Andes," in Julian Steward (ed.), *Handbook of South American Indians*, Smithsonian Institution, Bureau of American Ethnology, Bulletin 143 (Washington, 1948), vol. III, p. 528. For a slightly different pattern in North America, see Irving Goldman, "The Zuni Indians of New Mexico," in Margaret Mead (ed.), *Cooperation and Competition among Primitive Peoples*, rev. ed. (Boston: Beacon Press, 1961), p. 313.

76 Robert Lowie, "Social and Political Organization," in Steward, *Handbook*, vol. V, p. 345. For examples of this, see Steward, *Handbook*, vol. III, pp. 85, 355, 419, and 478. See also Steward and Faron, p. 244.

77 See, for example, Alfred Métraux, *Native Tribes of Eastern Bolivia and Western Matto Grosso*, Smithsonian Institution, Bureau of American Ethnology, Bulletin 134 (Washington, 1942), p. 39, on the Araona; or Leopold Pospisil, "Kaupauku Papuan Political Structure," in F. Ray (ed.), *Systems of Political Control and Bureaucracy in Human Societies, Proceedings of the 1958 Meetings of the American Ethnological Society* (Seattle), p. 18.

78 For a more detailed discussion of these bases of status, see Gerhard Lenski, *Power and Privilege* (Chapel Hill, N.C.: University of North Carolina Press, 1984, originally published 1966), pp. 126–131.

79 See Steward and Faron, pp. 302–303, on the former, and pp. 213–214, 243, and 248–249, on the latter.

80 Marvin Harris, *Cows, Pigs, Wars, and Witches: The Riddles of Culture* (New York: Random House, 1974), pp. 75–80.

81 William Divale, "Systemic Population Control in the Middle and Upper Paleolithic," *World Archaeology*, 4 (1972), fig. 9, p. 228.

82 Data provided by Leo Simmons, *The Role of the Aged in Primitive Society* (New Haven, Conn.: Yale, 1945), show that scalp taking or headhunting was a frequent practice in only one of five hunting and gathering societies but in thirteen of fourteen horticultural societies.

83 Alfred Métraux, "Warfare-Cannibalism-Trophies," in Steward, *Handbook*, vol. V, pp. 400–401. Quoted by permission of the Bureau of American Ethnology.

84 See, for example, Margaret Mead, *Coming of Age in Samoa* (New York: Morrow, 1928).

85 Bruce Knauft, "Reconsidering Violence in Simple Human Societies," *Current Anthropology*, 28 (Aug./Oct., 1987), p. 462.

86 Ibid., table 2, p. 464; also Napoleon Chagnon, *Yanamamö: The Fierce People* (New York: Holt, Rinehart, Winston, 1977).

87 Sonia Cole, *The Prehistory of East Africa* (New York: Mentor, 1965), pp. 46 and 299–301.

88 Meyer Fortes, in Meyer Fortes and E. E. Pritchard (eds.), *African Political Systems* (London: Oxford, 1940) p. 5.

89 In one study of twenty-two African horticultural societies, a correlation of 0.67 (Kendall's tau) was found between level of political development and level of social inequality (see

Lenski, p. 163). See also Basil Davidson with F. K. Buah, *A History of West Africa: To the Nineteenth Century* (Garden City, N.Y.: Doubleday Anchor, 1966), p. 174.

90 See Lucy Mair, *Primitive Government* (Baltimore: Penguin, 1962), especially chap. 4. The discussion that follows is based largely on her work. See also Lenski, chaps. 6 and 7; Morton Fried, *The Evolution of Political Society* (New York: Random House, 1967); and Elman Service, *Origins of the State and Civilizations: The Process of Cultural Evolution* (New York: Norton, 1975).

91 Estimated from the map in Davidson, p. 68.

92 I. Schapera, *Government and Politics in Tribal Societies* (London: Watts, 1956), p. 169. See also the Swazi proverb that "nobles are the chief's murderers."

93 See, for example, Davidson, chap. 14.

94 See, for example, George Peter Murdock, *Africa: Its Peoples and Their Culture History* (New York: McGraw-Hill, 1959), p. 37.

95 See, for example, P. C. Lloyd, "The Yoruba of Nigeria," in James Gibbs (ed.), *Peoples of Africa* (New York: Holt, 1965), pp. 554–556.

96 For an example of a multicommunity society, see P. R. T. Gurdon, *The Khasis* (London: Macmillan, 1914). This author reports that these people were divided into fifteen small states averaging 15,000 in population and controlling about 400 square miles apiece (pp. 1 and 66).

97 Lenski, pp. 160–162. See also Davidson, pp. 76–77.

98 See, for example, the writings of Count Joseph A. deGobineau or Houston Stewart Chamberlain.

99 See, for example, Charles Singer, "Epilogue: East and West," in Charles Singer (ed.), *A History of Technology* (Oxford: Clarendon Press, 1956), vol. II, pp. 754–772, or William H. McNeill, *The Rise of the West* (Chicago: University of Chicago Press, 1963), Parts I and II.

100 Robert W. Steel, "Africa: Natural Resources," in *Encyclopaedia Britannica*, vol. 1, p. 258; Philip L. Wagner, "Tropical Agriculture," ibid., vol. 22, p. 255; Andrew Kamark, "The Resources of Tropical Africa," *Daedalus*, III (Spring, 1982), p. 159; Andrew Kamark, *The Tropics and Economic Development* (Baltimore: Johns Hopkins Press, 1976); and Frederic Pryor, "The Invention of the Plow," *Comparative Studies in Society and History*, 27 (1985), pp. 727–743.

101 William H. McNeill, *Plagues and Peoples* (Garden City, N.Y.: Doubleday Anchor, 1976); Kamark, "Resources," pp. 159–160; Matt Clark, "Blight of the Tropics," *Newsweek*, June 26, 1978, pp. 83–84; Paul Harrison, *Inside the Third World* (Harmondsworth: Penguin, 1982), chap. 16; and Erik Eckholm, "River Blindness," *New York Times Magazine*, Jan. 8, 1989, p. 20ff.

Chapter 7

1 V. Gordon Childe, *What Happened in History* (Baltimore: Penguin, 1964), p. 77.

2 Ibid., chap. 4.

3 This paragraph and the one that follows are based on B. H. Farmer, "Agriculture: Comparative Technology," in *International Encyclopedia of the Social Sciences* (New York: Macmillan and Free Press, 1968), vol. 1, pp. 204–205.

4 See Gudmund Hatt, "Farming of Non-European Peoples," in E. Cecil Curwen and Gudmund Hatt, *Plough and Pasture: The Early History of Farming* (New York: Collier Books, 1961), pp. 217–218.

5 Childe, p. 89.

6 V. Gordon Childe, *Man Makes Himself* (New York: Mentor Books, 1951), p. 100.

7 Farmer, p. 205.

8 E. Cecil Curwen, "Prehistoric Farming of Europe and the Near East," in Curwen and Hatt, pp. 64–65; or C. W. Bishop, "The Origin and Early Diffusion of the Traction Plow," *Antiquity*, 10 (1936), p. 261.

9 Samuel Noah Kramer, *The Sumerians* (Chicago: University of Chicago Press, 1963), p. 123.

10 Childe, *Man Makes Himself*, pp. 143–144.

11 See, for example, Sir Leonard Woolley, *The Beginnings of Civilization*, UNESCO History of Mankind, vol. 1, part 2 (New York: Mentor Books, 1965), pp. 116, 119, 198, and 449ff.

12 Sir Leonard Woolley, *Prehistory* (New York: Harper & Row, 1963), vol. 1, part 2, p. 127.

13 Margaret Murray, *The Splendour That Was Egypt* (London: Sidgwick & Jackson, 1949), p. 174.

14 On Mesopotamia, see Woolley, *Beginnings*, p. 356; or A. Leo Oppenheim, *Ancient Mesopotamia: Portrait of a Dead Civilization* (Chicago: University of Chicago Press, 1964), pp. 84–85. On Egypt, see Ralph Turner, *The Great Cultural Traditions: The Foundations of Civilization* (New York: McGraw-Hill, 1941), vol. 1, p. 187; or George Steindorff and Keith Seele, *When Egypt Ruled the East*, rev. ed. (Chicago: Phoenix Books, 1963), p. 83.

15 Robert Adams, "Factors Influencing the Rise of Civilization in the Alluvium: Illustrated by Mesopotamia," in Carl Kraeling and Robert Adams (eds.), *City Invincible: A Symposium on Urbanization and Cultural Development in the Ancient Near East* (Chicago: University of Chicago Press, 1960), p. 33.

16 See, for example, Kramer, pp. 88–89; Woolley, p. 125; or Kingsley Davis, "The Origin and Growth of World Urbanism," *American Journal of Sociology*, 60 (1955), p. 431. See also Oppenheim, p. 140, who, though declining to estimate size, reports Nineveh to have been larger than Ur (generally thought to have been over 100,000) and Uruk nearly as large; or Mason Hammond, *The City in the Ancient World* (Cambridge, Mass.: Harvard, 1972).

17 Woolley, *Beginnings*, p. 185ff; or Steindorf and Seele, pp. 89–90.

18 Woolley, ibid., p. 188. Later armies were even larger.

19 Turner, p. 312.

20 McNeill, p. 68; Turner, pp. 310–311; Steindorff and Seele, chap. 9; Pierre Montet, *Everyday Life in Egypt: In the Days of Rameses the Great*, trans. A. R. Maxwell-Hyslop and Margaret Drower (London: E. Arnold, 1958), chap. 10; Oppenheim, pp. 70ff., 230ff., and 276–277.

21 Oppenheim, p. 276. As one writer reports, "Sumerian bureaucracy has left us a staggering number of texts; we are unable to venture a guess as to how many tablets beyond the far more than 100,000 now in museums may be buried in southern Mesopotamia."

22 Childe, *Man Makes Himself*, pp. 148–149, or Childe, *What Happened in History*, p. 144.

23 See especially Kramer, p. 231, or Samuel Noah Kramer, *It Happened at Sumer* (Garden City, N.Y.: Doubleday, 1959), p. 3.

24 See Turner, p. 263, or Childe, *What Happened in History*, p. 118.

25 Childe, *What Happened in History*, pp. 118–119.

26 See Turner's excellent treatment of this topic, pp. 317–323.

27 Adolf Erman, *Life in Ancient Egypt*, trans. H. M. Tirard (London: Macmillan, 1894), p. 128.

28 Childe, *Man Makes Himself*, p. 180, quoted by permission of C. A. Watts & Co., Ltd. See also McNeill, p. 53, or Childe, *What Happened in History*, p. 183ff.

29 *Man Makes Himself*, p. 181. Elsewhere, Childe adds a third innovation (or a fifth to the total list), the invention of glass in Egypt. See *What Happened in History*, p. 183.

30 See Childe, *Man Makes Himself*, chap. 9, for a classic discussion of this subject. The analysis that follows is heavily indebted to Childe's provocative discussion but varies in some details and emphasis.

31 See Childe, *What Happened in History*, p. 184.

32 For a classic statement of this principle, see Gaetano Mosca, *The Ruling Class*, translated by Hannah Kahn (New York: McGraw-Hill, 1939), p. 53.

33 For a good summary of the early history of iron, see Leslie Aitchison, *A History of Metals* (London: MacDonald, 1960), vol. 1, pp. 97–110. The discussion that follows is based largely on Aitchison.

34 Ibid., p. 113.

35 See, for example, Charles Singer's comparison of the level of technology in the ancient empires of Egypt and Mesopotamia prior to 1000 B.C. and later in Greece and Rome, in "Epilogue: East and West in Retrospect," in Charles Singer (ed.), *A History of Technology* (Oxford: Clarendon Press, 1956), vol. II, pp. 754–755.

36 Ibid., pp. 754–772.

37 This estimate was based on the known boundaries of these societies and on the fact that the Roman Empire, which was much larger and contained a much smaller percentage of uninhabitable land, had a maximum population of only about 70 million. See *The Cambridge Ancient History* (London: Cambridge, 1939), vol. XII, pp. 267–268. It is also noteworthy that in Roman times Egypt had a population of only 6 to 7 million. Even if allowance is made for the greater size of the Egyptian empire in the days of Egypt's independence, it is difficult to imagine a total population much in excess of 15 million. See Charles Issawi, *Egypt in Revolution: An Economic Analysis* (New York: Oxford, 1963), p. 20.

38 Chung-li Chang, *The Chinese Gentry: Studies on Their Role in Nineteenth-Century Chinese Society* (Seattle: University of Washington Press, 1955), p. 102.

39 On India, see Kingsley Davis, *The Population of India and Pakistan* (Princeton, N.J.: Princeton University Press, 1951), pp. 24–25; on Rome, see *The Cambridge Ancient History*, pp. 267–268, or UNESCO, *History of World Population Growth*, p. 15; on Russia, see Blum, p. 278.

40 See, for example, Tertius Chandler and Gerald Fox, *3000 Years of Urban Growth* (New York: Academic Press, 1974).

41 Warren Thompson and David Lewis, *Population Problems*, 5th ed. (New York: McGraw-Hill, 1965), p. 386; O. Andrew Collver, *Birth Rates in Latin America: New Estimates of Historical Trends and Fluctuations* (Berkeley, Calif.: Institute of International Studies, 1965), pp. 26–30; D. V. Glass and D. E. C. Eversley, *Population in History* (Chicago: Aldine, 1965), pp. 467, 532, 555, and 614. One of the lowest rates for an agrarian society prior to the twentieth century was for eighteenth-century Sweden, and it was nearly 36 per 1,000 (Glass and Eversley, p. 532).

42 See, for example, Horace Miner, *St. Denis: A French-Canadian Parish* (Chicago: Phoenix Books, The University of Chicago Press, 1963), p. 65; Coulton, *The Medieval Village*, p. 322; Manning Nash, *The Golden Road to Modernity: Village Life in Contemporary Burma* (New York: Wiley, 1965), pp. 265–266.

43 See, for example, John Noss, *Man's Religions*, rev. ed. (New York: Macmillan, 1956), pp. 227, 304ff., and 420–421; and Miner, pp. 65–66.

44 John Boswell, *The Kindness of Strangers: The Abandonment of Children in Western Europe from Late Antiquity to the Renaissance* (New York: Pantheon, 1989).

45 Harrison Brown, *The Challenge of Man's Future* (New York: Viking Compass, 1956), p. 75.

46 H. Hollingsworth, "A Demographic Study of the British Ducal Families," in Glass and Eversley, tables 2 and 5, pp. 358 and 360.

47 Brown, p. 75.

48 Warren Thompson, *Population Problems*, 3d ed. (New York: McGraw-Hill, 1942), p. 73.

49 M. C. Buer, *Health, Wealth, and Population in the Early Days of the Industrial Revolution, 1760–1815* (London: Routledge, 1926), pp. 77–78. Quoted by permission of Routledge & Kegan Paul, Ltd.

50 D. E. C. Eversley, "Population, Economy, and Society," in Glass and Eversley, p. 52; and William H. McNeill, *Plagues and Peoples* (Garden City, N.Y.: Doubleday Anchor, 1976).

51 Robert S. Gottfried, *The Black Death* (New York: Free Press, 1983), p. xiii.

52 K. F. Helleiner, "The Vital Revolution Reconsidered," in Glass and Eversley, p. 79.

53 Turner, p. 911.

54 F. R. Cowell, *Cicero and the Roman Republic* (London: Penguin, 1956), p. 79. Quoted by permission of Penguin Books.

55 See, for example, Jerome Blum, *Lord and Peasant in Russia from the Ninth to the Nineteenth Century* (Princeton, N.J.: Princeton University Press, 1961), pp. 126 and 394–395, on Russia; or Ralph Linton, *The Tree of Culture* (New York: Vintage Books, 1959), p. 231, on China.

56 S. B. Clough and C. W. Cole, *Economic History of Europe* (Boston: Heath, 1941), p. 25.

57 Ibid. See also Blum, pp. 16 and 126.

58 Marc Bloch, *Feudal Society*, trans. L. A. Manyon (Chicago: University of Chicago Press, 1962), p. 192. See also Robert Heilbroner, *The Making of Economic Society* (Englewood Cliffs, N.J.: Prentice-Hall, 1962), p. 27; H. R. Trevor-Roper, "The Gentry 1540–1640," *The Economic History Review Supplements*, no. 1 (n.d.).

59 Heilbroner, pp. 9–44.

60 A. H. M. Jones, *The Later Roman Empire 284–602: A Social, Economic and Administrative Survey* (Oxford: Blackwell, 1964), vol. 1, p. 465.

61 See page 186 on peasant revolts. See also G. G. Coulton, *The Medieval Village* (London: Cambridge, 1926), chaps. 11 and 24–25.

62 Gerhard Lenski and Jean Lenski, *Human Societies*, 4th ed. (New York: McGraw-Hill, 1982), table 7.2, p. 190.

63 Blum, pp. 356–357.

64 Gideon Sjoberg, *The Preindustrial City* (New York: Free Press, 1960), p. 215.

65 See, for example, Chung-li Chang, *Income of the Chinese Gentry* (Seattle: University of Washington Press, 1962), pp. 37–51.

66 For a survey of these obligations, see Gerhard Lenski, *Power and Privilege* (New York: McGraw-Hill, 1966), pp. 267–270.

67 Ibid., p. 228.

68 See, for example, Blum, p. 232, or W. H. Moreland, *The Agrarian System of Moslem India* (Allahabad, India: Central Book Depot, n.d.), p. 207.

69 George Sansom, *A History of Japan* (Stanford, Calif.: Stanford Press, 1963), vol. III, p. 29.

70 H. S. Bennett, *Life on the English Manor: A Study of Peasant Conditions, 1150–1400* (London: Cambridge, 1960), pp. 232–236.

71 Robert Darnton, *The Great Cat Massacre and Other Episodes in French Cultural History* (New York: Basic Books, 1984), p. 24. Quoted by permission of the publisher.

72 Ibid., p. 29.

73 Robert K. Douglas, *Society in China* (London: Innes, 1894), p. 354.

74 Blum, pp. 424 and 428, on Russia; and Gunnar Myrdal, *An American Dilemma* (New York: McGraw-Hill, 1964), p. 931, on the American South.

75 See Coulton, pp. 80 and 464–469; Blum, pp. 426–427; G. M. Carstairs, "A Village in Rajasthan," in M. N. Srnivas (ed.), *India's Villages* (Calcutta: West Bengal Government Press, 1955), pp. 37–38.

76 Bennett, p. 196; Coulton, pp. 190–191, 248–250, and 437–440.

77 G. G. Coulton, *Medieval Panorama* (New York: Meridan Books, 1955), p. 77, or Thompson, p. 708.

78 William Stubbs, *The Constitutional History of England* (Oxford: Clarendon Press, 1891), vol. 1, p. 454n.; Wolfram Eberhard, *A History of China*, 2d ed. (Berkeley: University of California Press, 1960), p. 32; and Yosoburo Takekoshi, *The Economic Aspects of the History of the Civilization of Japan* (New York: Macmillan, 1930), vol. 1, pp. 60–63.

79 See Boak, *A History of Rome*, p. 127, or Cowell, *Cicero and the Roman Republic*, p. 64. For an example of the application of Cato's principle in medieval Europe, see Bennett, p. 283.

80 See, for example, Bloch, p. 337; or George Homans, *English Villagers of the 13th Century* (Cambridge, Mass.: Harvard, 1942), p. 229.

81 See, for example, Morton Fried, *The Fabric of Chinese Society: Study of the Social Life of a Chinese County Seat* (New York: Praeger, 1953), pp. 104–105; Moreland, pp. 168 and 207; and Bennett, pp. 100–101, 112–113, and 131ff.

82 See, for example, the franklins in thirteenth-century England (Homans, pp. 248–250).

83 May McKisack, *The Fourteenth Century* (Oxford: Clarendon Press, 1959), pp. 331–340; Philip Lindsay and Reg Groves, *The Peasants' Revolt, 1381* (London: Hutchinson, n.d.), pp. 30, 34, and 63; Charles Langlois, "History," in Arthur Tilley (ed.), *Medieval France* (London: Cambridge, 1922), pp. 150–151; and Paul Murray Kendall, *The Yorkist Age* (Garden City, N.Y.: Doubleday, 1962), p. 171ff.

84 Sjoberg, p. 83; Lynn White, *Medieval Technology and Social Change* (Oxford: Clarendon Press, 1962), p. 39; Henri Pirenne, *Economic and Social History of Medieval Europe* (New York: Harvest Books, n.d., first published 1933), p. 58; J. C. Russell, *British Medieval Population* (Albuquerque: University of New Mexico Press, 1948), p. 305; Blum, pp. 268 and 281.

85 See Sjoberg, p. 108–116; or Samuel G. Stoney, *Plantations of the Carolina Low Country* (Charleston: Carolina Art Association, 1938), p. 36.

86 Kendall, p. 157.

87 Jerome Carcopino, *Daily Life in Ancient Rome* (New Haven: Yale University Press, 1940, p. 70.

88 See, for example, Sjoberg, p. 183ff. For an interesting example of the persistence of this pattern into the latter part of the nineteenth century in England, see W. Somerset Maugham, *Cakes and Ale* (New York: Pocket Books, 1944), p. 29.

89 On acquisition by marriage, see Elinor Barber, *The Bourgeoisie in 18th Century France* (Princeton, N.J.: Princeton University Press, 1955), p. 89, or Sansom, vol. III, pp. 128–129. On confiscation, see B. B. Misra, *The Indian Middle Classes* (London: Oxford, 1961), pp. 25–27; Takekoshi, vol. II, p. 251ff.; Kendall, p. 181; or Sir James Ramsay, *A History of the Revenues of the Kings of England: 1066–1399* (Oxford: Clarendon Press, 1925), vol. I. p. 58.

90 Clough and Cole, p. 442.

91 John Lossing Buck, *Secretariat Paper, No. 1, Tenth Conference of the Institute of Pacific Relations* (Stratford on Avon, 1947), reprinted in Irwin T. Sanders et al., *Societies around the World* (New York: Dryden Press, 1953), p. 65.

92 Clough and Cole, p. 445. See also R. J. Unstead, *The Rise of Great Britain: 1688–1837* (London: A. & C. Black, 1978), pp. 97, 81, and 92.

93 See, for example, John Nef, *The Conquest of the Material World* (Chicago: University of Chicago Press, 1964), p. 69.

94 Cowell, p. 80. See also William Woodruff, *Impact of Western Man: A Study of Europe's Role in the World Economy* (New York: St. Martin's, 1966), p. 254.

95 Sylvia Thrupp, *The Merchant Class of Medieval London* (Ann Arbor: Ann Arbor Paperbacks, University of Michigan Press, 1962), p. 9.

96 See, for example, Nef, p. 78.

97 Sidney Gamble, *Peking: A Social Survey* (New York: Doran, 1921), pp. 183–185.

98 Thrupp, pp. 19, 30, etc.

99 Ibid., pp. 23 and 29–31; James Westfall Thompson, *Economic and Social History of Europe in the Later Middle Ages, 1300–1530* (New York: Century, 1931), p. 398.

100 Gamble, p. 283.

101 In Asia many were sold into prostitution by their parents. See Gamble, p. 253. Many more, in every part of the world, were ignorant country girls seeking work in the city who were trapped by hired procurers, while still others were driven into prostitution by unemployment and lack of funds. See M. Dorothy George, *London Life in the XVIIIth Century* (London: Kegan Paul, Trench, Trubner, 1925), pp. 112–113.

102 See, for example, Frederick Nussbaum, *A History of the Economic Institutions of Modern Europe* (New York: Crofts, 1933); Frank Aydelotte, *Elizabethan Rogues and Vagabonds* (Oxford: Clarendon Press, 1913), p. 4; or A. L. Beier, *Masterless Men: The Vagrancy Problem in England 1560–1640* (London: Methuen, 1985), chap. 2.

103 Lenski, pp. 197–198.

104 For the effect of war on the forms of government, see Herbert Spencer, *The Principles of Sociology* (New York: Appleton, 1897), vol. II, part 5, chap. 17; Pitirim Sorokin, *Social and Cultural Dynamics* (New York: Bedminster Press, 1962), vol. III, pp. 196–198; or Stanislaw Andrzejewski, *Military Organization and Society* (London: Routledge, 1954), pp. 92–95.

105 These figures were calculated from A. E. R. Boak, *A History of Roman Imperial Civilization* (Garden City, N.Y.: Doubleday Anchor, 1959), using Mattingly's list of emperors, pp. 351–355.

106 For figures on several other societies, see Lenski, p. 235.

107 Wolfram Eberhard, *Conquerors and Rulers: Social Forces in Medieval China* (Leiden, Netherlands: Brill, 1952), p. 52; and Blum, p. 558.

108 Sorokin, vol. II, chap. 10, especially p. 352. Quincy Wright, *A Study of War* (Chicago: University of Chicago Press, 1965), p. 653, reports wars on average in nearly two-thirds of the years from 1500 to 1699 for five European powers and Turkey.

109 See, among others, Lenski, pp. 210–242 and 266–284, for more detailed documentation.

110 Douglas, p. 104.

111 See Max Weber, *The Theory of Social and Economic Organization*, trans. A. M. Henderson and Talcott Parsons (New York: Free Press, 1947), pp. 341–348; and Max Weber, *Wirtschaft und Gesellschaft*, 2d ed. (Tübingen: Mohr, 1925), vol. II, pp. 679–723.

112 Mattingly, p. 137. See also Turner, vol. II, p. 620, or Michael Rostovtzeff, *The Social and Economic History of the Roman Empire*, rev. ed. (Oxford: Clarendon Press, 1957), p. 54.

113 Hans Rosenberg, *Bureaucracy, Aristocracy, and Autocracy: The Prussian Experience 1660–1815* (Cambridge, Mass.: Harvard, 1958), pp. 5–6. Quoted by permission of Harvard University Press.

114 Chang, *The Income of the Chinese Gentry*, Summary Remarks, supplement 2, and chap. 1.

115 On the king's income, see Ramsay, vol. I, pp. 227 and 261. For the income of the nobility, see Sidney Painter, *Studies in the History of the English Feudal Barony* (Baltimore: Johns Hopkins, 1943), pp. 170–171. For the income of field hands, see Bennett, p. 121.

116 Lenski, pp. 219 and 228.

117 See, for example, Albert Lybyer, *The Government of the Ottoman Empire in the Time of Suleiman the Magnificent* (Cambridge, Mass.: Harvard, 1913); or Moreland, op. cit.

118 F. Pelsaert, *Jahangir's India*, trans. W. H. Moreland and P. Geyl and quoted by Misra, p. 47. Quoted by permission of W. Heffer & Sons, Ltd.

119 Lybyer, pp. 47–58, and 115–117.

120 See, for example, James Westfall Thompson's statement that "the medieval state was a loose agglomeration of territories with rights of property and sovereignty everywhere shading into one another," in *Economic and Social History of the Middle Ages* (New York: Appleton-Century-Crofts, 1928), p. 699. See also Bloch, especially chaps. 14–24; Blum, chap. 2; or Sidney Painter, *The Rise of the Feudal Monarchies* (Ithaca, N.Y.: Cornell, 1951), and *Studies in the History of the English Feudal Barony*, op. cit.

121 See Kenneth Scott Latourette, *A History of Christianity* (New York: Harper, 1953), pp. 15–16.

122 See Robert Bellah, "Religious Evolution," *American Sociological Review*, 29 (1964), pp. 367–368.

123 See, for example, Lenski, pp. 7–9. See also Kendall, p. 232ff.

124 Lenski, pp. 257–258.

125 Ibid., pp. 262–266, gives a more detailed treatment of this aspect of religion.

126 J. W. Thompson, *Economic and Social History of the Middle Ages*, p. 684.

127 See, for example, Carlo Levi, *Christ Stopped at Eboli* (New York: Farrar, Straus, 1947), chap. 11ff., for a good description of the role of magic in one agrarian community. On fatalism, see, for example, Edward Banfield, *The Moral Basis of a Backward Society* (New York: Free Press, 1967), pp. 36–37, 41, and 107ff.

128 Sjoberg, *The Preindustrial City*, p. 146ff.

129 Ibid., p. 155.

130 Ibid., p. 163ff.; Henry Orenstein, *Gaon: Conflict and Cohesion in an Indian Village* (Princeton, N.J.: Princeton University Press, 1965), pp. 53–57; Kendall, chaps. 11 and 12; L. F. Salzman, *English Life in the Middle Ages* (London: Oxford University Press, 1927), pp. 254–256.

131 Bennett, p. 260. For other descriptions of the uses of leisure in agrarian societies, see Margaret Wade Labarge, *A Baronial Household of the Thirteenth Century* (New York: Barnes & Noble, 1966), chap. 10; Bennett, chap. 10; or Coulton, *Medieval Panorama*, chaps. 8 and 44.

132 F. R. Cowell, *Everyday Life in Ancient Rome* (New York: Putnam, 1961), p. 173.

133 The data in this paragraph are drawn from Lenski, p. 212.

134 For further details on the expendables, see ibid., pp. 281–284.

135 See, for example, H. van Werveke, "The Rise of the Towns," in *The Cambridge Economic History of Europe* (London: Cambridge Press, 1963), vol. 3, pp. 34–37; L. Halphen, "Industry and Commerce," in Tilley, pp. 190–192; or Pirenne, *Economic and Social History of Medieval Europe*, pp. 187–206.

136 Amos H. Hawley, *Human Ecology* (New York: Ronald, 1950), pp. 242 and 387.

137 For important new analyses of the origins of ancient Israel, see Marvin Chaney, "Ancient Palestinian Peasant Movements and the Formation of Premonarchic Israel," in David Freedman and David Grof (eds.), *Palestine in Transition: The Emergence of Ancient Israel* (Sheffield: Almond Press, 1983), pp. 39–90; Norman K. Gottwald, "Two Models for the Origin of Ancient Israel: Social Revolution or Frontier Development," in E. B. Huffmon et al. (eds.), *The Quest for the Kingdom of God: Studies in Honor of G. E. Mendenhall* (Winona Lake, Ind.: Eisenbrauns, 1983), pp. 5–24; and Volkmar Fritz, "Conquest or Settlement?: The Early Iron Age in Palestine," *Biblical Archaeologist*, 50 (June, 1987), pp. 84–100.

138 See, for example, Richard Tomasson, *Iceland: The First New Society* (Minneapolis: University of Minnesota Press, 1980), chaps. 1 and 8; and Philip Longworth, *The Cossacks* (New York: Holt, Rinehart, 1970).

139 For the classic statement of the effect of frontier life, see Frederick Jackson Turner, *The Frontier in American History* (New York: Holt, 1920).

140 See James G. Leyburn, *Frontier Folkways* (New Haven, Conn.: Yale Press, 1936).

141 William T. Sanders and David Webster, "The Mesoamerican Urban Tradition," *American Anthropologist*, 90 (1988), p. 543.

142 Chung-li Chang, *The Chinese Gentry* (Seattle: University of Washington Press, 1955), p. 102; *The Cambridge Ancient History*, pp. 267–268; and Blum, p. 278.

Chapter 8

1 According to Murdock's data, the Manus of New Guinea come as close to full dependence on fishing as any people in the world. See *Ethnology*, vol. 6, no. 2 (April 1967), pp. 170–230. Yet, as Margaret Mead indicates in her report, these people also depend heavily for their subsistence on garden products that they obtain through trade from neighboring peoples and to a lesser degree on pigs that they raise or obtain through trade. See Margaret Mead, *Growing Up in New Guinea* (New York: Mentor Books, 1953, first published 1930), especially pp. 173–174.

2 For an earlier discussion of this point, see Gordon Hewes's excellent paper, "The Rubric 'Fishing and Fisheries,'" *American Anthropologist*, 50 (1948), pp. 241–242.

3 Our calculation.

4 See Hewes, pp. 240–241.

5 For an interesting account of one such group, see Wilmond Menard, "The Sea Gypsies of China," *Natural History*, 64 (January 1965), pp. 13–21.

6 See, for example, Lawrence Krader, "Pastoralism," in *International Encyclopedia of the Social Sciences* (New York: Macmillan and Free Press, 1968), vol. II, pp. 456–457; or Carleton Coon, "The Nomads," in Sydney Fisher (ed.), *Social Forces in the Middle East* (Ithaca, N.Y.: Cornell, 1955), pp. 23–42.

7 John L. Myres, "Nomadism," *Journal of the Royal Anthropological Institute*, 71 (1941), p. 20.

8 Krader reports that the average density of population in Mongolia was less than 1 per square mile, and among the Tuareg of Africa it was even lower (op. cit., pp. 458–459).

9 It is found in 61 percent of these societies compared to 2 to 35 percent of other types.

10 This is found in 88 percent of these societies, compared to 37 to 82 percent of other types.

11 This requirement occurs in 97 percent of herding societies, compared to 72 to 87 percent of other types.

12 See William McNeill, *The Rise of the West: A History of the Human Community* (New York: Mentor Books, 1965), p. 126ff.; or Ralph Turner, *The Great Cultural Traditions* (New York: McGraw-Hill, 1941), p. 259.

13 For a good discussion of this important subject, see McNeill, p. 256ff.

14 Ibid., p. 111.

15 Charles Boxer, *The Dutch Seaborne Empire, 1600–1800* (London: Hutchison, 1965); and Peter Burke, *Venice and Amsterdam: A Study of Seventeenth Century Elites* (London: Temple Smith, 1974).

16 On the less familiar Carthaginian empire, see Donald Harden, *The Phoenicians* (New York: Praeger, 1963), chaps. 5 and 6. The British empire, it might be noted, was also an *overseas* empire.

17 The Netherlands changed from a republic to a monarchy in the nineteenth century because of decisions made by foreign powers at the Congress of Vienna, not because of internal Dutch preference (Wout Ultee, personal communication, Dec. 2, 1988).

18 Compare, for example, the status of merchants and the rate of innovation for Europe during the sixteenth, seventeenth, and eighteenth centuries with the situation in India. Both were higher in Europe. Although this could have been coincidence, the evidence suggests a causal link.

Chapter 9

1 Charles Singer et al. (eds.), *A History of Technology* (Oxford: Clarendon Press, 1954–1956), vols. 1 and 2. See also Terry S. Reynolds, "Medieval Roots of the Industrial Revolution," *Scientific American*, 251 (July, 1984), pp. 123–130.

2 Michael Mann, *The Sources of Social Power* (Cambridge: Cambridge University Press, 1986), vol. I, p. 445.

3 William H. McNeill, *The Rise of the West* (Chicago: University of Chicago Press, 1963), pp. 570–571.

4 S. B. Clough and C. W. Cole, *Economic History of Europe* (Boston: Heath, 1941), pp. 127–128.

5 Ibid.

6 R. H. Tawney, *Religion and the Rise of the West* (New York: Mentor Books, 1947), p. 117.

7 Immanuel Wallerstein, *The Modern World-System* (New York: Academic Press, 1974), especially chap. 2.

8 Tawney, p. 257.

9 Elizabeth Eisenstein, *The Printing Press as an Agent of Change* (Cambridge: Cambridge University Press, 1979), vols. I and II.

10 James M. Wells, "The History of Printing," *Encyclopaedia Britannica*, vol. 18, p. 541.

11 Wells, pp. 541–542; and N. F. Blake, *Caxton: England's First Publisher* (New York: Barnes & Noble, 1976), chap. 1.

12 Ann Stanford, "A Link with the Past," *Endeavors*, vol. 2, no. 2 (Spring 1985), p. 8; Michael Clapham, "Printing," in Singer, op. cit., vol. II, p. 27.

13 See, for example, Arthur G. Dickens, *Reformation and Society in 16th Century Europe* (New York: Harcourt, Brace, 1966).

14 See, especially, Max Weber, *The Protestant Ethic and the Spirit of Capitalism*, trans. Talcott Parsons (New York: Scribner, 1958); or Reinhard Bendix, *Max Weber: An Intellectual Portrait* (Garden City, N.Y.: Doubleday, 1960), chaps. 3–8.

15 Ernest Gellner, *Plow, Sword and Book: The Structure of Human History* (Chicago: University of Chicago Press, 1989), chaps. 4 and 5.

16 Tawney, pp. 92–93.

17 Neil Smelser and S. M. Lipset (eds.), *Social Structure and Mobility in Economic Development* (Chicago: University of Chicago Press, 1967), p. 29ff.

18 Clough and Cole, pp. 185–194.

19 Ibid., pp. 308–315.

20 See, for example, Robert Heilbroner, *The Making of Economic Society* (Englewood Cliffs, N.J.: Prentice-Hall, 1962), pp. 101–102.

21 See, for example, John Nef, *The Conquest of the Material World* (Chicago: University of Chicago Press, 1965), especially part 2.

22 Paul Mantoux, *The Industrial Revolution in the Eighteenth Century*, rev. ed. (London: Cape, 1961), pp. 243–244.

23 Reynolds, op. cit.

24 Mantoux, p. 312.

25 Earlier in the century, Thomas Savery and Thomas Newcomen invented the atmospheric engine, which laid the foundation for Watt's work. Its only practical use, however, was to pump water out of mines.

26 Phyllis Deane and W. A. Cole, *British Growth 1688–1959: Trends and Structure* (London: Cambridge, 1962), p. 212.

27 For 1788, see Clive Day, *Economic Development in Europe* (New York: Macmillan, 1942), p. 134; for 1845, see Deane and Cole, p. 225.

28 Deane and Cole, pp. 55 and 216.

29 W. S. Woytinsky and E. S. Woytinsky, *World Population and Production: Trends and Outlook* (New York: Twentieth Century Fund, 1953), p. 1147.

30 *British Historical Statistics* (Cambridge: Cambridge University Press, 1988), p. 822.

31 U.S. Department of Commerce, Bureau of the Census, *Historical Statistics of the United States, Colonial Times to 1970*, series F238–239.

32 J. H. Clapham, *An Economic History of Modern Britain*, 2d ed. (London: Cambridge, 1930), vol. 1, pp. 391–392.

33 Clough and Cole, pp. 594–595.

34 Ibid., pp. 535–537.

35 Deane and Cole, p. 225.

36 Ibid., p. 216.

37 *Historical Statistics of the U.S.: Colonial Times to 1970*, p. 500.

38 Alfred D. Chandler, Jr., *The Visible Hand: The Managerial Revolution in America* (Cambridge, Mass.: Belknap Press, 1977), part II.

39 Ibid., p. 232.

40 Clough and Cole, p. 538.

41 Calculated from Woytinsky and Woytinsky, p. 1003.

42 Alfred D. Chandler, "Industrial Revolutions and Institutional Arrangements," *Bulletin of the American Academy of Arts and Sciences*, 33 (May, 1980), pp. 40–45.

43 This figure is an estimate based on Clough and Cole's report of French production in 1902 (p. 773) and Woytinsky and Woytinsky's report of American production in 1900 and 1902 (p. 1168). See also James M. Laux, *In First Gear: The French Automobile Industry to 1914* (Liverpool: Liverpool University Press, 1976), fig. 5.

44 Woytinsky and Woytinsky, pp. 1165–1166, including fig. 328.

45 Ibid., p. 1164.

46 Ibid., p. 966.

47 The 1900 figure is estimated from information provided by Woytinsky and Woytinsky, pp. 897–900; the 1940 figure is from fig. 257, p. 897.

48 J. Frederic Dewhurst and Associates, *America's Needs and Resources* (New York: Twentieth Century Fund, 1955), p. 317; and U.S. Department of Commerce, Bureau of the Census, *Statistical Abstract of the United States, 1963*, p. 516.

49 Woytinsky and Woytinsky, p. 1171.

50 *Statistical Abstract of the U.S., 1963*, p. 586, and projections to 1990 based on U.S. Department of Commerce, Bureau of the Census, *Statistical Abstract of the U.S., 1989*, p. 611.

51 The 1938 figure is from United Nations, *Statistical Yearbook*, 1951, p. 261; the 1978 figure is from *UN Statistical Yearbook*, 1981, table 154. For more recent years, see *Statistical Abstract of the U.S.*, 1989, p. 832.

52 The figure for the late 1930s is based on Woytinsky and Woytinsky's statement about output in the United States and other countries in that period (p. 1201); the current figure is based on United Nations, *Statistical Yearbook, 1983/84*, but translated into short tons.

53 United Nations, *Statistical Yearbook, 1965*, p. 353.

54 *Statistical Abstract of the U.S., 1989*, p. 571; and "The Global Grid," *Newsweek*, May 12, 1986, p. 44.

55 Associated Press, Feb. 15, 1989.

56 Figures for 1940 are from Woytinsky and Woytinsky, pp. 897, 966, and 1167; estimates of current figures are based on *Statistical Abstract of the U.S., 1989*, p. 811.

57 Calculations based on data in World Bank, *World Tables*, 3d. ed., vol. I (Baltimore: Johns Hopkins Press, 1983), p. 486; and World Bank, *World Development Report, 1987* (New York: Oxford University Press, 1987), table 2.1, p. 16.

58 *Historical Statistics of the U.S.*, series W–109; and *Statistical Abstract of the U.S., 1989*, table 972.

59 See the high percentage of all research and development expenditures coming from the U.S. Department of Defense, *Statistical Abstract of the U.S., 1989*, table 972.

60 See, for example, Max Weber and Karl Marx.

61 See, for example, William H. McNeill, *Plagues and Peoples* (Garden City, N.Y.: Doubleday Anchor, 1976).

62 J. L. Hammond and Barbara Hammond, *The Town Labourer: 1760–1830* (London: Guild Books, 1949, first published 1917), vol. I, ch. 3.

63 Ibid., chs. 2 and 6–9; or J. T. Ward (ed.), *The Factory System* (New York: Barnes & Noble, 1970), vols. I and II.

64 Hammond and Hammond, vol. I, pp. 32–33.

65 Compare and contrast the work of Hammond and Hammond, op. cit., or Eric Hobsbawm, "The British Standard of Living, 1790–1850," *Economic History Review*, 2d series, 10 (1957), pp. 46–61, with Thomas Ashton, "The Standard of Life of the Workers in England, 1790–1830," *Journal of Economic History*, 9 (1949), supplement, pp. 19–38.

Chapter 10

1 U.S. Department of Commerce, Bureau of the Census, *Historical Statistics of the United States: Colonial Times to 1970*, series D–152–153; and U.S. Department of Commerce, Bureau of the Census, *Statistical Abstract of the United States, 1989*, table 1074.

2 J. Frederic Dewhurst and associates, *America's Needs and Resources* (New York: Twentieth Century Fund, 1955), p. 1116; and *Statistical Abstract of the U.S., 1967*, table 752.

3 *Historical Statistics of the U.S.*, series S–1; and *Statistical Abstract of the U.S., 1988*, table 903.

4 The 1750 figure is from W. S. Woytinsky and E. S. Woytinsky, *World Population and Production: Trends and Outlooks* (New York: Twentieth Century Fund, 1953), p. 1100; the 1970 figure is from *United Nations, Statistical Yearbook, 1971*, tables 121 and 122, and is converted to short tons.

5 The 1820 figure is from Woytinsky and Woytinsky, p. 1101; the 1974 figure is from *Statistical Abstract of the U.S., 1989*, table 1182.

6 Production figures are from the *Statistical Abstract of the U.S., 1989*, table 1177. Per capita calculations are our own.

7 *British Historical Statistics* (Cambridge: Cambridge University Press, 1988), pp. 837–841.

8 *Historical Statistics of the U.S.*, series F–3; and World Bank, *World Development Report, 1989* (New York: Oxford University Press, 1989), table 1.

9 *Index to International Public Opinion, 1982–83* (Westport, Conn.: Greenwood), p. 533.

10 Ibid., *1980–81*, pp. 526–537.

11 *World Opinion Update*, 12 (June, 1988), p. 71.

12 *The Gallup Poll: Public Opinion, 1988*, p. 270.

13 Hugh Lefler, *North Carolina History* (Chapel Hill, N.C.: University of North Carolina Press, 1934), pp. 108–109. For the net worth of free southerners in 1774, see *Historical Statistics of the U.S.*, p. 1175. The median would almost certainly be lower than the average reported here.

14 Robert Heilbroner, *The Worldly Philosophers*, rev. ed. (New York: Time Books, 1961), ch. 3; and Jacob Viner, "Adam Smith," in *International Encyclopedia of the Social Sciences*, vol. 14, pp. 322–329.

15 Heilbroner, p. 47.

16 See, for example, Daniel Bell, "Socialism," in *International Encyclopedia of the Social Sciences*, vol. 14, pp. 506–532.

17 Maurice Duverger, *Political Parties: Their Organization and Activity in the Modern State*, trans. Barbara North and Robert North (London: Methuen, 1959), pp. 118–119.

18 Hedrick Smith, *The Russians*, rev. ed., (New York: Ballantine Books, 1984), pp. 367–376. In Polish Party headquarters Lenin's picture, not Marx's, was displayed prominently in offices.

19 Lewis Feuer (ed.), *Marx and Engels: Basic Writings on Politics and Philosophy* (Garden City, N.Y.: Doubleday, 1959), p. 127.

20 V. I. Lenin, *State and Revolution* (New York: International Publishers, 1932), p. 73. See also Basile Kerblay, *Modern Soviet Society*, trans. Rubert Swyer (New York: Pantheon, 1983), p. 242.

21 See, for example, Alvin Gouldner, *Against Fragmentation: The Origins of Marxism and the Society of Intellectuals* (New York: Oxford University Press, 1985), p. 41ff.

22 See, for example, Michael D. Kennedy, *Professionals, Power and Solidarity in Poland: A Critical Sociology of Soviet-Type Society* (Cambridge: Cambridge University Press, 1989), ch. 6. See also Sergei Y. Andreyev, "The Power Structure and the Problems of Society," *Neva* (Leningrad), Jan., 1989, English translation in *Federal Broadcast Information Service* (Washington), Feb. 13, 1989.

23 Hans Kohn, "Nationalism," *International Encyclopedia of the Social Sciences*, vol. II, pp. 63–70.

24 John H. Kautsky, *The Politics of Aristocratic Empires* (Chapel Hill, N.C.: University of North Carolina Press, 1982), part IV.

25 Robert Bellah, "Civil Religion in America," *Daedalus*, 96 (Winter), pp. 1–21. See also Will Herberg, *Protestant-Catholic-Jew* (Garden City, N.Y.: Doubleday, 1955).

26 See Gerhard Lenski, *Human Societies: A Macrolevel Introduction to Sociology*, 1st ed. (New York: McGraw-Hill, 1970), pp. 354, 359, 375–376, and 393.

27 Ibid., pp. 427–428.

28 Thomas McKeown, *The Modern Rise of Population* (New York: Academic Press, 1976), p. 2.

29 Rudolf Andorka and István Harcsa, *Modernization in Hungary in the Long and Short Run Measured by Social Indicators* (Budapest: Karl Marx University of Economic Sciences, Department of Sociology, 1988), Working Paper No. 1, p. 158.

30 Lori Heise, "Life and Death in the USSR," *World Watch*, vol. 2 (Jan/Feb., 1989), p. 36.

31 Andorka and Harcsa, part IV, tables 9 and 12.

32 Vladimir Treml, "Alcohol Consumption in the USSR," *Journal of Alcohol Studies* (April, 1975).

33 Dmitri Shalin, "Sociology for the Glasnost Era," *Social Forces*, forthcoming.

34 Nick Eberstadt, "The Health Crisis in the USSR," *New York Review of Books*, Feb. 19, 1981, pp. 23–31; Christopher Davis and Murray Feshbach, *Rising Infant Mortality in the USSR in the 1970s*, U.S. Bureau of the Census, Series P–95, No. 74 (Sept., 1980).

35 Alan Riding, "Prosperity Draws Migrants to Spain," *New York Times*, Aug. 24, 1989.

36 Paul Montgomery, "Luxembourg, a Ripe 150, Kicks Up Its Heels," *New York Times*, Apr. 19, 1989.

37 New York Times News Service, Nov. 28, 1986.

38 Pranay Gupte, "Germany's Guest Workers," *New York Times Magazine*, Aug. 19, 1984, p. 88ff.

39 "How Would You Vote?" *Charlotte Observer*, July 13, 1986.

40 Craig Whitney, "For Asia's Children, Hard Knocks," *New York Times*, Sept. 19, 1989.

41 David Sanger, "Japan to Deport Chinese Refugees," *New York Times*, Sept. 12, 1989; Steven Weisman, "Toward Fellow Asians, a Lack of Fellowship," ibid., Jan. 3, 1990.

Chapter 11

1 *World Development Report, 1989*, table 3.

2 Associated Press, August 7, 1972.

3 For statistical analysis of data from contemporary societies, see Erich Weede, "Beyond Misspecification in Sociological Analyses of Income Inequality," *American Sociological Review*, 45 (June, 1980), pp. 497–501; for historical evidence, see Gerhard Lenski, *Power and Privilege* (Chapel Hill, N.C.: University of North Carolina Press, 1984, originally published 1966), chaps. 8–13.

4 Based on recent company reports.

5 Dan Morgan, "New Farming Frontier," *Washington Post*, Oct. 20, 1974. The value has been adjusted for inflation.

6 U.S. Department of Commerce, *1987 Census of Agriculture*, vol. I, parts 5 and 15, table 50. Values have been adjusted upward about 10 percent to cover value of livestock, seed, etc.

7 U.S. Bureau of the Census, *Historical Statistics of the U.S.: Colonial Times to 1970*, series D–182–232; and *Statistical Abstract of the U.S., 1989*, table 668.

8 Ibid. A similar trend is reported in the Soviet Union. See T. Anthony Jones, "Work, Workers and Modernization in the USSR," *Research in the Sociology of Work*, 1 (1981), p. 251.

9 *Statistical Abstract of the U.S., 1989*, tables 480 and 544.

10 Ibid., tables 485 and 488.

11 Recent company reports.

12 U.S. Department of Labor, *Dictionary of Occupational Titles* (Washington, D.C.: Government Printing Office, 1977).

13 *Newsweek*, Mar. 26, 1973, p. 79.

14 Pehr Gyllenhammar, "Volvo's Solution to Blue Collar Blues," *Business and Society* (Autumn, 1973).

15 Esther Fein, "Read Their Lips! Soviet Legislators Vote No to Proposal for New Sin Taxes," *New York Times*, Nov. 1, 1989; Dmitri Shalin, "Sociology for the Glasnost Era," *Social Forces*, forthcoming.

16 See, for example, Lindley Clark, "Japan's Sinking Unions," *Wall Street Journal*, July 27, 1989; R. W. Apple, "Steep Fall in Power and Influence Hampers Labor Unions in Europe," *New York Times*, Jan. 20, 1985; and *Statistical Abstract of the U.S., 1989*, table 683.

17 Esther Fein, "Soviets Approve Some Strike Rights," *New York Times*, Oct. 10, 1989.

18 S. B. Clough and C. W. Cole, *Economic History of Europe* (Boston: Heath, 1941), pp. 693–698.

19 G. D. H. Cole, *A Short History of the British Working Class Movement* (New York: Macmillan, 1927), vol. II, p. 202; and Carroll P. Daughterty, *Labor Problems in American Industry* (Boston: Houghton Mifflin, 1941), p. 405.

20 See, for example, "Chrysler Says GM Sets U.S. Car Prices," *Raleigh News and Observer*, Sept. 13, 1979, a report of testimony at a congressional hearing by the chairman of the Chrysler Corporation.

21 G. Warren Nutter, "Industrial Concentration," *International Encyclopedia of the Social Sciences* (New York: Macmillan and Free Press, 1968), vol. 7, p. 221.

22 Ben Bagdikian, "Why Newspapers Keep Dying," *Washington Post*, July 23, 1972.

23 John Kenneth Galbraith, *The New Industrial State* (New York: Signet, 1968), pp. 38–39.

24 Michael P. Allen, "The Structure of Interorganizational Elite Cooptation: Interlocking Corporate Directorates," *American Sociological Review*, 39 (1974), pp. 393–406.

25 Our own computation based on data in *Historical Statistics of the U.S.: Colonial Times to 1970*, series F–1 and Y–533; and *Statistical Abstract of the U.S., 1984*, tables 449 and 735.

26 *The Economist*, Dec. 30, 1978.

27 Clough and Cole, p. 148ff.; or Edward S. Mason, "Corporation," in *International Encyclopedia of the Social Sciences*, vol. 3, pp. 396–403.

28 Statistics based on data in *Statistical Abstract of the U.S., 1989*, table 847.

29 *Forbes*, May 12, 1980, pp. 214 and 236.

30 See Robert A. Gordon, *Business Leadership in the Large Corporation* (Berkeley: University of California Press, 1961); or Edward S. Mason (ed.), *The Corporation and Modern Society* (Cambridge: Harvard Press, 1959), on American corporations; and P. Sargant Florence, *Ownership, Control, and Success of Large Companies* (London: Street and Maxwell, 1961); or David Granick, *The European Executive* (Garden City, N.Y.: Doubleday Anchor, 1964), on European corporations.

31 "The Soviet Economy," *The Economist*, Apr. 9, 1988, pp. 8–9; and James Jackson, "Inching Down the Capitalist Road," *Time*, May 4, 1989, p. 42.

32 Mark D'Anastasio, "Soviets Now Hail China as a Source of Ideas for Reviving Socialism," *Wall Street Journal*, Sept. 18, 1987. See the case of the taxi drivers' cooperative in Krasnovarsk.

33 "The Soviet Economy," *The Economist*, p. 8. See, also, Peter Gumbel, "Soviet Union Plans to Let Entrepreneurs Fill Gap Left By Creaky State Sector," *Wall Street Journal*, May 26, 1988.

34 New York Times News Service, May 29, 1986. See, also, Jackson, op. cit.

35 John Tagliabue, "Wider Capitalism to be Encouraged by Polish Leaders," *New York Times*, Aug. 24, 1989.

36 Henry Kamm, "The Man Solidarity Could Not Beat," *New York Times*, July 6, 1989; Barry Newman, "How Many People Does It Take to Fix a Broken TV Set?" *Wall Street Journal*, May 1, 1987.

37 R. István Gabor, "Masodik gazdasag" ["The Second Economy"], *Valosag*, 28, no. 2 (1985), pp. 20–37.

38 Peter Keresztes, "In Hungary, Taxes and Tears," *Wall Street Journal*, Dec. 16, 1987.

39 Frederick Kempe, "Open Markets: Some Hungarians Enjoy the Limited Free Enterprise," *Wall Street Journal*, Aug. 28, 1985.

40 Galbraith, chap. 9.

41 Szczepański, p. 125. Quoted by permission.

42 "The Soviet Economy," *The Economist,* op. cit.

43 See, for example, Elrad Parkhomoovsky, "Can't Anybody Here Make Shoes?" *Izvestia*, reprinted in *World Press Review*, July, 1982, p. 36.

44 Kamm, op. cit.

45 Steven Greenhouse, "Can Poland's Steel Dinosaur Evolve?," *New York Times*, Nov. 27, 1989.

46 Paul Hollander, *Political Pilgrims: Travels of Western Intellectuals to the Soviet Union, China, and Cuba, 1928–1978* (New York: Oxford University Press, 1981).

47 Tim Stone, "Wall St. on the Danube," *New York Times*, Dec. 18, 1988; Sarah Bartlett, "Soviets and Chinese Seek Uncapitalist Stock Markets," ibid., and "Yugoslavia Proposes to Let Citizens Buy Stocks, Bonds," *Wall Street Journal*, June 3, 1988.

48 "The Soviet Economy," *The Economist*, p. 11.

49 Ibid.

50 Ibid., p. 5.

51 Ibid., p. 11.

52 Richard Easterlin, "Economic Growth," in *Encyclopedia of the Social Sciences*, vol. 4, p. 405.

53 Calculations based on United Nations, *Statistical Yearbook, 1965*, table 148; and *Statistical Abstract of the U.S., 1979*, table 1539.

Chapter 12

1 Kenneth A. Bollen, "Political Democracy and the Timing of Development," *American Sociological Review*, 44 (August, 1979), pp. 572–587.

2 Many studies have documented the relationship between high rates of literacy and education on the one hand and democratic government on the other. See, for example, Daniel Lerner, *The Passing of Traditional Society: Modernizing the Middle East* (New York: Free Press, 1958), especially pp. 63–64 and 86–89; or S. M. Lipset, *Political Man* (Garden City, N.Y.: Doubleday, 1960), pp. 53–58.

3 On the relationship between democracy and the development of the mass media, see Lerner, op. cit., and Lipset, pp. 51–52.

4 W. L. Guttsman, *The British Political Elite* (London: Macgibbon & Kee, 1963), pp. 18 and 41.

5 A. Todd, *On Parliamentary Government* (London: Longmans, 1887), p. 622; and W. L. Guttsman (ed.), *The English Ruling Class* (London: Weidenfeld and Nicolson, 1969), p. 154.

6 U.S. Department of Commerce, Bureau of Census, *Historical Statistics of the U.S.: Colonial Times to 1970*, series Y–83.

7 U.S. Department of Commerce, Bureau of the Census, *Statistical Abstract of the U.S., 1989*, tables 447 and 566.

8 Judith Ryder and Harold Silver, *Modern English Society* (London: Methuen, 1970), p. 74; Dankwort Rustow, *The Politics of Compromise: A Study of Parties and Cabinet Government in Sweden* (Princeton: Princeton University Press, 1955), pp. 84–85.

9 "Is Europe Turning Green?" *New York Times*, June 22, 1989.

10 James Markham, "Greening of European Politicians Spreads . . . " ibid., Apr. 12, 1989.

11 Ivo Feierabend and Rosalind Feierabend, "Aggressive Behaviors within Polities, 1948–1962: A Cross-National Study," *Journal of Conflict Resolution*, 10 (1966), table 3. Results of this study suggest that rates of political instability are greatest in societies making the transition from agrarian to industrial, though results were not statistically significant. See also Douglas Hibbs, *Mass Political Violence: A Cross-National Causal Analysis* (New York: Wiley, 1973), chap. 3.

12 The figures shown in Table 12.3 are based on our own calculations, using the following sources: Robert Alford, *Party and Society* (Chicago: Rand McNally, 1963), pp. 136, 202–203, 234–235, and 274–275; Richard Rose (ed.), *Electoral Behavior: A Comparative Handbook* (New York: Free Press, 1974), pp. 147, 294, 334 and 398; Hannu Uusitalo, "Class Structure and Party Choice: A Scandinavian Comparison," Research Report No. 10 (1975), Research Group for Comparative Sociology, University of Helsinki, p. 21; Roy Pierce, *French Politics and Political Institutions* (New York: Harper & Row, 1968), table 10; Richard Rose, "Class and Party Divisions: Britain as a Test Case," *Sociology*, 2 (1968), pp. 129–162; Erik Allardt and Yrjo Littunen (eds.), *Cleavages, Ideologies and Party Systems: Contributions to Comparative Political Sociology*, in a series entitled *Transactions of the Westermarck Society* (Helsinki: The Academic Bookstore, 1964), vol. 10, pp. 102 and 212; S. M. Lipset, *Political Man* (Garden City, N.Y.: Doubleday, 1960), pp. 225 and 227; *Gallup Political Index*, Report No. 17 (October, 1966), p. 15 and inside back cover; S. M. Lipset, "Industrial Proletariat in Comparative Perspective," in Jan Triska and C. Gati (eds.), *Blue Collar Workers in Eastern Europe* (London: Allen & Unwin, 1981), figure 1.1; Walter Korpi, *The Democratic Class Struggle* (London: Routledge & Kegan Paul, 1983), figure 5.3; and *Index to International Public Opinion 1985–86*, pp. 410, 411, and 439.

13 Rosa Luxembourg, *The Russian Revolution and Marxism or Leninism?* (Ann Arbor: University of Michigan Press, 1961), p. 62.

14 Ibid., p. 71.

15 "Hungarian Parliament Rewrites Constitution," *New York Times*, Oct. 19, 1989.

16 Ann Cooper, "Opposition Dream," ibid.

17 See, for example, Lipset, chaps. 2 and 4.

18 *Statistical Abstract of the U.S., 1989*, table 479; and *Historical Statistics of the United States: Colonial Times to 1970*, series Y–308. Similar trends are reported in other countries. In France, for example, civil servants increased from 3.7 percent of the labor force in 1866 to 16.7 percent in 1962. See Jacques Lecaillon, "Changes in the Distribution of Income in the French Economy," in Jean Marchal and Bernard Ducros (eds.), *The Distribution of National Income* (London: MacMillan, 1968), pp. 45 and 47.

19 *Statistical Abstract of the U.S., 1989*, tables 2 and 479; and *Historical Statistics of the United States: Colonial Times to 1970*, series A–6 and Y–332.

20 Gallup poll published July 14, 1983.

21 See, for example, the statements of Lenin and Trotsky, quoted by David Lane, *The End of Inequality?: Stratification under State Socialism* (Baltimore: Penguin, 1971), p. 41; and Robert Osborn, *The Evolution of Soviet Politics* (Homewood, Ill.: Dorsey, 1974), p. 281.

22 Urii Davydov, "Technology and Bureaucracy," *Sotsiologicheskie Issledovaniia*, 5 (1988), pp. 116–127, and "The Weberian Renaissance," ibid., 3 (1986), pp. 56–68.

23 *Encyclopaedia Britannica*, 23, pp. 716 and 800.

24 *Washington Post*, Nov. 9, 1976.

25 See, for example, Harrison Brown, *The Challenge of Man's Future* (New York: Viking Press, 1954), pp. 222–228.

Chapter 13

1 Michael Voslensky, *Nomenklatura: The Soviet Ruling Class*, trans. Eric Mossbacher (Garden City, N.Y.: Doubleday, 1984); and Tatyana Zaslavskaia, "Perestroika as a Social Revolution," *Izvestia*, Dec. 23, 1988.

2 Ibid., p. 95.

3 Aleksander Smolar, "The Rich and the Powerful," in Abraham Brumberg (ed.), *Poland: Genesis of a Revolution* (New York: Random House, 1983), p. 43.

4 Voslensky, chap. 5, or Mervyn Matthews, *Privilege in the Soviet Union* (London: Allen & Unwin, 1978).

5 New York Times News Service, July 1, 1988.

6 Michael Kennedy and Ireneusz Białecki, "Power and the Logic of Distribution in Poland," *Eastern European Politics and Societies*, 3 (1989), pp. 300–328.

7 Roy Medvedev, *Let History Judge: The Origins and Consequences of Stalinism* (New York: Knopf, 1971); or Aleksandr Solzhenitsyn, *The Gulag Archipelago* (New York: Harper & Row, 1973).

8 Kennedy and Białecki, pp. 316–318.

9 Ivan Szelenyi, *Urban Inequalities Under State Socialism* (London: Oxford University Press, 1983).

10 Gerhard Lenski, "Income Stratification in the United States," *Research in Social Stratification and Mobility*, 3 (1984), table 1; and the World Bank, *World Development Report, 1989*, table 30.

11 Basile Kerblay, *Modern Soviet Society*, trans. Rupert Swyer (New York: Pantheon, 1983), p. 218.

12 Voslensky, ch. 5. See also Lenski, pp. 198–203, on the Polish-American comparison.

13 Carl Hall, "Socialists Say East Bloc Moves No Capitalist Victory," *San Francisco Chronicle*, Nov. 19, 1989.

14 Henry Kamm, "Hungarians Shocked by News of Vast Poverty in Their Midst," *New York Times*, Feb. 6, 1989; and Adrian Karatnycky, "Poles Daily Grind: Bad and Worsening," *Wall*

Street Journal, May 10, 1988. See also Agnes Bokor, "Modern Poverty-Deprivation: The Case of Hungary," *Research in Social Stratification and Mobility*, 5 (1986), pp. 245–260.

15 *Statistical Abstract of the U.S., 1989*, table 44.

16 Greg J. Duncan et al., *Years of Poverty, Years of Plenty* (Ann Arbor: Institute for Social Research, University of Michigan, 1984), table 2.1.

17 Robert Osborn, *The Evolution of Soviet Politics* (Homewood, Ill.: Dorsey, 1974), p. 382ff.

18 Alex Inkeles, "Social Stratification and Mobility in the Soviet Union," *American Sociological Review*, 15 (1950), p. 476n. A recent study of savings in a single unidentified region of the Soviet Union found that 3 percent of the accounts held more than 50 percent of the savings (London Observer News Service, August 14, 1985).

19 Zaslavskaia, op. cit.

20 *Statistical Abstract of the U.S., 1985*, table 775.

21 Ibid.

22 Edward Regan, "Pension Funds: New Power . . . ," *Wall Street Journal*, Nov. 2, 1987.

23 *Statistical Abstract of the U.S., 1989*, table 691.

24 Personal communication by Włodzimierz Wesołowski.

25 On the reversal in Soviet society, see Kerblay, table 38; on the United States, see *Historical Statistics of the U.S.: Colonial Times to 1957* (1960), Series G–169–190.

26 See, for example, Christopher Jencks et al., "The Wisconsin Model of Status Attainment," *Sociology of Education*, 56 (1983), pp. 3–19.

27 *Statistical Abstract of the U.S., 1989*, table 729.

28 Ibid., table 71.

29 Ibid., table 723.

30 Members of minority groups usually adopt the dominant group's prestige evaluations for groups other than their own. Sometimes they even adopt its evaluation of their own group. See, for example, Emory Bogardus, *Social Distance* (Yellow Springs, Ohio: Antioch Press, 1959), pp. 26–29.

31 See, for example, Everett C. Hughes, *French Canada in Transition* (Chicago: University of Chicago Press, 1943), especially chap. 7. See also John Porter, *The Vertical Mosaic: An Analysis of Social Class and Power in Canada* (Toronto: University of Toronto Press, 1965), chap. 3.

32 John Burns, "Separatists Vying for Quebec Power," *New York Times*, Sept. 24, 1989.

33 Our calculation based on *The Almanac of American Politics, 1988* (Washington, D.C.).

34 Our calculation based on a listing in *Forbes*, June 8, 1981, pp. 114–116.

35 Calculated from Morris Janowitz, *The Professional Soldier* (New York: Free Press, 1960), p. 63.

36 David Lane, *State and Politics in the USSR* (New York: New York University Press, 1985), p. 165. On China, see *Newsweek*, July 15, 1985, p. 32.

37 New York Times News Service release, Sept. 2, 1979.

38 Janet Schwartz, "Women Under Socialism," *Social Forces*, 58 (1979), p. 83.

39 This is also true in the Soviet Union. See Kerblay, pp. 127–128.

40 *Historical Statistics of the U.S.: Colonial Times to 1970*, series G–394 and 395; and Francine Blau and Marianne Berber, *The Economics of Women, Men, and Work* (Englewood Cliffs, N.J.: Prentice-Hall, 1986), table 10.2.

41 Hilary Land, "The Changing Place of Women in Europe," *Daedalus*, 108 (Spring, 1979), p. 84.

42 See, for example, *Statistical Abstract of the U.S., 1988*, table 723.

43 William J. Goode, *World Revolution and Family Patterns* (New York: Free Press, 1963), p. 55.

44 Gerhard Lenski, *Power and Privilege: A Theory of Social Stratification* (Chapel Hill, N.C.: University of North Carolina Press, 1984, originally published 1966), p. 412.

45 Lenski, p. 228.

46 Ibid., pp. 313–318, for a more thorough discussion of this subject.

47 L. J. Zimmerman, *Poor Lands, Rich Lands: The Widening Gap* (New York: Random House, 1965), table 2.8, p. 38; and *World Development Report*, 1982 (Washington, D.C.: World Bank, 1982), table 3.2.

Chapter 14

1 Our calculation, based on U.S. Department of Commerce, Bureau of the Census, *Statistical Abstract of the U.S., 1989*, tables 21 and 61.

2 Urie Bronfenbrenner, "The Disturbing Changes in the American Family," *Search* (Fall, 1976), pp. 11–14.

3 See, for example, U.S. Department of Commerce, Bureau of the Census, *Historical Statistics of the United States: Colonial Times to 1970*, p. 53.

4 *Statistical Abstract of the U.S., 1989*, table 83.

5 Edward L. Kain, *The Myth of Family Decline: Understanding Families in a World of Rapid Social Change* (Lexington, Mass.: Lexington Books, 1990).

6 Calculations based on Warren Thompson and David Lewis, *Population Problems*, 5th ed. (New York: McGraw-Hill, 1965), p. 374; J. Bourgeois-Pichat, "The General Development of the Population of France Since the Eighteenth Century," in D. V. Glass and D. E. C. Eversley (eds.), *Population in History* (Chicago: Aldine, 1965), p. 498; and W. S. Woytinsky and E. S. Woytinsky, *World Population and Production: Trends and Outlooks* (New York: Twentieth Century Fund, 1953), p. 181.

7 *Statistical Abstract of the U.S., 1989*, table 71.

8 Ibid., table 70.

9 Ibid., table 741.

10 In this section we have drawn heavily on suggestions provided by Joan Huber in two of her papers, "Toward a Socio-Technological Theory of the Women's Movement," *Social Problems*, 23 (1976), and "The Future of Parenthood: Implications of Declining Fertility," in Dana Hiller and Robin Sheets (eds.), *Women and Men* (Cincinnati: University of Cincinnati Press, 1976), pp. 333–351.

11 *Statistical Abstract of the U.S., 1989*, table 621.

12 Hilary Land, "The Changing Place of Women in Europe," *Daedalus*, 108 (Spring, 1979), p. 83.

13 Hedrick Smith, *The Russians* (New York: Ballantine, 1984), chap. 5.

14 Lisa Collins, "More Firms Giving Fathers Time Off . . . " *Wall Street Journal*, July 5, 1985.

15 United Press International news release, June 1, 1980; and Robin Morgan, "The First Feminist Exiles from the U.S.S.R.," *Ms.* (November, 1980), pp. 49–108.

16 Michael Getler, "Emancipation for E. German Women," *Washington Post*, Apr. 24, 1979.

17 Joann Lublin, "As Women's Roles Grow More Like Men's, So Do Their Problems," *Wall Street Journal*, Jan. 14, 1980. See also the *New York Times* series of articles, "Women's Lives: A Scorecard of Change," Aug. 20–22, 1989.

18 Ibid.

19 *Historical Statistics of the U.S.: Colonial Times to 1970*, series H–1004 and H–1005; and *Statistical Abstract of the U.S., 1989*, table 292.

20 Calculation based on *Statistical Abstract of the U.S., 1989*, table 206.

21 See, for example, Randall Collins, "Functional and Conflict Theories of Educational Stratification," *American Sociological Review*, 36 (1971), pp. 1002–1019.

22 *Statistical Abstract of the U.S., 1989*, tables 93 and 104.

23 Lynn Langway and William Schmidt, "A Youthquake in Russia," *Newsweek*, July 7, 1980, p. 46. See also Smith, chap. 7.

24 Walter Connor, *Deviance in Soviet Society: Crime, Delinquency, and Alcoholism* (New York: Columbia, 1972), p. 153.

25 *Statistical Abstract of the U.S., 1989*, table 293.

26 See, for example, Richard Quinney, *The Social Reality of Crime* (Boston: Little, Brown, 1970).

27 Connor, p. 93ff.

28 Ibid.

29 Bronfenbrenner, op. cit.

30 On Japan, see New York Times wire service story dated July 25, 1982; on the U.S., see A. C. Nielsen Co. report, 1987.

31 Robert Kalaski, "TVs Unreal World of Work," *American Federationist*, December, 1980.

32 Thomas E. Patterson, *The Mass Media Election: How Americans Choose Their President* (New York: Praeger, 1980).

33 For example, David Halberstam, "The Media: The Powers That Be," public lecture, University of North Carolina at Chapel Hill, April 5, 1982.

34 *Washington Post*, June 25, 1989.

35 Harry Waters, "Brave New Documentary," *Newsweek*, June 10, 1985, p. 71.

36 For a more detailed, though somewhat dated, discussion of one aspect of this subject, see Gerhard Lenski, "Marxist Experiments in Destratification: An Appraisal," *Social Forces*, 57 (1978), pp. 364–385.

37 Gail Lapidus, "Gorbachev and the Reform of the Soviet System," *Daedalus*, 116 (Spring, 1987), p. 9.

38 Michael Kennedy and Ireneusz Białecki, "Power and the Logic of Distribution in Poland," *Eastern European Politics and Societies*, 3 (1989), pp. 316–318.

39 For an earlier prediction of this, see Gaetano Mosca, *The Ruling Class*, trans. Hannah Kahn (New York: McGraw-Hill, 1939), especially p. 281ff.

40 Mark Zakharov, "A Glimpse in 1990: Politics and Democracy," *Literaturnaya Gazeta* (international edition), March, 1990, p. 5.

Chapter 15

1 See Gerhard Lenski and Patrick Nolan, "Trajectories of Development: A Test of Ecological–Evolutionary Theory," *Social Forces*, 63 (September, 1984), pp. 1–23.

2 World Bank, *World Development Report, 1988* (New York: Oxford University Press, 1988) tables 3 and 31.

3 Ibid., *1989*, table 1.

4 Ibid., table 2. Our calculation.

5 Manfred Halpern, *The Politics of Social Change in the Middle East and North Africa* (Princeton, N.J.: Princeton, 1963), p. 80.

6 Ibid.

7 Gladwin Hill, "View of the World's Shantytowns Less Grim," *New York Times*, June 9, 1976.

8 Olga Tellis, "India Proposes Sterilization," *Washington Post*, Mar. 31, 1976.

9 Barry Kramer, "The Politics of Birth Control," *Wall Street Journal*, May 8, 1978. See also Stuart Auerbach, "Family Planning—India's New Orphan," *The Washington Post*, Aug. 7, 1980.

10 Jay Matthews, "China Pressures Couples to Have Only One Child," *The Washington Post*, Feb. 28, 1980.

11 Ibid. See also Chen Muhua, "Birth Planning in China," *Family Planning Perspectives*, 11 (Nov/Dec., 1979), pp. 348–354.

12 June Shaplen and Robert Shaplen, "Taking on the Tide," *New York Times Magazine*, Aug. 27, 1976, p. 62.

13 Alex Inkeles and David Smith, *Becoming Modern: Change in Six Developing Countries* (Cambridge, Mass.: Harvard, 1974); or Alex Inkeles, "Making Men Modern," *American Journal of Sociology*, 75 (1969), pp. 208–225.

14 Ray Vicker, "Arab Industrialization Adds to the Problems of Western Producers," *Wall Street Journal*, July 9, 1980.

15 United Nations, *Yearbook of International Trade Statistics, 1982*, vol. 1, Cuba, table 5; and Roger Lowenstein, "Sugar is Cuba's Triumph and Failure," *Wall Street Journal*, Aug. 3, 1984.

16 John F. Burns, "Let a Million Businesses Bloom, The Chinese Cry," *New York Times*, Oct. 3, 1985.

17 "Deng's Quiet Revolution," *Newsweek*, Apr. 30, 1984, pp. 40–55; Victor Fung, "China Allows Rebirth of Some Private Corporations," *Wall Street Journal*, Aug. 10, 1984, p. 28; or Christopher Wren, "China's Cities to Get More Capitalism," *New York Times*, Oct. 14, 1984.

18 See, for example, the unsigned editorial in Peking's *People's Daily*, Dec. 7, 1984.

19 Paul Hollander, *Political Pilgrims: Travels of Western Intellectuals to the Soviet Union, China, and Cuba* (Oxford: Oxford University Press, 1981).

20 See note 18 above and Martin K. Whyte, "Destratification and Restratification in China," *Amsterdams Sociologisch Tijdschrift*, 5 (October 1978), pp. 242–243; Jay Mathews, "China Propagandizes in Favor of Material Incentives," *The Washington Post*, Dec. 30, 1977.

21 *World Development Report, 1989*, table 31.

22 See, for example, Myron Weiner, *Party Building in a New Nation: The Indian National Congress* (Chicago: University of Chicago Press, 1967).

23 Neil Smelser and S. M. Lipset (eds.), *Social Structure and Mobility in Economic Development* (Chicago: Aldine, 1966), p. 29ff. Other statistics cited in this paragraph are from the same source. See also Herbert Passin, *Society and Education in Japan* (New York: Columbia University Press, 1965), p. 57.

24 John Meyer et al., "National Economic Development, 1950–70," in John Meyer and Michael Hannan (eds.), *National Development and the World System* (Chicago: University of Chicago Press, 1979), chap. 6.

25 Smelser and Lipset, p. 37; and Jan Szczepański, *Polish Society* (New York: Random House, 1970), table 15, p. 115.

26 Smelser and Lipset, p. 37. See also June Kronholz, "In Third-World India College Students Study Humanities, Not Skills," *Wall Street Journal*, May 7, 1982.

27 Halpern, p. 122.

28 Henry A. Landsberger (ed.), *Latin American Peasant Movements* (Ithaca, N.Y.: Cornell University Press, 1969).

29 For Latin America, see Robert E. Scott, "Political Elites and Political Modernization: The Crisis of Transition," in S. M. Lipset and Aldo Solari (eds.), *Elites in Latin America* (New York: Oxford University Press, 1967), p. 133.

Chapter 16

1 See, for example, F. G. Bailey, *Tribe, Caste, and Nation* (Manchester, England: Manchester University Press, 1960), on the assimilation of hill tribes in India.

2 For a much more detailed discussion of this subject, see Gerhard Lenski and Patrick Nolan, "Trajectories of Development: A Test of Ecological–Evolutionary Theory," *Social Forces*, 63 (September 1984), pp. 1–23.

3 Median values based on *World Development Report, 1989*, table 31.

4 Ibid., table 1.

5 Ibid.

6 See, for example, Es'kia Mphahlele, "Africa in Exile," *Daedalus*, III (Spring 1982), pp. 29–48; George B. W. Ayittey, "Black Tyranny: A Deafening Silence," *New York Times*, Mar. 28, 1989; James Brooke, "Historian Tries to Fight Longtime African Ruler," ibid., Feb. 27, 1989; Kenneth Noble, "New Hope in Guinea, A Land That Hope Forgot," ibid., Nov. 29, 1989, and "Doe Leads the Good Life as Liberia Grows Poorer . . ." ibid., Mar. 26, 1990; Jane Perlez, "African Elder Trims One-Party Stand," ibid., Feb. 27, 1990; Jonathan Spivak, "In Nigeria, Payoffs are a Way of Life," *Wall Street Journal*, July 12, 1982; Lee Lescaze and Steve Mufson, "Angry New Leaders in Africa Are Trying to Right Past Wrongs," ibid., July 18, 1985; David Ottaway, "Ghana's Prosperity Feeds Corruption," *The Washington Post*, Jan. 29, 1978; or Leon Dash, "IMF Seeks to Aid Ruined Economy," ibid., Jan. 1, 1980.

7 See, for example, Steve Mufson, "Little is Being Done to Control Explosive Growth of Africa's Population," *Wall Street Journal*, July 31, 1985. For a slightly more optimistic view, see Jane Perlez, "Birth Control Making Inroads in Populous Kenya," *New York Times*, Sept. 10, 1989, and Philip Hilts, "Plan Offered to Stabilize Birth Rate in the 1990s," ibid., Feb. 26, 1990.

8 Lenski and Nolan, table 5.

9 Daniel Bell, "Socialism," *International Encyclopedia of the Social Sciences* (New York: Macmillan and Free Press, 1968), vol. 14, p. 529.

10 *World Development Report, 1989*, table 20. See also David Ottaway, "Tanzania Struggles in Vain to Meet the Needs of Its Poor," *Washington Post*, Feb. 3, 1979.

11 See, for example, Gwendolen Carter (ed.), *African One-Party States* (Ithaca, N.Y.: Cornell, 1962), pp. 371ff, and 461ff; Guy Hunter, *The New Societies of Africa* (New York: Oxford University Press, 1964), chap. 9, especially p. 223ff; International Bank for Reconstruction and Development, *The Economic Development of Uganda* (Baltimore: Johns Hopkins, 1962), pp. 23–24; or Ken Post, *The New States of West Africa* (Baltimore: Penguin, 1964), chap. 6.

12 *World Development Report, 1989*, table 29.

13 Based on Inter-African Labour Institute, *The Human Factors of Productivity in Africa*, as summarized in William H. Lewis (ed.), *French-speaking Africa: The Search for Identity* (New York: Walker, 1965), p. 168. Many of these propositions were supported in papers presented to a subsequent conference on competing demands for labor in traditional African societies, cosponsored by the Joint Committee on African Studies of the Social Science Research Council, the American Council of Learned Societies, and the Agricultural Development Council. See William O. Jones, "Labor and Leisure in Traditional African Societies," *Social Science Research Council Items*, 22 (March 1968), pp. 1–6.

14 See, for example, J. L. Hammond and Barbara Hammond, *The Town Labourer*, 1760–1832 (London: Guild Books, 1949, first published 1917), especially chap. 2.

15 On the latter, see, for example, J. A. K. Leslie's fascinating study, *A Survey of Dar es Salaam* (New York: Oxford University Press, 1963).

16 Hunter, p. 85.

17 Ibid., p. 94.

18 See, for example, June Kronholz, "In Africa Tribal Power Wanes, But Still Rivals Governments'," *Wall Street Journal*, June 15, 1981.

19 See Leslie, p. 32; or Merran Fraenkel, *Tribe and Class in Monrovia* (London: Oxford University Press, 1964), especially chap. 3.

20 Kronholz, op. cit.

21 Ayittey, op. cit.

22 David Lamb, "Africans Find Independence a Hard Road," *Los Angeles Times*, story reprinted in *Wall Street Journal*, Feb. 15, 1979. See also Ayittey, op. cit.

23 Ibid. See also Ray Vicker, "Arab Nations Growing More Cautious About Dispensing Aid to Third World," *Wall Street Journal*, Sept. 4, 1980.

24 *World Development Report, 1989*, table 30.

25 John Paxton (ed.), *The Statesman's Yearbook, 1980–81* (New York: St. Martin's Press, 1980).

26 The figure for Dar es Salaam is from Leslie, p. 210, and that for Tanzania from Bruce Russett et al., *World Handbook of Political and Social Indicators* (New Haven: Yale University Press, 1964), tables 74 and 75.

27 Fraenkel, p. 154; and Russett et al., tables 74 and 75.

28 From *A Survey of Dar es Salaam*, p. 211, by J. A. K. Leslie, published by Oxford University Press, 1963. By permission of the Oxford University Press.

29 Ibid., pp. 210–211.

30 Fraenkel, pp. 158 and 162.

31 Hunter, p. 74, provides numerous examples.

32 Carter, pp. 433–434. Copyright 1962 by Cornell University. Used by permission of Cornell University Press.

33 See, for example, Vittorio Lanternari, *The Religions of the Oppressed: A Study of Modern Messianic Cults*, trans. Lisa Sergio (New York: Knopf, 1963), chap. 1; or Mair, p. 171ff.

34 The same was true of Sekou Touré's Democratic Party in Guinea. See, for example, David Apter, *The Politics of Modernization* (Chicago: University of Chicago Press, 1965), p. 299, note 36.

35 L. A. Fallers (ed.), *The King's Men: Leadership and Status in Buganda on the Eve of Independence* (New York: Oxford University Press, 1964), p. 99.

36 Leslie, pp. 27–29.

37 Ibid., pp. 60–61; or Fraenkel, p. 127ff.

38 See, for example, June Kronholz, "Kenyans Say Missionaries Who Tried to Stop Polygamy Caused Baby Boom," *Wall Street Journal*, Apr. 11, 1983.

39 See, for example, Andre Gunder Frank, *Capitalism and Underdevelopment in Latin America* (New York: Monthly Review Press, 1969); Theotonio Dos Santos, "The Structure of Dependence," *American Economic Review,* 60 (1970), pp. 231–236; or Celso Furtado, *Economic Development of Latin America* (Cambridge: Cambridge University Press, 1970).

40 Compare, for example, Frank, op. cit., with Johan Galtung, "A Structural Theory of Imperialism," *Journal of Peace Research*, 8 (1971), pp. 81–117.

41 See, for example, W. W. Rostow, *The Process of Economic Growth* (New York: Norton, 1962); Wilbert Moore and David Feldman, *Labor Commitment and Social Change in Developing Areas* (New York: Social Science Research Council, 1960); S. N. Eisenstadt, *Modernization* (Englewood Cliffs, N.J.: Prentice-Hall, 1966); Talcott Parsons, *The System of Modern Societies* (Englewood Cliffs, N.J.: Prentice-Hall, 1971); or Alex Inkeles and David Smith, *Becoming Modern* (Cambridge, Mass.: Harvard, 1974).

42 Robert Fox, "The World's Urban Explosion," *National Geographic*, 166 (Aug. 1984), p. 182.

Chapter 17

1 See, for example, Jacques Ellul, *The Technological Society*, trans. John Wilkinson (New York: Vintage Books, 1967).

2 George R. Scott, *The History of Capital Punishment* (London: Torchstream Books, 1950), pp. 39–40.

3 Dover Wilson, *The Essential Shakespeare*, as quoted by Ivor Brown, *Shakespeare* (New York: Time Books, 1962), p. 112.

4 See, for example, Colin Turnbull, *The Forest People* (New York: Simon & Schuster, 1961); or John Garvan, *The Negritos of the Philippines* (Vienna: Ferdinand Berger, 1964).

5 René Dubos, *So Human An Animal* (New York: Scribners', 1968), p. 270.

6 See, for example, Friedrich Engels, as cited by D. G. Brennan in Foreign Policy Association (ed.), *Toward the Year 2018* (New York: Cowles, 1958), p. 2.

7 *ZPG* [Zero Population Growth] *Reporter*, 12 (Sept., 1980), p. 1. Italics added.

8 *The Global 2000 Report to the President*, vol. 2, table 6–12.

9 *ZPG Reporter*, p. 2.

10 Robert W. Fox, "The World's Urban Explosion," *National Geographic*, 166 (Aug., 1984), p. 181.

11 *The Global 2000 Report* . . ., vol. 2, p. 417.

12 See, for example, Lester Brown and Christopher Flavin, "The Earth's Vital Signs," in Lester Brown et al., *The State of the World 1988* (New York: Norton, 1988), pp. 16–18. For a skeptical view, see S. Fred Singer, "Fact and Fancy on Greenhouse Earth," *New York Times*, Aug. 30, 1988. For summaries of the controversy, see William K. Stevens, "Skeptics are Challenging Dire Greenhouse Effects," ibid., Dec. 13, 1989; or Bill McKibben, "Is The World Getting Hotter?" *New York Review of Books*, Dec. 8, 1988, p. 7ff.

13 Ibid.

14 *The Global 2000 Report* . . ., vol. 2, table 9–5.

15 Clifford P. Case, III, "Why Do We Refuse to Recycle?" *Washington Post*, Apr. 12, 1980.

16 Jay Mathews, "China Opts for Progress," ibid., Jan. 26, 1980; and "Chinese Metals Plant is Fined $1.3 Million for Water Pollution," *Wall Street Journal,* Mar. 18, 1980.

17 Stephen Yoder, "Japan Persists in Costly Energy Research," *Wall Street Journal*, June 2, 1987.

18 Our calculations based on reserves as reported in Lester Brown et al., *State of the World, 1987* (New York: Norton, 1987), table 1–3; and consumption as reported in U.S. Department of Commerce, Bureau of the Census, *Statistical Abstract of the U.S., 1989*, table 1400.

19 Elias P. Gyftopoulous, "Energy: Everybody's Business," *Forbes*, Oct. 27, 1980, p. 86.

20 Ibid., p. 88.

21 *Statistical Abstract of the U.S., 1989*, table 349.

22 William K. Stevens, "When Trash Leaves the Curb: New Methods Aid Recycling," *New York Times*, May 2, 1989.

23 *Newsweek*, Sept. 22, 1980, p. 90.

24 Harrison Brown, *The Challenge of Man's Future* (New York: Viking, 1954), p. 114.

25 Jean Mayer, "The Dimensions of Human Hunger," *Scientific American*, 235 (September, 1976), pp. 46–47.

26 John Saar, "Japan Looks to Future of Fish Farms," *Washington Post*, June 1, 1977; and *The Global 2000 Report* . . ., vol. 2, p. 112.

27 Nevin Scrimshaw and Lance Taylor, "Food," *Scientific American*, 243 (September 1980), p. 85.

28 Doug McInnis, "How Technology Altered NCR and Dayton," *Washington Post*, Jan. 8, 1978.

29 Jessica Tuchman Mathews, "Factories Too Tiny to See," ibid., Jan. 23, 1980.

30 Sandra Blakeslee, "Human Genes Turn Plants Into Factories for Medicines," *New York Times*, Jan. 16, 1990.

31 World Bank, *World Development Report, 1989* (New York: Oxford University Press, 1989), table 1.

32 Robert Heilbroner, *An Inquiry Into the Human Prospect* (New York: Norton, 1974).

33 Ibid., pp. 121–122.

Picture Credits

Cover   Steve Raymer © National Geographic Society.

1.2   Marc and Evelyne Bernheim/Woodfin Camp & Associates.

1.3   Baron Hugo Van Lewick/National Geographic Society.

2.1   T. D. Lovering/Stock, Boston.

2.2   George Malave/Stock, Boston.

2.4a   The American Museum of Natural History.

2.4b   Lynn McLaren/Photo Researchers.

2.5   Courtesy of Department of Antiquities, Ashmolean Museum, Oxford.

2.6   Henri Cartier–Bresson/Magnum.

2.7   Rene Burri/Magnum.

2.8   Martha Swope Photography, Inc.

3.1   By permission of John Marshall, Peabody Museum, Harvard University.

3.2   Peter Southwick/Stock, Boston.

3.3   Ed Fisher, by permission of the artist.

3.5   The Bettmann Archive.

3.9   Omikron/Photo Researchers.

4.1   Australian Information Service/Photo Researchers.

4.2   United Nations.

5.1   The Spectator.

5.2   From Grahame Clark, *The Stone Age Hunters,* copyright 1967 by Thames and Hudson, ltd., London.

5.4   American Museum of Natural History.

5.5a   From Hugo Obermaier, *Fossil Man in Spain,* plate XIV.

5.5b   Copyright Prehistoric Division, Museum of Natural History, Vienna.

5.5c   With permission from Peter J. Ucko and Andrea Rosenfeld, *Paleolithic Cave Art,* 1967, Wiedenfeld Publishers.

5.6   By permission of John Marshall, Peabody Museum, Harvard University.

5.7   National Anthropological Archive, Smithsonian Institution.

5.8   By permission of John Marshall, Peabody Museum, Harvard University.

5.9   By permission of John Marshall, Peabody Museum, Harvard University.

5.10   Courtesy of Department of Library Services, American Museum of Natural History.

5.12   Colonel Charles W. Furlong.

6.1   Courtesy of Department of Library Services, American Museum of Natural History.

6.2   Courtesy of Department of Library Services, American Museum of Natural History.

6.4   Courtesy of Department of Library Services, American Museum of Natural History.

6.6   From W. Watson, *Early Civilization in China,* copyright 1970, Thames & Hudson, Ltd., London.

6.7   United Nations.

6.8   Courtesy of the University Museum, University of Pennsylvania, Philadelphia.

6.10   From Napoleon A. Chagnon, *Yanamamö: The Fierce People,* © 1988 by Holt, Rinehart, & Winston Inc. Reprinted by permission of CBS College Publishing.

6.11   Courtesy of Department of Library Services, American Museum of Natural History.

6.12   United Nations.

6.13   Courtesy of Department of Library Services, American Museum of Natural History.

6.15   From Jacques Maquet, *Africanity, The Cultural Unity of Black Africa,* Oxford University Press, 1972, p. 112.

6.17   Courtesy of Stanford University Press, copyright 1946, 1947, 1956, and 1983. Reprinted from *The Ancient Maya,* 4/e by Sylvanus Griswold Morley and George W. Brainerd; revised by Robert J. Sharer.

7.1   Courtesy of the Metropolitan Museum of Art.

7.2   Evans/Three Lion Photos, Inc.

7.3   Courtesy of the Metropolitan Museum of Art.

7.4   Courtesy of the Metropolitan Museum of Art, Museum Excavations, 1919–1920; Rogers Fund, supplemented by contribution of Edward S. Harkness.

7.6   Courtesy of the Metropolitan Museum of Art, Museum Excavations, 1919–1920; Rogers Fund, supplemented by contribution of Edward S. Harkness.

7.7   United Nations.

7.8   Courtesy of Exxon Corporation.

7.10   United Nations.

7.11   From F. R. Crowell, *Everyday Life in Ancient Rome,* G. P. Putnam's Sons, copyright © 1961. By permission of B. T. Batsford, Ltd., London.

7.12   United Nations.

7.13   Courtesy of the Metropolitan Museum of Art, Bashford Dean Memorial Collection, Funds from various donors, 1929.

7.14   United Nations.

7.15   United Nations.

7.16   From F. R. Crowell, *Everyday Life in Ancient Rome,* G. P. Putnam's Sons, copyright © 1961. By permission of B. T. Batsford, Ltd., London.

8.1   United Nations.

8.2   Pietro F. Mele/Photo Researchers.

8.3   Paolo Koch/Photo Researchers.

8.4   By permission of Institut Français d' Archéologie, Beirut, Lebanon.

8.5   Courtesy of the Metropolitan Museum of Art, Rogers Fund, 1906.

9.1   The Granger Collection.

9.2   From Fritz Rorig, *The Medieval Town.* Courtesy of the University of California Press.

9.4   The Smithsonian Institution.

9.5   Historical Picture Service.

9.6   National Anthropological Archives, The Smithsonian Institution.

9.7   The Bettmann Archive.

9.8   Courtesy of Hershey Foods Corporation.

9.10   The Edward L. Bafford Photography Collection, Albin O. Kuhn Library & Gallery, University of Maryland, Baltimore County.

10.1   USDA/Science Source/Photo Researchers.

10.2   Craig Aurness/Woodfin Camp & Associates.

10.3   The Bettmann Archive.

10.4   Courtesy of the New York Public Library—Astor, Lenox, & Tilden Foundations.

10.5   The Granger Collection.

10.6   German Information Center.

10.7   Louis Goldman/Photo Researchers.

11.1   Peter Menzel/Stock, Boston.

Name Index

Subject Index